Man & Music

THE CLASSICAL ERA

THE CLASSICAL ERA

From the 1740s to the end of the 18th century

EDITED BY NEAL ZASLAW

PRENTICE HALL
ENGLEWOOD CLIFFS, NEW JERSEY 07632

First North American edition published 1989 by Prentice Hall Inc,
a Division of Simon & Schuster, Englewood Cliffs, New Jersey 07632

First published in the United Kingdom 1989 by
The Macmillan Press Limited

ISBN 0-13-136920-2 (hardback)

ISBN 0-13-136938-5 (paperback)

Typeset by Florencetype Ltd, Kewstoke, Avon
Printed in Hong Kong

Contents

Illustration Acknowledgements

The publishers would like to thank the following institutions and individuals who have kindly provided photographic material for use in this book.

1, 25, Kunsthistorisches Museum, Vienna; 2, Verlag das Musikinstrument, Frankfurt-am-Main: after Jürgen Meyer, *Acoustics in the Performance of Music* (1980); 3, 31, 34, Historisches Museum der Stadt Wien; 4, Institut für Theater–Film und Fernsehwissenschaft, University of Cologne; 5, 39, Civicae Raccolte Stampe 'A. Bertarelli', Castello Sforzesco, Milan; 6, Trafalgar Galleries, London; 7, Museum des Kunsthandwerks, Leipzig; 8, Museo Civico d'Arte Antica, Turin; 9, Art Institute of Chicago, Gift of Emily Crane Chadbourne, 1922.4790; 10, 68, 69, 70, 74, Trustees of the British Museum, London (68, 70 The Fotomas Index); 11, Musée du Louvre/Giraudon; 12, Jane Berdes/photo Georgio Dimatore, Venice; 13, Museo Correr, Venice/photo Federico Arborio Mella, Milan; 14, Trustees of the British Library, London, Additional MS 32676, f.158r; 15, Richard Macnutt, Withyham, Sussex; 16 Société Française de Musicologie, Paris; 18, Musée Condé, Chantilly/Giraudon; 20, 21, 22, Bibliothèque Nationale, Paris; 23, Bibliothèque Municipale, Besançon; 24, Oxford Illustrators; 29, 30 (Hofburg, Vienna), 33, 35, 36, 37, 40, Österreichisches Nationalbibliothek, Vienna; 38, Staatsarchiv, Vienna (Kabinettsarchiv, Protocollum seperatum aller Handbillets, vol.40 (X), 1786, nr.112); 41, Museum Carolino Augusteum, Salzburg; 42, Verlag St Peter, Salzburg; 43, Internationale Stiftung Mozarteum, Salzburg; 44, Archív Hlavního Města, Prague/photo Muzeum České Hudby; 45, Národní Muzeum, Prague/photo Olga Hilmerová; Muzeum Hlavního Města, Prague /photo Miroslav Jarošík; 47 Private Collection/photo Chemigrafie, Prague; 48 Národní Galérie (Uměleckoprůmyslové Muzeum), Prague/photo Miroslav Jarošík; 49, 50, Reiss Museum, Mannheim; 51, photo Robert Häusser, Mannheim; 52, Bayerisches Nationalmuseum, Munich; 53, Royal College of Music, London; 54, Museum für Kunst und Gewerbe, Hamburg; 55, Gemäldegalerie, Berlin/Archiv für Kunst und Geschichte; 56, Museum der Bildenden Künste, Leipzig; 57, Nationale Forschungs-und Gedenkstätten der Klassischen Deutschen Literatur, Weimar; 58, Burgenländisches Landesmuseum, Eisenstadt/photo Forstner; 59, photo A.F. Kersting, London; 60, 61, 62 Magyar Nemzeti Múzeum, Budapest; 63, Deutsches Theatermuseum, Munich; 64, Yale Center for British Art (Paul Mellon Collection)/photo Royal Academy of Arts, London; 65, Civico Museo Bibliografico Musicale, Bologna; 66, Victoria Art Gallery/Bath City Council; 67, 72, Courtesy of the Board and Trustees of the Victoria and Albert Museum, London; 73, Trustees of the National Gallery, London; 75, Drottningholms Teatermuseum, Stockholm; 76, Kunliga Teatern, Stockholm/photo E. Rydberg; 78, 79, Nationalmuseum, Stockholm; 80, Statens Konstmuseer, Stockholm; 81, Calcografia Nacional, Real Academia de Bellas Artes de San Fernando, Madrid; 82, Museo del Prado, Madrid; 83, Museo de Arte Moderno, Barcelona; 84, University of California, Berkeley.

List of Abbreviations

AMZ	*Allgemeine musikalische Zeitung*
BurneyH	C. Burney: *A General History of Music from the Earliest Ages to the Present* (London, 1776–89)
CMc	*Current Musicology*
DDT	Denkmäler deutscher Tonkunst
DTB	Denkmäler der Tonkunst in Bayern
EDm	Das Erbe deutscher Musik
Grove6	*The New Grove Dictionary of Music and Musicians*
GroveA	*The New Grove Dictionary of American Music*
GSJ	*The Galpin Society Journal*
HawkinsH	J. Hawkins: *A General History of Science and Practice of Music* (London, 1776)
IMSCR	*International Musicological Society Congress Report*
JAMS	*Journal of the American Musicological Society*
MAB	Musica antiqua bohemica
MGG	*Die Musik in Geschichte und Gegenwart*
ML	*Music and Letters*
MQ	*The Music Quarterly*
MT	*The Musical Times*
PRMA	*Proceedings of the Royal Musical Association*
RdM	*Revue de musicologie*
RIM	*Rivista italiana di musicologia*
RMARC	*R[oyal] M[usical] A[ssociation] Research Chronicle*

List of Abbreviations

Preface

The *Man and Music* series of books – eight in number, chronologically organized – were originally conceived in conjunction with the television programmes of the same name, of which the first was shown by Granada Television International and Channel 4 in 1986. These programmes were designed to examine the development of music in particular places during particular periods in the history of Western civilization.

The books have the same objective. Each is designed to cover a segment of Western musical history; the breaks between them are planned to correspond with significant historical junctures. Since historical junctures, or indeed junctures in stylistic change, rarely happen with the neat simultaneity that the historian's or the editor's orderly mind might wish for, most volumes have 'ragged' ends and beginnings: for example, the Renaissance volume terminates, in Italy, in the 1570s and 80s, but continues well into the 17th century in parts of northern Europe.

These books do not, however, make up a history of music in the traditional sense. The reader will not find technical, stylistic discussion in them; if he wants to trace the detailed development of the texture of the madrigal or the rise and fall of sonata form, he should look elsewhere. Rather, it is the intention in these volumes to show in what context, and as a result of what forces – social, cultural, intellectual – the madrigal or sonata form came into being and took its particular shape. The intention is to view musical history not as a series of developments in some hermetic world of its own but rather as a series of responses to social, economic and political circumstances and to religious and intellectual stimuli. We want to explain not simply *what* happened, but *why* it happened, and why it happened when and where it did.

We have chosen to follow what might be called a geographical, or perhaps a topographical, approach: to focus, in each chapter, on a particular place and to examine its music in the light of its particular situation. Thus, in most of these volumes, the chapters – once past the introductory one, contributed by the volume editor – are each devoted to a city or a region. This system has inevitably needed some modification when dealing with very early or very recent times, for reasons (opposite ones, of course) to do with communication and cultural spread.

These books do not attempt to treat musical history comprehensively. Their editors have chosen for discussion the musical centres that they see as the most significant and the most interesting; many lesser ones inevitably escape individual discussion, though the patterns of their musical life may be discernible by analogy with others or may be separately referred to in the opening, editorial chapter. We hope, however, that a new kind of picture of musical history may begin to emerge from these volumes, and that this picture may be more accessible to the general reader, responsive to music but untrained in its techniques, than others arising from more traditional approaches. In spite of the large number of lovers of music, musical histories have never enjoyed the appeal to a broad, intelligent general readership in the way that histories of art, architecture or literature have done: these books represent an attempt to reach such a readership and explain music in terms that may quicken their interest.

★

The television programmes and books were initially planned in close collaboration with Sir Denis Forman, then Chairman of Granada Television International. The approach was worked out in more detail with several of the volume editors, among whom I am particularly grateful to Iain Fenlon for the time he has generously given to discussion of the problems raised by this approach to musical history, and also to Alexander Ringer and James McKinnon for their valuable advice and support. Discussion with Bamber Gascoigne and Tony Cash, in the course of the making of the initial television programmes, also proved of value. I am grateful to Celia Thomson for drafting the chronologies that appear in each volume and to Elisabeth Agate for her invaluable work as picture editor in bringing the volumes to visual life.

London, 1989 STANLEY SADIE

Chapter I

Music and Society in the Classical Era

NEAL ZASLAW

The period of history encompassed by this volume begins in about 1740, the year in which Frederick the Great ascended the Prussian throne and Maria Theresa became head of the Austrian Empire: events that had far-reaching effects in European history and in the history of music. It ends towards the close of the eighteenth century: the French Revolution in 1789 and its sequelae, the Napoleonic Wars and the collapse of the Holy Roman Empire among them, and what may be called the end of the beginning of the industrial revolution, all combine to form a natural watershed, in political, social and cultural history alike.

Such limits chime naturally – which may not be wholly coincidental – with the traditional periodization of musical history. The so-called 'Classical' period in Western music is often construed as beginning in the 1740s, when a new style of opera and (to some extent) of instrumental music swept out of Italy and conquered all of Europe, and as ending with the death of Haydn and with Beethoven's evolution from his first to his middle period, both in the first decade of the nineteenth century. Some historians prefer to include all of Beethoven's production and, adding two more years, Schubert's as well. In any case, such beginning and ending points in music history represent perceived disjunctions in the evolution of musical styles – disjunctions that must be taken into account even by those historians who might prefer to treat the whole of the eighteenth century as a more-or-less coherent unit (the period of the 'Enlightenment'), or by those who might choose to put the so-called late Baroque, Classical and Romantic periods together as a single, larger musical phenomenon (the 'common-practice' period), or even by those who would urge avoidance of all such artificially imposed periodization.

If meaningful periodization is to be attempted, however, our criteria for deciding when important musical trends began and ended must include other factors along with those derived from the stylistic disjunctions based on the work of leading composers. If, for instance, one defines the Classical period as that in which public concerts arose, improvised ornamentation was suppressed in orchestral music,[1] liturgical music declined, the national anthem came into existence[2] and the *opera seria opera buffa* dichotomy was replaced by a mixed genre, or as that in which traditional aristocratic patronage was gradually supplanted by bourgeois patronage, then the boundaries of the period will vary widely from one region of Europe to another. That is why the chronological limits in this book differ from chapter to chapter: in England, for instance, in some degree a parliamentary democracy, the industrial revolution and a capitalist economy were already in place, whereas in most of eastern Europe feudalism still reigned supreme. In France the Revolution terminated long-standing musical institutions, while in many other parts of continental Europe older forms remained intact until Napoleon swept through in the first decade of the nineteenth century, causing the demise of the Holy Roman Empire. The changes in musical culture that signal the end of the era chronicled here were not autonomous but an integral part of broad political, social and economic developments.

Failure to recognize the extent to which various parts of Europe differed and were out of phase with one another has sometimes led to confusing interpretations of the interconnections between styles, genres and social changes. A striking instance is the intriguing proposal that the rise of the symphony and the rise of the novel, which occurred roughly simultaneously, could both be explained as the production of new art forms to satisfy the needs of a newly empowered middle class.[3] This makes sense for England, where the outpouring of novels by such authors as Richardson, Fielding, Smollett, Sterne, Goldsmith and Fanny Burney coincided with the growth of public concerts in the larger cities and towns and of amateur orchestral societies in the smaller ones. But a large portion of the 16,558 symphonies known to have been written between roughly 1720 and 1810[4] were written in or for the courts, the stately homes, the monasteries, the cities, the towns and the villages of central and eastern Europe, where the audience was mostly not middle class and was one for whom novels represented a largely foreign, relatively unimportant literary genre.

There is the further objection that the subject of novels, broadly speaking, was the presentation of middle-class secular life for its own sake, whereas the 'subjects' of symphonies were those of the aristocratic *opera seria*: the conflict between love and honour (first movement), the pastoral (andante), the courtly (minuet) and the anti-courtly (trio) and the rustic (finale).[5] The popularity of symphonies, and of Italian opera, in two such disparate circumstances as those represented by London and, for instance, Haydn's Eszterháza, suggests that the forces creating an international style could to some degree cut across social, political and economic systems – much as in recent decades the styles of American popular music have invaded all countries on all continents, without regard to wealth or politics.

In the history of styles, as usually written, emphasis is placed upon stylistic innovations (sometimes by 'minor' figures or *Kleinmeister*) brought to fruition by great 'masters'. When emphasis is on innovation and 'masterworks', vast geographical and social musical landscapes may be, and usually are, passed over virtually in silence. The broader approach of the social historian of music, on the other hand, permits what may be a revelatory view of the transmission and transformation of musical styles, genres and (in the widest sense) institutions, irrespective of the presence of musical genius. In theory, at least, one may learn as much about musical culture from discussions of provincial Stockholm or Philadelphia as from discussions of cosmopolitan Vienna, Paris or London.

Stylistic and social approaches to Western music do, however, share a common principle: the notion of a centre and a periphery. From time to time the locations of centres and peripheries shift. Very little is known about music in the Roman Empire, but since Charlemagne's codification and promulgation in the ninth century of a uniform body of plainsong for Catholic worship, the phenomenon has never entirely ceased to operate. Following Charlemagne, principal centres of international influence have included the Notre Dame school of Paris in the twelfth and thirteenth centuries, Provence and the troubadours in the same period, the Franco-Flemish school of the early Renaissance, and the Italian school of the sixteenth, seventeenth and early eighteenth centuries.

Evidence for the existence of such a centre is straightforward: music and musicians radiate outwards from it to much of the rest of Europe, exported, sometimes at considerable expense, even to places that have strong local traditions of their own. Often, in addition, young musicians and even older ones from the periphery are sent to serve an apprenticeship, or to hone or modernize their skills, in the centre. It was, therefore, no coincidence that Heinrich Schütz, Georg Muffat, George Frideric Handel, Jean-Marie Leclair *l'aîné*, Johann Christian Bach, Johann Adolf Hasse, Christoph Willibald Gluck, André-Ernest-Modeste Grétry, Wolfgang Amadeus Mozart and Felix Mendelssohn among transalpine composers each spent part of his apprenticeship in Italy. At the same time, Italians were found staffing opera houses in countless European cities and courts in a kind of musical diaspora.

The causes of change in the locations of the centre and periphery have been the subject of much debate. An economic determinist would maintain that the most desirable music is likely to go where the money is, and it is true that international cultural centres are often places that are also prosperous. But there are too many counter-examples and exceptions for the economic theory alone to explain the shifts of centre and periphery. Even in periods of extreme upheaval, for instance in Germany during the Thirty Years War or in Britain during the Interregnum, music continued, although on a smaller scale and sometimes privately. And Britain's vast wealth in the eighteenth and nineteenth centuries, while paying for noteworthy amounts of imported music, did not guarantee that country an indigenous flowering of great native music (although neither was it ever 'das Lande ohne Musik' as suggested by jingoistic German historians). Conversely, Italy in the eighteenth century, as its political, social and economic decline accelerated, poured forth unprecedented torrents of opera to fill not only its own opera houses but also those of the rest of Europe.

Explanations offered for the puzzling lack of firm connection between wealth and musical creativity are partial and not entirely satisfactory. Among educated and wealthy German and English speakers, there was a well-documented trend during the eighteenth century to favour French or Italian music and musicians over native talent. Thus London became a place of pilgrimage for continental musicians seeking their fortunes,[6] and in the correspondence of Leopold and Wolfgang Mozart one reads bitter complaints about the preferential treatment accorded to Italian musicians. The beliefs of the 'enlightened' Prussian monarch, Quantz's employer Frederick the Great, starkly illustrate this situation:

> In 1780, Frederick the Great (1712–86) published one of his many treatises in French. It presented his views on cultural activity in the German lands, concentrating on the literary and performing arts. Frederick aimed to show that his fellow countrymen were so totally lacking in genius as well as taste that they could not possibly compete with the French and the Italians. German, which Frederick is said to have eschewed using, except in the stables with his horses and hounds, was 'still a half-barbaric language . . . A German singer? I should as soon expect to receive pleasure from the neighing of my horse!'[7]

As Frederick was not alone in his prejudices, it should cause no surprise that wealthy German speakers spent their money on French and Italian music.

On the other side, as the political and economic decline of Italy continued, the emerging contrast between northern wealth and southern poverty would have been sufficient reason for Italian musicians to seek employment across the Alps. Yet far from declining in its native habitat, Italian opera flourished. One explanation put forward for this apparent anomaly is that, as things became worse, people became increasingly inclined to flee, as one of them put it, from their 'nausea delle cose cotidiane' – their 'disgust with daily life' – into the idealized fantasy world of the opera house.[8]

The British and German tendency to neglect indigenous music and musicians, usually portrayed as snobbery or as a sense of cultural inferiority, may have deep roots, going as far back as the antagonisms between the Greco-Roman mediterranean culture of the ancient world and the invading 'barbarian' tribes; this continued with the leap forward in learning and culture represented by the Italian Renaissance and was confirmed by the mid-seventeenth-century cultural hiatuses caused by the Thirty Years War in Germany and the Interregnum in Britain, during which important musical developments in France and Italy temporarily left those regions provincial backwaters.

What were the musical developments with which the German and English speakers felt they had to catch up in the late seventeenth and early eighteenth centuries? They included French dancing and dance music and the orchestral innovations embodied in the *ouverture*; also Italian operas, and especially the singing and composition styles of the solo aria, as well as the new genres of sinfonia, concerto and sonata; and finally, from both France and Italy, new expressive means for homophonic, treble-dominated music.

A later step in the same direction – the new sounds considered at the beginning of this volume – issued especially from Italian operatic styles of the 1730s and 1740s: a melodic style of short segments with frequent cadences came to replace the more continuous, motivically-based passage-work with avoided cadences; the rhythms of harmonic change grew slower; inner parts became unimportant or vanished entirely, leading to an even greater dominance by the treble (the solo singer in vocal music, usually the violins in instrumental); bass lines diminished in contrapuntal interest but increased in motoric and harmonic force. All these developments can be heard in the operas of such composers as Leo, Vinci, Feo, Pergolesi and other members of their generation and the next, in which one repeatedly hears, especially in rapid instrumental pieces and comic arias, the drive to the cadence outlined by a harmonic-rhythmic bass line on the scale-degrees 3–4–5–6–3–4–5–1.

In several parts of Europe, fortunes were spent to import the necessary musicians to present this new international style of opera. From Ljubljana to London, from Lisbon to St Petersburg, opera houses were usually staffed by Italian composers, instrumentalists and singers (along with some local forces) and French dancing-masters and dancers. In such an establishment, the Italian composer provided the overture, arias and ensembles for the opera, while the dancing-master supplied the music and choreography for the ballet *entrées* that appeared sometimes in each act, sometimes between acts and sometimes as after-pieces.

Table I.1 ITALIAN MAESTROS IN ST PETERSBURG

composer	*tenure*	*own operas given**
Araja	1735–58	19
Manfredini	1762–5	13
Galuppi	1765–8	14
Traetta	1768–75	8
Paisiello	1776–83	31
Sarti	1784–6	14
Cimarosa	1787–91	19
Martín y Soler	1790–94	15
Sarti	1793–1801	21

* Source: R.-A. Mooser, *Opéras, intermezzos, ballets, cantates, oratorios joués en Russie durant le XVIIIe siècle* (Basle, 3/1964). Of the 154 works chronicled here, 36 are serious operas, 55 comic operas, 5 operettas, 40 cantatas and 5 ballets.

We may take St Petersburg as an example.[9] Several internationally successful Italian opera composers served as *maestro* at the court (see table I.1). These composers presided over a house staffed by Italian, German, French and of course Russian instrumentalists, dancers and singers. In addition to their own operas, they performed operas by other Italian composers as well as operas from other countries given in Russian and French, especially the *opéras comiques* of such composers as Dalayrac, Duni, Gluck, Grétry and Philidor. Works by native composers and librettists were also given.

The eighteenth century was also the century of the 'mixed style' (as Quantz called it in 1752).[10] Musical styles in Europe were almost always 'mixed', in the sense that melodies, instruments and musicians had always travelled widely. But it is one thing for styles to co-exist or to influence one another and quite another to find protracted attempts at synthesis or hybridization. Earlier in the century François Couperin was already concerned with what he dubbed 'les goûts réunis',[11] and in the middle of the century there were many calls, at least north of the Alps, for a fusion of what were seen as the most successful features of French and Italian (or sometimes French, Italian and German) music. Stylistically, then, the high Classical synthesis must be viewed as arising from an amalgam of melodies, harmonies, textures, forms and techniques drawn especially from Italian vocal music, from French dance music and from Germanic instrumental music and mastery of *stile antico* counterpoint. Once achieved, this synthesis proved to be nothing less than the birth of a new international musical language centred on German-speaking lands and spoken, in a variety of local and sometime autonomous dialects, in all Western countries from the second half of the eighteenth century until at least World War I.

Why the synthesis should have found its strongest expression in the music of the Viennese Classical style is a question without clear answers, but three possible factors may be mentioned. The Austrian Empire included within its own boundaries the Germanic culture of central Europe, the brilliant wind playing of Bohemia, the music and the vocal culture of northern Italy and a strong French connection for reasons of political expediency as well as through control of part of the Low Countries and the marriage of Joseph II's sister Marie Antoinette to Louis XVI. Thus none of the principal ingredients of the synthesis was entirely foreign.

Further, the political and economic structure of Austria combined features of both the relatively centralized arrangements of France and Britain and the highly fragmented ones in Italian- and German-speaking areas. Paris and London provided 'advanced' models for urban music because in them were brought to bear the resources of an entire nation. The decentralization of Germany and Italy, on the contrary, provided a certain hybrid vigour by creating a large number of cities, towns and courts, each with its own musical establishment. But Austria had both: numerous provincial cities, towns, noble estates and monasteries with musical cultures, yet members of the nobility from all over the Empire lived in Vienna for part of the year, imparting to it a concentration of resources comparable to those of London and Paris.

Finally, there may have been a subtle shift among Austrian patrons from emphasis upon quantity to emphasis upon quality.[12] Such a shift might help to explain why the symphonies, operas and chamber works of the most distinguished nineteenth-century composers are longer, more complicated and fewer in number than the same types of work by Mozart or Haydn. Corresponding with a trend of this kind was a change in the *Zeitgeist*, dictating a movement among composers away from producing a large amount of ephemeral music for daily use as an ornament in aristocratic establishments, towards the creating of a few masterpieces to speak to a wider public and indeed to posterity in a fixed repertory of 'classics'.

The process by which this synthesis occurred is reflected in the order of chapters in the present volume. Beginning with two main centres of the dominant musical culture at the beginning of the period, Naples and Venice, and then moving to Paris, the home of the only other style then considered to provide a serious alternative, one reaches the formerly provincial but now culturally rising regions of central Europe. Here we examine musical life in the largest urban centre (Vienna), in two provincial centres (Salzburg and Prague), at a large court (Mannheim) and a small one (Eszterháza), before moving northwards to Prussia and Saxony. Next, a visit to the not-so-insular musical society of London, where the (psychologically) equal distance from France, Germany and Italy, combined with the most advanced political, economic and social arrangements in Europe, led to an array of musical activities that strikingly prefigure many aspects of twentieth-century musical life. From there we move further into the periphery to glimpse flourishing musical cultures in Stockholm and Madrid (it could as well have been Copenhagen, St Petersburg, Warsaw, Lisbon or Dublin – or, indeed, any of a number of provincial centres in Italy, France, Germany or Austria), eventually reaching Philadelphia (it could have been Boston, New York, Baltimore or Charleston), which may stand for the spread of Western culture to other parts of the world in the age of colonization.

The rise of central European, German-speaking musical culture to a position of international prestige and dominance coincided with several long-range trends: the growth of purely instrumental music from a subsidiary position, the increase in orchestras and concert halls, the gradual replacement of the *bel canto* ideal in serious opera by a more symphonic approach to both voices and instruments, and the

1. Court musicians at the festivities for the wedding of Archduke Joseph of Austria and Princess Isabella of Parma, 1760: detail of a painting by Martin van Meytens the younger and his workshop

decline of Italian *opera buffa* and the rise of operetta in the vernacular – the ballad opera, *opéra comique*, Singspiel or zarzuela.

Underlying many of these social and stylistic changes in musical culture was one extraordinary fact: in the course of the eighteenth century, the famines and plagues that had periodically ravaged Europe throughout recorded history ceased, as a result of improvements in sanitation, medicine and nutrition. With the death rate falling, the population of Europe began to increase markedly. As improvements in agriculture made it possible for fewer farmers to feed larger numbers, and as the beginnings of the industrial revolution created new forms of employment, the growing population accumulated especially in urban centres, many of which evolved from overgrown villages to true cities. While the nobility retained much of their wealth and power in most places, in some it was now joined by a steadily increasing upper middle class. Despite the extreme difficulty of distinguishing the behaviour and tastes of upper and middle classes, and despite the fact that for every era from the Middle Ages to the end of the nineteenth century important cultural changes have been all too glibly attributed to the middle class, always said to be 'rising',[13] certain changes in the musical culture of the eighteenth century can be explained in no other way. Taken together, the flourishing of public concerts, the appearance of a market for cheap sheet music and self-tutors, and the gradual replacement of small concert halls and court-sponsored opera houses by larger venues supported in good part by ticket receipts, are the unmistakable consequences of the appearance of a new, mostly urban audience for music.

These changes had profound implications for musical style. A new class of amateurs required technically and conceptually easy music to play and sing. Simultaneously, however, an increased professionalism among musicians, demonstrated in the founding of conservatories in Paris (1795), Prague (1811), Vienna (1817), London (1822), Milan (1824) and Brussels (1832), gave rise to new levels of virtuosity among orchestras and soloists, leading in turn to both new artistic possibilities and excesses of vulgar exhibitionism 'pour épater les bourgeois'.

Among the consequences of these developments, professionals and amateurs mostly ceased to perform together, as they had done regularly in the eighteenth century in orchestral and chamber music concerts, and the roles of composer and performer became separated. In the public arena, increased dependence on income derived from ticket sales to the general public – in fact largely from the upper and upper middle classes – eventually led to larger halls and auditoriums, which in turn encouraged composing, playing and singing styles that would make an effect in such large spaces. This, as much as anything else, may have been responsible for key aspects of what in retrospect is

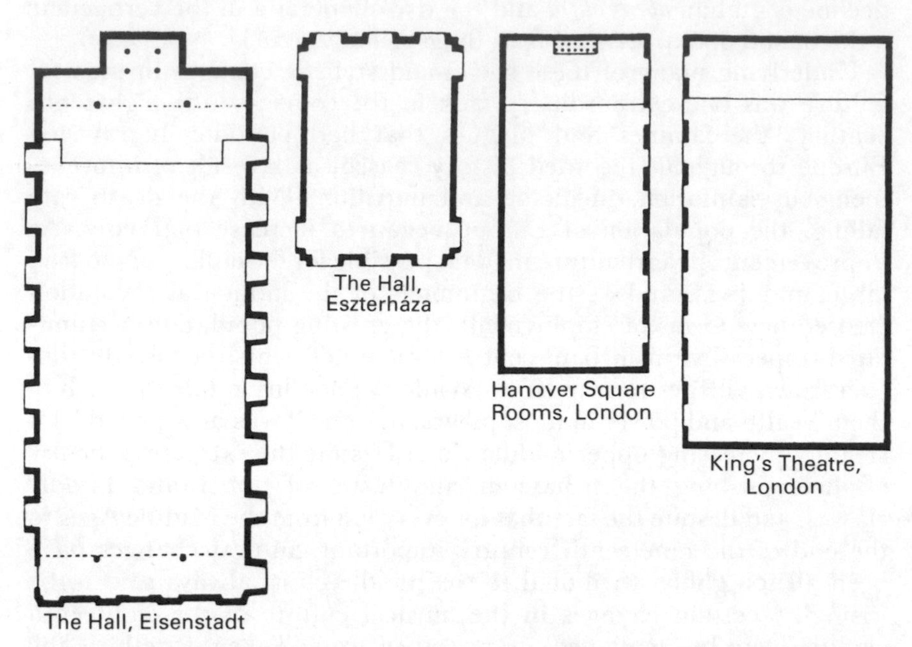

2. Comparative scale plans of the concert halls for which Haydn composed his music (courtesy of Dr Jürgen Meyer)

considered the shift from the Classical to the Romantic styles of composing, playing and singing. It is worth noting that the same period that saw the enlargement of halls and theatres (the first half of the nineteenth century) also saw a new style of interior decorating in which the hard furniture and bare floors and walls of the salons and halls of palaces and town houses were replaced by the rugs, drapery and heavily upholstered furniture of bourgeois living-rooms or parlours, providing, in place of an acoustically live space, an acoustically dampened one to which the more muscular composing and playing styles of nineteenth-century chamber music were appropriate.

The most significant and lasting stylistic or formal 'invention' of the Classical period, and the one that most powerfully facilitated the shift from a melody-orientated vocal conception to a symphonically-orientated instrumental conception as the basis for most music, vocal and instrumental, was sonata form. The power of sonata form – a particular organization of a single movement in any kind of composition, whether or not called 'sonata' (not, as the name might seem to suggest, the form of a multi-movement sonata) – resides in its ability to present and develop musical ideas and 'arguments' at unprecedented length while imparting a convincing aural unity to the whole.[14]

In the Renaissance no such means existed, and composers setting long texts and wishing to avoid purely strophic procedures simply strung together two or more related madrigals or motets, labelling them *prima pars*, *seconda pars* and so on. In the Baroque period, composers of large-scale movements resorted to recursive forms: the ostinato bass of the chaconne and passacaglia, theme and variations, the fugue with many expositions, the unifying refrain of the rondeau or the punctuating ritornello of the concertante style. These technical means and the prevailing aesthetic theory of the day (the so-called doctrine of the Affections) both required that strongly contrasting ideas and emotions be dealt with in separate movements. In the mid-eighteenth century the widespread use, for increasingly extended movements, of the two-part or binary form in which thousands of dances and other pieces were cast led gradually to the expansion of that form into what in the nineteenth century came to be called 'sonata form'. It is the peculiar genius of this formal design – which is more a procedure or set of principles for organizing and developing musical ideas than a rigid form – that a series of ideas can be presented and developed, and a dialectic among them sustained, without incoherence and without their disintegrating into so many autonomous segments related merely by contrast from one to the next, like the movements in a suite.

Charles Rosen has made a bold attempt to explain the social function of sonata form – to explain the interactions between the parallel developments of the growing middle-class audience, the rising prestige of purely instrumental music and the predominance of sonata form as the preferred means of organizing music of many types:

> For the public concert . . . proper and apt vehicles were needed, and they were provided by the sonata forms . . . When the London audiences flocked to hear Haydn in the early 1790s . . . it may have been partly Haydn himself that they were paying to see; nevertheless, it was not Haydn the performer or even Haydn the conductor, but Haydn the composer. Now pure instrumental music alone could be the principal attraction without the seductions of spectacle, the sentiments of poetry, and the emotions of drama, or even the dazzling technical virtuosity of singer and performer. The symphony could take over from drama not only the expression of sentiment but the narrative effect of dramatic action, of intrigue and resolution.
>
> The sonata forms made this possible by providing an equivalent for dramatic action, and by conferring on the contour of this action a clear definition . . .
>
> The sonata was new, above all, in its conception of a musical work as an independent musical object. It was completely written out (unlike the *da capo* aria which left the decoration to the singer), its shape was always definable by a simple contour (unlike the additive and easily extensible forms of the concerto grosso and the variation), and it was totally independent of words (unlike the madrigal and the opera). It is this status of the sonata as an independent musical

3. A scene from Act 2 of Mozart's 'Die Zauberflöte': engraving (c1793) by Joseph and Peter Schäfer, probably representing an early Czech production

> object, this reification that made possible the commercial exploitation of pure instrumental music.[15]

In the visual arts, the second half of the eighteenth century was a neo-classical period, strongly influenced by the art and architecture of ancient Greece and Rome. In music of the period certain classicizing tendencies appear that seek formal clarity and balance and the avoidance of excessive ornamentation.[16] These musical preferences arose from the same *Zeitgeist* as did contemporary neo-classical art and architecture, though primarily by means of aesthetic parallels with those sister arts, for virtually no music survived from ancient times. Sonata form may be regarded, therefore, as doing for music something analogous to what the neo-classical façade did for architecture: creating order and symmetry, balancing tension and resolution, in a medium that (unlike a façade) can be perceived only over time.

But an opposing tendency was also in evidence. The *Empfindsamer* or 'sensitive' style of C. P. E. Bach and other north German composers, the so-called 'Sturm und Drang' works of south German and Austrian symphonists and opera composers, and other proto-Romantic approaches exerted a powerful force on critical thinking about music. This is clear from, for example, the popularity of Shakespeare, whose plays only a generation earlier had been considered barbaric and 'Gothic'. Now they were read everywhere in translation. The conflict between classicizing and romanticizing approaches to music can be seen earlier in the century in the bitter antagonism between Rameau and Rousseau.[17] And it is embodied in the two operas that Mozart wrote in the last year of his life: the Metastasian *La clemenza di Tito* presents one eighteenth-century response to Aristotelian beliefs about theatre, whereas *Die Zauberflöte* could scarcely have been conceived without reference to Shakespearean, anti-classicist values.

Another cultural trend that germinated in the Classical period, even if it reached full flower only later, was the philosophy known as 'art for art's sake' (*l'art pour l'art*), which entailed collecting works and appreciating them for their purely aesthetic values, divorced from original contexts. In the fine arts this meant that artefacts that originally functioned as parts of architecture, as icons of worship, as tools or as objects of ritual use, were removed from their contexts and placed in salons, galleries or museums to be viewed purely as objects of aesthetic contemplation. In music it meant that compositions originally intended for worship, civic ceremonies, fraternal organizations, military occasions, marriages, coronations, funerals, dancing, social gatherings and so on, were now heard in concert halls.

This new use for music originally intended for other purposes had two profound effects. New music came more and more to be written for concerts rather than for daily life. Old music which had been

4. Mozart's 'La clemenza di Tito': stage design by G. Fuentes for the second scene of Act 2 in the 1799 Frankfurt production

replaced and, so to speak, had lost its function, could now be resuscitated for use in concert halls as an object of aesthetic contemplation. This represents a startling departure in the history of Western music, and many of what must be recognized as the strengths and weaknesses of modern and post-modern Western art music and concert life can be traced to this fateful metamorphosis. Much that is now taken for granted about the conditions of present-day music, opera and concert life first appeared in the period studied in this volume, lending it special interest for modern music-lovers trying to understand aspects of their own musical culture.

NOTES

[1] J. Spitzer and N. Zaslaw, 'Improvised Ornamentation in Eighteenth-Century Orchestras', *JAMS*, xxxix (1986), 524–77.

[2] Thomas Arne's version of *God Save the King* (1745), Claude-Joseph Roget de Lisle's *La Marseillaise* (1792) and Joseph Haydn's *Gott erhalte Franz den Kaiser* (1797).

[3] M. H. Abrams, 'From Addison to Kant: Modern Aesthetics and Exemplary Art', in *Studies in Eighteenth-Century British Art and Aesthetics*, ed. R. Cohen (Berkeley, 1985), 16–48; idem, ' "Art-as-Such": the Sociology of Modern Aesthetics', *Bulletin of the American Academy of Arts and Sciences*, xxxviii/6 (1985), 8–33.

[4] J. LaRue, *A Catalogue of 18th-Century Symphonies*, i (Bloomington, 1988).

[5] N. Zaslaw, 'Meanings for Mozart's Symphonies', *Mozart's Symphonies: Context, Performance Practice, Reception* (Oxford, 1989).

[6] R. Fiske, *English Theatre Music in the Eighteenth Century* (Oxford, 2/1983) contains documentation of, and complaints against, the favouritism accorded to foreign musicians; see also F. Petty, *Italian Opera in London 1760–1800* (Ann Arbor, 1980).

[7] G. Flaherty, 'Mozart and the Mythologization of Genius', in *Studies in Eighteenth-Century Culture*, ed. J. W. Yolton and J. E. Brown (East Lansing, 1988), 289–309, especially 289.

[8] D. Burrows, 'Music and the *nausea delle cose cotidiane*', *MQ*, lvii (1971), 230–40.

[9] The following remarks about St Petersburg are based on J. von Staehlin, *Zur Geschichte des Theaters in Russland; Nachrichten von der Tanzkunst und Balletten in Russland; Nachrichten von der Musik in Russland* (Riga, 1769–70), repr. with an afterword and index by F. Stöckl (Leipzig, 1982); and three monographs by R.-A. Mooser: *Annales de la musique et des musiciens en Russie au XVIIIme siècle* (Geneva, 1948–51); *L'opéra comique français en Russie au XVIIIme siècle* (Geneva, 2/1954); and *Opéras, intermezzos, ballets, cantates, oratorios joués en Russie durant le XVIIIe siècle* (Basle, 3/1964).

[10] J. J. Quantz, *On Playing the Flute* (1752), trans. and ed. E. Reilly (New York, 2/1988), 321–42.

[11] This refers to Couperin's *Les goûts réünis* (Paris, 1724), a collection of suites for two instruments and harpsichord.

[12] A. Ringer, 'Mozart and the Josephian Era: some Socio-Economic Notes on Musical Change', *CMc*, no.9 (1969), 158–65.

[13] W. Weber, 'The Muddle of the Middle Classes', *19th-Century Music*, iii (1979–80), 175–85.

[14] For the best summary of the history of this form, see J. Webster, 'Sonata form', *Grove 6*.

[15] C. Rosen, *Sonata Forms* (New York, 1980), 8–15, especially 9–10.

[16] The painter Jacques-Louis David described the strict avoidance of Baroque and Rococo ornamentation in his neo-classical canvases as 'removing the chicory'; see T. Crow, '*The Oath of the Horatii* in 1785: Painting and Pre-Revolutionary Radicalism in France', *Art History*, i (1978), 424–71.

[17] C. Kintzler, *Jean-Philippe Rameau: splendeur et naufrage de l'esthétique du plaisir à l'âge classique* (Paris, 1983).

Chapter II

Italy: Two Opera Centres

DENNIS LIBBY

One of the striking aspects of eighteenth-century music is the antagonism that often marks the relations between its leading national varieties – French, German and Italian. This is particularly true of the confrontation between German and Italian music. Partisans of one were not often willing to recognize the worth of the other, formulating their condemnation in terms that reveal a good deal about the conflicting aesthetic principles of each. For Italians, the very term 'musica tedesca' was one of reproach, signifying an inability to write properly for the human voice – a crucial failing in Italian eyes, which recognized only the voice and vocal melody as agents of true expression. Then there was the German fondness for excessive complexity, learnedness and forwardness in the use of musical elements such as harmony, tonal structure and texture; if these were not kept strictly subordinate to vocal melody there could be none of the naturalness and clarity that were essential to good taste and beauty. Partisans of German music often regarded Italian music as shallow and insipid, flimsy in construction and shoddy in workmanship; in their opinion its emphasis on the voice had led to an excess of vocal virtuosity at the expense of true musical substance and interest.

The judgment of history, both figuratively and literally, has come down resoundingly on the German side. The Italian music that dominated so much of musical culture in this period disappeared with the period itself, and occasional attempts at resuscitation have not enjoyed the success of the revivals of Vivaldi or even of Rossini. Music history has still not completely freed itself from attitudes prevailing in its formative days as a scholarly discipline in nineteenth-century Germany. A moral tone and vocabulary tend to enter the discussion when eighteenth-century Italian music is at issue. It was a period of decadence, we often read, in which composers sacrificed their artistic integrity to satisfy singers' demands for empty virtuoso display. As a result of such 'abuses', there arose the need for reform, which was provided by Gluck, whom, however, the Italians, much to their discredit, largely ignored. In this formulation we can still hear the echoes of eighteenth-century polemics on topics that were again passionately argued in the debates about Wagnerism, leading to an orthodox view of the proper relation of music, words and drama so strong that the changing intellectual and artistic currents of several generations have not yet completely swept it away.

Is later eighteenth-century Italian music – or more specifically its central genre, *opera seria* – most profitably approached in terms of 'decadence', 'abuse', 'reform' and the like? We shall begin to reject such concepts when we recognize how profoundly Italian musical practice was performer-orientated; the creative function was not exercised by the composer alone, but was divided between composer and performer. (This is clearly unlike more composer-orientated music, such as much German music of the eighteenth and nineteenth centuries, in which the performer's function is to realize or at most to interpret, the composer's 'intentions', as they are often called.) In Italian music of this period, as practice was systematized by theory, the composer determined the general character and structure of the composition and filled in its main outlines, leaving the surface detail to be supplied spontaneously by the performer in the heightened state induced by performance. This division of function was conceived of as complementary, with the contributions of composer and performer both essential to the final result; the reflective creativity of the composer was reinforced by the spontaneous creativity of the performer, thus combining the powers unique to each.

For this to work, a close rapport – almost a symbiotic relationship – had to exist between composer and performer. The composer did not react solely to inner urges or to words and dramatic situations and then hand on the result to the performer for his contribution. Rather he wrote for the performer from the outset as for a specific instrument of a highly defined technical and temperamental character. The performer was expected to be sensitive to the character of the music as the composer had determined it, for it was the performer's task to intensify that character. This is especially true of the improvised ornamentation that was one of the primary performance techniques of the period, ranging from the intensification of a single note by more or less conventional ornamental figures to the melodic diminution and free variation that could considerably alter the surface of the music (see fig.14 below). From a later, composer-orientated point of view performers' ornamentation has often been dismissed as extraneous, even impertinent, decoration; for Italian music it was an essential agent of expression.

In effect, then, the singer's contribution to an aria in performance is to be regarded not as post-compositional but as the final stage in the act of composition itself. It follows that it was not the composer's score but the performed music that embodied the finished work of art, one that was both fluid – varying with each realization – and ephemeral, not directly recoverable. This concept of performance as work of art can profitably be regarded as the central principle of this musical practice. It makes clear that the score alone (the final stage of the work that remains) cannot appropriately be analysed, judged, performed or listened to in the same way as a score of composer-centric music. It also allows much that from a later perspective may seem unusual or problematical (contributing to judgments about 'decadence', 'abuse' and the like) to be comprehended as coherently related elements of a musical system. For example, patterns of conventionality and individuality, and of what might be called familiarity and unfamiliarity, are in this system rather different from those that now tend to be considered normal.

Because composers wrote specifically for their singers, taking into account, as far as they were able, their character and abilities as performers, singers were not only permitted but encouraged to develop (within general limits of style and taste) their full individuality. It is clear from contemporary sources, both written and musical, that the resulting interplay between singers' physical instruments and their musical temperaments produced a great range of vocal styles comparable in their way to composers' styles. This is more akin to what is found today among performers of popular music and jazz (for example) than in classical music, where performers tend to be shaped and restricted by the demands of a classic repertory. In the performance-orientated genres of eighteenth-century Italian music a classic repertory had no chance of forming. Once an *opera seria* company dispersed, an opera composed for it was unlikely to be performed again, at least not without considerable alterations to fit it to the new company. This is in strong contrast to the different circumstances of the opera libretto, many of which, particularly those of Metastasio, became classics and were produced many times but usually with new music.

As a result, audiences could generally assume that the music they heard in the opera house would be new music. Indeed, the perception by the public that a composer's or performer's style was old-fashioned or *passé* was likely to be fatal. At the same time, because of the importance of the opera house as a gathering place for society, the audience throughout the often lengthy run of an opera consisted to a large extent of the same people. This meant that even new music was soon extremely familiar, and this in turn helps to explain the emphasis on spontaneity and fluidity of performance. They served to maintain the music's freshness over repeated hearings.

In general, most performer-orientated music that includes an element of improvisational freedom seems to balance this with a measure of conventionality of some sort. These conventional procedures create a framework of familiarity that serves as the basis for improvisation and for the listener's perception of it. Eighteenth-century Italian music was indeed highly conventionalized. That this should be so was largely taken for granted in an age whose general aesthetics still had their deepest roots in the kind of classicism that divided art into standard genres with sharply defined boundaries and internal procedures. This conventionality has, however, been decried by later historians, particularly with regard to opera; the orthodox view, especially since Wagner, has stressed the paramount importance of moulding the music on every level from large structure to small detail as closely as possible to the dramatic action. It was precisely in this respect that the *opera seria* composer was most bound by convention: it determined the structure of the opera as a succession of recitatives and arias and little else, and the structure of the aria itself, limited in the first part of this period to the da capo form. The number of arias in an opera had been steadily decreasing since the seventeenth century, as their individual length increased. As a result, a mid-century composer had considerably less flexibility than one of the generation of Alessandro Scarlatti when it came to arranging the succession of arias for some dramatic or musical purpose. By this time even the star singers were seldom allotted more than five arias, later often only three. Further, they were expected to demonstrate in every opera their mastery of the three principal styles of Italian singing – the cantabile, the *grazioso* and the bravura or *brillante* – by singing one aria in each style. Even their ordering became subject to convention. The primo uomo (first castrato) usually sang his *aria di bravura* in the first act, his aria cantabile in the second and his *aria grazioso* in the third. Obviously, dramatic action was to a large extent moulded to a standardized operatic format rather than the reverse.

For the most part, this format varied little from place to place, and the constant circulation of composers and singers among the theatres of Europe – which had the effect of producing ever new combinations in the creative interaction of composers and singers, a major factor in maintaining the genre's vitality – helped to enforce a homogeneity of musical practice. It also ensured that innovations in style, the area in which composers were most free to demonstrate originality, rapidly became known everywhere and available for absorption into the common musical language.

This does not mean that there were no variations of local taste to which composers and singers had to adjust. Local musical culture took its direction from a city's general culture and from its dominant institutions, musical and otherwise. For example, the presence of a court was an important factor. In a small city such as Turin, court music tended to monopolize musical life and to give it an intensity and brilliance that it would not otherwise have had. The influence of a court with foreign tastes was especially noticeable, as in the Frenchify-

5. The castrato Manzuoli as Theseus, fighting the Minotaur in Giuseppe Ponzo's 'Arianna e Teseo', performed at the Teatro Regio, Milan, in Carnival 1762: engraving by Marc' Antonio dal Re after Fabrizio Galliari

ing tendency of operas at the court of Parma in the 1750s and 1760s. Foreign rule could be highly influential, as it was at Milan where the Austrian presence almost certainly had something to do with the continued cultivation of instrumental music at a time when it had sunk to insignificance in the rest of Italy. In Bologna the Accademia Filarmonica had evolved into the central institution in the city's musical life, giving it a tone of serious purpose and high professionalism that was further enhanced by the presence of Padre Martini, whose reputation for profound musical knowledge was universal and enormous.

Some cities had more distinctive musical tastes than others. Rome, for example, had the reputation of being highly discriminating and given to extremes of enthusiasm and disapprobation. This was apparently due to the army of clerics in minor orders who infested the city, hangers-on of the papal bureaucracy and the entourages of prelates, many of them with little to do, it would seem, except to hone their aesthetic sensibilities and to pass judgment on works of art. In 1770 the castrato Manzuoli, near the end of a long and brilliant career, was reported to be reluctant to accept an engagement in Rome because, having been esteemed everywhere, 'he did not wish to end by being hissed by four abbés'. In the end he came, and it was decided 'that he does not sing from the heart, and that he knows little of music, and that he has no style'.[1]

A correspondent for Cramer's *Magazin der Musik* implies that Mysliveček's failure as an opera composer in Rome in 1780 gave particular satisfaction because he had long been a great favourite in Naples, and his Roman failure thus demonstrated the greater discrimination of Roman taste.[2] (Neapolitan taste was viewed with suspicion elsewhere in Italy. While it gave rise to the boldness and originality of Neapolitan music and, according to Burney, the 'energy and fire'[3] of Neapolitan musical performance, it was also considered at times to infect the arts with a touch of what another writer called the 'Capriccioso and Stravagante'.[4] By contrast Burney saw the essential quality of Venetian music as 'delicacy of taste'.[5])

Somewhat paradoxically, the music favoured by Roman audiences does not seem always to have been characterized by as refined an expression as one might have expected. Alessandro Verri, in 1768, described the Roman taste in *opera seria* as follows: 'The style that pleases at Rome is to make a great play of instruments under the voice, great contrasts, vigorously to reinforce or reduce the sound, much novelty'.[6] Some of these predilections appear to have long been prevalent in Rome. A correspondent of the *Allgemeine musikalische Zeitung* in 1807 refers to the Roman liking for 'usciti di stromenti di fiato' in opera accompaniments,[7] and Pergolesi's addition of fanfare-like passages for wind and brass to the sinfonia of a Naples opera when he re-used it in *L'Olimpiade* for Rome in 1735 suggests that composers were already taking this into account.

The city, therefore, is the context into which this music needs to be fitted – a framework of social, institutional and aesthetic factors that helped to determine its character. In what follows, Italian music will be examined in the context of Naples and Venice. These two cities cannot fully represent the diversity of Italian musical life in this period, but they can suggest some of its richness.

NAPLES

Naples in the eighteenth century was by far the largest city in Italy and more than twice the size of Venice, which ranked second. Our image of Naples derives largely from travellers' accounts. The city often made a powerful and exotic impression: streets choked with people; extreme contrasts of wealth and poverty (the latter somewhat tempered, in northern eyes, by the mild climate, the picturesque setting and the ease with which the necessities of life were obtained); strange and colourful customs and superstitions. Little sense is usually conveyed of the economic and social structures that supported Neapolitan life. Naples was a pre-industrial, even a pre-capitalist city, and the increase in its population in this period (from 295,000 in 1742 to 437,000 in 1802) was more the result of greater misery in the somewhat feudal countryside than of opportunities in the capital. In the absence of extensive commerce and manufacturing there was a relatively small middle class, which seems to have been dominated by government functionaries and a plague of lawyers.

Given a city of such size, strangeness and confusion, it is not surprising that travellers' impressions of the character, condition and way of life of the Neapolitans varied greatly. This is exemplified by what they said about music. By the beginning of this period Naples had achieved the reputation of being the leading musical centre of Italy, and many visitors described the streets as resounding with music:

> The common sort . . . work till evening; then take their lute or guitar (for they all play) and walk about the city, or upon the seashore with it, to enjoy the fresco. One sees their little brown children jumping about stark-naked, and the bigger ones dancing with castenets, while others play on the cymbal to them.[8]

On the other hand another Englishman maintained with the enthusiasm of a debunker that:

6. Music and dance by the Bay of Naples: painting (c1770) by Pietro Fabris

> there is no place where music seems to be in less esteem than Naples, or where so little is heard; no one ever attends to it, even from the finest singers and performers, and even the common people appear utter strangers to it. There is no national music, and, except for a few drawling kind of *sequadillas*, probably bequeathed to them by the Spaniards, you never hear any such things as vielles, organs, guitars, etc. in the streets.[9]

This writer does allow that musicians were often 'sent for to entertain the parties that in summer sup on the shore of Posillipo', and it appears from all accounts that the outdoor recreations that took place in summer along the shore of the Bay of Naples at Chiaja, Mergellina and Posillipo supported the city's musical reputation.

From 1782 a summer fair was held at Chiaja (now part of central Naples): 'Every summer for about two months the night is illuminated by an infinitude of torches, and in the middle is erected an orchestra on which students of the three music conservatories of our city play most beautiful sinfonias and notturnos until after midnight'.[10] On the water itself 'until the beginning of autumn, one sees little boats [*barchette*] in abundance which cover the sea full of musicians and people enjoying themselves; and in Mergellina there abounded at one time serenades, night music [*musiche notturne*] and suppers'.[11] Many of the surviving collections of canzonettas and notturnos (the latter, when applied to vocal music, designating canzonettas for two voices) from this period were probably sung by amateurs and professionals on such occasions. Indeed, some specify that they were 'made for Posillipo', some of them probably for concerts at the royal villa, the Casino di Delizia, which the king and queen often used in the summer from the early 1770s. In summer 1780, for example, the press reported that on one occasion the violinist Nardini played for them there; on another they heard the great soprano Anna De Amicis and the castrato Luigi Marchesi, who was then engaged at the Teatro San Carlo.

There were no public concerts in the modern sense in eighteenth-century Naples, nor in Italy generally. From 1777 the Accademia de' Cavalieri, devoted to gambling, dancing and music, gave brilliant concerts for members and guests. Membership was restricted to the nobility and to military officers and the like. However, any respectable citizen or well-recommended tourist could attend the many concerts in private houses in celebration of weddings, baptisms, name days and other such occasions, often with specially composed music. The greatest religious festivals of the Neapolitans were the two for S Gennaro in May and September and Corpus Christi in June, celebrated with great ceremony, processions through the streets, a specially constructed *apparato* or *macchina* and often a cantata on an appropriate Italian text by a more or less well-known composer.

Of the forces that powered Neapolitan music, perhaps the most essential was the presence of the musical conservatories, for it was they that produced the majority of the composers and many of the male performers who carried on the city's intense professional musical activity and spread its reputation throughout Europe. Indeed, relatively few of the important figures of this period generally thought of as Neapolitan composers were native Neapolitans (although some, such as Jommelli and Cimarosa, both of whom were born in Aversa, came from very close by). Cimarosa grew up in Naples, as did Sacchini, who was born in Florence. Many of the others – among them Piccinni, Paisiello and Traetta – were Neapolitans in the sense that they came from within the kingdom. From an early period the conservatories attracted students from other parts of Italy (and eventually beyond). There were virtually no institutions like these conservatories elsewhere in Italy at this time. In the later part of the century, particularly, it is obvious from many composers' biographies that even though they may have received most of their musical education elsewhere, the final polish resulting from a few years in Naples was considered very desirable.

It was possible for a composer to have a distinguished career outside the theatres, in the church or as a conservatory master. Francesco Durante, one of the great figures of the second quarter of the century, never got closer to dramatic music than the oratorio. However, the opera house was the centre of musical life and success there caused a composer to be sought after for every other genre as well. *Opera seria* was the most prestigious theatrical genre. The king had the final choice of composers for the Teatro San Carlo, and a system developed whereby a composer proved himself by writing successfully for the comic theatres before being given a commission for the San Carlo. It was possible to circumvent this system, however. In 1778 the Spanish composer Martín y Soler composed and directed an outdoor symphony with a part for twenty cannons performed by the king himself, who took a great delight in all things military (except for actual fighting). Although Martín had previously written nothing for the theatres of Naples but ballet music, he was given a San Carlo commission the next day.[12]

The connection between *opera seria* and the ruler was a close and important one. After the Spanish Bourbon prince Charles drove out the Austrians and established himself as King of Naples in 1735, one of the early concerns of the new reign was a building programme. This was standard royal practice. Great public buildings and palaces demonstrated the semi-divinity of the ruler through his ability to create beyond the power of ordinary men, and often further allowed the king to be viewed in grand settings that enhanced the royal presence. (The Bourbons of Naples needed as much enhancement as possible. Thomas Gray described Charles and his queen as being 'as ugly a little pair as one can see',[13] while their son Ferdinand's lack of regal attributes of any kind was legendary.)

That one of the first of Charles's building projects should have been a grand new opera house bearing his own name and placed next to his palace is indicative of the importance of *opera seria* as an appurtenance of royalty. The political purpose of the opera is especially evident in Charles's case, for the only art he is known to have enjoyed was hunting. The Teatro San Carlo opened on 4 November 1737, the king's name day, and for the rest of the century its schedule of three or (from 1746) four operas a year was determined by Bourbon birthdays and name days. Premières were a part of gala court celebrations in which the theatre was fully illuminated and remained so throughout the performance. Mirrors hung in front of the boxes multiplied the effect. In the age before gas and electric lighting brilliant artificial light was an expensive luxury, and providing copious quantities of it was an act of royal magnificence.

Spectacle and magnificence were as much in evidence on the San Carlo stage as in its auditorium. This is not surprising. Absolutist monarchs had long used quasi-theatrical techniques in the display of power and the rituals of monarchy, and the same human susceptibilities made them effective in both spheres. The French traveller de Brosses wrote that the Italians:

> fill their [operas] with a great display of marches, of sacrificial rites, of ceremonies of all sorts, which they render with a detail that is authentic, curious and amusing . . . Processions are numerous, sometimes with a hundred or a hundred and fifty participants . . . The spectacle of these triumphal chariots, of this crowd, of all this apparatus makes an impression of pomp and magnificence . . . The public especially loves fights, mêlees; to please the parterre there has to be such a show in every opera.[14]

The surviving account books of the San Carlo provide further details. The production in 1741 of Metastasio's *Ezio* with music by Sarri is typical. It begins with a triumphal procession and features an uprising of the Roman people in Act 3. The accounts refer to a grand triumphal chariot full of trophies, eight horses, four camels, lions, 60 supernumeraries dressed *alla Romana*, four leaders of the supernumeraries, sixteen freed slaves dressed in silk of different colours, six slaves dressed as soldiers of Attila the Hun, a stage band of eight members, 37 swordsmen representing the Roman people, twelve swordsmen playing soldiers of the emperor and twelve Praetorian guards. There were also fourteen pages and maids attending the principal characters.

Scenic effects were often spectacular. The accounts for *Il trionfo di Camilla* (1740; music by Porpora) describe how a river was constructed on stage with water flowing down a hill, under a real bridge and into a

7. The theatre in the Palazzo Reale, Naples, during a performance (6 November 1747) of Giuseppe de Majo's serenata 'Il sogno d'Olimpia': engraving by Giuseppe Vasi after Vincenzo Re, from 'Narrazione delle solenni reali feste fatte per celebrare in Napoli . . . la nascita di . . . Filippo Principe della Due Sicilie' (1748)

tank large enough for a battle to take place on the water. Real fire was provided for *Didone abbandonata* and *Adriano in Siria*, for which 200 imitation building stones as well as pieces of cornice, columns and balustrades were manufactured to represent the collapse of a building.

The mutual reflection of auditorium and stage went beyond spectacle and magnificence to a more precise political message. The arrangement of the audience was a paradigm of society itself, compartmentalized and hierarchical. The ordering of the boxes radiated out from the royal box at the centre, each representing a social unit – primarily noble families but also foreign ambassadors, court functionaries and the like – all ranged above the lower orders spread across the floor below.

The dramas presented on stage, especially those of Metastasio, had as a central concern the functioning of that order and its consequences. Their characters represent a hierarchical society dependent on a quasi-feudal system of mutual ethical prerogatives and obligations defined by society's roles and relationships, those of ruler and subject – and its familial parallel of father and child – of consanguinity, of friendship and of love. The harmony of this system is disturbed when obligations conflict, and the affected character, because of an inability to master the passions within himself, balks at observing the proper priorities, usually by giving unsanctioned precedence to a love relationship.

Following the classical (or neo-classical) aesthetic, the drama sought to delight and move the onlooker as a means of making him virtuous – virtue here being the observance of a certain code of social conduct. The opera house and its auditorium had the complementary goal of dazzling and impressing the onlooker to reinforce his belief in the power and stability of the existing social order. These influences were largely subliminal; to those who frequented it, the opera's social function was as a gathering place for the upper classes:

> In the fashionable world, the morning is spent in a slovenly deshabille, that prevents their going out, or receiving frequent visits at home. Reading, or work takes up a very small portion of this part of the day; so that it passes away in a yawning sort of nonchalance. People are scarcely wide awake, till about dinner-time. But, a few hours after, the important business of the toilette puts them gently into motion; and, at length, the opera calls them completely into existence. But it must be understood, that the drama, or the music, do not form a principal object of theatrical amusement. Every lady's box is the scene of tea, cards, cavaliers, servants, lap-dogs, abbés, scandal, and assignations; attention to the action of the piece, to the scenes, or even to the actors, male, or female, is but a secondary affair. If there be some actor, or actress, whose merit, or good fortune, happens to demand the universal homage of fashion, there are pauses of silence, and the favourite airs may be heard. But without this cause, or the presence of the sovereign, all is noise, hubbub, and confusion, in an Italian audience. The hour of the theatre, however, with all its mobbing and disturbance, is the happiest part of the day, to every Italian, of whatever station; and the least affluent will sacrifice some portion of his daily bread, rather than not enjoy it.[15]

This intermittent attention given to an opera was not conducive to making the integration of a work or a uniformly high level of quality a priority for composers. In terms of material success the composer was better advised to concentrate on producing two or three arias with the power to stop conversation. These circumstances had predictable consequences. Several writers of the later part of the century mention that it had become common for a busy and successful composer not to write operatic recitative but to give the task to an assistant or apprentice. Extant autograph scores of some composers seem to confirm this; in many of those of Paisiello, for example, the recitative appears to be in another hand. To the extent that such practices represent a lack of concern for the quality of certain parts of an opera, they can be said to be a falling away from the genre's own ideals. At the same time, criticism in terms of such now familiar concepts as the 'integrity' of the work of art or its 'organic unity' should be carefully considered in the light of the nature of the genre itself, many of whose salient characteristics point in a somewhat different direction.

Operatic stage deportment required extremes of formality and informality. Acting involved using highly stylized gestures and statuesque poses. However, the actors were not expected always to be 'in character', especially when they were not themselves reciting, and this convention sometimes led them to a freedom of behaviour that, in at least some cases, was deliberately provocative. This convention, though, was not an unreasonable one in a kind of drama in which realism, in the usual sense of the word, and the creation of characters as individuals were not the goals of either dramatist or performer. The neo-classical aesthetic saw the individualization of character as diminishing rather than increasing dramatic power. Instead of seeking the universal in the individual, as in Shakespeare and the Romantic drama, neo-classical drama sought the universal in the universal. From this results an emphasis on generic types. A king, for cxample, should act like a king, with no contrary traits. A king of what in the eighteenth century was considered a barbarian country should behave differently from one who was the legatee of Greek civilization, as in the confrontation of the Indian King Porus and Alexander the Great in Metastasio's *Alessandro nell'Indie*; but the neuroses of the Spanish Bourbons were not acceptable dramatic material, however much they might have appealed to Shakespeare.

Similarly, costumes and scenery did not aim at authenticity of time or place; at most they alluded to them while adhering to a largely self-sufficient tradition of theatrical design. The actors were usually positioned towards the front of the stage rather than within the set, which in scenes of long perspective was necessarily out of proportion when they moved very far into it (as they must have done in crowd scenes). Scenery thus had an essentially referential function rather than creating the illusion of a real place.

Some of these procedures have led many later writers to claim that *opera seria* was undramatic ('a concert in costume' has become a critical cliché for this genre). This may be so according to certain definitions of 'dramatic', but at the same time these practices were all highly theatrical in the sense that their frame of reference was a self-contained theatrical practice that created its own world and its own rules rather than aiming at the illusion of something that passes for everyday reality. In this, of course, *opera seria* belongs to an older phase of European drama that was being challenged and gradually supplanted in this period by a new orientation towards authenticity (in scenery and costumes), realism (in characterization and situation) and naturalism (in acting).

8. Interior of the Teatro Regio, Turin, during a performance of Feo's opera seria 'Arsace': painting (1740) by Pietro Domenico Olivero

This all has great relevance to the relation between music and drama in *opera seria*. The suggestion of individualized character is no more the aim of the composer than of the dramatist. The arias create strongly delineated expressions of feeling, but of a generic sort. It was indeed in relation to the general stylistic categories of Italian singing – the cantabile, *grazioso*, bravura, *parlante* – that the individuality and expression of an aria was likely to be judged rather than dramatic characterization. Further, aria form was highly standardized as well. Just as poets shaped aria texts almost exclusively in two stanzas, usually quatrains, so composers during much of this period not only set them in the well-known da capo form, but employed internal formal procedures that were in many respects equally predetermined.

It was because of this that arias could be transferred rather freely from one opera to another, a practice found shocking by some later critics with different views of dramatic characterization and organic unity.

Similarly, the anti-realism of acting and staging – the prominence of procedures that call attention to themselves as theatrical devices – has a parallel in the musical-dramatic method of alternating recitatives, in which the dialogue was set, and arias, moments of greater musical expressiveness. This was a system that stressed disjunction rather than a minute ebb and flow of dramatic tension and emotion. Indeed, the degree of disjunction actually increased as the arias became longer and more elaborate in the course of the century.

From this perspective it can be seen that the tailoring of *opera seria* arias to the temperament and technique of their singers was not necessarily detrimental to dramatic values – in terms of the dramatic values that the genre itself embodied – but actually constituted one of the genre's principal sources of real individuality, acting as a counterweight to its generic characterization, situations and aria types.

A good example of how these elements worked together in practice is provided by the *opera seria* duet. Until the 1780s the duet was always sung by the primo uomo and prima donna and had a highly conventionalized format. It began (after the orchestral introduction) with a lyrical solo that was immediately repeated with different words by the other singer. A short passage of dialogue followed and then a lengthy section in which the singers shared material of various sorts, much of it involving florid passage-work, sometimes together in parallel thirds or sixths, sometimes in the overlapping alternation of short phrases. This format was subject to minor variation (and developed from da capo to through-composed form), but it had relatively little dramatic potential from a later point of view. Apart from the relatively insignificant passage of dialogue, the singers mostly shared the same musical material, so there was little opportunity for creating conflict or dynamic dramatic interaction between the characters, on which later styles place such emphasis.

There was, however, the potential for considerable 'dramatic' interaction of the singers *qua* singers, and this was almost certainly a principal factor in the way the duet developed. In a solo aria the singer reacted to what the composer had written and to the feeling of the moment. The duet added a further dimension in that two singers also reacted spontaneously to each other. Their sharing of so much common material sharpened the confrontation. When kept within the bounds of art the results must have been sometimes exhilarating, at others disappointing. Ill-will could bring catastrophe, of which Croce recorded an amusing example from an official report, once in the San Carlo archives, involving Caffarelli and the prima donna Astrua in the performance of the duet in Hasse's *Antigono* on 4 January 1745:

> The castrato Caffarelli began by employing in the first two verses a manner of singing different from that which was written in the part composed by Hasse; and although Astrua, who had to respond to it, was caught unawares, she nevertheless acquitted herself in the best manner possible so that the first and second parts [of the three-part da capo form] ended peacefully; but then in repeating the first part Caffarelli used still another manner [of singing] rather different from the first, full of offbeats and syncopation, and even with the anticipation of the bar by a beat, and when Astrua in responding to him was attempting to find her way back into the correct time, which had gone wrong, Caffarelli had the audacity not only to indicate with his hands how she should manage the time, but also suggested vocally the [correct] manner of responding to the [melodic] proposal that he had made. This was seen and heard by everyone, and I cannot fully express how scandalous was its result, because immediately there was a general murmur and outcry because of the reaction of the people in the boxes and on the floor. All the more since there were those who said that Caffarelli had come with some intention of attacking Astrua in this way on stage and had warned the orchestra players to pay strict attention when playing the arias and especially the duet.[16]

On this occasion the performance had succumbed to one of the great perils inherent in the Italian musical system: Caffarelli was a great singer but an equally impossible person, and this was not an unusual combination. The ideal on which the genre rested, that of the delicate balance and sympathetic creative interaction of composer and performers, must sometimes have received rough treatment in practice, often from those who had been responsible for its greatest triumphs.

The aesthetic principle that had justified and encouraged the course of Italian music in the eighteenth century was that the voice was the only agent of true expression. However, this principle had as a corollary the old idea that music in itself had no self-sufficient meaning or expression; these were imparted to it by the words that were sung. Therefore the only proper function of music was to intensify the meaning and expression embodied in words. For most eighteenth-century Italian writers on the subject, who were generally men of letters not musicians, this meant through the intensification of the declamatory properties of the text. However, the general direction of Italian music, especially in the decades following the 1720s, was towards varied and often elaborate vocal and compositional techniques in which the relation between text and music became increasingly varied as well, and the notion that the music rested on a basis of text declamation became more difficult to maintain. This represented a *de facto* rejection by musicians of this aspect of traditional aesthetics and an intuitive recognition (and demonstration) by them that the possible relations between text and music were actually much more complex.

Interestingly, this did not lead to a rethinking of aesthetic doctrine to bring it into line with practice, but rather to a vigorous critical opposition to current operatic practice that is usually characterized by historians as 'operatic reform'. Although new aesthetic approaches to the meaning of music were being put forward outside Italy, there is little sign of them in the debates over Italian opera until near the end of the century. Men of letters were not likely to give up the primacy of the word, and therefore of the poet, in the relation of words and music, even had they been able to grasp the possibility. Their position was reinforced by other contemporary trends.

The 1750s, when reform became an important issue, also saw the rise of neo-classicism, one of the arts' periodic returns to classical antiquity for renewal. The innovatory aspect of neo-classicism was that it was a return directly to Greek rather than Roman antiquity, leading to a positive reappraisal of what had previously been regarded as the excessive starkness of older Greek art and architecture and the brutality of Greek tragedy. These were now reinterpreted as an ideal of harmonious simplicity and tragic strength. As for music, there was a natural association between neo-classicism and the principle that music should serve text declamation, since that principle, supported by classical authorities, was closely associated with an ideal of simplicity. This association was to be embodied in practice in the so-called reform operas of Gluck and Calzabigi, which, especially in *Alceste*, sought a tone of classical tragedy and musical restraint, both in conscious reaction to the contemporary *opera seria*.

These questions of art took on a wider scope through the tendency of much Enlightenment thought to see presumed decadence in the arts as symptomatic of the decadence and irrationality of society and its institutions. This tendency was particularly strong in Naples because of the continuing influence on local intellectuals of Vico's thought, in which the close interconnection of a society's culture, institutions and arts is a basic premise. The result was a powerful alliance of forces that made opera reform both modern and moral, and therefore of considerable appeal to idealists – especially young ones – as an end in itself and as an instrument of larger cultural and political goals.

In fact, reform was really revolution, both in music and in its broader implications. In opera it looked towards an artistic system that was hierarchical rather than collaborative. The composer served the poet, and the performer served the composer. Further, its largely negative attitude towards decoration closed off, or at least greatly limited, one of the performer's principal means of expression and individuality. Reform thus proposed not just a change of tone, format and style for the musical drama, but a rejection of the Italian musical system.

This did not happen, but a change in the balance of the relationship between composer and performer is apparent in the second half of the century. Before that, conventions had attained a pervasiveness and rigidity that severely limited the composer's freedom. A mid-century opera often consisted entirely of the alternation of da capo arias and recitatives, unvaried even by a duet. However, as the pendulum gradually swung towards the composer, duets became more common, then act-ending trios and quartets; eventually more varied aria forms replaced the earlier uniformity. These developments were very noticeable by the 1770s, and by the mid-1780s the genre was in the process of transformation. However, change seems to have been guided by regulating elements of public taste that were permissive in some respects but highly conservative in others. The case of Nicolò Jommelli is illuminating in this respect.

Probably no Italian of this period is more easily recognizable by modern eyes as a great composer than Jommelli. During a fifteen-year service as music director at Stuttgart, and thanks to the complete artistic control he had there, Jommelli had vigorously asserted the composer's role in opera. He took great pains with recitative, tried to compensate for the deficiencies of secondary singers by increasing the interest of the non-vocal elements of their arias, such as textures and the interplay of instruments among themselves and with the voice. He also did it in the star arias without sacrificing his obligation to provide opportunity for the creative participation of the great singers. All this was within a format that often included dancing in the opera or other spectacular elements. As a result, the concept of organic unity of the opera as a whole is appropriately applied to his work.

On returning to Naples in 1769, Jommelli found himself in an equivocal position. A group of partisans that included some of the city's musical connoisseurs seems to have seen him as the means of changing the direction of *opera seria* and to have prevailed upon him to produce three operas at the San Carlo in quick succession. Jommelli was a generally respected figure, and the first of these, *Armida abbandonata* (1770), was well received, the second, *Demofoonte* (1770), somewhat less so, and the third, *Ifigenia in Tauride* (1771), a complete fiasco, even though it contained some of Jommelli's most wonderful music. Rather than recognizing Jommelli as having revitalized the traditional composer-performer relation of Italian music, the general opera-going public seems to have considered him to have fallen victim to the dread perils of excessive complexity and learnedness, and to have rebelled against the zeal of his supporters. The prevailing opinion has probably left a trace in the reaction to *Armida abbandonata* of the young Mozart, who was then in Naples. After the dress rehearsal he wrote of how much he liked the music, but after the première he added a caveat: the music was 'beautiful, but too serious and old-fashioned for the theatre'. (This is ironic in that Jommelli had achieved a stylistic synthesis in some ways comparable with that of Haydn, and of Mozart himself in the 1780s.)

In 1784 Paisiello returned to Naples, after eight years as music director to Catherine the Great, to extraordinary marks of royal favour including appointments and emoluments that made him the dominating figure in Neapolitan music. Among these was a post created for him as composer to the San Carlo with the obligation to produce one opera a year there. Before his virtual retirement from opera in the mid-1790s, he composed nine operas for the San Carlo between 1785 and 1794 and another in 1797. Taste was changing in these years and this led to considerable experimentation, sometimes of a rather contradictory kind. There is evidence that Paisiello had earlier become receptive to some aspects of reformist dogma, and there are signs of it in these operas (an inclination to do away with lengthy vocal coloraturas, for example). But the overriding impression is of pragmatism and accommodation, though Paisiello might be considered to have been in a position to have imposed his will on the public or on singers. (It is apparent, for instance, that the prima donna Brigida Banti demanded coloratura passages when the rest of the company of which she was a part was willing to do without them.)

Paisiello's *Fedra* (1789) is a Frenchifying opera with choruses, ballets and the like, whose ultimate source is Rameau's *Hippolyte et Aricie*. It appears to have been unsuccessful, the Neapolitan public having developed an aversion to choruses in opera, and Paisiello never again attempted anything similar for Naples. In contrast, *Pirro* (1787) was a great success, partly because of its adoption from *opera buffa* of a concerted introduction and act-ending finales, an innovation that aroused much favourable comment. Yet Paisiello did not go on to make finales a standard feature of later operas, although his composing the last act of *Catone in Utica* (1789) as a highly organized musical whole with only five bars of simple recitative in the entire act suggests an interest in extending musical continuity. Equally successful, somewhat surprisingly (except that the unsettled state of taste must have made success or failure difficult to predict or explain), was *Elfrida* (1792), a gloomy medieval subject with a tragic ending, derived from William Mason's English tragedy by Calzabigi, who tried to adapt some of his reform ideas to Italian realities by doing away with solo arias for secondary characters, but not the characters themselves, who are compensated by parts in concerted ensembles.

However, for the last two operas in the series Paisiello returned to Metastasio in *Didone abbandonata* (1794) and an even older libretto, Salvi's *Andromaca* (1797), although with significant revisions. *Andromaca*, for example, opens with a poetic added scene in which the curtain rises on Andromache alone and asleep, dreaming of the dead

Hector, whose ghostly voice is represented by a melody in the horn. This creates an atmosphere entirely foreign to Metastasian rationalism, one looking back to the *ombra* scenes of pre-Metastasian opera but also ahead to the super-naturalism of the Romantics. This scene reveals the complex situation that was created once the barriers of the old conventions were broken down but no new synthesis had yet been formed.

The Teatro di San Carlo, like the king whose name it bore, stood at the top of a hierarchy. Beneath it were ranked the theatres of the comic opera, often called *teatrini*, a diminutive suggesting both their size and their prestige in relation to the San Carlo. These were the Fiorentini, where Neapolitan comic opera had first appeared in public in 1709; the Nuovo, opened in 1724; the Pace, intermittently tolerated from 1724 until it was definitively closed as a threat to public morals in 1749; and the Fondo, opened in 1779. At the bottom came the locales of the *commedia dell'arte*. These ranged from a proper theatre with boxes, the Teatro di San Carlino, to another that was a grubby hole beneath the steps of a church, to the outdoor spaces where companies sometimes performed in summer.

Obviously, the lowest reaches of the hierarchy descended into a lowly milieu, and the comic opera itself edged into the socially unacceptable, the Teatro della Pace being, if one accepts the reports of the authorities, as much a brothel as a theatre. The aristocracy was completely at home at the better comic-opera theatres and had been a presence there from the genre's beginnings. Burney in 1770 described the comic-opera audience as behaving much like that of the San Carlo – talking, playing cards and sleeping (the latter because, according to Burney, of the lack of ballets, which were permitted only at the San Carlo). Casanova spent one stimulating evening chatting with the mistress of the Duke of Maddaloni at the San Carlo and the next evening did exactly the same in her box at the Fiorentini.[17] There had been a royal (or vice-regal) box at the Nuovo, which had apparently been used by the Austrian viceroys. King Charles, whether because of decorum or lack of interest, did not attend the comic theatres, but Ferdinand resumed the practice in 1776.

Ticket prices were lower at the comic theatres than at the San Carlo, allowing a broader range of the public to attend them. It is clear that in this sense the comic opera was a more popular kind of theatre than the *opera seria*, but whether it was dominated by a particular class or the lower classes in general is more open to debate. It is even more questionable whether it can be called an 'expression' of one class or another. This is a point of some importance because of the interpretations that have been applied to the comic opera by later critics and historians.

Intense historical interest in this genre was awakened in the late nineteenth century among Neapolitan intellectuals, including

9. *Commedia dell'arte performance on a temporary stage in the Verona amphitheatre: painting (1772) by Marco Marcola*

the historian and philosopher Benedetto Croce and the local-colourist writer Salvatore di Giacomo. The principal work on the subject was *L'opera buffa napoletana* by Michele Scherillo. Scherillo's point of view is reflected in the following characteristic passage:

> The serious opera [*melodramma*] had nothing about it that was alive, or of the real world, and little that was human, but among the common people there was taking shape a kind of drama that was human, of the people, and peculiarly Neapolitan, namely the *opera buffa*, which little by little acquired the standing of an art form, and gloriously entered the most sumptuous European theatres.[18]

By 'melodramma' Scherillo was here referring to the seventeenth-century opera, but the unfavourable comparison with the comic opera was also extended to the eighteenth-century *opera seria* and became a standard historical attitude. It was based on the nineteenth-century view of the serious genre as trivial, decadent and artificial, like the aristocratic society that it reflected. The comic opera, in contrast, is said to have originated among the common people and for that reason to embody a vitality and the somewhat mysterious but much prized 'humanity' that are assumed to reside in the 'folk'. In spite of its evident (and in some respects debatable) ideological content, various forms of this comparison between the supposedly artificial, moribund *opera seria* and the supposedly more natural, vital *opera buffa* remain a standard feature of much music history.

10. Nicola Logroscino directing an opera from the harpsichord (and apparently beating time on the sides of the instrument): caricature (1753) by Pier Leone Ghezzi

For Scherillo and his fellow Neapolitan historians, the principal attraction of *opera buffa* was the picture it offered of eighteenth-century Naples – its daily life and customs, the language (dialect being a common feature of some roles) and the Neapolitan character. This they saw primarily from the perspective of the late nineteenth-century literary orientation towards realism and naturalism. Since realism of this sort is most prominent in the earliest Neapolitan librettos of the 1710s and 1720s, Scherillo regarded the latter development of the genre in somewhat negative terms as a debasement of realism and the popular origin of the genre through the accretion of elements antagonistic to both.

This development was parallel in a general way to that of analogous genres, the *opéra comique* and the Singspiel, around the same time, all evolving towards greater literary respectability and regularity of subject matter and structure, as well as towards musical complexity. The literary reached fulfilment in the librettos of Giambattista Lorenzi, who dominated the last third of the century, the musical in the great composers of the same period, Piccinni, Paisiello and Cimarosa.

The mature Neapolitan *opera buffa* was a genre that resists one-dimensional characterization. Much of its interest lies in the degree to which it absorbed and balanced artistic polarities. It was both realistic and highly artificial.The vignettes of everyday life relished by Scherillo are for the most part contained within plots which are as intricate and improbable as those of *opera seria*, which often use similar devices of mistaken identity, mixed-up babies, transvestite disguises and unlikely coincidences. Further, in classically orientated aesthetics, both tragedy and comedy had the same goal: to teach virtue. Only their means were different, tragedy working by positive example, comedy by exposing and ridiculing vice. Both therefore tended to exaggeration of characterization, tragedy by idealization and comedy by caricature. The generic characters of *opera seria* were paralleled in *opera buffa* by conventionalized character types, often descended from classical comedy or from the *commedia dell'arte*, including the cunning servant, the stupid servant, the foolish and easily deceived parent or guardian, the blustering soldier and so on.

The presence of Neapolitan dialect and the taking up of expressions and rhythms of everyday speech is one of the most striking aspects of the genre, but it is balanced by the evocation, for various comic purposes, of the high style of *opera seria* verse, often in the form of allusions to specific passages, usually well-known aria texts, in Metastasio. This polarity has a parallel in the music: allusions to contemporary Neapolitan songs on the one hand and the exceedingly common use of the musical styles of *opera seria* on the other. The latter takes a variety of forms. The arias of the *parti serie*, the 'serious roles', high-minded characters who usually do not knowingly stoop to comedy, are almost always in a straightforward serious style, both in text and music, often resembling the arias of the secondary roles in *opera seria*. Other characters – *buffo* or *mezzo carattere*, to use the terminology of the genre, indicating degrees of comic characterization – often begin an aria in what seems to be a serious vein, but which is gradually transformed into a comic idiom. However, a considerable variety of tone was available, depending on the relation between text and music, mock-serious music being set to serious texts, and the opposite, indicating general types of procedures capable of almost infinite gradations. A similar range of effects may well have been produced in the use of popular songs and dances, but so little is known about this material that even the identification of such allusions is now difficult.

Ironically, the tendency to oversimplify the nature of the *opera buffa* kept Scherillo and others like him from fully appreciating the richness and variety of the genre – a reflection of the wealth and diversity of Neapolitan culture itself – and the artistic achievement in the synthesis of such a range of elements; similarly, the usual comparison of the *opera seria* and *opera buffa* by music historians oversimplifies both genres, thereby diminishing the eighteenth century's achievement generally.

It is likely that none of Paisiello's late operas, *buffa* or *seria*, had the success of his *Nina, o sia la pazza per amore* (1789), which was neither, but an *opera semiseria*, the operatic equivalent of the sentimental *drame bourgeois*, in which the French had created a new dramatic genre outside the Classical system. The difference in tone from the *opera buffa* is here manifested in the pathetic treatment of mental aberration, so often a source of comedy in the older genre. The title role was played by the great Celeste Coltellini, who dominated the Neapolitan comic stage in the 1780s. By the early nineteenth century some writers were declaring *opera buffa* to be dead, so great had been the inroads of the *semiseria* on it. This declaration was premature, but the vogue for the new genre did change the topography of the Italian operatic world.

From a historical perspective, there was little reason to laugh in Naples in the 1790s. Times were hard, with inflation and unsettled political and economic conditions arising from the French Revolution. This changed the whole atmosphere of life. The fate of the king's Bourbon cousin and the queen's sister in Paris struck close to home and created a somewhat paranoid fear of subversion very different from the tolerance of earlier times. Piccinni was one of the victims. Initially very well received on his return in 1791 after many years in Paris, he fell under suspicion in 1794, living under the most difficult conditions until he was allowed to leave in 1798.

The conservatories were in decline, shrinking to two in 1797 and later to one. The generation of composers born around the middle of the century, that of Cimarosa and Zingarelli, was the last to produce figures fully equal to the great ones of the past. The age of the castrato was ending: Cresentini was the last of the stars to sing at the San Carlo, in 1788–9. The calamity came at the end of 1798 when the royal government fled to Palermo in the face of a French army, which established a republic manned by local idealists and liberals. The republic lasted less than six months and the royalist return was vindictive, resulting in a long parade to the scaffold that put a bloody seal on the old Naples and took it a long step into the modern world.

Previously a change of regime, even by force, often meant little to those in the arts. When Charles drove the Austrians from Naples in 1735, the royal chapel went on serving him as it had the viceroys. Both Paisiello and Cimarosa served the short-lived republic as they had King Ferdinand, Paisiello as its music director, Cimarosa by taking part in a great republican celebration in the French manner that included dancing round a Liberty Tree, ritual burning of royalist symbols and the singing of republican hymns. Paisiello hastened to celebrate the royalist victory with a *Te Deum*, Cimarosa with a cantata, but both were disgraced and in danger. Cimarosa spent four months in prison and probably escaped harsher punishment only through influential admirers; he died in Venice less than a year later. Paisiello, more adroit, was eventually restored to favour and went on to desert Ferdinand once again when the French returned in 1806.

VENICE

In the eighteenth century, Venice was in the final phase of its long and often glorious career as an independent city-state. The monuments of that glory remained, but little of the substance. Between the Peace of Utrecht (1718), which ended Venice's involvement as an active participant of any significance in international affairs, and the republic's self-dissolution in 1797, a capitulation to the threats of Napoleon, there were 80 years which are usually regarded by historians as a sad, if piquant, period of political decline and social decadence. In respect to what Venice had been, this is an understandable assessment, but in other ways it is not quite a fair one.

The great days when Venice had been Europe's principal commercial gateway to the Near and Far East were long over, and she could no longer enforce even her earlier monopoly of Adriatic trade, but she remained a busy and prosperous port none the less, increasingly so in the second half of the century. The sometimes pusillanimous neutrality that Venice maintained throughout this period may not contrast at all favourably with her former assertiveness, but it did allow her, virtually powerless as she was, to preserve her independence and what remained of her empire through an often troubled time of European wars and shifting alliances.

In this sense Venice's policy was based on realism, but one that permitted an illusion: the outer forms and attitudes of a great power were maintained with considerable effort and expense almost to the end. The play of appearance and reality is a recurring theme of eighteenth-century Venetian life. Ostensibly a republic, Venice was in reality a despotic oligarchy with important posts restricted to 42 noble families. Wealth was increasingly concentrated in the hands of a commercial bourgeoisie, but the political status quo, which by denying that class access to power became ever more irrelevant, was rigidly maintained.

Venice was primarily known in this period for its way of life. The regime seems to have permitted a certain freedom, even licence, of personal behaviour (always carefully watched and kept within limits) as an outlet for energies denied political freedoms. The extraordinarily varied and sophisticated assortment of pleasures and pastimes that this policy produced attracted great numbers of visitors, Italian and transalpine, and has continued to fascinate later generations through the arts that memorialized them and through the magical, magnificent city in which it all took place. Much Venetian art and literature of this period took Venice itself, either its reality or its illusion, as its subject, from the allegorical paintings of Tiepolo, designed to brighten the fading glory of the great noble families, to the views of the city produced by the *vedutisti* for rich visitors, to Goldoni's dissection of Venetian society and mores in his comedies, and finally to Casanova, who added a further dimension through the vivid glimpse he allows us into the city's demi-monde. It was through this final burst of artistic achievement that Venice recaptured some of its former glory. Although its monuments are now little known, music rightfully deserves a full share of the credit in this, and many musical works were as characteristically Venetian as those of the visual arts and literature.

Venetian church music for important feasts and other special occasions had always been especially grand, reinforced by the city's rather selfconscious sense of theatricality; and in the eighteenth century, despite economic and political decline, the republic managed to maintain the major public ceremonies, religious and civic intertwined, that reinforced the illusion of greatness and attracted tourists. On his visit in 1770, Charles Burney attended a special service at St Mark's, with the doge present, when the orchestra was divided into six parts, the two principal ones placed in the two main galleries with the two large organs, the two smaller ones on each side of the church.[19] However, the most spectacular sacred music was heard not in church services but in the all-female sacred concerts of the four conservatories. Growing out of institutions for the education of foundlings and orphan girls, the Mendicanti, Pietà, Incurabili and Ospedaletto had seen music become the focus of their activities in the

11. Venetian Carnival scene: painting by Giovanni Battista Tiepolo (1696–1770)

seventeenth century and the early eighteenth under such distinguished masters as Francesco Gasparini and Vivaldi, and had maintained their brilliant reputation under Hasse and Porpora among others.

Their concerts were customarily in the form of Vespers on Saturday and Sunday, but were not actually sacred services. The girls also performed on great feast-days and often gave Latin oratorios. The Vesper concerts consisted of Vesper psalms and canticles and solo motets, as well as the instrumental solo concertos that seem to have been a common feature of musically elaborate sacred services in the eighteenth century. From the frequency with which they are mentioned by travel writers in this period, it is clear that the conservatory concerts retained their hold on the imagination and remained one of the attractions not to be missed by the tourist. A typical description is offered by de Brosses, whose visit to Italy was made in 1739–40:

> The transcendent music here is that of the conservatories . . . [The girls] are raised at the expense of the state and are uniquely trained to excel in music. They both sing like angels and play the violin, the flute, the organ, the oboe, the cello, the bassoon; in short, there is no instrument big enough to daunt them. They are cloistered like nuns. They perform entirely by themselves, and each concert is composed of about 40 girls. I assure you that there is nothing so pleasing as to

12. Concert in one of the Venetian conservatories, probably the Pietà: fresco by Francesco Battagliuoli (1742–99) in the Sala della Musica of the Villa Strà

> see a young and pretty nun, in a white habit, with a bouquet of grenadins over her ear, conduct the orchestra and beat time with all the grace and precision imaginable. Their voices are exquisite in character [*tournure*] and agility . . . Zabetta of the Incurabili is especially astonishing for the range of her voice and the bow strokes she has in her throat. It seems to me that she must have swallowed Somis's violin . . . The Pietà . . . is pre-eminent in the perfection of instrumental works. What firmness of execution! It is only here that one really hears that *premier coup d'archet* so boasted of at the Paris Opéra.[20]

This passage puts into relief the combination of elements that contributed to the girls' appeal. In an age when few women apart from opera singers were professional musicians, an all-female ensemble, including choir and orchestra, was truly exotic. Female opera singers were more or less *déclassée*, a situation which many of them exploited in the freedom of their behaviour, but these girls were, if not actually nuns, then at least 'pious virgins' as the printed programmes of their concerts often designate them (a condition which the post-conservatory activities of some of them left far behind). Most travellers reported (though the evidence is contradictory) that the girls performed unseen by their audience, thereby creating another analogy with the cloister, and even though the women of Venice had a reputation for being the most beautiful in Italy, their invisibility allowed the imagination to work more freely, for it seems certain that there was a sensual element in all this, especially in an age when the fancied sexual behaviour of nuns was one of the favourite topics of erotic literature. We have here, then, a typically Venetian formula for pleasure: a subtle, sophisticated intertwining of sensuality, spirituality and aesthetic delight.

The latter was dazzling. The circumstances of the conservatories permitted the achievement of a quality of performance of which there were few equals at the time. It is the perfection of the ensemble and the technical abilities of individual soloists that are usually praised in the accounts. These abilities were so overpowering that descriptions often create the impression that performances were entirely in a bravura mode. Surviving scores reveal considerably more balance of expressive elements – in the vocal music, for example, the same distribution of vocal styles as in *opera seria*, not only the *brillante* and bravura but also the cantabile and *grazioso*. The comparison with opera is appropriate and occurred to many at the time. For example, the cadenzas of some of the singers that Burney heard in 1770 for 'compass of voice, variety of passages, or rapidity of execution . . . would have merited and received great applause in the first opera houses of Europe'. This is sacred music of the most worldly and brilliant sort. It therefore required, for its maximum effect, the participation of the most worldly, brilliant and modern composers.

Burney, who left one of the most detailed and informed (if opinionated) accounts of the conservatories, compared performances at all four. At that time three of them were under the musical direction of local figures. One of these was the greatest Venetian composer of the period after Vivaldi and Albinoni, Baldassare Galuppi (1706–85), and Burney was fully aware of his genius, praising the originality of his ideas, his 'spirit, taste, and fancy', as well as his 'good harmony and good sense', the latter manifested in his treatment of the touchy matter of accompaniments to the voice. Galuppi's were ideal, 'always ingenious, but, though full, free from that kind of confusion, which disturbs and covers the voice' (which was, it will be remembered, the only agent of true 'expression').

The *maestro* at the Mendicanti was Ferdinando Bertoni (1725–1813), who in spite of a rather distinguished career as an opera composer in Italy (and several seasons at the King's Theatre, London) and as successor to Galuppi at St Mark's, was never considered to belong to the first rank of composers. Burney's judgment reflects this. He allowed that there were 'some pretty passages' in the music that he heard, but found the rest wanting in originality ('not new'), quality of ideas ('trite') and workmanship ('but slightly put together').

This was, however, much more favourable than his judgment of Bonaventura Furlanetto (1738–1817), *maestro* at the Pietà. Furlanetto was a Venetian musician-priest, whose career, restricted to church music and oratorios, was primarily a local one, but long and distinguished (he succeeded Bertoni as *maestro di cappella* at St Mark's). Burney reacted strongly to his music, which he admitted was not badly written but found extremely 'tiresome' because devoid of imagination, going so far as to refer to its composer as an 'ecclesiastical dunce'.

The situation at the Ospedaletto was quite different. It was in the hands of one of the most acclaimed of the younger generation of opera composers, Antonio Sacchini (1730–86), who had established himself during the previous decade with a string of brilliant successes. Such an appointment was common at the conservatories. It had become traditional to fill vacancies with the stars of the opera house, either rising or just risen. In the period under consideration Jommelli, Cocchi, Ciampi, Latilla, Sarti, Traetta, Anfossi and Cimarosa were among those appointed to a conservatory post under similar circumstances. Few of these were strongly associated with Venice (all except Sarti were trained in Naples) and few remained for long; most were probably often absent on operatic commissions (and this may help explain why the conservatories sometimes turned to more stable, if less exciting, local figures), but in fact the rather rapid turnover was in keeping with the principal reason for engaging this kind of *maestro* in the first place. In a period when music aged quickly, they ensured that their conservatory would be in the vanguard of musical style, availing itself of the latest developments of the opera house and so maintaining the modernity and brilliance that were essential to the kind of effect that the conservatories sought to achieve (or, at least, that was expected of them). Burney's reaction to the music of Sacchini that he heard at the Ospedaletto illustrates this: 'It was new, spirited, and full of ingenious contrivances for the instruments, which always *said* something without disturbing the voice. On the whole there seemed to be as much genius in this composition as in any that I had heard since my arrival in Italy'.

The conservatories' formula for maintaining themselves in fashion was thus to combine singers and players of the highest technical accomplishments (both individually and in ensemble) with composers representing the last word in successful modernity. Both elements of the formula were essential; composer and performer were so intimately connected in Italian music that deficiencies in one tended to redound to the other. (Burney seems to illustrate this when expressing his dislike for Furlanetto's music; he also condemned its performance as 'not exceed[ing] mediocrity'.)

In the long and, by most accounts, highly successful application of this formula may also lie the conservatories' primary significance to the history of music (taken in its usual sense as the history of musical style). The activities of the conservatories represent an important point of contact between sacred music and opera, the genre that fertilized the others. The conservatories were served by many of the principal figures in the development of operatic style, in circumstances that promoted the maximum degree of transference of those developments to sacred music, virtually without restrictions.

One of the reasons why Burney devoted so much attention to the conservatories was that his visit to Venice took place at a time when the theatres were closed. Unlike Naples, where opera was given nearly all the year (to the extent that the church calendar allowed), opera in Venice was confined to three seasons – the famous Venetian Carnival, the rather brief Ascensiontide fair (when Venice annually wedded the sea, a ceremony kept up at this time mainly as a tourist attraction) and the autumn season, which began in October or early November and introduced the companies of performers who remained through the following Carnival.

Venice was rich in theatres, and the amount of theatrical activity there seems to have been greater, in proportion to the population, than elsewhere in Italy. Since data that would allow the character of opera audiences to be analysed apparently do not exist for Venice in this period, one can only suggest possible reasons: the avidity, often mentioned by travel writers, of the Venetian public for spectacles; the prosperity that permitted the indulgence of this inclination; the many tourists; and the ownership of the theatres by noble families keen to make a conspicuous display of *noblesse*.

In the 1740s opera was heard at six Venetian theatres: the San Giovanni Grisostomo, the San Angelo, the San Samuele, the San Moisè, the San Cassiano and the San Salvatore. In any season usually two or three, occasionally four, theatres presented opera, while the others offered spoken drama, entertainments such as acrobatic exhibitions or nothing. With the opening in 1756 of the Teatro San Benedetto, the largest and most splendid in the city, that house became the principal seat of *opera seria* until the new Teatro La Fenice assumed that position (which it retains) in 1792. The number of operas given each year remained fairly constant throughout this whole period; from around 1740 until the end of the century it was usually between seven and nine. (A larger number did not necessarily reflect greater operatic activity; sometimes unsuccessful operas were replaced by others.) The character of the repertory, however, underwent great change.

In 1740 the theatrical world of Venice was dominated by *opera seria* and the comedy of masks. By the end of the decade both genres had begun to share primacy with another, *opera buffa* and the fully written comedy of Goldoni. The rise of a new operatic genre was a most

13. Interior of a typical Venetian theatre during the performance of an opera seria: engraving from the satire 'I viaggi d'Enrico Wanton' (1749) – note the masked audience, shuttered boxes and general lack of attention

important development that profoundly changed the structure of the Italian musical world. The dynamics of that change have sometimes been interpreted in purely musical terms, and sometimes in terms of such changes as the rise and fall of social classes. Much of this interpretation rests upon a simultaneous rise of *opera buffa* and decline of *opera seria*. Since in Venice the total number of operas of any kind given each year did not change appreciably with the appearance of *opera buffa*, the new genre seems to have reduced the audience for the old. However, this does not necessarily mean that *opera seria* was losing its vitality. The two genres were so different in so many respects that they cannot be regarded in simple terms as having been in competition. Even the data are open to varying interpretations. In other cities, where the market for opera was less saturated than in Venice, *opera buffa* did not always cut into the audience for *opera seria*; rather it supplemented it. In any case, one of the principal mysteries is why it took so long for a full-length comic genre to develop.

Although before the 1740s it was only in Naples that comic opera was fully established, a local product that did not travel, there was intermittent activity elsewhere, for example in the 1720s and 1730s at Bologna, where the works of the librettist-composer Buini constituted a one-man comic genre. G.M. Ruggieri's *Elisa* (1707), performed in 1711, is often called the first Venetian comic opera. It had a direct connection with Naples through its librettist Domenico Lalli, who settled in Venice, but the Venetian ground did not prove receptive to transplantation and *Elisa* had no immediate successors. A number of comic operas were given at the Teatro di San Fantino in 1717–19, and Buini's works were occasionally performed in Venice, as well as examples of other comic genres such as the comic pastorale and the burlesques of *opera seria* given by *commedia dell'arte* companies. The short, two- or three-character comic intermezzo was continually popular, but a sustained appetite for full-length comic opera did not develop.

The first appearance of the kind of work that would stimulate such an appetite, first in Italy and then throughout Europe, occurred at Rome. In Carnival 1738 three full-length comic operas were performed there, composed by Neapolitan musicians to locally produced librettos: *La commedia in commedia* by Rinaldo di Capua, *La finta cameriera* and *Madama Ciana*, both by Latilla. In 1741 these three works, together with another Roman opera of the same type, Rinaldo di Capua's *La libertà nociva* (1740), began to travel widely. In that decade *La finta cameriera*, the most popular of the four, was performed in at least fifteen Italian cities and crossed the Alps (Graz, 1745; London, 1748; Barcelona, 1750; Brunswick, 1751). In Venice it was given in Ascension season 1743 and revived in 1744 and 1745, suggesting that it caused a considerable furore. In autumn 1743 Venice heard the comic opera *Orazio*, a rather mysterious work at times ascribed to both Pergolesi and Latilla until recently when it was traced to a Neapolitan comic opera by Auletta (1737).[21] The widespread circulation of a Neapolitan comic opera (which underwent radical transformation along the way), contrary to the usual inability of that genre to travel, suggests that there was a growing demand for such material.

In 1744 the other three Roman operas also reached Venice, together with another Neapolitan comic opera, *Origille* by Palella, performed by a travelling company with a Neapolitan impresario. The vogue for comic opera had started earlier at Florence than at Venice, nourished by the company of one of the great *buffo* singers of the century, Pietro Pertici. All four Roman operas, as well as *Orazio*, were given in Florence before they reached Venice, and many Florentine singers (including Pertici in 1744–5) appeared in Venice, probably bringing with them the three comic operas of Florentine origin that were heard there in 1744–6.

From all this it is clear that there was fertile ground all over Italy for full-length comic opera and that Rome, through the musical agency of Neapolitan composers, had provided a viable model for it (although curiously Rome did not participate further in the early development of the new genre, instead cultivating the intermezzo for three and four characters). It is also evident that composers and performers in several cities contributed to comic opera in its early stages and by their movements helped to spread it to others. Venice did not participate in the earliest of these stages, but it was there that comic opera reached what might be called its mature phase. The principal reason for this was the presence of Carlo Goldoni and Baldassare Galuppi.

In the 1730s Goldoni had written a series of intermezzo texts, using Venetian local colour, for *commedia dell'arte* companies, and two of the burlesques of *opera seria* that such companies liked to perform occasionally. His first real full-length *opera buffa*, *La contessina*, was given in Carnival 1743. There is nothing to suggest that *La contessina* aroused much interest, and in any case Goldoni could not immediately follow it up since he spent the next several years practising law in Pisa. When Goldoni returned to Venice and to the stage, engaged to write for a comic company, the vogue for comic opera was in full flood there, and from late 1748 he threw himself into it, soon virtually monopolizing the field in Venice. His early ventures were undertaken in collaboration with a young Neapolitan composer Vincenzo Ciampi, but in Ascension season 1749 he began working with Galuppi.

Galuppi was an *opera seria* composer of twenty years' standing. In the mid-1740s he had become interested in the new comic genre, revising imported works and composing one himself, apparently without sufficient results to lead him to continue at that time. Goldoni and Galuppi presented *L'Arcadia in Brenta*, a satire on contemporary Venetian life, with great success, and it must have been immediately apparent that the two were made for each other. From Carnival 1749–50 to the end of 1750 they produced a virtual explosion of comic opera – five works, several of them highly successful and performed over much of northern Italy and beyond the Alps, thereby ensuring the continuation of the genre and determining the character of its next phase of development.

The pace of the collaboration slowed thereafter. There were five more joint operas in 1755, the year that marked the end of the period of their most significant work, together and apart, and also of the formative period of Venetian comic opera generally. In the later 1750s Galuppi devoted himself more to *opera seria* than to *opera buffa*, and with the production of Piccinni's *La buona figliuola* in Rome in Carnival 1760 (to a libretto by Goldoni) the role of standard bearer of the genre passed back to a Neapolitan, where it was to remain (though Galuppi produced a few very successful comic works in the years before his engagement at the Russian court in 1765–8).

Opera buffa, through its emphasis on satire and social criticism in the pursuit of comedy's classical justification of exposing and chastising vice, was potentially subversive. In practice, however, its influence was often highly conservative because of its tendency to focus on characters whose primary 'vice' was an inclination to move outside the places in life into which they had been born. This encompassed a wide range of behaviour, including any kind of alienation from social norms. (It was this attitude that could see mental aberration as a subject for comic treatment, as a kind of social alienation.) One prominent element of this genre was thus conducive to social conformity and social immobility.

A subversive potential was always there, however, and Goldoni's work has a broad vein of it, particularly in the political context of Venice's rigid oligarchy, through its embodiment of rationalist ideas current in contemporary Enlightenment thought. This is already evident in *La contessina*, in which the absurd pretensions of a noble and his daughter (the Contessina) are humbled by a worthy merchant. But the circumstances are equivocal: the count is newly ennobled and his excesses are presented as those of the *arriviste*, a traditional attitude and, for its author, a relatively safe approach to the criticism of a powerful class. The direction of Goldoni's thinking is, however, perfectly clear in the context of his work as a whole, which continually stresses, either explicitly or implicitly, industriousness (seen as leading to material success), individual worth and achievement in any station of society, disapproval of social parasites of various sorts, and the value of rational thinking free of sham, pretentiousness and shibboleth. This quality of rationalism is embodied most notably in the title character of Goldoni and Galuppi's best-known collaboration, *Il filosofo di campagna* (1754), the prosperous peasant Nardo who, devoid of false pride and false honour, freely takes the ready and willing serving-maid as his wife after learning that her mistress, who had been promised to him, prefers another. These are all Enlightenment virtues and, as exemplified by the characters who embody them, bourgeois ones as well. This puts the Goldonian comic opera into direct opposition to the Metastasian *opera seria*, which taught the rather different virtues of a rigid and authoritarian social hierarchy.

The spirited, occasionally farcical, but graceful and highly rational comic tone of Goldoni's librettos was paralleled by the equally spirited but graceful music of Galuppi, music highly rational in its regular periodicity of phrasing, expansiveness of harmonic rhythm and transparency of texture, all enlivened by a notable gift for lyrical melody. These were all to be constituent elements of later eighteenth-century style, and Galuppi appears to have been of historical significance in embodying and (to an extent still to be determined) initiating an earlier stage of that style. Burney repeatedly stressed the originality of Galuppi's ideas and their subsequent absorption into the musical language as universal idioms.

Because of the rapid development of that language, and of that of the *opera buffa* in particular, Galuppi's earlier and historically most important comic operas began to seem somewhat outmoded by the early 1760s, as Piccinni and, a few years later, Paisiello raised the level of brilliance and complexity in the genre. They did this, at least in part, by building on what Galuppi had begun. Some continued to prefer what they felt to be the greater grace and charm of Galuppi's simpler style, but this simplicity should not obscure the elegant but unobtrusive craftsmanship of Galuppi's work, which is evident in his ability to expand the short act-ending ensembles of Neapolitan comic opera into the much larger structures of finales in several connected but contrasting tempos. One should also not overlook the sophistication of Galuppi's style, particularly in the relation of words and music. While a straightforward, seemingly naive setting of text is sometimes the goal, this was only one of the composer's options, which also included techniques more 'mannered' in the musical articulation and melodic intonation of words. This once again underlines the intrinsic sophistication and variety of *opera buffa* and the inadequacy of comparisons between the serious and comic genres of opera in terms of 'naturalness' as opposed to 'artificiality'.

Goldoni presented himself, and has often been presented by historians, as a 'reformer' of comedy, one who fought to replace the low, disreputable (as he saw it) improvised *commedia dell'arte* with rational and well-regulated fully written comedy, bourgeois in its decorum as well as in its values. Goldoni often referred to this as comedy of character replacing comedy of situation. It can also be regarded as a performer-orientated art giving way to an author-orientated one, analogous in that respect to the 'reforms' of Gluck and Calzabigi. The greater flexibility of aria forms, turning away from the da capo pattern that had earlier dominated comic opera as well as *opera seria*, and the development of the possibilities of vocal ensembles in the expanded finales, greatly increased the composer's range of creative choices. At the same time it did not abrogate the old relation between composer-librettist and performer but recognized and took advantage of the nature of the performer's art in this genre. Goldoni several times indicated in his memoirs and elsewhere that he conceived his spoken comedies for the company of actors for which he was writing, and there is no reason to suppose that he (or Galuppi) worked any differently in comic opera. His willingness to alter a libretto for a different cast indicates this, as does the substitution of arias for different singers, a practice that seems to have been as common in this genre as in *opera seria*. In short, what Goldoni and Galuppi achieved was an art form in which the traditional Italian concept of a work of art as a creative collaboration was not only preserved but realized more fully in keeping with the potential of the genre itself.

As was pointed out above, *opera seria* underwent an analogous transformation in the second half of the century, but much more slowly. When radical changes finally began to be unmistakable in *opera seria* in the mid-1780s, it appears that they were the result of more changes of taste in the culture as a whole than by the internal evolution of the genre itself or by the influence of reformers. In *opera seria* this change of taste is most immediately apparent in the decline of the Metastasian libretto after half a century of dominance and the very different tone of much of what replaced it.

Typical of the Venetian libretto in this period is *Calto*, given at the Teatro San Benedetto in 1788, with music by Francesco Bianchi, perhaps the most prominent opera composer then based in the city. In the preface to its printed libretto the poet, a local one named Giuseppe Foppa, revealed one of the new quarters to which Italian literary and dramatic attentions were being directed by acknowledging Ossian as his source. The modern reader is more likely to be reminded of *Hamlet*. Duntalmo has usurped the throne by murdering Sirmo. In the first act Calto (sung by the great alto castrato Giovanni Rubinelli) engages in a dialogue with a chorus of ghosts, while 'the dead Sirmo . . . majestically advances, shows the wound in his breast, and follows with gestures in keeping with the situation'. He is of course seeking vengeance. Act 2 scene vi is set in a 'Vast *sotterraneo* [subterranean construction], reached by stairways on the sides. Tomb in the middle'. The scene opens with a chorus 'Lugubri gemiti solo qui risuonino' ('Lugubrious groans only here resound'), accompanied by a 'dance around the tomb'. The scene progresses to a *giuramento* (oath-swearing ceremony).

This atmosphere of ghosts, crypts and lugubrious groans is entirely foreign to the Metastasian libretto. It had slowly been gaining ground for some time. The subterranean setting, which allowed the painter to create an effect of oppressive gloom (recalling Piranesi's *Prigioni* of mid-century), had been popular for years. This 'Gothic' tendency in late eighteenth-century taste can be linked to the seemingly rather different neo-classical tendency that also began to gather strength just after mid-century. In seeking what was considered to be a more authentic tragic tone in the Greek manner (as in the librettos of Calzabigi, Gluck's collaborator in 'reform'), neo-classicism similarly moved away from the tone and range of feeling encompassed by the taste of the first half of the century towards more extreme emotional expression and dramatic situation. Both styles passed at their extremes into the melodramatic, the horrific and (as it may seem to modern eyes) the neurotic.

Venetian opera of the period reflects the progress of these tendencies. A good indicator is the tragic ending. In *Calto*, for example; the morbid tone that pervades the drama is not carried through to the tragic conclusion that it seems to prefigure. The tyrant is overthrown but pardoned, and the social mechanism restores itself to working order in Metastasian fashion. By the second half of the 1790s, however, the violent death onstage of one of the principals had become a common manner of ending an opera. This is sometimes managed in a sensational fashion that suggests a librettist straining to satisfy an audience's predilection. Perhaps the most outré example is found in Vittorio Trento's *Bianca de' Rossi* (1797). At the extremity of despair, hounded by a cruel and villainous tyrant (an operatic stereotype of this period), the noble Bianca orders that her husband's tomb be opened so that she may embrace his corpse one last time (this gruesome inclination being itself a sign of the taste of the 1790s). As the libretto describes it, she then 'approaches the tomb, and with a hand pushing away the support, places her head beneath the fall of the stone'.

The decline of the Metastasian libretto constituted a major change of circumstances for the genre, creating the need for a greater volume of new material to fill the void and thereby establishing favourable conditions for more significant participation by practising librettists than had long been the case. Indeed, in Venice, which at this time lacked a dominating composer comparable to Paisiello in Naples, librettists can be considered in some respects the central figures in operatic developments. One of the most interesting was Count Alessandro Pepoli (1757–96), who epitomizes Venetian life in this period through his seemingly obsessive drive to try his hand at almost everything. As one contemporary memorialized him:

> Count Pepoli was one of those phenomena which nature from time to time provides to give an idea of vices and virtues in bizarre mixture: in a word he was a new Alcibiades: poet in the comic, tragic and lyric genres, master swordsman, dancer, musician, man of letters, publisher, horseman, lover of debauchery, of the fine arts, of luxury, of women. Perhaps in another century he would have passed for a philosopher; in ours he passed for a madman. I do not know which of his so many passions was most fatal to him. He died in the flower of his years, lamented by many, but principally by his creditors.[22]

As this suggests, Pepoli often cut a somewhat ridiculous figure (of which he appears to have been completely unaware), and this is as true in the artistic sphere as elsewhere, especially in the disparity between the loftiness of his artistic pretensions and his actual talent, which was small. However, his librettos provide a good example of the artistic cross-currents of the time.

Pepoli began working as a librettist in the late 1780s, very much in the classicizing, reformist mode of Calzabigi, whom he then regarded as the restorer of Greek tragedy to the modern theatre, characterizing him at one point as the Aeschylus to whom he himself hoped to become the Sophocles. His writings of this period are typical of this school of thought in their emphasis on the association between Greek drama and religion and the resulting seriousness with which the Greeks themselves took tragedy, compared with the frivolous, decadent milieu of the contemporary opera house. The Metastasian libretto is charged with unworthily catering to the tastes of that public.

Ironically, Pepoli's most important libretto, *I giuochi d'Agrigento*, written for the inauguration of the Teatro La Fenice in 1792 and set by Paisiello, reflects the pervasiveness of Metastasio in Italian literary culture that made it difficult to escape his influence even when the writer, like Pepoli, was anxious to do so. The plot device of the athletic contest, in which the prize is the king's daughter, is a variation on Metastasio's *L'Olimpiade*, while the incest motif recalls *Demofoonte*. Pepoli modernized it by having his characters react with near hysteria and self-loathing rather than with Metastasio's tearful pathos. There are also Gluckian and Calzabigian elements – a spectacular storm with near shipwreck that colours part of the first act, as in *Iphigénie en Tauride*, and a temple scene recalling the oracle episode in *Alceste* in the second. The elaborateness and spectacle of this work (there are eight solo roles, two more than was customary) probably reflect the gala occasion for which it was written, as does the happy ending, where the presumed incest turns out to have been an illusion, resulting (as in *Demofoonte*) from the tendency of operatic babies to find their way into the wrong nursery.

No doubt for the same reason Paisiello provided an unusually elaborate and carefully written score, but one in other respects representative of the time. There are spectacular scenes in which Paisiello uses the chorus as an important architectural element, since the Venetian public, unlike the Neapolitan, seems to have welcomed choruses. Temple rituals are especially favoured for scenes of this sort in classicizing operas such as this, but one of Paisiello's more interesting constructions is the storm sequence in Act 1, which continues through a change of scene with unbroken music. Certain types of musical-dramatic numbers, while relatively new to the genre, were already so frequent as almost to qualify as conventions. One is the *preghiera* (prayer), of which this opera has an example for chorus interspersed with solos for the primo uomo. (Another is the *giuramento*, found in *Calto* but not here.) Many operas of this period have a dialogue for the chorus and one of the principals in the middle of Act 1, and there is one here for the prima donna after she disembarks from the storm-tossed ship on which she had made her entrance. Substantial solo ensembles close the first two acts and there is a septet within the second act. Even so, solo singing remains all-important and the arias are treated with considerable formal and stylistic diversity.

I giuochi d'Agrigento was a moderate success, revived in Venice in 1794 and 1801 and also produced in Verona, Florence, London and

Lisbon. Pepoli's later work radically shifts its aesthetic allegiance from neo-classicism to the proto-Romanticism that found one of its most potent models in English literature, especially 'divine Shakespeare', as Pepoli referred to him. Under this influence he rejected classical subjects and the unities of time and place and advocated the mixing of genres, of comedy and tragedy, prose and verse, mime and speech – procedures justified as more 'natural' than classical ones. All this was not new, even in Venice, when Pepoli took it up. Paisiello's *Nina*, an *opera semiseria*, had been performed there in 1792 in its original version with spoken prose dialogue; and the Venetian librettist Foppa had produced two similar works, both also based on French sources, before Pepoli brought out his *Belisa*, a *dramma tragicomico* of the same character, in 1794. Pepoli's radical change of direction reflects the unsettled state of the genre in this period.

The most widely performed and long-lived Venetian serious opera of the 1790s was *Gli Orazi e i Curiazi* (1797) by Cimarosa and the house poet of La Fenice, P.A. Sografi, which was given until well into the next century and even, most unusually, published in full score. *Gli Orazi* was in some ways a very stark work, styled a *tragedia* on the libretto and justifying this designation by ending with the same shocking and bloody dénouement as Corneille's great tragedy *Les Horaces* on which it is based (probably via a French operatic version produced in Paris in 1786). Absolute devotion to the state as the noblest of virtues is the subject of this work, a not uncommon one in this period of revolutionary governments and nascent nationalism. The wide applicability of this theme (exemplified by the revival of this opera, first performed in the last months of the old Venetian Republic, immediately after the installation of the new French-dominated regime) probably played a part in the work's success, but it was more likely the opera's synthesis of disparate stylistic elements that created the enthusiasm with which it was received. The stern heroes of the ancient Roman republic were balanced by the traditional Italian lyricism of Cimarosa's melodic style, more sensuous and ornate than Paisiello's, while moments of strongly characterized serious musical expression were mixed with others in a popular, patriotic style of march-like rhythm and triadic melodies.

In the late 1790s Venice had a commanding figure among its composers. Like many Venetian composers, he was not a native. Giovanni Simone Mayr (1763–1845) was a Bavarian who lived most of his life in Bergamo, but soon after arriving in Italy he came to Venice where he studied with Bertoni, played the viola in La Fenice's orchestra and first attracted notice with his oratorios for the girls at the Mendicanti. His first opera was *Saffo* (La Fenice, 1794), to a curious libretto by Sografi, which aims at being a classicizing tragedy in the Calzabigian manner. Secondary characters are omitted, as are the usual amorous intrigues. Frustrated sexual passion is the theme, everyone being in love with a different person. This is presented by Sografi at such a high and unrelenting emotional pitch that the impression made by the libretto is less one of classical tragedy than of neurotic obsession (a not uncommon effect of librettos of this time, straining for an emotional intensity that is not always sufficiently supported by the rest of the dramatic mechanism).

The music of this period did not seek a comparable degree of emotional abandon, and *Saffo*'s music cools the over-heated libretto. It is composed with solid craftsmanship and close attention to musical and dramatic values. This is particularly evident in the orchestration, which contains a good deal of solo wind writing, and in the recitative. Much of the latter is accompanied, but even the simple recitative has considerable dramatic force. (German critics would no doubt attribute these qualities to Mayr's national origins.) He also possessed a good sense of Italian vocal style and dutifully subordinated accompaniments to voice; he was also willing to write flashy bravura arias for the prima donna, Brigida Banti. The deficiency that made Mayr one of the near-misses of opera history (and the possession of which allowed his pupil Donizetti to succeed where he had failed) was a lack of distinction in his ideas and of the nearly indefinable attribute that gives lyrical élan to a melody and makes it memorable. (Italian critics would no doubt attribute this failing also to Mayr's German origins.)

Saffo seems not to have been a success; its first production was its last, and Mayr did not have another opera performed for two years. His next was *Lodoiska*, which was a great success, and Mayr went on to produce seventeen more operas in Venice in the next four years. Although ten of these were slight, one-act farces, five were full-scale, serious operas, making Mayr the most active opera composer in the city. *Lodoiska* is very different from *Saffo*. The libretto, by a Florentine, Francesco Gonella, has its source in the *opéra comique*, the subject having been composed in that form by both Kreutzer and Cherubini. With its Polish knights among the Tartars, it is far from the classical milieu, but this somewhat Romantic topic had been treated by the French from an eighteenth-century rationalist perspective, the Tartars becoming another of the many manifestations of the noble savage, intuitively living by principles more right and natural than the Europeans.

Much of this was toned down in the Italian libretto and the Tartars' role was reduced. *Lodoiska* was designed as a vehicle for the great castrato Luigi Marchesi (see fig.39 below), who played the Polish hero. He appeared in at least twelve further productions of it, including two Venetian revivals. Indeed, there were few other productions, so it appears that the work that established Mayr as a major figure (which he remained until the vogue for Rossini swept away the

14. Niccolò Antonio Zingarelli: manuscript of 'Pirro, re d'Epiro' (La Scala, Milan, 26 December 1791), showing part of the aria 'Cara negli'occhi tuoi', with an ornamented alternative vocal line, possibly by the castrato Luigi Marchesi (it is written in the treble clef; the basic text is in the soprano)

older generation) owed as much to the genius of a singer as to its composer. This again raises the subject of Italian music as a creative collaboration between composer and performer and the question of the extent to which this relationship continued to function during the transformation that the genre was undergoing in the 1790s. This tranformation was concurrent with the last great flowering of the art of the castrato, concentrated in a few remaining major figures in northern Italian theatres, primarily La Scala, Milan, and the theatres of Venice. The Teatro La Fenice opened with the final stage appearances of Pacchiarotti, and through most of the decade Marchesi and Crescentini, the last two giants, virtually alternated engagements in the city.

There is contemporary testimony that *Lodoiska* was written expressly for Marchesi and at his instigation. Further, a letter (now in the British Library) from Marchesi to the librettist Gonella in Florence, reporting on the première and sending a payment from the impresario for the libretto, does not state that he had commissioned it, but the circumstances and tone suggest as much. Indeed, Marchesi had done the same in the past. In the late 1780s he had applied to Pepoli for a libretto on the death of Hercules, specifying that it be an 'opera a cori . . . colla morte obbligata', and Pepoli had responded with a *tragedia per musica* in the most ponderous and solemn classicizing manner of the over-enthusiastic disciple of Calzabigi that he then was.[23] Marchesi was appalled. There were too many choruses; Marchesi's rondò was in his death scene in Act 3 rather than in the second where convention required it. Worse, since Hercules was dying, Pepoli had directed that the rondò be sung sitting. Finally, Marchesi had approved of ending the opera with an apotheosis in the French manner, in which he would appear with Jupiter on a cloud, but as the perverse Pepoli wrote the scene, he was given nothing to sing.

In the ensuing battle of wills, Pepoli's only concession was to allow Marchesi to sing his rondò standing (supported by attendants), but this was his only substantial concession. Marchesi turned elsewhere for another libretto on the same subject; this was eventually given in Venice in 1791. Pepoli in the meantime published his rejected libretto, which was never set to music, together with a satire on Marchesi in the form of a dialogue between an ignorant, vain, unreasonable castrato and a high-minded librettist (who is, however, not above a few pointed references to his opponent's 'neutered' condition).

Marchesi, it is clear, was not attracted to the notion of an 'opera a cori . . . colla morte obbligata' by any reformist or aesthetic principle. Rather, he had grasped that a Frenchified opera of this sort could effectively be combined with the *opera seria*'s traditional emphasis on solo singing, enhancing his own performance. In Pepoli he met a librettist imbued with reformist notions about the primacy of the poet and who rejected collaboration with the performer as debasing. Marchesi seems to have learnt from this experience. His letter to Gonella shows that he informed him of the changes made in *Lodoiska* only after the première, and it was probably not by chance that he chose a librettist in Florence to write an opera for Venice.

Marchesi's activities suggest that the castrato was not beginning to fade from opera at this very time because he was some sort of operatic dinosaur unable to adapt to new conditions. It is even likely that the evolution of the two-tempo (slow–fast) vocal rondò that came into vogue in the late 1770s into the cantabile-cabaletta aria format that was to dominate much of early nineteenth-century Italian opera owed a great deal to Marchesi. In one passage of Pepoli's satire the poet attacks the castrato's claim to 'know the theatre', this knowledge consisting, in the poet's view, of cheap theatrical tricks, of which one was 'to recommend to the poet and the composer the celebrated *cabaletta*', which is defined in a footnote as 'the repeat of a short theme [*motivo*], both facile and interesting, which is likely to have pleased the first time'. This is the first appearance in print that has so far come to light of this etymologically mysterious term, which probably originated as singers' slang. A later appearance of it is also associated with Marchesi. In an assessment of the singer published in 1803, one of his attributes is said to be the singing of rondòs 'with cabalettas . . . of a new character [*modulazione*] and difficult execution'. In the first passage Marchesi is represented as urging the use of cabalettas on librettists and composers and in the second as seeking novelty of style (*modulazione* does not here refer to key changes, as it usually does today, but to melodic and vocal character).

Marchesi's rondò in *Lodoiska* can serve as an example. The fast concluding section of the rondò form seems to have originated as a coda to the earlier one-tempo (slow) rondò, perhaps as a single brilliant stroke by some as yet unknown composer that caught on to become a standard feature and eventually transform the genre. In the *Lodoiska* rondò the final section is more than four times as long as the slow beginning and much more complex in form and musical-dramatic expression. A principal reason for this is the presence of *pertichini*, other characters who intrude into the aria with bits of dialogue or ensemble. This practice, which began in the 1780s, dramatizes and diversifies the aria form and highlights the soloist. It therefore has an effect within the rondò analogous to those that Marchesi encouraged in the opera generally, and it thus seems reasonable to assume that he was also involved in this development of rondò form. In this way the Italian musical system's central principle of the shaping of the work of art through creative interaction of poet, composer and performer is reasserted within the new conditions arising from the evolution of this genre.

In that evolution, then, the *opera seria* remains true to its traditional nature. The adoption of tragic subjects and dénouements, the use of choruses and diversified musical-dramatic format do not reflect the inroads of opera 'reform' in the sense that the Calzabigian-Gluckian reform represented an artistic system dominated by poet and composer. Throughout this period Italian opera persistently resisted such a reorientation, taking from such sources only what could be adapted to its traditional orientation. This should not be taken to mean, as it sometimes has, that *opera seria* was too fossilized or too decadent to reform itself. *Opera seria* did change in this period and, significantly, did so at the very time that the society and culture that produced it were also in a state of change after a long period of relative stability. This is evidence of the close link between *opera seria* and the culture of which it was a part and of its evolving primarily through that relationship. In this, *opera seria* and the Italian musical system prove their continuing vitality as cultural expressions.

NOTES

[1] *Carteggio di Pietro e di Alessandro Verri dal 1766 al 1797*, ed. E. Greppi, A. Giulini and others (Milan, 1910–40), iii, 165, 188.
[2] *Magazin der Musik*, ii (1784), 50ff.
[3] C. Burney, *The Present State of Music in France and Italy* (London, 2/1773/*R*1969), 369.
[4] [P. J. Grosley], *Nouveaux mémoires, ou Observations sur l'Italie et sur les italiens par deux gentilshommes suédois* (London, 1764), iii, 92.
[5] Burney, *Present State*, 194.
[6] *Carteggio di Pietro e di Alessandro Verri*, i, pt.2, 174.
[7] *AMZ*, x (1807), col.205.
[8] *The Letters of Thomas Gray*, ed. D. C. Tovey (London, 1900), i, 67.
[9] H. Swinburne, 'Letters at the End of the Eighteenth Century', in *Secret Memoirs of the Courts of Europe*, ix (n.p. [George Barrie & Sons], n.d.), 161.
[10] G. Sigismondo, *Descrizione della città di Napoli e suoi borghi* (Naples, 1788), ii, 136.
[11] Pietro Napoli-Signorelli, *Vicende della coltura nel regno delle Due Sicilie* (Naples, 2/1810–11), viii, 273–4.
[12] U. Prota-Giurleo, 'Un compositore spagnuolo Vincente Martín y Soler', *Archivi d'Italia e rassegna internazionale degli archivi*, xxvii (1960), 146.
[13] *The Letters of Thomas Gray*, i, 74.
[14] C. de Brosses, *Le Président de Brosses en Italie: lettres familières écrites d'Italie en 1739 et 1740*, ed. R. Colomb (Paris, 5th edn., n.d.), ii, 342.
[15] *The Travel Diaries of William Beckford of Fonthill*, ed. G. Chapman (Cambridge, 1928), i, 252.
[16] B. Croce, *I teatri di Napoli* (Naples, 1891), 414.
[17] G. Casanova, *History of my Life*, trans. W. Trask (New York, 1969), vii, 210ff.
[18] M. Scherillo, *L'opera buffa napoletano durante il Settecento* (Milan, 2/1917), 52.
[19] The extracts by Charles Burney in the Venice section are all from his *Present State*, 149–90 passim.
[20] C. de Brosses, *Le Président de Brosses en Italie*, i, 194.
[21] F. Walker, '*Orazio*: the History of a Pasticcio', *MQ*, xxxviii (1952), 369–83.
[22] *Antologia* [*di Firenze*], xxxiv, no.100 (April 1829), 61.
[23] A. Pepoli, *La morte d'Ercole* (Venice, 1790). All the information in the text is derived from this source.

BIBLIOGRAPHICAL NOTE

For the general reader, the voluminous eighteenth-century travel literature can be one of the most agreeable means to familiarity with the life of the time. A list of such works containing significant references to music can be found in E. Surian's *A Checklist of Writings on 18th Century French and Italian Opera (Excluding Mozart)* (Hackensack, 1970), which is also useful for other aspects of bibliography. C. Burney's *The Present State of Music in France and Italy* (London, 2/1773/*R*1969) is special in having music as its central focus. Among modern editions, *An Eighteenth-Century Musical Tour in France and Italy*, ed. P. A. Scholes (London, 1959), is the most widely available. C. de Brosses's *Lettres familières*, available in several nineteenth- and twentieth-century editions, has also been an important source for historians. The English translation by Donald Schier of its letter on spectacles and music (n.p., *c*1978) is not easily found.

Most travel writings record the impressions of visitors relatively unfamiliar (and sometimes unsympathetic) with what they are describing. The private letters of Italians provide a native point of view. The large correspondence of the brothers Pietro and Alessandro Verri, *Carteggio di Pietro e di Alessandro Verri dal 1766 al 1797*, ed. E. Greppi, A. Giulini and others (Milan, 1910–40), includes many references to music, as do the *Lettere* of the great architect Luigi Vanvitelli, ed. F. Strazzullo (Galatina, 1976). Renato Bossa has made a selection from the latter in 'Luigi

Vanvitelli spettatore teatrale a Napoli', *RIM*, xi (1976), 48–70.

Italian musicians of this period wrote relatively little of either an aesthetic or technical nature on music. Two important books by singing masters, both intended primarily as guides for other singing teachers, are exceptions likely to interest the modern reader. These are P. F. Tosi's *Opinioni de' cantori antichi e moderni* (Bologna, 1723/*R*1968), which pre-dates this period but remained influential in it, and G. Mancini's *Riflessioni pratiche sul canto figurato* (Vienna, 1774, 2/1777). Both have been translated into English. Among modern writings on this art, P. Duey's *Bel Canto in its Golden Age: a Study of its Teaching Concepts* (New York, 1951), is a good epitome and synthesis of the older writers. F. Haböck's *Die Kastraten und ihre Gesangskunst* (Stuttgart, 1927), although in need of updating, remains the major study of the castrato singers. In English, A. Heriot's *The Castrato in Opera* (London, 1956/*R*1975) is largely biographical and anecdotal and, being based mostly on secondary sources, is often factually incorrect, though frequently amusing.

For readers of Italian, the works of the Neapolitan archivist-historians present a mass of often interesting historical data, usually unshaped by any wider historical perspective and unrelated to any specific discussion of music. Most significant among these are *I teatri di Napoli* (Naples, 1891), a youthful work of the great philosopher Benedetto Croce, largely based on archival material destroyed in World War II (later editions of this book contain corrections and additions, but also considerable abbreviations of the original). The well-known local-colourist writer Salvatore di Giacomo produced two similar volumes on *I quattro antichi conservatorii musicali di Napoli* (Palermo, 1924–8). This tradition was carried on by Ulisse Prota-Giurleo, whose many writings tended to be published in obscure periodicals, difficult of access outside Naples. No comparable group of writers exists for Venice. *Venezia e il melodramma nel Settecento*, ed. M. T. Muraro (Florence, 1978), is a collection of scholarly papers resulting from a conference on eighteenth-century opera in Venice. D. Arnold's 'Orphans and Ladies: the Venetian Conservatoires (1690–1797)', *PRMA*, lxxxix (1962–3), 31, surveys the history of the Venetian conservatories.

The question of whether eighteenth-century references to a Neapolitan school of composers can be taken as indicative of a Neapolitan style of composition has interested modern scholars: H. Hucke, 'Die neapolitanische Tradition in der Opera', and E. Downes, 'The Neapolitan Tradition in Opera', both in *IMSCR*, viii *New York 1961*, i 252–84, and is of relevance to M. Robinson's *Naples and Neapolitan Opera* (London, 1972).

In recent years, this period (and especially Italian opera) has been a fertile source of American doctoral dissertations, mostly studies of individual composers. These have clarified many problems of chronology and attribution and begun to amass the kind of analytical data that will be necessary in large quantities before a broader outline of the development of musical style can be attempted. Among those published, M. McClymonds's *Nicolò Jommelli: the Last Years, 1769–74* (Ann Arbor, 1980) may interest the general reader through its inclusion (in Italian and English translation) of many of Jommelli's letters, very revealing of artistic attitudes, while E. Weimer's *Opera Seria and the Evolution of Classical Style 1755–1772* (Ann Arbor, 1984) takes a step towards a broader view by tracing the evolution of a few stylistic elements through the work of several composers.

Chapter III

Paris: the End of the Ancien Régime

JEAN MONGRÉDIEN

Music acquired a new status in France in the eighteenth century, moving from the limited circle of specialists, where until then it had remained, to take its place at the centre of the aesthetic discussions of the Enlightenment philosophers. If the seventeenth had been a century of literary disputes, the eighteenth was to be one of musical altercation. However, the moving spirits – with the possible exception of Rousseau – were neither composers nor even very knowledgeable about musical technique itself. For all that, the art of music inspired heated polemics, and it often crystallized aesthetic and ideological differences. It is therefore particularly important, in the discussion of French eighteenth-century music, to distinguish between the study of theoretical writing about music and the study of the music itself – the more so in that the influence of the first on the second is not always clear. Sometimes, indeed, the activity of composers and performers, as well as public taste, seems to move in a direction quite contrary to the ideas developed by the theorists of the time.

In France the eighteenth century was marked by the progressive weakening of the absolute monarchy established in the previous century by Louis XIV. Under repeated attack from the philosophers, who shook the foundations of power by ceaselessly questioning social, political and religious principles, the monarch's power waned. Reasoned criticism denounced the excesses, injustices and incoherence of the regime which was to collapse after 1789. The intellectual ambition of the bourgeoisie, often encouraged by increasing material prosperity, was to give the French cultural landscape new contours. The musical life of the period undeniably bears the mark of these profound upheavals.[1]

In establishing himself symbolically at the Palais Royal in Paris after the death of Louis XIV in 1715, the regent, during the minority of Louis XV, was striking a blow against the almost exclusive monopoly hitherto held by Versailles on the country's intellectual life. In this sense it is no exaggeration to say that the eighteenth century would belong to Paris. Rameau was to owe much less allegiance than had Lully to the life of Versailles, and composers of subsequent generations owed even less than Rameau. An art of the court was succeeded by one belonging to society. Artists no longer worked primarily for the king, but for a new clientèle which, in establishing itself in the comfortable Parisian town houses, sought not so much luxury as the comfort of privacy. At the end of the century they would liberate themselves even from the protection of patronage, becoming answerable to public opinion alone. In this respect the career of a composer such as Gossec might serve as a model.

MUSIC AND AESTHETIC THEORY

Music, then, occupies a prominent place in the great aesthetic debates that shook eighteenth-century France.[2] One of the commonplaces of eighteenth-century thought, present in all of the innumerable treatises which stand out like landmarks of the century from the famous *Réflexions critiques* of the Abbé Dubos in 1719 onwards, is to draw a parallel, if rather an artificial one, between literature, painting and music: words, colour and sound. The common denominator in the construction of these misleading parallels is the Aristotelian doctrine of imitation, adopted since the Renaissance by men of letters and literary aestheticians. In the eighteenth century, painting and music were integrated into this theory, which may be summarized thus: music, like literature and painting, is an imitative art – that is to say, its essence consists of reproducing a model that already exists in nature. Musical imitation may be either physical (depicting natural phenomena: storms, the murmuring of water etc) or psychological (all the human passions). This principle, which makes the artist not a demiurge, the creator out of nothing of a work without a model and having no end but itself, but a copyist who depicts – a word continually used of music in the eighteenth century – is perfectly defined in the Abbé Batteux's work, *Les beaux arts réduits à un même principe* (1746). In this treatise, regarded as gospel truth in its day, such statements might be found as 'The function of genius is not to imagine that which may be, but to find out that which is. Even those men of genius who dig the deepest will find nothing but what already existed'.

The more discerning of the philosophers, however, soon realized that there was a danger here, and that forcing music to imitate a model slavishly limited its aims. Thus Diderot – who was in no way a practical musician yet still devoted long passages of aesthetic reflection to it – soon became aware of the specific character of the musical phenomenon. He was one of the first in the eighteenth century to try thinking of music and defining it without reference to any exterior object, taking music itself, its structure and the effects peculiar to it as his starting-point. A little later in the century, Jean-Jacques Rousseau, most notably in the entries 'Imitation' and 'Opera' in his *Dictionnaire de musique* (1768), also tried to avoid the impasse even while retaining the imitative principle; the gist of his argument is that music does not directly imitate natural phenomena, but makes that impression on us which we would feel if confronted with such and such a phenomenon: it acts symbolically. Thus the philosopher can explain, for example, that music, which in essence is sound and movement, may yet depict 'the stillness of a quiet night'.

On the eve of the French Revolution, Michel de Chabanon, a writer and member of the Académie who was also an excellent musician (he led the second violins in the Concert des Amateurs), put an end to the tyranny of the theory of imitation. In *De la musique considérée en elle-même et dans ses rapports avec la parole, les langues, la poésie et le théâtre* (1785), he wrote that 'Nothing is as dubious as the necessity to imitate, claimed as one of the essential propositions of music', and put forward a new theory, asserting that, unlike painting, music 'pleases without imitation, by means of the sensations it produces'.

These expositions of the theory of imitation, repeated in mutual emulation by the best minds of the time, might have had formidable consequences for the development of music in France. Fortunately, they did not; composers were drawn to follow the taste of the public and respond to its requirements rather than obey the theorists' precepts. In fact, the proponents of the principle of imitation, in claiming that all music must have a strictly rational meaning and must be supported by a literary argument exterior to itself, might well have succeeded in side-tracking composers of instrumental music. One recalls the famous remark attributed to Fontenelle: 'Sonate, que me veux-tu?'[3] Towards the end of the century, in 1785, the curse still sometimes weighed heavy; it is surprising to find a writer as fine as the Count of Lacépède devoting a volume of over 700 pages to *La poétique de la musique*, but content to study instrumental music – symphony, concerto, quartet, trio and sonata – in no more than sixteen pages. The few pages dealing with the symphony are obviously conceived with vocal music in mind. It would almost appear as if the symphony suffered *a priori* from some deficiency. Instead of trying to discover wherein its originality lies, Lacépède constantly sought to define it by reference to something else, to something which it is not and by definition cannot be: 'vivid as the pictures offered by a symphony may be, it will be easy to see that they are only vague images'. It is thus the composer's business to paint with energy and to try 'to compensate with brighter colours and a greater number of images for the pleasures given by an exact representation'. Each of the three movements of the symphony must be devised like an air on a large scale 'in which one or more voices may seek to express feelings of

15. Title-page of the 'Sei sextuor' by Luigi Boccherini, published by La Chevardière in 1775 as op.15 (Boccherini's op.16)

a more or less lively nature'. The ensemble of three movements must be conceived 'as three acts of a play' and the whole should compose 'a kind of drama'.

At exactly the time when the symphony had just established itself as a genre and was attaining, in the works of Haydn and Mozart, true perfection of form, it is surprising that a musical aesthetician should persist in analysing it in strictly literary and dramatic terms, as if unaware of the requirements of a purely musical, harmonic and thematic work. Lacépède's book contains no more precise reflections on the symphony, implying that in his view the structure of a movement must depend on some literary argument imposed upon it, generating a superficial picturesqueness of style.

THE CULTIVATION OF INSTRUMENTAL MUSIC

Despite these theories, instrumental music in France was in a state of exceptional vitality from 1730 to 1789, evident equally among composers, performers and the public. As genres and forms evolved, the change from the Baroque to Classicism took place by degrees – although it is not always possible to determine the exact stages of these far-reaching developments.

Two factors favoured the growth of instrumental music: the great activity in music publishing in Paris, and the proliferation of concerts, both public and private, which allowed soloists to perform before increasingly large (if not necessarily increasingly knowledgeable) audiences.

Music publishing flourished in eighteenth-century France.[4] First, the practice of engraving music on copper or pewter plates (replacing the use of movable type), still new at the beginning of the century, made faster reproduction of texts possible. Second, the number of publishers increased considerably, particularly after 1750. They played an essential part in the musical life of the period; they acted as intermediaries between composers and the public and, anxious to seek out the best talents, they offered their customers catalogues (many of which survive) which constitute some of the earliest evidence of written musical publicity. For instance, Louis-Balthazar de La Chevardière (not afraid to follow the profession of music publisher, although of noble birth), supplied music for fifteen years to people in fashionable society, most notably the Prince of Conti, whose musical salon was famous. A publisher of this type performed an important social function: he discovered talented musicians and made them known to the public or presented them to patrons.

Paris was one of the European capitals of music publishing during this period and many foreign composers had their works published there: Boccherini, for instance, published sonatas, trios, quartets and symphonies. His publishers were La Chevardière and Jean-Baptiste Venier, a violinist who in 1755 took over the publication of the important collection *Sinfonie da varii autori*. These works, published in instalments, were to play a crucial part in the distribution of contemporary Italian and German symphonies.

Soon, for commercial reasons, spurious texts were also published, including symphonies falsely attributed to Haydn or Pleyel. Composers and publishers thus had to be alert for forgeries and counterfeits. The little world of music publishing of the time was a body of some importance and was very much a world unto itself; in Paris, where the population was about 500,000 in the second half of the century, there were 150 music engravers (most of whom, incidentally, were women). The *Almanach musical* of 1783 lists 97 music publishers, a figure that bears out the international role played by Paris in this field.

Throughout the eighteenth century, authors had not only to defend themselves against the danger of counterfeits and pirated editions, but from the moment when they began to work independently, living on their own incomes, they had to fight for their rights. Beaumarchais, after his dispute with the actors of the Théâtre Français in 1777, was behind the foundation of the Société des Auteurs et Compositeurs Dramatiques, which would ensure the recognition of authors' rights, a measure reaffirmed by ratification of the Revolutionary Convention in the 1790s. Librettists and composers profited by this new legislation which gave them, for instance, prompt remuneration for performances of their works in the provinces. The archives of the society, although very incomplete, are an interesting source for the study of a musician's way of life at the time.

In April 1727, the *Mercure de France* significantly noted: 'Musical taste has never been so universal. In Paris and in the smallest of provincial towns, we see concerts and academies of music maintained at great expense, and more are being set up every day'. Like the flourishing state of music publishing in Paris, this marked proliferation of concerts, which accelerated after 1750, was a sign of intense musical activity and of an increasing audience for music.[5] We can conclude from surviving programmes that there was a great vogue for virtuosos, both French and foreign. Another important development was the increasing popularity of wind instruments: flute, oboe, bassoon and horn, followed by the clarinet and trumpet. Solos for these instruments were often performed by German players. Among the strings, the violin and the other instruments of the violin family finally superseded the viol. Although in 1740 the jurist Hubert le Blanc published his treatise *Défense de la basse de viole contre les entreprises du violon et les prétentions du violoncelle*, in which he praised the great viol players of the previous generation and berated 'Sultan Violin, undersized, a pygmy' which 'not content with Italy, its inheritance, proposed to invade the neighbouring states . . . and hopes to win the day with torrents of voluptuous notes', his cause was lost. As Ancelet wrote in his *Observations* (1757): 'The bass viol is now relegated to the studies of elderly partisans of ancient music'.

All the instruments of the violin family, on the other hand, were to benefit from the refinements to the bow introduced during the eighteenth century by the various members of a family of Parisian violin makers, the Tourtes. In modifying the curve of the bow and the position of the fingers on the nut, they gave rise to the finely mannered style of playing, made expressive by the execution of accents, which Classical composers were frequently to enhance with a sudden interruption or a moment of silence. This new style of writing for the string quartet, with its constant indications of dynamics and its breaks in the continuity of phrasing, was unlike the often uninterrupted flow of Baroque musical discourse.

The most important innovation in instrument making at the time was of course the appearance of the pianoforte, which for a while co-existed with the harpsichord; this topic will be discussed later. We should now turn to the great Parisian concert organizations and to the private concerts.

The institution which through its influence, durability and the frequency of its concerts easily dominated Parisian musical life was the famous Concert Spirituel.[6] It was the first important society to

CONCERT SPIRITUEL,
AU CHATEAU DES TUILERIES,
Aujourd'hui MARDI 2 Février 1779, JOUR DE LA PURIFICATION.

CE Concert commencera par une nouv. lle Symphonie à grand Orcheſtre de la Compoſition del Signor HA EN.

M. MOREAU, de l'Académie-Royale d Muſique, chantera un Motet de M. CANDEILLE.

M. VOUNDERLICH, exécutera un Conc de Flûte.

Mde TODI, chantera un nouvel Air Ita PICCINI.

MM. PALSA & TIERSCHEMIEDT exécutero ncerto de Cors de Chaſſe. On exécutera un nouvel Oratorio (ON) Paroles de VOLTAIRE, Muſique de M. CAMBINI, dans lequel . DUCHASTEAU, MM. MOREAU & LE GROS chanteront.

M. CHARTRAIN, exécutera un nouv. Concerto de Violon de ſa compoſit.

Le Concert finira par un nouvel Air Italien del Signor GUGLIELMI, chanté par Mde TODI.

On commencera à ſix heures. Les Voitures entreront par toutes les Cours.
On s'adreſſera, pour louer des Loges, à la Dlle SOUBRA, Cour des Suiſſes.

16. Handbill for a Concert Spirituel at the Palais de Tuileries on 2 February 1779

organize public concerts for a paying audience in France. The initiative came from the composer Anne-Danican Philidor, who was granted a royal privilege for the purpose in 1725. The name 'Concert Spirituel' is explained by the intentions of its founders, whose initial aim was to offer Paris concerts of sacred music on those days of the church calendar (Lent, Corpus Christi, All Saints etc) when the theatres were closed. Philidor undertook not to put on performances of vocal works with French words. The concerts were at first given in the Salle des Suisses of the Palais des Tuileries; in 1784 they moved to the Salle des Machines in the same building. In 1750, 87 solo musicians performed at the Concert Spirituel, 39 instrumentalists and 48 singers. A quarter of a century later, in 1775, these figures were considerably larger: 58 instrumentalists and 55 singers were heard that year.

Originally, the staple repertory of the Concert Spirituel consisted of religious and instrumental music. It was the first time the Parisian public had been given a chance to hear certain artists who had not previously performed outside Versailles. As early as 1727, however, and contrary to the terms of the privilege, concerts including secular vocal music were advertised (cantatas and extracts from operas sung in French). The Concert Spirituel retained its name, although, giving way to public pressure, its organizers were changing direction. There were concerts twice weekly in winter and once in summer from 1730. They continued until the Revolution, drawing large audiences from an increasingly wide social range, and with the Opéra they were the centre of Parisian musical life. The enterprise ran into operational problems at various times, but it never foundered; only the first upheavals of the revolutionary period could put an end to so splendid an institution, one successively led by several of the best musicians of the time.

In many ways, the Concert Spirituel played a crucial part in the musical life of the whole of France. It gave young provincial composers the chance of being heard in Paris, and it soon opened its doors to works from abroad as well. Thus the Parisian public must quickly have become acquainted with the contemporary Italian and German schools, and this first experience of other repertories proved fertile, especially in the instrumental field. In 1733 music by the Italian composer Giovanni Bononcini, then staying in Paris, was played at the Tuileries; December 1736 saw the first appearance on the concert programmes of a name still unknown to Parisians, that of George Frideric Handel. A concerto grosso by the same master was heard in 1743, while Johann Stamitz, who was in Paris from 1754, was applauded both as composer (his symphonies were played at the concerts) and as performer (of his own works for violin). Ten years later, in 1764, the first French editions of Haydn's symphonies appeared, and these masterpieces immediately became part of the Concert Spirituel repertory. One of the institution's most glorious claims to fame was surely to have commissioned a symphony from Mozart on his visit to Paris in 1778, although Mozart's style may have been too rich for the Parisian palate – the *Mercure* of June 1779 wrote of the finale of one of his symphonies that it must be left 'to the lovers of a kind of music which may interest the mind without ever going to the heart'.[7] The Italian school also figured large in the Concert Spirituel programmes, with music by Corelli, Vivaldi and Geminiani. It was the first time works by these composers, who were to exercise great influence on the French school, had been heard publicly in Paris.

We can thus see how important a position the Concert Spirituel occupied. The supreme aim of a composer was to be played there, and that of an artist to perform there. Certain instrumentalists of great talent never dared offer themselves to the judgment of this select and critical audience; among them was the violinist Louis-Gabriel Guillemain, of whom Ancelet recalled in his *Observations*, that 'his great timidity prevented him from performing at the Concert Spirituel, which is, without doubt, the best and most advantageous place to be heard. Several other very clever people attached to the Musique du Roi were in the same predicament'.

The success of the Concert Spirituel encouraged the formation of other societies. About 1770, further concert organizations appeared in Paris: a series known as the Concert des Amateurs, for example, whose performances were held in the Hôtel de Soubise and which was dissolved in 1781. The greatest French soloists and others from abroad played there, and Mozart mentioned the institution in his letters from Paris. In January 1771 the *Journal de musique* announced that this concert organization was 'composed almost entirely of amateurs whose great talents are in no way inferior to those of the cleverest professors', adding: 'Here one may enjoy the all too rare pleasure of hearing the symphonies concertantes of Messieurs Gossec and the younger Stamitz'. The *Almanach musical* of 1775 was to go even further in its praises, declaring that this orchestra of nearly 48 musicians was 'the best orchestra for symphonies that there is in Paris and perhaps in Europe'.

When the Concert des Amateurs was dissolved, another organization was formed, the Société de la Loge Olympique, which, like the Concert Spirituel, held its performances in a hall in the Palais des Tuileries;[8] the composer and violinist Giovanni Battista Viotti became its conductor when he settled in Paris. It was for this institution that Haydn's six 'Paris' symphonies of 1784 (nos.82–7) were intended. The Société is interesting in relation to the history of freemasonry in France just before the Revolution. A considerable number of musicians were freemasons during the reign of Louis XVI, many of them members of the Musique du Roi. Several lodges devoted a large proportion of their activities to music. The Loge Olympique was primarily set up to allow its members to meet and make music together. The *Annuaire de la Société Olympique pour 1786* clearly indicates its objectives: 'Its principal aim, of interest to the large number of masons who united to form it and to those who have since joined, is the establishment in Paris of a concert organization which may in some respects replace the loss of the Concert des Amateurs'.

There were other public associations about which we have little information: a Concert des Associés is mentioned in the December 1770 issue of the *Journal de musique*, which approved of the setting up of the association, a kind of trial ground intended to help young artists 'still too weak to bear the judgment of a severe public'. There was the Société Académique des Enfants d'Apollon, which dates back to 1741 and which gave one concert of solemn music each year until 1789; Gossec's *Messe des morts* was heard there in 1770. Nor should this outline of Parisian concert organizations omit to mention the proliferation, in the last years of the *ancien régime*, of 'pleasure gardens' and cafés such as the Vauxhall described by Louis-Sébastien Mercier in his *Tableau de Paris*, which employed small orchestral groups to play light music, tunes from fashionable light operas and medleys, for the first time allowing the working-class public of Paris, which attended neither theatres nor grand concerts, to hear the music it liked at a reasonable cost.

The *Tableau de Paris pour l'année 1759* lists a number of those who organized private concerts at their own houses. Any description of these private concerts must naturally begin with the court of Versailles. If Louis XV was not especially well versed in music, the queen, the king's acknowledged mistress Mme de Pompadour, the dauphin, the dauphine and all the royal princesses, Louis XV's daughters, were not content merely to enjoy music; they all practised it too, and several of them were accomplished performers. The dauphine, for

17. Concert in the home of Comtesse de St Brisson, 1773: engraving by A. de St Aubin after Antoine Jean Duclos

instance, Marie-Josephe of Saxony (whose birth had occasioned Rameau's harpsichord piece *La dauphine*), organized several concerts a week in her apartments at Versailles, where on one occasion she received her compatriots, the famous Hasses, husband and wife, he a composer and she a famous singer. Even the greatest of the foreign artists who triumphed at the Concert Spirituel valued the favours of the court: Farinelli was twice fêted there, in 1737 and 1752, and another Italian castrato, Caffarelli, enjoyed success at Versailles.

The great salons of the nobility were also increasingly opening their doors to music. The brilliance of the musical performances at the house of the Prince of Conti, where the child Mozart played with his sister on his first visit to Paris, is well known. The salons of the Prince of Guéménée, the Duke of Aiguillon, Louis XV's minister, and of the Princes of Condé at Chantilly should also be mentioned. Concerts were more popular than ever among the French nobility in the reign of Louis XVI. In her *Mémoires*, the Baroness von Oberkirch recalls the distinguished concerts given at his house in Paris by the Count of Albaret, 'a very rich Piedmontese, whose own musicians lived in his house and never went out without his permission'. Such private bands were characteristic of musical patronage of the time. The musicians were maintained entirely by their master and patron, but they forfeited their freedom when they agreed to wear his livery. The two most famous musical salons were those of the Baron of Bagge and of the wealthy *fermier général* Le Riche de La Pouplinière. The former, a colourful character who came from Courland (Latvia), settled in Paris in 1751. A composer, a virtuoso violinist, an aesthete and a teacher, he was an original known all over Europe. The *Tablettes de renommée des musiciens* of 1785 recount that:

> the Baron of Bagge holds one of the finest private concerts in this capital at his house every Friday during the winter. It pleases him to patronize all the foreign and amateur virtuosos who wish to make their début in this capital and to make their talents known here.

Three years later, in his *Mémoires secrets*, Bachaumont noted: 'People generally make their débuts at his house before appearing at the Concert Spirituel'. The many dedications of instrumental works to the Baron of Bagge, most notably by Boccherini (who stayed at his house) and by Gossec, give an idea of his importance in the musical life of the time.

However, the outstanding musical salon in eighteenth-century Paris was that of the financier Le Riche de La Pouplinière.[9] He kept an entire orchestra, conducted by such eminent musicians as Rameau, Johann Stamitz and Gossec. This was a great expense, even for someone as wealthy as this epicurean financier. Theatrical performances and literary evenings alternated at his house with concerts in which instrumental music always predominated. La Pouplinière's salon, unimaginable in French life in the preceding century, was to some extent the realization of the hedonist universe imagined by Voltaire in his poem *Le mondain*:

> J'aime le luxe et même la mollesse,
> Tous les plaisirs, les arts de toute espèce,
> La propreté, le goût, les ornements:
> Tout honnête homme a de tels sentiments . . .
> Quel est le train des jours d'un honnête homme?
> Entrez chez lui: la foule des beaux-arts,
> Enfants du goût, se montre à vos regards . . .

> (I love luxury, even softness, all pleasures, arts of every kind, propriety, good taste, embellishment; all gentlemen feel such sentiments . . . How does a gentleman spend his days? Enter his house, and the whole host of fine arts, children of taste, will meet your eye . . .)

In 1754, the year of Johann Stamitz's arrival in Paris (he was soon to succeed Rameau as conductor of La Pouplinière's orchestra), the group consisted of some twenty players; the presence of instruments still unusual in France at this time (horns, clarinets and harps) meant that the repertory of the Mannheim school could be performed. There was a great musical flowering here, and it had a decisive influence on a composer like Gossec. Unfortunately, the sudden death of La Pouplinière in 1762 brought his high-flying patronage to an end.

Various contemporary reports show that the further the century advanced, the more widely the performance of music spread among the Parisian bourgeoisie. The great development of private concerts after the Revolution, under the Directoire, the Consulate and the Empire, had actually begun in the last days of the *ancien régime*. Among the accounts, that of the English music historian Charles Burney, who travelled to Paris in 1770, is particularly interesting. In his diary for 20 June, he described a dinner at the house of the amateur composer Madame Brillon de Jouy, wife of a civil servant. Burney was impressed by the luxury of the house and the excellent dinner, obvious signs of the social rise of the bourgeoisie before 1789. 'After coffee', he wrote, 'we went into the music room, where I found an English pianoforte which Mr [J. C.] Bach had sent her'. Mme Brillon was an accomplished musician:

> This lady not only plays the most difficult pieces with great precision, taste, and feeling, but is an excellent sightswoman: of which I was convinced by her manner of executing some of my own music, that I had the honour of presenting to her . . . She played the second of my sonatas very well at sight on the pianoforte accompanied by M. Pagin – and for want of a violoncello I played that part on the harpsichord.

This excellent player had also composed sonatas for piano and violin obbligato. Burney wrote:

> But her application and talents are not confined to the harpsichord; she plays on several instruments; knows the genius of all that are in common use . . . To this lady many of the famous composers of Italy and Germany, who have resided in France at any time, have dedicated their works; among these are Schobert and Boccherini.

This salon was certainly not the only one of its kind; the middle classes were passionately fond of performing music. But records of private concerts are, understandably, very rare.

THE ORCHESTRAL REPERTORY

France was not exclusively the country of opera in the eighteenth century, as one is still inclined to think. Instrumental music also flourished; and it provides excellent material for the study of the profound upheavals taking place which were gradually to lead from Baroque to Classical aesthetics. Unfortunately, the abundant repertory is still unfamiliar and not easy of access; there are few modern editions and the music historian seeking to study the texts meets the problem of sources. Up to the beginning of the nineteenth century, few instrumental works were available in full score; the repertory has survived in the form of separate parts. To understand the structure of a work, and to judge its merits, it is thus necessary to construct a full score, which requires considerable labour.

The term 'symphony'[10] retained the general sense of 'instrumental piece' until well into the eighteenth century, even after 1750; that is how Rousseau defined it in his *Dictionnaire*. Just before 1750 the first true Classical French symphonies appeared. They are the work of a musician forgotten today, and about whom little is known: the cellist François Martin, a protégé of the Duke of Gramont. He was the first to write symphonies showing some of the features that were to be the hallmarks of the Classical school, before the first masterpieces of the Mannheim composers were heard in Paris. It is not known exactly where Martin found his model, for the orchestral works performed in Paris from 1730 to 1750 were influenced by the style of the Baroque suite or by the French taste for imitative or programme music.

This was the period when Jacques Aubert, first violin of the Académie Royale de Musique, published several collections of *Concerts de symphonies pour les violons, flûtes et hautbois* (1730–37) divided into suites, each beginning with an overture and presenting a succession of minuets, rondos, sarabandes, tambourins, chaconnes etc. Curiously, Aubert often associated the name of the dance with the tempo designation; thus one finds 'Sarabande adagio' or 'Gavotte grazioso', proof of the growing abandonment of Baroque terminology for movement titles in favour of tempo indications, the only kind of title that would be retained in the Classical period.

Les élémens, symphonie nouvelle (1737) by Jean-Féry Rebel, conductor of the orchestra of the Académie Royale de Musique, is for two violins, two flutes and a cello. Divided into two parts, respectively entitled 'Le cahos' and 'Les élémens', it endeavours, in strict obedience to the principle of imitation in music, to depict the efforts made by the elements to separate themselves from each other. 'I have ventured', wrote Rebel, 'to undertake to join to the idea of the confusion of the elements that of the confusion of harmony. I have dared to have all the sounds heard first mingled together, or rather all the notes of the octave united in a single sound.' From the initial jarring dissonance to the final common chord, the work runs a harmonic course which makes this symphony – almost a symphonic poem – one of the most original pieces of its time.

But François Martin cannot have found his models here. It is more likely that they came from abroad, and that the influence of Italian or German symphonies was crucial. In any case, the presence in Paris (1754–5) of Johann Stamitz, the Mannheim Konzertmeister, confirmed French composers in their course. They vied in writing this new form of symphony, which gradually developed the characteristics of a new style – the Classical style. There was a progressive reduction of the symphony to three or four movements, while works still inspired by the spirit of the Baroque suite might contain more than ten. The architecture of sonata form was progressively elaborated – most notably with the appearance of a second subject in the initial Allegro movement – and the figured bass, still present in the 1750s, became less common. The influence of the German model can be seen, particularly in the importance and autonomy given to the woodwind sections, their music being generally for pairs of instruments; flutes, oboes and bassoons no longer merely echoed the violins and bass line. They had won their independence and could converse on equal terms with the strings, producing pleasing contrasts of timbre. Contrasts, of dynamics as well as timbre, are emphasized yet further by the highly thematic character of the musical discourse, which brings tonal relationships to the fore. Modulation acquired a power that it had lacked in Baroque music. In this sense, Classical composition marked the success – for at least a century – and the supreme power of that tonality whose universality Rameau had proclaimed, revealing what he saw as its natural foundations.

For the 40 years from 1750 to 1789, Paris, together with Vienna and London, was to be one of the European shrines of the Classical symphony. Several hundreds of symphonies were published and played in Paris during this period. François-Joseph Gossec alone, sometimes (rightly) called 'the father of the French symphony', and one of the leading figures in French musical life up to the end of the century, wrote 50 symphonies. A Fleming from Hainaut, he had come to Paris as a young man in 1751. He began his career as conductor of La Pouplinière's orchestra and was thus able to hear the masterpieces of the Mannheim school when they were first performed in France. Gossec's model, once established, was used by all his followers up to the Revolution: Marie-Alexandre Guénin, Jean-Baptiste Davaux, Henri Rigel and the Chevalier de Saint-Georges, to name only the principal figures. Many of their symphonies, through the quality of their orchestration, the delicacy of their colouring and particularly the indefinable sense of equilibrium and felicitous strength that emanates from them, often convey a sense of perfection attained, though they only rarely contain those anguished resonances found at the same period in the works of Haydn and Mozart.

The symphonie concertante, which came into being a little later than the symphony – it appeared in Europe towards 1770 – is also a manifestation of the Classical spirit. Paris is the uncontested capital in the history of the genre. Mozart, staying in Paris in 1778, followed the dictates of fashion in composing his double concerto for flute and harp (K299/297*c*), despite its title a symphonie concertante, and then his lost sinfonia concertante for four wind instruments (K297*B*) which was intended for the Concert Spirituel. Between 1770 and 1800 the French alone wrote as many symphonies concertantes as all other European composers combined; more than 150 were composed between 1768 and 1789.

This outpouring of symphonies concertantes came in response to a clear public demand. The development of instrumental virtuosity at the time, for strings as well as for woodwind, was such that increasing pleasure was taken in the interplay between soloists; for the symphonie concertante was actually a concerto, in the modern sense of the word, for several instruments. The number of solo instruments varies from two to seven. Most of the symphonies concertantes were for two soloists, but they may offer the most varied combinations: some 40 have been enumerated. Any instrument may serve as soloist; there is even one example for harpsichord, clarinet and horn, by Emilie-Julie Candeille.

There was scarcely a concert in Paris from 1770 onwards at which no symphonie concertante was performed. Again, the aesthetic of pleasure lies behind this fashion. In his *Dictionnaire de musique* (1787), the Chevalier de Meude-Monpas considered the symphonie concertante 'a perpetual struggle', and added, amusingly, 'It resembles a large double-sided ladder, with the performers two schoolboys competing to see who can climb it better'. Typically, the symphonie concertante is in two movements, an initial Allegro and a rondo; the omission of a slow movement represents a conscious limitation of the music's expressive scope. Similarly, minor keys are avoided. The form is tailored to the taste of a society that requires diversion and for which all kinds of variety, beginning with a variety of timbre, are a way to banish monotony and boredom. In the realm of art, it is equivalent to the polite conversation of the salon.

The masters of the genre were mostly those of the symphony: Gossec, Davaux and Saint-Georges, also Jean-Baptiste Bréval, Simon Leduc and above all the Italian Giuseppe Cambini, who settled in Paris in 1770 and was always in the forefront of the Parisian musical scene. Unlike the symphony, the symphonie concertante, which continued to flourish under the Revolution and the empire, disappeared for good in the 1820s. Born for a well-defined society, that of the close of the eighteenth century, it could not survive the passing of that era.

The history of French chamber music during this period remains imperfectly understood; entire sections of the repertory are still almost unknown. Classification by genre is often difficult; the frontiers between what we now regard as symphonic music and chamber music often remain blurred. The composers of this period did not hesitate to delegate responsibility to the performers. It seems clear that in some circumstances, especially when performances were given in the provinces or in domestic amateur contexts, players felt free to interpret the music in their own way. The titles composers assigned to their works may mislead the modern performer. In 1766 in Paris, for instance, La Chevardière issued six symphonies by the German composer Johann Christoph Cannabich under the title: 'Six symphonies, the first three of which may be played as octets or quartets and the three others by full orchestra obbligato'. Nothing is fixed; the interpreter has a comfortable margin of freedom which, at its furthest, may considerably modify the character of the music.

The violin holds pride of place in the history of eighteenth-century French chamber music.[11] At this period some of the most brilliant virtuosos of the time were in Paris, all of them excellent composers. It was no matter of chance that at least three, Jean-Pierre Guignon, Louis-Gabriel Guillemain and Jean-Marie Leclair, had been pupils in Italy of the famous Giovanni Battista Somis, himself a disciple of Corelli; we know of the enthusiasm of the French at this time for the sparkling virtuosity of Italian instrumental music (the concerto and sonata). D'Alembert and Rousseau were in correspondence with Tartini, whose works enjoyed much success in Paris during the second half of the eighteenth century. This was when new performers appeared, notably the famous Pierre Gaviniès, the leading virtuoso of the time and soon to be director at the Concert Spirituel with Gossec and Simon Leduc. In the last years of the *ancien régime* Giovanni Battista Viotti, a musician of the first rank, established himself in Paris, whence his influence spread throughout Europe.

Today, Jean-Marie Leclair is indisputably the most famous name of the years 1725–60. He was universally admired in his own time; Marpurg (*Abhandlung von der Fuge*, 1753–4) did not hesitate to place him alongside Handel and Telemann. He was the first to display to his dazzled contemporaries the full resources of his instrument. He was also unusually interested for the time in matters of style. In the preface to his second book of violin sonatas (*c*1730), he pertinently wrote: 'All who wish to be able to perform this work must try to find out the character of each piece, as well as the true tempo and quality of sound suitable for the different movements' – a distinctly 'modern' sentiment. Leclair's violin works may exemplify the evolution of forms in the course of the century. His first sonatas, published before 1730, are still in the spirit of the Italian *sonata da camera*. The works of his maturity, on the other hand, are truly Gallic as much in form as in the spirit which animates them, whether they are sonatas for one or two violins, with or without a bass, quartets in sonata form or concertos.

These remarks on the history of forms and the violin apply equally to the cello – an instrument increasingly popular from 1760, with such masters as the brothers Jean-Pierre and Jean-Louis Duport, and Jean-Baptiste Bréval – and to wind instruments. Moreover, it was wind rather than string instruments which had been the first to introduce the concerto to France (*Concertos pour cinq flûtes* by Joseph Bodin de Boismortier, 1727). The titles that composers gave their works are sometimes enough to show the evolution of the form. Thus the flautist Michel Corrette wrote first a *Concerto en quatuor pour une flûte et deux violons avec la basse continue*; a little later, he published a *Concerto pour la flûte avec deux parties de violon et la basse continue*; the second obviously denotes opposition between a soloist (the flute) and the other instruments. The independence acquired by all the orchestral instruments between 1750 and 1789 is well gauged by Pierre-Louis Ginguené in his article on the concerto in the *Encyclopédie méthodique* (1791):

> Instrumental performance has now reached so advanced a state of perfection that there is no instrument that cannot claim to shine in a concert . . . The flute, the oboe and the clarinet have long had their concertos. Even the horn has concertos, and the sad bassoon has not forgone that advantage. I have heard the nephew of the great Stamitz play concertos for the viola; concertos for the violoncello have made the reputation of more than one famous artist, and concertos have now been composed for the double bass.

During this period, and in step with the progressive elimination – or rather, transformation – of the basso continuo, the instrumental writing known as 'en trio', popular in Europe during the Enlightenment, gradually gave way to a new genre: the instrumental quartet,

18. Quartet of horn, cello, violin and oboe, played by Rodolphe, Duport, Vachon and Vernier: watercolour by Louis Carrogis de Carmontelle (1717–1806)

more precisely the string quartet.[12] French composers were early to be attracted by the balance of this ensemble, and on 1 December 1768, the *Annonces, affiches et avis divers* advertised the publication of six quartets (unfortunately now lost) by a composer whose reputation has not survived, Antoine Baudron. These were the first French quartets published in Paris. Nearly 1000 quartets (including works by foreign composers who chose to be published in Paris) were to be issued between 1770 and 1800. Such abundance is positive proof of the widespread private performance of music, since there were no public chamber music concerts at the time.

The string quartet described as 'concertant' or 'dialogué', in which all four instrumental roles play equal roles, was the most popular. Rousseau, who liked a striking phrase, wrote in the entry on the quartet in his *Dictionnaire*: 'There are no true quartets, or if there are they are not worth anything', suggesting that it was dangerous to claim that four different parts could be on an equal footing. Such reservations did not prevent the French taking enthusiastically to the new genre; Pierre Vachon alone, a protégé of the Prince of Conti, published five sets, each of six quartets, and among others who worked in the genre are such composers as Bréval, Gossec and the Chevalier de Saint-Georges.

Towards 1780 another form of quartet, in which the flute or oboe could replace a violin, was devised: the *quatuor d'airs variés*. A kind of music that might now be described as 'functional', it consisted of arrangements of fashionable tunes, making theatre music available to the chamber musician. Such transcriptions indicated the presence, among amateurs, of at least as many string and wind players as harpsichordists or fortepianists.

The first decades of the eighteenth century had been the heyday of the French harpsichord school, culminating in the works of François Couperin and Jean-Philippe Rameau. Rameau's three solo harpsichord collections antedate 1730. His last collection for harpsichord is called *Pièces de clavecin en concerts* (1741), for harpsichord obbligato, viola da gamba and violin or flute. These are true instrumental trios, with the leading role assigned to the harpsichord while the other two instruments sometimes act as accompanists. Their form is that of the suite but, like many of the works already discussed, they are a musical turning-point, for some of the *concerts* have a three-movement structure characteristic of the concerto. As in Couperin's harpsichord music, there is a typically French psychological colouring in the choice of titles based in images: portraits of great men, artists or patrons (*La Forqueray, La Pouplinière*), or the depiction of a character, or genre painting (*La timide, Les cyclopes*).

Rameau's *Pièces de clavecin en concerts*, in using string and wind instruments to accompany the keyboard, follow up a new and distinctively French development. In 1734, J. J. Cassanéa de Mondonville had published *Pièces de clavecin en sonates avec accompagnement de violon*: a new kind of sonata, as Mondonville himself noted, fusing French and Italian keyboard and string styles; he followed them up in 1748 with a set of sonatas in which the player could accompany himself by singing, or could assign the vocal part to a violin. Several composers, including Boismortier and Corrette, pursued the idea of the keyboard sonata with string accompaniment. After the middle of the century, with the influx of German keyboard players into Paris, the accompanied sonata became increasingly international and one of the most popular genres not only in Paris but in all the main commercial musical centres of Europe, serving a genuine need in amateur music-making.

In about 1760 the influence of foreign models helped the French harpsichord sonata to become established. The catalogues of the Parisian publishers of the time are full of foreign harpsichord sonatas, especially by Germans: Wagenseil, Johann Schobert and the sons of

J.S. Bach. The year 1765 even saw the publication in Paris of some harpsichord sonatas with violin *ad libitum* by W. A. Mozart (aged nine). From this period it becomes more difficult to speak of a typically French harpsichord school. Artists were travelling more; there were increased exchanges between countries, and many reciprocal influences were becoming established in Europe: this led to a certain hybridization of national schools. In France writing for the harpsichord changed gradually after the death of Rameau in 1764 and began to show a new expressive style. For instance, in his fourth book of *Pièces de clavecin* (1768), Jacques Duphly, organist at Rouen, still gave all his pieces the names of people, in the manner of Couperin or Rameau. Yet his style is not the same; throughout this collection there are simple, unornamented melodic lines sustained by an Alberti bass or triplet arpeggios, nearer to the Rococo style than the ornate melody dear to the previous generation of harpsichordists.

These expressive ventures in musical language of the 1760s developed together with the emergence of a new sensibility in French society. After two centuries of Classicism, which had proclaimed the universality of Cartesian reason, 'the best apportioned thing in the world', the heart was gradually reclaiming its rights. This development is naturally discernible in contemporary painting and particularly in literature: Rousseau's *La nouvelle Héloïse* is the first important landmark in the return to sensibility which was to mark the late eighteenth century.

The harpsichord, with its inability to convey the light and shade of dynamics, was no longer appropriate to these expansive and spare melodies, sustained solely by a few bass arpeggios. In this connection an article by the Abbé Trouflaut which appeared in the *Journal de musique* of 1773 (no.5) is revealing. He wrote in particular: 'Despite the inexhaustible resources that the harpsichord offers to genius, the equality of its sounds is undeniably a real fault'. The aim of musicians at this time was precisely the pursuit of light and shade. When, in 1768, Pascal Taskin 'perfected' the harpsichord by adding an extra row of jacks fitted with buff leather, it was considered a great step forward. The Abbé Trouflaut commented:

> The effect of this leather on the string of the instrument is to give delicious, velvety sounds; one swells these sounds at will by pressing harder or less hard on the keyboard . . . The mere touch of the harpsichordist is enough to operate these charming vicissitudes alternately, without any change of either the keyboard or the register.

The phrase 'charming vicissitudes' might almost come from a novel by Rousseau or Bernardin de Saint-Pierre.

In short, the stage was set for composers, interpreters and the

19. A sonata for harpsichord with violin: engraving from La Borde, 'Choix de chansons', ii (1773)

public to give an enthusiastic reception to a new instrument, the fortepiano, which by replacing the jack with the hammer, and striking instead of plucking the strings, would make possible the most subtle varieties of musical light and shade. The fortepiano was first offered to the audience of the Concert Spirituel in 1768.[13] The instrument's success quickly grew, and publishers, with an eye to publicity, began advertising sonatas or concertos 'for the harpsichord or fortepiano'. Despite understandable hesitations, the new instrument increasingly asserted itself in time to satisfy the highest aspirations of the generation of the 1780s. *L'art du faiseur d'instruments de musique et de lutherie* (1785) contains these comments on the fortepiano: 'The amount of pressure by the finger determines the strength or weakness of the sound. It lends itself, consequently, to expression'.

The first school of French fortepianists was to consist of harpsichordists and organists (J. F. Tapray, C. B. Balbastre, Nicolas Séjan) and also of very young composers just starting their careers on the eve of the Revolution. Etienne Méhul, for example, who was soon to shine on the *opéra comique* stage, published several collections of sonatas between 1783 and 1788, and there was also Jean-Louis Adam, who would be professor of piano at the Paris Conservatoire ten years later, and Nicolas Hullmandel. These were the years when some of the great virtuosos of the coming generation made their mark for the first time in Paris: Daniel Steibelt, J.B. Cramer, J.L. Dussek. In less than twenty years, a radical revolution had come about in the world of the keyboard.

By contrast, the history of the organ in the eighteenth century was marked by a slow decline. In aiming too exclusively at virtuosity, the French organ school impoverished itself. The organ came to be heard less in churches and more often at the Concert Spirituel. Louis Daquin, organist of the chapel at Versailles and of Notre Dame, left several books of noëls. In his organ loft, or at the Concert Spirituel, he enjoyed success as a virtuoso when he improvised. Rameau's pupil, Claude Balbastre, also organist at Notre Dame, attracted so many people to the cathedral with his improvisation that the archbishop had to intervene; it was also Balbastre who introduced the organ concerto to France. Whatever the talent of these masters, it is plain that in their hands religious music secularized itself; on the eve of the Revolution, even transcriptions of fashionable *opéras comiques* would be heard played on the organ. The best representative of the French school in the second half of the eighteenth century was Nicolas Séjan, who was also a fortepianist of note; he composed organ noëls, sonatas and fugues. At the beginning of the next century he was organ professor at the Conservatoire, and Choron, in his *Dictionnaire* (1810), regarded him as the last descendant of the school of Couperin and Marchand.

RELIGIOUS MUSIC

The century of Voltaire was not a religious one; the fierce and frequent attacks made by many philosophers on the church and the clergy are well known. In this eminently critical context, religious music could find a place only on condition that it adapted itself to the underlying tendencies of the times – and that was what it did. As early as 1713 Johann Mattheson had emphasized, in *Das neu-eröffnete Orchestre*, the particular character of French religious music as compared with that of Italy and Germany.

French composers tended to take dramatic music as their model for religious music, rather than employ the learned or severe style currently developing in Germany. No doubt the great majority of the French people remained deeply Christian throughout the century; but religious sentiment often took on new expression. There were increasing endeavours to reconcile the observation of Christian duty with the pleasures of a man of the world. There were attempts to make the practice of religion easier and more agreeable; the requirements of the faith did not forbid human intercourse, nor demand renunciation of secular delights. A new kind of piety – it might be described as humanist piety – came into being, and religious music was well able to adapt itself to such sentiments. At the end of the century, an aesthetician as subtle as Chabanon did not hesitate to write, in his treatise *De la musique considérée en elle-même et dans ses rapports avec la parole, les langues, la poésie et le théâtre* (1785): 'The difference between the sacred and the secular does not exist for the composer . . . The opening of the *Stabat* sung in chorus and very softly by the tomb of Castor would suit the situation perfectly'. We need not, therefore, expect to find the strict style developing in eighteenth-century French religious music. Rousseau recommended 'the banishing from our temples' of fugue and counterpoint; even the style of *opéra comique* might sometimes invade the church. The *Journal de Paris* praises a pretty motet, heard at Communion in the church of the Madeleine, which was an *O salutaris* arranged to the music of the trio in Grétry's *opéra comique Zémire et Azor*.

The establishment of the principle of absolute monarchy by Louis XIV in the second half of the seventeenth century had obvious consequences for literature and the arts, and for music in particular. The king's personal tastes had guided the genius of artists, and it was primarily due to to Lully that a new genre in religious music appeared, a brilliant and sumptuous genre perfectly suited to the royal ideology and indelibly marked from the first with the seal of Versailles: the *grand motet*. This genre, which took definitive shape in the earliest years of the eighteenth century, scarcely developed thereafter until the Revolution. It quickly spread through the French provinces, a positive propaganda tool, taking the unimpaired image of royal splendour to all parts of the country; significantly, it would never go beyond the frontiers of France itself.

A *grand motet*[14] (thus named to distinguish it from a *petit motet*, a short piece lasting a few minutes written for a soloist, usually with a simple violin and bass accompaniment) is a work lasting some twenty minutes, a setting of a Latin text from the psalms, the *Te Deum* or the *Magnificat*. It calls for a large orchestra (the *symphonie*), sometimes including trumpets and drums, a choir and an ensemble of soloists, who sing alternately, in a succession of numbers, the various verses or parts of verses of the Latin text. This music, festive and sparkling – an effect heightened by the contrast of its successive parts – was heard daily at divine service at Versailles, and its strength of character was such that it overshadowed the actual text of the Mass Ordinary. The latter was probably recited in a low voice by the priest at the altar, while from the choir loft came brilliant musical commentaries on a verse of a psalm. This practice, which spread rapidly through all the main French cities, explains why mass composition was at a low ebb in France during the eighteenth century.

Recent research has shown that there was enormous 'consumption' of *grands motets* for almost a century; a thousand have been listed (most of them still in manuscript), and that represents only a small part of the total repertory. The uncontested master of the genre at the beginning of the century was Michel-Richard de Lalande. After his death in 1726, the recently founded Concert Spirituel was to play a determining role in the history of French religious music. Indeed, it became usual to perform *grands motets* at the organization's concerts, first during Lent and then throughout the year. In coming to the concert platform, religious music had of necessity to become secularized. This process was accentuated by the already highly decorative nature of the genre. Composers sought worldly success in writing religious music for concert performance. Those psalms whose texts lent themselves to picturesque effects of representational music were set dozens of times: for example, *Super flumina Babylonis*, with what became a traditional evocation of the waters of the Euphrates.

The best composers of the time distinguished themselves in the genre: André Campra, Henri Madin and Esprit Blanchard, not forgetting Rameau, who composed four *grand motets*, or Mondonville. About 1760, however, the Parisian public showed that it was tiring of this kind of religious music, which could be heard indiscriminately either in church or in the concert hall and was tending to lapse into the merely facile. In his *Spectacle des beaux-arts* (1763) Lacombe could write: '*grands motets* arouse no interest now'. Help came not from Versailles but from Paris. Indeed, despite the presence of an outstanding musical director of the Chapel Royal, François Giroust, in the last years of the *ancien régime* Versailles and the court were stagnating. In Paris, interesting experiments were underway at the Concert Spirituel where composers presented a kind of drama on French texts taken from the Old Testament. These attempts came to nothing; no doubt the poetry of the Old Testament was not amenable to pre-Romantic sensibility. Gossec, known as a composer of symphonies, was more fortunate when his *Messe des morts* of 1760 was performed to great acclaim; the effect of the trombones, a novelty at the time, in the 'Tuba mirum' was much admired, and the 'Dies irae' with its horns, clarinets and drums was given several times at concerts. His *Nativité*, performed at the Concert Spirituel in 1774, a kind of Christmas oratorio with spatial effects using contrasting groups, was an important landmark: it reintroduced the figure of Christ to French religious music.

But the decisive step in this direction was taken by a young Parisian choirmaster, who came into prominence overnight with a phenomenal triumph at Notre Dame. This was Jean-François Le Sueur,[15] later the teacher of Berlioz. On Easter Monday 1787 he presented his *Histoire suivie de la Résurrection*, a Latin oratorio. The score is lost, but the composer left a long commentary on the work, from which his intentions are clear. Sentence of death was passed on the *grand motet* that day; after a century in which the Old Testament held sway, with the dominant image of a terrible, avenging God, the touching and merciful figure of Christ reappeared. The Latin oratorio, until then unknown to the French of the eighteenth century, had been created and it was to have a tremendous success in France in the nineteenth century. In Le Sueur, with his images of touching simplicity and his poetic treatment of religious sentiment, we may see a foreshadowing of the Romantic century which Chateaubriand's *Le génie du christianisme* was to inaugurate in 1802.

OPERA

Vocal music between 1730 and 1789 was almost entirely limited to opera and *opéra comique*. The secular cantata, which had flourished at the turn of the century and which had then been the most sophisticated form of vocal chamber music, scarcely survived after 1730. At the other end of the eighteenth century, another genre of vocal music appeared: the solo song known as the *romance*, perhaps the only musical genre to be both popular and aristocratic at the same time. Queen Marie-Antoinette sang the same *romances* as the humble peasant woman. To interpret the *romance*, said Rousseau in his *Dictionnaire*, all that was needed was 'a true, clear voice, good pronunciation and a simple style of singing'. Accompaniments, generally within the capability of amateurs, were written for the harpsichord and the fortepiano, or for the harp, an instrument which was fashionable in the last decades of the century. The simplicity of the *romance*, its naivety, often tinged with melancholy (it was no coincidence that the new genre began to develop in the pre-Romantic period), gave it universal appeal. The *romance* sang of love, usually unrequited. At the time of the Revolution, the best example was indubitably Martini's famous *Plaisir d'amour*.

French opera had, of course, been the creation of Jean-Baptiste Lully, an Italian by birth and a naturalized Frenchman, who had successfully anticipated the tastes of the young Louis XIV in obtaining the foundation of the all-powerful Académie Royale de Musique in 1672. In their privileged position, Lully and his successors were able to confine the repertory to French works. When the whole of Europe – from Lisbon to St Petersburg, from Vienna to London – was in the grip of Italian *opera seria*, France was still hermetically sealed against this foreign form of art. Up to the Revolution, only the *tragédie lyrique* held sway. It is important, in considering opera in eighteenth-century France, to emphasize the extremely specific character of the French stage, analogous to the tyrannical omnipresence of that essentially Gallic genre, the *grand motet*, in the realm of religious music.

Tragédie lyrique had been conceived in relation to classical tragedy;[16] and Lully's greatest success was to have created a French manner of recitative which, perfectly adapted to the metre of the alexandrine line, allowed perfect understanding of it. This happy equilibrium between words and music was completed by the presence of dance, an important element in the genre. It was difficult to follow Lully, as many French composers found to their cost, and Rameau must have needed to feel very sure of himself to venture into the arena for the first time at the age of 50 in 1733.[17] The most eminent figure in eighteenth-century French music, he was born at Dijon in 1683, trained as an organist, and after a visit to Italy was an organist in several towns before settling in Paris. For a time he worked for La Pouplinière, conducting his private orchestra; Rameau and his wife, an excellent singer and harpsichordist, lived in the financier's house.

Throughout his career Rameau was anxious to explain his ideas, producing some 30 prose works, of which the earliest was the *Traité de l'harmonie réduite à ses principes naturels* (1722). His theories were based on a reconciliation between art and science: 'Music is a science which must have certain rules; these rules must be drawn from an evident principle, and this principle can hardly be known to us without the help of mathematics'. He worked out the famous theory of the 'sounding body', which he represented to the Académie des Sciences in 1749. The whole thesis is summed up in one magisterial sentence, in which technical and aesthetic applications are explicitly linked to theoretical propositions. Rameau's entire harmonic system was to rest on the discovery of the establishment of strictly physical relationships of order between the fundamental sound and its harmonics:

> The sounding body, which I will accurately call fundamental sound, that unique principle, generator and controller of all music, that immediate cause of all its effects – the sounding body, I say, does not so much resound as engender, at the same time, all the continuing proportions whence are born harmony, melody, the modes, the forms, everything down to the very least of the rules necessary for the practice of music.

From these ideas, one gains above all an impression of the erudite nature of Rameau's thought and music, and of his predilection for harmony, whose supremacy he had just proclaimed in supporting it by his theory of natural resonance – this at a time when most Frenchmen, beginning with Rousseau, were asserting that it was only melody that could touch the heart. In a sense, Rameau was indeed a 'difficult' musician; we know, for instance, that the enharmonic writing of the famous 'Trio des Parques' in *Hippolyte et Aricie* disconcerted the singers so much that the composer had to give up its performance. But he was not austere or dull.

From the moment of Rameau's début on the French stage, opera was to occupy an increasingly important place not only in the musical but also in the social life of Paris. An evening at the Opéra was a landmark for a whole intelligentsia of subscribers who were not necessarily musical but who liked to see and be seen, to talk and exchange ideas. However, not until 1770 was a theatre designed with its specific needs in mind. From its beginnings until 1763 it had used the narrow hall in the Palais Royal where Molière and his troupe and then Lully had created their masterpieces. Destroyed by fire in 1763, it was rebuilt on the same site, but now enlarged and specially designed for opera. After a brief period in the Salle des Machines in the Palais des Tuileries (1763–70), the opera finally had a theatre worthy of it. This building was the first 'Italian' theatre in Paris. Contemporary accounts tell of the richness of its interior decoration; intended for a sophisticated society who regarded attendance at a performance as a social occasion, it had a large foyer, for the first time in the history of the Opéra. The *Mercure de France* commented on the innovation: 'The foyer is meant for those who are attracted less by the exigencies of the spectacle than by the pleasure of meeting friends in an agreeable setting'. Unfortunately this theatre, which held an audience of 2000, had only a short existence: it was just able to stage the triumphs of Gluck before it, in turn, was destroyed by fire in 1781. That year, a new theatre was built in a few months, close to the Porte Saint-Martin; the Opéra was to stay there until the Revolution. Between the columns of the neo-classical façade, four busts were placed, showing the musicians who were seen as the celebrities of operatic history at the end of the *ancien régime*: Quinault, Lully, Rameau and Gluck. It is to the works of these last two that we now turn.

Recalling the 1733 première of Rameau's *Hippolyte et Aricie*, the *Almanach des spectacles* of 1765 said that this opera marked the date of 'the revolution which then occurred in France, and of the progress it was making'. *Hippolyte et Aricie* spoke a language to which contemporaries were not yet accustomed. Once the first surprise was over, all was enthusiasm and also – the natural consequence of a real triumph – controversy. There was a feeling that this was a modern work, and at the same time that the whole Lully repertory appeared ancient. In a letter of 1 May 1743, the librettist Antoine Danchet, who had worked for André Campra early in the century, deplored the oblivion into which the old masters had so suddenly been cast: 'You know how much musical taste has changed. Even the works of the divine Lully are now regarded as if they were plainchant'. He added, nostalgically, 'Perhaps there will be a return to those scenes drawn from nature at her most beautiful'.

A dispute thus ensued between the modern 'Ramistes' and the traditional 'Lullistes', though Rameau himself declared: 'I have

20. Interior of the Comédie-Italienne, Paris: pen and ink drawing with wash (1772)

always considered Lully a great master'. Paris was divided, the philosophers entered into the argument, and in his free-thinking novel *Les bijoux indiscrets* (1748) Diderot was to set two characters briefly against one another: Utmiutsol (i.e. the common chord), or Lully, and Utremifasollasiutut (i.e. the seven degrees of the scale), or Rameau. With the perspective of time, we can now see the richness of the music and the dramatic force of *Hippolyte et Aricie*, and also that its structure remained faithful to the Lullist model. For Rameau, *tragédie lyrique* represented the greatest of all genres, the equivalent of what tragedy, the epic and the ode were to the poets of the time.

In fact, Rameau continued to write for the theatre until the year of his death.[18] He left 25 important works of varying dimensions. Those pieces whose common characteristic is that they have a single plot may be classed together. They are the five great *tragédies lyriques*: *Hippolyte et Aricie* (1733), *Castor et Pollux* (1737), *Dardanus* (1739), *Zoroastre* (1749) and *Les boréades* (1764), all on mythological or ancient subjects and having recourse to the marvels of the pagan world. The *pastorales héroïques* are in the same category, and differ from the *tragédies* only in having pastoral settings. Next come the *opéra-ballets*, works in several acts with a unifying theme, but with each act consisting of a different *entrée* (i.e. a new strand of plot); the most famous of these is *Les Indes galantes*, which transports the spectator from continent to continent in the course of its four acts. Finally, in this considerable body of work, there are Rameau's one-act pieces, which his contemporaries generally called *actes de ballet*. Even in the great *tragédies lyriques*, dance is one of the basic components of Rameau's art. Rameau's operatic works were perfectly adapted to the tastes and requirements of the French society of the Enlightenment for which they had been created, a society both cultivated and profoundly hedonistic, as avid for enjoyment as for thought, as responsive to the pleasure of the text, the spectacle and the dance as to the attractions of the music itself, a society for which the opera, with its mythological splendours, was primarily a feast for the mind and the senses.

Rameau's prominent position in the musical life of Paris in the middle of the century, and the nature of the reproaches addressed to him, may partly explain the famous Querelle des Bouffons which broke out in 1752. The affair was so called because an Italian *opera buffa* troupe had come to Paris, achieving a tremendous success with various comic intermezzos in Italian, including Pergolesi's famous *La serva padrona*. The principal episodes in this dispute, which divided the court and all Paris, are well known.[19] A show was made of believing that this little *opera buffa* of Pergolesi's represented the whole of Italian opera, and Rameau's *tragédie lyrique* was, absurdly, set up in opposition; for any comparison to be valid, *opera buffa* should have been paralleled with the contemporary spectacles of the Théâtre de la Foire

21. Theatre (Salle de la Belle-Cheminée) at Fontainebleau, with a rustic set such as would have been used for the première of Jean-Jacques Rousseau's 'Le devin du village', given there in 1752: engraving (c1778)

and the nascent *opéra comique*. However, the French of the eighteenth century, or at least those who had not travelled abroad, knew little about Italian *opera seria* (for all that Metastasios's writings were published in Paris), which might well have been the subject of a fruitful comparison with French *tragédie lyrique*.

This dispute, claiming to make comparisons where none could be made, was lame from the start. That made it only the more violent, however, with the rival supporters of Italian and French music rending one another savagely in pamphlets and leaflets. From this large body of polemical literature, the material most interesting to read today is Rousseau's *Lettre sur la musique française* (1753), an impassioned plea against Lully, Rameau and French music in general, in which the philosopher, then at the outset of his career and already not afraid of paradox, stated: 'French music is as ridiculous on examination as it is insupportable on being heard'. Despite these crushing remarks, his own *Le devin du village* was performed very successfully in 1752 and may in many ways be considered one of the prototypes of French *opéra comique*.

Whatever the real stakes in this dispute were, implications were clear: the Parisians, on hearing *La serva padrona*, had breathed a gust of fresh air. Asphyxiated not so much by the works of Rameau, whose exceptional merit the more discerning and musical among them had quickly recognized, as by the works of his mediocre imitators, they perhaps wished for art to be more 'true to life'. In clumsy hands, the

Lully model tended to become fixed in a dull and sterile convention. The accounts of foreigners who visited Paris, such as the Englishman Charles Burney and the Italian Carlo Goldoni, agree in this respect, and when *Zoroastre* was revived for the last time in 1770 a Paris critic pronounced a disillusioned verdict (*Journal de musique*, February 1770):

> The dances, although very fine, break up the sequence of events too much and too often with their long and frequent repetitions. They quite prevent one from perceiving that *verisimilitude of action* which, despite the element of the marvellous in opera, is as necessary there as in any other spectacle.

A foreign composer, Gluck, soon to come to Paris, was to make this 'verisimilitude of action', seen as a priority in opera by the critic, an essential article of faith in his own aesthetic creed. But before we turn to the works of Gluck and the significance of his reforms, we need to trace the birth of another lyric genre, *opéra comique*, which was establishing itself at the time of the Querelle des Bouffons. It was soon to attract the attention of several important composers, to the detriment of *tragédie lyrique*.

Opéra comique had its roots in the musical spectacles performed at the traditional Paris fairs. The term 'opéra comique' goes back only to the first years of the eighteenth century. The popular gatherings at the Foires St Germain and St Laurent had always been the occasion for entertainment, in which music played a part; French and Italian artists (the latter returning to Paris under the regency in 1721) performed vaudevilles, parodies of famous operas, plays with interpolated songs and sometimes original music. Some of the best writers and artists of the time worked for this little world, a clear indication that the popular theatre was not scorned by intellectuals in the capital; among them were the writer and playwright Alain-René Lesage, the librettist Charles Favart and the composer Jean-Joseph Mouret, a musician of the *chambre du roi*. In 1723 Rameau himself had composed music (which now is lost) to a play by Alexis Piron. These popular spectacles were described on the posters of the two Théâtres de la Foire with the generic term 'opéra comique'.

Several series of performances of Italian *opera buffa* in Paris, notably the one which sparked off the Querelle des Bouffons in 1752, gave a fresh impetus to popular spectacle, showing the possibilities of a form of musical drama made up of short numbers with a simple plot and only two or three characters. The librettist Favart began to arrange parodies of *opera buffa* for the Fair performers. With a view to exploiting all possibilities, French composers tried their hand at intermezzos in the Italian style; and in 1753 the Fair performers put on *Les troqueurs*, claiming that it was the work of an Italian composer living in Vienna. It was in fact by the Frenchman Antoine Dauvergne, the musical director of Louis XV's *chambre du roi*. This imitation of *opera buffa* was a great success: '*Les troqueurs* appeared', wrote Framery in the *Journal de musique* (May 1770), 'and all was decided. The Italian genre, very well imitated, did not seem too far removed from our own language'.

At that point, *opéra comique* was decisively established. Though typically French in spirit, it owed much to the Italian model, and an Italian, Egidio Duni, who settled in Paris shortly after 1750, was one of the first to have French *opéras comiques* performed at the Comédie-Italienne. This intermingling of the Italian and French styles was officially sanctioned, so to speak, in 1762, when the Comédie-Italienne merged with the Opéra-Comique of the Théâtre de la Foire. The date marks the creation of a second musical French stage beside the previously all-powerful Académie Royale de Musique. The Opéra-Comique was closely supervised by the Opéra, which, to avoid competition, imposed strict limits on the newcomers; its singers were not to perform 'pieces in one or more acts which are works of uninterrupted music'. The compulsory alternation of speech and singing was thus from the first statutorily imposed upon the Opéra-Comique.

In the 1760s, two composers won fame on this new stage: François-André Danican Philidor, brother of the founder of the Concert

22. Scene from André-Modeste Grétry's opéra-comique 'Richard Coeur-de-Lion' (Comédie-Italienne, 1784) showing the assault on Linz Castle in Act 3: engraving (1786) by Claude Bornet

Spirituel, and Pierre-Alexandre Monsigny. These musicians collaborated with literary men of talent, Favart and Michel-Jean Sedaine. Their librettos generally depict humble social settings, with peasants, the lower classes and soldiers for characters. They extol middle-class virtues and sometimes partake of a superficial and sentimental sensibility entirely in accord with the times (one may be reminded, for instance, of the innumerable 'village scenes' in contemporary painting). Melody reigns supreme; it defines the musical style, with harmony sometimes very sparse in the genre's *ariettes* which are often strophic. The orchestra, usually limited to strings but sometimes with supporting woodwind, accompanies discreetly. Originally a popular art, but not a minor one, *opéra comique* was soon successful at court. It espouses if not a philosophy of life then at least a morality which is always on the side of bourgeois wisdom and good sense. Philidor's *Sancho Pança* ends with these lines, surprising in a period of intense social ferment: 'Il faut, quoi qu'il arrive,/Que chacun vive/Dans son état' ('It is necessary, come what may, for everyone to live in his proper station').

In his *Mémoires ou Essais sur la musique*, André-Modeste Grétry, [20] born in Liège in 1741 and eventually to become the uncontested master of *opéra comique*, wrote of his initial reservations about a genre with which he was not yet well acquainted at the time of his return from Italy:

> *Tom Jones*, *Le Maréchal*, *Rose et Colas* [*opéras comiques* by Philidor and Monsigny] gave me great pleasure when I had once got into the way of hearing French sung, which had struck me at first as disagreeable. I needed yet more time to get used to hearing speech and singing in the same piece.

However, arriving in Paris in 1767, he attracted great attention the next year with *Le Huron*, after Voltaire. His popularity was to be considerable and up to the beginning of the nineteenth century he produced some 40 *opéras comiques*, among them the famous *Richard Coeur-de-Lion* (1784). A true export product, *opéra comique* carried a certain image of French art far beyond its country's borders; in 1783, for the inauguration of the new Kraków Opera in Poland, Grétry's *Zémire et Azor* was performed. His works were soon to be translated into every European language – and we know what the German Romantics were to make of French *opéra comique*.

The extraordinary popularity of *opéra comique* in France from the 1770s onwards had not, however, obliterated the French public's interest in serious opera. Just after Rameau's death in 1764, as we have seen, a certain lassitude came over the *tragédie lyrique*. It was now for a German to rescue French opera from its stagnation, giving it a powerful momentum. On his arrival in Paris in 1774, Gluck already had a long career as a composer behind him. In Vienna, where he had lived for many years, his works, mostly in Italian but including some *opéras comiques*, had been successfully performed at court and in the city and had done much towards the 'reform' of Italian opera. His ambition was to continue his Viennese reforms in Paris and for French operas. His first Paris opera, *Iphigénie en Aulide* (1774), brought him outstanding triumph, which its immediate successors, *Orphée* (1774), *Alceste* (1776), *Armide* (1777) and *Iphigénie en Tauride* (1779) would merely confirm. The elderly Rousseau, who had said twenty years earlier at the time of the Querelle des Bouffons, that there could never be a French opera, retracted. Gluck's reform was dramatic rather than musical. The objectives he had set out in the preface to the Italian version of *Alceste* included intensity of expression, concentration and sobriety, strictly classical qualities. There were no more danced divertissements, none of those pagan marvels with gods bedecked with plumes descending from the flies to mingle with mortals. The French found in Gluck the purity of Greek tragedy and the plays of Racine: the strength of the emotions, the tragedy of man facing his destiny alone. 'To hold the audience's attention for five acts with a straightforward plot, sustained by the violence of the passions, the beauty of the sentiments and the elegance of the expression': Racine's objectives as stated a century earlier in the preface to his *Bérénice*, are exactly the same as Gluck's in *Alceste* or *Iphigénie en Aulide*.

In eighteeenth-century Paris there was no triumph without its attendant intrigues. Gluck's enemies set up a rival to him in the Italian composer Niccolò Piccinni, who had settled in Paris in 1776, writing French *tragédies lyriques* for the Opéra. For a while the two composers were even in competition, composing operas on the same subject, *Iphigénie en Tauride*. The 'Querelle des Piccinnistes et des Gluckistes'[21] produced much empty verbiage, all the more so in that the two composers, who were good friends, were not as far apart in their aesthetic positions as their supporters tried to maintain. Like Gluck, Piccinni disliked ornate and dramatically inexpressive vocal lines and considered music the auxiliary of poetry, supporting it while always remaining subordinate to the action.

Unlike Rameau, who founded no school of imitators and sank into oblivion on the eve of the Revolution, Gluck had followers, and his works remained alive. Several Italian masters, abandoning the model of Metastasian opera, came to Paris at the end of the eighteenth century to gather laurels by presenting French operas in the tradition of Gluck: Antonio Salieri (*Les Danaïdes*, 1784; *Tarare*, 1787), Antonio Sacchini (whose *Oedipe à Colone*, 1786, was perhaps the most frequently performed serious opera up to 1830), Cherubini and of course Piccinni himself, who stayed in Paris until the Revolution. It was upon the well-springs of this Gluckian tradition that the masters of French

23. Sketch by Pierre-Adrien Paris of the 'palais enchanté' for the 1784 production of Gluck's 'Armide' at the Grande Théâtre, Versailles

opera in the first years of the nineteenth century would draw, proudly owning their debt to it.

*

In the almost unparalleled intellectual ferment of eighteenth-century France, music had its place. It was central to some of the greatest debates of the century, where the true issues often transcended mere aesthetic theorizing.

During the 60 years between 1730 and the Revolution, the creative activity of French composers was intense, but not – sometimes despite appearances – ill-regulated. The Classical style was established in Paris during the 1760s. In 1789 the musical scene was radically different from that in 1730: the Classical genres had been established (symphony, concerto, quartet and sonata), the Gluckian opera had reigned supreme since 1780, *opéra comique* was firmly ensconced, and 'ancient' music was nearly forgotten. Here we may see a salient characteristic of the musical life of the time: Parisian society of the eighteenth century lived in a constant spirit of modernity. The programmes of the Concert Spirituel or the Opéra show that the great majority of works performed were contemporary; since 1760 there had been scarcely any interest in the Baroque repertory. In the same way, the triumph of Gluck overshadowed the operas of Lully and Rameau. Rameau, the genius of the century, was forgotten twenty years after his death (the last revival of one of his operas, *Castor et Pollux*, was in 1785); that repertory would have to wait more than a century, for the first research in music history, before interest in it began to be felt again.

It was precisely that sense of the past, and of history, that was lacking in the composers and audiences of the eighteenth century. They were not concerned to establish any continuity between yesterday and today; none took any interest in studies of the past, and public taste was almost exclusively for the works of the day, which were the subject of eager discussion. Such a state of affairs – a society unaware of its musical past – encouraged the production of an enormous volume of music; it was inevitable that not everything in this repertory would be equally inspired, and that once the grain was separated from the chaff only a few masterpieces would remain.

The Revolution of 1789 was to cause immense political and social upheavals. If one excludes the religious domain (with the disappearance for ever of the *grand motet* as inspired by Versailles), these violent convulsions would in the end have only a small impact on French music. The new genres established just before 1789 remained, evolving imperceptibly into other forms. The history of music would see none of those sudden ruptures which, in so many other fields, marked the passage from the *ancien régime* to the nineteenth century. Perhaps music is, after all, a privileged art.

NOTES

[1] W. Weber, 'Learned and General Musical Taste in Eighteenth-Century France', *Past and Present* (1980), 58–85; Weber, 'The Muddle of the Middle Classes', *19th-Century Music*, iii (1979–80), 175–85.

[2] G. Snyders, *Le goût musical en France aux XVIIème et XVIIIème siècles* (Paris, 1968).

[3] M. R. Maniates, ' "Sonate, que me veux-tu?": the Enigma of French Musical Aesthetic in the 18th Century', *CMc*, no.9 (1969), 117–40.

[4] A. Devriès, *Edition et commerce de la musique gravée à Paris dans la première moitié du XVIIIème siècle* (Geneva, 1976).

[5] M. Brenet, *Les concerts en France sous l'ancien régime* (Paris, 1900).

[6] C. Pierre, *Histoire du Concert Spirituel, 1725–1790* (Paris, 1975).

[7] N. Zaslaw, 'Mozart's Paris Symphonies', *MT*, cxix (1978), 753–7.

[8] J.-L. Quoy-Bodin, 'L'orchestre de la Société Olympique en 1786', *RdM*, lxx (1984), 94–107.

[9] G. Cucuel, *La Pouplinière et la musique de chambre au XVIIIème siècle* (Paris, 1913).

[10] B. S. Brook, *La symphonie française dans la seconde moitié du XVIIIème siècle* (Paris, 1962).

[11] L. de La Laurencie, *L'école française de violon de Lully à Viotti* (Paris, 1922–4/*R*1971).

[12] J. M. Levy, *The Quatuor Concertant in Paris in the Latter Half of the Eighteenth Century* (diss., Stanford U., 1971).

[13] A. de Place, *Le pianoforte à Paris entre 1760 et 1822* (diss., Ecole Pratique des Hautes-Etudes, Paris, 1978).

[14] J. R. Mongrédien and Y. Ferraton, *Le grand motet français (1663–1792)* (Paris, 1986).

[15] J. R. Mongrédien, *Jean-François Le Sueur, contribution à l'étude d'un demi-siècle de musique française (1780–1830)* (Berne, 1980), 52–9, 121–56.

[16] C. Girdlestone, *La tragédie en musique considérée comme genre littéraire (1673–1750)* (Geneva, 1972).

[17] N. Zaslaw, 'Rameau's Operatic Apprenticeship: the First Fifty Years', *Jean-Philippe Rameau: Dijon 1983*, 23–50.

[18] P.-M. Masson, *L'opéra de Rameau* (Paris, 1930); and C. Girdlestone, *Jean-Philippe Rameau: his Life and Work* (London, 1957/*R*1969).
[19] D. Launay, *La Querelle des Bouffons: textes des pamphlets* (Geneva, 1973).
[20] D. Charlton, *Grétry and the Growth of Opéra Comique* (Cambridge, 1986).
[21] G. Desnoiresterres, *Gluck et Piccinni, 1774–1780* (Paris, 1872/*R*1971).

BIBLIOGRAPHICAL NOTE

At present there is no comprehensive survey of music in Paris during the years 1730–89: too much detailed work remains to be done for such a synthesis to be possible. Various works of an older generation deal with the problems of musical aesthetics in France: L. de La Laurencie, *Le goût musical en France* (Paris, 1905/*R*1970), L. Striffling, *Esquisse d'une histoire du goût musical en France au XVIIIème siècle* (Paris, 1912), and G. Snyders, *Le goût musical en France aux XVIIème et XVIIIème siècles* (Paris, 1968). To these should be added the recent study by B. Didier, *La musique des lumières* (Paris, 1985), which contains an excellent bibliography and deals admirably with the links between musicians and philosophers. In B. Durand's *Diderot et la musique* (diss., U. of Paris-Sorbonne, 1986), there is some brilliant interpretation (if sometimes, perhaps, a little cursory) within a structuralist frame of reference, relating to a subject that is still far from exhausted. M. R. Maniates's '"Sonate, que me veux-tu?": the Enigma of French Musical Aesthetic in the 18th Century', *CMc*, no.9 (1969), 117–40, is also valuable.

At present the role played by Paris in the diffusion of European music during this period is better understood, both as far as concerns publication and commerce. See A. Devriès, *Edition et commerce de la musique gravée à Paris dans la première moitié du XVIIIème siècle* (Geneva, 1976); and A. Devriès and F. Lesure, *Dictionnaire des éditeurs de musique français*, i: *Des origines à environ 1820* (Geneva, 1979).

The musical life of concert societies in France is well understood since the work of M. Brenet, *Les concerts en France sous l'ancien régime* (Paris, 1900/*R*1969). The early study, though recently published, of C. Pierre, *Histoire du Concert Spirituel, 1725–1790* (Paris, 1975), includes a list of all the concert programmes produced by that famous society. The evidence concerning the performance of music in private circumstances in Paris during the eighteenth century is sparse and fragmentary. The most important of these salons is the object of a comprehensive study that is still useful today, G. Cucuel's *La Pouplinière et la musique de chambre au XVIIIème siècle* (Paris, 1913). No doubt discoveries remain to be made in private archives, diaries in manuscript and the like; such finds would help to define the repertory of the smaller salons more precisely and would cast light particularly on the circumstances in which the music was performed.

On the origins and evolution of the symphony and the symphonie concertante, the magisterial work of B. S. Brook, *La symphonie française dans la seconde moitié du XVIIIème siècle* (Paris, 1962), has shed new light on a subject that is still obscure in many respects. For a comprehensive treatment of the violin in France in the eighteenth century consult the three volumes of L. de La Laurencie, *L'école française de violon de Lully à Viotti* (Paris, 1922–4/*R*1971), which brings together a considerable body of indispensable primary sources. For the cello, the fundamental work today is S. Millot's *Le violoncelle en France au XVIIIème siècle* (Lille, 1981). Research into the origins of the quartet in the eighteenth century in France is currently in progress; awaiting the results, one may profit from J. M. Levy's *The Quatuor Concertant in Paris in the Latter Half of the Eighteenth Century* (diss., Stanford U., 1971), even though the period referred to in this work is slightly later. There is still no comprehensive study of keyboard music in France during the eighteenth century. However, for the early history of the pianoforte and a catalogue of its repertory, there is an authoritative work by A. de Place, *Le pianoforte à Paris entre 1760 et 1822* (diss., Ecole Pratique des Hautes-Etudes, Paris, 1978).

For the history of the *grand motet* at Versailles, the bibliographical essentials are available in *Catalogue thématique des sources du grand motet français (1663–1792)*, published under the direction of J. R. Mongrédien (Munich, 1984); and Mongrédien and Y. Ferraton, *Le grand motet français (1663–1792)* (Paris, 1986). To these volumes may be added the recent work of J.D. Eby, *François Giroust (1737–1799) and the Late Grand Motet in French Church Music* (diss., U. of London, 1986). The importance of the reform at Notre Dame de Paris brought about by Le Sueur has been studied in detail by J. R. Mongrédien, *Jean-François Le Sueur, contribution à l'étude d'un demi-siècle de musique française (1780–1830)* (Berne, 1980), 52–9 and 121–56.

Tragédie lyrique in France has given rise to many works of synthesis. On the genre itself see C. Girdlestone's *La tragédie en musique considérée comme genre littéraire (1673–1750)* (Geneva, 1972); C. Kintzler's *Jean-Philippe Rameau: splendeur et naufrage de l'esthétique du plaisir à l'âge classique* (Paris, 1983) is a brilliant literary and aesthetic analysis of the subject. The two fundamental studies on the works of Rameau are P.-M. Masson's *L'opéra de Rameau* (Paris, 1930) and C. Girdlestone's *Jean-Philippe Rameau: his Life and Work* (London, 1957/*R*1969). The texts relative to the Querelle des Bouffons have been published by D. Launay, *La Querelle des Bouffons: textes des pamphlets* (Geneva, 1973). On the quarrel of the Gluckistes and the Piccinnistes, the fundamental study is still G. Desnoiresterres's *Gluck et Piccinni, 1774–1780* (Paris, 1872/*R*1971). On Grétry, and principally on the analysis of his works, see D. Charlton's *Grétry and the Growth of Opéra Comique* (Cambridge, 1986), which contains much new information.

Finally there are two general works, one historical, one aesthetic. These are R. Cotte's *Les musiciens francs-maçons à la cour de Versailles et à Paris sous l'ancien régime* (diss., U. of Paris-Sorbonne, 1983) and W. Weber's 'Learned and General Music Taste in Eighteenth-Century France', *Past and Present* (1980), 58–85.

Chapter IV

Maria Theresa's Vienna

BRUCE ALAN BROWN

A number of pleasant shocks of recognition await the student of the musical life of Vienna in the middle years of the eighteenth century – if he is familiar with Richard Strauss's opera *Der Rosenkavalier*. In the director of the city's theatres, for instance, he will find a real-life 'Quinquin' – Franz Esterházy, a member of the family closely associated with Haydn. The Marschallin's 'Bub', Octavian Rofrano, is brought to mind by the name of a Viennese musical landmark dating from that time, the Palais Rofrano, where not only Italian tenors and flautists but also renowned soloists from all over Europe could be heard along with an orchestra directed by Gluck. And in the macaronic blend of bureaucratic German, French, Italian and Latin in the diary of the Empress Maria Theresa's chamberlain Johann Joseph Khevenhüller – a main source of information on Viennese theatre and music – all but the notes of Strauss's and Hofmannsthal's sound-world lie revealed. It will come as no surprise, then, to learn that Khevenhüller's diary, the first volume of which was published in 1907, served as a main source for the opera's libretto.[1] A more fundamental inspiration for *Rosenkavalier* was the prevalence of a certain theatricality and cosmopolitanism in the Austrian capital during the personal reign of Maria Theresa (1740–65) which the composer and the librettist recognized as a natural setting for a twentieth-century opera. Under Maria Theresa's son, Joseph II, Vienna became a more enlightened, purposeful city, and its culture more Germanic in orientation. Yet the peculiar mix of nationalities, ideas and institutions in the years before 1765 were the necessary soil for the outstanding musical fruits of Joseph's reign.

Beethoven's 'Eroica' Symphony and *Wellingtons Sieg* (the 'Battle Symphony') are perhaps the best-known musical responses to political forces that confronted Austria. There were similarly inspired pieces before 1800 – settings of the *Te Deum* for victories in battle, *opere serie* for imperial weddings, and the like – but during that era political reality tended to impinge on Viennese musical life more broadly, in collective responses to shifts in the political winds. The death in 1740 of Charles VI and, with him, of the old Spanish ceremonial was the

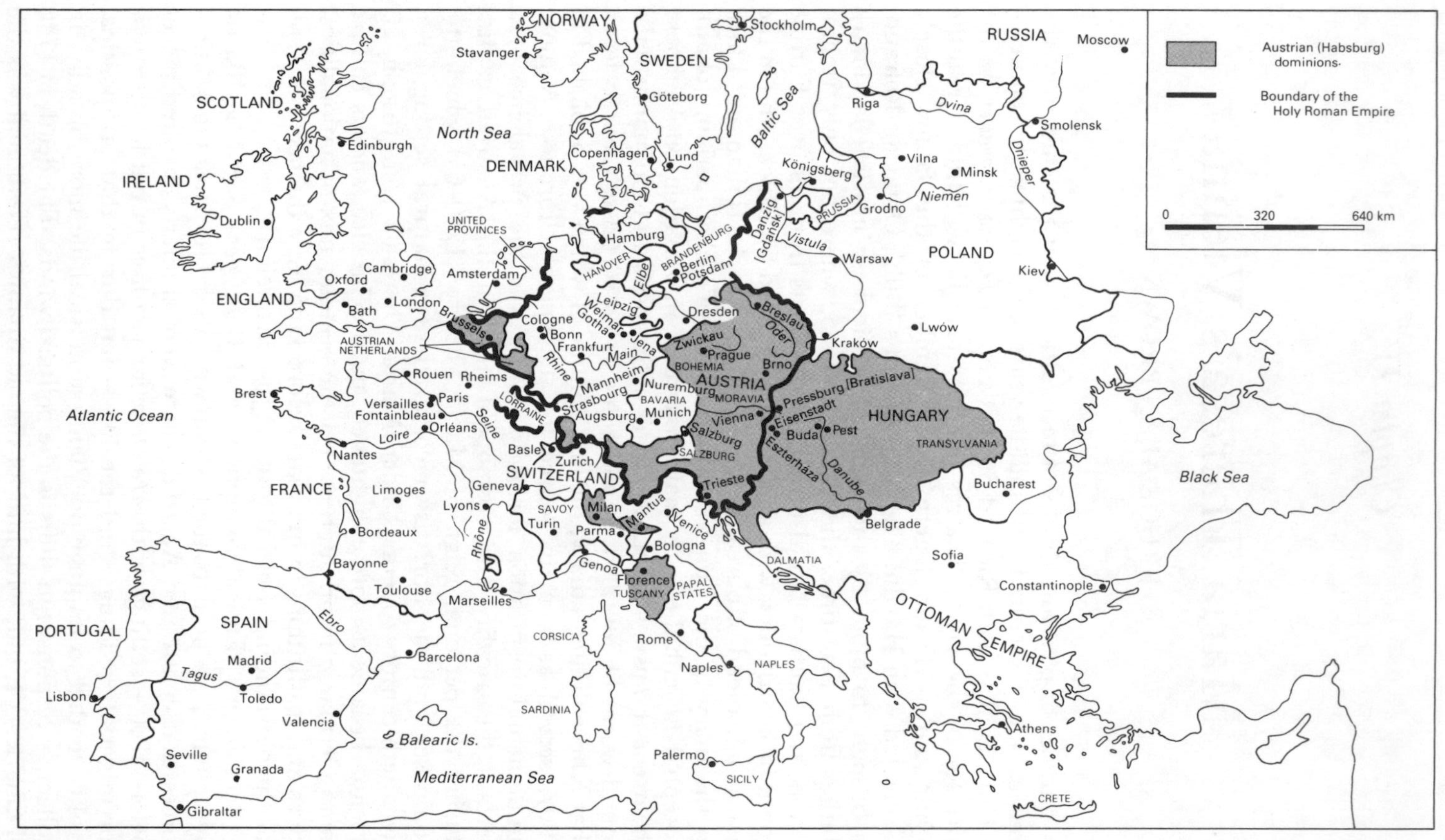

24. *Map of Europe (showing the Habsburg dominions) in the mid-late 18th century*

occasion for a reform of the ballets given at court, and especially of the by now old-fashioned *ballo serio*. The accession of Maria Theresa and her husband Francis Stephen, dispossessed Duke of Lorraine, brought an influx of French culture to court that, periodically reinforced by direct political ties with France, had a determining influence on Austrian theatrical life for decades. And only with the maturity of the native-born Archduke Joseph, and the death of his father in 1765, did there begin to be a consensus as to what should constitute Austrian literary or musical style.

Changes in Viennese music during this period had humble as well as courtly origins. Noble and well-to-do citizens enjoyed farces – often with music – involving the characters Hannswurst and Bernardon and others of the partly improvised *Stegreifkomödie* (the local version of the *commedia dell'arte*) in the German theatre, but Maria Theresa complained about their lewdness. The young Joseph Haydn made his début as a composer for the theatre with just such a piece (*Der krumme Teufel*) in 1753. By the last years of the century the musical language we call Viennese Classicism had managed to absorb the folk style so thoroughly that it could rub shoulders with the most sublime counterpoint – whether in a string quartet by Haydn, or an opera by Mozart – with perfect ease.

ITALIAN OPERA: THE METASTASIAN MODEL

European monarchs have not infrequently turned their attention to musical or theatrical matters soon after ascending the throne – for example, Louis XIV's founding of the Académie Royale de Musique and Charles II's reorganization of the Chapel Royal after the Restoration. Maria Theresa had little opportunity to attend to such diversions, for the precarious (and humiliating) Pragmatic Sanction that her father had so painstakingly negotiated on her behalf began to unravel almost as soon as he was dead, with the seizing of Austria's northern province of Silesia by Frederick the Great, King of Prussia, and his support, along with his allies, of a Bavarian pretender to her throne. The remodelling early in her reign of the old *Ballhaus* (tennis court) adjacent to the palace as a theatre was quite a modest undertaking, financed primarily by the manager of the city's theatres, Joseph Selliers.[2] Italian opera, by far the costliest of the court spectacles to maintain, disappeared altogether for several years, except for a single work, Metastasio and Johann Adolf Hasse's *Ipermestra*, staged in honour of the marriage of the empress's sister in January 1744. Thereafter the sumptuous Baroque opera house in the Burg was abandoned to the cobwebs, eventually to be transformed into a ballroom (the Redoutensaal).

In spite of the severe restrictions imposed on Italian opera during the early part of Maria Theresa's reign, in many ways this genre represents most clearly the prevailing musical aesthetic at court. Nearly every composer in the imperial employ found himself setting words by Pietro Metastasio (the imperial poet, or *poeta cesareo*), whether in a full three-act opera, an oratorio or merely an occasional cantata, and the lessons in musicality imparted by his verses were easily transferred to domains other than vocal music. Italian opera in Vienna was an instrument of state, celebrating Habsburg victories, marriages and anniversaries, and allowing (in occasional *gratis* performances) the general populace to view its monarchs in full splendour – and it was a favourite recreation of the young Maria Theresa, who after 1740 regretted being no longer able to participate (on account of her position) in amateur productions.

By 1730, when he was called to Vienna by Charles VI, Metastasio's reputation rested securely on half a dozen librettos notable for their supremely poignant situations and polished diction. Once he was established in the imperial capital, *drammi per musica* continued to flow from his pen at the rate of about one per year – not only for Viennese composers, but also for Italy, Germany and Spain, and wherever Italian opera flourished. In his new 'nest', as he called Vienna, Metastasio found a congenial group of patrons and admirers, led by the Countess Althann; in 1769 the young Vittorio Alfieri was disgusted by just how perfect a courtier the poet was, describing the 'servile and

25. Maria Theresa with her husband Francis Stephen and family on the terrace of Schönbrunn Palace (Joseph, heir to the throne, stands in the centre of the star pattern): painting (1750) by Martin van Meytens the younger

adulatory manner' in which he 'perform[ed] the customary genuflexion' to the empress in the gardens of Schönbrunn Palace.[3] For the period to about 1760, Metastasio's letters to distant friends and relations offer some of the most revealing glimpses of Viennese theatrical life and of his own art.

Table IV.1 THE POSITIONS ON STAGE FOR THE CHARACTERS IN THE FINAL SCENE OF 'DEMOFOONTE', AS SPECIFIED BY METASTASIO

We gain a notion of just how stylized the performance of an *opera seria* could be from a letter of 10 February 1748 in which, in answer to a query from Dresden, Metastasio lays out the positions on stage of all the characters in his *Demofoonte* (set by Hasse), in a manner that makes apparent the relative rank of each.[4] The arrangements of the final scenes (see table IV.1) are of a symmetry suggesting that of a da capo aria, or of the painted architecture against which the actors sing. Yet Metastasio did not expect that the musical effect would be cold. 'When I hear someone sing', he once wrote, 'I am not content to be astonished, but wish for the heart to share the profits with the ears.'[5] And in the text of *Le cinesi* (1735, revised 1754), the poet demonstrated how fully he expected his audience to enter into the emotions of the characters he presented. As Lisinga is acting out in accompanied recitative a scene from the tragedy *Andromaca* (in a contest of different dramatic genres with which she and her sisters pass the time), Tangia cannot refrain from interjecting:

> LISINGA: . . . Oh god, Pirro, have pity! What great triumph is the death of a child to the victor of Troy? . . . Leave us in peace! I entreat you, by the generous shade of your great father, by that hand

which makes Asia tremble, by these streams of bitter tears . . . Ah! the evil one hears not the plaints of others.
Tangia: I'd kill him.

As Austria's fortunes improved in the War of Austrian Succession, it again became possible to stage Italian opera at court. In the ensuing years, particularly after the management of the theatres was taken over by the Genoan diplomat Count Giacomo Durazzo, there came to be two distinct camps in Viennese *opera seria*. The conservative faction was led by Metastasio and Hasse, nicknamed the 'mellifluous Sassone', who, though employed at the court of Dresden, was a frequent guest in Vienna. The progressive camp centred on Durazzo, and the chief instrument of his agenda for theatrical reform was Gluck. In the distribution of *scritture* (commissions) for works celebrating the birthdays and name days of the imperial couple, we see a somewhat less pronounced version of the operatic rivalry in Paris which congealed into a *coin du roi* and a *coin de la reine* – Maria Theresa tending to prefer Hasse, Francis favouring the works of Gluck. The empress's interest was less direct than her husband's; a Prussian observer at court wrote in 1755 that 'she formerly loved hunting, gaming and theatre: the only thing to her taste now is the governing of her state and the education of her children'.[6] Francis died in the theatre (in 1765), after having seen an *opera buffa* and a ballet by Gluck.

Hasse provided the music for two of the *opere serie* presented during the 1746–7 season, but it was to Gluck that a more prestigious honour fell: it was his opera *La Semiramide riconosciuta* with which the Burgtheater reopened in 1748 after a thorough remodelling by Nicolas Jadot, an architect from Lorraine who had followed the emperor to Vienna (fig.26).[7] It was somehow fitting that a work by Gluck should inaugurate this edifice in the latest Parisian style, for he was to become director of its music once a resident company of French actors had been installed. In nearly all his music there was a roughness that corresponded to his origins (he was the son of a Bohemian forester) and his patchy training in counterpoint. Metastasio noted it in the 1748 opera, writing to a friend that '*Semiramide* is exalted to the stars, thanks to the excellence of the performers, and the magnificence of the decorations, in spite of an *archivandalian* music, which is insupportable'.[8] But the fertile musical soil of Bohemia also supplied Gluck with a sureness of instinct that more than made up for any technical deficiencies.

Musical barbarisms are not difficult to find in Gluck's score to *La Semiramide riconosciuta*, a resetting of Metastasio's poem of 1729. Errors of part-writing abound (appropriately) in Ircano's aria 'Maggior follia non v'è'. Gluck several times chafes at the rigidity of the da capo structure, changing metre and tempo even within sections – for example, in another aria, when Ircano turns to the Assyrian queen

26. The Burgtheater (right) in the Michaelerplatz, Vienna: engraving (1783) by Carl Schütz

and asks 'And canst thou, tyrant, look upon me without blushing?' What must have struck the *poeta cesareo* as most 'vandalian' of all was the composer's manipulation of the text. Twice within the dénouement, for which Metastasio had supplied no lyric verse, only recitative, the characters break into arioso (music more like an aria), that is not in the printed libretto. (One thinks of Gluck's crucial additions – four lines at the end of Act 3 – 30 years later, to the otherwise unaltered *Armide* of Quinault.)

Gluck was not alone in tampering with a Metastasian text. The poet's recitatives were routinely abridged and arias were replaced, even by Hasse. In 1749 a reworking still more radical than Gluck's was carried out by Galuppi on the poet's *Artaserse*, again under Metastasio's nose, in the Viennese Burgtheater.[9] Tastes having evolved, it was not long before the poet's librettos in their entirety were found wanting: in ensembles, spectacle and concision.

SACRED MUSIC: THE LEGACY OF FUX

For the late twentieth-century visitor to Vienna, the masses of Haydn and Mozart, resounding in the Augustinerkirche, the Carlskirche and elsewhere, are among the principal glories of the city's musical life. A papal dispensation in this era of the vernacular liturgy keeps them so, in the context of the service itself. How ancient is this tradition is suggested by an eighteenth-century visitor to the Austrian capital, the Prussian bookseller Friedrich Nicolai, who noted that since 'the starting time for each church was different, I could certainly hear the music for three or four Masses on Sundays and holidays'.[10] Yet the music Nicolai heard was not likely to have been composed by Haydn or Mozart for they were only peripherally involved with Viennese church music. Their fame, however, has largely eclipsed a host of lesser figures whose industry and imagination kept the city's churches supplied with great quantities of music – much of it of high quality – for the Mass and other liturgical Offices.

The prodigious amount of sacred music that survives in Austrian churches, monasteries and libraries reflects the large place accorded to figural (orchestrally accompanied) music, as opposed to Gregorian chant, in the liturgy of the Austrian Catholic Church. Rousseau could use the epithet 'plainchant' to express his dissatisfaction with French operatic singing and know that his readers would have had long experience of that genre. Chant was certainly not unknown in the Catholic German states and Austria – indeed, composers could embed it into masses, and even into symphonies, and count on its being recognized – but the musical elaboration of the concerted mass was as essential to the Bavarian and Austrian religious experience as the exuberant Baroque stuccoes and frescoes of church interiors. Within this area of music, Viennese citizens enjoyed an especially rich diet; Charles Burney, arriving in the Habsburg capital after having passed through Augsburg, Munich, Passau and Linz, was impressed enough to note that 'there is scarce a church or convent in Vienna, which has not every morning it's *mass in music*: that is, a great portion of the church service of the day, set in parts, and performed with voices, accompanied by at least three or four violins, a tenor and base, besides the organ'.[11] Religious music outside the church was likewise plentiful. Burney claimed to have witnessed five or six processions in a single morning, the first of them 'two or three miles long', with a three-part hymn being passed from head to tail and back again.[12]

Types of music which German Protestants like Nicolai would associate with the church – independent organ music and congregational singing – were not much favoured in the south. On Burney's first visit to St Stephen's Cathedral in Vienna he found the main organ long since fallen into disrepair and the smaller ones, which were 'used occasionally', 'as usual, . . . much out of tune'.[13] When Joseph II, as part of his religious reforms of February 1783, tried to institute the singing during the service of simple devotional songs in German, protests were not so much over the type of music as over the requirement that the congregation participate.[14]

The stance of the Austrian monarchy, and of Joseph II in particular, towards the church and church music has been a source of much

27. Performance of a mass with orchestra and soloists: engraving by J.E. Mansfeld from J. Richter's 'Bildgalerie katholische Missbrauche' (1784), a work criticizing the use of concerted music in the Roman Catholic Church on account of its tendency to distract.

confusion. The emperor's 1783 reforms did not eliminate all concerted music from the service, as has sometimes been claimed, but rather regulated its use and the expense it entailed. Nor did his actions constitute the first government intervention in this area. Attempting to control excesses both of piety and impiety in quick succession at the beginning of the 1750s, Maria Theresa substantially curtailed the number of religious processions and increased the number of religious holidays on which the city's theatres would be closed. Around the same time she promulgated a decree limiting the use of clarino trumpets and timpani in the Mass. Noting their absence from a service in December 1753, the court diarist Khevenhüller wondered how 'the poor trumpeters and timpanists' would earn their bread. In fact, the ban was only on the intradas that came at the beginning and close of the service on high feast-days; the prohibition against 'bruyante Musique' did not extend to obbligato parts in concerted masses, which one indeed still finds after this date.

The death of Charles VI in 1740 was followed early in 1741 by that of his Hofkapellmeister (and organist at St Stephen's), Johann Joseph Fux. The emperor had been signally negligent in failing to prepare his daughter to succeed him, but no similar charge can be made against Fux, who trained several generations of church musicians – either personally or through his classic treatise on composition, *Gradus ad Parnassum* (1725). This servant of three Habsburg emperors (starting with Leopold I in 1698) was in large measure responsible for the lasting Viennese taste for counterpoint among composers and amateurs alike, the latter including notably Joseph II.

The most successful of Fux's musical heirs was Georg Reutter (1708–72), who in 1738 began assembling an impressive collection of musical posts in the principal Viennese churches and at court. (For less exalted church musicians this simultaneous wearing of different hats was a matter of economic necessity; Haydn related to one of his biographers how, in his youth, on Sunday mornings he had had to play the violin for the Brothers of Mercy at eight o'clock and the organ in Count Haugwitz's chapel at ten, and sing at St Stephen's at eleven.)[15] Reutter's many positions and long tenure account for the survival of some 72 masses bearing his name, a circumstance which has led to his being given both the credit and the blame for whatever happened in Viennese church music during his time. Thus the scurrying violin parts found in Allegro movements of almost all Viennese composers' masses have been labelled 'rauschende Violinen à la Reutter', and a falling off in performing standards in sacred music around mid-century has likewise been laid at his door. This decline was due mainly to institutional factors beyond his control,[16] not the least of these being the conflicting demands on his court musicians by Durazzo, the superintendent of the court's chamber and theatrical music.[17]

Unlike most composers of sacred music, Reutter was not also a composer of opera. But his music was none the less progressive; indeed, some of his masses exhibit both sonata procedure and the unifying of movements by motivic means – which Mozart later used to such good effect in his 'Coronation' Mass.[18] With the various sections of the Ordinary of the Mass separated by other portions of the service, this latter feature was particularly welcome – as it was also in symphonies, whose individual movements could similarly be interspersed with other items in a concert programme.

The author of the 1766 article 'Über den Wienerischen Geschmack in der Musik' in the *Wienerisches Diarium* (the semi-official weekly newspaper of the court)[19] gave Reutter pride of place in his survey of local composers:

> Herr Georg von Reutter, Imperial Royal Kapellmeister, . . . is unquestionably the composer most capable of singing God's praises,

> and the model of all men working in this sphere locally. For, who knows better than he how to express, when the music requires it, magnificence, happiness, rejoicing, without falling into the profane and the theatrical? Who is more pathetic, richer in harmony, when the music calls for sadness, a prayer, pain? The music of his masses always attracts a throng of listeners, and each goes away edified, convinced and wiser.

A touchy issue is raised in these lines: the infiltration of theatrical (i.e. operatic) style into church music. The problem was not unique to Vienna or to Austria; a 1749 encyclical *Annus qui* by Benedict XIV addressed it generally to the Catholic lands. But local examples are not difficult to find. For instance, the music of the *air* 'Tendre Agathe' from Gluck's first comic opera for Vienna, *La fausse esclave*, was reset as an *Ave regina caelorum* for the church of St Leopold (many listeners would have heard both versions). And the Agnus Dei from Mozart's 'Coronation' Mass (written for Salzburg in 1779) served unmistakably as the model for the Countess's aria 'Dove sono i bei momenti' in *Le nozze di Figaro*. The Viennese worshippers' 'undertone of *Bravo*, *schön* and *che viva*', reported by an anonymous critic in 1781, was hardly different from theatre-goers' noises of approval.[20]

THEATRICAL LIFE: RIVALRY WITH PARIS

If church music in Vienna borrowed from theatrical style and musicians, the city's theatres were in turn continually casting envious glances at a model and rival: Paris. This was especially true after 1752, when a French theatrical company was brought into the Burgtheater, but the comparison between capitals ran deeper. In the 1757 *Répertoire des théâtres de la ville de Vienne* one reads that:

> Even in courts where the Spectacle is run at the expense of the Sovereign, the theatres are not open all year . . . because of the enormous costs of those things which one calls accessories: the *composers*, the *costumes* of the *actors* and *dancers*, the *decorations*, the *illumination*, the *extras*, the handyman, etc . . .
>
> It is only in VIENNA and PARIS that one is not subject to this inconvenience, and during the entire course of the year the public never has the displeasure of seeing the Spectacles shorn of the brilliance and of the decency proper to them.

The mutual attraction of these two poles remained strong for the whole of Maria Theresa's personal rule and beyond, to Gluck's successful siege in the 1770s of the Paris Opéra itself.

In 'the first years of Maria Theresa's reign', the time specified in *Der Rosenkavalier*, the courtiers did indeed stage many a 'Wienerische Maskarade', in the form of elaborate costume balls at Carnival. But rather more often they entertained themselves with amateur productions of French plays, on the model of Parisian *théâtres de société*;

one piece was even written especially for them by the salon hostess Mme de Graffigny. Among the 'Dames und Cavalliers' participating were Count Franz ('Quinquin') Esterházy, Count Giacomo Durazzo (who was to succeed the former as theatrical intendant) and Count von Harrach, who, according to Khevenhüller, died of over-exertion after one such performance. Perhaps because these amateur theatricals were so taxing, there soon arose a desire for a professional French theatre, in which nobles could witness a wider repertory than they could themselves mount and be free to converse and to carry on all the other activities ancillary to an evening in the theatre. For such pursuits the German theatre was not an acceptable alternative, on account of the licentiousness of its offerings. When pleading for the re-establishment of the French theatre in 1765, the state chancellor Prince Wenzel Kaunitz argued that 'to confine this [select] society to the national [i.e. German] theatre would be almost to deprive it of all spectacle'.

And it was Kaunitz who engineered the acquisition of a permanent French troupe, at the time of his departure for Paris to begin preparations for a diplomatic coup: the 'renversement des alliances' which ended nearly a century of emnity between Austria and France. In the coming years the Viennese French troupe (recruited from The Hague) distinguished itself from the many others like it scattered across Europe in that, besides the classics of the Parisian stages, it also gave important new creations: comic operas by Gluck and dramatic ballets by Franz Hilverding and Gasparo Angiolini.

Around the same time, Maria Theresa overhauled the city's theatres generally, addressing matters at once financial, moral and artistic. Both German (city) and French (court) theatres were put under the direct control of the court, and henceforth the former would in effect help subsidize the latter. The empress also promulgated a 'Norma' (1752, revised 1753) which prohibited theatrical performances on a great many religious feasts and vigils, and all Fridays. And she sought to quash the largely improvised farces by the local actor Joseph von Kurz (also known as Kurz-Bernardon, or Bernardon, the character he played), permitting only 'those pieces [adapted] from the French, Italian or Spanish theatres', and perhaps a few written by the more high-minded F. W. Weiskern. Even these were to be 'carefully read through' for '*équivoques* and dirty words'.

The presentation in 1753 at the Kärntnertortheater, or German Theatre, of Kurz's *Der krumme Teufel*, with music by Haydn, shows how ineffective was the empress's attempt to suppress the indigenous popular entertainment. Had she succeeded, the world might never have seen Mozart's *Die Zauberflöte*, which is a direct descendant of this form and particularly of the so-called *Maschinenkomödien*. This type of piece could contain substantial amounts of music, both borrowed (often from recent Italian *opere buffe*) and newly composed. Late in life

Haydn recounted to his biographer Griesinger how he gained entrée to the author's home by serenading his actress wife below their window, and how he came to compose the music for one of the scenes in *Der krumme Teufel*: Kurz, playing Bernardon, 'lay down at full length over several chairs and imitated all the movements of a swimmer. "See how I swim! See how I swim!", Kurz called out to Haydn, who was sitting at the clavier and who at once, to the poet's great satisfaction, fell into six-eight time'.[21] None of Haydn's music for this piece, or for its sequel (performed in 1758), has survived, but in two manuscript volumes of *Teutsche Comoedie-Arien* from this period are several numbers with strong affinities to his style.[22] The music of the oddly cheerful-sounding 'Wurstl mein Schatz'rl, wo wirst du wohl sein' is especially akin to the finale of the early keyboard sonata in A attributed to Haydn (HXVI:5). Haydn, Joseph Paul Ziegler and other composers were paid one gulden per aria – much as the actors received fixed fees for pratfalls, slaps or other *Accidenzien*.[23]

For at least one bourgeois spectator the antics of Bernardon and his companions hardly differed from what one could see in the Burgtheater. After the début of the French company, he described the mannerisms of the actors in the following terms:

> Imagine: in taking leave of her lover the actress makes an oriental-Christian-French *Révérence*, both hands crossed over her breast, her body deeply bent forward, the right knee also forward, the left backward. From every step she makes the stage shudders. Her lover embraces her, full of tenderness, with his head on her breast, his left leg across her entire belly – who wouldn't sp[it]?[24]

Even for aristocratic spectators like Khevenhüller the French style of acting was unnatural and it is not surprising to see the French players, soon after their arrival in Vienna, adding a lighter, more modern entertainment to their offerings: *opéra comique*. Increasingly over the next decade it was this genre around which the constitution of the troupe revolved.

Opéra comique, and especially the pastorales by Charles Favart, matched perfectly the temperament of the empress, her consort and their courtiers, and became the principal fare at the theatre of the pleasure palace at Laxenburg to which they retired each spring or summer. But the triumph of the genre in the public theatre was due to the efforts of two men on the fringes of Viennese theatrical life who were now given more central roles. Maria Theresa appointed Giacomo Durazzo as assistant to Franz Esterházy (and later as *cavagliere di musica*), but only after much vacillation, for she regarded him as a dangerous 'intriguer'. With Esterházy's resignation from the theatrical directorship in 1754 Durazzo moved to the fore, and immediately began laying the groundwork for his own theatrical agenda, in which he envisaged a cross-

28. Frontispiece to Charles Simon Favart's 'La chercheuse d'esprit' (1741), from the 'Théâtre de M. et Mme Favart', vi (Paris, 1763)

fertilization of French and Italian opera. One of his first acts was to name Gluck as director of music of the French theatre.

What most probably brought Gluck to Durazzo's attention was his music for an Italian opera – the above-mentioned *Le cinesi* – into which a large dose of French text had been infused. Metastasio, in updating his old text for the lavish outdoor festivities in 1754 at Schlosshof (the estate of Gluck's employer, Prince Joseph Friedrich of Saxe-Hildburghausen), drew upon recent Parisian *opéras comiques* such as *Le chinois poli en France* in which the foppery of French *petit-maîtres* is satirized. Gluck's musical characterization of the Frenchified dandy the poet had added to the cast was fully convincing and Durazzo soon gave the composer a chance to try his hand at French characters in *opéra comique*.

Though Durazzo had engaged several new singer-actors for the 1754–5 *opéra comique* season, the musical demands of the genre were in fact minimal at this time, consisting mainly of vaudevilles (French popular songs) to which new texts – often with humorous or salacious double meanings – had been fitted. Of the *ariettes* or parodied Italian arias (or imitations of them) that were beginning to infiltrate *opéra comique*, Durazzo wrote that 'one isn't especially curious about them here . . . We prefer a pretty, tuneful vaudeville, pretty minuets or contredanses, etc, such as . . . "Les niais de Sologne" '.[25] This last was a harpsichord piece by Rameau that Favart had used in *Les amours de Bastien et Bastienne*, a work later reset by the twelve-year-old Mozart. But before long the *ariettes* also had caught the fancy of Viennese audiences and Durazzo responded accordingly. He gave Gluck the task of writing original music to replace a certain number of the vaudevilles (until these disappeared altogether), and in the autumn of 1759 he visited Paris – not for the first time – and arranged for Favart to be his theatrical agent there. Over the next five years the playwright sent a steady stream of scores, librettos, actors and other personnel, and theatre news – in effect making the Viennese Burgtheater an extension of Parisian theatrical life.

From the start, *opéra comique* in Vienna had to adapt to local circumstances. Durazzo had told Favart in no uncertain terms that 'any *équivoque* . . . corrupts morals, or supposes them corrupt'; accordingly, Favart pruned any *doubles entendres* from texts he sent to the count. Local censors added heavy-handed moralizing as extra insurance. In the Viennese version of Favart's *Les amours champêtres*, for instance, the heroine was given the following lines, which directly contradicted the *timbre* (tune), 'De l'amour tout subit les loix', to which they were sung:

> I flee from dangerous lovers
> Because, I hear, they're too cunning;
> The sort of love they're interested in,
> Which presents us with its perfume,
> Is only meant to inebriate our senses.
> They're always trying
> To take advantage of our weakness . . .

At the time, Gluck's *airs nouveaux* were described alternately as 'brilliantly Italianate' and as completely in accord with the rules of French prosody. In truth, the composer was using any and every style that was within the capabilities of his singers, feeling his way in a genre that changed shape with every dispatch from Paris. More than most Parisian composers, whose comic operas were seen in Vienna within months of their premières, Gluck gave a coherent, almost architectural form to his works. In perhaps the finest of these, *L'ivrogne corrigé*, the mock funeral and punishment of the protagonist by Pluto stretch nearly unbroken across several musical numbers. The opera also contains some of Gluck's most vaudevillian and most unrestrainedly lyrical melodies to date.

Shortly after turning to *opéra comique* in 1758, Gluck also took on the composition of ballet music for both theatres (later dropping the German one). Here there was ample precedent to follow in the work of the choreographer Franz Hilverding and the composer Joseph Starzer, both of whom had just left for the court of St Petersburg. Through the writings of his student Gasparo Angiolini we know how Hilverding, single-handed, transformed ballet from a grotesque, disjointed display of acrobatics into a 'complete pantomime action with a beginning, middle and an end'.[26]

It has recently become possible to gain a better idea of Viennese ballet in the years immediately preceding Gluck and Angiolini's *Don Juan* (1761), with the discovery of the music to some three dozen ballets by Hilverding and Starzer, and of published eyewitness accounts by a resident foreigner. The former reveal an unsuspected wealth of instrumentation (pairs of chalumeaux, trios of bassoons, for example) and of musical gesture. The latter confirm Angiolini's claims on behalf of his master, but also make clear the extent of Durazzo's role in choosing the subjects and sketching the dramatic plans of ballets, 'without sharing in the glory'. The correspondent is particularly warm in his praise of *La force du sang* of 1757 which, like *Don Juan*, features a young Spaniard serenading a beautiful girl on a balcony and a duel. For the serenades both Starzer and Gluck respond with ardent oboe solos (in sarabande and siciliana rhythm, respectively). Hilverding's duel is 'an interesting pas de trois', in which 'everyone must express a different sentiment', but which nevertheless forms a 'tableau which is easily grasped by the spectators'.[27] Starzer's music, alternately fierce and tender, no doubt aided in the comprehension of the scene. In other ballets he follows every twist and turn of the action in through-composed finales of several hundred bars, even daring to let the music die away, *piano*, in the minor mode.

Hilverding and Angiolini's success in creating the danced equivalent of spoken theatre was partly a result of ballet's privileged role in both Viennese theatres. At the Paris Opéra dance was an essential ingredient, but always linked to and explained by song. In Vienna ballets were generally independent works given between and after the two spoken or sung pieces on the programme. In fact, Durazzo once explained that they were there precisely in order 'to attract those [spectators] who don't understand French well enough'.[28]

Don Juan differed from its predecessors on the Viennese stage not in length or form, but rather in subject matter (its source is an actual play, by Molière) and in its sheer power. Don Juan's flaming descent to hell, tormented by furies and accompanied by sepulchral blasts from the trombones, elicited a long, excited description in the diary of the avid theatre-goer Count Johann Karl Zinzendorf and, later, musical homage in Mozart's operatic version of the tale – only one of several instances where the younger genius trod a path taken first by Gluck. The catalyst for Gluck's masterpiece was a newcomer to the capital: the poet, schemer, editor and critic of Metastasio, Ranieri de' Calzabigi. Coming from Paris via the Low Countries, Calzabigi

29. Scene from Hilverding's pantomime ballet 'Le turc généreux' (from Rameau's 'Les Indes galantes') given at Schönbrunn in 1758: engraving (1759) by Canaletto

quickly fell in with Durazzo and Kaunitz and their circle, and aided in drafting the scenario of *Don Juan*. With his participation Gluck and Angiolini were able now to take Italian serious opera into the uncharted regions Durazzo had in mind.

For all its novelty, *Orfeo ed Euridice* (1762) is really the culmination of a long process of reform, supported at key moments by Durazzo. Durazzo had come to Vienna with an outline for an Italian Armida opera based on that of Quinault and in 1755 he used his own poetic skills in the first major task he gave Gluck, *L'innocenza giustificata*. In this work he put assorted aria texts by Metastasio into a dramatically fluid context, with significantly more chorus than Metastasio ever used. The next year saw Durazzo furthering the cause of opera reform in another way, paying for the publication of the anonymous *Lettre sur le méchanisme de l'opéra italien*,[29] a French counterpart to Francesco Algarotti's famous *Saggio sopra l'opera in musica* (published in 1755). And in 1761, for the birthday of Archduke Joseph's new bride, Isabella of Parma, Durazzo realized his *Armida* on the stage of the Burgtheater.[30] His prose sketch, versified by another hand, was set to music (appropriately) by the Parma court composer Tommaso Traetta, known for his resettings of *tragédies lyriques* by Rameau. *Armida* included some of the spectacle recommended by the *Lettre* and the *Saggio*: a ballet and chorus of furies and the destruction of the enchantress's palace, but the main weight still fell on the solo arias, treated flexibly and with great psychological insight. A year and a half later, in *Orfeo*, a more experienced chorus could be entrusted with a role rivalling that of the protagonist himself.

In the introduction to his edition of Metastasio's works, Calzabigi had tactfully questioned whether the overall plan of the works was the best imaginable. Calzabigi's libretto for *Orfeo* was criticism far more bold. As if thumbing his nose at the *poeta cesareo*, he included but a single simile (about a turtle-dove) in the opening chorus and thereafter abandoned this favourite Metastasian technique entirely. His characters expressed their feelings directly, and they were only three in number; gone were the usual secondary intrigues and parallel sets of

30. Performance of Gluck's 'Il Parnaso confuso' at Schönbrunn, 24 January 1765 (Archduke Leopold is at the harpsichord): painting by Johann Franz Griepel

31. Gluck and his wife Marianne: portrait by Barbara Krafft (1764–1825)

lovers. By returning to myth, and such a well-known one at that, Calzabigi was able to dispense with narration to a large degree and instead construct his opera in a series of monumental tableaux – a scale favourable to the skills of his collaborator.

Orfeo is rightly viewed as a product of Vienna's French theatre, despite the language of its text. True, the two principals were played by Italians, but the performers also included the French singer Lucile Clavereau (as Amore) and the orchestra, dancers and choristers of the French troupe. Musically the work can trace its ancestry to French opera both serious and comic. The opening scene of mourning recalls that in Act 1 of Rameau's *Castor et Pollux*, and nearly all the solo numbers have their origins in *opéra comique* style. This was natural in the case of Mlle Clavereau, whose normal repertory this was. For the character of Orpheus, simple song was arguably more efficacious in swaying the furies than ornate *arie di bravura* would have been, but the casting of this role was also crucial in determining its musical treatment. The alto castrato Gaetano Guadagni had learnt from David Garrick, the best possible model, the art of sustaining dramatic illusion.[31] 'The Music he sung was the most simple imaginable; a few notes with frequent pauses . . . were all he wanted', wrote Charles Burney,[32] and this sounds very much like a description of his threefold cry of 'Euridice' in the opening chorus. His more ample expression of sorrow, in a three-strophe song, is an example of the French *romance*, a form then ubiquitous in *opéra comique*. The *air* was called by this name when the composer Philidor plagiarized it a year later in a comic opera. That he had seen the piece was due to Durazzo's decision to have the score of *Orfeo* engraved in Paris – a clear indication of its affinities.

The next landmark in the Viennese reform was again by Traetta, his *Ifigenia in Tauride* of 1763. As in *Orfeo*, the full forces of chorus and ballet were deployed. Zinzendorf commented: 'There are a great many choruses in it. Orestes' dream of his mother is represented, naturally, and that brings on the furies, who since the ballet *Don Juan* have really arrived in the French theatre of Vienna'. Zinzendorf's noticing of this tradition (which actually stretches back to Traetta's *Armida* of 1761, and even to Gluck's *L'ivrogne corrigé* of 1760) helps us to see another: that of the musical 'Sturm und Drang'. Luigi Boccherini, a young cellist in Vienna around the time of the première of *Don Juan*, later turned its finale into the last movement of a symphony entitled 'The House of the Devil'. The outbreak in the late 1760s of minor-mode symphonies exhibiting the same vocabulary of scales, tremolo and leaps may well have owed something to this vogue for furies on the Viennese stage, even where there is nothing in the title to suggest it.[33]

The ascendancy of French theatre in Vienna was dealt two severe blows, with the dismissal of Durazzo in 1764 (for reasons never entirely explained) and the death of Emperor Francis the following year. The loss of these two advocates made it easier for the new emperor, Joseph II, to dismiss the expensive French players, but he could not erase the impact that French theatre, opera and ideas had exercised on Viennese music over the preceding decades.

INSTRUMENTAL MUSIC AND CONCERT LIFE

Most research into Vienna's concert life has been concentrated on the period after Mozart's arrival as a permanent resident in spring 1781. Even today writers on the subject generally pass in silence over the rich fare offered to Viennese citizens during the 1750s and 1760s, which rivalled that available in many other European capitals. In public and in private the city lived and breathed music, every bit as much as in the era of Schubert.

The autobiography of the violinist and composer Carl Ditters von Dittersdorf tells of an important musical establishment in the (still-existing) Palais Rofrano (fig.32). In 1751 this twelve-year-old prodigy joined the orchestra of Prince Joseph Friedrich of Saxe-Hildburghausen, which gave concerts there for the high nobility 'all through the winter'.[34] Led by the court composer Giuseppe Bonno, and later also by Gluck, these concerts featured the most accomplished local soloists. In addition, 'whenever any *virtuoso*, [whether] singer, or player came to Vienna, and deservedly succeeded in winning the applause of the public, Bonno was ordered to arrange the terms, and to secure him for the prince'.[35] Dittersdorf's list reads like a 'who's who' of mid-eighteenth-century music: Caterina Gabrielli, protégée of

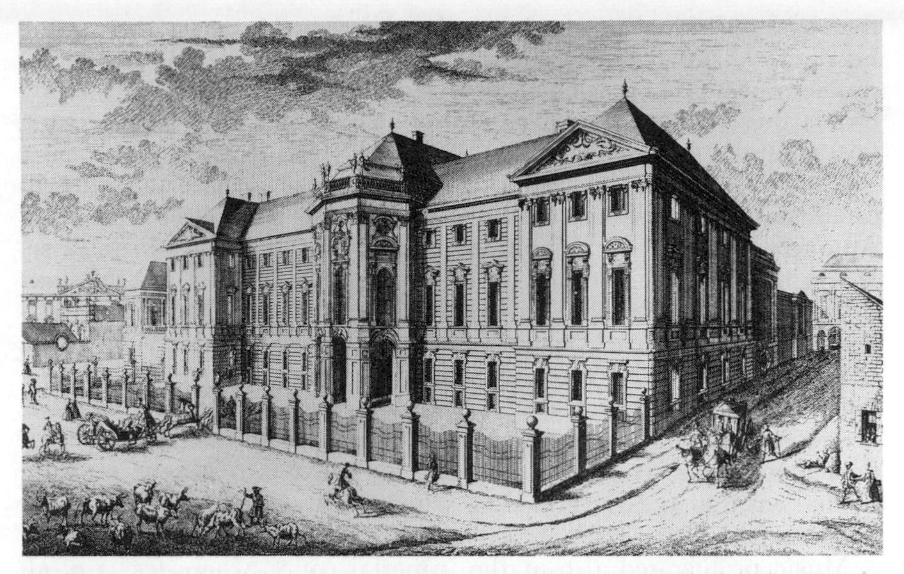

32. The Palais Rofrano (Auersperg), where concerts were held: engraving by J.A. Corvinus after Salomon Kleiner

Chancellor Kaunitz and possessed of the most astonishing vocal technique of any soprano of her era; the Turinese violinist Gaetano Pugnani, famous as much for his prominent nose as for his expressive playing; the Belgian violinist and pioneer composer of symphonies Pierre van Maldere; a member of the Besozzi family of oboists who toured the Continent for decades; and Joseph Ignaz Leutgeb, for whom Mozart later wrote his horn concertos (in different colours of ink). As Dittersdorf implies, these artists also appeared in concerts that were more truly public – in the Mehlgrube and, most notably, at the Burgtheater.

When Hildburghausen's declining fortunes forced him to disband his Kapelle, Dittersdorf and his younger brother were taken into the orchestra of the French theatre. Its concerts, too, were led by Gluck (after 1756) during Lent, and eventually on Fridays all through the year. The manuscript chronicle of theatrical activities kept for Durazzo by Philipp Gumpenhuber yields intriguing information on concert activity. On 13 May 1763 we find listed a concerto played by Johann Baptist Schmid 'on his new instrument called a piano and forte', five years before Londoners heard the instrument in public.[36] And throughout there are descriptions of lavish stage decorations against which the musicians performed during Lent. In 1758, for instance, an oratorio by Galuppi was heard against a backdrop showing 'Telemachus led by Minerva, and covered by her shield, advancing on a rocky path toward the temple of immortality . . . One sees falling into the abyss of Pride, Envy and the other Vices or Monsters obstructing his path'. Virtue was also inculcated by a 1763 poster addressing the problem of 'noise occasioned by the gaming tables' in the adjoining room; those taking part were admonished that this was proving 'disturbing to the amateurs of music'.

Various other nobles besides Hildburghausen supported musical establishments, and among them should be counted Prince Paul Anton Esterházy, who maintained a residence in the Wallnerstrasse. It was here in 1761 that Haydn received one of his first commissions from the prince: a trilogy of symphonies on the times of the day. The last, 'Le soir', depicts a specific evening in April of that year, when Esterházy presumably attended a performance of Gluck's *Le diable à quatre*, an *opéra comique* one of whose *airs*, 'Je n'aimois pas le tabac beaucoup', Haydn transplanted intact as the main theme in the first movement of his symphony.[37] What better way to relive the pleasure of that visit to the Burgtheater, when back at his main palace at Eisenstadt?

Music proliferated also at the imperial court, where feasts of all sorts were marked by 'vortreffliche Tafel-Musique' performed by salaried musicians. Virtually all the archdukes and duchesses were musically accomplished enough to appear in private theatrical or musical productions; several large canvases by court painters show them so doing. Their harpsichord instructors – Georg Christoph Wagenseil, Joseph Steffan (Štěpán) and Wenzel Raimund Pirck (or Birck) – kept them well supplied with compositions answering to a number of names: sonata, divertimento, *trattenimento*, concerto and so on. Collected into sets and dedicated appropriately, these were also some of the earliest and most handsome examples of Viennese music engraving.

Viennese amateurs had a wide choice of music available to them from publishers all over Europe, plus a horde of local copyists. In this mixture Vienna shows her position midway between Italian and north-European practices; in eighteenth-century Italy nearly all music circulated in manuscript. One very common form of music which very rarely saw editions was keyboard reductions of ballets, comic operas and other theatre pieces. That these could influence the composition of original music is suggested by the movement titles of Pirck's *Tratteniment* 'per pantomimi', which included two 'Pierot's, 'Ninfe e Pastori', a 'Zinghera', a Contredanse and a Finale.[38]

The string quartet is a genre of instrumental music especially closely associated with Vienna and Viennese Classicism. Though strictly speaking not its inventor, Haydn deserves credit as one of the quartet's earliest and most assiduous cultivators. The first of his works in this form date from the late 1750s and were composed for Baron Karl Joseph von Fürnberg at his country estate. These light and winning miniatures, generally in five movements (with a pair of minuets with trios framing a central slow movement), represent the so-called divertimento type of chamber music. Such pieces were also scored for various wind and mixed ensembles and often played out of doors (Haydn must have used something of this sort in serenading the young wife of Joseph von Kurz). While the divertimento lived on into modern times, a more learned, citified and conversational variety of string quartet eventually replaced the earlier type. Its wit and the equality in its part-writing (which could include strict counterpoint) were a reflection of its players: skilled amateurs, professionals and even composers. In 1772, during a Viennese soirée at the residence of Lord Stormont, Charles Burney heard 'some exquisite quartets, by Haydn' – surely from op.20, his most recent set – 'executed in the utmost perfection' by the ballet composer Joseph Starzer, the instrumental (largely symphonic) composer Carlo d'Ordonez, Count Brühl (an amateur) and Joseph Weigl, a cellist in the employ of Prince Esterházy: 'All who had any share in this concert, finding the company attentive, . . . were animated to that true pitch of enthusiasm . . . so that the contention between the performers and hearers, was only who should please, and who should applaud the most'.[39]

THE REGENCY

The period between the death of Francis Stephen in 1765 and that of Maria Theresa in 1780 is hardly comparable to the years following the demise of Louis XIV in France, though both carry the name 'regency'. The 24-year-old Joseph of Austria became co-ruler immediately (though still under considerable parental constraint), and the shadow cast by the exaggerated mourning of the empress (who wore black for the rest of her days) is in sharp contrast to the outbreak of gaiety and loose living which greeted the five-year-old Louis XV. Similar, however, was the relative chaos that reigned in the theatres during these two regencies. Out of the battles between royally privileged and fairground theatres in Paris there came the potent new genre of *opéra comique*; in Vienna a popular form of lyric drama was also the main product of a conflict between theatrical traditions.

In the wake of Durazzo (who was given the post of ambassador to Venice), theatrical impresarios followed one another in rapid succession. An outward appearance of order – as in the elaborate new regulations on dancers' conduct, for instance – masked an essentially rudderless quality to theatrical life. Kaunitz and the nobility succeeded twice in obtaining new companies of French actors for the Burgtheater, but these concentrated almost exclusively on spoken productions and in any case were short-lived. In the area of dance, Jean-Georges Noverre dazzled the Viennese public with his full-length pantomime ballets, while claiming in their prefaces that he had invented the genre. An outraged Angiolini protested from Milan, saying 'This you say, write and publish in the year 1772 in Vienna, in the very city where was born, lived and died the true restorer of the art of pantomime, Monsieur Hilverding'.[40] The German theatre was no less embroiled in dispute than the French, as Kurz fought vainly to reinstate the traditional popular comedy against authors of more 'regular' pieces.

And yet the music of this period is not without masterpieces. One thinks first of Gluck's *Alceste*, whose heroine was meant to recall the widowed empress and whose music was as unrelievedly sombre as she. Ideas on the reform of opera left largely unsaid at the time of *Orfeo* were now expressed without reserve: in the dedication to Archduke Leopold of the published score – signed Gluck, but drafted by Calzabigi – and privately in a letter from the latter to Kaunitz, in which the poet heaped scorn on Metastasio and his way of making opera. The fact that the score was printed in Vienna is itself significant; recourse to Paris, as with the publication of *Orfeo*, was no longer the first instinct of Viennese artists.

Viennese music publishing was pursued only sporadically until the founding of the firm of Artaria in 1778, but the 1760s did see the birth of serious music criticism. In an article published in 1764 the *Wienerisches Diarium* apologized for its earlier neglect of this area, explaining that although much of merit had been seen on Viennese stages, 'native citizens have had so little part in this, that it could hardly have been credited to our account'.[41] Most such criticism, in fact, was bound up with the issue of nationalism, and in the essay on the Viennese taste in music from 1766 (mentioned above, p.108) it is easy to see a foreshadowing of the Viennese Classical style in these terms. The author declares first that '[t]wo or three good authors can remake the literary taste of a nation, and just as many good compositions can do the same in music', and goes on to call Haydn:

> the darling of our nation . . . His compositions have beauty, order, purity, an elegant and noble simplicity, which are all the more quickly felt when the listener is prepared for them. In his cassations, quartets and trios he is a pure and clear stream, which is now and then rippled by a southern breeze . . . In his symphonies he is as manly and strong as he is inventive. In cantatas charming, engaging, flattering; and in minuets natural, joking, alluring. In short, Haydn is in music what Gellert is in poetry.[42]

One is struck by the use of 'noble simplicity' – since Johann Winckelmann (1717–68) a term almost synonymous with classical antiquity – and also by the large amount of Haydn's music known to the author. Haydn's compositions were starting to become part of the cultural property of the Austrian nation, in spite of the infrequency of his visits to the capital and his contract's stipulating that his music was for the personal use of his employer. Praise such as this must surely have been a factor in Prince Esterházy's decision in 1780 to loosen restrictions on the dissemination and publication of Haydn's music, after which it penetrated to the far corners of Europe.

The press was used as a powerful tool also in shaping opinion on the theatre and theatrical music. Assuming the guise of a Frenchman in his *Briefe über die wienerische Schaubühne*, Joseph von Sonnenfels chided his fellow citizens for their enthusiasm for French plays and Italian *opere buffe*: 'I have always maintained that one owes the greater attention and encouragement to the national theatre'. By this he meant not burlesque farces, but plays (or operas) of some literary pretensions (whether serious or comic), independent as far as was possible of foreign models. It proved to be more difficult than Sonnenfels imagined to break free of these last, but Emperor Joseph's proclamation of a 'Nationaltheater' in spring 1776 – putting the German company in the Burgtheater, formerly the domain of foreigners – was none the less a triumph for German literature. As Mozart's commission to write *Die Entführung aus dem Serail* was a direct result of this new arrangement, we can call Joseph's action a triumph for Viennese music as well.

NOTES

[1] A. Jefferson, *Richard Strauss: Der Rosenkavalier* (Cambridge, 1985), 12–13.

[2] See D. Heartz, 'Nicolas Jadot and the Building of the Burgtheater', *MQ*, lxviii (1982), 1–31, especially p.4.

[3] V. Alfieri, *Memoirs*, anon. trans., 1810, rev. E. R. Vincent (London, 1961), 96.

[4] *Tutte le opere di Pietro Metastasio*, ed. B. Brunelli (Milan, 1943–54), iii, 340.

[5] Letter of 8 Dec 1756, in *Tutte le opere*, iii, 1153.

[6] Prince Carl Joseph Maximilian von Fürst's MS *Lettres sur Vienne écrites en 1755*, excerpts trans. L. von Ranke in *Historisch-politische Zeitschrift* (Berlin, 1832–6), ii, 672.

[7] See Heartz, 'Nicolas Jadot'.

[8] Letter of 29 June 1748, in C. Burney, *Memoirs of the Life and Writings of the Abate Metastasio, in which are incorporated Translations of his Principal Letters* (London, 1796), i, 230.

[9] See D. Heartz, 'Hasse, Galuppi and Metastasio', in *Venezia e il melodramma nel settecento*, ed. M. T. Muraro (Florence, 1978), 309–39.

[10] F. Nicolai, *Beschreibung einer Reise durch Deutschland und die Schweiz, im Jahre 1781* (Berlin and Stettin, 1784), iv, 544; quoted in B. MacIntyre, *The Viennese Concerted Mass of the Early Classic Period* (Ann Arbor, 1985), 13.

[11] C. Burney, *The Present State of Music in Germany, the Netherlands, and United Provinces* (London, 2/1775), i, 226–7.

[12] ibid, i, 308.

[13] ibid, i, 218–19.

[14] F. Riedel, 'Liturgie und Kirchenmusik', in *Joseph Haydn in seiner Zeit*, ed. Gerda Mraz, Gottfried Mraz and G. Schlag (Eisenstadt, 1982), 121–33, especially pp.123–4.

[15] G. A. Griesinger, *Biographische Notizen über Joseph Haydn* (Leipzig, 1810); trans. V. Gotwals, in *Haydn: Two Contemporary Portraits* (Madison, 1968), 14.

[16] MacIntyre, *The Viennese Concerted Mass.*

[17] The relevant documents on the dispute are quoted from at length by R. Haas in *Gluck und Durazzo im Burgtheater* (Vienna, 1925).

[18] MacIntyre, *The Viennese Concerted Mass*, 85.
[19] It has recently been suggested that the author was the violinist and composer Carl Ditters von Dittersdorf; see D. Heartz, ' "Wagenseils würdigster Nachfolger": Štěpán and his Sonatas opp.1–3', in *Czech Music and its Influence on the Development of European Classicism in Music* (in preparation).
[20] *Ueber die Kirchenmusic in Wien* (Vienna, 1781), 9; quoted in MacIntyre, *The Viennese Concerted Mass*, 53.
[21] *Haydn: Two Contemporary Portraits*, 14.
[22] See E. Badura-Skoda, 'The Influence of the Viennese Popular Comedy on Haydn and Mozart', *PRMA*, c (1973–4), 185–99.
[23] See F. Hadamowsky, 'Das Spieljahr 1753/54 des Theaters nächst dem Kärntnerthor und des Theaters nächst der k. k. Burg', *Jb der Gesellschaft für Wiener Theaterforschung*, xi (1959), 3–21, especially p.4.
[24] Reproduced by O. Teuber in *Das k. k. Hofburgtheater seit seiner Begründung* (Vienna, 1896), 69.
[25] Letter of 2 June 1756 to Count Starhemberg, Austrian ambassador in Paris, quoted by Haas in *Gluck und Durazzo*, 31–2.
[26] G. Angiolini, *Lettere a Monsieur Noverre sopra i balli pantomimi* (Milan, 1773), 13–14.
[27] *Journal encyclopédique* (15 Nov 1757), 137–8.
[28] Letter of 10 Aug 1763, in *Mémoires et correspondance littéraires, dramatiques et anecdotiques de C.S. Favart*, ed. A. P. C. Favart (Paris, 1808), ii, 137.
[29] See G. Gentili-Verona, 'Le collezioni Foà e Giordano della Biblioteca Nazionale di Torino', *Vivaldiana*, i (1969), 31–56.
[30] See D. Heartz, 'Traetta in Vienna: *Armida* (1761) and *Ifigenia in Tauride* (1763)', *Studies in Music from the University of Western Ontario*, vii (1982), 65–88.
[31] See D. Heartz, 'From Garrick to Gluck: the Reform of Theatre and Opera in the Mid-Eighteenth Century', *PRMA*, xciv (1967–8), 111–27.
[32] C. Burney, *A General History of Music from the Earliest Ages to the Present Period*, ii (London, 1782), 876.
[33] See H. C. Robbins Landon, *Haydn: Chronicle and Works*, ii: *Haydn at Eszterháza, 1766–1790* (London, 1978), chap.4, 'Crisis Years: *Sturm und Drang* and the Austrian Musical Crisis'.
[34] *Autobiography of Karl von Dittersdorf*, trans. A. D. Coleridge (London, 1896/*R*1970), 7.
[35] ibid, 47.
[36] See E. Badura-Skoda, 'Prolegomena to a History of the Viennese Fortepiano', *Israel Studies in Musicology*, ii (1980), 77–99.
[37] See D. Heartz, 'Haydn und Gluck im Burgtheater um 1760: Der neue krumme Teufel, Le diable à quatre und die Sinfonie "Le soir" ', *Kongressbericht: Bayreuth 1981*, 120–35. Gluck's opera had its origins in English stage plays dating back to 1686; the 1731 reworking by Charles Coffey as *The Devil to Pay*, in which magical transformations and trenchant social commentary were very effectively intertwined, gained wide circulation on the Continent, inspiring versions in both German and French.
[38] A. P. Brown, *Joseph Haydn's Keyboard Music* (Bloomington, 1986), 185.
[39] Burney, *Present State*, i, 294.
[40] Angiolini, *Lettere*, 8–9.
[41] *Wienerisches Diarium* (7 Jan 1764), no.2, appx.
[42] ibid (18 Oct 1766), no.84, appx.

BIBLIOGRAPHICAL NOTE

Historical-political background

The standard documentary biography of the empress is the ten-volume *Geschichte Maria Theresia's* (Vienna, 1863–79) by A. von Arneth. A shorter, more interpretative account in English is given by E. Crankshaw in *Maria Theresa* (New York, 1969). Students of this period will also profit much from D. Beales's *Joseph II*, i: *In the Shadow of Maria Theresa* (Cambridge, 1987). E. Wangermann focusses more specifically on administrative, intellectual and cultural developments in the two monarchs' reigns in *The Austrian Achievement* (London and New York, 1973). The German-speaking reader is referred to the diaries published as *Aus der Zeit Maria Theresias: Tagebuch des Fürsten*

Johann Joseph Khevenhüller-Metsch, kaiserlichen Obersthofmeisters 1742–1776, ed. R. Khevenhüller-Metsch and H. Schlitter (Vienna, 1907–25), for a vivid impression of life at court, its etiquette, linguistic mix and entertainments. An outside perspective from the time is provided by excerpts from the Prussian Prince Carl Joseph Maximilian von Fürst's manuscript *Lettres sur Vienne écrites en 1755*, translated by L. von Ranke in his *Historisch-politische Zeitschrift* (Berlin, 1832–6), ii, 667–740.

Literature and the arts

The 200th anniversary of Maria Theresa's death was the occasion for a richly illustrated, comprehensive overview of her reign (with much emphasis on culture) and contributions by virtually all major Austrian historians of the period, *Maria Theresia und ihre Zeit*, ed. W. Koschatzky (Salzburg and Vienna, 2/1980). Of more limited scope are A. Novotny's excellent *Staatskanzler Kaunitz als geistige Persönlichkeit* (Vienna, 1947), which gives ample evidence of the intermingling of statecraft and the arts, and H. Wagner's 'Die Höhepunkt des französischen Kultureinflusses in Österreich in der zweiten Hälfte des 18. Jahrhunderts', *Österreich in Geschichte und Literatur*, v/10 (1961), 507–17. J Schmidt's *Die alte Universität in Wien und ihr Erbauer Jean Nicolas Jadot* (Vienna and Leipzig, 1929) contains an interesting chapter on the wave of French influences brought to Vienna by Francis Stephen of Lorraine in 1740.

Theatre, opera and ballet

Fundamental contemporary sources include G. Angiolini's polemical *Lettere a Monsieur Noverre sopra i balli pantomimi* (Milan, 1773); J. von Sonnenfels's manifesto against foreign domination of Vienna's theatres, *Briefe über die wienerische Schaubühne* (Vienna, 1768); and the exchange of letters (somewhat pruned, and inaccurately edited) between the theatre director Durazzo and his agent in Paris, C.S. Favart, in the latter's *Mémoires et correspondance*, ed. C. N. Favart (Paris, 1808).

G. Croll considers the Austrian sovereigns and music in 'Anmerkungen zu Musik, Theater und Musikern in Wien zur Zeit Maria Theresias und Josephs II', *Österreich im Europa der Aufklärung* (Vienna, 1985), 663–72. A documentary study of Vienna's theatres has been undertaken by G. Zechmeister, in *Die Wiener Theater nächst der Burg und nächst dem Kärntnertortheater von 1747 bis 1776* (Vienna, 1971). A mixed narrative and archival approach is taken by R. Haas in *Gluck und Durazzo im Burgtheater* (Vienna, 1925), a pioneer book that new finds have made out of date. Music for the stage is put in the larger contexts of court, city and continent in a series of articles by D. Heartz, among which are: 'From Garrick to Gluck: the Reform of Theatre and Opera in the Mid-Eighteenth Century', *PRMA*, xciv (1967–8), 111–27; 'Haydn und Gluck im Burgtheater um 1760: Der neue krumme Teufel, Le diable à quatre und die Sinfonie "Le Soir" ', *Kongressbericht: Bayreuth 1981*, 120–35; and 'Traetta in Vienna: *Armida* (1761) and *Ifigenia in Tauride* (1763)', *Studies in Music from the University of Western Ontario*, vii (1982), 65–88. In a similar vein, E. Badura-Skoda traces 'The Influence of the Viennese Popular Comedy on Haydn and Mozart', *PRMA*, c (1973–4), 185–99. On ballet, see R. Haas's 'Die Wiener Bühnentanz von 1740 bis 1767', *JbMP*, xliv (1937), 77–93, and M. H. Winter's *The Pre-Romantic Ballet* (London, 1974), which uses recent archival finds of major importance.

Instrumental music

The following will provide a general orientation to non-theatrical music in Vienna during the latter part of the century: N. Tschulik, 'Musikartikel aus dem Wienerischen Diarium von 1766', *SMw*, xxx (1979), 91–106 (primarily concerned with an anonymous survey of Viennese composers); O. Biba, 'Concert Life in Beethoven's Vienna', *Beethoven, Performers, and Critics: Detroit, 1977*, 77–93 (useful for earlier periods as well); and J. Webster, 'Towards a History of Viennese Chamber Music in the Early Classical Period', *JAMS*, xxvii (1974), 212–47.

Chapter V

Vienna under Joseph II and Leopold II

JOHN A. RICE

I assure you that this is a splendid place – and for my *métier* the best one in the world.

(Mozart to his father, 4 April 1781, shortly after arriving in Vienna.[1])

THE 1770S AND 1780S: THE TRADITION OF EXCELLENCE MAINTAINED

The conditions under which Viennese musicians worked in the 1770s and 1780s differed little from those described in Chapter IV. The court dominated Viennese musical life, as it had for centuries. The court theatres, under close supervision of court officials and of the sovereigns themselves, remained Vienna's principal theatres, and, as such, the centre of the city's musical life. Many of the musicians active in Vienna during the 1750s and 1760s continued to shape musical life during the succeeding decades. Audiences that heard them perform in the 1780s included many who had heard them perform in the 1760s. And Vienna continued to fascinate young, ambitious musicians, attracting them to perform and to compose there, and convincing many of them to settle there. When the 22-year-old Beethoven travelled from Bonn to Vienna in 1792, moving from one edge of the German-speaking part of Europe to the other, he did so for many of the same reasons that had brought Gluck to Vienna more than a generation earlier and that had emboldened Mozart to establish himself in Vienna in 1781, breaking free of his job, his father and his home.

Vienna in the 1780s maintained the position it had long enjoyed of principal city of the German-speaking part of Europe.[2] With a population of roughly 230,000 in 1789, Vienna was by far the largest German-speaking city. Berlin, with a population of 172,000 in 1800, was a distant second; many of the cities from which Vienna drew its most talented musicians – like Prague, Salzburg, Munich and Bonn

– were even smaller. But compared to Europe's largest cities – London (861,000 in 1800), Paris (547,000) and Naples (430,000) – the Habsburg capital was still medium-sized.

Vienna consisted of two quite distinct parts: a walled city of some 52,000 residents, surrounded by rapidly growing suburbs where most of the people lived – 140,000 of them in 1772, 165,000 in 1785. The court dominated the inner city and all its activities. Around the court clustered the offices of government, the ministries and treasuries and the law-courts, and, around these, the palaces of the nobility, the churches, the homes of court officials, bureaucrats, lawyers, accountants and secretaries, and the homes of their servants and other employees.

The Viennese nobility numbered perhaps 8000 during most of the 1780s, roughly three per cent of the city's total population. What might be defined as an 'upper middle class' of affluent professional people – doctors, bankers, lawyers, wealthier merchants – was still relatively small in the 1780s; one recent study defines a class of Viennese 'Beamten und Bürger' (civil servants and, presumably wealthier, townspeople) as four per cent of the population, or only a little bigger than the nobility.[3] These figures are admittedly problematic. The boundary between the groups was hazy, because many of the richest and most influential members of the bourgeoisie were ennobled by the emperor; nor can a clear distinction be made between the 'Beamten und Bürger' and the bulk of the middle class below them. Yet the figures, however imprecise, suggest that Viennese society was one of many eighteenth-century societies in which most of the wealth and power was concentrated in the hands of a few.

Together with the court and the Catholic Church, the Viennese nobility and, to a lesser extent, the 'Beamten und Bürger' supported and enjoyed those aspects of Viennese musical life with which this chapter is primarily concerned. A recent sociological analysis of Mozart's only extant concert subscription list provides a clear idea of the social background of Mozart's musical patrons. Of Mozart's 174 subscribers to a concert series in 1784, 50 per cent came from the high nobility, 42 per cent from the lesser nobility or from wealthy commoners with purchased titles and a mere eight per cent from the bourgeoisie.[4]

During the 1770s and 1780s the imperial court continued to keep for itself the privilege of operating public theatres within the walls of Vienna. Minor remodelling did not greatly change the size or shape of the Burgtheater between 1760 and 1790; nor were the number and arrangement of its seats, or the social composition of its audience, much altered. The Burgtheater of the 1780s was still an intimate space, with room for a maximum of about 1350 spectators. By comparison, the King's Theatre in London, as rebuilt in 1789–91,

33. Cross-section through the Burgtheater, Vienna: engraving

and La Scala in Milan, both among Europe's largest theatres, had capacities of about 3300.

The Burgtheater (fig.33) continued to segregate its audience along class lines. The *parterre noble*, directly in front of the stage, was reserved for members of the nobility, as were the first two tiers of boxes, except for those belonging to the imperial family or reserved for foreign ambassadors. The second parterre (behind the *parterre noble*), parts of the third tier of boxes and the upper gallery were open to anyone who could pay the substantial ticket prices. These were for the most part wealthier members of Vienna's middle class, along with foreign visitors. The price of the cheapest seats – those in the uppermost section of the theatre, the so-called 'Paradies' – was sharply reduced during the 1770s, from twenty kreuzer to seven, but even at seven kreuzer the tickets were out of reach of many Viennese. A mason would have to work a full day to buy such a ticket. It has been estimated that the nobility and the 'Beamten und Bürger', although together they may have made up only about seven per cent of the population, represented 90 per cent of the Burgtheater's audience.[5]

It is likely that among those who saw Mozart's operas and concertos performed in the Burgtheater during the 1780s were many who had seen performances there for a generation or more. A major source of income for the court theatres was the rental of boxes to members of the nobility. They paid dearly for their privilege. The annual fee for a box in the Burgtheater ran from 700 to 1000 gulden (1 gulden = 60 kreuzer), or about the same as the annual income of a lower-ranked court official. (Mozart, as Kammermusiker, earned an annual salary of 800 gulden.) Yet many noblemen renewed their subscriptions year after year. Count Johann Karl Zinzendorf attended concerts and theatrical performances in Vienna several times a week whenever he was in Vienna, over a period of more than 40 years, from the early 1760s until his death in 1813. His feat is remembered today because he recorded it in his diary; but there is no reason to believe that there were not others in the audience who went to the theatre as often as Zinzendorf and for as many years. A composer writing in the 1780s could thus probably count on a large part of his audience recognizing references to music that had been performed in Vienna much earlier. A stormy D minor episode in the first-act finale of Dittersdorf's *Doktor und Apotheker* (1786) may well have reminded Zinzendorf and his music-loving friends of the dance of the furies in Gluck's *Don Juan* (1762); they may have enjoyed Mozart's references to the traditions of *opéra comique* – so much a part of Viennese musical culture during the 1750s and 1760s – in *Le nozze di Figaro* (also 1786).[6]

With its long exposure to some of Europe's finest music and musicians, the audience of the Burgtheater was an educated one. Having become accustomed to music of high quality through performances of the works of Gluck, Traetta, Gassmann and Haydn, it expected the same level of quality from composers and performers during the 1780s. Thus the audience helped maintain the Burgtheater's tradition of musical excellence.

Music 'is the only thing about which the nobility shows taste', according to an account of Viennese musical life published in 1784.[7] The wealthy, music-loving Viennese aristocracy, willing and able to spend large amounts of money on music, contributed much more to musical life than the price of their Burgtheater boxes. Although Prince Joseph Friedrich of Saxe-Hildburghausen, patron of Dittersdorf and Haydn in the 1750s, had to dismiss his orchestra when he left Vienna for his estates in 1761, his place was taken up by other generous and knowledgeable patrons. Methods by which patronage was bestowed, on the other hand, changed gradually during the second half of the century. A mid-century patron might employ musicians on a full-time basis and require that they work for him alone, as when Haydn agreed, on joining the musical establishment of Prince Paul Anton Esterházy in 1761, that his compositions would be reserved 'wholly for the exclusive use of his Highness'.[8] Such strict, long-term agreements became less common later in the century; they were replaced to a large extent by arrangements whereby a patron would engage a musician for a single concert or a series of concerts, for the composition of a single work or a series of works. The transition from the one kind of patronage to the other was not always easy. Mozart's confrontation with Archbishop Colloredo of Salzburg in 1781 was fundamentally a conflict between the older style of patronage and the newer, between steady employment and the many restrictions that it entailed and the riskier life of a freelance musician. The two styles were incompatible, Mozart found out quickly; without much hesitation he chose the second.

Prince Dimitri Golitsïn (Galitzin), the Russian ambassador in Vienna from 1762 to 1792, was a generous bestower of the new kind of patronage. For many years Golitsïn gave weekly concerts in his Viennese palace at which the leading musicians of the city were invited to perform. During Lent 1784 Mozart appeared almost every Thursday at the palace. He must have welcomed the opportunity to earn cash and gain access to the high nobility without having to go through the difficult and time-consuming process of organizing his own concerts, and without having to give up his freedom to make music where and when he pleased.

Mozart had a more discerning patron in Baron Gottfried van Swieten, perhaps the most influential Viennese musical patron of the late eighteenth century. Van Swieten was a composer himself and an enthusiastic performer. A well-travelled diplomat early in his career, he got to know the music of Handel and Johann Sebastian Bach in Berlin and he brought his knowledge back to Vienna. In the 1780s he became one of the chief architects of Joseph's reforms in education, religion and censorship; but that did not keep him away from music. He invited musicians to the imperial library for weekly music-making. Mozart joined van Swieten's circle soon after establishing himself in Vienna and it was not long before he too became fascinated by the Baroque polyphony that was the centre of attention at these musical gatherings.

Van Swieten continued to enrich Viennese musical life in the 1790s. He invited a newcomer to his music-making, one who had no need to be convinced of the value of Bach's and Handel's fugues; it was to van Swieten that Beethoven dedicated his first symphony when it was published in 1800. Without van Swieten at his side, the aged Haydn probably would not have written the oratorios *The Creation* and *The Seasons*: van Swieten encouraged Haydn to undertake the projects, supplied him with texts, and may even have provided some of the musical ideas. In short, the *Jahrbuch der Tonkunst für Wien und Prag, 1796* does not seem to have been exaggerating when it described van Swieten as:

> practically a patriarch in music. His taste is only for the great and elevated. Many years ago he wrote twelve beautiful symphonies.

> When he is present at a concert, our half-connoisseurs do not take their eyes off him, so that they can read from his expression (which, however, may not be so easily understood) what opinion he might have about the work in question. Every year he gives some very large and magnificent concerts, in which only pieces by old masters are given. He especially loves the Handelian style, and mostly gives large choral works by him.[9]

Viennese orchestras were of particularly fine quality. The 1784 account of Viennese musical life quoted above praises the orchestras of Vienna at length:

> Many [noble] houses have their own bands of musicians, and all the public concerts bear witness that this aspect of art is in high repute here. One can put together four or five large orchestras, all of which are incomparable. The number of real virtuosi is small, but as far as the orchestral musicians are concerned, one can hardly imagine anything in the world more beautiful. I have heard 30 or 40 instruments playing together, and they all produce one tone so correct, clean and precise that one might think one is hearing a single, supernaturally powerful instrument. One stroke of the bow animated all the violins and one breath, all the wind instruments. An Englishman next to whom I sat thought it miraculous that throughout an entire opera there was – I won't say no mistake, but nothing of all that which generally occurs in large orchestras: a hasty entrance, dragging, or too strong a bowing or attack. He was enchanted by the purity and correctness of the harmony, and he had just come from Italy.[10]

The orchestra of the Burgtheater, to which the writer was probably referring in the latter part of this description, increased in size only a little during the 1770s and 1780s. In 1773 it was the size of a typical twentieth-century chamber orchestra, with 32 players: fourteen violins, four violas, three cellos, three double basses and pairs of oboes, flutes, bassoons and horns (presumably the horn players also played trumpets and some other member of the orchestra also played timpani when needed). By 1791 the orchestra had expanded, but only to 37 players: twelve violins (six firsts and six seconds), five violas, three cellos, four double basses and pairs of oboes, flutes, clarinets, bassoons, horns and trumpets, and timpani.[11] It is interesting to note that the string section remained, at 24 players, exactly the same size that it had been eighteen years earlier, with only a slight shift in the balance from the violins to the lower strings. It is also worth noting that many of the musicians playing in the Burgtheater orchestra in 1773 were still members in 1791; this continuity in personnel must have been partly responsible for the fine sense of ensemble achieved by the orchestra.

The Burgtheater orchestra was much larger than many in Vienna and in the Viennese cultural orbit. The enormously wealthy

Hungarian Prince Nikolaus Esterházy was satisfied with an orchestra that rarely exceeded 25 players. At the same time larger orchestras than the Burgtheater's were occasionally gathered. Perhaps the largest ensembles in Vienna, often exceeding 150 instrumentalists and singers, were those gathered by the Tonkünstler-Sozietät for their semi-annual concerts, to be discussed later in this chapter. Mozart wrote to his father on 11 April 1781 that one of his symphonies, possibly the 'Paris', K297/300*a*, was performed at a Tonkünstler-Sozietät concert by an orchestra of 40 violins, ten violas, eight cellos, ten double basses and six bassoons, with all the other wind parts doubled. This amounted to an orchestra of 85 or thereabouts. Though Mozart was pleased with the performance, there is no reason to accept one scholar's conclusion that this was 'the orchestra that Mozart preferred' for the performance of his works.[12] He probably preferred that of the Burgtheater, an ensemble representing the middle ground between the small private orchestras of Vienna and the giant public ensembles of the Tonkünstler concerts. Remarkably stable in size, composition and personnel, it offered Viennese composers a dependable and familiar means of bringing their music to life.

One of the violinists who played in the Burgtheater orchestra during the first performances of Gluck's *Orfeo* (1762) was young Carl Ditters, who, in addition to his duties as an orchestral player, also delighted the Viennese during the early 1760s wth his virtuoso violin concertos. He returned to Vienna in the 1780s, now styling himself Ditters von Dittersdorf, and won applause as a composer of German opera and Italian oratorio. Dittersdorf was one of many musicians active in Vienna in the 1750s and 1760s who contributed to Viennese musical life later in the century. Haydn was another. He received his musical training in Vienna during the 1740s and worked as a musician and composer there during the following decade. Although his service to the Esterházy princes kept him away from Vienna for most of the next 30 years, Haydn remained in touch with Viennese musical life, composing much of his music for Viennese musicians and musical institutions. And it was in Vienna that he spent the last years of his life, there that he created two of his last and greatest masterpieces, *The Creation* and *The Seasons*.

Dittersdorf was a native of Vienna; Haydn was born nearby. But Vienna also attracted musicians from elsewhere, and the most successful of these often made it their home. Vienna was especially attractive to Bohemian musicians: Gluck, Florian Gassmann, Leopold Kozeluch and Adalbert Gyrowetz are among the many Bohemians who enriched Viennese musical life during the second half of the eighteenth century and the first half of the nineteenth. Italians came to Vienna too. Most of the Burgtheater's greatest singers had enjoyed successful careers in Italy before coming north to Vienna, where they

34. Fanfare to the special performance of Haydn's 'The Creation' given in the hall of the Old University, Vienna, on 27 March 1808 to mark the composer's 76th birthday (he is seated centre foreground): copy of a miniature by Balthasar Wigand painted on a box lid (lost)

helped to shape the characters, the dramatic situations and the music created for them. But Vienna's leading Italian musician was in many ways more Viennese than Italian. Antonio Salieri arrived in Vienna in 1766 as a teenager and studied with Gassmann; he must have absorbed not only Gassmann's music but also that of Gluck's late Viennese works, for his first big operatic success, in 1771, was a Gluckian *Armida*. As music director for Joseph II, Salieri, perhaps more than any other musician, influenced the course of Viennese musical theatre during the next generation.

Mozart, though younger than Salieri, reached Vienna before him. Mozart's first visit, in 1762, coincided with the first run of Gluck's *Orfeo*. Like Salieri and Dittersdorf, Mozart remembered the sound of Gluck's Viennese operas. As mentioned in Chapter IV, one can hear an echo of the music Gluck wrote to accompany the furies in *Don Juan* and *Orfeo* in the demonic violence of the second-act finale of *Don Giovanni* (first performed in Prague in 1787 and presented the following year in the Burgtheater); in the monumental choruses of *La clemenza di Tito* (Prague, 1791) one can hear some of the solemn grandeur achieved by Gluck more than twenty years earlier in the choruses of *Alceste* (1767).[13]

JOSEPHINIAN REFORM AND OPERA

The second half of the eighteenth century was clearly an age of continuity in Viennese musical life, but it was also an age of change, much of that change connected with the reforms instituted by Maria Theresa and, to an even greater extent, by her son, co-regent and successor Joseph II. The humiliating military defeats suffered by Austria at the hands of Prussia during a series of mid-century wars encouraged Maria Theresa to embark on a series of reforms that had as their goal the transformation of the Habsburg dominions into a modern, centralized state capable of competing, economically as well as militarily, with Prussia, France and Great Britain. Joseph continued and accelerated the reformist drive. His reforms changed fundamentally the character of Viennese society; Viennese music, as a reflection of the society that created it, changed too.

Even before his mother's death in 1780 Joseph made important changes, including one with a dramatic impact on Viennese musical life. During the first decade of Joseph's co-regency (1765–75) Maria Theresa maintained much of her authority; as she grew older, Joseph's share of responsibility and power increased. During the 1760s and early 1770s it is difficult to see Joseph as predominant decision maker concerning the court theatres; with his reorganization of the theatres in 1776 Joseph made it clear that he, not his aged mother or court officials appointed by her, was in charge of the theatres, and that henceforth he would supervise them closely.

The first decade of Joseph's co-regency saw the administration of the court theatres in flux. A succession of impresarios attempted to present opera, ballet and spoken drama according to the specifications of the court; most of these impresarios suffered financial ruin in the process. The court itself was buffeted by contradictory pressures: intellectuals like Joseph von Sonnenfels (who, despite the fact that his father had been ennobled in 1746, still represented middle-class ideals that were foreign to most of the Viennese nobility) wanted to see the court theatres transformed into a 'national theatre' dedicated to the performance of serious spoken drama in German; Prince Wenzel Kaunitz, the powerful minister of state, led a party consisting mostly of nobles that called for the performance of more *opéra comique* and *opera buffa*. Since the nobility's financial support of the court theatres was essential, their preferences carried a good deal of weight.

In 1776 Joseph decided to take the situation into his own hands. His theatrical reorganization bears all the features characteristic of his reforms. The changes he made were, typically, sudden and drastic. Dissolving the contract with the impresario who was then struggling to manage the theatres, the emperor brought all aspects of theatre management under the direct supervision of the court. He ordered that the *opera buffa* and ballet troupes be dismissed, together with the orchestra of the Kärntnertortheater. All that remained were a troupe for the performance of spoken dramas in German and the Burgtheater orchestra to play overtures and entr'acte music. Following the advice of Sonnenfels and his partisans, and imitating the example set by the founding of the Nationaltheater in Hamburg in 1767, Joseph commanded that the Burgtheater henceforth be called 'das teutsche National Theater'.[14]

Joseph's reorganization was consistent with three of the most important aims of his reforms in general, all related to the ultimate goal of transforming the Habsburg domains into a modern state. To increase the efficiency of his government Joseph initiated a programme of Germanization, increasing the use of German throughout his polyglot empire, in schools, in churches and in government business. The establishment of a theatre for the performance of German spoken drama was a powerful symbol of the pre-eminence of German. At the same time it allowed the court to save money – another important goal for Joseph – for spoken drama was much cheaper to produce than opera and ballet. Finally, it represented a short-lived victory for the monarchy in a long struggle that lay at the heart of the Theresian-Josephinian reforms: the monarchy's efforts to bring the nobility under the authority of the central government, to hasten and complete the transition from a feudal to a modern state. Since the nobility had made plain its preference for French and Italian opera, the transformation of the Burgtheater into 'das teutsche National Theater' must have been regarded as a blow to the nobility's prestige and a slight but symbolically important shift in the balance of power.

As was often the case with his reforms, Joseph seems to have disregarded the practical implications of his theatrical reorganization: that many of his most powerful subjects loved opera and ballet; that he needed the cooperation of the nobility, not their hostility; and that his reorganization, while financially beneficial to the court, caused financial ruin for many: over 100 people (singers, dancers, instrumentalists and administrators) lost their jobs as a result of Joseph's theatrical reform.[15] No ruler could afford to make so many enemies among those with close connections with the court. It is not surprising that Joseph's reorganization of the court theatres, like so many of his reforms, had to be modified and to some extent reversed.

The first of these modifications was the re-establishment in the Burgtheater of an opera troupe organized and subsidized by the court. In 1778 Joseph put together a troupe for the performance of German opera. Although this action represented a reversal of one aspect of his reorganization, it was still in keeping with its spirit. The performance of German opera was consistent with the idea that the court theatre should serve as a centre for the promotion of German language and culture (although it is true that many of the 'German' operas presented

35. Ignaz Umlauf's 'Die Bergknappen' (scene xii), first performed at the Burgtheater, 17 February 1778: engraving by Carl Schütz

by Joseph's troupe were German only in language). It was also consistent with Joseph's goal of saving money. Most German operas of the 1770s were Singspiels (spoken plays with songs), which required much less virtuosity from their performers than Italian operas, and the German singer-actors who performed them were easier to find and cheaper to employ than Italian opera singers.

The German troupe made its début on 17 February 1778 with an opera by Ignaz Umlauf, *Die Bergknappen* (fig.35).[16] The work is typical of the operas written for Joseph's troupe in that it borrows freely from several theatrical traditions. The plays with music of north Germany – operas by Johann Adam Hiller, Georg Benda and others – provided one important source of inspiration. French *opéra comique*, so popular in Vienna during the 1750s and 1760s, influenced Viennese German opera both directly and by way of north German opera, which itself was largely inspired by *opéra comique*. Nor had the Viennese composers forgotten Italian opera, both serious and comic, for there is much of both in their German operas. *Die Bergknappen* is a spoken play with musical numbers interspersed: in this it is similar to both *opéra comique* and north German opera. There are simple, folklike melodies such as one might find in an opera by Hiller. But the big trio 'Erinnere dich stets meiner Schwüre', which has several changes of tempo, resembles an *opera buffa* finale; and Sophie's accompanied recitative is clearly inspired by *opera seria*, as is the virtuoso coloratura of her aria 'Wenn mir der Himmel lacht'. Rounding out the musical smorgasbord is the finale, a very French vaudeville in which each of the principal characters sings one verse (the hero and heroine sing one verse together) and the rest join in for the refrain.

In view of the eclectic quality of *Die Bergknappen* it is not surprising to find that many of the operas presented by Joseph's troupe were not German operas at all, but French and Italian operas in German translation. When Count Zinzendorf attended a performance of a work billed as *Diesmal hat der Mann den Willen*, with music by the Viennese composer Carlo d'Ordonez, he recognized its libretto as a reworking of an *opéra comique*, set by Monsigny (although he mistakenly attributed it to Grétry): *Le maître en droit*, a work that had been performed by Vienna's French troupe in the Burgtheater in 1763. Zinzendorf may have had Monsigny's music still in mind when he criticized Ordonez's as 'trop difficile, trop peu chantante'. Many more *opéras comiques* followed, mostly with the original, French music; other 'German' operas included *Robert und Kalliste oder Der Triumph der Liebe*, which turned out to be a reworking of *La sposa fedele*, an *opera buffa* by Pietro Alessandro Guglielmi.

On freeing himself from the Archbishop of Salzburg in 1781 the young Salzburg musician Wolfgang Amadeus Mozart enthusiastically entered the musical life of Vienna. He was not particular about which kind of music he composed; he was eager to show off his extraordinary talents in any genre. What Mozart wanted above all was the recognition of Emperor Joseph. He had written to his father, only eight days after arriving in Vienna: 'Well, my chief object here is to introduce myself to the emperor in some becoming way, for I am absolutely determined that he shall *get to know me*' (24 March 1781). It was natural that he should be drawn to the theatrical genre then in official favour. Mozart's *Die Entführung aus dem Serail*, begun a few months later, represents a culmination of the short-lived tradition of German opera in the Burgtheater.

Mozart combined in *Die Entführung* the same generic elements, the same national styles, that Umlauf, Ordonez and others had combined in their German operas; but Mozart, though younger than Umlauf and Ordonez, had much more experience as a dramatic composer than either and he had composed works in many of the genres from which he was expected to draw as a composer of German opera for the Burgtheater. Mozart's harsh criticism of one of Umlauf's later German operas, *Welches ist die beste Nation?*, suggests the basic assumptions behind his own approach to the genre. In a letter to his father Mozart called Umlauf's work 'a new opera, or rather a comedy with ariettas' (21 December 1782). For Mozart such a work was not an opera at all; and the Viennese public must have agreed with Mozart's assessment, for it rejected Umlauf's opera after two performances. Clearly aware of what worked in the theatre and what did not, Mozart collaborated with his librettist, Gottlieb Stephanie the younger, in recasting a German libretto by Christoph Friedrich Bretzner of Leipzig. Bretzner's libretto was a typically north German 'comedy with ariettas'; Mozart and Stephanie transformed it with the addition of many new musical numbers, both solo and ensemble, some of which replace spoken dialogue. The changes increased Mozart's opportunities for musical characterization and for the musical depiction of relationships between the characters; it allowed him, in short, to write a real opera, not just a comedy with ariettas.

Eager to win over the Viennese public and the emperor, Mozart calculated his music carefully to please his audience, but at the same time he filled his score with a richness of musical ideas and of musical technique that Umlauf, Ordonez and their colleagues could not match. It was doubtless to this abundance that Joseph alluded when he jokingly commented to the composer: 'Too beautiful for our ears, and far too many notes, my dear Mozart'. But he must have agreed with Mozart's response, 'Just as many, Your Majesty, as are needed', if for no other reason than that *Die Entführung* was a great popular success. The Viennese greeted the première, on 16 July 1782, with loud applause and the work was given many more performances during the short time that remained for the German opera troupe in the Burgtheater.

Vienna had not lost its taste for Italian opera as a result of Joseph's theatrical reorganization and his establishment of German opera in his 'Nationaltheater'; and the occasional performance of *opere buffe* in German translation was no substitute for the real thing sung by Italian singers. Popular support for the German troupe was weak. Umlauf's *Welches ist die beste Nation?* failed miserably, as we have seen; so did a German version of Gassmann's *La notte critica* of 1768, which likewise received only two performances. *Die Entführung* brought enthusiastic crowds into the theatre whenever it was performed, but the German troupe could not survive on one work alone, or on the works of one composer. That is probably why Mozart was not asked to write another German opera for the Burgtheater; nor is there any indication in his letters that he had an interest in writing such an opera. In late 1782, as he continued to enjoy the success of *Die Entführung*, Mozart had already turned his attention to Italian opera.

Following the death of Maria Theresa in 1780 the pace and nature of governmental reform in Vienna changed. Joseph II was less diplomatic than his mother, more headstrong and impulsive; in short, he was less of a statesman. Where Maria Theresa pushed her reforms forward slowly, compromising with those who opposed her wishes, cajoling and negotiating, Joseph tried to rule by fiat. He had no interest in half measures and had already made this clear with his theatrical reorganization of 1776. His reforms came in the form of sweeping proclamations; and this was especially the case after his mother's death. 'The Josephinian decade' is a suitable term for the ten years during which Joseph ruled alone and during which he changed the face of Viennese society.

Among the most pervasive of Joseph's reforms were those he promulgated as part of his attempt to limit the power, wealth and influence of the Catholic Church. In 1781 he issued his Edict of Toleration, a revolutionary decree that did away with many of the laws restricting the rights of Protestants within the Habsburg lands. He repealed many but by no means all of the laws that restricted the rights of Jews. He ordered that hundreds of monasteries be dissolved so that the church's wealth and resources could be put to more constructive use: for the building of parish churches and schools and for the salaries of teachers. Joseph's interest in supervising the lives of his subjects down to the smallest detail led him naturally to prescribe their religious ceremonies, which were to be as simple as possible, both to reduce expense and to discourage the spread of what he considered 'superstitious' ritual. He restricted the number of processions, of statues and of candles, and he restricted the kind of music that could be performed in church.

The reign of Maria Theresa had been a period of rich accomplishment in Viennese church music, as we have seen in Chapter IV. Georg Reutter (Maria Theresa's Hofkapellmeister), Hasse, Gassmann and Haydn were among the first-rate composers whose brilliant music echoed through the churches of Vienna during the 1750s, 60s and 70s. But during the early 1780s Joseph issued a series of decrees that limited the occasions when the most elaborate church music could be performed. His regulations never completely forbade such performances, but the spirit of his regulations, and his anti-clerical stance in general, seems to have discouraged the composition, performance and dissemination of elaborate church music (see fig.27 above). As early as 1782 a report from Vienna could state, probably with a good deal of exaggeration, that 'orchestrally accompanied music [*Figuralmusik*] has now been entirely eliminated from the churches, except for very important feast-days'.

It cannot be an accident that from 1783 to the end of Joseph's reign in 1790 little church music was written by the best Viennese composers. Mozart and Haydn, who had been productive composers of church music during the 1770s, suddenly turned away from the genre after 1783; both returned to it in the years following Joseph's death. Church music they had written before the Josephinian restrictions were imposed does not seem to have circulated much during the years 1783 to 1790. This is clearly the case with Haydn's fine *Missa Cellensis* ('Mariazeller Messe') of 1782, few copies of which are dated earlier than 1791.[17]

Between 1783 and 1790 Mozart and Haydn could do what they had never been able to do earlier in their careers: they could focus all their creative energy on secular music. The success that Mozart achieved in Italian opera and the concerto and that Haydn achieved in the symphony during the 1780s may well owe something, indirectly, to Joseph's religious reforms: the decline of Viennese church music left Haydn and Mozart free to concentrate on other genres.

That Mozart turned to *opera buffa*, after a period of several years in which he had written no such works, can similarly be connected to the emperor and his policies. For in 1783 Joseph reversed yet another part of his theatrical reorganization of 1776 and re-established an Italian *opera buffa* troupe in the Burgtheater.

PUBLIC CONCERTS: SYMPHONY, CONCERTO AND ORATORIO

Concert life in late eighteenth-century Vienna was nowhere near as highly developed as it was in the much larger city of London during the same period. Although the Viennese court did not maintain a monopoly in the organization of public concerts within the walls of Vienna, as it did in the public performance of opera, the Burgtheater nevertheless remained the central focus of the city's concert life during the late eighteenth century and into the nineteenth. Individual concerts and series of concerts were organized at other places, but these rarely developed into long-lasting institutions like the Professional Concerts or the Academy of Ancient Music in London, partly because Vienna seems to have lacked the aggressive and imaginative impresarios like Johann Peter Salomon – a fine musician as well as a skilful businessman – who brought Haydn to London and organized his concerts there.

London's much larger population allowed public concerts to continue throughout the winter and spring, competing for audiences with operas and spoken plays. In Vienna public concerts were mostly limited to the last few days of Advent and to Lent, during which the performance of opera was forbidden. The imperial court made its theatres available to individual virtuosos, who organized their own concerts, engaging musicians and selling tickets. The programmes they put together were surprisingly uniform in their structure and content. The typical concert consisted of seven or eight items, including both vocal and instrumental works. It opened and closed with symphonies, or movements of symphonies; it included arias and often vocal ensembles as well. If the virtuoso organizing the concert was an instrumentalist he would display his prowess with one or more concertos and possibly with a solo fantasy or theme and variations.

The performance of chamber music such as string quartets, an important part of many concerts in London, was rare in Burgtheater concerts, although wind ensembles sometimes made appearances.

When Mozart arrived in Vienna in 1781 the public concert was one of the aspects of Viennese musical life that excited him the most. In letters to his father he expressed his frustration at not being allowed by his employer, the Archbishop of Salzburg, to take part in public concerts: 'I told you in a recent letter that the Archbishop is a great hindrance to me here, for he has done me out of at least a hundred ducats, which I could certainly have made by giving a concert in the theatre' (4 April 1781). It was largely his eagerness to take part in such concerts, and his confidence that he could make a financial success of them, that encouraged Mozart to seek his dismissal from the archbishop's service and to settle in Vienna.

The concert seasons became periods of hectic activity for Mozart. Like other virtuosos he had to move quickly from public concerts in the Burgtheater to subscription concerts in other halls, to appearances in the private salons of wealthy patrons like Prince Golitsïn and Baron van Swieten. Leopold Mozart visited his son in Vienna during Lent 1785; in a letter to his daughter (12 March 1785) he described vividly the exhausting activity of the Lenten season:

Heute Sonnabends den 16. — und Sonntags den 17. April 1791.
wird
im. kaiserl. königl. Nazional- Hof- Theater
von der errichteten Tonkünstlergesellschaft
zum Vortheil ihrer Wittwen und Waisen
eine große musikalische Akademie,
gehalten werden, die aus folgenden Stücken bestehet:

1) Eine große Sinfonie von der Erfindung des Hrn. Mozart.

2) Ein Auszug aus der Oper: Phedra.

Es werden dabey singen:
Die Rolle der Arizia .... Mad. Lange.
Die Rolle des Ippolits .... Herr Kalvesi.
Die Rolle des Tescus .... Herr Nenzini.
Chor.
Die Musik ist vom Hrn. Johann Paisello, mit Ausnahme der Arie, welche Mad. Lange singt, und von der Komposition des Hrn. Mozart ist.

3) Ein Konzert auf dem Violonzell von der Komposition des Hrn. Pleyel, welches Hr. Kajetan Gottlieb, ein unlängst aus Florenz angekommener Virtuose, spielen wird.

4) Der sehr beliebte große Chor: Alleluja! vom Hrn. Georg Albrechtsberger, k. k. Hofmusikus und Mitglied dieser Gesellschaft.

5) Zum Beschluß eine neue Harmonie aus 21 blasenden Instrumenten bestehend, von Erfindung des Hrn. Druschetzki, die in Presburg bey der Krönung Sr. Maj. des Kaisers aufgeführet wurde, und von beyden Kapellen J. J. Durchlauchten der Herren Fürsten Esterhazi und Graschalkowich ausgeführet wird.

Die Musik, Instrumenten und Singstimmen gerechnet, wird von mehr denn 180 Personen ausgeführet.

Die Eintrittspreise sind folgende:

	fl.	kr.		fl.	kr.
Erster Parterre	1	25	Gesperrter Sitz im dritten Stock	—	50
Gesperrter Sitz	1	42	Vierter Stock	—	20
Zweyter Parterre	—	24	Eine Loge	4	30
Dritter Stock	—	40			

Die Herren Offiziers von der Garnison werden ersucht, jeder für das Eintrittsbillet 30 kr. zu bezahlen.

Jene von der hohen Noblesse, welche vielleicht ihre bey den sonst gewöhnlichen Schauspielen abbonirten Logen nicht beybehalten wollen, werden ersuchet, es dem Logenmeister beyzeiten melden zu lassen.

Die Bücher vom Auszug sind beym Logenmeister das Stück für 10 kr. zu haben.

Der Anfang ist um 7. Uhr.

Oggi Sabbato il 16, e Domenica il 17. Aprile 1791.
nel Teatro Nazionale
si darà
DALLA SOCIETÀ DI MUSICA
A BENEFIZIO DELLE LORO VEDOVE ED ORFANI
UNA GRANDE
ACADEMIA DI MUSICA,
nella quale si eseguirà

1) Una grande Sinfonia della composizione del Sig. *Mozart*.

2) Un'Estratto dell'Opera: FEDRA, dove canteranno nella Parte
dell' *Aricia* .... la Sigra. *Lang*.
dell' *Ippolito* .... il Sigre. *Calvesi*.
dell *Teseo* .... il Sigre. *Nencini*.
CORO.
La Musica è del Sig. Giov. Paisiello *fuori dell'Aria, che canta la Sigra.* Lang, *ch'è del Sig.* Mozart.

3) Un Concerto sul Violoncello, composto dal Sigre. *Pleyel*, ed eseguito dal Sigre. Cajet. *Gottlieb*, un Virtuoso nuovamente arrivato di Fiorenza.

4) Il tanto gradito gran Coro: ALLELUJA del Sigre. *Albrechtsberger*, Musico di questa Cesarea Corte, e membro di questa Società.

5) Pel Finale sarà prodotta dai Virtuosi in attual servizio di l. l. A.e i *Signori Principi d'Esterhazi e Grassalkowich* UNA NUOVA ARMONIA, consistente in 21 instrumenti da fiato della composizione del Sigre. *Druschetzki*, che fù eseguita in Presburgo in occasione dell incoronazione di S. M. I. e R.

La Musica fra Cantanti e Suonatori sarà eseguita da più di cento ottanta Persone.

I prezzi per l' ingresso sono i seguenti:

	fior.	kr.		fior.	kr.
Al Parterre nobile	1	25	Sedia chiusa al terzo piano	—	50
Sedia chiusa	1	42	Al quarto Piano	—	20
Al secondo Parterre	—	24	Una Loggia	4	30
Al terzo piano	—	40			

Li Signori Offiziali della Guarnigione si compiaceranno di pagare per l'intrata ciascheduno 30 kr.

Quelli però della Nobiltà, che non sono intenzionati di tener loro Balchi abbonati, sono ricercati, di avvisarne a tempo il Maestro delle Loggie.

I libretti dell'Estratto si trovano dal Maestro delle Loggie a 10 car. l'uno.

Si comincerà alle ore 7.

36. Bilingual handbill for a Tonkünstler-Sozietät concert at the Burgtheater on 16 and 17 April 1791

> We never get to bed before one o'clock and I never get up before nine. We lunch at two or half past. The weather is horrible. Every day there are concerts; and the whole time is given up to teaching, music, composing and so forth. Where am I to go? If only the concerts were over! It is impossible to describe the trouble and commotion. Since my arrival your brother's fortepiano has been taken at least a dozen times to the theatre or to some other house.

In another letter from Vienna (16 February 1785) Leopold described one of Wolfgang's subscription concerts in the Mehlgrube, a hall often used for musical events. The concert contained the typical mixture of symphonies, arias and concertos; typical too is the way in which the musician had to involve himself in every aspect of the concert, from renting the hall to overseeing the music copying:

> Each person pays a souverain d'or or three ducats for the six Lenten concerts. Your brother is giving them at the Mehlgrube and pays only half a souverain d'or each time for the hall. The concert was magnificent and the orchestra played splendidly. In addition to the symphonies a female singer of the Italian theatre sang two arias. Then we had a new and very fine concerto by Wolfgang [K466, in D minor], which the copyist was still copying when we arrived, and the rondo of which your brother did not even have time to play through, as he had to supervise the copying.

Leopold Mozart referred only casually to the symphonies in his son's concert. As a piano virtuoso Mozart specialized in the composition and performance of piano concertos, and these were the *pièces de résistance* of his concerts. The symphonies served a different purpose. Closely related to the opera overture in form and style, the symphony was composed with the aim of attracting the attention of an audience, of stimulating excitement and expectation at the beginning of a theatrical event and of providing a rousing, applause-generating finale to the same. Composers usually wrote their symphonies quickly and in a style that required little or no rehearsal. A difficult, complicated symphony was cause for comment, as when the Viennese composer Johann Baptist Vanhal published three in 1781. A north German critic likened them to Haydn's latest symphonies, and warned: 'they are more difficult than easy, and it would not be advisable to perform them without having played them through first with all the instruments at least once'.[18] Haydn himself wrote in a similar vein of his own Symphonies nos.95 and 96, when, in 1791, he sent copies from London to Vienna: 'Please tell Herr von Keess that I ask him respectfully to have a rehearsal of both these symphonies, because they are very delicate, especially the last movement of that in D major, for which I recommend the softest *piano* and a very quick *tempo*'.[19]

During the years Mozart was busiest as a composer for and a performer in Viennese concerts (1782–5), he wrote no symphonies for those concerts. His casual attitude towards the genre is clear from his letters. When his father sent him the score of the Haffner Symphony (K385) so that he could have it performed during one of his Vienna concerts, Mozart expressed pleasant surprise, claiming (certainly with much exaggeration) that he could not remember a note of this symphony that he had written less than a year before (letter of 15 February 1783). A year later he sent his father scores of the Linz Symphony (K425), written within the space of a few days for a concert in Linz, and of the Piano Concerto in E flat (K449); in the accompanying letter (20 February 1784) he made clear how differently he felt about the works:

> The symphony is in the original score, which you might arrange to have copied some time. You can then send it back to me or even give it away or have it performed anywhere you like. The concerto is also in the original score and this too you may have copied; but have it done as quickly as possible and return it to me. Remember, do not show it to a *single soul*, for I composed it for Fräulein Ployer, who paid me handsomely.

In line with their festive, public purpose, Viennese symphonies of the 1780s were rarely in the minor mode. They achieved their aims with simple, grand gestures, brilliant passage-work and pleasing melodies. During the 1780s Viennese composers wrote hundreds of such works, many of them effectively fulfilling the purpose for which they were written. The 35 or so symphonies of Adalbert Gyrowetz, many of them written during the 1780s, certainly do. The Bohemian Gyrowetz visited Vienna for the first time in 1785 or 1786; he later returned to make Vienna his permanent home, and during the first two decades of the nineteenth century enjoyed great success as a composer of operas and ballet music. During his first visit in the mid-1780s the young Gyrowetz was delighted when Mozart decided to have one of his symphonies performed at a subscription concert, possibly one of the Mehlgrube concerts which Leopold Mozart described in the letter quoted above.

Which of the symphonies (around 30) that Gyrowetz wrote during the 1780s Mozart chose to perform is unknown. The Symphony in C that was later published by Imbault in Paris as *3e Sinfonie périodique* and by André in Offenbach (near Frankfurt) as *Grande sinfonie* op.3 no.1 would have been a suitable work.[20] It is in the normal four movements, with two fast ones framing a slow movement and a minuet. The opening movement is an energetic Allegro con spirito, brilliant in texture and straightforward in construction. The vigorous opening theme, with conventional, busy accompanimental figures in the lower parts, gives way in the second theme area to a pretty, sentimental tune, which is suddenly interrupted by an abrupt entrance of the full orchestra in the minor mode, *fortissimo* – a surprise that Gyrowetz delighted in and used often. The development treats a version of the opening theme in five-part counterpoint, giving an impression of hectic activity rather than complex artifice. The flurry of counterpoint is over quickly, and with the expected recapitulation Gyrowetz brings his movement to an animated and satisfying conclusion. This kind of music would have made a fine opening for one of Mozart's subscription concerts. Simple and easy to appreciate, it would have left Mozart's audience ready to tackle the more complex and sophisticated fare later in the programme.

Mozart was a prolific composer of symphonies before he came to Vienna, but he wrote relatively few keyboard concertos; in Vienna the reverse is true. The concert seasons in Vienna were short and the court theatres were in great demand by performers, who rarely received permission to use them more than twice during the season. Performers saved their best for such occasions. Mozart did, quite consciously: 'Vienna is certainly the land of the clavier!', he wrote excitedly to his father on 2 June 1781, and during the years in which he devoted himself to the Viennese concert stage he put special effort into the music he played at the keyboard. Of his Quintet for piano and wind K452, which he performed during one of his Burgtheater concerts in 1784, Mozart wrote to his father: 'I myself consider it to be the best work I have ever composed' (10 April 1784). The same care, the same richness of invention that Mozart lavished on that quintet went into the seventeen piano concertos he wrote during his Viennese decade.

Mozart's Viennese piano concertos are patently theatrical. As such they admirably satisfied a specific need. Since opera was not given in Vienna during Lent, opera-loving Viennese looked to concerts as a substitute for the forbidden pleasures of the operatic stage. They wanted and expected the music performed in such concerts to be theatrical in effect. One of Mozart's greatest achievements in the piano concertos was his introduction of operatic drama into the genre. These works do not tell a story, of course; yet they vividly convey all the passion and violence, all the gaiety and laughter of the Viennese stage.

One aspect of the concertos crucial to their dramatic effect is their wide variety of keys. Choosing a key was one of the first and most important decisions that a late eighteenth-century composer had to make before beginning a large-scale composition – particularly one that involved an orchestra. This decision had implications for the music's texture, instrumentation, dynamics and melodic style, and, consequently, for its expressive and dramatic character.[21] Mozart wrote concertos in many different keys, as if eager to explore the full potential of the piano concerto as a dramatic genre and to insure that his audiences would not tire of the genre on which the success of his concerts largely depended.

G major, a key in which the lowest string of the violin (the G string) could be used as a tonic drone and in which eighteenth-century flutes and oboes could be played with greater ease than in many other keys, was often used by Mozart in his operas as a pastoral or rustic key; he associated it with joyful peasants in *Le nozze di Figaro* and *Don Giovanni*, with Papageno and Papagena in *Die Zauberflöte*. In his G major Piano Concerto (K453) the rustic connotations of the key led Mozart to accompany his cheerful opening melody with a bagpipe-like drone and to echo the melody with bird-like twittering in the woodwind. One wonders what, besides the dotted rhythm in the first bar, could have led one critic to include this movement among Mozart's 'military allegros'![22] The G major concerto is Mozart's 'pastoral' concerto.

Composers often associated E flat, on the other hand, with things serious and sombre, perhaps partly because the same open G string that sometimes gave music in G major a rustic sound encouraged composers to write rich, sonorous E flat major chords, with the violin's lowest note providing a low and resonant third degree. Mozart chose to write *Die Zauberflöte* in E flat; the Piano Concerto in E flat K482, with its sumptuous writing for clarinet, evokes the calm nobility of Sarastro's realm.

Mozart's C major concertos K467 and 503 both project the confidence, the grandeur, that he associated with the key. These are brilliant works, evocative of royal celebration and triumph; they belong to the expressive world of *La clemenza di Tito*, Mozart's opera (also in C) for the coronation of Leopold II as King of Bohemia (1791); Mozart's use of trumpets and drums (instruments traditionally associated with music in C and D, and missing from many of the concertos in other keys) adds to the majestic, festive effect of the C major concertos.

If the C major concertos evoke the imperial pomp of a coronation opera, the Concerto in D minor (K466) evokes the tragic stage at its most dramatic. Mozart could hardly have made a more adventurous choice for a piano concerto than D minor, a key strongly associated in operas and ballets of the period with vengeance and violence, especially supernatural violence, the underworld and the furies.[23] Gluck's Don Juan is dragged down to hell to the sound of D minor; so is Mozart's. And when the Queen of Night invokes 'der Hölle Rache' she does so in D minor. Mozart's introduction of such associations into the genre of the piano concerto was a daring and brilliant stroke.

As one might expect, violence and anger pervade the D minor concerto, written by Mozart for his Lenten concerts of 1785 and admired by Leopold Mozart when his son performed it in the Mehlgrube. The quiet opening is awe-inspiring: menacing syncopations in the violins, low in their register, sinister rumblings in the bass. But the full fury of the music is held back until the full orchestra enters, *forte*, with trumpets and drums, the violins playing fiery arpeggiation. When the soloist enters, it is as if he were Orpheus confronting an orchestra of furies, playing a new, pleading melody, or rather a melancholy fragment of melody. We must imagine the intensity of the drama at this moment as Mozart, performing the concerto for the first time, seemingly improvised this passage, reaching an expressive climax as he stretched to play his piano's highest note, F above high C.

An anonymous letter in doggerel verse, written from Vienna during Advent 1777, provides a pleasing glimpse of life in the Habsburg capital at that time of year; here is part of the poem, loosely translated:

> It's Advent time, and though it snows all day,
> One cannot see a single horse-drawn sleigh.
> Because the theatres are all shut down,
> One cannot even find a comic clown
> To rock the crowd with laughter's jolly note.
> An oratorio, *Des Heilands Tod*
> Of Metastasio, is sung; what's more,
> Salieri has contributed the score.
> Whoever hears this score and does not melt,
> His heart most certainly has never felt.
> Imagine this: together with the heavenly song,
> An orchestra one hundred-sixty strong.[24]

The oratorio to which the poet alludes is Salieri's *La passione di Gesù Cristo*, with a libretto by Metastasio; the performance was one of a series organized by the Tonkünstler-Sozietät, a society for the support of musicians' widows and orphans. Near the end of every Lenten and Advent concert season the Tonkünstler-Sozietät presented a large concert, usually consisting of the performance of an Italian oratorio. The finest Viennese musicians provided music for the society: not only Salieri, but Gassmann, Hasse, Haydn, Mozart and Dittersdorf, among others. Haydn wrote his big oratorio *Il ritorno di Tobia* for performance during Lent 1775; Mozart worked his unfinished C minor Mass into the oratorio or cantata *Davidde penitente* a decade later. Virtuosos both vocal and instrumental contributed their efforts to the worthy cause. The concerts typically included at least one concerto in addition to the oratorio. During one performance of *Tobia* the leader (Konzertmeister) of the Esterházy orchestra, Alois Luigi Tomasini, played a violin concerto between the acts; during another performance Xavier Marteau, a cellist in the Esterházy orchestra, played a cello concerto.

To perform their oratorios the Tonkünstler-Sozietät customarily amassed the large performing forces to which the poet alludes.

Dittersdorf mentioned in his memoirs that the first of the Tonkünstler oratorios, Gassmann's setting of Metastasio's *Betulia liberata* (1772), was performed by an orchestra of 200. Mozart arrived in Vienna during Lent 1781, and in a letter to his father (24 March 1781) he wrote that the Tonkünstler orchestra for that Lent would number 180 players. These figures probably include chorus, soloists and orchestra, but these are still extraordinarily large ensembles for Vienna and it seems that the Tonkünstler-Sozietät was able to assemble them year after year. For the concerts during Lent 1791, when the customary oratorio was replaced with excerpts from an *opera seria* by Paisiello, the programme announced that performers, vocal and instrumental, would number more than 180.[25]

Most Italian oratorios of the eighteenth century differed little from serious operas – a series of arias interspersed with recitatives, occasional ensembles and even fewer choruses. But Viennese audiences and musicians, introduced to the grandeur of Handel's choral works in the early 1770s with performances of *Alexander's Feast* (an abbreviated version with Italian text), favoured a mixing of the Italian and Handelian types of oratorio. Viennese oratorios in Italian have more choruses than most Italian oratorios, and these choruses sometimes adopt the polyphonic style associated with Handel's choruses. It is an interesting indication of Viennese taste that a review of Haydn's *Tobia* should report that his choruses 'glowed with a fire that was otherwise only in Händel'.[26]

Dittersdorf's *La liberatrice del popolo giudaico nella Persia, ossia L'Ester*, composed for the Tonkünstler-Sozietät in 1773 and revived by the society during Advent 1785, is a fine example of the Viennese oratorio. In his memoirs Dittersdorf mentioned the figure of 200 musicians in connection with the first performance of the oratorio, the same number that he said executed Gassmann's *La Betulia liberata*. For one of the performances of *Ester* in 1785 Mozart provided the traditional entr'acte music: he performed one of his recently composed piano concertos.

Ester is typical of the Viennese oratorio in its wide variety of musical styles. The Italian heritage of the genre is clearly evident in the many operatic arias, including a rondò very much like those sung by primi uomini and prima donnas in the *opere serie* of the 1780s. (The rondò, 'Ah, se in vita, o mio tesoro', is not in all manuscript copies of the oratorio and was perhaps added by Dittersdorf for the 1785 performance, to bring his oratorio up to date.)[27] In some numbers the chorus alternates with a soloist, in the manner of a Gluckian operatic tableau like the one that opens *Orfeo*. A short, homophonic chorus in the style of a Lutheran chorale, 'Fra le sventure estreme', brings the first part to a close. And in several polyphonic choruses Dittersdorf, to the best of his ability, takes up the Handelian style. Perhaps most effective of these – though to our ears it is no longer Handelian in sound – is the fugal section of the chorus 'Per noi quel core s'agita', which boldly takes as its subject a minor scale descending in long notes through an entire octave. A completely different kind of piece, but equally beautiful, is the love duet for Esther and Ahasuerus, 'Ester, cara mia vita', in which the tenor Ahasuerus presents a tender opening melody, with graceful three-bar phrases. Esther responds to Ahasuerus's questions as to the cause of her distress; later they sing together, their voices intertwined in sequential suspensions. Listening to such passages one can believe Dittersdorf when he said in his memoirs that Joseph II was particularly fond of *Ester*, preferring it to the oratorios by Gassmann and Hasse that had been performed earlier by the Tonkünstler-Sozietät.

MUSIC IN THE HOME

Michael Kelly, the Irish tenor who sang in the Burgtheater from 1783 to 1787, and whose *Reminiscences* are an important source of information about Viennese musical life during the 1780s, was impressed by the musicality of the Viennese: 'All ranks of society were doatingly fond of music, and most of them perfectly understood the science' – doubtless an exaggeration, but it is true that music was an important part of daily life for many. In the taverns one could drink to the sounds of Haydn minuets; in the Redoutensaal during Carnival an orchestra played dance music by Starzer or Mozart or Haydn from nine in the evening until five in the morning. And in the private apartments and palaces of Vienna a great many of its residents spent their leisure hours engaged in a wide variety of music-making.

Vienna's small but growing upper middle class demanded music that could be played in the home. Many could not afford to engage professional musicians to play for them, but they could buy music and many were well-trained musicians themselves. Haydn's friend and patron Marianne von Genzinger is a case in point. Her husband was a doctor who had accumulated enough wealth and social connections by 1780 to be ennobled by Maria Theresa. Marianne, a fine musician, organized musical soirées in her home for her friends. They played pleasant, light music on such occasions – piano sonatas, both solo and accompanied by violin or by violin and cello, songs and piano reductions of larger works like symphonies and opera arias; they sipped coffee, tea and chocolate, and no doubt they engaged in casual conversation. In its increasingly elaborate musical endeavours, the Viennese bourgeoisie played a role of growing importance in Vienna's musical life, although it was not until the nineteenth century that it surpassed the court and the nobility as patrons of music and shapers of musical taste.[28]

Closely connected with the spread of music-making in the home was the development of a Viennese music-publishing industry.[29] Before the 1780s little music was published in Vienna; little, that is, compared to the quantities produced by the flourishing music businesses of Paris and London. Most music circulated in manuscript, when it circulated at all. We have seen earlier in this chapter that Haydn's contract of 1761 stipulated that he should retain all his new compositions 'for the exclusive use of his Highness'. How could Haydn be of any use to publishers if he honoured such a contract? He found ways to get round it, but the fact that the contract existed at all is symptomatic of a society that did not favour the mass dissemination of the best music.

As the number of amateur musicians increased, publishers were quick to see the profitable possibilities of music publishing. The Italians Carlo and Francesco Artaria were among the first to do so; they were joined by the Bohemian composer and pianist Leopold Kozeluch and the composer Franz Anton Hoffmeister. These and other Viennese publishers specialized in the music that appealed to amateur musicians – the kind of music that Marianne von Genzinger could perform at her soirées. Compared to those in Paris and London, Viennese publishers were provincial in their tastes, limiting much of

37. Chamber music: engraving from J. Richter's 'Bildgalerie weltlichen Missbrauche' (1785)

their output to music by Viennese composers; the music from elsewhere that they published had often been performed in Vienna. It is unlikely that any Viennese composer of the late eighteenth century could make a living from having his music published in Vienna, but the growth of Viennese music publishing offered composers an important way to supplement their income and it made the music of the best composers available to more musicians than ever before.

Disappointed by the performance of one of Mozart's piano quartets by unskilled amateur musicians at a private concert, a critic writing in the *Journal des Luxus und der Moden* (Weimar, 1788) concluded that both the performers and the setting of the performance were unsuitable. He recommended that such works be performed 'by four talented musicians, who have probably studied it, in a quiet room where not even the suspension of each note escapes the ear, in the presence of three or four attentive people'.[30] The circumstances that the critic envisaged for the proper performance of a piano quartet would have suited a string quartet just as well. He could not have imagined a more perfect setting for quartet playing than that recalled by Kelly in his *Reminiscences*. Kelly described a party that took place in Vienna some time during 1784, in which some of the finest musicians in Vienna entertained themselves and a few friends with string quartets:

> The players were tolerable; not one of them excelled on the instrument he played, but there was a little science among them, which I dare say will be acknowledged when I name them:
> The First Violin . . . HAYDN.
> " Second Violin . . . BARON DITTERSDORF.
> " Violoncello . . . VANHALL.
> " Tenor [Viola] . . . MOZART.
>
> The poet Casti and Paesiello formed part of the audience. I was there, and a greater treat, or a more remarkable one, cannot be imagined.
>
> On the particular evening to which I am now specially referring, after the musical feast was over, we sat down to an excellent supper, and became joyous and lively in the extreme.[31]

The Viennese string quartet of the 1780s was a genre for connoisseurs. If composers usually wrote symphonies with the assumption that they could be rehearsed little or not at all and performed before a large and not particularly attentive or knowledgeable audience, by musicians who played not because they wanted to on that particular occasion but because they needed to earn a living, they wrote quartets with the assumption that they would be played by skilful musicians who played for their own amusement and who might have practised their parts carefully. Descriptions of quartet playing rarely mention an audience of more than a few, and these were often themselves fine musicians who listened attentively and appreciatively, as Kelly did.

The six quartets of Mozart that Artaria published as op.10 in 1785 are perfect examples of the intricacy and sophistication attained by the Viennese quartet in the 1780s. It is no accident that Mozart dedicated these works to Haydn, whose op.33 quartets of 1781 supplied Mozart with an important source of ideas for his own set. In his dedication, Mozart wrote of the labour these works had cost him; Haydn could, and did, appreciate the craft, the attention to detail and the originality that distinguish Mozart's quartets. Haydn expressed his opinion to Leopold Mozart during the performance of three of the 'Haydn' quartets in Mozart's apartment in Vienna during Lent 1785. Here was another typically intimate setting. As few as five people were in the room at the time; Leopold, in a letter to his daughter, mentioned only Haydn and 'die 2 Baron Tindi' (Anton and Bartholomäus von Tinti), to whom we can add the Mozarts, father and son. Four played, leaving an audience of possibly no more than one; perhaps the musicians took turns listening while the others played. It may have been after listening carefully to one of the quartets, or after playing one of the beautifully fashioned inner parts, that Haydn said to Leopold Mozart: 'Before God and as an honest man I tell you that your son is the greatest composer known to me either in person or by name. He has taste, and, what is more, the most profound knowledge of composition' (quoted in Leopold's letter of 16 February 1785).

Mozart assembled his set with the same care and ingenuity that characterize the music itself. The 'Haydn' quartets were originally published in the following order: no.1, G major; no.2, D minor; no.3, B flat major; no.4, E flat major; no.5, A major; no.6, C major. Mozart chose six different keys for his quartets, balancing flat keys with sharp keys; there are two major-mode quartets with sharp keys, two with flat keys, together with one quartet in C major and one minor-mode quartet. Tonal relationships between the works bind the set together in an intricate symmetrical filigree (see table V.1).

There is plenty that Haydn could have admired in the quartet published first in the set (K387), though this was not one of those performed on the night he made his famous statement. The opening movement, Allegro vivace assai, begins with a melody in the first violin, accompanied by the lower strings. The lower parts are at first subordinate, and yet they are full of melodic interest; there are none of the stock accompanimental figures so prominent in Gyrowetz's symphony referred to above, and in many other symphonies of the period. A short motif is passed from part to part, then the melody is presented again, this time shared by all the parts in imitation. Counterpoint is characteristic of Viennese quartet writing, but Mozart is careful to keep his contrapuntal passages from sounding academic or ecclesiastical; his counterpoint sounds casual, natural and unobtrusive. When the opening melody returns later in the movement, at the beginning of

Table V.1 THE TONAL RELATIONSHIPS BETWEEN MOZART'S SIX 'HAYDN' QUARTETS

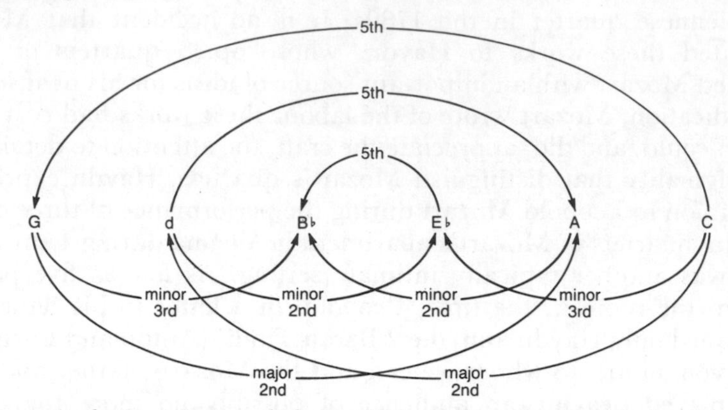

the recapitulation, it is subtly varied, and so is the fabric of accompanying parts. The performers must have appreciated the witty touch of an extra bar, *pianissimo*, a false echo of the bar it follows, that extends the phrase unexpectedly. The movement ends in an understated way: no loud fanfares, no busy passage-work, nothing to excite applause. This is light, cheerful music that does not call attention to its sophistication, and indeed sometimes seems purposely to mask it. But the connoisseurs for whom it was written must have appreciated its richness, variety and subtlety when they performed it.

OPERA BUFFA IN THE JOSEPHINIAN DECADE: 'BUFFA E SERIA UNITE A MERAVIGLIOSA INSIEME'

Joseph II assembled in Vienna in 1783 a troupe of comic-opera singers second to none in Europe; he seems for once to have spared no expense. Already in Vienna were two first-rate composers, Salieri and Mozart, both experienced in the composition of Italian opera, serious and comic. Joseph preferred Salieri, a composer he had known personally for seventeen years, but he had the musical sophistication to appreciate the newcomer as well and the generosity to support him with commissions, and, from 1788, with a salary from the court. Two talented librettists, Giambattista Casti and Lorenzo Da Ponte, inspired Joseph's composers. True to his character, the emperor maintained control over the whole complex enterprise. Joseph's letters to his High Chamberlain and opera director Count Rosenberg show clearly that Joseph, not Rosenberg, was in charge of the opera, with the emperor making decisions about every aspect of the production of comic operas. In his *Reminiscences* Kelly remembered his employer fondly:

> As the theatre was in the palace, the Emperor often honoured the rehearsals with his presence, and discoursed familiarly with the

> performers. He spoke Italian like a Tuscan, and was affable and condescending. He came almost every night to the opera [. . .]. He was passionately fond of music, and a most excellent and accurate judge of it.[32]

Without Joseph's direction Viennese opera in the 1780s would certainly have developed differently from the way it did; we have Joseph as well as Da Ponte and Mozart to thank for *Le nozze di Figaro* and *Così fan tutte*.

That Joseph's Italian troupe specialized in comic rather than serious opera is itself a product of the emperor's interests. The finest Italian composers of the 1780s – Paisiello, Cimarosa and Sarti among them – put as much energy and creativity into their *opere serie* as into their *opere buffe*; in most cities where Italian opera was cultivated, both in Italy and northern Europe, serious as well as comic works were performed. But Joseph preferred comic opera. As part of the preparations for the visit to Vienna of the Grand Duke and Duchess of Russia in 1781 Prince Kaunitz, Joseph's state chancellor, urged the emperor to arrange for the performance of 'a magnificent *opera seria*'; this would be an effective means of impressing the Russian visitors with 'the power of this monarchy', according to Kaunitz. But Joseph rejected the idea of *opera seria*, and in doing so made his opinion of the genre perfectly clear: 'In regard to *opera seria* from Italy it is too late to arrange something good; and anyway, it is such a boring spectacle that I do not think I will ever use it'.[33] If Italian opera was to be performed on a regular basis in the Burgtheater, it would have to be comic.

This did not keep Viennese librettists and composers from introducing serious elements into their comic operas. 'Ho fatto ciò che non parea possibile', boasts the poet in Salieri's *Prima la musica e poi le parole* (Vienna, 1786; libretto by Casti), 'ho buffa e seria unite a meravigliosa insieme' ('I have done what seemed to be impossible: I have brought the comic soprano and the serious one miraculously together'). This can be taken as a kind of motto for Viennese comic opera during the Josephinian decade. *Opera buffa* had long included elements borrowed from *opera seria*, but Viennese opera made a speciality of combining comedy and pathos. At its best Viennese *opera buffa* was tragi-comedy. Here again the emperor's tastes may have played a role. Joseph liked serious opera when it was mixed with comedy, as it was in his favourite work, Salieri's *Axur, rè d'Ormus* (1788). This *dramma tragicomico*, written for Joseph's *opera buffa* troupe on a libretto by Da Ponte, was weighted so heavily to the serious side that one Austrian admirer called it 'the greatest Italian serious opera, even better than Mozart's *La clemenza di Tito*'. A German critic praised Salieri as one who could 'bind all the power of German music to the sweet Italian

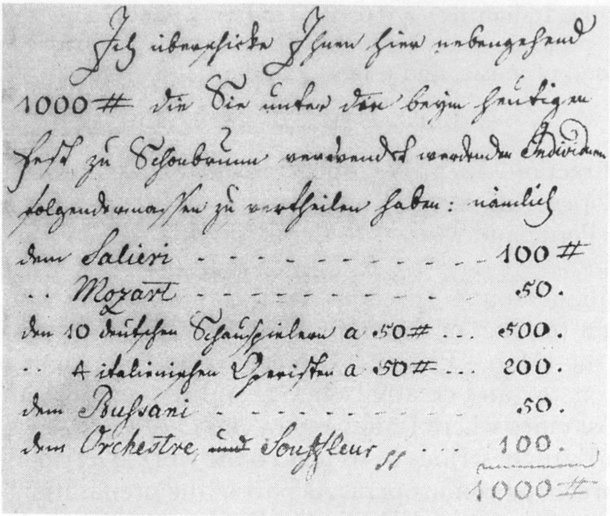
Ich überschicke Ihnen hier nebengehend
1000 # die Sie unter den beym heutigen
Fest zu Schönbrunn verwendet werdenden Individuen
folgendermassen zu vertheilen haben: nämlich
dem Salieri . . . . 100 #
.. Mozart . . . . 50.
den 10 deutschen Schauspielern a 50# ... 500.
.. 4 italienischen Sängern a 50# ... 200.
dem Bussani . . . . 50.
dem Orchestre und Souffleur ... 100.
1000 #

38. Joseph II's memorandum to Rosenberg about how to distribute payment for the premières of Salieri's 'Prima la musica' and Mozart's 'Der Schauspieldirektor', 7 February 1786

style', and doubtless this ability helped him to combine serious and comic.[34]

Mozart too used Italian comic opera as a vehicle for the expression of passion and jealousy, of anger and grief. In the last opera written for Joseph's *opera buffa* troupe, Mozart's *Così fan tutte* (1790), comic and serious are held in delicate balance; the audience is rarely allowed to laugh out loud, except in a few sustained *buffo* sections like the first-act finale, but neither is it encouraged to weep. The symmetrical layout of the plot recalls Metastasio's *drammi per musica*, as does Da Ponte's use of six characters, common in Metastasio and his followers, neatly arranged in pairs. In the trio 'È la fede delle femmine', Da Ponte has Don Alfonso sing a parody of an aria by Metastasio, 'È la fede degli amanti' (from *Demetrio*, Act 2); and the decorous vocabulary and diction of *opera seria* is maintained through most of the opera, with the major exception of Despina's part. And yet Da Ponte chose for his characters names that clearly suggest *opera buffa*: Dorabella, Fiordiligi and Despina must have sounded to Viennese audiences like a scrambling of Doralba and Fiordispina, two characters in Cimarosa's *L'impresario in angustie*, an *opera buffa* that had recently been performed in Vienna.

Mozart's music reflects the text's mixture of comic and serious. The very first sound of the opera, a C major chord with the first violins playing double-stopped E and high C, has the majestic, serious quality that Mozart often associated with the key of C major. Although the slow introduction is labelled 'Andante' in his autograph, Mozart, fully aware of its expressive implications, entered it as 'Andante maestoso' in his own catalogue. Mozart later used a

C major chord almost identical in orchestration and voicing to open *La clemenza di Tito*. Yet this majestic opening to *Così fan tutte* is prelude to the scurrying Presto that just as vividly evokes light-hearted playfulness.

A similar balancing of effect is to be found throughout the opera. The terzetto 'Una bella serenata', again in C major, begins with a grand Allegro in serious style; Mozart used a similar idea and the same key to begin the ensemble with chorus that brings *La clemenza di Tito* to a triumphant close. But here Alfonso soon undercuts the serious tone with his mocking question 'Sarò anch'io de' convitati?', accompanied by unison strings in a laughing figure. It is again Alfonso who introduces a *buffo* element in the tender, sad quintet, 'Di scrivermi ogni giorno'. As the lovers bid one another a heart-breaking farewell, Alfonso is highly amused; he murmurs to the audience, with a disjunct melodic line clearly *buffo* in character, that he will burst if he does not laugh: 'Io crepo se non rido'.

Mozart was aided in his compositional task by the special background and skills of his prima donna, Adriana Ferraresi del Bene, who sang the role of Fiordiligi. Before coming to Vienna in 1788, Ferraresi had sung *opera seria* in Italy; among her roles were many of the greatest tragic heroines – Alcestis (in Gluck's *Alceste*), Dido, Iphegeneia and Semiramis. But Ferraresi, unlike most *opera seria* singers, was also interested in comic opera. In London in 1785–6 she sang both serious and comic operas, winning praise for her performances; the following quotation from the *Morning Herald* of 30 January 1786 refers to her singing of the aria 'Per salvarti o mio tesoro' in Paisiello's *opera buffa Il marchese Tulipano*:

> From the nature of its composition it gave this lady an opportunity, which she properly improved, of shewing that her talents are equally conspicuous in the serious and comic, and that she can with unabated abilities, accompany the lyre of Melpomene [the muse of tragedy], and the reeds of Thalia [the muse of comedy].[35]

One of the dramatic highpoints of *Così fan tutte*, the great duet 'Fra gli amplessi in pochi istanti', took full advantage of Ferraresi's talents. Fiordiligi's dilemma, her conflict between love for her 'Albanian' suitor and her fidelity to Guglielmo, must be resolved before the opera ends; so must the imbalance, the asymmetry of having only one of the two women give in to the charms of the 'Albanians'. The duet is preceded by a recitative in which Fiordiligi resolves to dress up as a soldier and seek Guglielmo on the field of battle; although she has come close to admitting to herself that she loves Ferrando (in the recitative preceding her rondò 'Per pietà ben mio perdona'), her sense of duty and propriety has not left her. The duet begins like an aria for Fiordiligi. Her words are completely serious in character: 'Fra gli amplessi in pochi istanti/Giungerò del fido sposo' ('In a few moments I will reach the embraces of my faithful husband'). The words 'amplessi' and 'sposo' in Da Ponte's text might have reminded Mozart of an important aria in one of the most popular *opere serie* of the late eighteenth century, and one of the few that had been performed in Vienna (in 1785), Giuseppe Sarti's *Giulio Sabino* (fig.39).[36] In 'Cari figli, un altro amplesso', the hero Sabino, about to be taken off to prison, bids farewell to his wife and children: 'Cari figli, un altro amplesso,/Dammi, o sposa, un altro addio' ('Dear children, another embrace; my wife, give me another farewell'). Fiordiligi's tender melody, like her words, recalls Sabino's in rhythm and outline.

We have seen how Alfonso undercuts the serious mood in two of Mozart's ensembles; here it is Ferrando who interrupts, his sudden entrance accompanied by a sudden switch from E major to E minor. A change in the dramatic situation is reflected in a tonal shift and a new melody: this is a typical *opera buffa* technique, especially common in finales as far back as Piccinni's *La buona figliuola* of 1760. Indeed the first-act finale of Piccinni's celebrated *opera buffa* treats an analogous event with exactly the same musical procedure.[37] Poor Cecchina, the heroine, sings a melody in F major. The Marchese, thinking that she is abandoning him, enters, singing in F minor. The effect of the modal switch is all the more powerful in *Così fan tutte*, because Mozart has set up the expectation of a conventional *opera seria* aria, in which such sudden shifts rarely occur. The tonality begins to shift towards the

39. Luigi Marchesi and Catarina Cavalieri in a scene from Giuseppe Sarti's opera seria 'Giulio Sabino' (Vienna, 1785): engraving

ultimate return of the tonic A that will coincide with Fiordiligi's capitulation; and it is Fiordiligi, not her suitor, who sets up most of the shifts in tonality, seemingly prompting Ferrando to continue and to intensify his siege. Fiordiligi moves from E minor to C major and Ferrando follows her lead. The melody he sings is full of irony for the audience. He sang it earlier in the opera, in the same key, to the words 'Una bella serenata far io voglio alla mia dea'; now he serenades another goddess, very likely with more passion than he had ever mustered for Dorabella. Fiordiligi steers the tonality towards the dominant of A, encouraging Ferrando with questions to which she already knows the answer: 'Per pietà da me che chíedi?'. She realizes now, repeating Zerlina's 'Non son più forte' in *Don Giovanni*, that she has succumbed. Fiordiligi can only give the dominant of A one final reiteration, asking the gods for advice. But it is of course Ferrando, sensing now that she is ready to be convinced, who answers her plea, in the gorgeous A major Larghetto, 'Volgi a me pietoso il ciglio'.

This is Viennese *opera buffa* at its best, the product of a complex combination of genres, of the collaboration of some of Europe's finest librettists, singers and composers, all under the direction of an experienced musician and patron of music, the emperor himself. It is music like this that makes the Italian comic operas written and performed in Vienna during the 1780s perhaps the finest artistic achievement of the Josephinian decade.

LEOPOLD II AND THE END OF THE JOSEPHINIAN DECADE

The emperor's tastes and policies shaped Viennese musical life to such an extent that when Joseph II died, on 20 February 1790, a few weeks after the successful première of *Così fan tutte*, his subjects must have known that with the new emperor would come changes in the kind of music they could hear and in the musicians who would compose and perform it. In July 1790 an anonymous critic evaluated musical life in Vienna under Joseph; turning to Leopold II, Joseph's brother and successor, the critic continued:

> The present king has not been in the theatre, nor has he had his music in private, nor has he shown any other sign of being a music-lover. *Malum signum*, cry our pseudo-prophets. But I believe that once the enormous burdens of statesmanship that lie on his shoulders are reduced to minor difficulties, once he has bestowed golden peace on his dominions, then too will we have a new golden age of music.[38]

The writer's hopes were to some extent fulfilled. Leopold's short reign (1790–92) was a period of intense musical activity and of dynamic change, a period of transition away from the most characteristic aspects of the Josephinian decade and towards the musical culture of early nineteenth-century Vienna.

We have seen that Viennese musical life in the 1780s was in many respects moulded by Joseph's artistic direction. Characteristic features were the hegemony of a particularly complex and sophisticated kind of *opera buffa*, the virtual absence from Vienna of *opera seria* and ballet, a turning-away from church music by the best composers and the cultivation of a rich and highly developed language of instrumental music – the high-Classical symphony, concerto and quartet. The years following Leopold's reign present a very different picture. The brilliant comic operas of Mozart were absent from the court theatres for most of the 1790s, replaced by Italian works of a simpler kind. Comic opera, instead of dominating the stage, shared it with other genres. Italian serious opera vied with comic opera on equal terms. Ballet enjoyed the prestige it had won during the days of Angiolini and Noverre. Outside the theatre, church music regained its former attraction to composers.

In short, Viennese musical life was transformed, and much of the transformation took place during Leopold's reign. The departure from Vienna in mid-1791 of Lorenzo Da Ponte signalled the end of an era in Viennese comic opera; Mozart's death later that year removed from the scene the author of the greatest musical achievements of the Josephinian decade. The débuts of Leopold's Italian ballet and *opera seria* troupes less than a month before Mozart's death introduced the Viennese to new genres and new musicians. A decree promulgated by Leopold in March 1791 permitting the performance of orchestrally accompanied church music was one manifestation of a revival of church music, of which Mozart's Requiem, commissioned a few months later, was but one product. The year of Leopold's death saw the arrival in Vienna of two musicians who would do more to shape Viennese music during the next decade than any others. Haydn, still to write his late masses and oratorios, returned from his first trip to London, and Beethoven arrived from Bonn.

When Leopold arrived in Vienna in early March 1790, crises on every side threatened the monarchy. Joseph had not managed all aspects of his reign as successfully as he had managed his theatres. By his despotically imposed reforms, by his arrogant and autocratic behaviour, he had succeeded in alienating himself from large numbers of his subjects, even from those, such as the peasants and the urban lower class, who had in general benefited from his reforms. His unpopular Turkish war was going badly for the Austrians. War taxes and forced conscription increased discontent. The nobility of Bohemia and Hungary, alarmed by Joseph's attempts to better the peasants' lot, threatened to rebel; and the Prussians, old enemies, threatened to come to the aid of the Hungarian nobility. Already the Austrian Netherlands were in open revolt. With the outbreak of the French Revolution in 1789 a dynasty closely allied to the Habsburgs by marriage, and the tradition of absolute monarchy in general, faced a dangerous, and ultimately fatal, challenge.[39]

Leopold's response to the crises inherited from his brother was vigorous and effective. An important element was his use of carefully chosen concessions to appease and win over various groups adversely affected by Joseph's reforms. By means of such concessions Leopold was able to preserve some of the most important of Joseph's achievements.

Among the most unpopular of Joseph's reforms were his restrictions of Catholic ceremony. Religious rituals, especially in the countryside, provided many of Joseph's subjects with a rare and treasured diversion from the drudgery of daily life. The peasants, who should have been grateful to Joseph for his efforts to abolish the hated *robot* (the system, associated with serfdom, which forced peasants to work for their landlord in exchange for the privilege of farming the land), instead resented Joseph because he limited the number of candles and the kinds of music that could be used to dramatize religious ceremonies.

Leopold saw the problem clearly. When his younger brother Ferdinand, governor of Milan, wrote to the emperor asking if he had done the right thing to permit a particular religious procession to take place (one evidently forbidden by Joseph's policies), Leopold expressed his approval; his letter reveals his pragmatic, somewhat cynical approach to politics:

> As for the village that wanted the procession for the Feast of God, you have done well to keep them happy in the present, rebellious circumstances; it is necessary to proceed gently, and to take care not to offend people at the wrong time; it is better to concede or dissemble.[40]

Leopold recognized that he would have to make concessions concerning certain unpopular details of Joseph's policies if he was to make progress towards the ultimate goals of the Theresian-Josephinian reforms, to which he subscribed with as much conviction as had his mother and his older brother.

What applied to religious processions applied to church music as well. On 17 March 1791 Leopold issued a decree that in effect did away with many of Joseph's restrictions: 'The High Mass and the litanies can also be performed with instrumental music, as long as the church's resources are able to pay for it'.[41] About four months after Leopold issued his decree a stranger is said to have delivered to Mozart a commission to write a requiem mass, to be accompanied by full orchestra. During a period of almost ten years, since he left unfinished the C minor Mass about the time that Joseph issued his restrictions on church music, Mozart had not completed a single large-scale composition for the church (with the possible exception

40. Te Deum performed in the Vienna Hofkapelle as part of the ceremony in which Leopold's sovereignty over Austria was confirmed: engraving by Löschenkohl.

of the Kyrie in D minor, K341/368*a*, which may date from the late 1780s). Yet when he received the commission for the requiem, he accepted it.

Leopold's decree and the requiem commission are connected in that both were responses to, and manifestations of, a new interest in church music that followed the death of Joseph II. In 1790, elaborate church music closely associated with Leopold had already been composed and performed. A *Te Deum*, possibly by Salieri, was performed as part of the ceremony in April 1790 in which Leopold's sovereignty over Austria was confirmed (fig.40). A *Missa solemnis* by Vincenzo Righini, in D minor like Mozart's Requiem of the following year, was performed later in 1790 as part of celebrations surrounding the election of Leopold as Holy Roman Emperor. As new works were written old ones were revived. A requiem of Georg Reutter was performed in St Stephen's Cathedral in November 1790 to mark the tenth anniversary of Maria Theresa's death; Mozart's 'Coronation' Mass, written in Salzburg in 1779, was probably performed in Baden, near Vienna, in 1790 or 1791. It has been suggested that the Coronation Mass earned its name in connection with its possible performance during the celebrations of Leopold's coronation as King of Bohemia in September 1791.[42]

The revival of Viennese church music during Leopold's reign bore rich fruit. It is unlikely that the aged Haydn would have composed his six late masses between 1796 and 1802 if the genre had not returned to public and governmental favour. From the 1790s we can follow into the nineteenth century a thriving tradition of Viennese church music that was to produce the masses of Beethoven and Hummel, of Schubert and Diabelli.

'Iam redeunt saturnia regna' – 'Now the golden age returns'. These words from Virgil's *Eclogues* were among the principal mottos of Leopold's reign; they are emblazoned below a portrait of the emperor published as the title-page of the *Journal von und für Deutschland*, 1791; they figured too in an illuminated inscription erected in Frankfurt in celebration of Leopold's coronation as Holy Roman Emperor: 'Plaude Germania felix. Imperatorem tenes bonitate Trajanum, clementia Titum, sapientia Aurelium. Jam redeunt Saturnia regna!' (Celebrate, fortunate Germany. You have an emperor who is Trajan in his goodness, Titus in his clemency, [Marcus] Aurelius in his wisdom. Now the golden age returns!'). A commentary on the first year of Leopold's reign, Joseph von Sartori's *Leopoldinische Annalen* (1792), begins with the same idea: 'Germany has embarked on a new golden age'. Nowhere did Leopold project this theme more convincingly than on the stage of the court theatres. His theatrical reorganization of 1791 did away with the last traces of Joseph's theatrical policies; it brought back to Vienna the opulence of an earlier era, the golden age of Maria Theresa.

'Adesso sono io direttore ed impresario' – 'Now I am director and impresario. I want to command, and we will see if things get any better'. Thus, according to Da Ponte's memoirs, Leopold announced his intention of taking charge of the court theatres in July 1791. Leopold kept his word. During the last few months of his reign the emperor completely reorganized the theatres, their personnel and their repertory.

Leopold brought to his job as theatre director many years of experience as a patron of music. He was a competent musician himself, good enough in his youth to lead from the harpsichord the first performance of Gluck's *Il Parnaso confuso*, early in 1765 (see fig.30 above). A few months later he was installed in Florence as Grand Duke of Tuscany, and there he spent the next 25 years, thoroughly absorbing Italian musical culture. Leopold's Italian background played a crucial role in his musical patronage in Vienna; his transformation of Viennese musical theatre was in many ways an Italianization, involving the establishment in Vienna of genres and performers with which he had become familiar in Florence.

Leopold's theatrical programme was inaugurated on his name day, 15 November 1791, about three weeks before Mozart's death. The Burgtheater presented a new 'patriotic play' by F. W. Ziegler, *Fürstengrösse*, with an overture and incidental music by Joseph Weigl, a protégé of Salieri. The few Viennese who may have missed the allegorical reference to the Habsburg sovereign in the title would have understood what was intended once they saw that one of the principal characters in Ziegler's historical drama was Leopold the Praiseworthy, Duke of Austria and Swabia. *Fürstengrösse* was followed on the same evening by the inauguration of Leopold's newly-formed ballet troupe, with a performance of the ballet-master Antonio Muzzarelli's *Il Capitano Cook agli Ottaiti*, a work that Muzzarelli had presented in Florence to great applause several years earlier. The next night the Kärntnertortheater, which had not been used for operas or plays on a regular basis since 1788, reopened its doors, offering another performance of *Fürstengrösse*, while in the Burgtheater a comic opera, by the recently engaged composer Pietro Dutillieu, was followed by a performance of *Capitano Cook*.

During the remainder of Leopold's reign the two court theatres offered the Viennese a nightly choice of entertainment, with evenings of ballet, opera and spoken drama alternating between the theatres. Later in November Empress Maria Luisa's birthday was celebrated with the return to Vienna of *opera seria*, and the first performance of Sebastiano Nasolini's *Teseo a Stige*. During the following Carnival season, on 7 February 1792, old Count Zinzendorf was in the Burgtheater audience that listened in delight to the first performance of Cimarosa's *Il matrimonio segreto*, an *opera buffa* that represented a shift away from the complex tragi-comedies produced by Salieri and Mozart on the Burgtheater stage during the previous decade. Rarely had Vienna witnessed so lavish and varied a series of spectacles; certainly nothing like this had been seen in Vienna since Joseph's reorganization of 1776.

Leopold died on 1 March 1792, before he had had a chance fully to enjoy the fruits of his theatrical management; but the effects of his reorganization of the court theatres and his introduction of new genres and new personnel continued to be felt into the nineteenth century. Italian ballet, Italian serious opera and Italian comic opera of the kind championed by Leopold all enjoyed success in Vienna during the 1790s and beyond. Leopold's establishment of an Italian ballet troupe led soon to the arrival of the great Salvatore Viganò, the choreographer for whom Beethoven wrote his ballet score *Die Geschöpfe des Prometheus*, and within a few years Vienna had become one of the leading centres of Romantic ballet. Ballet has remained an integral part of the Burgtheater/Staatsoper repertory to the present day. Italian serious opera too has maintained an important place in the Burgtheater repertory; the Viennese have welcomed in turn the serious operas of Paer, Rossini, Bellini and Verdi. The reign of Leopold II represents an important turning-point in the evolution of Viennese musical life. His theatrical reorganization brought the Josephinian decade to a sudden close and it helped to shape the musical milieu in which Beethoven and Schubert and their contemporaries thrived.

NOTES

[1] *Mozart: Briefe und Aufzeichnungen*, ed. W. A. Bauer, O. E. Deutsch and J. H. Eibl (Kassel, 1962–75), iii, 102. Subsequent references to and extracts from the Mozarts' correspondence will be identified by date only. The translation used here and in most extracts is that of E. Anderson, *The Letters of Mozart and his Family* (London and New York, 3/1985).

[2] The following demographic data are derived from T. Chandler and G. Fox, *3000 Years of Urban Growth* (New York, 1974), and O. G. Schindler, 'Das Publikum des Burgtheaters in der Josephinischen Ära: Versuch einer Strukturbestimmung', in *Das Burgtheater und sein Publikum*, ed. M. Dietrich (Vienna, 1976).

[3] Schindler, 'Das Publikum des Burgtheaters', 91–2.

[4] H. Schuler, *Die Subskribenten der Mozart'schen Mittwochskonzerte im Trattnersaal zu Wien anno 1784* (Neustadt an der Aisch, 1983).

[5] See D. Heartz, 'Nicolas Jadot and the Building of the Burgtheater', *MQ*, lxviii (1982), 1–31; Schindler, 'Das Publikum des Burgtheaters'; and Schindler, 'Der Zuschauerraum des Burgtheaters im 18. Jahrhundert', *Maske und Kothurn*, xxii (1976), 20–53.

[6] Burgtheater subscription prices are listed by Schindler in 'Das Publikum des Burgtheaters'. R. Fink has drawn my attention to the Gluckian passage in Dittersdorf's opera; on the influence of *opéra comique* on *Figaro* see B. A. Brown, 'Beaumarchais, Mozart and the Vaudeville: Two Examples from "The Marriage of Figaro"', *MT*, cxxvii (1986), 261–5, and D. Heartz, 'Constructing "Le nozze di Figaro"', *JRMA*, cxii (1987), 78–98.

[7] Quoted, in translation, by H. C. Robbins Landon in his monumental study of Haydn's life, music and times, *Haydn: Chronicle and Works* (London, 1976–80): ii *Haydn at Eszterháza, 1766–1790*, 214.

[8] Quoted by Landon, i: *The Early Years, 1732–1765*, 351; see also Chapter X below, p. 272.

[9] Quoted by Landon, iv: *The Years of 'The Creation', 1796–1800*, 28.

[10] Quoted by Landon, ii: *Haydn at Eszterháza, 1766–1790*, 214.

[11] The Burgtheater players in 1773 are listed in a document reproduced in facsimile in G. Zechmeister, *Die Wiener Theater nächst der Burg und nächst dem Kärntnerthor von 1747 bis 1776* (Vienna, 1971), 356. The players for 1791 are listed in the theatre account book for that year in *Vienna, Haus-, Hof- und Staatsarchiv, Generalintendenz der Hoftheater*.

[12] C. Rosen, *The Classical Style: Haydn, Mozart, Beethoven* (New York, 1971), 143.

[13] Compare, for example, the opening phrase of Mozart's magnificent chorus 'Che del ciel, che degli dei' to the opening of Gluck's chorus 'A di questo afflitto regno', near the beginning of *Alceste*.

[14] On Joseph's theatrical reform see F. Hadamowsky, 'Die Schauspielfreiheit, die "Erhebung des Burgtheaters zu Hoftheater" und seine "Begründung als Nationaltheater" im Jahr 1776', *Maske und Kothurn*, xxii (1976), 5–19; and Hadamowsky, *Die Josefinische Theaterreform und das Spielzeit 1776/77 des Burgtheaters* (Vienna, 1978). On the role played by Sonnenfels see E. Wangermann, *The Austrian Achievement* (London, 1973), 121–4; Wangermann sees Sonnenfels as 'the chief protagonist of bourgeois culture in Austria'. See also R. A. Kann, *A Study in Austrian Intellectual History* (New York, 1960), 208–24.

[15] Hadamowsky, 'Die Schauspielfreiheit', 11.

[16] Ed. R. Haas, DTÖ, xxxvi, Jg.xviii/1 (1911). See A. A. Abert's perceptive comments (with music examples) in *NOHM*, vii (1973) 91–4.

[17] On Joseph's restrictions on church music and their effect on church music in Vienna during the 1780s see C. M. Brand, *Die Messen von Joseph Haydn*, (Würzburg, 1941), 187ff; R. G. Pauly, 'The Reforms of Church Music under Joseph II', *MQ*, xliii (1957), 372ff; O. Biba, 'Die Wiener Kirchenmusik um 1783', *Beiträge zur Musikgeschichte des 18. Jahrhunderts* (Eisenstadt, 1971); and Landon, ii: *Haydn at Eszterháza, 1766–1790*, 555–6.

[18] *Magazin der Musik*, i (Hamburg, 1783), 92.

[19] Quoted by Landon, iii: *Haydn in England, 1791–1795*, 107.

[20] *Adalbert Gyrowetz: Four Symphonies*, ed. J. A. Rice in The Symphony 1720–1840, B/xi: 1 (New York, 1983).

[21] See R. Steblin, *A History of Key Characteristics in the Eighteenth and early Nineteenth Centuries* (Ann Arbor, 1983); and, for Mozart in particular, S. Sadie, *The New Grove Mozart* (London, 1983), 132–3, and A. Einstein, *Mozart: his Character, his Work* (New York, 1945), 157–63.

[22] Rosen, *The Classical Style*, 221.

[23] M. Chusid, 'The Significance of D Minor in Mozart's Dramatic Music', *MJb 1965–6*, 37ff.

[24] [. . .] Wir haben starken Schnee/jedoch es ist Advent,/deswegen auch kein Schlitten

rennt./Die Schauspielhäuser sind geschlossen,/nun machen keine komische Possen/der Lacher grosse Menge froh;/das Oratorium von Metastasio:/*Des Heilands Tod* genannt, wird uns izt aufgeführet,/und Salieri hat die Musik componiret;/Wer da nicht Schmelzen will, der muss ganz fühllos seyn,/man bilde sich nur einmal ein,/zum Accompagnement der himmlischen Accenten/ sind hundert sechszig Instrumenten., in *Konstanzisches Wochenblatt*, 12 Jan 1778 (photocopy, Stadtarchiv, Konstanz).

[25] On the performance of Haydn's *Il ritorno di Tobia* see Landon, ii: *Haydn at Eszterháza, 1766–1790*, 215; on the performance of Gassmann's *La Betulia liberata*, see *Karl von Dittersdorfs Lebensbeschreibung*, ed. N. Miller (Munich, 1967), 197–8. For a reproduction of a playbill for the Tonkünstler-Sozietät's concerts during Lent 1791 see 'Vienna', *Grove 6*, xix, 725.

[26] Quoted by Landon, ii: *Haydn at Eszterháza, 1766–1790*, 215.

[27] *Ester* has been published in a facsimile of an early manuscript score, ed. H. E. Smither, in The Italian Oratorio, 1650–1800, xxiv (New York, 1987). The rondò 'Ah, se in vita' is not included in this score, but can be heard in a recording of excerpts from the oratorio conducted by Ferenc Szekeres on Hungaroton HCD 11745–2.

[28] Glimpses of Marianne von Genzinger's musical salon can be found in the correspondence between Genzinger and Haydn; see Landon, ii: *Haydn at Eszterháza, 1766–1790*, 720ff.

[29] On the beginnings of music publishing in Vienna and its relationship to middle-class music-making see R. Flotzinger and G. Gruber, 'Die Wiener Klassik und ihre Zeit', in *Musikgeschichte Österreichs* (Graz, 1979), ii, 152–3.

[30] Quoted in translation by M. S. Morrow, *Concert Life in Vienna, 1780–1810* (diss., Indiana U., 1984), 22–3.

[31] *Reminiscences of Michael Kelly of the King's Theatre and Theatre Royal Drury Lane* (London, 2/1826, ed. R. Fiske, 1975), 122.

[32] ibid, 103.

[33] *Joseph II., Leopold II., und Kaunitz. Ihr Briefwechsel*, ed. A. Beer (Vienna, 1873), 101.

[34] *Antonio Salieri: Prima la musica poi le parole*, vocal score ed. J. Heinzelmann and F. Wanek (Mainz, 1972), 92. *Axur* is said to have been Joseph's 'Lieblingsoper' in the anonymous article 'Auszug eines Schreibens aus Wien vom 5ten Jul. 1790', in *Musikalische Korrespondenz der teutschen filarmonischen Gesellschaft* (1790), cols.27–31, reprinted in R. Angermüller, *Antonio Salieri* (Munich, *c*1971–4), iii, 55ff. *Axur* is compared favourably to *La clemenza di Tito* by I. F. von Mosel, in *Ueber das Leben und die Werke des Anton Salieri* (Vienna, 1827), 113. The Berlin *Musikalisches Wochenblatt* (1791), 15, had warm words for Salieri when expressing regret at a report (later proved to be erroneous) that Salieri had been dismissed from his position as Hofkapellmeister in Vienna.

[35] Quoted by C. Petty in *Italian Opera in London, 1760–1800* (Ann Arbor, 1980), 232.

[36] On Sarti's *Giulio Sabino* see D. Heartz, 'Mozart and his Italian Contemporaries: "La clemenza di Tito"', *MJb 1978–9*, 275–93, and J. A. Rice, 'Sarti's "Giulio Sabino", Haydn's "Armida", and the Arrival of Opera Seria at Eszterháza', *Haydn Yearbook*, xv (1984), 181–98.

[37] *La buona figliuola*, vocal score ed. G. Benvenuti, CMI, vii (1941), 141.

[38] 'Auszug eines Schreibens aus Wien'; see n.34 above.

[39] The crisis of 1789–90 is discussed in detail by E. Wangermann, *From Joseph II to the Jacobin Trials* (London, 2/1969), 5–55; see also R. J. Kerner, *Bohemia in the Eighteenth Century* (New York, 1932), 82–95, and A. Wandruszka, *Leopold II* (Vienna, 1963–5), ii, 249–61.

[40] Leopold to Ferdinand, 7 June 1790, *Vienna, Haus-, Hof- und Staatsarchiv, Sammelbände*, Karton 19.

[41] 'Hofdekret an gesammte Erblande vom 17 März 1791', in *Sammlung der Gesetze . . . Leopold des II.*, ed. J. Kropatscheck (Vienna, [1791–2]), iii, 247.

[42] On the *Te Deum* performed in April 1790, see the lavishly illustrated souvenir book *Beschreibung der Huldigungsfeyerlichkeiten Seiner königlichen apostolischen Majestät Leopolds II. Königs von Hungarn und Böheim, Erzherzogs von Oesterreich, welche von den Nieder-Oesterreichischen Landständen zu Wien am 6ten April 1790 gehalten wurden* (Vienna, 1790). On Righini's D minor Mass, see *Die Krönung Leopold des II. zum römischen Kaiser beschrieben von einem Augenzeugen* (Frankfurt, 1790). On the performance of Reutter's Requiem, see Zinzendorf's diary, 29 Nov 1790, *Vienna, Haus-, Hof- und Staatsarchiv*. On the revival of Mozart's 'Coronation' Mass in the early 1790s and the origins of its name, see K. Pfannhauser's important article, 'Mozarts "Krönungsmesse" ', *Mitteilungen der Internationalen Stiftung Mozarteum*, xi/3–4 (1963), 3ff.

BIBLIOGRAPHICAL NOTE

For a general introduction to Austrian politics, society and culture in the eighteenth century, E. Wangermann's *The Austrian Achievement* (London, 1973) is highly recommended. D. Beales's *Joseph II* (Cambridge, 1987–) will, on its completion, almost certainly be the biggest and best biography of Joseph II in any language; the second volume (in preparation) deals with the last ten years of Joseph's life. E. Wangermann's *From Joseph II to the Jacobin Trials* (London, 2/1969) is an excellent source for the last years of Joseph's reign and its aftermath; P. P. Bernard's *Joseph II* (New York, 1968) is a good short biography. The standard work on Joseph's religious policy is F. Maass's, *Josephinismus: Quellen zu seiner Geschichte in Österreich, 1760–1790* (Vienna, 1951–61). On Joseph's successor see A. Wandruszka's *Leopold II* (Vienna, 1963–5), the only full-length biography of Leopold.

For interesting letters of Joseph II concerning the management of the Burgtheater see *Joseph II. als Theaterdirektor*, ed. R. Payer von Thurn (Vienna, 1920); surprisingly, there is no thorough study of Joseph II as patron of music. On Leopold's musical patronage see J. A. Rice's *Emperor and Impresario: Leopold II and the Transformation of Viennese Musical Theater, 1790–1792* (diss., U. of California, Berkeley, 1987).

One of the richest and most vivid sources of information on musical life in Vienna during the 1780s is the correspondence of the Mozart family, *Mozart: Briefe und Aufzeichnungen*, ed. W. A. Bauer, O. E. Deutsch and J. H. Eibl (Kassel, 1962–75), available in an English translation by E. Anderson, *The Letters of Mozart and his Family* (London and New York, 3/1985). Also of primary importance are the memoirs of the Irish singer Michael Kelly, a member of the Burgtheater's Italian troupe during the mid-1780s, in *Reminiscences of Michael Kelly of the King's Theatre and Theatre Royal Drury Lane* (London, 2/1826, ed. R. Fiske, 1975).

On the Burgtheater and its audience, two long articles by O. G. Schindler are useful: 'Das Publikum des Burgtheaters in der Josephinischen Ära: Versuch einer Strukturbestimmung', in *Das Burgtheater und sein Publikum*, ed. M. Dietrich (Vienna, 1976), and 'Der Zuschauerraum des Burgtheaters im 18. Jahrhundert', *Maske und Kothurn*, xxii (1976), 20–53. See also D. Heartz's fine study, 'Nicolas Jadot and the Building of the Burgtheater', *MQ*, lxviii (1982), 1–31. On the repertory of the Burgtheater during the late eighteenth century see O. Michtner, *Das alte Burgtheater als Opernbühne von der Einführung des deutschen Singspiels (1778) bis zum Tod Kaiser Leopolds II. (1792)* (Vienna, 1970). Michtner's book, although sometimes inaccurate, is an indispensable guide to Viennese opera of the 1770s and 1780s.

On Viennese concert life, both public and private, M. S. Morrow, *Concert Life in Vienna, 1780–1810* (diss., Indiana U., 1984, published as *Concert Life in Haydn's Vienna: Aspects of a Developing Musical and Social Institution*, New York, 1988) supersedes earlier studies.

Chapter VI

Salzburg under Church Rule

CLIFF EISEN

Salzburg – sometimes called 'the German Rome' because of its numerous churches, open squares and fountains – owes its post-Roman origin to the founding of the Abbey of St Peter by St Rupert of Worms in 696 and of the cathedral by St Virgil in 774. In the eighth century, the bishopric of Salzburg was elevated to an archdiocese and the Archbishop of Salzburg was made a papal legate; in 1278 Rudolph of Habsburg made the archbishops of Salzburg imperial princes. During centuries of relative peace – except for the Peasants' War of 1525–6 – the power and prestige of Salzburg increased until it was perhaps the most important and influential archdiocese and sacred state in German-speaking Europe. In 1700, some 55 years before Mozart was born, its boundaries stretched north and west into what is today Bavaria and east and south as far as Wiener Neustadt and Graz. Salzburg was a profoundly conservative state, predicated on a severe Catholic orthodoxy: the Jews were expelled from Salzburg in 1498 and the Protestants in 1731–2.[1]

The city had a distinguished musical history. Although there is little evidence for the practice of early polyphony there, a twelfth-century manuscript copy of the treatise *De musica* by Aribo Scholasticus (*fl* 1068–78) survives at St Peter's and records show that the population of the city included instrument makers, bell founders and musicians. The Monk of Salzburg, the first poet-musician to write in German, was active there during the late fourteenth century, and both Heinrich Finck, a well-known composer of German songs, and Paul Hofhaimer, who was considered the foremost organist of his time, were attached to the court during the sixteenth century.[2]

A formally constituted court music was established in 1591 by Archbishop Wolf Dietrich von Raitenau (1587–1612). At first its duties were limited to service in the cathedral. From the time of Archbishop Marcus Sitticus von Hohenems (1612–19), however, dramatic music also came to the fore, at the Benedictine university founded in 1622 (the Gymnasium was founded in 1617) and at court, where a stage on the Italian model was erected in 1614 and inaugurated with the first known opera performance outside Italy, an *Orfeo* sometimes said to be Monteverdi's. Later archbishops, including Guidobald Thun (1654–68), Max Gandolf von Kuenburg (1668–87) and Johann Ernst von Thun (1687–1709), expanded the activities of the court music, in particular with regard to secular music; Max Gandolf's Kapelle included the internationally known Georg Muffat, famous for his cultivation of current French and Italian musical styles, and the Bohemian Heinrich von Biber, one of the most prominent violin virtuosos of the time. During the reign of Franz Anton, Prince of Harrach (1709–27), the Viennese deputy Hofkapellmeister Antonio Caldara was a regular visitor to Salzburg and between 1716 and 1727 many of his works were performed for the first time there, including the *feste Il giubilo della Salza* (1716) and *Dafne* (1720) and the oratorio *Il morto redivivo ovvero S Antonio* (1726).

Harrach was succeeded by Leopold Anton Eleuthnerius, Baron of Firmian (1727–44), Jakob Ernst, Count of Liechtenstein (1745–7), and Siegmund Christoph, Count of Schrattenbach (1753–71). Of these, Schrattenbach was the most important: he was lavish in his support of the court music, exhibited a keen interest in instrumental music, sent his composers and performers to Italy to study and rewarded composition with generous presents. He was also the Mozarts' strongest supporter in Salzburg: Leopold advanced rapidly in the court music establishment during Schrattenbach's reign, and during the 1760s and 1770s, when Wolfgang and his father travelled to Vienna, Paris, London and Italy, the archbishop subsidized their travels, at least in part.

As a result, the last Archbishop of Salzburg, Hieronymus, Count of Colloredo (1772–1803), inherited a court music of considerable talent and accomplishment which boasted the regular composition of works for both cathedral and court, and included among its members Anton Cajetan Adlgasser, Michael Haydn and Leopold and Wolfgang Mozart. Colloredo pursued radically different political and social policies from his predecessors, designed to modernize and secularize the archdiocese. In many respects these changes favoured cultural life in Salzburg. A new sense of toleration and freedom of the press attracted several prominent writers, scientists and teachers to the court.[3] The court music, however, suffered. Its traditions were predominantly sacred and Colloredo's reforms, together with a severe fiscal policy, restricted or eliminated most of the traditional venues for composition and performance in Salzburg. The important university theatre was permanently closed in 1778, a loss that was keenly felt and not compensated for by the establishment of a public theatre; German hymns were made obligatory at church services, replacing some traditional liturgical compositions which themselves had already been restricted; and instrumental music was limited at the court and abolished at the cathedral. A foundling secular music tradition was

41. Interior of Salzburg Cathedral during the celebrations to mark the 1100th anniversary of the founding of the Archbishopric of Salzburg: engraving (c1680) by Melchior Küsel

left to fend for itself, supported for the most part by a small and only moderately affluent minor nobility. Not surprisingly, many performers and composers left Salzburg for elsewhere, among them Mozart, who took up permanent residence in Vienna in 1781. By 1806, when Salzburg was secularized, musical life in the archdiocese had declined to provincial unimportance.

THE REIGNS OF THREE ARCHBISHOPS, 1745–71

When Leopold Mozart joined the Salzburg court music establishment as fourth violinist in 1743, the organization of the Hofkapelle was much the same as it had been at the time of its founding in 1591. In general, it was divided into four distinct and independent groups: the court music proper, which performed in the cathedral, at the Benedictine university and at court; the court- and field-trumpeters, together with the timpanists (normally ten trumpeters and two timpanists), who performed in the cathedral and at court entertainments and provided special fanfares before meals and at important civic functions; the cathedral music (Dommusik), which consisted of the choral deacons (Domchorvikaren) and choristers (Choralisten) and performed in the cathedral; and the choirboys of the Kapellhaus, usually ten sopranos and four altos, who also performed in the cathedral and who were instructed in music by the court musicians.[4]

The chief duty of the court music proper, together with the Dommusik and choirboys, was to perform in the cathedral. For elaborate performances the musicians numbered about 40, sometimes more. (Fig.41 shows the disposition of musical forces in the cathedral at a service *c*1680.) The Kapellmeister, vocal soloists, trombones and bass instruments played in the first choir, with ten to twelve strings in the second. The trumpeters and timpanists occupied the third and fourth choirs, while the fifth, which was below by the altar, contained the vocal ripienists, a bass player and another organ; the fifth choir played only in tutti passages. On less important occasions, the performing forces were reduced: for the Festis praepositi et decani, for example, there were no trumpets or timpani, and for the Festis canonici, only the 'principal choirs' performed.[5] Often the court musicians did double duty: because the woodwind players, trumpeters and timpanists performed less frequently than the string players and vocalists, they were also expected to perform on the violin; when needed, they filled out the ranks of the orchestra both at court and in the cathedral.

Performance at the cathedral also represented the primary venue for Salzburg's composers, foremost among them Johann Ernst Eberlin (1702–62, Hofkapellmeister from 1749 to 1762). Leopold Mozart, who is presumed to be the author of a 1757 report on the archbishop's musical establishment (*Nachricht von dem gegenwärtigen Zustande der*

Musik Sr. Hochfürstlichen Gnaden des Erzbischoffs zu Salzburg im Jahr 1757), had a high regard for Eberlin; according to the report:

> Ernst Eberlin, from Jettenbach in Swabia, is also archiepiscopal Lord High Steward. He was previously court organist, and if anyone deserves to be called a thorough and accomplished master of composition, it is indeed this man. He is entirely in command of the notes, and he writes with such quickness that many people would take for a fairy-tale the manner in which this profound composer brings this or that important work to the music-stand. With regard to the number of his compositions, one can compare him to the two very industrious and famous composers, Scarlatti and Telemann.[6]

Some of Eberlin's sacred works – which include several hundred masses, as well as requiems, motets, litanies, sequences, hymns, vesper psalms and settings of the *Te Deum* – are composed in a learned, late-Baroque *stile antico*; others are written in a harmonically unadventurous but rhythmically complex *stile moderno*.[7] They represent fine examples of mid-century German rather than Italian counterpoint and because they were performed at least until the late 1770s they served as models for succeeding Salzburg composers, including Adlgasser (Eberlin's son-in-law and presumed to be his pupil), Leopold and Wolfgang Amadeus Mozart and Michael Haydn.[8] Eberlin's compositions far outstrip in quality those of his contemporary, Giuseppe Lolli (1701–78; deputy Hofkapellmeister from 1743 to 1763 and Hofkapellmeister from 1763 to 1778), who composed several masses and vespers as well as about a dozen church sonatas.

The post-Eberlin generation of Salzburg composers is best represented by Adlgasser (1729–77; court and cathedral organist from 1750 to 1777) and Leopold Mozart (1719–87; deputy Hofkapellmeister from 1763 to 1787). Adlgasser was a fairly prolific composer of sacred works, although after an Italian journey of 1764–5 he seems more or less to have given up composition in this area and concentrated on stage works. Leopold Mozart's sometimes eccentric works, on the other hand, are less numerous but generally of higher quality; several of them were long thought to be by Wolfgang, including the *Missa brevis* in C and the *Missa brevis* in F (K115/166*d* and 116/90*a*). Contemporary with Adlgasser and Leopold Mozart was Franz Ignaz Lipp (1718–98, court and cathedral organist from 1754 to 1798), whose works are little known; according to Leopold Mozart, Lipp composed 'not badly'.[9]

A final generation of church composers in Salzburg included Michael Haydn (1737–1806), who joined the court music as Hofkonzertmeister in 1763, and Wolfgang Amadeus Mozart (1756–91). Haydn, whose sacred works number more than 600, received his earliest training at St Stephen's in Vienna, and he brought to Salzburg some elements of the current Viennese style. More important, however, is his adoption of contemporary Salzburg practice, not least in its external features – among them local textual variants, the traditional concluding of Gloria and Credo mass sections with fugues, and the disposition of the orchestra, which on special occasions included trumpets and oboes but not other winds.[10] In general, his masses for Advent and Lent are composed in a *stile antico* similar to that of Johann Joseph Fux; others, however, are in a more modern style, with some extensive vocal coloratura or, in the case of his graduals, in a harmonically simple, homophonic style with few solos.

To some extent, Mozart stands outside this tradition. His sacred works, not nearly as numerous as Michael Haydn's, are more Italian in style, almost certainly a result of his contact in the early 1770s with Padre Martini in Bologna and Eugène, Marquis of Ligniville, in Florence, and his composition of Italian opera, a genre that was not cultivated in Salzburg. Similarly important is the influence of Leopold Mozart. Several of Wolfgang's early works, including the masses K66 and 139/47*a* and the Litany K125, are apparently modelled on compositions by his father. Leopold was probably the first in Salzburg to write parts for horns in sacred music, an orchestral disposition later followed by Mozart.[11]

Contemporaries of Michael Haydn and Mozart included Joseph Hafeneder (1746–84; court violinist from 1769 to 1784), who composed several dozen masses, litanies and offertories, and Anton Ferdinand Paris (1744–1809; cathedral and court organist from 1762 to 1809), whose works were poorly regarded. In general, sacred music in Salzburg was a local affair; a contemporary catalogue shows that during the 1780s more than 90 per cent of the cathedral repertory consisted of works by local composers.[12]

In addition to their services at the cathedral, the court musicians also performed at the Benedictine university, where school dramas were regularly given. These belonged to a long tradition of spoken pedagogical Benedictine plays which during the seventeenth century developed into an opera-like art form. Salzburg University, the most important Benedictine educational institution in south Germany at the time, played a leading role in this development.[13] At first, music in the dramas was restricted to choruses which marked the beginnings and ends of acts. By the 1670s, however, the works consisted of a succession of recitatives and arias, based at least in part on the model of Italian opera. Because there was little opera in Salzburg at this time, the school dramas, which included elements of Italian opera and German comedy, represented the most important dramatic genre in Salzburg. A description from 1670 of the anonymous *Corona laboriosae heroum virtuti* shows to what extent the Salzburg school dramas represented an important fusion of dramatic genres:

> The poem was Latin but the stage machinery was Italian. . . . The work could be described as an opera. The production costs must have been exceptionally great. It drew a huge crowd. Part of the action was declaimed, part was sung. Gentlemen of the court performed the dances, which in part were inserted in the action as entr'actes. It was a delightful muddle and a wonderful pastime for the audience.[14]

At mid-century, the most prolific composer of school dramas was Eberlin – more than 50 such works by him are known. His last, *Sigismundus, Hungariae rex* (1761), is typical of the genre. Its main subject, the wooing of Maria, daughter of King Ludwig of Hungary, by Sigismund, later emperor, was presented as a spoken play. Combined with it was a second play, set to music. The music is largely in the current Italian style with a predominance of extended da capo arias. Among the dancers was the five-year-old Wolfgang Amadeus Mozart who in this production may have made his first public appearance.

After Eberlin the composition of school dramas fell to younger composers attached to the court, especially Adlgasser, Joseph Meissner (?1725–1795; a court bass from 1747 to 1795) and Michael Haydn. Mozart's contribution to the genre was limited to a single work, *Apollo et Hyacinthus*, which was performed between the acts of Rufinus Widl's Latin tragedy *Clementia Croesi* in 1767. According to a contemporary document, the orchestra at the school dramas consisted of twelve violins, two violas, one cello, two double basses, one bassoon, two oboes and two horns, altogether 22 players.[15]

Secular music was less important at court than sacred music or school dramas. Although Schrattenbach is said to have been a supporter of Italian opera, there is little evidence to suggest that such works were much performed in Salzburg at this time. Librettos survive for only about half a dozen, including Sarti's *Vologesco* (1766) and Sacchini's *L'Olimpiade* (1768). Orchestral music, which was needed for court concerts and performance during meals, was not seriously cultivated before about 1740, a long-standing tradition of first-rate chamber music, including the sonatas of Biber and Muffat, notwithstanding.

Almost certainly there was a qualitative difference in the performances of church music and orchestral music. The repertory of sacred works remained fairly constant (it has already been noted that works by Eberlin, who died in 1762, were performed in Salzburg at least until the late 1770s) and the court musicians had opportunities to play the same work often. Instrumental music, however, was often composed for special occasions and there is little evidence that works were repeated; hence the repertory was constantly new. This may be behind Louis de Visme's criticism of the Salzburg orchestra as 'too harsh'[16] and Mozart's complaints about the poor quality of the performances, which he also blamed on over-work and, by implication, the inexperience of the players.[17]

Apart from overtures to stage works and numerous church sonatas of the 1730s and 1740s, the creation of an important repertory of independent orchestral music in Salzburg must be credited to Leopold Mozart. Almost 70 symphonies are attributed to him; other orchestral works, described in contemporary documents and including more than 30 orchestral serenades, concertos for flute, oboe, bassoon, horn and trumpet, occasional works (like *The Musical Sleigh Ride* and *The Peasant Wedding*) and hundreds of minuets and other dances, are for the most part lost. Among Leopold's contemporaries, both Ferdinand Seidl (*c*1700–1773; court Konzertmeister from 1745 to 1773) and Caspar Cristelli (*c*1706–1766; court cellist from 1726 to 1766) were also active as composers of symphonies and other orchestral works, but few compositions by them survive.

Composers of the younger generation cultivated instrumental and orchestral music more assiduously. Michael Haydn composed numerous symphonies and serenades during his first years of service in Salzburg and Mozart turned out dozens of works during the first ten years of his compositional career; even though many of them were composed when he was away from Salzburg, it may be presumed that they were performed there as well. Other composers of instrumental music in Salzburg at this time included Wenzel Hebelt (*c*1736–1769, court violinist from 1757 to 1769); Georg Scheicher (*fl c*1768–1775), who was not attached to the court but to St Peter's; Joseph Griner (*c*1745–before 1807; subordinate court musician from 1766 to 1772); Joseph Leutgeb (1732–1811; court horn player and violinist from 1763 to 1773), for whom Mozart later composed his horn concertos (K412/386*b*, 417, 447 and 495); and Andreas Pinzger (1740–1817; court violinist from 1766 to 1807). The most prolific of them, however, was Joseph Hafeneder, whose extant works include close to a dozen symphonies and orchestral cassations.

Diversity of style characterizes Salzburg orchestral music. Eberlin's few symphonies not composed as introductions to stage works are based largely on the model of the Italian opera overture. Cristelli's three extant symphonies, on the other hand, have the character of church sonatas. Leopold Mozart's numerous orchestral works include elements of the contemporary south German concert symphony and the Italian overture; some of them approach chamber music and were probably performed one to a part, while others are for a larger orchestra, including oboes and horns and sometimes trumpets and timpani. Only a few of his works are programmatic, using local melodies and instrumentation (among them the so-called 'Toy' symphony). From about 1760 Leopold's symphonies seem to be influenced by contemporary Viennese fashion: they have recapitulations marked by a simultaneous return of the main theme and tonic key, and a greater lyricism than previously. Michael Haydn's symphonies are steeped in the Viennese tradition, and it may have been their general character that influenced the younger Mozart more than any specific compositional procedures.

Part of the reason for the diversity of style in Salzburg orchestral music – a diversity best characterized by Mozart's eclectic works – may be that in contrast to church music, which was mostly of local origin, orchestral music by other composers was widely disseminated and performed in Salzburg. Symphonies and concertos by Wagenseil, Stamitz and Mysliveček are mentioned in the Mozart family letters; manuscripts of Salzburg origin survive for works by Joseph Haydn, Aumann, Leopold Hofmann, Dittersdorf, J. C. Bach and Vanhal; and the estate inventory of Martin Bischofreiter (1762–1845; active at St Peter's from 1786) includes dozens of symphonies and chamber works primarily by Viennese composers of the second half of the eighteenth century. As a result, Salzburg's composers appear never to have developed a unique and identifiable orchestral style; at least this was the opinion of C. F. D. Schubart, who visited the archdiocese in the 1770s.[18]

One orchestral genre, however, was unique to Salzburg: the serenade. Like the important Benedictine school drama, the serenade owes its origin to the university. Every year in August, in connection with the university's graduation ceremonies, the students had a substantial orchestral work performed for their professors. Typically, these serenades consisted of an opening and closing march and eight or nine other movements, among them two or three concerto-like movements for various instruments. Although the origin of this tradition is not known, serenades were certainly established as a regular fixture of the academic year by the mid-1740s. Leopold Mozart, who composed more than 30 such works by 1757, was the most important early composer in the genre. There are later examples by Michael Haydn, Wolfgang Amadeus Mozart and Joseph Hafeneder.

The importance of the serenade stems mainly from its fusion of symphony and concerto movements, which were often extracted from the main works and given separately: examples from Mozart's works include K185/167*a* and 204/213*a*, movements of which were given as symphonies; and K320, the concerto-like movements of which were performed independently as a sinfonia concertante. The close association of serenade and concerto also explains the outward form of several otherwise atypical works. The recent discovery of a serenade by Leopold Mozart shows that his trumpet concerto of 1762, unusual for its two-movement form – a slow movement and a fast movement – represents only two movements extracted from a parent work. Two Michael Haydn concertos for solo trumpet (P34 and *deest*) also consist of two movements, probably from lost serenades. What is more, unlike symphonies, which were known as independent works at least as early as the earliest serenades, there appears to have been little or no independent development of the concerto in Salzburg. The genre's cultivation there may owe its origin to the serenade as much as to independent concertos by other composers that may have circulated in Salzburg during the 1750s and 1760s.

The Salzburg court musicians were also active at other institutions in and around Salzburg as well as at the homes of the local nobility. Mozart is supposed to have composed the offertory *Inter natos mulierum*

42. Interior of the Abbey Church of St Peter, remodelled in the Rococo style in 1770

(K72/74*f*) for P. Johannes Hassy of Seeon, a monastery not far from Salzburg; about 1780 he revised his motet *Exsultate jubilate*, composed in Milan in 1773, for performance at the Salzburg Dreifältigkeitskirche; and it was possibly for the 100th anniversary of the pilgrimage church Maria Plain that he composed the *Missa brevis* K194/186*h*.[19]

At St Peter's, the important Benedictine monastery in the heart of Salzburg itself,[20] the Mozarts and Michael Haydn were welcome guests. There the Musikkapelle consisted largely of students; only a few musicians at the abbey were professionals, among them the *chori figuralis inspector*, who was also responsible for the music archive. Nevertheless, St Peter's offered the court musicians opportunities for both performance and composition. In 1753, for instance, Leopold Mozart composed an *Applausus* to celebrate the anniversary of the ordination of three fathers, and some years later, in 1769, Wolfgang composed the Mass K66 for Cajetan Hagenauer, son of the Mozart's landlord, Johann Lorenz Hagenauer. Cajetan, who took the name Dominicus, was also the dedicatee of two of Michael Haydn's works, the *Missa S Dominici* and a *Te Deum*, both composed to celebrate his election as abbot in 1786. Haydn established close ties with St Peter's almost immediately after his arrival in Salzburg in 1763 and it was the source of his most important students and closest friends, for whom he composed his innovatory lieder for men's chorus.

Similarly important for the court musicians were the minor nobility and wealthy merchants of Salzburg, who required music for private occasions, especially weddings and name-day celebrations.[21] The Mozarts, about whom we are better informed than other musicians in the archdiocese, composed numerous works for the nobility and other prominent townspeople. As early as 1754, for example, Leopold composed twelve minuets for the wedding of a local merchant, Francesco Spangler. And some of Wolfgang's finest orchestral and chamber works were composed for the family's friends, including the Serenade K185/167*a*, for the graduation of Judas Thaddäus von Antretter; the Divertimento K247, for the name day of Countess Lodron; the 'Haffner' Serenade K250/248*b*, for the marriage of Elisabeth Haffner and Franz Xaver Späth; and the Divertimento K334/320*b*, for Georg Sigismund Robinig on the occasion of his law examination. Occasionally these private performances had disastrous results, as the history of a Nachtmusik composed by Hafeneder and Count Czernin for Countess Lodron shows. Leopold Mozart wrote to his son on 29 June 1778:

> I wrote to you about Czernin's Nachtmusik . . . it had a tragi-comic asinine end. Czernin wanted to perform it on the same evening for the Countess Lodron and for his own sister. Now his first idiocy was to play first for his sister and then for the countess, not only because

> the wife of a land marshall takes precedence by far over the wife of a palace director, but because his sister, the Countess Lützow, with her innate modesty would gladly have left this honour to another lady. The second idiocy was even more incomprehensible. The music had begun outside Countess Lodron's. Czernin looked up at the windows, shouting all the time. Then came the minuet and trio, only once, then an Adagio which he worked very diligently to play abominably badly – he talked constantly to the Konzertmeister, Brunetti, who was standing behind him, shouting throughout: and then 'allons! marche!' and he went off with the musicians in a flash, as one might do if he intended to insult someone publicly with a Nachtmusik, for half the town was there. And why? Because he imagined that the Countess had not come to the window, in which impression Brunetti confirmed him: but the countess and Prince Breuner were at the window and were seen by everybody else. A couple of days later the countess . . . gave Brunetti a terrible telling-off, and since then the archbishop will not speak to him.[22]

THE REIGN OF HIERONYMUS COLLOREDO, 1773–1806

When Schrattenbach died in 1771, the Salzburgers reasonably expected as their next prince one of a number of popular, locally known candidates: Count Spaur, Bishop of Seckau; Count Auersperg, Bishop of Lavant; or Leopold Ernst Firmian, Bishop of Passau. For the first time in Salzburg's history, however, the imperial court in Vienna interfered with an archbishop's election, and after five days of bitter debate and 30 votes, Hieronymus, Count of Colloredo, Prince-Bishop of Gurk and second son of the imperial state vice-chancellor, was elected Archbishop of Salzburg by an unpopular majority. Colloredo, true to his Viennese origins and in keeping with the policies of Joseph II,[23] embarked almost immediately on an ambitious course to modernize the archdiocese.

In 1773 the school system was overhauled along Viennese lines. Among other changes, the university theatre was closed in 1778 with the performance of Michael Haydn's *Abels Tod*, itself an unusual event since there had been no performances at the theatre during the previous three years. The gap in Salzburg's musical-theatrical life created by the demise of the university theatre was only partly made good by the establishment of a public theatre in 1775, when Colloredo ordered the Ballhaus in the Hannibalgarten (today the Makartplatz and site of the Landestheater) be rebuilt at the city's expense as a theatre for both spoken drama and opera. The first troupe to play there, directed by Carl Wahr, included in its repertory Regnard's *Der Zerstreute*, with entr'actes by Joseph Haydn (Symphony no.60, 'Il distratto'),[24] Gebler's tragedy *Thamos, König in Aegypten*, which may have been performed with incidental music by Mozart, and Michael

43. The Mozart Family: portrait (c1780) by Johann Nepomuk della Croce; Mozart's mother (d 1778) is depicted in her portrait (c1775) (probably by Lorenzoni or Franz Joseph Degle)

Haydn's incidental music to Voltaire's *Zaire*. Otherwise, however, there is scant evidence that Salzburg's composers were active in the theatre which offered little in replacement of the former Benedictine drama. Hence a significant venue for Salzburg's composers was lost.

Instead, the theatre was occupied by visiting troupes, including those of Wolfgang Rössl, Johann Heinrich Böhm (who became friendly with the Mozarts during his stay in Salzburg in 1779–80) and Emanuel Schikaneder, who was later the librettist of Mozart's *Die Zauberflöte*. Schikaneder's repertory included German Singspiels and German versions of French *opéras comiques*, among them Egidio Duni's *Les deux chasseurs et la laitière* as *Das Milchmädchen*, Johann Adam Hiller's *Löttchen am Hofe*, Ignaz Umlauf's *Die schöne Schusterin, oder Die pücefarbenen Schuhe* and Georg Joseph Vogler's *Der Sklavenhändler*.[25] Karl Ludwig Schmidt, who played in Salzburg from September 1784 to February 1785, included in his repertory Mozart's *Die Entführung aus dem Serail*.

It was not until 1797 that a local standing troupe was established under the direction of Lorenz Hübner, editor of the *Salzburger Intelligenzblatt* and the *Oberdeutsche allgemeine Literaturzeitung*, and the court tenor Giuseppe Tomaselli.[26] The troupe, under the musical direction of the court Konzertmeister Franz Joseph Otter, included in its repertory Mozart's *Die Entführung*, *Die Zauberflöte*, *Le nozze di Figaro* and *Don Giovanni* (the last two not in Italian, but in German), while the spoken dramas were dominated by the works of Goethe and Schiller. Theatre represented the most important form of public entertainment in Salzburg at this time and contemporary descriptions leave little doubt that the Salzburgers had an almost inexhaustible appetite for the productions, even if Mozart's works were – at least according to one observer from 1803 – played more out of respect for his Salzburg background than for the works themselves:

> Among German cities of similar population, I have hardly found such an overwhelming partiality, especially among the lower classes, for theatrical entertainments, as here. . . . The taste of the public has for many years been corrupted by self-serving entrepreneurs through Schikaneder's senseless and tasteless operas and farces. . . . Players, who set pleasure aquiver most crudely with hand, body and voice, are applauded and encored, and scarcely enough astounding happenings, ghostly apparitions, battles and *double entendres* can be brought to the stage in order to win the applause of the public . . . To be sure, in recent years some more cultivated entrepreneurs have ventured, with the approval of the Theatre Commission, to bring some better plays and operas to the boards; but it is only recently that some of Iffland's, Kotzebue's and Schiller's masterpieces have had the anticipated success. For Mozart's operas the public seems more to affect taste than really to feel it; for this immortal composer was born and brought up in Salzburg.[27]

In addition to overhauling the school system, Colloredo also instituted numerous church reforms, many of them intended to make the liturgy more comprehensible. While in Vienna similar reforms were part of Joseph II's efforts to shift the balance of power in favour of the state at the expense of the church, in Salzburg – not a secular but a church state – the reforms represented Colloredo's attempts to modernize the archdiocese along Enlightenment principles and his increasing desire to rule as a secular prince. Indeed, in 1787 Colloredo changed his coat of arms and local coinage to include a sword on the right side, a gesture which has been interpreted as a sign that he considered his secular rule paramount.

Among the earliest reforms was a shortening of the Mass, which is described by the Mozarts in a letter of 4 September 1776 to Padre Martini in Bologna:

> Our church music is very different from that of Italy, since a mass with the whole Kyrie, the Gloria, the Credo, the Epistle sonata, the Offertory or Motet, the Sanctus and the Agnus Dei must not last longer than three quarters of an hour. This applies even to the most

> Solemn Mass said by the Archbishop himself. So you see that a special study is required for this kind of composition. At the same time, the mass must have all the instruments – trumpets, drums and so forth.[28]

By 1782 the reforms were more or less worked out and publicized by Colloredo in a pastoral letter which did not attack matters of faith, but was directed against the liturgy and the excessive ornateness and ostentation of parish churches.[29] Numerous local traditions, including the firing of cannons and the carrying of pictures and statues during church processions, as well as the famous pilgrimage to Pinzgau, were abolished. These changes prompted a local saying: 'Our Prince Colloredo has neither Gloria nor Credo'. Other reforms were directed against church music: purely instrumental music, as well as some instrumentally accompanied sacred vocal music, was abolished, at least in theory. The pastoral letter was harsh on this point: '[in our common city and country churches] . . . every good thought is driven out of the heart of the common people by the miserable fiddling; and horrible howling only invites stupidity and inattention'.[30] In place of purely instrumental pieces traditionally performed at the gradual, Colloredo ordered the performance of choral composition based on liturgical texts; and in place of Latin hymns he ordered German hymns that were to be sung by the congregation.

At least one contemporary witness – who described the symphonies performed in the cathedral as an 'annoyance to pious souls and musical ears'[31] – thought that the abolition of purely instrumental music was a good thing. And it is thanks to Colloredo's reforms that Michael Haydn composed more than 100 offertories and graduals during the 1780s and later published his *Heilige Gesang*. In general, however, the reforms were not popular: congregations passively resisted the introduction of German hymns by not singing them, and worshippers in parishes near the border attended services in Bavarian churches where instruments were still allowed.

For fiscal reasons, the number and length of concerts at court were also curtailed. When Mozart was in Paris in 1778, Leopold wrote to him:

> Yesterday I was for the first time [this season] the director of the great concert at court. At present the music ends at around a quarter past eight. Yesterday it began around seven o'clock and, as I left, a quarter past eight struck – thus an hour and a quarter. Generally only four pieces are done: a symphony, an aria, a symphony or concerto, then an aria and with this, 'Addio!'[32]

Possibly as a result of these restrictions, during the late 1770s the lesser nobility in Salzburg began to organize private orchestras and give private concerts. One of the first of these, sponsored by the archbishop's nephew Johann Rudolf, Count Czernin, was described by Leopold Mozart in a letter of 12 April 1778:

> Count Czernin is not content with fiddling at Court, and as he would like to do some conducting, he has collected an amateur orchestra who are to meet in Count Lodron's hall every Sunday after three o'clock . . . A week ago today, on the 5th, we had our first music meeting. There was Count Czernin, first violin, then Baron Babbius, Sigmund Lodron, young Weinrother, Kolb, Kolb's student from the Nonnberg, and a couple of young students whom I did not know. The second violins were myself, Sigmund Robinig, Cusetti, Count Altham, Cajetan Andretter, a student and Ceccarelli la coda dei secondi. The two violas were the two ex-Jesuits, Bullinger and Wishofer; the two oboes were Weiser, the lacquey, and Schulze's son, who acted in the Linz play. Two watchman's apprentices played the horns. The double basses were Cassl and Count Wolfegg, with Ranftl doing duty occasionally. The cellos were the new young canons, Count Zeill and Spaur, Court Councillor Mölk, Sigmund Andretter and Ranftl. Nannerl accompanied all the symphonies and she also accompanied Ceccarelli who sang an aria per l'appertura della accademia di dilettanti. After the symphony Count Czernin played a beautifully written concerto by Sirmen alla Brunetti, and doppo una ultra sinfonia Count Altham played a frightful trio, no one being able to say whether it was scraped or fiddled, whether it was in 3/4 or common time, or perhaps even in some newly invented and hitherto unknown tempo. Nannerl was to have played a concerto, but as the Countess wouldn't let them have her good harpsichord (which is Casus reservatus pro summo Pontifice), and as only the Egedacher one with gilt legs was there, she didn't perform. In the end the two Lodron girls had to play. It had never been suggested beforehand that they should do so. But since I have been teaching them they are always quite well able to perform. So on this occasion too they both did me credit.[33]

A later private orchestra, which performed at the house of Dr Silvester Barisani, physician to the archbishop, gave the first Salzburg performance of Mozart's Linz Symphony (no.36) in September 1784.

It was a small step from the private orchestras and concerts of Czernin and Barisani to the establishment of public subscription concerts, which were first given in Salzburg in 1781 and, again, at the archbishop's instigation, in 1786. Leopold Mozart described one of these concerts to his daughter, Nannerl:

> Because the *Redouten* turned out so well, the archbishop has had the idea of having something also during Lent, and, thinking of the *Casino* concerts that were given in 1781 during his absence, he informed the town council that he wished such [concerts] to be organized for five Wednesdays in Lent. The first concert was

> yesterday . . . Those who subscribe pay one ducat and can bring their entire family . . . There are more than 70 subscribers. It was surprisingly full because a number of visiting tradesmen were there. There were gaming-tables for the nobility and city officials in the assembly room, the tradesmen played in the long hall, and in the first room there was Faro – and where there was Faro, there were cavaliers. One could have all sorts of refreshments and confections. In short, it was splendid![34]

The repertory at these concerts was increasingly dominated by the works of non-local composers. Although Michael Haydn continued to write symphonies throughout the 1780s, with the departure of Mozart for Vienna in 1781 and the death of Hafeneder in 1784, Salzburg composers seem more or less to have abandoned instrumental music. Not surprisingly, perhaps, the decline of instrumental music in Salzburg was coincidental with a sudden and dramatic flowering of music-printing and -copying shops in Vienna.

Although the history of the performance of music in Salzburg is clear in its broad outlines, it is by no means certain what the court musicians' obligations were with respect to composition or how they arranged to have their works performed. When Mozart was appointed cathedral organist in 1779, succeeding Adlgasser who had died in 1777, his contract stated only that '[he] shall as far as possible serve the Court and the Church with new compositions made by him'.[35] And according to the *Nachricht* of 1757, the choice of works to be performed at court depended entirely on the Kapellmeister or the court composers – Eberlin, Leopold Mozart, Caspar Cristelli and Ferdinand Seidl – who directed the court music a week at a time in rotation.[36] Consequently, other than for special occasions when specific works were commissioned, composition and performance in Salzburg were apparently ad hoc affairs.

The authority exercised by the Kapellmeister and the court composers begins to explain some irregularities in the output of Salzburg composers. It is striking that most of Michael Haydn's orchestral works were composed when the Mozarts were absent from Salzburg. Between 1763 and 1766, the first three years of his appointment at the court, Haydn composed at least eight symphonies, an orchestral divertimento and an orchestral cassation. Between 1767 and 1769, however, he composed only one symphony (P7) and a serenade (P87), while Mozart produced the four cassations K100/62*a*, 63, 99/63*a* and *deest* (referred to in a letter of 18 August 1771), and probably performed in Salzburg the symphonies composed on the grand tour of 1763–6 and in Vienna, where he spent part of 1767 and all of 1768 (K16, 19, A223/19*a*, 22, A221/45*a*, 43, 45 and 48). In 1770 and 1771, when the Mozarts were in Italy, Haydn produced at least four more symphonies. But from 1772 to 1774, when the Mozarts were mostly in

Salzburg, he composed only one cassation (P90) and three symphonies (P9, 10 and 11). During these years Mozart composed eighteen symphonies (from K73 to K200/189*k*), the Divertimento K131 and the Serenades K185/167*a* and 203/189*b*.

Leopold Mozart – who for 30 years was partly responsible for running the court music – was no doubt better disposed towards performing his own and Wolfgang's works than Haydn's: his personal antipathy to Haydn is well known. A letter of Nannerl Mozart's puts the blame for their poor relations squarely on Haydn's shoulders. In 1778, when the Kapellmeister's post was vacant, she wrote to her mother and brother in Paris:

> When things fare well or badly with you, think of us, who are obliged to live sadly here, separated from you both. I only wish that what Herr Cassel came to congratulate us about were true, that is, that you and Papa were appointed to Munich and were to draw 1600 Gulden. I am sure it is Haydn's wife and her vulgar set who concoct these lies, for they would like to see Papa leave Salzburg, so that her husband might be certain of the post of Kapellmeister.[37]

In fact, there is little reason to suppose that Leopold Mozart considered himself a candidate for the post: he had already written to Wolfgang that the archbishop intended to engage an Italian. The irony is that Leopold never advanced beyond the post of deputy Kapellmeister, nor Michael Haydn beyond the post of Konzertmeister and court organist. Although at times the Mozarts' letters have more than a touch of paranoia, an earlier example from 1743 shows that their troubles in Salzburg were not necessarily of their own making:

> At the archbishop's order, Eberlin's promotion to deputy Kapellmeister had already been drawn up and was considered by everyone to be a closed matter. Then his rival, Herr Lolli (Eberlin's inferior by far in musical experience), grasped a last means, threw himself at the prince's feet, and promised that, should he take over the office, he would serve without [additional] pay. And so the archbishop, who was determined to economize in every possible way, appointed him to the post, to [Eberlin's] detriment and much grumbling of almost the entire court and others.[38]

In this context it is worth noting that Cajetan Hagenauer wrote in his diary on the day of Leopold's death (17 May 1787) that '[he] had the misfortune of always being persecuted here'.[39]

*

The election of Hieronymus Colloredo as archbishop in 1772 marked a fundamental break with Salzburg's centuries-old political and cultural traditions. Music in particular suffered. The restrictions of church music and the closing of the university theatre deprived composers of their principal compositional venues. Dramatic music was put on a new footing with the establishment of a public playhouse, but local composers had little experience with opera and did not compose works for the new theatre. Although the archbishop encouraged the establishment of public subscription concerts, the local nobility was too small and insufficiently affluent to support orchestral and chamber music as it was supported in Vienna and elsewhere. Not surprisingly, many musicians left Salzburg, among them Leopold Mozart's and Michael Haydn's most important pupils of the 1780s and 1790s, Heinrich Marchand, Anton Diabelli and Sigismund Neukomm.

As for the younger Mozart, he had always stood outside Salzburg's important musical traditions, even as they were known during Schrattenbach's reign. It has already been noted that his early church music differed from the church music of other Salzburg composers of the 1760s and early 1770s and that he was the foremost composer of orchestral and chamber music in the archdiocese. His other chief compositional interest, opera, found outlet only in Italy and in Vienna and Munich. He wrote to his friend Joseph Bullinger in 1778:

> Salzburg is no place for my talent. In the first place, professional musicians there are not held in much consideration; and secondly, one hears nothing, there is no theatre, no opera; and even if they really wanted one, who is there to sing? For the last five or six years the Salzburg orchestra has always been rich in what is useless and superfluous, but very poor in what is necessary, and absolutely destitute of what is indispensable.[40]

Three years later he took up permanent residence in Vienna.

The secularization of the archdiocese and the social and political upheavals of the early nineteenth century put a virtual end to Salzburg's musical importance. The Peace of Luneville brought Salzburg under the rule of Archduke Ferdinand of Tuscany (1803–5) and with the Peace of Pressburg the court was abolished. By then, most professional musicians had left for the Vienna Hofkapelle or elsewhere. Salzburg remained a place of pilgrimage for people like Vincent and Mary Novello, but it was not until the 1840s that it regained some of its musical prestige, with the founding of the Dommusikverein and the Stiftung Mozarteum.

NOTES

[1] In general, see *Geschichte Salzburgs: Stadt und Land*, ed. H. Dopsch, i (Salzburg, 1981); H. Widmann, *Geschichte Salzburgs* (Gotha, 1914); and F. Martin, *Salzburgs Fürsten in der Barockzeit 1517–1812* (Salzburg, 1949).

[2] For the early history of music in Salzburg, see G. Croll, 'Die Musikpflege', in *Geschichte Salzburgs: Stadt und Land*, 1137–42; H. Spies, 'Beiträge zur Musikgeschichte Salzburgs im Spät-Mittelalter und zu Anfang der Renaissancezeit', *Mitteilungen der Gesellschaft für Salzburger Landeskunde*, lxxxi (1941), 41–96; and C. Schneider, *Geschichte der Musik in Salzburg* (Salzburg, 1935), 7–79.

[3] See H. Wagner, *Die Aufklärung im Erzstift Salzburg*, Salzburger Universitätsreden, no.26 (Salzburg and Munich, 1968).

[4] For further concerning the organization of the court music establishment in Salzburg see E. Hintermaier, 'Die Fürsterzbischofliche Musik in Salzburg zur Zeit Mozarts', *ÖMz*, xxvii (1972), 395–400, and E. Hintermaier, *Die Salzburger Hofkapelle von 1700 bis 1806: Organisation und Personal* (diss., U. of Salzburg, 1972).

[5] For contemporary descriptions of performing forces at Salzburg Cathedral see W. Rainer, 'Anton Cajetan Adlgasser: ein biographischer Beitrag zur Musikgeschichte Salzburgs um die Mitte des 18. Jahrhunderts', *Mitteilungen der Gesellschaft für Salzburger Landeskunde*, cv (1965), 210; [L. Mozart], 'Nachricht von dem gegenwärtigen Zustande der Musik Sr. Hochfürstlichen Gnaden des Erzbischoffs zu Salzburg im Jahr 1757', in F. W. Marpurg, *Historisch-kritische Beyträge zur Aufnahme der Musik* (Berlin, 1757), iii, 195.

[6] 'Nachricht', 183.

[7] See R. G. Pauly, 'Johann Ernst Eberlin's Motets for Lent', *JAMS*, xv (1962), 182–92; K. A. Rosenthal, 'Zur Stilistik der Salzburger Kirchenmusik von 1600–1730', *SMw*, xvii (1930), 77–94, and xix (1932), 3–32.

[8] During the 1770s, Leopold Mozart copied several of Eberlin's works, presumably as models to be studied by Wolfgang; see KAnh. A 1–5, 72–9 and 81–8.

[9] 'Nachricht', 188. For a list of Lipp's extant compositions, see T. Aigner, 'Wenn Mozart mit aller Kunst des Lipp fugierte', *Wiener Figaro*, xlv (1978), Dec, 3–10.

[10] M. H. Schmid, 'Mozart und die Salzburger Kirchenmusik', *MJb 1978–9*, 26–9; K. A. Rosenthal, 'Mozart's Sacramental Litanies and their Forerunners', *MQ*, xxvii (1941), 433–55.

[11] In general, see K. G. Gellerer, 'Mozarts Kirchenmusik und ihre liturgischen Voraussetzungen', *MJb 1978–9*, 22–6; M. H. Schmid, *Mozart und die Salzburger Tradition* (Tutzing, 1976); K. A. Rosenthal, 'Der Einfluss der Salzburger Kirchenmusik auf Mozarts kirchenmusikalische Kompositionen', *MJb 1971–2*, 173–81; W. Senn, 'Das wiederuafgefundene Autograph der Sakramentslitanei in D von Leopold Mozart', *MJb 1971–2*, 197–216; K. A. Rosenthal, 'The Salzburg Church Music of Mozart and his Predecessors', *MQ*, xviii (1932), 559–77; and W. Kurthen, 'Studien zu W. A. Mozarts kirchenmusikalischen Jugendwerken', *ZMw*, iii (1921), 194–222 and 337–74.

[12] W. Senn, 'Der Catalogus Musicalis des Salzburger Doms (1788)', *MJb 1971–2*, 182–96.

[13] H. Boberski, *Das Theater der Benediktiner an der alten Universität Salzburg (1617–1778)* (Vienna, 1978); A. Isnenghi, 'Das Theater an der alten Salzburger Universität', in *Universität Salzburg 1622–1962–1972: Festschrift* (Salzburg, 1972), 173–92; S. Dahms, M. C. Schneider and E. Hintermaier, 'Die Musikpflege an der Salzburger Universität im 17. und 18. Jahrhundert', in *Universität Salzburg . . . Festschrift*, 193–201; T. Antonicek, 'Das Salzburger Ordensdrama', *ÖMz*, xxv (1970), 377–84; R. Tenschert, 'Zur theatralischen Musikpflege der Salzburg Alma Benedictina', *Musikerziehung*, vi (1952–3), 373–6.

[14] Dahms and others, 'Die Musikpflege an der Salzburger Universität', 197.

[15] W. Rainer, 'Anton Cajetan Adlgasser: ein biographischer Beitrag zur Musikgeschichte Salzburgs um die Mitte des 18. Jahrhunderts', *Mitteilungen der Gesellschaft für Salzburger Landeskunde*, cv (1965), 220.

[16] 'I passed lately some days at Salsburg and had a great deal of Musick at the Archbishop's as he is a Dilettante & plays well on the Fiddle. He takes pains to reform his Band, which, like others, is too harsh', quoted in C. B. Oldman, 'Charles Burney and Louis De Visme', *MR*, xxvii (1966), 95–6.

[17] 'Ah, how much finer and better our orchestra might be, if only the Archbishop desired it. Probably the chief reason why it is not better is that there are far too many performances. I have no objection to the chamber music, but only to the concerts on a larger scale.'; letter of 3 Dec 1778, in *Mozart: Briefe und Aufzeichnungen*, ed. W. A. Bauer, O. E. Deutsch and J. H. Eibl (Kassel,

1962–75), i, 517, and *The Letters of Mozart and his Family*, trans. and ed. E. Anderson (London, 1938, 3/1985), 638.

[18] C. F. D. Schubart, *Ideen zur Ästhetik der Tonkunst*, ed. L. Schubart (Vienna, 1806), 146.

[19] E. Hintermaier, 'Die Familie Mozart und Maria Plain', *ÖMz*, xxix (1974), 350–56. Concerning the practice of music at other institutions in the Salzburg region, see T. Aigner, 'Der letzte geistliche Landesfürst Salzburgs, Hieronymus Graf von Colloredo, und das Stift Nonnberg', *MJb 1980–83*, 278–83; E. Hintermaier, 'Zur Musikpflege in der Wallfahrtsbasilika Maria Plain im 18. Jahrhundert', *Studien und Mitteilungen zur Geschichte des Benediktinerordens*, new ser., lxxxv (1974), 228–39; H. Federhofer, 'Zur Musikpflege im Benediktinerstift Michaelbeuren (Salzburg)', in *Festschrift Karl Gustav Fellerer zum sechzigsten Geburtstag am 7. Juli 1962* (Regensburg, 1962), 106–27.

[20] In general, see *St Peter in Salzburg (3. Landesausstellung 15. Mai–26. Oktober 1982): Schätze europäischer Kunst und Kultur* (Salzburg, 1982).

[21] E. Hintermaier, 'Bürgerliche Musikkultur des 18. Jahrhunderts am Beispiel der Stadt Salzburg', in *Städtische Kultur in der Barockzeit*, ed. W. Rausch (Linz, 1982), 151–7.

[22] *Mozart: Briefe und Aufzeichnungen*, ii, 383; not in *Mozart Letters*, ed. Anderson.

[23] See Chapter V above, pp.134ff.

[24] See R. Angermüller, 'Haydns "Der Zerstreute" in Salzburg (1776)', *Haydn-Studien*, iv (1978), 85–93.

[25] In general, see E. Hintermaier, 'Mozart und das Theater am Salzburger fürsterzbischöflichen Hof', *MJb 1978–9*, 144–8; S. Dahms, 'Das musikalische Repertoire des Salzburger Fürsterzbischöflichen Hoftheaters (1775–1803)', *ÖMz*, xxxi (1976), 340–55; E. Hintermaier, 'Das Fürsterzbischöfliche Hoftheater zu Salzburg (1775–1803)', *ÖMz*, xxx (1975), 351–63; A. Kutscher, *Vom Salzburger Barocktheater zu den Salzburger Festspielen* (Düsseldorf, 1939).

[26] For Hübner, see H. Ruby, 'Lorenz Hübner (1751–1807): Leben und Werk als Publizist, Topograph und Historiker in Salzburg', *Österreich in Geschichte und Literatur*, x (1966), 345–56.

[27] F. Spaur, *Nachrichten über das Erzstift Salzburg nach der Säkularisation* (Passau, 1805), i, 155–6.

[28] *Mozart: Briefe und Aufzeichnungen*, i, 532–3; *Mozart Letters*, ed. Anderson (3/1985), 265–6.

[29] See Martin, *Salzburgs Fürsten in der Barockzeit*, 229.

[30] R. G. Pauly, 'The Reforms of Church Music under Joseph II', *MQ*, xliii (1957), 381.

[31] [G. Schinn and F. Otter], *Biographische Skizze von Michael Haydn* (Salzburg, 1808), 38.

[32] Letter of 17 Sept 1778, in *Mozart: Briefe und Aufzeichnungen*, ii, 372–3; *Mozart Letters*, ed. Anderson (1938), ii, 809–10.

[33] *Mozart: Briefe und Aufzeichnungen*, ii, 338–9; *Mozart Letters*, ed. Anderson (3/1985), 526–7.

[34] Letter of 9 March 1786, in *Mozart: Briefe und Aufzeichnungen*, iii, 512–13; not in *Mozart Letters*, ed. Anderson.

[35] O. E. Deutsch, *Mozart: a Documentary Biography* (London, 2/1966), 182.

[36] 'Nachricht', 186.

[37] Letter of 23 Oct 1778, in *Mozart: Briefe und Aufzeichnungen*, ii, 79–80; *Mozart Letters*, ed. Anderson (1938), ii, 492.

[38] Based on a German translation after the Latin original in D. Pellegrini-Rainer and W. Rainer, 'Giuseppe Lolli (1701–1778): ein biographischer Beitrag zur Musikgeschichte Salzburgs', *Mitteilungen der Gesellschaft für Salzburger Landeskunde*, cvi (1966), 285.

[39] Quoted in Deutsch, *Mozart*, 293.

[40] Letter of 7 Aug 1778, in *Mozart: Briefe und Aufzeichnungen*, ii, 439; *Mozart Letters*, ed. Anderson (3/1985), 594.

BIBLIOGRAPHICAL NOTE

History and politics

English-language literature on Salzburg is virtually non-existent. The best survey of Salzburg's political history, from the Renaissance to the secularization of the archdiocese, is F. Martin's *Salzburgs Fürsten in der Barockzeit 1517–1812* (Salzburg, 1949); a briefer survey, stretching back to the twelfth century, is H. Wagner's 'Salzburgs Geschichte im Überblick', *Österreich in Geschichte und Literatur*, vii (1963), 204–16. For extensive coverage of all aspects of Salzburg's social, political and cultural history, the multi-volume *Geschichte Salzburgs: Stadt und Land*, ed. H. Dopsch (Salzburg, 1981–) is excellent.

Individual institutions in Salzburg have an extensive literature. For the university, see in particular *Universität Salzburg 1662–1962–1972: Festschrift* (Salzburg, 1972); for the cathedral, *Festschrift 1200 Jahre Dom zu Salzburg*, ed. H. Spatzenegger (Salzburg, 1975); and for St Peter's, *St. Peter in Salzburg (3. Landesausstellung 15. Mai–26. Oktober 1982): Schätze europäischer Kunst und Kultur* (Salzburg, 1982). Other articles of interest are published regularly in the *Mitteilungen der Gesellschaft für Salzburger Landeskunde* (*MGSLK*) and in the *Jahresschrift des Salzburger Museum Carolino Augusteum.*

Music

The only available survey of the history of music in Salzburg, now out of date, is C. Schneider's *Geschichte der Musik in Salzburg* (Salzburg, 1935), though some more recent books and articles deal with specific musical and theatrical institutions, including H. Boberski's *Das Theater an der alten Universität Salzburg (1617–1778)* (Vienna, 1978) and S. Dahms's 'Das musikalische Repertoire des Salzburger Fürsterzbischöflichen Hoftheaters (1775–1803)', *ÖMz*, xxxi (1976), 340–55. The organization and personnel of the Salzburg court music is thoroughly described in E. Hintermaier's dissertation *Die Salzburger Hofkapelle von 1700 bis 1806: Organisation und Personal* (Salzburg U., 1972). Other important sources of information about music and musicians include R. Angermüller, 'Musiker der Erzabtei St. Peter, Salzburg, von 1586 bis 1922', *Mitteilungen der Internationalen Stiftung Mozarteum*, xxxi (1983), 61–102; J. Gassner, *Die Musikaliensammlung im Salzburger Museum Carolino Augusteum* (Salzburg, 1962); and M. H. Schmid, *Die Musikaliensammlung der Erzabtei St. Peter in Salzburg: Katalog I: Leopold und Wolfgang Amadeus Mozart, Joseph und Michael Haydn*, Schriftenreihe der Internationalen Stiftung Mozarteum, iii–iv (Salzburg, 1970).

Without question, the most interesting accounts of music in Salzburg from 1755 to 1787 – incomplete and biassed as they may be – can be found in the Mozart family correspondence. A complete edition of the German-language originals is available in *Mozart: Briefe und Aufzeichnungen*, edited by W. A. Bauer and O. E. Deutsch, with an extensive commentary by J. H. Eibl (Kassel, 1962–75). English translations of many of the letters appear in *The Letters of Mozart and his Family*, ed. E. Anderson (London, 1938, rev. 2/1966, rev. 3/1985). For the best straightforward biography of Mozart, see S. Sadie's *The New Grove Mozart* (London and New York, 1982). Some aspects of the relationship between the church music of Mozart and his contemporaries are discussed in K. A. Rosenthal, 'The Salzburg Church Music of Mozart and his Predecessors', *MQ*, xviii (1932), 559–77, and M. H. Schmid, *Mozart und die Salzburger Tradition* (Tutzing, 1976). An extensive bibliography by R. Angermüller and O. Schneider of writings about Mozart to 1970 is in *MJb 1975*, and supplements appear regularly.

Despite the interest focussed on Salzburg by Mozart, his contemporaries have been studied less than might be expected. The most important biography of Michael Haydn remains H. Jancik's *Michael Haydn: ein vergessener Meister* (Vienna, 1952). Other useful works on Salzburg composers and their music include R. G. Pauly, 'Johann Ernst Eberlin's Motets for Lent', *JAMS*, xv (1962), 182–92; K. A. Rosenthal, 'Zur Stilistik der Salzburger Kirchenmusik von 1600–1730', *SMw*, xvii (1930), 77–94, and xix (1932), 3–32; M. Cuvay, 'Beiträge zur Lebensgeschichte des Salzburger Hofkapellmeister Johann Ernst Eberlin', *MGSLK*, xcv (1955), 179–88; W. Rainer, 'Anton Cajetan Adlgasser: ein biographischer Beitrag zur Musikgeschichte Salzburgs um die Mitte des 18. Jahrhunderts', *MGSLK*, cv (1965), 205–37; and W. Rainer and D. Pellegrini-Rainer, 'Giuseppe Lolli (1701–1778): ein biographischer Beitrag zur Musikgeschichte Salzburgs', *MGSLK*, cvi (1966), 281–91.

Chapter VII

The Bohemian Lands

CHRISTOPHER HOGWOOD and JAN SMACZNY

In autumn 1787, while preparing the first performance of *Don Giovanni*, Mozart and the impresario Bondini were alarmed to find that the Archduchess Maria Theresa was due to visit Prague and would attend the première of the opera planned for 14 October. According to the composer's own account to von Jacquin,[1] not only would the performance have been under-prepared, but the subject matter was unlikely to find favour with the royal visitor. The situation was saved by a royal command to the effect that if the new opera was not ready, *Le nozze di Figaro* would serve. The archduchess was honeymooning in Prague with her new husband, Prince Anton of Saxony, and left a few days later. The anecdote serves less to illuminate an uncomfortable, if slightly risible, episode in the composer's career than as an illustration of the status of Prague in the Austrian empire. For the aristocracy of Vienna, who were to a large extent the raison d'être for large-scale musical performance in the Bohemian capital, Prague was less a second home than a place to stay on the way to further destinations, or a refuge for holidaying.

For the late eighteenth-century virtuoso, Prague was one stop on a route as likely to take in Pressburg (now Bratislava) and Dresden as the Bohemian capital. Most significantly, for Czech composers in the second half of the eighteenth century, Prague was usually the start of a journey to the other musical centres of Europe. Charles Burney's happy description of Bohemia as the 'Conservatoire of Europe' was based as much on his encounter with Czech musicians in nearly every important court and capital he visited as on his observations of domestic music-making. Yet it would be wrong to paint a picture of Prague and Bohemia simply as a training-ground for talents who found their true *métier* outside their native land. The abundant supply of musicians for the excellent and extensive educational institutions which were such an outstanding feature of eighteenth-century Bohemia requires explanation. Far from being a musical ghost town, Prague had a fully developed cultural life, and music for theatre, church and home flourished along with an exceptional proficiency in basic musical education.

If the Czechs did not produce a composer of the first rank, musicians of Bohemian birth or ancestry were responsible for some of the most interesting developments in the music of the late eighteenth century. As will be discussed in Chapter IX, Georg (Jiří Antonín) Benda (1722–95) was in large part responsible for the development of melodrama. Taking a lead from Rousseau's *scène lyrique*, *Pygmalion* (1770), he produced works which were a considerable advance on their model and much admired at the time as revealed by the comments of Mozart, among others, and by the numerous parodies of *Ariadne auf Naxos* and *Medea* (both 1775), in particular, which spread to Vienna in the 1790s. The symphonic school of Mannheim would be unthinkable without the initial impetus of Johann Stamitz (1717–57) and the second generation of Carl Stamitz (1745–1801), Anton Fils (*c*1730–60) and Franz Xaver Richter (1709–89); the history of musical thought would be much the poorer without the definitions of sonata form and the penetrating speculation of Antonín Rejcha (1770–1836).[2]

Significantly, these achievements needed the soil of a foreign country to flourish. For Benda, it was the stimulus of Abel Seyler's theatre group which led to his development of melodrama; for the Stamitzes, it was the superb orchestral resources of Mannheim that permitted the forging of a distinctive style; for Rejcha, it was the experimental environment of post-revolutionary Paris which provided the background for his own philosophical and musical development. While Bohemia could furnish the human material for some of the most characterful advances of the Classical era, the musical establishments of a country with an aristocratic population which was absent for much of the year were inadequate to provide the stimulus and financial reward for indigenous talent.

The social and economic circumstances which produced the vigorous national revival of the later nineteenth century in Bohemia and Moravia were inconceivable in an age when the most significant historical events were bound up almost entirely with the fate of the Austrian monarchy. The process of cultural, linguistic and religious colonization which followed the Battle of the White Mountain in 1620 supplanted a flourishing artistic heritage, based to a large extent on self-determination by the Bohemian Estates, religious freedom and the Czech language. The Land Ordinance of 1627 vested all legislative power in the Habsburg emperor, Ferdinand II, and his successors, a state of affairs which persisted throughout the eighteenth century. In many senses it was a penal document, placing the blame for the events leading to the Battle of the White Mountain firmly on the shoulders of the disloyal Bohemian nobility and people. It also removed religious tolerance. This led directly to the expulsion of the nobility who did not profess Roman Catholicism, followed by any member of the common populace who wished to remain Protestant. By the time of the Treaty of Westphalia in 1648, Bohemia had lost nearly 80 per cent of its native aristocracy and over 30,000 families. Even without the determined efforts of the Jesuits to stamp out religious and cultural heterodoxy, the sense of national identity had received a crushing blow.

Within two generations of 1620 the Czech language had become largely the province of the lower classes. The 1627 Ordinance had given German equal status with Czech, and in official documents, both languages co-existed until the Bohemian Court Chancery was abolished and the administration centralized in Vienna in 1749. However, as a literary language Czech lost ground steadily throughout the seventeenth century. The language was virtually unknown among the upper classes until the turn of the eighteenth century. It did, however, remain the language of the musicians educated in the village schools: as a ten-year-old chorister, Franz (František) Benda (1709–86) recalled that on arriving in Dresden in 1720, 'I found some of my future colleagues playing ball. As I could not speak German, I addressed them in Czech'.[3] Some 50 years later, Burney, in his account of Bohemia, noted that, 'It was with much difficulty that I acquired information from the Bohemian musicians, as even the German language is of little use in that kingdom, throughout which the Sclavonian dialect is generally used'.[4] Two generations later still, Carl Maria von Weber attempted to learn Czech during his tenure as musical director of the Estates Theatre (Ständetheater) in Prague (1813–17), the better to communicate with the musicians in the theatre orchestra.

Settings of the language in the eighteenth century are by no means the rule. The prevalence among these of Christmas carols (*koledy*), folksongs and, in the latter half of the century, market songs (the equivalent of the English broadside ballad) on popular and frequently lurid themes, suggests that they circulated among the common populace. The relatively few art-music settings of Czech indicate that it had more the status of a curiosity than a language with any real currency among the upper classes. A much-quoted example is an opera by František Antonín Míča (1694–1744), *L'origine di Jaromeriz in Moravia* (1730), whose libretto comprises texts in Italian, Czech and German by different authors. The vernacular settings in the opera (Act 2) suggest little attempt to alter the conventions of Neapolitan style to suit the requirements of Czech stress and quantity.

In an effort to create greater strength and uniformity in the Czech crown lands, both Maria Theresa and Joseph II attempted to Germanize the peasantry. German became compulsory in elementary schools under Maria Theresa (1774), and Joseph II's abolition of the Czech language in the gymnasia (1780) was followed by the requirement that pupils had to know German to secure entry (1788). From 1784 all lectures at the University of Prague had to be in German, apart from those in theology and law which continued to be in Latin. These apparently draconian measures were ameliorated by the easing of regulations for entry into the priesthood. Thus many parish priests towards the end of the eighteenth century were Czech speakers and did much to foster a love for the native language. Joseph's reform of the educational system, with the help of Gerhard and his better-known son Gottfried van Swieten, produced an educated class of Czech with a more than antiquarian interest in the vernacular.

One of the main initiatives of Joseph's reform was the dissolution of the Jesuit order in the Austrian Empire in 1775 and the replacement of an old-fashioned curriculum with one based on the study of natural sciences, general and national history, as well as the classics. The Jesuits were the principal instrument of Austrian cultural domination in the seventeenth and early eighteenth centuries, but by the 1750s their influence was widely regarded as reactionary and deleterious to the unity of Austria. Nevertheless, their pervasive presence is evident in generations of educated Czechs and in the Baroque architecture so typical of Bohemia and Moravia. Nearly every major town in Bohemia had a Jesuit church and seminary, dominating the cultural development of the community as it dominated the skyline. In Prague the evidence of the Jesuit foundations is to be found everywhere. Franz Benda recorded his education at their hands, and the enormous domed church of St Nicholas in the Lesser Town (Malá strana) dominates the centre of this loveliest part of Prague. The architect, Christoph Dientzenhofer, completed the nave in 1711 but the rest of the church was finished by his son Kilian in 1753. Nearly twenty years later, Burney marvelled at the beauty of the church and its furnishings; the organ, he said, was:

> divided into two parts, placed one on each side of the gallery; and the keys, with a *positif*, or small choir organ, are in the middle, but placed so low, as to leave the west window clear: instead of wood, the frame-work, pillars, base, and ornaments of this instrument, in front, are of white marble; the organ and church seem quite new. I never saw a more rich or noble front to an organ than this; it was constructed by one of the Jesuits [Thomas Schwarz, 1695–1754], and it is well-toned; but has a very heavy touch.

The eighteenth century was not particularly tranquil for Bohemians, given the conflict with Prussia in the reign of Maria Theresa and the French wars towards the end of the century after the relative stability of Joseph II's reign. The former resulted in the loss of Silesia from the Czech crown lands by the treaties of Breslau (1742) and

Dresden (1745). In 1742 Prague was occupied by Bavarian and French soldiery, and came again under threat in 1757 from the artillery of Frederick the Great, an event commemorated, if not immortalized, in *The Battle of Prague* (*c*1788) by Kocžwara (*c*1750–91).

Burney's social observations also encompassed the indignity of serfdom, still widely practised in central Europe in the eighteenth century, 'as, in many parts of Bohemia and Saxony, the Gothic power over vassals still subsists, these people have seldom any ambition to excel in music, as they have no opportunities of mending their condition by it'. The burden of serfdom had indeed been heavy during the eighteenth century, although by the 1770s, when Burney was writing, Maria Theresa had taken measures to limit the requirements made by landlords. For the Rejcha family the release from their status as serfs by Count Prokop Černín in 1764 was a decisive opportunity:[5] Simon, the father of the composer Antonín Rejcha, became a piper in the Old Town in Prague and his brother, Josef (1752–95), was able to pursue a successful career as a cellist, composer and conductor. Two edicts of 1781 in the reign of Joseph II reintroduced religious toleration and effectively abolished serfdom. This relaxation of previously stringent rules did much to release talented Czech peasants from crippling labour requirements. The possibility of improvement under the previous, severe regime was slight, and many musicians of humble birth chose the path of flight rather than servitude, as Burney pointed out: 'now and then, indeed, a man of genius among them, becomes an admirable musician, whether he will or no; but, when that happens, he generally runs away, and settles in some other country, where he can enjoy the fruit of his talents'.

Burney also touched upon the major cause for the emigration of many of Bohemia's finest musicians, which had been taking place throughout the eighteenth century: 'their first nobility are attached to the court of Vienna, and seldom reside in their own capital'. Musical employment available to those who remained to serve the needs of the wealthy was seasonal, and conditions of performance were probably less than inspiring: 'The nobility were now, for the most part, out of town; but in winter, they are said to have great concerts frequently at their hotels, and palaces, chiefly performed by their own domestics and vassals, who have learned music at country schools'. The replacing of native nobility with a more pliant, new aristocracy in the seventeenth century was the prelude to a gradual gravitation of the more important families to Vienna. The coronation of Charles VI in 1723, celebrated with much pomp in the Czech capital and including visits by Fux, Tartini, Gottlieb Muffat, Sylvius Weiss, Jan Dismas Zelenka, François Francoeur, Quantz and Francesco Conti, effectively marked the end of a resident nobility in Prague.

After Prague, the natural paths for composers and performers of promise led south and east to Vienna, or north to the German-speaking towns of Silesia. This phenomenon would not be exceptional had Czech musicians confined their perambulations to the Austrian Empire and Germany, but in the eighteenth century they can be found as far east as Moscow and Kiev, and as far west as Dublin. The settlements of the Moravian Church in Georgia, and later Pennsylvania, in the early eighteenth century brought the effects of Czech musical training to the New World.

By far the largest concentration of Czech composers was in Vienna. Between the early eighteenth century and the death of Jírovec (Adalbert Gyrowetz, 1763–1850), 27 Czech composers either visited or made their home in the Austrian capital, including Jelínek (Josef Gelinek, 1758–1825), Leopold Kozeluch (1747–1818), František Kramář (Franz Krommer, 1759–1831), Jan Křtitel Vaňhal (Johann Baptist Vanhal, 1739–1813), Jan Václav Voříšek (Johann Hugo Worzischek, 1791–1825) and Antonín and Pavel Vranický (Anton and Paul Wranitzky, 1761–1820, 1756–1808). Berlin, Dresden, Mannheim, London, Paris and Warsaw[6] all had a respectable number of Czech composers even without including the large number of Bohemian orchestral musicians. While religious intolerance, the deprivation consequent upon Prussian and French occupation and the oppressive system of serfdom undoubtedly played their part in this diaspora, the principal criterion seems to have been the availability of opportunities in other musical centres. In a society where dynastic considerations counted for so much, the process of movement away from the Bohemian heartland was often effected by family connections. A senior member of the family would establish a bulwark in an important musical centre and quite often other relations would follow. After a career as a chorister in which he followed a fairly well-worn path to Dresden, Franz Benda eventually became a member of the musical establishment of Frederick the Great, following him to Potsdam on his accession in 1740. Franz's brother Johann Georg (1713–52) was also a violinist in Frederick's orchestra and later other members of the family were brought to the court, as the composer related:

> When after the death of Charles VI [in 1740], war broke out and His Majesty found himself in the neighbourhood of my native town, he sent to my parents and asked to see my brothers . . . My youngest brother presented himself to His Majesty, who immediately decided to engage him, even without having heard him play. I was informed about it by letter and also that he would be sent to me and I was supposed to give him violin instructions. In my answer I pointed out that this was such a good occasion to have my parents sent too, who always expressed great longing to be near me; thus I begged His Majesty for my whole family. The decision was immediately made.

The move of the Bendas may have been one of the largest musical migrations by a single family, but, in essence, their case was not exceptional. Associations with a court or, as was the case with Franz Benda, a specific prince led to further moves. Depending on the attitude of the prince to music, a composer might find numerous opportunities for travel and study. After some eight years in Prussia with his brother and the rest of his family, Georg Benda (1722–95) became Kapellmeister to Duke Frederick III of Saxe-Gotha. This enlightened prince gave Benda the opportunity of travelling in Italy (1765) where he had the chance to meet such composers as Hasse and imbibe the musical style of Galuppi, Traetta, Piccinni, Paisiello and Gluck. The early careers of Antonín Rejcha and Georg Benda followed similar patterns. After the death of his father, Antonín went to live with his uncle, the cellist and composer Josef Rejcha, who was principal cellist in the orchestra of Count Kraft Ernst von Oettingen-Wallerstein at Harburg in Swabia. In 1785, Josef Rejcha was appointed initially to the post of Konzertmeister in the orchestra of the court of Maximilian Friedrich, the new Elector of Cologne, at Bonn. He then became instrumental director and began to assemble an orchestra in which his nephew Antonín was both violinist and flautist. After the flight of the elector's court in the face of the invading Napoleonic army in 1794, Antonín Rejcha became a freelance musician, in accordance with the times and in common with Beethoven, his colleague from Bonn.

Emigration has been a major focus of attention in assessing the significance of Bohemia in the eighteenth century, but the Czechs had a fair measure of musical immigrants. Bohemia was not exceptional in the Austrian Empire in having a number of small country seats and churches in rural towns which offered opportunities for appointment. While Haydn's stays at Count Karl Morzin's estate at Lukavec were temporary, since the orchestra only functioned there during the summer months, other composers made their home in Bohemia. One such was Mauritius Vogt (1669–1730). Born in Bavaria, he studied for the priesthood in Bohemia and later studied music in Italy and Germany. Although a monk, he was also musical director at the home of Countess Marie Gabriela Lažanská at Manětín, and later took charge of the pilgrimage church at Mariánská Týnice, where he died. Among the visitors to Prague who found a certain degree of fame and fortune in the first half of the eighteenth century was Giovanni Marco Rutini (1723–97) whose first opera, *Semiramide*, was given by the impresario Giovanni Battista Locatelli (1713–after 1790) at the city theatre in Prague in 1753. He also worked as a conductor in Prague, performing works by Galuppi and Fischietti, and produced there his first three sets of harpsichord sonatas.

If the 'first nobility' was often absent from Prague, there were enough enlightened aristocrats of the second rank to sustain a flourishing musical life in the capital and in their Bohemian estates. Among the most active were the Questenbergs. Count Adam von Questenberg (1678–1752), a fine lutenist, and his wife, Maria Charlotte, who played the harpsichord, kept a substantial musical establishment at their castle in Jaroměřice where F.A. Míča was Kapellmeister.

Few of the lesser nobility surpassed the musical interests of Count Franz Anton Šporck (1662–1738), who travelled widely in Europe and had broad cultural affinities. His three palaces in Prague and his country seats at Kuks and Lysa housed much fine art, including paintings by Petr Brandl and sculpture by Braun. His musical interests focussed on the horn and its music, and opera. He seems to have been in contact with J. S. Bach who sent him the Sanctus of the B minor Mass in 1735 and quoted a favourite theme of Šporck's (*Brandeiser Jägerlied*) in the 'Aria col corne de chasse' (to the words 'Es nehme zenntausend Dukaten') in the *Peasant Cantata*. More important for Czech musical life, Šporck attracted a considerable amount of opera to his private theatres. He built the first of these at one of his palaces in Prague in 1701. Between 1718 and 1720, Antonio Lotti and his musicians from Dresden produced operas there. In 1724 Šporck employed the singer and impresario Antonio Denzio and his musical director Antonio Bioni (1698–after 1739) to perform Italian opera at Kuks and later that year at his palaces in Prague. Between 1724 and 1737 a wide repertory of Venetian and Neapolitan opera was performed in the various Šporck establishments, including works by Albinoni, Bioni, Leo, Lotti and Vivaldi.

Šporck's interest in the hunting-horn and the use of the horn in orchestral and chamber music also had an important effect on the music of Bohemia. He encountered the French *cor de chasse* about 1680 at Versailles during his travels. It is likely that he brought examples back with him and later had copies made. His servants were taught to play the instruments and Šporck commissioned the publication of French hunting airs set to German words (1701 and 1708). As well as introducing the horn into Bohemia, Šporck seems to have cultivated ensembles of horns and wind instruments in chapel services, a precursor of the Bohemian predilection for wind ensembles and Harmoniemusik.[7] An author of theological tracts, Šporck was also responsible for the publication of a large collection of Bohemian hymns, both tunes and texts, made by the Czech priest Jan Josef Božan (1644–1716) entitled *The Nightingale of Paradise on the Tree of Life* (Hradec Králove, 1719).[8]

If the mantle of Šporck fell on the shoulders of any successor, it was Franz Anton Nostitz (also Nostitz-Rhienek, 1725–94). Apart from a musical establishment, including a substantial orchestra and library,

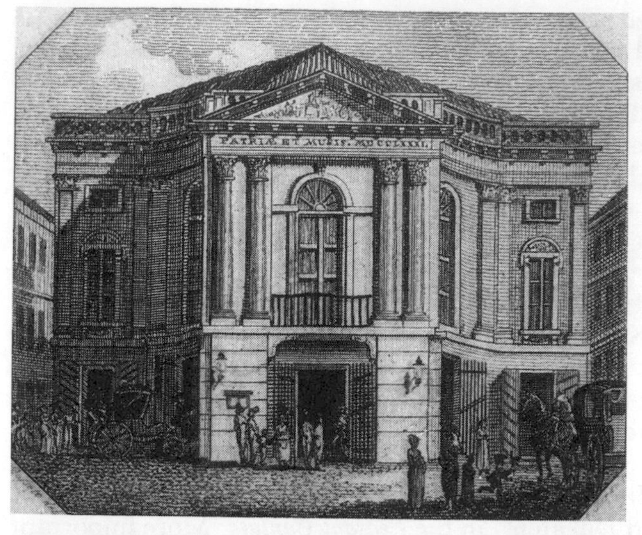

44. The Nostitz Theatre, Prague, built 1781–83: title-page engraving from the Prague 'Theater-Almanack' (1801)

Nostitz commissioned the architect Anton Haffenecker to design a large theatre. This was built between 1781 and 1783 at the count's expense and became the most important theatre for opera in Prague. Taking the place of the smaller municipal Kotce Theatre, it saw the first Prague performances of *Le nozze di Figaro* and the premières of *Don Giovanni* and *La clemenza di Tito* (figs.44 and 46).

The absence of greater nobility for much of the year may have caused Prague to sparkle less than Vienna, but the aristocrats who remained were nevertheless the source of important local musical developments and in the case of Šporck and Nostitz ones on which most of the Austrian Empire could look with gratitude. As is often the case with major provincial cities, the desire to be seen not to fall too far behind the capital could lead to considerable efforts at cultural betterment. Mozart, with commissions for *Don Giovanni* and *La clemenza di Tito* and an ever attentive and discriminating audience among the Czechs, was one who had cause to thank the city's musical population and institutions, as Leopold Mozart noted: '*Le nozze de Figaro* was performed there with such success that the orchestra and a company of distinguished connoisseurs and lovers of music sent him letters inviting him to Prague and also a poem which was composed in his honour' (12 January 1787).

EDUCATION

The astonishing abundance of musical excellence among the Czech peoples of Bohemia was a fact Burney often encountered: 'I had frequently been told, that the Bohemians were the most musical people of Germany, or, perhaps, of all Europe; and an eminent German composer, now in London, had declared to me, that if they enjoyed the same advantages as the Italians, they would excel them'. Whatever the inherent abilities of the Czechs, the prevalence of musical education among the common people, whether destined for a career in music or not, was an important factor. In the town of Czaslau (Čáslav), Burney recorded the following account:

> I went into the school, which was full of little children of both sexes, from six to ten or eleven years old, who were reading, writing, playing on violins, hautbois, bassoons, and other instruments. The organist had in a small room of his house four clavichords, with little boys practising on them all.

This was by no means exceptional, as Burney observed earlier in his account of Bohemian music: 'I found out at length, that, not only in every large town, but in all villages, where there is a reading and writing school, children of both sexes are taught music'. This flourishing tradition of rural musical education is corroborated in Franz Benda's autobiography. Born in the village of Staré Benátky, northeast of Prague, he went to school in the market town of Nové Benátky, where, 'I learned how to read, to write and to sing and thus laid the first musical foundation with the help of the skilled schoolmaster'.

While Prague could offer the benefits of an advanced musical training in the three major Jesuit foundations, the fundamental education at a primary level seems to have been carried out largely in the provinces. The overwhelming majority of Bohemian composers in the eighteenth century were born outside the capital. František Xaver Brixi (1732–71) and Antonín Rejcha were exceptional in being born in Prague. The role of the village schoolmaster was vital in producing this broad base and accounts of the numerous cantors in the eighteenth century suggest a high level of musical accomplishment with a broad range of instrumental skills to their credit. František Šebesta, who taught in Velvary from 1738, gave tuition in the violin, viola, cello, trumpet and hunting-horn and could sing tenor and bass as well as possessing skill in arithmetic.[9] The musical expertise of the Bohemian cantor did not stop at performance: a rich literature of compositions remains from the eighteenth and the nineteenth centuries.

Jiří Ignác Linka (also Linek, 1725–91), cantor in the small town of Bakov (slightly further into the mountains than Nové Benátky), if more prolific than most of his contemporaries, was not atypical. The son of a town cantor, Linka composed some 40 masses, numerous requiems, motets, pastorellas, concertos, instrumental and organ music. His early musical education follows a comparable path to that of his fellow pupil Georg Benda. After an early introduction to music in the locality, both studied at the Piarist high school in Kosmonosy. While Benda went on to the Jesuit college in Jičín in 1739, Linka stayed closer to home, studying in Mladá Boleslav before finally going to Prague. In 1742 Georg Benda and the remaining members of his family joined his brothers in Germany, thus rejecting the well-worn path to Prague. The excellence of the musical training in rural areas was not only a vital factor in providing Prague with a steady flow of talent but, as Burney noted, it supplied a reservoir of musically literate servants:

> It has been said by travellers; that the Bohemian nobility keep musicians in their houses; but, in keeping servants, it is impossible to be otherwise, as all the children of the peasants and trades-people, in every town and village throughout the kingdom of Bohemia are taught music at the common reading schools, except in Prague, where, indeed it is no part of school-learning; the musicians being brought thither from the country.

This tradition was of sufficient strength to last throughout the eighteenth century and well into the nineteenth. For Antonín Dvořák in the 1840s and 1850s, the path to a musical education was not materially different from that followed by Benda and Linka.

OPERA

Notwithstanding the efforts of Šporck and Nostitz, the history of musical theatre in Bohemia is more a succession of notable moments than a continuous tradition of distinction. Before Šporck's increasingly varied operatic activities, opera in Bohemia was a distinctly sporadic entertainment. Between 1703 and 1705 the impresario Giovanni Francesco Sartorio gave performances of Bartolomeo Bernardi's opera *La Libussa* for the members of an Italian opera society in Prague of which he was director. The next major event involving opera was the coronation of Charles VI in 1723, for which Fux composed *Costanza e Fortezza* (fig.45). This *opera seria* was staged in the open air on the castle height with lavish set designs by the architect Giuseppe Galli-Bibiena (1696–1756). Another celebratory performance was mentioned by Franz Benda: 'The Jesuits also performed a kind of Latin comedy for the Bohemian nobility. Arias were interspersed. The music was composed by Zelenka, who was then church composer at the Dresden court'. This was the allegorical play, *Melodrama de Sancto Wenceslao* (1723) by J. D. Zelenka (1679–1745).

In the years following this spectacular efflorescence most of the notable activity took place in Count Šporck's theatres, including the performance of another opera on a Czech theme *Praga nascente da Libussa e Primislao* (1734), given with considerable success. The composer may have been Antonio Bioni, several of whose works had received their first performances in Šporck's theatres.

45. Arena of Prague castle during the performance of Fux's opera 'Costanza e Fortezza', given as part of the festivities celebrating the coronation of Charles VI as King of Bohemia in 1723: engraving by Birckart after Giuseppe Galli-Bibiena

It would be wrong, however, to suggest that Šporck's establishments were the only purveyors of opera in the first part of the century. In 1738 the municipal Kotce Theatre was opened in the Old Town in Prague. The operatic output of the theatre was dominated by a succession of Italian impresarios. Between 1748 and 1757 G. B. Locatelli hired the Kotce Theatre to mount entirely Italian operas, including works by the young Gluck who had studied in Prague. In 1750 Gluck directed performances of his opera *Ezio* during Carnival, and two years later *Issipile*. Other impresarios included Pietro Mongotti (*c*1702–59), Gaetano Molinari and, from 1764, Giuseppe Bustelli. Bustelli leased the Kotce Theatre until 1778. He inherited his musical director, Domenico Fischietti (1725–1810), from Molinari's company, opening on 4 October 1764 with *Vologeso, re de parti*, an *opera seria*. In later years, however, Bustelli showed a distinct predilection for *opera buffa*, performing works by Galuppi. He also presented works by Czech composers, although these were entirely in the contemporary Italian style, including *Gli uccellatori* (performed 1765)

46. Ball in the Nostitz Theatre to mark the coronation of Leopold II in September 1791: engraving by Kaspar Pluth

by Florian Gassmann (1729–74), Mysliveček's *Bellerofonte* (1768) and J. A. Kozeluch's *Alessandro nell'Indie* (1769).

The business of opera production was not solely the preserve of Italians. In 1753 the Austrian Joseph von Kurz (1717–84) sublet the Kotce Theatre from Locatelli and later Carl Wahr who gave performances of Singspiels from 1781 to 1783, including the first Prague performances of *Die Entführung aus dem Serail*. This première was the beginning of the rise of Mozart's popularity in Prague. František Xaver Němeček (Niemetschek, 1766–1849), who published the first biography of the composer in 1798, spoke about its reception in the following terms:

> I cannot speak from my own experience of the applause and the sensation which it aroused in Vienna – but I was witness of the enthusiasm which it caused among cognoscenti and amateurs alike when it was performed in Prague! It was as if all that we had previously heard and known had not been music![10]

The Czech passion for Mozart was important in shaping the major musical events of the remaining seventeen years of the century. In 1781 one of the most active of all Italian impresarios in central Europe, Pasquale Bondini (?1737–89), took over the musical direction of the theatre of Count Václav Joseph Thun. Shortly after the opening of Count Nostitz's theatre in 1783, Bondini took on a three-year lease running from Christmas 1784 to Christmas 1787. One year before the lease expired, Bondini had an enormous success with *Le nozze di Figaro* which led the following year to the commissioning of *Don Giovanni*, given in the Nostitz Theatre on 29 October 1787. For the coronation celebrations of Leopold II in 1791, Bondini's erstwhile partner and successor Domenico Guardasoni (1731–1806) commissioned *La clemenza di Tito* on behalf of the Bohemian Estates. He continued to be a dominant force in opera in Prague until his death, marshalling his resources in the cause of Italian opera against growing hostility to the style, and he even went to the length of having Italian works translated into Czech. In 1798 the Nostitz Theatre was sold to the Bohemian Estates after which it became the only place for the public performance of opera in Prague. Outside the capital there were a number of new theatres built in the second part of the eighteenth century, including the castle theatres at Český Krumlov, built by Prince Schwarzenberg between 1766 and 1767, and Litomyšl, built by Count Jiří Josef Valdstejn-Vartenberk between 1796 and 1797. Both still survive intact, with full scenery and machines at Krumlov.

While Italian opera occupied most of the attention of Prague audiences in the eighteenth century, there was still room for performances of Singspiel. The history of the Czech Singspiel in the eighteenth century is somewhat hazy. Most performances took place in what was known as the Patriotic Theatre (Vlastenské divadlo) which opened in 1789. Among the Singspiels performed there were the works of Ondřej František Holý (*c*1747–83), who worked in Bruniani's troupe in the Kotce Theatre, František Xaver Partsch (1760–1822), who worked under the direction of the German director and singer Franz Spengler at the Nostitz Theatre in the early 1790s, and Jan Tuček (*c*1743–83). Tuček's music for plays constitutes an important early stage in the rise of Czech opera in the vernacular. Although modest in scope, such works as *Opilý muž* ('The drunkard') were popular in Bohemia. Tomášek gave a picture of a performance of this and another work (presumably before 1790) at his home in Skuteč:

> One day my father, who was always passionate about music, brought home two Czech Singspiels. For production they were given to the collection of musical friends in the town who met every Sunday. The first Singspiel was called *Opilec* [*Opilý muž*] and the second *The Silesian Rebellion* . . . [*Selské povstání*]. Both were written to Czech words with music by Tuček.[11]

MUSIC IN CHURCH

The huge number of religious foundations in Prague fostered a distinctive school of church music in the eighteenth century. The religious orders in the city were not, of course, limited to the Jesuits, despite their predominant role. Important foundations included St Francis of the Order of the Cross, Our Lady Mary of the Strahov Premonstratensians (possessing one of the largest and loveliest of Prague's libraries), the Order of the Sacred Heart, St Martin and the Minorite chapel of St Ann. Jan Zach (1699–1773), later Kapellmeister to the Prince-Elector of Mainz, was organist for all of these, and for the Minorites at the church of St James in the Old Town, where Bohuslav Matěj Černohorský (1684–1742), František Tůma (1704–74) and Josef Ferdinand Norbert Seger (1716–82) played and studied. In addition, both the Cathedral of St Vitus and the Lobkowicz foundation of Our Lady of Loretto on the castle height had strong musical traditions with large libraries.

While Černohorský was undoubtedly a major figure, with numerous composers and performers claiming his tuition, his true stature is difficult to assess. Very little of the organ music published under his name is by him. The handful of choral works which are incontrovertibly authentic show a robust, contrapuntal style, softened by a fondness (quite general in central Europe) for Italianate coloratura. Establishing the credentials for the pupils of Černohorský is no easy matter. Josef Seger, organist of the Týn and Crusader's churches and, according to Burney 'the best player in this city', was, on the evidence of his pupil Václav Pichl (1741–1895), taught by Černohorský, and recently it has been shown that Tartini was also a pupil.

Judging from the organ works of those who might have been pupils of Černohorský, the fruits of his teaching seem to have been the imparting of a secure, if not particularly imaginative, contrapuntal technique. The preludes and fugues of Josef Seger show considerable harmonic ingenuity and a variety of figuration, but it is the work of Brixi that shows the greatest individuality. By all accounts, Brixi was one of the most brilliant musicians of his day in Prague. After what appears to have been a highly successful school career at the Piarist Gymnasium in Kosmonosy, he arrived in 1749 in Prague, where he acquired the post of organist in several churches including St Nicholas in the Lesser Town. At the age of 27 he became organist of St Vitus, thus securing the pre-eminent musical post of the capital. His early death from tuberculosis cut short one of the most promising careers of any Czech musician resident in Bohemia. His extreme musical facility – he composed over 500 pieces including 100 masses – led to a somewhat dilute musical style. His frequent incorporation of folk music, especially Christmas carols, into his church music reflects a trend which was common among Bohemian composers in the late seventeenth, eighteenth and early nineteenth centuries. While this tendency imparts the charm of the vernacular to his style, it does not conceal the fact that his music owes much to Neapolitan opera and the Italian-influenced work of Viennese contemporaries.

Another composer who showed similar musical affinities was Brixi's older contemporary, František Tůma. After 1741, through a series of appointments, Tůma lived mostly in Austria. Although more inclined towards stricter styles of counterpoint than towards Brixi's more robust musical language, Tůma's work none the less takes an approach fundamentally similar to Brixi's. In much the same mould, though of more cosmopolitan tendency, was František Habermann (1706–83) who travelled widely in Europe. Six of his masses, printed as *Philomela pia* (1747), were of sufficient interest to Handel for the latter to copy and incorporate passages into his oratorio *Jephtha*. An important local figure in the church music of Prague was Habermann's pupil Franz Joseph Oehlschlägel (1724–88), often known as Joannes Lohelius, the name he took after entering the holy orders of the Premonstratensians at the Strahov monastery in Prague. He was not only a competent composer, whose music shows strongly elements of early Classical style, but also a distinguished organ builder whose instrument at Strahov was used by Mozart to improvise on a theme by Brixi, according to an account by Norbert Ignaz Loehmann.[12]

If the history of church music in Prague and Bohemia in the eighteenth century tends to lack unity, that is largely because of its diversity. When certain musical institutions, such as the Cathedral of St Vitus, are examined a more consistent picture appears. The cathedral archives reveal a large collection of Italian music including works by Aldrovandini, Conti, Durante, Leonardo Leo, Lotti, Mancini, Alessandro Scarlatti, Vinci, Vivaldi and particularly Antonio Caldara. Both Fux and Hasse are well represented, as is the music of Czech musical emigrants such as Zelenka, Tůma and Mysliveček.[13]

Between the early 1690s and 1705 the choirmaster was Mikuláš František Xaver Wentzely (*c*1643–1722) who came to the cathedral from the Church of Our Lady of Loretto. It is interesting to note that the Archbishop of Prague recommended the study of Wentzely's publication *Flores verni* of 1699 (containing five masses, one requiem and a *Salve regina*) to all clerics of the archdiocese. His successor (also organist of the Loreta church), Kryštof Karel Gayer (?1668–1734), did much to raise standards of performance and to increase the size and scope of the cathedral's collection of music. He improved and modernized the old instrumental ensemble, removing the trombones and bassoon and later adding an oboe. Gayer's period in office coincided with an increase in funding for the cathedral and a consequent improvement in standards. The introduction of a Baroque altar, sepulchres, statues and ornamental furnishings was the final part of a process towards re-Catholization which had begun in the years following the Battle of the White Mountain.

Gayer was succeeded by two relatively undistinguished musicians, Johann Anton Görbig (?1684–1737) who served from 1734 until his death and Jan František Novák (*d* 1771) who was replaced in 1759 by F. X. Brixi. Towards the end of Novák's incumbency the Prussian bombardment of Prague had a serious effect on the castle and cathedral; musically the most serious depredation was the destruction of the large Renaissance organ. By the late 1750s the musical establishment of the cathedral had grown to a considerable size comprising nine lay clerks, nine ecclesiastical clerks (nine priests who could sing psalms), 32 permanent musicians including instrumentalists and six bonifantes. A younger man was needed to run such an organization and F. X. Brixi made the best of his advantages.

A principal task was replacing the organ. Costing some 13,400 florins, it was built by Antonín Gartner (Gärtner) of Tachov, and, with nearly 3000 speaking pipes, was the largest organ in Bohemia. Brixi was clearly a man of determination. Since the early eighteenth century and before, the use of trumpets had been (and still is) a popular part of ecclesiastical music-making in Bohemia. In 1754 Maria Theresa banned the use of trumpets and drums during fanfares, processionals and recessionals in church. Brixi took advantage of their continued use in concerted music by performing a repertory which included Caldara, Fux, Gluck, Graun, Handel, Hasse, Porpora and Rutini. Brixi left his large body of compositions to the Convent of St George (behind the cathedral on the castle height), but many of his works returned to the cathedral under the conductorship of his successor Anton Laube (1718–84). Between 1771 and 1784, Laube did much to improve the standard of singing in the cathedral, though his music, noted for its simplicity and extreme homophony, disappeared soon after his death.

The last sixteen years of the century and the first decade of the next were dominated by Leopold Kozeluch's elder brother Johann Antonín (1738–1814). His collection of music was very extensive and incorporated works by his predecessor. In contrast to Laube, Kozeluch was a fine contrapuntist and his music eschews Rococo ornament in favour of the more solid virtues of developing Classicism. At the turn of the century Kozeluch could call upon an instrumental ensemble comprising an organist, seven violins, two violas, two oboes and two clarinets (the post of cellist and bassoonist were still vacant) and a choir of three basses, three tenors and eight boy choristers. Kozeluch built upon the heritage of Brixi to leave a strong establishment and a substantial library including 439 works of his own for his successor, Augustin Vitásek (1770–1839).

Like opera in Prague, a local tradition of oratorio, sepolcri and religious plays with music flourished throughout the eighteenth century. As with Zelenka's *Melodrama de Sancto Wenceslao*, great occasions called for such works as much as for opera, and for the coronation of Maria Theresa as Queen of Bohemia in 1743, Sehling provided the music for a play, commissioned and sponsored once again by the Jesuits, on the subject of the constancy of Judith (*Firma in Deum fiducia ... in Judith ... exhibita*). He composed music for a number of other such works, as did F.A. Míča, F. X. Brixi, Habermann, Jacob, Oelschlägel and, later in the century, Johann Antonín Kozeluch, both of whose known Easter oratorios were to Italian rather than Latin texts. Unfortunately, too little of the music survives for one to assess the merits of the tradition.

Far more evidence is available pertaining to one of the few examples of a vernacular art form and one related to religious observance – the pastorella. If the use of the Czech language was something of a curiosity in opera and other art music, it was an integral part of this charming and characteristic vocal form. Although it appears to have originated in Slavonic-speaking countries, the pastorella is also to be found in Austria. Its main characteristics are a use of folksong (composers would have had access to a number of collections from the late seventeenth century and Božan's *Nightingale of Paradise* among others in the eighteenth) and a text based on the Christmas story. Although the earliest-known pastorella from the Czech lands is by Fux (*Pastores evangelizo vobis*, copied in 1725) the form was taken up by a wide variety of composers in both towns and cities. The accent of the pastorella is rural, with the use of drones, folk instruments and the simple fanfares of the *tuba pastoralis*, but there are examples from composers working predominantly in Prague, including Sehling and F. X. Brixi. Nevertheless, the principal exponent of the form was the village cantor, and examples of purely instrumental music as well as vocal settings abound. The instrumental *Pastorella a 3*[14] by Daniel Alois František Milčinský (1732–1808) is interesting for the breadth of its modulation, including a long drone section in B flat major as the central part of a fugue, based on the carol *Narodil se Kristus Pán*. Robust vocal settings were, however, more the norm and after the middle of the century the vogue for troping the Mass became widespread. A large literature of Christmas masses exists in which the text of the Ordinary is entirely supplanted by folk verse and dialogues. The best-known example, by Jakub Jan Ryba (1765–1815), is *Hej, mistře* of 1796. Abounding in folk references, drones, the fanfares of the *tuba pastoralis*, quotations ranging from folksong to Mozart, it is testament to the vigour of the single, clearly defined native tradition of Bohemia in the eighteenth century.

INSTRUMENTAL MUSIC

As with church music, the history of instrumental music in Bohemia may be traced as effectively through the musical establishments of the

47. Open air wind music at a feast of the Prague Civic Guard on Strelecky Island, Prague, in 1794: engraving

nobility and the collections of the amateur as through the works of the composers themselves. That the nobility who maintained groups of musicians were alive to musical changes can be seen from the large quantity of eighteenth-century copies of Haydn's music in private collections.[15]

Understandably, much attention has been given to the pioneering work of the Stamitzes in Mannheim, but it would be wrong to assume that the Czechs were without resident symphonists. It is no longer possible to sustain the claims, defended by several authorities, that F. A. Míča anticipated the Classicism of Haydn in a D major symphony reputed to have been written before 1744,[16] but a number of Czech composers produced symphonies and concertos in due measure. However the palm must go to the expatriates, in particular F. A. Rösler (Rosetti, ?1746–92), Franz Xaver Richter, if indeed he was of Czech origin, Jiří Čart (1708–88) and, of course, the Stamitzes. Even the delicate and imaginative symphonies of Rejcha were composed outside Bohemia for Parisian or Viennese audiences.

The case is similar with the solo and accompanied sonatas and piano miniatures. In general, the latter was best cultivated by Tomášek and Jan Václav Voříšek in the nineteenth century. The finest Czech exponent of the piano sonata and indeed one of the finest composers for the instrument of his day in Europe was Jan Ladislav Dussek (1760–1812), but again virtually all his works in the genre were composed outside Bohemia. Isolated examples of sonatas by F. X. Brixi and František Xaver Dušek (1731–99) do not suggest a strong or independent tradition of writing in Prague. The string quartet and quintet fared rather better, but there is nothing in the native repertory to rival the works of the émigrés Antonín Rejcha, Josef Mysliveček, F. X. Richter, least of all Franz Krommer, whose quartets and quintets were among the most widely published in Europe.

If the instrumental music composed by the residents of Bohemia did not often rise above the common run, one outstanding feature which rarely escapes comment about music-making in the Czech-speaking lands was the predilection for wind groups or Harmoniemusik. The practice of grouping wind instruments in pairs (two horns, two bassoons, two oboes and two clarinets or more rarely two english horns, particularly in Bohemia and Vienna towards the end of the eighteenth century) was well known throughout Europe and connects with the military tradition of regimental wind music. Divertimentos, serenades, Feldparthie and arrangements of operas formed a popular part of the musical background to balls and dinner parties in the homes of the nobility in the late eighteenth century and early nineteenth. Burney described his frequent encounters with groups of wind instruments in his European travels, though in Vienna he was quick to censure their poor tuning. Once across the border into Bohemia, Burney noted that 'the Bohemians are remarkably expert in the use of wind instruments, in general; but M. Seger says, the instrument upon which their performers are most excellent, on the Saxon side [of] the kingdom, is the hautbois; and on that of Moravia, the tube, or clarion'.

The Bohemian interest in pairings of wind instruments may go back as far as Count Šporck's introduction of a pair of *cor de chasse* already mentioned. Horns were certainly used in groups for hunting and ceremonial occasions, and the horn's combination with other wind instruments, in common with its introduction into the orchestra, was an inevitable development. The fact that these combinations had passed beyond the province of ceremonial and military Feldmusik by the middle of the century is clear from the establishment kept by Count Morzin at Lukavec, his estate near Plzeň (Pilsen). Here, as Kapellmeister between 1759 and 1761, Haydn wrote a number of divertimentos for the count's Harmonie which comprised a standard grouping of pairs of oboes, bassoons and horns. There is

48. Wind quintet (flute, oboe, bassoon and two horns): painting on glass by B. Egerman (c1810)

also a divertimento (HII:16) for the less usual grouping of two english horns, two bassoons, two horns and two violins.

Other wind groups were employed in the aristocratic seats of Bohemia and Prague, but none was quite so well provided for as that of the Schwarzenberg family in Český Krumlov. It has also one of the biggest collections of music from a Czech estate including a large amount of Harmoniemusik. The group which Prince Schwarzenberg founded in the mid-1770s was particularly strengthened by the Bohemian oboist Johann Went (1745–1801), who later went on to a career of distinction with the Viennese Hofkapelle, as first english horn player. Apparently, owing to a shortage of clarinettists in Bohemia, Schwarzenberg opted for an ensemble with two english horns. Went's transcriptions of Mozart operas, together with a large number of original compositions, are still in the castle library of Český Krumlov.

*

Isolated examples of works on aspects of musical theory and the history of music suggest a lively if sporadic interest in musical culture in Bohemia beyond composition and performance. The principal source of knowledge about native Czech composers before the nineteenth century is Jan Bohumír Dlabač's *Allgemeines historisches Künstler-Lexikon* of 1815 which was a pioneering attempt to outline the cultural history of his native Bohemia. Dlabač (1758–1820) had had material from the composer and writer Václav Pichl who as early as the 1770s had assembled a history of Czech musicians working in Italy. Němeček's *Leben des k k Kapellmeisters Wolfgang Gottlieb Mozart nach Originalquellen beschrieben* of 1798 (see p.200) was the first biographical study of Mozart and is still valuable as an indicator of Czech interest in the composer.

The major work of music theory in Bohemia in the eighteenth century, *Clavis ad thesaurum magnae artis musicae* by Tomáš Baltazar Janovka (1669–1741), published as early as 1701, set out to define a broad range of musical terms. Janovka began but did not finish a second treatise. In some senses his work was continued in Mauritius Vogt's posthumous publication *Conclave thesauri magnae artis musicae* (1719), but rather than defining terms it sets out to summarize the rules of harmony and the doctrine of the Affections as it applies to music. Vogt also included a section on organs and organ building.

By the turn of the eighteenth century Prague was a city of great musical enthusiasm and variety. It had taken a century for its citizens to accept their less than exalted position in the Austrian Empire but the compensations in terms of improved educational standards and a growing awareness of national identity were considerable. Their artistic life had also benefited from a steady growth in the number of musical establishments, an improvement in the standards of opera and church music and the development of an educated bourgeoisie. By the end of the century there were many orchestras of various sizes employed in the capital; the Nostitz Theatre had passed to the control of the Bohemian Estates and was mounting consistently good performances.

No-one better represents this period of musical well-being than the composer F. X. Dušek and his wife, the soprano Josefa Dušek (1754–1824). With the opportunities put before him by the patronage of Count Johann Karl Šporck he was educated at the Jesuit Gymnasium at Hradec Králové, thus following the lead of many of his Czech colleagues throughout the eighteenth century. In the more enlightened atmosphere of the late eighteenth century, however, he made a living as a teacher and pianist rather than by seeking employment as a court musician. He was also somewhat exceptional in settling in Prague, where he became an influential teacher and a performer of note. In his summer villa, Bertramka, in the hilly south-western outskirts of the capital, he entertained numerous musical friends, including Mozart. The connection with Mozart came from his wife, a native of Salzburg: the couple met the composer there in 1777 and were pleased to welcome him to Prague on several occasions in the 1780s.

Perhaps it is the relationship to Mozart of not just the Dušeks but all musical Czechs that reflects the characteristically cultured qualities of the Bohemians in the late eighteenth century. While the Austrians were happy to admit Mozart's greatness, his popularity in Vienna was never entirely secure. The Czechs, perhaps aided by a superior musical education and background, took instinctively to his works whenever they were offered. *Le nozze di Figaro* and *Don Giovanni* were near failures when first presented to the Viennese, but their enormous success in Prague gave the composer very considerable encouragement. Nothing better sums up the loss the Czechs felt at Mozart's death than the commemoration service mounted shortly after news of his demise had reached Prague. On 24 December the *Wiener Zeitung* published the following account:

> The Friends of Music in *Prague*, on the 14th inst. and in the Small Side parish church of St Nik[o]las, performed solemn obsequies for Wolfgang Gottlieb *Mozart*, Kapellmeister and Hofkomponist, who died here on the 5th. This ceremony had been arranged by the Prague Orchestra of the National Theatre, under the direction of Hr Joseph *Strohbach*, and all Prague's well-known musicians took part in it. On the appointed day the bells of the parish church were rung for half an hour; almost the entire city streamed thither, so that the Wälsche Platz could not hold the coaches, nor the church (which is, moreover, big enough to hold nearly 4000 people) the admirers of

> the dead artist. The Requiem was by Kapellmeister *Rössler* [Rosetti],[17] it was admirably performed by 120 of the leading musicians, first among whom was the well-loved singer Mad *Duscheck* . . .; solemn silence lay all about, and a thousand tears flowed in poignant memory of the artist who through his harmonies so often tuned all hearts to the liveliest feelings.[18]

Mozart's music continued to dominate the endeavours of Czech musicians over the next 40 years, his major champions being two influential residents of Prague, Václav Jan Tomášek and Jan August Vitásek. If the direct influence of Mozart's compositions waned after this, the popularity of his music continued throughout the nineteenth century. The Provisional Theatre in the 1860s and 1870s commemorated his death with performances of his operas, and the Czechs were the first to restore the recitatives and sextet finale to *Don Giovanni* in 1865, some 30 years before Vienna. Mozart's death cast a lengthy shadow for the Czechs and it was with a poignancy undiminished by the passage of some seventeen years that Franz Xaver Němeček recorded that the year which had given *La clemenza di Tito* to the Bohemians was also, 'destined to tear from us the pride of music'.[19]

NOTES

[1] All quotations from Mozart and his father are taken from *The Letters of Mozart and his Family*, trans. and ed. E. Anderson (London and New York, 3/1985).

[2] Except for composers who enjoyed an international reputation during their own lifetimes, we have preferred the local (i.e. Czech) orthography of proper names.

[3] All quotations from Franz Benda are taken from his *Autobiography* (1763), ed. in *Neue Berliner Musikzeitung*, x (1856); Eng. trans. in P. Nettl, *Forgotten Musicians* (New York, 1951), 204–45.

[4] All Burney quotations are from *The Present State of Music in Germany, the Netherlands, and United Provinces* (London, 1771), ed. P. A. Scholes as *Dr Burney's Musical Tours in Europe* (London, 1959).

[5] For further details see O. Šotolová, *Antonín Rejcha* (Prague, 1977), 6f.

[6] For further details see J. Racek, *Česká hudba od nejstarších dob do počátku 19. století* [Czech music from the earliest times to the beginning of the 19th century] (Prague, 1958), 327f.

[7] See H. Fitzpatrick, *The Horn and Horn-Playing and the Austro-Bohemian Tradition from 1680 to 1830* (London, 1970), 9–25.

[8] *Slaviček rajský na stromě života slávu tvorci svému prozpěvující.*

[9] See R. Fikrle, *Jan Ev. Ant. Koželuch* (Prague, 1946), 24.

[10] O. E. Deutsch, *Mozart: a Documentary Biography* (London, 2/1966), 505.

[11] *Vlastní Životopis V. J. Tomáška*, ed. Z. Němec (Prague, 1941), 17–18.

[12] Deutsch, *Mozart*, 518.

[13] For further details see J. Stefan, *Ecclesia metropolitana pragensis catalogus collectionis operum artis musicae*, Artis Musicae Antiquoris Catalogorum, iv/1 (1983).

[14] Published in *České vánoční pastorely*, ed. J. Berkovec, MAB, xxiii (1965).

[15] See H. C. Robbins Landon, *Supplement to the Symphonies of Joseph Haydn* (London, 1961).

[16] See Racek, *Česká hudba*, 143 and 153.

[17] Rosetti's Requiem in C minor was long thought lost but has survived in the archives of the Loreta church (no.569 in Pulkert's Catalogue, sign 194); it is scored for a large orchestra including a distinctly Mozartian wind grouping of bassoon, two basset-horns, two clarinets and two horns.

[18] Deutsch, *Mozart*, 427.

[19] ibid, 509.

BIBLIOGRAPHICAL NOTE

History and architecture

The most thorough consideration of Czech history in this period is R.R.J. Kerner's *Bohemia in the Eighteenth Century* (New York, 1932), and A.H. Hermann's *A History of the Czechs* (London, 1975) is a useful general survey of the nation's history. Brian Knox's two books, *The Architecture of Prague and Bohemia* and *Bohemia and Moravia: an Architectural Companion* (both London, 1962), provide an informative and engaging account of the rich architectural heritage of the country, and the plastic and graphic arts are covered by O. J. Blažíček's *Baroque Art in Bohemia* (Eng. trans., Prague, 1968).

Music

No comprehensive account of Czech music has yet appeared in English, and many reliable Czech sources are no longer in print. Individual articles in *Grove 6*, including 'Czechoslovakia' and 'Prague', provide the most recent assessment, together with the article 'Bohemia and Czechoslovakia' in the *New Oxford Companion to Music*, ed. D. Arnold (Oxford and New York, 1983). General studies of Czech eighteenth-century music include J. Němeček's *Nástin české hudby XVIII století* (Prague, 1955) and a portion of J. Racek's *Česká hudba od nejstarších dob do počátku 19. století* [Czech music from the earliest times to the beginning of the 19th century] (Prague, 1958). An indication of the high level of national research into the period is the increasing number of articles in Czech musicological publications such as *Hudební věda*, though this work is not available for the most part to the English reader.

More specific accounts of composers include R. Fikrle, *Jan Ev. Ant. Kozeluch* (Prague, 1946); M. Poštolka, *Leopold Koželuh* (Prague, 1964); and V. J. Sykora, *František Xaver Dušek* (Prague, 1958). E. K. Wolf's *The Symphonies of Johann Stamitz: a Study in the Formation of the Classic Style* (The Hague, 1981) is a comprehensive account of this composer's achievement and an analysis of his influence on the Mannheim style. H. Fitzpatrick's *The Horn and Horn-Playing and the Austro-Bohemian Tradition from 1680 to 1830* (London, 1970) provides a large amount of information concerning performing traditions in Bohemia in the period and H. C. Robbins Landon's *Supplement to the Symphonies of Joseph Haydn* (London, 1961) gives a limited but useful summary of archival material and monastic sources surviving from the eighteenth century. For an account of the repertory and development of Harmoniemusik see R. Hellyer's article, 'The Transcriptions for *Harmonie* of *Die Entführung aus dem Serail*', *PRMA*, cii (1975–6), 53.

For valuable historical insight and a lively account of music in Bohemia see C. Burney's *The Present State of Music in Germany, the Netherlands, and United Provinces* (London, 1771), edited by P.A. Scholes as *Dr Burney's Musical Tours in Europe* (London, 1959), and the autobiographies of Franz Benda, translated in P. Nettl's *Forgotten Musicians* (New York, 1951), and Tomášek (*Vlastní Životopis V. J. Tomáška*, ed. Z. Němec; Prague, 1941).

For iconographic reference the most valuable publication is T. Volek and S. Jareš, *Dějiny české hudby v obrazech* ('A history of Czech music in pictures') (Prague, 1977), in both Czech and English. In addition to these historical studies the series Musica Antiqua Bohemica (Prague, 1943–) and the more recent Musica Viva Historica (Prague, 1961–) provide a wide range of music, with editorial and historical commentary of variable reliability.

Chapter VIII

The Mannheim Court

EUGENE K. WOLF

> The musical Athens of the German-speaking world.
>
> The paradise of composers.
>
> That famous court whose rays, like those of the sun, illumine the whole of Germany, nay even the whole of Europe

These statements, by the eighteenth-century writer C. F. D. Schubart, the philosopher Friedrich Jacobi and the musician Leopold Mozart,[1] might well be thought to describe such famous centres as Vienna, Berlin or Dresden; but in fact they all refer to the electoral court-city of Mannheim in south-western Germany. For reasons that will become obvious in the course of this chapter, Mannheim never achieved the lasting renown of a city like Vienna. For a brief period, however, it represented a kind of musical Elysium unrivalled in many respects by larger and better-known centres.

The prominence of Mannheim in the eighteenth century owed much to politics. The ruling prince at Mannheim, known as the Elector Palatine, was one of the four original secular electors of the Holy Roman Empire and thus occupied an august position within the aristocratic hierarchy. Moreover, the Electoral Palatinate (*Kurpfalz*) or south-central Rhine region over which he reigned was important both for its size and its location. The capital of the Palatinate, Mannheim, was strategically situated at the confluence of the Rhine and Neckar rivers, controlling – and profiting from – several of the principal European trade and travel routes. At the same time, the proximity of Mannheim to France assured a continuing French influence at court, both politically and culturally.

While geo-political elements such as these gave Mannheim its wealth and power, its real renown derived from its position as one of the leading cultural centres of the Enlightenment. The foundation for this eminence was laid during the reign of Elector Carl Philipp, who ruled from 1716 until 1742. In Heidelberg, Carl Philipp's principal residence from 1718, the arch-Catholic elector found himself in constant dispute with the strong Protestant faction of the town. As a

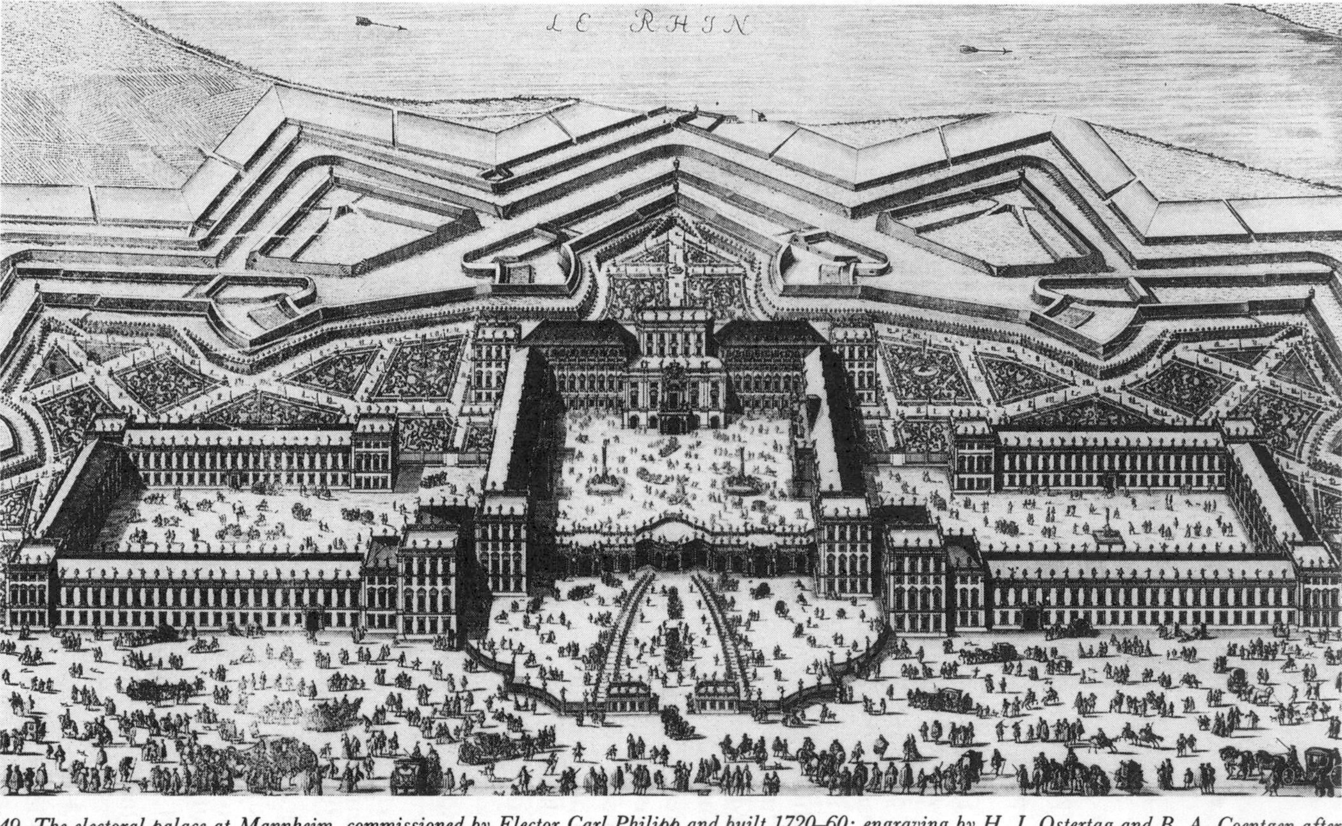

49. The electoral palace at Mannheim, commissioned by Elector Carl Philipp and built 1720–60: engraving by H. J. Ostertag and B. A. Coentgen after a drawing (1725) by the architect Jean Clemens de Froimont

result, he decided to transfer his court in 1720 from Heidelberg to Mannheim, then a town of minor importance in the marshes along the Rhine. There he began a lavish building programme, summoning many of the finest architects, sculptors, painters and craftsmen in Europe to his court. The major project was the huge electoral palace, the largest of the German Baroque (see fig.49). The first phase of construction was completed by 1737, at which point the elector was able to occupy the palace, and the second by early 1742, when the new opera house in the west wing, designed by the court architect Alessandro Galli-Bibiena, was dedicated (see fig.50).[2]

Carl Philipp possessed a strong interest in music, establishing a tradition that eventually gave Mannheim its most permanent claim to fame. His musical establishment, or Kapelle, was large for the time. During most of his reign it comprised about 50 musicians, some brought with him from his previous post in Innsbruck, some who had served his predecessor as Elector Palatine in Düsseldorf, and various new appointees, primarily singers from Italy. His most significant new acquisition was the Bohemian violin virtuoso Johann Stamitz (1717–57), who joined the court orchestra about 1741 and quickly rose to the rank of Konzertmeister.

Carl Philipp died on New Year's Eve 1742 at the age of 81, and was succeeded by his eighteen-year-old nephew Carl Theodor (1724–99). The wide difference in age between the two rulers provides one explanation for the personal contrast so evident between them. The older elector was the epitome of the Baroque absolutist, an intolerant military man who took Louis XIV as his ideal. By contrast, Carl Theodor was in most respects a typical Enlightenment ruler. Though a devout Catholic with powerful ties to the Jesuits, he promulgated – at least in his public pronouncements – a more tolerant approach to other religions. In addition, he was less repressive in the political sphere and fostered a number of modest economic and commercial reforms. His was not, however, the more thoroughgoing Enlightenment approach of Frederick the Great or, later, Joseph II, and few of his initiatives proved substantial or lasting. As Charles Burney wrote after visiting Mannheim in 1772, 'The expence and magnificence of the court of this little city are prodigious; the palaces and offices extend over almost half the town; and one half of the inhabitants, who are in office, prey on the other, who seem to be in the utmost indigence'.[3]

A more profound Enlightenment influence on Carl Theodor appears in his enthusiasm for science, philosophy and the arts. In the course of his reign he founded academies for the study of the fine arts (1757), the sciences (the Academia Theodoro-Palatina, 1763), physics and economics (1770) and German language and literature (1775). Similarly, his collections of engravings and drawings (established

1758), naturalia (1765) and especially antiquities (1767) were widely influential. He was also a friendly patron of philosophers and writers such as Voltaire, to whom he addressed his famous remark that the eighteenth century was like a siren or mermaid, whose beauty above concealed a repulsive fish-tail below. According to Schubart, who visited Mannheim in 1773, a statue of Voltaire stood outside the electoral library, 'as though he were a god presiding over all knowledge'.[4]

There can be little question, however, that of all Carl Theodor's interests, music ranked the highest; it was 'the chief and most constant of his electoral highness's amusements', according to Burney.[5] Like many other eighteenth-century rulers, he was a good performer on the flute. He also played the cello on occasion and was trained in theory and composition. The first few years of Carl Theodor's reign seem to have witnessed little musical activity, doubtless owing in part to his participation in the War of Austrian Succession (1740–48). But the season of 1747–8 marked the start of an extraordinary series of new opera and ballet productions that extended for 30 years – a time of unbroken peace in the Palatinate – and included important premières by the foremost composers of Europe.

At about the same date Carl Theodor began to increase the size and improve the quality of the Kapelle, which eventually came to number over 80 members. Appointments during this period brought many of the finest performers and composers in Europe to the Mannheim court, including the composer and bass singer Franz Xaver Richter, the flautist Johann Baptist Wendling and the oboist Alexander Lebrun (all *c*1747), the composer and Kapellmeister Ignaz Holzbauer (1753), the cellists Innocenz Danzi and Anton Fils (both 1754) and several notable Bohemian horn players. In addition, Carl Theodor carefully groomed the talented offspring of musicians already at court, often by financing an extended period of study in Italy for them. Such was the case, for example, for several outstanding singers as well as for the violinist Christian Cannabich (1731–98), who succeeded Johann Stamitz as Konzertmeister after the latter's death in 1757.

MUSIC IN THE LIFE OF THE COURT

For those accustomed to the modern tradition of the concert hall, in which music exists primarily as an aesthetic object, the pervasiveness and functional character of music at a large eighteenth-century Catholic court may be surprising. Court life was highly ordered, even ritualistic. Events at every level, from everyday occurrences such as meals to major celebrations spanning several days, were carried out – one is tempted to say choreographed – according to a set plan that remained unchanged for decades. This plan not only specified the order and content of each occasion; it also stipulated which members of the court were to participate – a clear reflection of the hierarchy of power on which any monarchy depends. At Mannheim, as at other large courts, the organization of court life was recorded in pocket-sized almanacs or 'calendars' issued annually, which contained a detailed listing of various events throughout the year as well as a roster of court personnel.[6]

Just as the palace at Mannheim provided the visual setting for this daily ritual, with its frescoes by Cosmas Damian Asam and its inner decoration by Nicole de Pigage, so music provided the aural setting. The ubiquity of music within the life of the court stands out clearly from the following statement by Cosimo Collini, Voltaire's secretary, who visited Mannheim with his master in 1753:

> The electoral court was at that time perhaps the most splendid in Germany. Fêtes followed upon fêtes, and the good taste developed thereby constantly gave them fresh charm. There were hunts, operas, French dramas, musical performances by the leading virtuosos of Europe. In short, the electoral residence [at Mannheim] offered the most pleasant sojourn imaginable for every person of fame and merit, who could always count on the most heartfelt and flattering reception there.[7]

Collini specifically mentioned the two most celebrated elements of musical life at Mannheim: opera and concert. In addition, both the hunts and the dramatic performances to which he referred had important musical components, the latter in the form of incidental music. To these categories we may add the following: music for the river excursions and water pageants popular at court, similar in function to music for the hunt; music for parades, processions and military exercises, featuring the elector's corps of twelve trumpeters and two drummers;[8] music for receptions, banquets and dinner (*Tafelmusik*); music for the many court balls; music for ballets and pantomimes, which normally appeared as intermezzos between the acts of operas or as afterpieces in the theatre; smaller vocal works such as pastorales, serenatas and secular cantatas, either staged or unstaged; and the many forms of sacred music. The most significant of these types will be discussed in greater detail below.

The cultural year at Mannheim was divided into three parts. Most important was the autumn and winter 'season', extending until Shrove Tuesday and encompassing the varied celebrations of Carnival. During a typical week virtually every evening was filled with a performance of one sort or another. Theatrical presentations occurred several times a week, usually on Sunday, Tuesday and Friday at 5.30. These included French comedies and tragedies or, after dismissal of the French troupe in 1770, works in German. A ballet or pantomime (a harlequinade mimed to music) often followed the principal work, which itself contained incidental music such as an overture and entr'actes. Dramatic performances generally took place in a theatre in the west wing of the palace, between the court chapel and the opera house. The second type of large evening event was opera, which occupied a position of special prominence at the electoral court. The opera season began with a gala performance in celebration of the elector's name day, 4 November, and thereafter operas were staged approximately twice weekly, normally beginning at four or five o'clock (six o'clock when the court was at the summer residence of Schwetzingen). After the theatre or opera would come *souper* and chamber music (known at Mannheim as *Kabinettsmusik*). The final principal type of evening performance was the 'academy' or concert, featuring the incomparable Mannheim orchestra. Academies were generally held twice weekly, typically on Wednesdays or Thursdays and Saturdays, at six o'clock in the Rittersaal (Knights' Hall) in the central tower of the palace (see fig.51 below). In addition to members of the court, the audiences for all these types of performance – drama, opera and academy – included guests of the elector, visitors to Mannheim and members of the Mannheim bourgeoisie.

The next major division of the year was Lent, during which all theatrical performance, including opera and ballet, was proscribed. Orchestral concerts still occurred, however, and it is likely that performances of smaller vocal works such as pastorales and serenatas, as well as instrumental chamber music of various kinds, helped to fill the gap. The third part of the cultural year was the summer and early autumn (until October), when the elector and his retinue occupied the nearby summer palace of Schwetzingen, the electress her palace at Oggersheim. During this period Schwetzingen, which boasted a lovely small opera house (still extant), an outdoor theatre in the form of a Greek temple and renowned gardens, resembled 'a magical island, where everything sounded and sang', according to Schubart.[9]

The height of pageantry at the Mannheim court came with the so-called galas or gala days, which were celebrations held in conjunction with major feast-days of the church year and the name days and birthdays of the elector and electress. The name days and birthdays of the Duke and Duchess of Zweibrücken, Carl Theodor's cousin and heir apparent, were also designated gala days, as were such occasional events as weddings and major state visits. The most important of these galas would last for several days and include various ceremonies, processions, church services, banquets, receptions and, in the evenings, balls, concerts, major dramatic presentations and operas. The name days of the elector and electress were often occasions for an important operatic première. When Mozart and his mother, Maria Anna, visited Mannheim in 1777–8, they arrived just in time for the name-day celebrations of the elector. In a letter to her husband, Mme Mozart provided an unusually detailed description of the various events:

> The gala days are now over. On the first day [Tuesday, 4 November 1777] there was a [church] service at eleven o'clock, during which cannons and rockets were fired off. . . . After that there was a splendid banquet and during the evening a magnificent reception. On the second day the grand German opera *Günther von Schwarzburg* [by the court Kapellmeister Ignaz Holzbauer] was performed . . . , [along with] a marvellously beautiful ballet. On the third day there was a grand academy at which Wolfgang played a concerto; then, before the final symphony, he improvised and gave them a sonata. He won extraordinary applause from the elector and electress and from all who heard him. On the fourth day there was a gala play, which we went to see with Monsieur and Madame Cannabich.[10]

The way in which pageantry, religion, might and music were woven together in court ritual could hardly be clearer than in the following description, taken from the court almanac for 1755, of a gala on the elector's name day. The stability of such rituals may be seen from the fact that the ceremony parallels almost exactly that described by Mozart's mother 22 years later.

> On the fourth [of November], the feast of St Charles Borromeo, there will be a large gala at court in honour of the high name day of his electoral highness, our most gracious ruler and lord, lord [*sic*]. On this high feast-day the entire nobility, ministers and cavaliers, as well as all [officials of the] law courts, will most graciously be allowed to appear in the electoral apartments to congratulate and kiss the hand [of the elector], after which at about eleven o'clock his electoral highness and the entire court will process between the electoral bodyguard and the Swiss Guard, arranged to the left and right of the palace corridor [*Schlossgesang*], to the High Mass [in the court chapel], wherein Communion will be celebrated and, after the Elevation, a *Te Deum laudamus* will be performed. During the Mass, at the *Gloria in excelsis*, again at the performance of the *Te Deum*, and finally at the last sign of the cross, cannons will be fired from the ramparts. Thereafter [there will be] an open banquet, served by the electoral chamberlains.
>
> That evening towards five o'clock an opera will be performed.[11]

While the almanac does not specifically mention music except in the case of the *Te Deum* and the opera, the Mass as a whole would have been performed by a full choir, soloists and orchestra (see below) Moreover, music would doubtless have graced the ceremonies in the elector's apartments, and the procession and firing of the cannons would have been accompanied by the trumpet and drum corps.

The passage just quoted, and especially the rather bizarre combination (as it may seem) of High Mass and cannon blasts, may serve as a reminder that the function of music at court was not merely to provide entertainment and aesthetic delight (important as these were), any more than the function of religion was merely to induce piety. These and other elements of court ritual served rather to symbolize, embellish and indeed enhance the power of the ruler. As has been noted in another context, 'Political symbols and rituals were not metaphors of power; they were the means and ends of power itself'.[12]

There were numerous ways in which ritual and music combined, consciously or unconsciously, to further political ends within a court environment. Most obviously, the magnificence and solemnity of a ritual like that described above would have been highly impressive, even awe-inspiring, to the noble participants, who felt privileged to be part of it, as well as to the court employees, visitors and townspeople who were encouraged to observe (and who could not in any event ignore the cannon shots). In this way the ritual, and the music which animated and controlled it, functioned in part as an instrument of power. In a less direct manner, the same is true of the explicitly musical sphere at court. For example, the magnificence of the elector's music brought him international fame, as when Burney wrote enthusiastically that at the opera he attended in Schwetzingen 'there was a greater number of attendants and figurers [figure-dancers] than ever I saw in the great opera, either of Paris or London; in the dance [i.e. the ballet] . . . there were upwards of a hundred persons on the stage at one time'.[13] Burney went on to call the Mannheim opera house 'one of the largest and most splendid theatres of Europe' and, like numerous visitors to Mannheim, to praise the orchestra in extravagant terms.[14] On the latter point, it is worth noting here that one of the things that distinguished Mannheim from other courts of the time was the emergence of the orchestra as a status symbol comparable to the opera.

In a similar fashion, the social and class distinctions inherent in events like the name-day celebration described above, with their highly exclusive character and carefully controlled rank-ordering of participants, helped to reinforce both the concept of monarchy and the power-structure at court. These elements are easily identified within court musical life. At the opera and theatre, for instance, the distribution of boxes was strictly determined by rank, position and influence, and the price of individual seats made the expense of attendance prohibitive for many.[15] Musical commissions and appointments at court were controlled by the elector, and the organization of the court musicians was strictly hierarchical, supervised by the Intendant, a nobleman who answered directly to the elector. Most court musicians were classed as skilled servants during this period, though Carl Theodor was well known for his friendly and respectful treatment of his musicians. At his court they enjoyed relatively high salaries, normally had tenure for life and received other benefits, including pensions upon retirement.

OPERA

Another way in which music can reflect and enhance princely power is through its subject matter or content and its style. This is most readily seen in the principal form of opera cultivated at Mannheim and courts throughout Europe: Italian *opera seria*. Its librettos, generally based on mythology and ancient history, deal with such traditional aristocratic themes and subjects as the conflict of love and duty, noble bearing in the face of a dire destiny, and the virtues of the clement ruler. In one sense, then, these operas are allegorical works with the same themes – and often the same stories and characters – as the large ceiling frescoes of Carl Theodor's palace and theatres. The allegories may be more specific in certain frescoes than they are in opera (the portrayal of the river Rhine and Carl Philipp's three granddaughters in C. D. Asam's frescoes for the monumental stairwell of the palace, for example), yet they are rarely ambiguous in either medium; indeed the heroic, elevated and dignified world of

50. Cross-section of the opera house in the west wing of the electoral palace, designed by Alessandro Galli-Bibiena and dedicated in 1742: drawing destroyed in World War II

both fresco and *opera seria* is a symbol of aristocratic ideals. It was partly for this reason that opera also figured significantly within formal court ritual. Before the opera, members of the court were expected to assemble in the electress's apartments in the west wing of the palace and then to process, again to fanfares of trumpets and drums, to their seats in the opera house. Only then could the overture begin.[16] In short, opera at Mannheim again demonstrates the interpenetration of artistic and socio-political elements so characteristic of court life.

Because there was no large theatre in Mannheim until 1742, the typical vocal works of the Carl Philipp era were not operas but serenatas, pastorales, cantatas and similar works, many of which were presented with costumes and staging. The great opera house at Mannheim (fig.50) was dedicated in January 1742 to celebrate the double wedding of the future elector Carl Theodor and the Duke of Bavaria to two of Carl Philipp's granddaughters. For that occasion the court Kapellmeister, Carlo Pietro Grua, wrote the opera *Meride* (also referred to as *Cambise*). The next opera known to have been presented at Mannheim was also by Grua, his setting of Pietro Metastasio's *La clemenza di Tito* for the birthday of the electress on 17 January 1748. The music for both these works is lost, but they almost certainly conformed to the Metastasian type common at the time: a prominent role given to the high voice (especially castrato), few choruses and ensembles and a generally invariant scene structure consisting of recitative (simple or accompanied) and da capo aria, followed by the singer's exit. The majority of the new *opere serie* produced at Mannheim during the next decade also fit this description, works by both Ignaz Holzbauer (1711–83), appointed Kapellmeister for the theatre in 1753, and illustrious outsiders like Baldassare Galuppi, Nicolò Jommelli and Johann Adolf Hasse.

During the 1750s, however, currents of change were already being felt in various European centres, antedating Gluck's well-known 'reforms' of the 1760s. Historians of opera commonly associate these changes with the courts of Stuttgart/Württemberg (where Jommelli succeeded Holzbauer as Kapellmeister in 1754) and Parma (where Tommaso Traetta was resident from 1758). Yet Mannheim also played a vital role. Mattia Verazi, court poet at Mannheim from 1756 and later Carl Theodor's private secretary, was Jommelli's favourite librettist and exerted a profound influence on him. Equally important, Carl Theodor commissioned five new operas between 1760 and 1774 on texts by Verazi, including works by Jommelli and Traetta as well as Johann Christian Bach.[17]

Verazi's librettos introduced numerous modifications to the traditional *opera seria* model, most of them reflecting the French influence prominent at Mannheim, Stuttgart and Parma. Spectacle became an important operatic ingredient, as alluded to by Burney in the passage quoted earlier; the large crowd scenes, ballets, choruses and scenic effects of French opera were perfectly suited to both the magnificent new theatre and to the cultural milieu of the Mannheim court. Typical spectacular scenes in Verazi include military processions (with horses and, in one case, elephants), storms, sacrificial rituals and battles. Verazi also increased the elements of suspense, horror and tragedy in his librettos, going so far in certain cases as to restore the original tragic endings of stories altered by Metastasio. From the musical standpoint, many of the changes evident in settings of Verazi's librettos prefigure those of Gluck: the grouping of recitatives, ariosos, ensembles, choruses and instrumental music into large scene-complexes; the extensive and dramatically flexible use of ensembles; the frequent replacement of the exit-aria convention with dramatically more viable alternatives; a reduction in the number of arias and the choice of more flexible forms; and, beginning in the early 1760s, integration of the overture with the first scene. Those familiar with Mozart's *Idomeneo*, commissioned by Carl Theodor and first performed in 1781 after the court moved to Munich, will realize that it conforms substantially to the Mannheim tradition of *opera seria* just described.[18]

Mannheim was also in the forefront of another momentous development: the establishment of serious opera in the German language. During the 1770s Carl Theodor showed an increasing interest in the German language and its literature, founding the Churfürstliche deutsche Gesellschaft (Electoral German Society) in 1775 and in the same year authorizing reconstruction of the former arsenal as a German theatre. By 1778 the latter had become the seat of an important new enterprise sponsored by the elector, a permanent German National Theatre under the direction of Wolfgang Heribert von Dalberg.

These developments left their mark upon music. In August 1775 the court opera gave two performances at Schwetzingen of the German opera *Alceste* (Weimar, 1773), with music by Anton Schweitzer and a libretto by Christoph Martin Wieland; these were followed by a production at Mannheim on 5 November as part of the elector's name-day celebrations. The success of this work led the elector to commission an original German opera, *Günther von Schwarzburg* (first performed at Mannheim, 1777), with music by Ignaz Holzbauer and a much-criticized libretto by the Mannheim poet Anton Klein. It was this opera that the Mozarts heard in conjunction with the name-day celebrations of November 1777. In place of the usual subject matter from ancient history or mythology, Klein chose his material from fourteenth-century German history. (In view of the comments made earlier about opera as aristocratic allegory, it is pertinent to note that two of the principal characters in *Günther* were ancestors of Carl Theodor: the Elector Palatine Rudolf and his daughter Anna.[19] Needless to say, both are treated sympathetically.) Holzbauer's music, praised by Mozart, hardly departs from the Mannheim *opera seria* style, but the work is none the less important as a further example of serious German opera outside the tradition of the comic Singspiel. Carl Theodor also commissioned a second original German opera, this time from Schweitzer and Wieland. The resulting work, *Rosemunde*, was to have been performed in January 1778, but the death of the Bavarian elector and Carl Theodor's sudden departure for Munich forced its cancellation. It was subsequently scheduled for production in Munich in November 1778 and at the Nationaltheater in Mannheim in 1780.

Comic opera at the electoral court, whether full-scale *opera buffa*, intermezzo or an occasional *opéra comique*, was particularly associated with the smaller Rococo opera house at Schwetzingen, completed in 1752. Numerous intermezzos have survived from the 1750s – a reflection, no doubt, of the prominence of this genre in the Querelle des Bouffons in Paris, witnessed by Johann Stamitz during the year he spent there in 1754–5. (Indeed, Stamitz was probably the prototype for the hero of Baron von Grimm's *Le petit prophète de Boehmischbroda* of 1753, one of the earliest contributions to the Querelle.) From 1769, with the production of Piccinni's *La buona figliuola* (based on Richardson's *Pamela*), even the name-day opera at the Mannheim theatre was frequently a full-length *opera buffa*.

SACRED MUSIC

Church music at Mannheim was generally performed in the court chapel, but after 1756 special celebrations often took place in the larger Jesuit church designed by Alessandro Galli-Bibiena and connected to the palace. At Mannheim, as at most Catholic courts, settings were normally for choir, orchestra and (often) vocal soloists. Mozart related that the performing forces for a major Mass service at Mannheim were quite large: 24 singers, an orchestra of nearly 50 and of course the organ.[20] Mozart praised the orchestra but severely criticized the singers and organists. Wieland, however, wrote in a letter of 1777 that he would 'rather lose several of my fingers than forgo Christmas Matins in the court church at Mannheim; that is for me a fête that surpasses all other fêtes and operas'.[21]

The sacred repertory at Mannheim consisted of masses as well as shorter works like the *Te Deum* mentioned in the almanac description above. A distinguishing characteristic of Mannheim Mass settings was omission of the Benedictus from the cycle; Mozart reported in 1777 that it was replaced with an organ solo.[22] The works of the Kapellmeister C. P. Grua, appointed during the reign of Carl Philipp, frequently employed a modified *stile antico*, with no vocal soloists and little independent writing for orchestra. During Carl Theodor's reign this conservative type quickly lost ground to the Italian *stylus mixtus*, which combines relatively homophonic music for chorus or soloists – often highly evocative of the opera house – with *stile antico* settings such as the conventional closing fugues of the Gloria and Credo. The most important representative of this trend was Holzbauer; his many masses contributed significantly to the development of a truly symphonic mass type, familiar to us from the late masses of Mozart and Haydn. Also important was the more conservative Franz Xaver Richter (1709–89), as well as many other Mannheimers known today primarily for their instrumental music, most notably Johann Stamitz and Anton Fils.

The last few years of the court's stay in Mannheim saw the ascendancy of the composer and theorist Abbé Georg Joseph Vogler (1749–1814), who became vice-Kapellmeister and spiritual adviser to Carl Theodor in 1775. Vogler opposed the Italian style represented by Mozart and J. C. Bach, and both Wolfgang and Leopold Mozart blamed him for Wolfgang's failure to secure a position at Mannheim during his sojourn there in 1777–8. In addition, Mozart would have threatened Vogler's position as the leading keyboard player at court.

The oratorio was also prominent at Mannheim. Oratorios were generally performed during Lent, when the opera house was closed, so it is hardly coincidental that they are essentially operatic in both their musical and dramatic style. Indeed, the traditional Good Friday performance of a new oratorio at Mannheim was almost as much of an occasion as the première of an opera. Held at nine o'clock in the evening in the court chapel, this performance represented the culmination of elaborate Holy Week rituals involving the entire court. For instance, the description of the ceremonies for Maundy Thursday requires one and a half pages in the court almanac; the rites include a complex evocation of the Last Supper in the Knights' Hall, during which the elector, taking the part of Christ, washes the feet of twelve old men in the presence of the court.

ORCHESTRAL MUSIC: THE SYMPHONY AT MANNHEIM

Mannheim is best known, of course, for orchestral music, especially the symphony. (The concerto at Mannheim was less extensively cultivated and was rather conservative in style.) As we have seen, the concerts or 'academies' featuring the Mannheim orchestra formed one of the three basic types of evening entertainment in the Mannheim social calendar, together with opera and theatre. Visitors to Mannheim were admitted free, as standees, and this description by an anonymous traveller in 1785 provides an idea of the special character of these concerts:

51. The Rittersaal (Knights' Hall) in the central tower of the Mannheim electoral palace

This evening there was an academy, or what I would call a concert at court. I therefore left my statues [in the antiquities collection] and hastened to the Knights' Hall, where the concert was to be given [see fig.51]. The court was to assemble after six o'clock, and I therefore had time to look around. The hall is large and oval-shaped, with four large windows and a fresco on the ceiling . . . Life-size paintings of former electors adorn the walls, . . . and there are two niches with life-size statues of the present elector and electress. The room is lit with eleven chandeliers, and the floor is inlaid.[23]

Around and to the right of the windows card tables had been set up, and to the left was the space for the orchestra, raised somewhat off the floor and encircled with a railing.[24] After six o'clock the court entered, the elector and electress, the dowager electress of Bavaria, and the ladies-in-waiting and cavaliers. Then the music began, and at the same time everyone began to play cards. The two electresses . . . and von Dalberg [Intendant of the Nationaltheater] played at the first table . . . [In the section for standees] there was such a crush of people that I at first gave up any hope of getting through to see their highnesses up close. But then I decided, together with some priests, to endure and also mete out some elbows in the ribs – and in this manner we finally came close to the two princely tables.

And what did I see there? Well, Carl Theodor in a new robe, just

> as in former times.[25] But the electresses . . . were seated so that I was unable to see their faces. The palatine electress had her back to me, while the Bavarian was placed behind her so that I could see nothing but her powdered red hair . . . So I waited patiently, and in the meantime listened to the orchestra, which through the magical tones of one Mamselle Schäfer reconciled me to my fate.[26] The elector stood up every now and then and went from table to table with a cheerful laugh. Finally, the two electresses had the honour to satisfy my curiosity by getting up from their seats and going up to the orchestra, giving me the opportunity to examine their faces to my heart's content . . .
>
> I stayed in the Knights' Hall until the last candle was extinguished, then went home – as satisfied, perhaps, as certain other visitors that night who indulged in a pastime I denied myself – stealing the place-cards from the tables as souvenirs.[27]

This gossipy description vividly depicts the essentially social character of an electoral academy. These were not concerts in the modern sense, but relatively informal occasions at which music was only one of the attractions, together with cards, conversation, seeing and being seen and (as we learn from other sources) tea. It would be going too far to consider the music presented on these occasions as merely background music, but it is clear that it did not enjoy the concentrated attention of music performed at a public concert – especially one to which the audience had paid admission. This is fundamental to a proper understanding of courtly music of the mid-eighteenth century. It is a commonplace that the music of this period lacks both the complexity and depth of expression found in, say, the late symphonies of Haydn or Mozart; but the occasional nature of these works – their partly social function – makes it apparent that stylistic complexity and expressive profundity would not only not have been expected in them, but might well have been deemed inappropriate. Conversely, the kinds of dynamic and orchestral effects for which Mannheim was famous, to be discussed below, were admirably suited to the type of audience, occasion and listening described by our anonymous visitor.

There are no surviving listings of the music played at electoral academies, but several extant programmes for closely related events allow us to reconstruct a typical evening's fare.[28] First would come a symphony, then several concertos alternating freely with vocal works such as arias and duets. The finale was usually a symphony or a larger vocal ensemble such as a trio or quartet. Maria Anna Mozart's description of the academy at which her son played, quoted earlier as part of her account of the gala days, conforms to this summary as regards the performance of a concerto and final symphony, but on that occasion Mozart, as a visiting virtuoso, also played a sonata and improvised.

Under Stamitz, and later Cannabich, the elector assembled an orchestra that Leopold Mozart – no mean judge of such things – called 'undeniably the best in Europe'.[29] In a famous passage Burney praised the disciplined playing of the orchestra and also referred to the large number of fine soloists and composers it contained:

> I cannot quit this article, without doing justice to the orchestra of his electoral highness, so deservedly famous throughout Europe. I found it to be indeed all that its fame had made me expect: power will naturally arise from a great number of hands; but the judicious use of this power, on all occasions, must be the consequence of good discipline; indeed there are more solo players, and good composers in this, than perhaps in any other orchestra in Europe; it is an army of generals, equally fit to plan a battle, as to fight it.[30]

Burney, who heard the orchestra in the theatre and not at an academy, went on to say that the only fault he noted was that the wind played out of tune; he added that this was so all over Europe. Schubart, characteristically, was more rhapsodic when he wrote about the Mannheim orchestra, which he heard one year after Burney, in 1773:

> No orchestra in the world has ever surpassed that of Mannheim in performance. Its *forte* is like thunder, its crescendo a cataract, its diminuendo a crystal stream burbling into the distance, its *piano* a breath of spring. The wind are all used just as they should be: they lift and support, or fill out and animate, the storm of the strings.[31]

The Mannheim orchestra was quite large for the time, rivalling a typical large theatre orchestra. In 1756, for example, when Stamitz was Konzertmeister, the almanac lists twenty violinists, four viola players, four cellists, two bass players, two flautists, two oboists, two bassoonists and four horn players (only two of which would be used at once); to this would be added two trumpeters and a timpanist when required; a harpsichord player would also have been present. By the 1770s the number of bass players and bassoonists had increased to four each (though only two bassoonists would probably have played at an ordinary academy), and clarinets appeared at least as early as 1758. Otherwise the totals are surprisingly consistent, remaining so until the departure of the court for Munich in 1778.[32] The Mannheim orchestra was thus about twice the size of Haydn's at Eszterháza.

The composers who wrote for this orchestra, often referred to as members of a unified Mannheim 'school', actually belong to two rather disparate generations. The first consists principally of Johann Stamitz, Holzbauer and Richter, who were born between 1709 (Richter) and 1717 (Stamitz). All three left a substantial number of instrumental works, especially symphonies, but only Stamitz devoted himself primarily to instrumental music; Holzbauer was mainly responsible for vocal music (both operatic and sacred), while Richter's interests lay in music for the church (he left Mannheim to become Kapellmeister of Strasbourg Cathedral in 1769). Richter's symphonies are far more conservative in style than those of Stamitz, retaining many Baroque textural and melodic traits, while Holzbauer's continue to reflect his early training in Austro-Bohemia and northern Italy.

The most important composers of the second generation were all born in the early 1730s Cannabich, the second Konzertmeister Carl Joseph Toeschi (1731–88) and the cellist Anton Fils (1733–60; also Filtz, Filz). This group is considerably more homogeneous than the former, for all its members were string virtuosos and composers who had been students of Stamitz. Hence, if there is a valid concept of a Mannheim school of composers (that is, not merely musicians resident at Mannheim or violin students of Stamitz), it would refer to the second generation and their teacher, Stamitz. To this group one might add Stamitz's sons Carl (1745–1801) and Anton (1750 – between 1796 and 1809), though both left Mannheim for Paris in 1770.

The precise importance of Mannheim in the history of eighteenth-century music has long been a subject of controversy. In 1902 the German musicologist Hugo Riemann announced that he had discovered in the Mannheim school the chief creators of the Classical style of Haydn and Mozart. His attention principally fell on the symphonies of Johann Stamitz, whom he proclaimed (in bold-face type) to be 'the long-sought forerunner of Joseph Haydn'.[33] Riemann's rather nationalistic claims were quickly challenged by musicologists in Austria, Italy and France, who in their turn tended to exaggerate the importance of their own country's contributions. The more objective present-day view assigns the leading position in the development of the early Classical style to Italy, and particularly to Italian opera. Similarly, it sees Mannheim as 'the residence of a talented, up-to-date, though not pre-eminent group of composers'.[34] The following discussion summarizes the principal characteristics of the Mannheim symphony, the genre for which Mannheim has always been most famous, and assesses the role of each within the history of the symphony.

Perhaps the clearest contribution of Mannheim to the history of the symphony is the addition of a minuet and trio to the original three-movement, fast–slow–fast plan, as the third movement of four. This expansion not only adds to the breadth and stylistic variety of the symphony, most notably by introducing the courtly dance style, but also orders the last three movements in a kind of large-scale accelerando: slow movement, then moderate-tempo dance movement, then *prestissimo* finale. This sequence was established as normal for the symphony by Johann Stamitz; the great majority of his symphonies after about 1745 make use of it, and these works circulated all over Europe. (This was at least a decade before Haydn's earliest symphonies.) It is striking that the composers of the second generation at Mannheim, probably reflecting French preferences, mostly returned in the course of the 1760s to the original three-movement form.

Mannheim is perhaps best known for its exploitation of musical dynamics, as seen in Schubart's comments about the Mannheim orchestra. Burney cited the same characteristics, explicitly distinguishing between the graded dynamics common in the Mannheim symphony and the older type of terraced dynamics:

> It was [at Mannheim] that the *Crescendo* and *Diminuendo* had birth; and [there] the *Piano*, which was before chiefly used as an echo, with which it was generally synonimous, as well as the *Forte*, were found to be musical *colours* which had their *shades*, as much as red or blue in painting.[35]

Dynamic effects of the type cited by Schubart and Burney are indeed common in the Mannheim symphony, forming one of the major components of its style. For example, many Mannheim symphonies begin with *forte* hammerstroke chords or a dramatic unison theme, followed by an abrupt drop to *piano* for the start of one of the crescendo passages for which the Mannheim orchestra was famous. Other works incorporate *forte–piano* contrast directly within the opening theme.

While dynamic effects of this sort are unquestionably central to the Mannheim style, recent research has shown that they were not, as Burney claimed, invented by the Mannheimers. Instead, they were taken over from the Italian opera overture, where they were also ubiquitous.[36] This is most obvious in the case of extended crescendo passages, known in German as *Walzen* or 'rollers' (*Walze* is often mistranslated as 'steamroller' – a rather blatant anachronism). Whereas Burney called Mannheim the birthplace of the crescendo, other authors of the time gave credit to Nicolò Jommelli. For example, Johann Friedrich Reichardt focussed on that composer when he described the remarkable effect of the new device, citing Mannheim only as a personal illustration: 'They say that when Jommelli first introduced [the crescendo] in Rome, the listeners gradually rose from their seats during the crescendo, and only at the diminuendo noted that it had taken their breaths away. I myself have experienced this phenomenon at Mannheim'.[37] Significantly, this passage is often cited as a description of a Mannheim crescendo, without any mention of Jommelli. Schubart told essentially the same story (though with Naples as the setting), this time specifically referring to Jommelli as the inventor (*Erfinder*) of the crescendo passage.[38]

In fact, crescendo passages comparable in every way to those of Mannheim appeared considerably earlier in Italian opera overtures, not merely those of Jommelli but also of many of his contemporaries.[39] Italian operas of the Jommelli generation were staple repertory at the Mannheim court theatre from the late 1740s and were thus well known to all the composers there. In addition, Christian Cannabich was a student of Jommelli in the early 1750s. What Stamitz and his colleagues did was not to create the crescendo passage from whole cloth, but rather to transfer it (and a host of related traits) from the overture to the symphony, from the opera house to the 'academy'.

Riemann also claimed that Mannheim composers invented a group of melodic clichés that he provided with picturesque names and labelled the 'Mannheim figures'.[40] The best known of these are the 'Mannheim sigh' and 'Mannheim rocket'. The former is merely a stepwise appoggiatura figure, usually in quavers. Such figures are common in the music of all countries during this period, and they unquestionably originated in Italy. This is not to say, however, that they do not form a major melodic resource of the Mannheim symphonists (especially those of the second generation), together with turn figures and related ornaments.[41] The case of the 'Mannheim rocket', a rapidly rising chordal theme, is somewhat different. Not only can such themes be found elsewhere, but they are not particularly common at Mannheim. (In one sense this is a shame, for the vividness of the metaphor has assured that it is the only thing many music-lovers remember about the Mannheim symphony!) In addition to the various 'figures' enumerated by Riemann, the Mannheim symphonists borrowed many basic thematic types, and sometimes even actual themes, from Italian opera.[42] In the same way, such characteristic traits of the Mannheim style as slow harmonic rhythm and the use of extended pedal points originated in the Italian overture.

Another element of the Mannheim symphony that deserves discussion is its use of the orchestra. Again taking a cue from the opera overture, the Mannheim symphonists preferred a large orchestra with full wind section, often including a pair of trumpets and timpani. To an extent the handling of these instruments is also rooted in practices developed in the opera overture. However, the variety and idiomatic treatment of the various instruments in a Mannheim symphony greatly surpasses that in a typical overture. Just as in the case of dynamics, the Mannheim composers took full advantage of the superb precision and fine soloists of the electoral orchestra. For example, contrasting secondary themes are often given to the wind as a solo or duet, and exposed horn passages of considerable difficulty are not uncommon.

This was an area in which Mozart clearly benefited from his extensive contacts with Mannheim in 1777–8. In letters to his father he frequently praised the quality of the Mannheim orchestra, often at the expense of that in Salzburg. Most notably, it was in Mannheim that Mozart first encountered the extensive use of clarinets in an orchestra; the Mannheim Kapelle was among the first to use these instruments on a regular basis (from at least 1758, and probably earlier). In a letter from Mannheim in December 1778, Mozart exclaimed to his father, 'Ah, if only we had clarinets [in Salzburg] too! You cannot imagine the glorious effect of a symphony with flutes, oboes and clarinets'.[43] Only three months after leaving Mannheim he had written his first symphony with that instrumentation – the 'Paris', K297/300*a*. Mozart's well-known proclivity for extensive wind writing thus derived in significant measure from his contact with Mannheim, whose wind players were among the most renowned in Europe.

In their form Mannheim symphonies depart somewhat from what we have come to regard as the norm. Before *c*1770 the fast movements of these works are likely to exhibit a variant of sonata form known as binary sonata form, in which the recapitulation begins with a restatement of the secondary rather than the primary material. Many of these movements omit double bars and repeat signs, a practice undoubtedly borrowed from the Italian opera overture. These and other characteristics give the quick movements of a Mannheim symphony – especially one by Johann Stamitz – a rather headlong, volatile quality that contrasts strikingly with the more articulated and formal structure of contemporary Viennese and Italian symphonies.

A recurrent theme of the preceding discussion has been that many of the fundamental components of the Mannheim symphonic style had their origin in the Italian overture of the time. Accordingly, the contribution of Mannheim in this area would be most accurately described not as innovation but as a transfer of the rather crude but highly effective opera overture style to the symphony performed at an academy – a major advance, if not quite the one Riemann and others have depicted. In the process, the Mannheim composers not only refined every element they adopted from the overture, but also greatly enhanced its aesthetic and expressive qualities. Burney provided a felicitous summary of the results, speaking in this case of Stamitz:

> His genius was truly original, bold, and nervous; invention, fire, and contrast, in the quick movements; a tender, graceful, and insinuating melody, in the slow; together with the ingenuity and richness of the accompaniments, characterise his productions; all replete with great effects, produced by an enthusiasm of genius, refined, but not repressed by cultivation.[44]

As vehicles for the dazzling virtuosity and discipline of the Mannheim orchestra, these symphonies must have seemed the very image of the brilliance and power distinguishing the elector's milieu. Indeed, it seems reasonable to suggest that the elements of operatic style prominent in the Mannheim symphony, which any listener of the time would have recognized as such, carried with them at least some of the iconographic significance attached to *opera seria* at Mannheim and elsewhere.

MUNICH

The glittering era of electoral Mannheim came to a close in 1778 with the dissolution of the court and its reluctant move to Munich. On 30 December 1777 – while Mozart and his mother were still in Mannheim – the Elector of Bavaria died without issue. According to long-standing treaty obligations, he was succeeded by Carl Theodor, and Bavaria and the Palatinate were united, with Munich as the capital. In order to cushion the blow, Carl Theodor gave his musicians the choice of remaining in Mannheim at full salary or

52. A Munich court musician with instruments of the Classical orchestra: painting (1762) by Peter Jakob Horemans

following the court to Munich, where the Kapellen of the two courts were to be amalgamated under the leadership of Cannabich and Carl Joseph Toeschi; about 60 per cent chose Munich, while the remainder stayed behind as members of the Nationaltheater and a Concert des Amateurs endowed by the elector. With the final move of the court to Munich in August and September 1778, Mannheim's brief golden age ended almost as abruptly as it had begun.

Music at Munich had been actively cultivated during the reign of Carl Theodor's predecessor, Maximilian III Joseph (ruled 1745–77), but it was substantially more conservative than at Mannheim. Continuing a tradition established by his father, Carl Albrecht (ruled 1726–45), Max Joseph showed a strong preference for Italian music and musicians; the principal composers at court were all northern Italians, including Giovanni Porta (Kapellmeister 1737–55), Giovanni Battista Ferrandini and Andrea Bernasconi (Kapellmeister 1755–84). *Opera seria* at Munich occupied the centre of attention, especially after the opening in 1753 of François Cuvilliés's splendid new Residenztheater (destroyed in World War II but since rebuilt). Both dramatically and musically, however, opera in Munich remained generally orthodox, showing few of the vigorous reformist tendencies so characteristic of Mannheim. Most of the court composers also left sacred and instrumental music of various kinds. Finally, as a large metropolitan centre, Munich had numerous churches and other institutions with their own musical establishments; in contrast to the situation at court, local Bavarian composers and performers were prominent in many of these.

Despite the presence of revered older musicians like Cannabich and excellent younger ones like Franz Danzi and Peter Winter, music at Munich after the merger of 1778 never attained quite the splendour it had possessed at Mannheim. Many reasons have been advanced for this decline, including the difficulties of the move and subsequent reorganization of the Kapelle, the necessity for financial constraint, the ineptitude of the Munich Intendant, Count von Seeau, and the general animosity of the Bavarians towards their new ruler. Whatever the explanation, the most noteworthy musical achievements of the period between 1778 and Carl Theodor's death in 1799 were arguably two works by Mozart: *Idomeneo*, given its première in January 1781, and the lovely Oboe Quartet K370, written for the Mannheim and by then Munich oboist Friedrich Ramm in 1781. It is a matter of some irony that two of the greatest works associated with Carl Theodor's long and brilliant reign should have been written by a composer to whom he had refused a permanent appointment, thereby securing for himself a position in history as a person of eminently bad judgment. It is an irony that would not have been lost on Mozart.

NOTES

[1] Sources for the above quotations are as follows: C. F. D. Schubart, *Deutsche Chronik*, i (Augsburg, 1774), i, 423; F. H. Jacobi, letter to C. M. Wieland of 8–11 June 1777, printed in *Friedrich Heinrich Jacobi, Briefwechsel: Gesamtausgabe*, 1st ser., ii: *Briefwechsel 1775–1781*, ed. P. Bachmaier and others (Stuttgart–Bad Cannstadt, 1983), 62; and L. Mozart, letter of 13 Nov 1777, after the translation in *The Letters of Mozart and his Family*, ed. E. Anderson (London, 2/1966, 3/1985), 367. All translations in the present chapter are my own unless otherwise indicated. An earlier version of portions of this chapter appeared in E. K. Wolf, *The Symphony at Mannheim*, The Symphony 1720–1840, ed. B. S. Brook and others, C/iii (New York, 1984), pp.xiii–xx.

[2] The electoral palace was almost totally destroyed in World War II but has since been reconstructed. It is used today as the University of Mannheim. The opera house had burnt to the ground during the Austrian bombardment of Mannheim in 1795, taking with it much of the music that had been left behind in Mannheim when the court moved to Munich; it was never rebuilt.

[3] Quoted from *Dr Burney's Musical Tours in Europe*, ed. P. A. Scholes (London, 1959), ii, 30.

[4] C. F. D. Schubart, *Leben und Gesinnungen*, i (Stuttgart, 1791), 200.

[5] *Dr Burney's Musical Tours*, ed. Scholes, ii, 36.

[6] At Mannheim these almanacs were issued in both German and French editions, the former with the title *Chur-Pfältzischer Hoff- und Staats-Calender*, the latter with the title *Almanach Electoral Palatin*. The best listing of extant Mannheim almanacs appears in R. Würtz, *Verzeichnis und Ikonographie der kurpfälzischen Hofmusiker zu Mannheim nebst darstel-lendem Theaterpersonal 1723–1803* (Wilhelmshaven, 1975), 30–33, which also includes a reproduction of the title-page of the 1760 *Calender* (p.21). The complete schedule of events from the *Calender* of 1749 is reprinted in F. Walter, 'Die Hof- und Kirchenfeste am kurfürstlichen Hof zu Mannheim', *Mannheimer Geschichtsblätter*, xiv (1913), 253–9.

[7] Quoted in F. Walter, *Geschichte des Theaters und der Musik am kurpfälzischen Hofe* (Leipzig, 1898/*R*1968), 101.

[8] The magnificent eighteenth-century trumpets used by the Mannheim trumpet corps are on display at the Music Instrument Museum in the Munich Stadtmuseum.

[9] C. F. D. Schubart, *Ideen zu einer Ästhetik der Tonkunst* (Vienna, 1806/*R*1969; written 1784–5). In his *Leben und Gesinnungen*, i, 208–9 and 218–19, Schubart described two encounters with Carl Theodor at Schwetzingen in 1773, at the first of which the elector played a flute concerto in the bath-house accompanied by the violinists Carl Joseph and Johann Toeschi and the cellist Innocenz Danzi.

[10] *Mozart Letters*, ed. Anderson, 361 (letter of 8 Nov 1777). Mozart and his mother arrived in Mannheim on 30 October 1777 and remained there for four and a half months, finally departing on 14 March 1778.

[11] *Chur-Pfältzischer Hoff- und Staats-Calender, auf das Jahr . . . MDCCLV* (Mannheim, 1755), entry for 4 Nov. Which opera was performed on this occasion is not known.

[12] L. A. Hunt, *Politics, Culture, and Class in the French Revolution* (Berkeley, 1984), 54; see also C. Geertz, 'Centers, Kings, and Charisma: Reflections on the Symbolics of Power', in *Local Knowledge: Further Essays in Interpretive Anthropology* (New York, 1983), 121–46 (with further citations). For a detailed consideration of this point as it relates to music, see A. Dunning, 'Official Court Music: Means and Symbol of Might', *IMSCR*, xiii *Strasbourg 1982*, 17–21. The symbolic aspects of ritual and ceremony have been the subject of numerous studies by anthropologists in recent decades, most notably Victor Turner and Geertz.

[13] *Dr Burney's Musical Tours*, ed. Scholes, ii, 34.

[14] ibid, 34–5.

[15] In a letter of 7 Dec 1777, Maria Anna Mozart stated that tickets to the theatre cost 45 kreuzer for a seat in the parterre and 1 gulden (60 kreuzer) for a seat in the poorer boxes (*Mozart Letters*, ed. Anderson, 409) – expensive when one considers that an ordinary musician at Mannheim earned only about 200 to 600 gulden per year. Walter, *Geschichte*, 104, gives a detailed description of the (strictly hierarchical) seating arrangements in the opera, including the information that the women of the court occupied boxes separate from the men and were not allowed in the parterre.

[16] See the description in Walter, *Geschichte*, 103–4. The parallel between the procession to the

opera and that described above from the elector's apartments to Mass should not go unremarked.

[17] For a review of Verazi's contributions see M. P. McClymonds, 'Mattia Verazi and the Opera at Mannheim, Stuttgart, and Ludwigsburg', *Studies in Music from the University of Western Ontario*, vii (1982), 99–136. Verazi was the librettist of Jommelli's influential opera *Ifigenia in Aulide* (Rome, 1751), which was given at Mannheim later in 1751 and may have led to his eventual appointment there.

[18] See D. Heartz, 'The Genesis of Mozart's *Idomeneo*', *MQ*, lv (1969), 17–18.

[19] The part of Rudolf was played by the outstanding bass Ludwig Fischer, for whom Mozart later wrote the part of Osmin in *Die Entführung aus dem Serail* (Vienna, 1782); the part of Günther was played by the famous tenor Anton Raaff, already well past his prime, for whom Mozart wrote the title role of *Idomeneo* (Munich, 1781). The personal contacts Mozart made with these and other musicians at Mannheim were of great significance in his later career. Equally important, of course, was the fact that he met his first love, the soprano Aloysia Weber (then sixteen), and his future wife Constanze Weber in Mannheim; they were daughters of the poor bass singer and copyist Fridolin Weber. The Weber family went with the court to Munich for a brief period and thence to Vienna, where Fridolin died in October 1779, two years before Mozart's arrival.

[20] *Mozart Letters*, ed. Anderson, 355–6 (letter of 4 Nov 1777). The performance Mozart described took place on All Saints' Day (Saturday, 1 November), at which a mass by Abbé Georg Joseph Vogler was given. The next day he heard a mass by Holzbauer.

[21] As quoted in Walter, *Geschichte*, 181.

[22] *Mozart Letters*, ed. Anderson, 356.

[23] In fig.51 the windows may be seen to the left, the paintings to the centre and right. The neo-classical statue of Carl Theodor, by the court sculptor Peter Anton Verschaffelt, appears to the rear at the right. The ceiling fresco, portraying a banquet of the gods and other mythological scenes, is by Cosmas Damian Asam.

[24] According to this description, the orchestra seems to have occupied approximately the position of the photographer in fig.51. At a concert of this type the orchestra would have played standing, with the obvious exception of the keyboard player(s) and the cellists.

[25] That is, when the court was still permanently in Mannheim, before the transfer to Munich in 1778; the present description, dating from 1785, depicts a visit made by Carl Theodor to his former residence.

[26] 'Mamselle Schäfer' was Josepha Schäfer or Schaefer (later Beck), a leading soprano with the Mannheim Nationaltheater. Concerts of the time typically included vocal as well as instrumental music (see n.28 below).

[27] Anon., *Lustreise in die Rheingegenden, in Briefen an Fr. J. v. Pf.* (Frankfurt and Leipzig, 1791), 102ff (letter of 11 May 1785), as reprinted in F. Walter, 'Ein Akademiekonzert im Rittersaale des Mannheimer Schlosses 1785', *Mannheimer Geschichtsblätter*, x (1909), 210–11. The informal nature of these academies is confirmed by Mozart's comment about the one at which he performed just after his arrival (see Mme Mozart's description of the gala days, p.219): 'On both occasions [during the concert] when I played, the elector and electress came up quite close to the clavier' (*Mozart Letters*, ed. Anderson, 362; letter of 8 Nov 1777).

[28] See the discussion of programme content at Mannheim in E. K. Wolf, *The Symphonies of Johann Stamitz* (Utrecht, 1981), 15 (with further citations). To the programmes listed there one should add a printed programme from Munich of 8 December 1785, published in facsimile in H. Bihrle, *Die Musikalische Akademie München 1811–1911: Festschrift zur Feier des hundertjährigen Bestehens* (Munich, 1911), 5, as well as the contents of Mozart's concert at the house of Christian Cannabich on 13 February 1778 (see *Mozart Letters*, ed. Anderson, 482; letter of 14 Feb 1778). The latter concert opened with a Cannabich symphony, after which came six works by Mozart: a keyboard concerto, an oboe concerto, an aria sung by Aloysia Weber, another keyboard concerto, another aria for Aloysia and finally the overture to *Il rè pastore*.

[29] Quoted from *Mozart Letters*, ed. Anderson, 25 (letter of 19 July 1763).

[30] Quoted from *Dr Burney's Musical Tours*, ed. Scholes, ii, 35.

[31] Schubart, *Ideen*, 130.

[32] These figures exclude known retirees, who were listed until their death. The size of the orchestra may have been augmented by the presence of *Akzessisten*, talented young performers awaiting a permanent position in the orchestra who drew little or no salary. However, Mozart's enumeration of the performers at the mass he heard at Mannheim (*Mozart Letters*, ed. Anderson, 355–6) happens to conform almost precisely with the figures for the 1770s given above. On that

occasion all four bassoons played, but only two horns. During the 1740s and early 1750s the string sections were somewhat smaller; in 1750, for example, there were only fourteen violins altogether and two violas.

[33] *Sinfonien der pfalzbayerischen Schule (Mannheimer Symphoniker)*, ed. H. Riemann, DTB, iii/1 (1902), p.xxiv.

[34] W. S. Newman, *The Sonata in the Classic Era* (Chapel Hill, 1963), 327. On pp.326–8 Newman provides a useful survey of the controversy over Riemann's claims.

[35] *Dr Burney's Musical Tours*, ed. Scholes, ii, 35.

[36] See E. K. Wolf, 'On the Origins of the Mannheim Symphonic Style', in *Studies in Musicology in Honor of Otto E. Albrecht* (Kassel, 1980), 197–239 (especially pp.206–16), and the slightly later treatment in Wolf, *Stamitz*, 231–9 and 298–302. Several articles in the volume *Mannheim und Italien: zur Vorgeschichte der Mannheimer*, ed. R. Würtz (Mainz, 1984), treat the relationship between the Mannheim and Italian styles in the realm of dynamics.

[37] J. F. Reichardt, *Briefe eines aufmerksamen Reisenden die Musik betreffend*, i (Frankfurt and Leipzig, 1774), 11n.

[38] Schubart, *Ideen*, 47. Abbé Vogler also specifically attributed the invention of the crescendo to Jommelli (*Betrachtungen der Mannheimer Tonschule*, i (Mannheim, 1778), 162).

[39] Wolf, 'Origins', 207–10, and *Stamitz*, 235 (with further citations).

[40] H. Riemann, 'Der Stil und die Manieren der Mannheimer', DTB, vii/2 (1906), pp.xv–xxv.

[41] An example of the latter type is the semiquaver figure consisting of two rising and two falling steps (e.g. C–D–E–D–C), which Riemann labelled a 'Bebung' (trembling, tremolo).

[42] See Wolf, 'Origins', 207–35. Several of Stamitz's secondary themes are transparently based on clichés found in Italian opera overtures and arias of the time, particularly those of Jommelli.

[43] *Mozart Letters*, ed. Anderson, 638 (letter of 3 Dec 1778). This letter was written on Mozart's return trip from Paris to Salzburg; he remained in Mannheim from 6 November until 9 December. The court, of course, had already moved to Munich by that time.

[44] *Dr Burney's Musical Tours*, ed. Scholes, ii, 134.

BIBLIOGRAPHICAL NOTE

Mannheim

There are no extended treatments in English of the general historical and cultural background at Mannheim; the most valuable studies, both in German, are F. Walter's *Geschichte Mannheims* (Mannheim, 1907, 2/1952 as *Aufgabe und Vermächtnis einer deutschen Stadt: drei Jahrhunderte Alt-Mannheim)* and M. Oeser's *Geschichte der Stadt Mannheim* (Mannheim, 1904). A comprehensive view of the cultural life of the court is presented in two major exhibition catalogues, both lavishly illustrated: Kurpfälzisches Museum der Stadt Heidelberg, *Carl Theodor und Elisabeth Auguste: höfische Kunst und Kultur in der Kurpfalz* (Heidelberg, 1979); and Badisches Landesmuseum Karlsruhe, *Barock in Baden-Württemberg* (Karlsruhe, 1981).

General studies in English of music at Mannheim are also sparse; they include Roland Würtz's article on Mannheim in *Grove 6* and the more popular treatment in C. Hogwood's *Music at Court* (London, 1977), 91–101. The indispensable work on this subject remains F. Walter's *Geschichte des Theaters und der Musik am kurpfälzischen Hofe* (Leipzig, 1898/*R*1968). Both Burney and Mozart provided eyewitness accounts of musical life at the electoral court; see C. Burney, *The Present State of Music in Germany, the Netherlands, and United Provinces* (London, 1773), ed. P. A. Scholes as *Dr Burney's Musical Tours in Europe*, ii: *An Eighteenth-Century Musical Tour in Central Europe and the Netherlands* (London, 1959), 30–36; and *The Letters of Mozart and his Family*, trans. and ed. E. Anderson (London, 2/1966, 3/1985), 347–510 and 630–39.

Opera at Mannheim under Carl Theodor is discussed in M. McClymonds, 'Mattia Verazi and the Opera at Mannheim, Stuttgart and Ludwigsburg', *Studies in Music from the University of Western Ontario*, vii (1982), 99–136; see also D. Heartz, 'The

Genesis of Mozart's *Idomeneo*', *MQ*, lv (1969), 1–19. Among studies in German one should again cite Walter's *Geschichte des Theaters und der Musik am kurpfälzischen Hofe* as well as various articles in *Mannheim und Italien: zur Vorgeschichte der Mannheimer*, ed. R. Würtz (Mainz, 1984). Holzbauer's *Günther von Schwarzburg* is the only Mannheim opera presently available in modern edition; see DDT, viii–ix, ed. H. Kretzschmar (1902).

A selection of sacred music by Mannheim composers may be found in *Kirchenmusik der Mannheimer Schule*, ed. E. Schmitt, DTB, new ser., ii–iii (1982, 1980 [*sic*]); the introduction to this edition (in German), which contains thematic catalogues of the entire repertory, is the only full discussion of this topic published to date.

Instrumental music at Mannheim has been the subject of numerous studies, with principal attention centring on the Mannheim symphony. The most detailed treatment of the latter subject is E. K. Wolf's *The Symphonies of Johann Stamitz: a Study in the Formation of the Classic Style* (Utrecht, 1981); see also J. LaRue and others, 'Symphony, I: 18th century', *Grove 6*, and the introductions to *The Symphony at Mannheim: Johann Stamitz, Christian Cannabich*, ed. E. K. and J. K. Wolf, The Symphony 1720–1840, ed. B. S. Brook and others, C/iii (New York, 1984). For a full discussion of Italian influence on the Mannheim symphonic style see E. K. Wolf's 'On the Origins of the Mannheim Symphonic Style', in *Studies in Musicology in Honor of Otto E. Albrecht: a Collection of Essays by his Colleagues and Former Students at the University of Pennsylvania* (Kassel, 1980), 197–239, reprinted in *The Garland Library of the History of Western Music*, ed. E. Rosand, vii: *Classic Music* (New York, 1985), 231–73, as well as several of the articles in *Mannheim und Italien*, ed. Würtz. Modern editions of Mannheim symphonies may be found in *Sinfonien der pfalzbayerischen Schule (Mannheimer Symphoniker)*, ed. H. Riemann, DTB, iii/1, vii/2, viii/2 (1902, 1907–8), reprinted *sans* introductory material as *Mannheim Symphonists* (New York, n.d.), and The Symphony, ed. Brook and others, C/iii–v. Both editions include introductory material and thematic catalogues of works by individual composers.

Among studies in English of other instrumental genres the following may be mentioned: P. Ward Jones, 'The Concerto at Mannheim *c.*1740–1780', *PRMA*, xcvi (1969–70), 129–36; E. K. Wolf, 'The Orchestral Trios, Op. 1, of Johann Stamitz', in *Music in the Classic Period: Essays in Honor of Barry S. Brook* (New York, 1985), 297–322; and W. S. Newman, *The Sonata in the Classic Era* (Chapel Hill, 1963, 3/1983), 326–42. The most extensive modern edition of Mannheim concertos is *Flötenkonzerte der Mannheimer Schule*, ed. W. Lebermann, EDM, li (1964), while that of music for soloistic ensemble is *Mannheimer Kammermusik des 18. Jahrhunderts*, ed. H. Riemann, DTB, xv–xvi (1914–15; with introductions and thematic catalogues).

There are, of course, many other specialized studies of individual Mannheim composers or genres, most in German and many unpublished; these may be located by consulting the bibliographies in *Grove 6* and *MGG* as well as the excellent classified listings in B. Höft's *Mannheimer Schule: Schriften–Schallplatten–Noten–Bilddokumente* (Mannheim, 1984). A bibliographical tool of a different sort, not always complete or accurate, is R. Würtz's *Verzeichnis und Ikonographie der kurpfälzischen Hofmusiker zu Mannheim nebst darstellendem Theaterpersonal 1723–1803* (Wilhelmshaven, 1975), which lists all known Mannheim musicians and theatre personnel together with biographical information gleaned from almanacs, archival documents and the like.

Munich

The literature on music in Munich during the eighteenth century is less prolific than that on Mannheim. The most useful general survey in English is H. Leuchtmann and R. Münster, 'Munich', *Grove 6*. Studies in German include E. Bücken, *München als Musikstadt* (Munich, 1925); O. Ursprung, *Münchens musikalische Vergangenheit von der Frühzeit bis zu Richard Wagner* (Munich, 1927); and several pertinent articles in *Musik* in Bayern, ed. R. Münster and H. Schmid (Tutzing, 1972; with detailed bibliographies).

As in the case of Mannheim, Burney provided an extensive description of music in Munich and at the summer palace of Nymphenburg under Max Joseph (*Dr Burney's Musical Tours*, ed. Scholes, ii, 45–62). Similarly, Mozart's letters written while he was in Munich for the preparation of *Idomeneo* (1781) present a vivid picture of the court after Carl Theodor's accession; see *Mozart Letters*, ed. Anderson, 657–710, and also the exhibition catalogue Bayerische Staatsbibliothek, *Wolfgang Amadeus Mozart: Idomeneo 1781–1981: Essays, Forschungsberichte, Katalog*, ed. R. Münster and R. Angermüller (Munich, 1981).

Chapter IX

Courts and Municipalities in North Germany

THOMAS BAUMAN

One of the difficulties in discussing musical activity, or any other kind of activity, in northern Germany during the eighteenth century lies in the problem of formulating an adequate concept of what we mean by the regional term 'North Germany'. The well-known political fragmentation of German-speaking lands at that time was especially marked in the north, perhaps because it was more Protestant than other regions and therefore lacked the social, political and spiritual cohesion the traditions and institutions of Catholicism still provided elsewhere.

Religion was merely one factor among many (although an important one) that effectively blocked the development of a strong sense of common culture among the small states that proliferated across northern and central Germany.[1] Products of German genius and the language itself were generally regarded as sources of national pride, but not so political or economic aspirations – even after the military and political triumphs of Frederick the Great (Frederick II) against virtually all of the rest of Europe. If a businessman in Leipzig used the term 'patriotic', he most probably referred either to his civic consciousness or to the less immediate ties of the free city of Leipzig to the electoral court of Saxony, resident in Dresden. A citizen of nearby Weimar would have conveyed by the same term an even narrower sense of personal allegiance to the Duke or Duchess of Saxe-Weimar, with the town itself representing but a pale, subservient extension of the all-important court.

By and large, the role of local rulers in Germany was patriarchal and paternal rather than remote or imperial. Respect for rank and an unchanging social order loomed large at all levels of society, and conservatism tended to dominate other arenas as well – commerce, agriculture, education and the arts. For the most part, musical activities were no exception. At court, music responded along with every other detail of life and manners to the sensibilities and ambitions of the monarch; in Germany's several sizable free cities, music's significance often stood in direct proportion to the city's commercial pre-eminence, and the forms it took usually reflected the rather narrow taste of the city's merchant class.

Larger courts, notably the electoral ones at Berlin, Dresden, Brunswick and Hanover, favoured Italian style in their musical fare and either sent promising young German composers to Italy or imported Italians. The smaller courts proved far more significant in fostering indigenous developments. The brilliant court of Duchess Anna Amalia and her son Duke Karl August at Weimar made contributions to the development of German literature, music and theatre far out of proportion to its modest size and political significance. On the other hand, many other courts had little use for civilizing refinements of any sort, the majority of German nobles confining their pleasures to gambling, card-playing and hunting.

Protestant schools did little to cultivate music beyond the rudimentary level and the churches were not much better, although they continued to support traditional liturgical uses of music. Much more than this was not to be expected, since Protestant churches did not own vast tracts of income-generating property or have any close connection with the upper class, which the Catholic Church enjoyed in many areas.

Although German cities during the eighteenth century by and large suffered some degree of economic decline, a few maintained strong commercial positions. Hamburg, blessed with a superb natural harbour and access to inland trade via the Elbe, led the way in developing a prosperous middle class. Frankfurt and, especially, Leipzig derived their economic significance during the century chiefly from trade, made manifest by the semi-annual fairs held in each city. Leipzig was the hub not only of the German book trade but also of German music publishing.

The diffusion of culture and commerce across northern Germany made travel an ingredient essential to the development of both. One travelled to ply a trade or craft, particularly as a journeyman, and this was equally true for musicians, music teachers and theatre or opera companies. Artistic tours were undertaken by many musicians and often led to employment as a private tutor or in a Kapelle, a court's musical household. Cultural diffusion also necessitated heavy reliance on correspondence as a means of communication – an eighteenth-century passion – especially for selling printed music by subscription.

A large body of middle-class merchants and officials proved to be the chief patrons of household music. Their children required keyboard, chamber and vocal pieces for domestic use; a ready market also lay at hand in German households for keyboard reductions of popular German operas; and private 'academies' and, after 1770, public subscription concerts generated public demand for concertos, symphonies, arias and other genres of concerted music. In all these areas, it must be acknowledged, music's role was not to challenge or provoke but to please. Take, for example, the following remark from Carl Philipp Emanuel Bach's autobiography: 'Because I have had to compose most of my works for specific individuals and for the public, I have always been more restrained in them than in the few pieces that I have written merely for myself. At times I even have had to follow ridiculous instructions'.[2] As the tone of Bach's remarks suggests, not all German composers were content with this reality, but its effects are clear in numerous publications directed at very specific audiences – collections of songs for masonic lodges, for example, or sonatas and concertos labelled 'à l'usage du beau sexe'.

BERLIN AND THE COURT OF FREDERICK THE GREAT

Berlin presents a situation found in no other north German centre – that of a true cosmopolitan capital, or at least the rudiments of one, with a record of significant contributions to virtually every aspect of musical life. Admittedly, it can in no way bear comparison with Vienna, Paris and London, or even the most important Italian cities of the century, in terms of setting a national tone through either sustained artistic leadership or monopolization of resources. Yet the picture of musical activity it presents exerted a certain amount of exemplary force in an otherwise diffuse musical culture.

The most striking example of the thoroughgoing local conditioning music underwent in north Germany was set by the court of Frederick the Great, an astonishing instance of artistic despotism, of an almost obsessive control by a monarch over the least detail of music-making for the gratification of his own firmly delineated and unvarying musical taste.[3] Like nearly every other aspect of life at the Prussian court, music in Frederick's hands became a regimen. Through sheer force of habit he cultivated and controlled it as carefully as his most important administrative measures, diplomatic manoeuvres and military exploits, even though he regarded music as innocent recreation and an avenue of escape from his duties.

In impressing his own personality so forcibly upon his musical establishment, Frederick merely offered an extreme case of what commonly occurred at many German courts. But there were also differences. Most important, Frederick's passion for music was that of a performer, not of a passive consumer. By all reports his mastery of the transverse flute was exceptional. Charles Burney heard him play in 1772:

> I was much pleased, and even surprised with the neatness of his execution in the *allegros*, as well as by his expression and feeling in the *adagio*; in short, his performance surpassed, in many particulars,

53. Concert with Frederick the Great as flute soloist: engraving by Peter Haas (1754–1804)

> any thing I had ever heard among *Dilettanti*, or even professors. His majesty played three long and difficult concertos successively, and all with equal perfection.[4]

Frederick employed a considerable household of musicians, some of them among the most distinguished in Germany, and in nearly every case the favour in which any one of them stood was directly proportional to his adherence to the king's every wish. Important female singers were forbidden to marry. Neither they nor even the greatest castratos in the king's service were to add a single note of embellishment to an aria. Frustrated musicians routinely saw their protests and entreaties for salary improvements, and even requests for dismissal, summarily rejected or simply ignored. If the king performed exceptionally, no-one was suffered to voice his admiration with a 'Bravo'.

Frederick made exception to this last rule for the one musician dearest to his heart – his flute teacher, Johann Joachim Quantz (1697–1773). So enamoured of Quantz's music was the king that he played nothing but sonatas and concertos composed by either Quantz or himself. By the time of the Seven Years' War these works had evolved into a corpus of Frederican order and thoroughness – two identical books of sonatas and two of concertos, one kept at the royal palace in Berlin, Schloss Charlottenburg, and one at the residence in nearby Postdam, Sans Souci. Methodically the king and his musicians worked their way through these cycles again and again.

Although none of this music merits much attention on its own, Frederick's compositions help illuminate his extraordinary personality and Quantz's shed some practical light on his most important contribution to eighteenth-century music, his *Versuch einer Anweisung die Flöte traversière zu spielen* of 1752. Much more than a treatise on flute method, it offers a broadly conceived if somewhat retrospective aesthetic of musicianship, taste and musical criticism.[5] Quantz's *Versuch* was one in a series of practical and theoretical works emanating from Berlin around the mid-eighteenth century that led C. F. D. Schubart to choose 'critical exactitude' as the feature most clearly distinguishing Berlin from other European musical centres.[6] One of Quantz's most important themes, and one that recurs in other Berlin writings of the period, involves national styles: Quantz tried to identify what is specific to Italian and French music and then to propose German music as a mixture of the best elements in both.

Quantz's *Versuch* is surpassed by an even greater essay from the mid-century court of Frederick the Great, Carl Philipp Emanuel Bach's influential *Versuch über die wahre Art das Clavier zu spielen* (i, 1753; ii, 1762). Most keyboard players of the day and many later ones owe something to Bach's lucid treatise. In the first part the chapter on fingering summarizes the practice of his father, Johann Sebastian Bach, and the one on embellishments seeks to systematize mid-century ornamentation and its notation. The second part presents the century's most important guide to the art of the accompanist, the role in which Bach himself served Frederick at Berlin and Potsdam.

Bach's *Versuch* is a work of eminent practicality; for instance, his advice to keyboard players is to listen to accomplished musicians, especially singers, rather than bothering with learned treatises. Perhaps most revealing of all in terms of Bach's own accomplishment as a composer and the aesthetic of his age is a passage on expression: 'A musician cannot move others unless he too is moved. He must of necessity feel all of the affects that he hopes to arouse in his audience, for the revealing of his own humour will stimulate a like humour in the listener'. And he added that the performer must communicate the piece with his body as well as his fingers: 'Those who maintain that all of this can be accomplished without gesture will retract their words when, owing to their own insensibility, they find themselves obliged to sit like a statue before their instrument'.[7] Burney left a famous description of Bach's own playing, indicating that he practised the physical manifestation of expression recommended to the performer here.

The treatises of Quantz and C. P. E. Bach represent the most enduring part of Berlin's critical legacy. Less impressive but perhaps more characteristic contributions tended towards extremes. The writings of J. S. Bach's devoted pupil Johann Philipp Kirnberger (1721–83), for instance, jealously brood over the style perfected by the 'Great Cantor'. That this patrimony of tonal counterpoint had no place at Frederick's court emphasizes the purely theoretical bent of Kirnberger's works, something we may glean as well from the title of his most important treatise, *Die Kunst des reinen Satzes* ('The Art of Pure Composition', 1771–9). Kirnberger no doubt thought of his works as the kind of theory Bach himself would have written in support of his music, but in spirit they embrace the pervasive rationalism that animated Berlin's intelligentsia throughout Frederick's reign.

Another major writer on music at Berlin, Friedrich Wilhelm Marpurg, was far more journalistic in tone and, certainly, less rigorous as a theorist than Kirnberger. The several journals on music that he kept going from 1749 to 1763 parallel similar endeavours in other fields in north Germany, ranging over every conceivable topic in a spirit of eclectic encyclopedism. He was no doubt among the figures foremost in Burney's mind when he wryly remarked of Berlin that 'there are more critics and theorists in this city, than practicioners; which has not, perhaps, either refined the taste, or fed the fancy of the performers'.[8]

Criticism is the one area in which Berlin rose above localism to exert an influence on all of German musical culture. Nothing of the sort could be said of the cultivation of Italian opera at Frederick's court, least of all by the time of the Seven Years' War, when the king's taste had completely ossified.[9] Changes which began to make themselves felt around mid-century were ignored at Berlin in favour of the music which had formed the young monarch's taste in the 1730s and 1740s, embodied in the serious operas of two Italian-trained Germans, Johann Adolf Hasse and Carl Heinrich Graun.

Immediately upon acceding to the throne in 1740, Frederick set about creating an operatic establishment at Berlin (along with French ballet and theatre). Graun, his Kapellmeister since 1735, was dispatched to Italy to engage first-rate singers. (As it turned out, using agents within Italy to contract singers proved more fruitful.) Once established, the company was run with Prussian order. Two new operas were normally mounted each season, the first given continually until New Year's Day, the second thereafter. Virtually every new opera was composed by Graun, supplemented by works of Hasse, who was resident at Dresden for most of the period from 1730 to 1763. The king criticized and sometimes sketched out the subjects of each new libretto Graun set and ordered him to recompose arias that failed to please him (everywhere else this was the prerogative of the singers).

A mark of the insularity of Graun's operas is the fact that only a couple among the dozens he wrote for the Berlin opera company were ever produced anywhere else. This puts in perspective the claims of priority for the use of the so-called 'cavatina' in *Montezuma* (1755) – basically just the first two parts of the five-part da capo aria form Graun favoured. Frederick, who himself wrote the libretto in French prose, enforced this supposed innovation on Graun, but before the present century these arias never saw print or reached ears in any opera house outside Berlin.

MUSIC AT OTHER ELECTORAL COURTS: DRESDEN, BRUNSWICK, HANOVER

Of the major north German courts that indulged themselves in Italian music, Dresden outshone all the others – even Berlin – in pomp and lavishness. Opera, of course, dominated completely, at least until 1763, when the death of the spendthrift Elector Frederick Augustus and the disastrous effects of the Seven Years' War forced austerity on all of Saxony. During this period Hasse made frequent trips to Italy, where his operas were nearly as popular as at Dresden and Berlin. To German composers who aspired to greatness, Hasse came to represent a living ideal of restraint, elegance and decorum – the very qualities that also surrounded the imperial poet (*poeta cesareo*) Metastasio at Vienna, who yielded to no-one in his admiration of Hasse as the perfect composer of his librettos. The immutability of Hasse is evident in his operas composed for Dresden – they betray virtually no significant stylistic change from the earliest to the latest.[10]

During Hasse's residence the standards of orchestral playing at Dresden were among the highest in Europe, and some of the finest Italian singers were also imported (at their head was Hasse's wife, Faustina Bordoni). The ideal embodied by Hasse left a decided mark on future generations of German-born, Italian-trained composers at Dresden (Johann Gottlieb Naumann and his pupils) but, unlike him, their Italian experiences helped move them in the direction of current operatic fashions. One important change after 1763 at Dresden duplicates a pattern seen at other courts where economic strictures forced the abandonment of expensive productions of *opera seria* – the installation of an Italian *opera buffa* troupe and the patronage of German comic opera (often in direct rivalry with each other). Even Vienna followed this path under Joseph II.

The Dresden court, unlike Frederick's, supported church music. Owing to the Elector of Saxony's conversion for political reasons earlier in the century, this meant Catholic church music. Some of Hasse's finest music went into the Neapolitan-style oratorios he wrote for the Dresden court, particularly his *Conversione di S Agostino* of 1750. The text for this work had been written in imitation of Metastasio by the wife of the Saxon crown prince, the Bavarian Princess Maria Antonia Walpurgis.[11]

Brunswick rivalled to some degree the lavish entertainments at the Dresden court from mid-century until it, too, set about economizing in 1770. A certain Nicolini, who first came to Brunswick as the head of a troupe of Dutch children who performed pantomimes and intermezzos (entertainments given between the acts of plays), rose to become *directeur des spectacles*. Beginning in 1753 Italian singers were imported, and eventually a young composer, Johann Gottfried Schwanenberger, was appointed Kapellmeister, having been sent to Italy for six years at the duke's expense. After 1770 German troupes came to prominence, bringing both spoken drama and comic operas. As was typical elsewhere, these companies were forbidden to perform in the opera house.

At Hanover, music and the other arts suffered from the absence of the monarch. After George I left for England in 1714, there was no equivalent to the self-indulgent Frederick Augustus of Saxony to squander vast sums on *opera seria* productions. From 1760 music sponsored by the court tended to follow much more middle-class patterns – a string of German theatrical companies, concerts and oratorios (including Handel's *Messiah* in 1775).

GERMAN CONCERT TRADITIONS: THE SYMPHONY AND CONCERTO

Perhaps in no other area did north German composers compile a worse record of receptivity to innovations from abroad than in the symphony. Their style leant heavily on intensely conservative, concerto-like ways of treating theme, texture and form in both independent symphonies and overtures, despite the dissemination of exciting new works from Paris, Mannheim and Vienna. Only C. P. E. Bach made a virtue of this insular tradition through his own original approach. Germans pointed with pride to the symphonies Bach composed at Hamburg. A set of six completed there in 1773 and dedicated to Baron van Swieten even found their way to Vienna, an unusual distinction for symphonies from the north.

Johann Friedrich Agricola, Frederick's Kapellmeister after Graun, set out north German attitudes towards symphonic styles from abroad in a review of 1766 castigating six symphonies of Ferdinand Fischer issued in 1765 and dedicated to Fischer's employer, Duke Ferdinand of Brunswick: 'We are truly astonished that [Fischer] has dedicated to a German hero symphonies that exhibit all the lame, unmelodic, base, waggish, fragmented features, all the (as Telemann once put it) feverish attacks of continuous rapid changes of *piano* and *forte*, etc, of the latest, fashionable Italian composers'. And he went on to uphold exemplary German composers and virtues against this tide:

54. Torchlight Concert by Jena Collegium Musicum: watercolour (1744) by an unknown German artist (the orchestra is presenting a professor with a festive musical greeting, while a congratulatory poem is borne on a cushion)

'Meanwhile, with two Grauns, a Hasse, a Bach, a Quantz etc at the head, we other Germans want to bend our efforts towards cultivating the sublime, the worthy, the tender, the touching, beautiful melody, pure harmony, noble expression and so forth in music according to our abilities'.[12]

The concertos composed in north Germany by the generation of C. P. E. Bach, most of them for keyboard and orchestra, made their peace with outmoded features of style far more readily than the symphony did, since it was by nature far easier for the concerto to maintain ritornello structure as an essential ingredient. Scarcely a single north German composer escaped the pervasive influence of Vivaldi in this genre. Again, one need look no further than C. P. E. Bach for the finest examples. All of his 52 concertos appear to have been written originally for keyboard and most of them date from his Berlin years. He preferred a structure having four ritornellos in his first movements, but developed a more modern sense of recapitulation than is found in Vivaldi. As was typical of the age Bach's concertos circulated both in manuscript and in print. His published concertos were not for his own use, but commercial ventures. A Hamburg newspaper announced in April 1771 that, 'at the request of many amateurs of music, six easy harpsichord concertos by Capellmeister C. Ph. E. Bach are to be published'.[13]

The flute concertos of Frederick the Great and Quantz mentioned above derive from an earlier style established by Hasse in the north – lyrical, clear of texture and modest in both length and technical demands. In what we recognize as true concertos, Hasse relies on the ritornello both as the main structural element and as the thematic foundation of a movement. The name 'concerto' was loosely applied in his day, however. The English publisher John Walsh issued in 1741 a set of 'Six Concertos' by Hasse that are actually overtures to six of his operas.[14]

By the 1780s most of northern Germany had finally embraced the new symphonic styles of the French and the Viennese, with Haydn belatedly acknowledged as the genre's leading exponent. The development of public concerts by several dedicated northerners had a lot to do with this change in taste. While it is true that by mid-century court concerts had become somewhat less exclusive and thus exerted a stronger influence on the large market that existed in the north for concerted music, it was from civic initiative that the most important institution, the independent subscription concert, arose.[15]

Berlin sponsored a great deal of concert activity, beginning with the founding of the Liebhaberkonzerte in 1770. During the last two decades of the century the innkeeper Corsica put on concerts in a large hall he owned; here several important productions of Handel's oratorios and concert versions of Gluck's operas took place. The penchant of Berliners for vocal music crystallized in the Singakademie established in 1792 by Carl Friedrich Christian Fasch; like many other concert series at Berlin, notably Johann Friedrich Reichardt's Concert Spirituel (1783), Fasch's emphasized earlier as well as current music.

Leipzig had had a public concert series since 1743, the Grosses Konzert, which did not take on great artistic significance, however, until the energetic Johann Adam Hiller reorganized the series as the Liebhaber-Concerte in 1763. In 1780 the municipality offered to build a concert room for the enterprise in the Gewandhaus, opened a year later. Here not just north German music but the best works of Austrian and Italian composers were cultivated. Most of these institutions, but especially the Gewandhaus concerts and the Berlin Singakademie, continued to play leading roles in north German musical life during the nineteenth century.

KEYBOARD MUSIC: CARL PHILIPP EMANUEL BACH AND THE CULT OF SENSIBILITY

In the age of Frederick II, the greatest composer produced by north Germany was one that Frederick treated with little respect – Carl Philipp Emanuel Bach, his first harpsichordist (1740–67). Bach was one of the supreme exponents of the most distinctively north German of eighteenth-century musical styles, the *emfindsamer Stil* (or 'style of sensibility'). It was most effective in smaller forms, where the exploration of expressive nuances in successive short, uncluttered phrases could speak in simple, heartfelt tones. Ornamentation was applied discreetly, especially in frequent, stock cadences. It has been suggested that about 1750 there was a dichotomy in European art music involving this expressive style on the one hand and the *style galant*, based on rational premises, on the other; they led seemingly contradictory existences, according to this theory, until the great Viennese masters brought them into Classical balance in the 1780s.[16] Actually, both styles were essential parts of music-making in the north as well as in the rest of Europe. The *galant* style, earlier and essentially counter-Baroque in spirit, was born in Neapolitan opera of the 1720s and 1730s. It found employment in elegant salons and courts, such as Frederick's, that were suffused with French cultural values, which is probably where its connection with rationalism arose.

The composers who best exemplified this style in north Germany also created the most admired works in the *empfindsamer Stil*. Graun, for example, created the epitome of the *galant* style in 1747 with his setting, twice revived at Berlin, of *Le feste galanti* for Frederick's opera (the very title brings to mind Watteau's *Les fêtes galantes*). Yet in 1755 he also composed the immensely popular and cloyingly sentimental oratorio *Der Tod Jesu* (see below) for the king's sister, Anna Amalia.

C. P. E. Bach also partook of both styles. His *Versuch*, along with Quantz's, offers a practical anatomy of the *galant* style's constituent parts. Some of Bach's keyboard music, too, shares fully in this tradition. His best keyboard works, however, embody a quality that the musicologist Arnold Schering sought to identify with the term 'das redende Prinzip' ('the rhetorical principle'). In dramatic passages this takes the form of proto-verbal, emotion-laden rhetoric similar in affective content to obbligato recitative. More often, Bach manages to create in more intimate contexts – especially his slow movements – an earnest sentimentality tinged with a certain element of the theatrical. The effect of the *empfindsam* style of Carl Philipp Emanuel's brother Wilhelm Friedemann 'is one of extreme, almost nervous volatility, like that of the mercurial facial expressions made by a highly sensitive actor'.[17]

The *galant* style was able to make its peace with aesthetic doctrines of affective unity and imitation of Nature, but with its abrupt shifts of

55. The Artist with his first Wife at the Clavichord: painting (1789) by Johann Heinrich Tischbein the elder

emotional state, textural variety and astonishing tonal somersaults, the language C. P. E. Bach perfected – especially after moving to Hamburg – could no longer do so. Bach's last keyboard works focus on three genres important to the *empfindsamer Stil* – the sonata, the rondo and the fantasia. Many of his later sonatas are actually revisions of earlier works; nearly all follow a fast–slow–fast movement pattern and on the whole they show his originality to least advantage. As noted earlier, they were not usually written for his own use, but for public consumption. This was less the case with his rondos and fantasias, genres which also offered him far more flexibility and constructive freedom.

Many reports of and rhapsodies on Bach's music and his playing have come down to us, but one of the most fitting portrayals of the emotional world this music served came in Schubart's description of the instrument Bach favoured most, the clavichord:

> tender and responsive to your soul's every inspiration, and it is here that you will find your heart's soundboard . . . Sweet melancholy, languishing love, parting grief, the soul's communing with God, uneasy forebodings, glimpses of Paradise through suddenly rent clouds, sweetly purling tears . . . [are to be found] in the contact with those wonderful strings and caressing keys.[18]

All three of the great Viennese masters acknowledged C. P. E. Bach's influence. In the north it was enormous, even among those who admired him as an inimitable original genius. The Weimar Kapellmeister Ernst Wilhelm Wolf put it most directly: 'I have long believed that there is nothing greater in the world than Bach, and a keyboard composer can and must not even think otherwise than to imitate him'.[19] Beethoven's teacher, Christian Gottlob Neefe, dedicated his first set of published sonatas to Bach with a fulsome preface (Leipzig, 1772). At Gotha, Georg Benda sought to imitate the more wilfully original aspects of Bach's style both in his solo keyboard works and in his concertos, prompting Burney to remark that 'his efforts at singularity, will by some be construed into affectation'.[20]

Sensibility as practised in music by Bach and his imitators had close parallels with German letters. Goethe's *Die Leiden des jungen Werthers* was the most successful and sensational of a stream of works conceived in the same emotional climate, most of them intense psychological studies of distraught youth. Music was included by many of these authors in important scenes.[21] In Hamburg Bach befriended several poets and translators keenly involved with the expressive world mirrored in his music, most notably the poet Klopstock, whose rhapsodic-meditative epic poem *Messias*, begun in 1748 and completed in 1773, treated German as freely as Bach handled musical sense and grammar. Both men, apart from their immediate aesthetic goals, must be considered seminal figures in the Romantic conception of the artist, for in creating a language apart from conventional modes of expression each explored in his own medium the possibility of a voice speaking from a separate, self-engendered creative sphere.

SACRED MUSIC

Some of Bach's poetic friends in Hamburg felt the press of rhetoric and programmatic implications in his music so strongly that they proposed setting texts beneath some of his works (including Hamlet's soliloquy in one case), but Bach himself usually resisted this or any other verbal explication. Word and tone were married in another genre important to the *empfindsamer Stil*, however – the oratorio. Bach again contributed significant and original works, setting his sensitive style in a more dramatic context with *Die Israeliten in der Wüste* and in a more introspective, meditative one with *Die Auferstehung und Himmelfahrt Jesu* (a divergence he may have noticed in his father's settings of the *St John* and *St Matthew* Passions).

But it was Graun and Johann Heinrich Rolle who offered enthusiastic north Germans the most popular and tearful examples. Graun's *Der Tod Jesu* was probably the most popular German oratorio of the entire century. It maintains some traditional features of Protestant church music – the structural placement of chorales in the architectural plan and use of rather stiff imitative counterpoint in the choruses – but its most memorable moments (for its early audiences) came in its arias and highly expressive obbligato recitatives. The poet Carl Wilhelm Ramler provided the inspiration by centring the drama not on Jesus but on several observers who describe events and their own empathetic reaction to his very human suffering. ('All at once the pent-up pain strikes furiously at the hero's soul', sings a bass voice in one recitative. 'His heart heaves within his strained breast. A dagger twists in every vein. His whole body flies up from the Cross. He feels the sevenfold horror of death. All Hell weighs down upon him.') Graun's da capo arias do not depart radically from his operatic style in the works he had written for Frederick the Great, but the soulful, expressive obbligato recitatives respond to every emotional nuance in Ramler's text.

A more fluid and dramatic spirit guided north Germany's greatest master of the oratorio, the Magdeburg music director Johann Heinrich Rolle. The best-known and best-loved of his 'music dramas', as he called his oratorios, was *Der Tod Abels*, based on a prose idyll by the Swiss writer and publisher Salomon Gessner (1730–88). Although much of the work dwells on the moral virtues of an idealized pastoral community familiar to audiences across Europe at the time, Rolle moves beyond C. P. E. Bach and Graun in his confrontation with the theme of fraternal strife and fratricide at the end of the oratorio. The raw dramatic power to which he responded here finds even greater latitude in several of his subsequent works, notably *Abraham auf Moria* (dealing with the sacrifice of Isaac) and *Thirza und ihre Söhne*.

Rolle developed a musical language of fluidity and expressive power for the most intense scenes in these music dramas. Just as the epistolary structure of *Werther* yields to a freer dramatic continuum in the final episodes (centred, appropriately, on readings of the poetry of Ossian), so Rolle departs from the *Empfindsamkeit* of concatenated pastoral arias in *Der Tod Abels* in order to follow each psychological step in the persecution of Cain. In this and similar episodes an overarching musical curve is clearly perceptible, involving arioso, obbligato recitative and strong choral pillars.

GERMAN LETTERS AND THE LIED

Before discussing any kind of north German vocal music, it is important to clarify the relationship of text and music in general, for during this period it was in some ways different in the north from the rest of western Europe, and it is essential to an understanding of the lines of development followed by German opera and the lied from mid-century to the age of Napoleon. The close connection is attested to by our way of describing German musical style by period labels during these years: the terms we use do not come from art history, as they do in other eras (Baroque, Renaissance, Mannerism, Impressionism, Expressionism, to mention a few), but from literature (*Empfindsamkeit*, 'Sturm und Drang'). Indeed, these terms, when applied to north German music, serve for ones derived from the visual arts that are applied to styles developed elsewhere (Rococo, *galant*).

Why was north German music so closely tied to literary currents? We have already mentioned one reason – the rhetorical element essential to the style of C. P. E. Bach and those he inspired. Another was the absence of strong traditions, outside the church, for either opera or non-dramatic secular music with German texts. In fact, Italy provided here the most compelling models, and German vocal music came to be defined as much by its avoidance of a perceived 'ear-tickling' emptiness of true content in Italian music as by its own traditions and tenets. Finally, the second half of the eighteenth century was the great coming of age of German literature and also the German theatre. Music was swept up into discussions of both, in the public press and in the clubs that flourished as centres of intellectual exchange in most German cities of any size.

Among the leading figures of German literature, those untrained in music tended to have only an indirect influence on musical practice and aesthetics – Klopstock and Lessing, for example. Poets especially popular with composers often supplied opera librettos as well as poems for lieder – Gellert, Weisse and Goethe among the most prominent. But it was through criticism, aesthetic discussion and polemics that issues and possibilities found sharpest focus.

German song became the object of an important movement that began around mid-century, the so-called First Berlin School of lieder. It received strong impetus from one of the spate of theoretical works emanating from the Prussian capital about this time, *Von der musikalischen Poesie* (1752) by the lawyer Christian Gottfried Krause. The aesthetic proposed here and actually followed by Berlin composers over the next two decades advocated artless strophic melodies, complete in themselves, with no need of accompanimental support, and singable by all. In Krause's essay the term 'volkstümlich' makes an early appearance, to remain an essential part of the lied's character down to the present. The high-water mark of this style came in Johann Abraham Peter Schulz's collection *Lieder im Volkston* (1782), which went through many editions. Songs in this style often circulated with no accompaniment at all, or one so spare that the old sense of the continuo no longer applied. Apart from the new emphasis on pure melody, these songs also stressed the absolute primacy of the poetry in expression and structure.

The aesthetic was not entirely new and in fact derived considerable inspiration from the French chanson. A more distinctively German voice emerged in settings for domestic use of sacred poems. In this arena C. P. E. Bach established himself as master with his collection of *Geistliche Oden und Lieder* based on poems of the beloved Christian Fürchtegott Gellert (Berlin, 1758) and his later settings of Christoph Christian Sturm's spiritual poems. The latter in particular include dramatic touches that push at the seams of the restrictive doctrine of the Berlin School.

In secular poetry several types established themselves as particular favourites – the ode, the fable and Anacreontic song, for example. Perhaps most fruitful for the eventual expansion of the north German lied was the *Romanze*, a narrative genre in deliberately naive style borrowed from the French but soon infused with English, Spanish and, especially, native German elements. In particular, the popular German tradition of the itinerant mountebank, or *Bänkelsänger*, lent a distinctive tone. (These singers travelled from town to town and set up platforms from which they sang grisly or sensational tales, often enlarging on current events, which were then sold to the onlookers.) By the 1770s, the *Romanze* had yielded to the more weighty, dramatic and serious *Ballade*. A classic early example, Gottfried August Bürger's *Lenore*, tells of a young girl carried off to a graveyard by the spectre of her fiancé.

The *Romanze* and its cousin, the *Ballade*, illustrate the mutuality of the lied and German opera during this era. Both poetic types found their way into opera as soon as it began to flourish, just as many of the most popular tunes from early German comic operas came to lead independent existences as folksongs. Some of Goethe's most important poems first appeared in his librettos, such as the *Romanze Das Veilchen* and the *Ballade Der Erlkönig*.

The *Ballade* also became a prime vehicle through which composers moved beyond the limitations of the First Berlin School. Johann André provided an early example in his through-composed setting of Bürger's *Lenore*. Freed of strophic stricture, composers could now follow the dramatic and emotional development of a poem as the poet's equal. Goethe and many other poets, however, regarded such

56. Scene from the opera 'Alceste' composed by Anton Schweitzer for the Weimar court in 1773: engraving by J.G. Geyser after Steinhauer

competition with suspicion, even after they had accommodated themselves to the idea of poetic subjugation to music in German opera.

GERMAN LETTERS AND OPERA

German writers debated the place of opera in their culture far more relentlessly and acrimoniously than the place of the lied.[22] From the Leipzig professor Johann Christoph Gottsched's excoriation of opera as a literary form in 1730[23] to the debate over Viennese magic opera in the last decade of the century, again and again the same themes were sounded: the roles of composer and librettist, verisimilitude, German versus Italian, the admissibility of the supernatural, dramatic structure, simplicity of plot, and so forth.

Three outstanding figures in German letters established practical ties with German opera as librettists – Wieland, Herder and Goethe. Christoph Martin Wieland, in so many ways a child of French Rococo art and thought, in matters of opera adored Metastasio above all other poets and sought to imitate his mellifluous verse, delicacy of expression, moderation in tone and simplicity of structure in his German text for the serious opera *Alceste* (*Alkeste*), composed for the Weimar court by Anton Schweitzer in 1773. Despite the opera's classical setting, Wieland's choice of a familial theme and the rather prissy virtue-vaunting of his Hercules reflect values already strong in German drama of the day under the influence of Diderot.

Wieland outlined his goals in writing *Alceste* and his underlying aesthetic of opera even before the work received its première.[24] Along with Metastasio he welcomed much of what refined audiences had admired most in *opera seria* around mid-century. If anything, Wieland wanted the plot kept even simpler and emotional content even more restricted. He did not believe music could adequately express extreme passions. Large-scale musical organization never enters his discussion; instead emphasis remains on the individual aria or recitative. Although Wieland admired Gluck's *Orfeo ed Euridice*, he showed little sympathy for the progressive edge of serious opera of the 1760s and 1770s. His unhappy attempt to write a stirring historical libretto incorporating spectacle, chorus and extreme passions for Mannheim in 1777 – his *Rosemunde*, again composed by Schweitzer – began and ended under an ill star. *Alceste*, meanwhile, enjoyed great popularity all over Germany and served as a model for others who later attempted *opera seria* in German.

Wieland's aesthetic of opera, embodied in *Alceste*, harmonized with his general literary outlook. Elsewhere in Germany, however, young voices were already being heard crying for quite a different aesthetic in all forms of literature, opera included. Johann Gottfried Herder had already set to work on a music drama conceived in this 'Storm and Stress' spirit when Wieland's libretto appeared. Eventually, Herder's *Brutus* was set to music by Johann Christoph Friedrich Bach and produced in 1774 at Bückeburg – a provincial location for such an experiment, which may in part explain why it remained a local phenomenon.

Herder's inspiration was not musical but literary, and one of the most important for German spoken drama during the coming decade – Shakespeare. But Herder was virtually alone among German librettists in seeking to kindle Shakespearean fire in his unruly verses, to inspire the composer as primary creative agent and to assemble as compelling a concatenation of scenes as possible without regard to the unities or other dramatic proprieties of the day. Shakespeare suffered little at Herder's hands – spiritually, at least – compared with the major revisions undertaken by many translators and dramatists in Germany (not to mention eighteenth-century English adapters). Writers under the influence of *bienséance* such as Wieland and Christian Felix Weisse worked major changes on his plays in their translations. Operatic versions, not surprisingly, went even further. Only a handful of young librettists and composers responded sympathetically to the new spirit suffusing Herder's *Brutus*. Most important among them was Goethe in his vagabond opera *Claudine von Villa Bella* (1776), filled with autobiographical layers of discontent over the bourgeois narrowness of his cultural world. Yet this libretto, like the brief, turbulent epoch in which it was conceived, marked only one stretch of the long path German opera followed from the end of the Seven Years' War to the turn of the century. During this period Goethe never lost interest in opera: he pursued it variously as librettist, critic, aesthetician and theatre director.

OPERA FROM HILLER TO REICHARDT

An era of German opera ended with the collapse of the Hamburg opera company in 1738. The years of the Silesian wars that followed saw only sporadic operatic activity in northern Germany, save for the Italian establishments discussed earlier. Works in German were performed from time to time, but now found their home mostly in travelling companies, where they shared the stage and often many of the same performers with German comedy and tragedy.

German opera – although quite a different brand from what Hamburgers had relished in the age of Reinhard Keiser – returned to prominence in German life at Leipzig in the early 1760s. It was the creation of three men. Each had a different agenda and as a result the fledgling genre they called 'komische Oper' had to try to satisfy competing and often conflicting goals. The organizing genius was the theatre owner and actor Heinrich Gottfried Koch. He fixed his attention first and foremost on his dangerously depleted cash-box, whose sole hope lay in finding a way to lure into his little theatre the sizable crowds who flocked to Leipzig during its semi-annual trade fairs. A cheerful tale enlivened with little German songs would be ideal, Koch decided. He was insistent 'that everything should be song-like, simple, and in such a manner that every spectator would be able to join in the singing if he wished'.[25]

The first great librettist of German comic opera, Christian Felix Weisse, also believed that simple, singable strophic songs were just the thing for the new genre, ones that could find their way into good company and form a wholesome part of the culture's social fabric. Weisse came to favour French plays and comic operas as the sources of the librettos he wrote for Koch's stage. The English connection of his first efforts is often pointed out (*Die verwandelten Weiber*, for example, based on Coffey's *The Devil to Pay*), but the earthy humour and structural irregularity of the ballad opera dwindled or disappeared early in the history of German comic opera, superseded by the naive sentimentality practised by the French.

Johann Adam Hiller is often considered the father of the Singspiel ('play with singing'), since we tend to regard composers as the prime movers in any operatic development. Yet he was brought into the enterprise only reluctantly. As it turned out, the delightful tunes he composed for Weisse's texts earned him the universal love and admiration of his countrymen and several became virtual folksongs. The young Reichardt noticed, however, that an artful guiding hand had produced their seeming artlessness: 'When he has, so to speak, drawn the theme of a song or aria out of the poetry, thereafter he draws everything out of the theme, or to put it more precisely, everything flows for him out of the theme'.[26]

Hiller succeeded as did no other composer in capturing musically the spirit of Weisse's texts, but only by virtue of necessity. He had been trained in the spirit of Hasse at Dresden and strove all his life to elevate musical taste in Germany towards an essentially Italianate ideal. In this enterprise comic opera was simply a preliminary step, beyond which he himself never progressed. But he does figure prominently in other areas: as an aesthetician and music journalist, as one of Germany's foremost singing masters, as a conductor and organizer in Leipzig concert life and as a teacher of several prominent composers of the next generation (chief among them Reichardt and Neefe).

The style of opera that Koch, Weisse and Hiller created at Leipzig moved quickly across Germany. Koch himself moved to Berlin, beginning an important new chapter in that city's operatic history even as Frederick's Italian establishment was slipping into utter stagnation. Travelling companies everywhere found Hiller's operas ideal; they filled the house night after night, unlike even the best spoken plays in their repertories, and in consequence saved more than one company from financial ruin.

The travelling company remained an institutional necessity for German opera to the end of the century and beyond, a fact that explains some of the limitations under which it laboured. One necessity was a large repertory, for the same pieces could not continue to fill theatres in the small towns and cities itinerant companies visited. Most troupes found it most prudent to mix opera and spoken drama in their repertories. This policy had repercussions on troupe composition: travel and economic realities enforced small numbers, so most members of the company were expected to sing in the operas as well as act in spoken works. As with French comic opera, this also kept German opera from seriously exploring the possibility of recitative rather than spoken dialogue except in certain works fashioned directly after Italian models.

The best companies were by no means limited to unsophisticated provincial audiences. Even the cultivated Duchess Anna Amalia of Weimar delighted in Hiller's operas. Before Koch moved to Berlin, his troupe had spent several winters at the Weimar court and it was there that Hiller's most enduring opera, *Die Jagd*, saw its première in 1770. A little later, at Berlin, Crown Prince Friedrich Wilhelm attended Koch's performances regularly. As a student, Goethe had included Koch's operatic performances as a part of his social life. 'Weisse's operas', he wrote later in his autobiography, 'enlivened in a light manner by Hiller, gave us much pleasure.' We may note his emphasis on the author, with the composer fulfilling a decorative role. Most writers at the time regarded German opera in this spirit – as spoken plays, essentially, interspersed with short songs.

The 1770s was a time of remarkable innovations in German

theatre and German opera, and in both categories northern and central Germany were the undisputed centre of activity. In terms of theatrical music, the locus is even more precise, for nearly all the decade's important innovations came into being at two relatively small, though enlightened, provincial courts in central Germany – the Weimar court of the music-loving Duchess Anna Amalia, and the one Baron von Grimm represented at Paris: the orderly, high-minded court of Ernst II of Gotha in neighbouring Thuringia. Perhaps even more remarkable, each of these experiments was brought to life by the same theatre company, a previously itinerant group under the direction of a Hamburg businessman, Abel Seyler.

The earliest of their operatic innovations has already been touched on – Wieland's *Alceste* of 1773, composed by the troupe's Kapellmeister Anton Schweitzer. With Seyler's blessing Schweitzer had recruited several first-rate singers for the company, something of a rarity at the time. This explains both the virtuoso character of most of the music in the opera and also the small number of characters Wieland allowed himself (just four singing parts). Both features recur in most subsequent German recitative operas modelled on *opera seria*.

A year earlier Schweitzer had embarked on another new project with even more far-reaching consequences for the German theatre, a new setting of Rousseau's *scène lyrique Pygmalion*, produced by the Seyler company in 1772. The genre – melodrama – consists of a single act or scene, dramatically unified and emotionally highly charged, declaimed by one or two actors with musical accompaniment in the style of obbligato recitative. Schweitzer's setting achieved

57. Madame Brandes as Ariadne in Georg Benda's melodrama 'Ariadne auf Naxos', 1775: engraving from the Gotha 'Theater-Kalender' (1776)

some distinction, but the German melodrama was catapulted to national and even international fame by Georg Benda, Kapellmeister to the Gotha court. He wrote his two great melodramas, *Ariadne auf Naxos* and *Medea*, in 1775 for the two leading ladies of the Seyler company. Both works, unlike Schweitzer's, trade in female heroines and tragic endings, eliciting from Benda some of the most remarkable dramatic music written in Germany during the era. Mozart professed unbounded enthusiasm for both works, which he carried around with him in the later 1770s. The technique left its mark on his unfinished opera known as *Zaïde* and in his incidental music to Gebler's drama *Thamos*.

Although the melodrama as a device does not appear in Mozart's two mature German operas, it found its chief use after about 1778 in the operas of other German composers as a way of enhancing an especially solemn, tense or chilling scene. Thus what in Benda's hands had taken listeners by storm as a highly improbable and yet completely unified and compelling independent genre devolved into an occasional operatic technique, a variant of the obbligato recitative from which it had sprung. This use – familiar from the dungeon scene in Beethoven's *Fidelio* and the Wolf's Glen finale in Weber's *Der Freischütz* – can obscure the compositional challenge posed by the melodrama as an independent entity. Here for once was a north German counterpart to the search for large-scale formal control essayed by Jommelli, Traetta and, above all, Gluck. The theatrical roots of the German melodrama, however, lay deep in the German troupe system, where the best singers plied their art in one part of a company's repertory while the best actors were absorbed in another. Now it was possible to unite the tragic actor at the pinnacle of his art, the dramatic monologue, with the most expressive and powerful language available to dramatic composers, obbligato recitative.

The final important musical innovation at Gotha again involved Benda. With *Alceste* before them, he and the poet Gotter began contemplating a different form of serious opera in German, one that – like the melodrama – made more sense in terms of the split repertories of spoken plays and operas common throughout Germany. The first attempt was the one-act 'ernsthafte Operette' *Walder*, produced in early 1776, a 'serious operetta' with the kind of happy ending familiar to audiences – recognition and reunion of father and son in a rustic environment. Later that year the two moved fully into the world of serious opera with a Shakespearean venture, their three-act *Romeo und Julie*. The opera was completely in the *seria* style musically, save that instead of recitative it used spoken dialogue.[27] Immediately, it won over listeners everywhere. Although a spate of similar works did not follow, German opera with spoken dialogue and songs could now claim pretensions to seriousness unthought of in Hiller's day.

In the later 1770s German opera's centre of activity shifted to Berlin. Johann André, the composer and friend for whom Goethe had written his first libretto in the Rhineland (*Erwin und Elmire*, 1774–5), now dominated German opera in the Prussian capital. While absorbing some of the exciting new possibilities coming out of Weimar and Gotha, he none the less stuck to a conception of German opera rooted fundamentally in popular song.

The period during which Mozart composed his greatest operas, from *Idomeneo* in 1780 to *Die Zauberflöte* in 1791, saw little happen in northern Germany to match the developments of the preceding decade. That Mozart's *Die Entführung aus dem Serail* had as its source the libretto of one of André's most popular Berlin operas (*Belmont und Constanze*, 1781) pointed clearly to the future domination of Austrian operas on north German stages.

Goethe went through something of a cultural crisis in the mid-1780s, and opera played a part. He was by now an outspoken partisan of *opera buffa*, particularly Paisiello. In late 1785 he found himself unaccountably put off by Mozart's *Die Entführung*; only when he was able to suppress the fact that it was a German opera by putting the text out of his mind could he at last grasp the impression the work was making on everyone else. A month later he abandoned the German libretto he was working on, which he had come to pity 'as one can pity a child that is to be born to a black woman in slavery'. His thoughts even turned to writing a libretto in Italian rather than in 'this barbaric tongue'.[28] By that autumn Goethe had embarked on his Italian journey, during which he undertook the project of rewriting his first two operas, not in Italian but completely in the Italian spirit. Both were eventually set by one of the most fascinating figures in the history of north German music, Johann Friedrich Reichardt.

REICHARDT AND THE END OF THE ENLIGHTENMENT

Reichardt was neither the most gifted composer nor the most incisive critical mind of his era, but he offers an apt illustration of the gradual transformation of the north German musical world during the age of the French Revolution. Reichardt applied his talents to virtually every field of musical endeavour available to him; in addition, his extensive travels brought him in direct contact with the music, musicians, intellectuals and ideas current in London, Paris, Venice and Vienna – a breadth of exposure no other north German composer of the time enjoyed. The effects of Reichardt's frequent travels were more apparent in his writings than in his music. The rationalist spirit dominant especially in Berlin around 1750 had produced musical writings that were systematic to a fault, a quality, in fact, that the rest of Europe came to regard as peculiarly German. Reichardt's early publications, written in his native Königsberg after travelling around northern

Germany, contrast sharply with this spirit. They abound in naive patriotism, overdrawn enthusiasm and spontaneous disorganization – qualities Reichardt retained to some degree in all his later writings. Travels abroad also served to stimulate his interest in older music (particularly Palestrina, Handel and Leo), bringing a new historical consciousness into his music journalism in the 1780s, which included the editing of examples of earlier music.

Reichardt was not a significant composer of instrumental music. His own literary bent seemed to have directed his compositional energies towards opera, the melodrama and, above all, the lied. In each case his experience was symptomatic of larger cultural tendencies around him. He began composing German operas in the early 1770s at Leipzig, apparently under Hiller's informal supervision. A little later, one of the boldest moves in his colourful career came on the death of Frederick the Great's Kapellmeister Johann Friedrich Agricola in 1774. With youthful brashness Reichardt proposed himself, barely 23 at the time, as Frederick's new Kapellmeister and laid at the king's feet an *opera seria* written in shameless imitation of Hasse and Graun and, what is more, one that set the same *Le feste galanti* that Graun had composed for the king's opera in 1747! Reichardt got the job, but Frederick would not suffer him to compose anything new for his Italian establishment. Reichardt composed several works for the German stage in Berlin, set up a concert series modelled after the French Concert Spirituel and travelled abroad as frequently as his employer would allow. In the mid-1780s two French operas were commissioned from him in Paris, attesting to a growing international respect for and interest in works of German composers.

The death of Frederick the Great in 1786 brought to the Prussian throne a monarch much more kindly disposed to German opera, Friedrich Wilhelm II. Eventually he set up a Nationaltheater in Berlin, whose operatic wing became the artistic equal of the Italian opera company he continued to maintain. Reichardt composed several heroic Italian operas for Friedrich Wilhelm, the most important of them his *Brenno*, first performed at the royal opera house (Königliches Theater) in 1789. Earlier the same year the court had also given official countenance to one of Reichardt's German operas, his setting of Goethe's newly revised *Claudine von Villa Bella*, produced at the Charlottenburg Palace.

Reichardt spent much of 1790 to 1792 in Paris and London. His outspoken republican sympathies during these years of turmoil did not sit well with the Prussian court and in 1794 Friedrich Wilhelm discharged him without pay. It was in that year that Reichardt set up a country home in Giebichenstein, which became a haven for forward-looking intellectuals such as Schlegel and Schleiermacher and for young Romantic writers like Jean Paul and E. T. A. Hoffmann. A new King of Prussia, Friedrich Wilhelm III, brought Reichardt back into favour in 1796. Two years later he composed his most important German opera, *Die Geisterinsel*, for the Nationaltheater. In the early nineteenth century, when most north German operas written during the last third of the eighteenth century had quickly sunk into oblivion, Reichardt's *Die Geisterinsel* remained in German repertories. It could do so because it had accommodated the new spirit of opera emanating from Italy and, more especially, Vienna. Yet in embracing the spectacle and magic in which *Die Zauberflöte* and its lesser confrères traded, Reichardt's opera also preserved what was most valuable in his northern heritage – folklike simplicity where appropriate, deference to the role of the spoken word and an essentially optimistic view of human nature.

Reichardt was also a dominant figure in the development of the lied during the decades before Schubert. He wrote over 1500 lieder in all and never forsook the essentially northern commitment to the strophic song. His association with Goethe encouraged him to set more of the poet's lyric poetry and librettos than any other composer before or since. A listener at a concert performance of Reichardt's setting of Goethe's *Erwin und Elmire*, given at Halle in 1798, praised his music in terms both composer and poet would have welcomed, saying that it was 'conceived wholly in the spirit of Goethe, and with Goethean simplicity'.[29]

NOTES

[1] On this point and on the general social context of German culture during the eighteenth century see W. H. Bruford, *Germany in the Eighteenth Century: the Social Background of the Literary Revival* (Cambridge, 1935).

[2] Quoted in W. S. Newman, *The Sonata in the Classic Era* (New York, 2/1972), 422.

[3] The relevant study in English remains E. Eugene Helm, *Music at the Court of Frederick the Great* (Norman, 1960); see also A. Yorke-Long, *Music at Court: Four Eighteenth-Century Studies* (London, 1954), chap. 4.

[4] *The Present State of Music in Germany, the Netherlands, and United Provinces* (London, 1773), ii, 152–3.

[5] Quantz's treatise is available in a carefully annotated modern English edition by E. R. Reilly, *On Playing the Flute* (New York, 2/1985).

[6] C. F. D. Schubart, *Ideen zu einer Ästhetik der Tonkunst*, ed. L. Schubart (Vienna, 1806/*R*1969), 129.

[7] *Versuch über die wahre Art das Clavier zu spielen*, trans. W. J. Mitchell as *Essay on the True Art of Playing Keyboard Instruments* (New York, 1949), 152.

[8] *Present State*, ii, 225.

[9] As Helm points out (*Music at the Court of Frederick the Great*, 39), 'the decline of [Frederick's] performing ability was accompanied by a decline of interest in all music'.

[10] See F. L. Millner, *The Operas of Johann Adolf Hasse* (Ann Arbor, 1979).

[11] On Maria Antonia see Yorke-Long, *Music at Court*, chap.3. Like several Austro-Bavarian rulers of the first half of the century, Maria Antonia was a gifted musician. In 1754 she had mounted a pastoral opera in three acts, *Il trionfo della fedeltà*. Not only had she composed both text and music, she also sang in the production.

[12] *Allgemeine deutsche Bibliothek*, ii/1 (Berlin, 1766), 270–71. This comprehensive periodical of book reviews, edited by Friedrich Nicolai, stood at the centre of the critical arsenal created by Berlin's champions of rationalism and Enlightenment.

[13] See L. Crickmore, 'C. P. E. Bach's Harpsichord Concertos', *ML*, xxxix (1958), 237.

[14] See P. Drummond, *The German Concerto: Five Eighteenth-Century Studies* (Oxford, 1980), 245.

[15] See P. M. Young, *The Concert Tradition* (London, 1965), where institutional similarities between German and English concert life are pointed out.

[16] E. Bücken, *Die Musik des Rokokos und der Klassik* (Wildpark–Potsdam, 1927).

[17] Newman, *The Sonata in the Classic Era*, 398.

[18] C. F. D. Schubart, *Musicalische Rhapsodien* (Stuttgart, 1786); quoted in 'Clavichord', *Grove 6*.

[19] Quoted by Newman, in *The Sonata in the Classic Era*, 383.

[20] *Present State*, ii, 237.

[21] In Karl Philipp Moritz's 'psychological novel' *Anton Reiser*, for example, the young hero shuts himself up during a rainy spell with scraps of poetry he has been scribbling and a rickety harpsichord, sitting at the instrument the whole day learning by heart the arias from Hiller's *Die Jagd* and Rolle's *Der Tod Abels*.

[22] On the entire subject see G. Flaherty, *Opera in the Development of German Critical Thought* (Princeton, 1976).

[23] In his *Versuch einer critischen Dichtkunst für die Deutschen* (Leipzig, 1730).

[24] 'Briefe an einen Freund über das deutsche Singspiel Alceste', published in 1773 in the January and March issues of Wieland's new journal, *Der teutsche Merkur*. The opera was first produced in May 1773.

[25] So wrote J.A. Hiller in his autobiography, *Lebensbeschreibungen berühmter Musikgelehrten und Tonkünstler neurer Zeit* (Leipzig, 1784), 312. Koch's ideal had a close parallel in the early stages of French *opéra comique*.

[26] J. F. Reichardt, *Über die deutsche comische Oper* (Hamburg, 1774), 12.

[27] On an essay Benda wrote defending this admixture see T. Bauman, 'Benda, the Germans, and Simple Recitative', *JAMS*, xxxiv (1981), 119–31.

[28] This important episode in Goethe's life is more fully explored in T. Bauman, *North German Opera in the Age of Goethe* (Cambridge, 1985), 253–5.

[29] *Der neue Teutsche Merkur vom Jahre 1798*, i/3, 349. The other works that earned 'undivided applause' at the winter concerts in Halle that season also reflect the taste for the earnest still quite characteristic in northern Germany – Salieri's *Axur, rè d'Ormus* and Mozart's *La clemenza di Tito*.

BIBLIOGRAPHICAL NOTE

Social-political background

A detailed history of Germany from around 1770 to the collapse of the Holy Roman Empire in 1806 is provided by K. Epstein's *The Genesis of German Conservatism* (Princeton, NJ, 1966), which addresses social and intellectual as well as political issues. See also the perceptive study by H. Brunschwig, translated by F. Jellinek as *Enlightenment and Romanticism in Eighteenth-Century Prussia* (Chicago and London, 1974); the original title is more telling: *La crise de l'état prussien à la fin du XVIIIe siècle et la genèse de la mentalité romantique* (Paris, 1947). On a broader front, W. H. Bruford's classic social history of the period, *Germany in the Eighteenth Century: the Social Background of the Literary Revival* (Cambridge, 1935), is still very useful; a work of equal stature more directly focussed on the area covered in the present chapter is H. Rosenberg's *Bureaucracy, Aristocracy and Autocracy: the Prussian Experience, 1660–1815* (Cambridge, Mass., 1958). It outlines the coalescence of a non-noble élite of executives in Prussia and its impact on class structure, social mobility and political power. G. Parry discusses the conflict between rationalism and traditionalism in German theories of government in his essay, 'Enlightened Government and its Critics in Eighteenth-Century Germany', *Historical Journal*, vi (1963), 178–92.

The importance of the role played in Germany by the Holy Roman Empire has been a source of scholarly disagreement in recent decades. In a review-article discussing several relevant monographs, G. Strauss argued that faith in the empire's institutions kept it reasonably effective throughout the eighteenth century: 'The Holy Roman Empire Revisited', *Central European History*, xi (1978), 290–301. J. G. Gagliardo has analysed the structure of the empire in both theory and practice in his *Reich and Nation: the Holy Roman Empire as Idea and Reality, 1763–1806* (Bloomington and London, 1980).

Intellectual history: the German Enlightenment

Most recent literature has tended to emphasize intellectual rather than social or political aspects of German culture in the eighteenth century. Part III of L. White Beck's *Early German Philosophy: Kant and his Predecessors* (Cambridge, 1969) discusses both the Berlin Enlightenment and counter-Enlightenment trends in German thought during the second half of the century. On the latter see also F. M. Barnard's *Herder's Social and Political Thought: From Enlightenment to Nationalism* (Oxford, 1965). The debate on the question, 'What is Enlightenment [Aufklärung]?', a preoccupation of the period itself, has also engaged many modern historians, for example J. Whaley, 'The Protestant Enlightenment in Germany', in *The Enlightenment in National Context*, ed. R. Porter and M. Teich (Cambridge, 1981), 106–17, and P. H. Reill, *The German Enlightenment and the Rise of Historicism* (Berkeley, Los Angeles and London, 1975). J. B. Knudsen presents a socialist view of an eighteenth-century conservative in *Justus Möser and the German Enlightenment* (Cambridge, 1986).

Literature and the theatre

A general survey of the earlier part of the period is provided by F. Radandt, *From Baroque to Storm and Stress, 1720–1775* (London, 1977), although for close-grained coverage one must still turn to H. Hettner's *Geschichte der deutschen Literatur im achtzehnten Jahrhundert*, rev. G. Erler (Berlin, 1961). Other useful surveys include R. Heitner's *German Tragedy in the Age of Enlightenment* (Berkeley, 1963) and R. M. Browning's *German Poetry in the Age of the Enlightenment* (University Park, Penn., 1978). Older studies that remain valuable include W. H. Bruford's *Theatre, Drama, and Audience in Goethe's Germany* (London, 1950) and R. Pascal's *The German Sturm und Drang* (Manchester, 1953), as well as the latter's topical work, *Shakespeare in Germany, 1740–1815* (Cambridge, 1937). E. Purdie's *Studies in German Literature of the Eighteenth Century: some Aspects of Literary Affiliation* (London, 1965) contains essays on English influence, Herder, Hamann and Klopstock. J. W. van Cleve has published an interesting composite of social history and literary criticism focussing on the mid-century figures Gellert and Lessing, *The Merchant in German Literature of the Enlightenment* (Chapel Hill and London, 1986).

Music

General studies of north German music in the Enlightenment are not plentiful. For opera, see T. Bauman's *North German Opera in the Age of Goethe* (Cambridge, 1985), a comprehensive survey from a theatrical as well as musical perspective; and G. Flaherty's monograph on German theory and criticism of opera in the eighteenth century, *Opera in the Development of German Critical Thought* (Princeton, NJ, 1978). Two works on music at major German courts during the period are E. Eugene Helm's *Music at the Court of Frederick the Great* (Norman, 1960) and A. Yorke-Long's *Music at Court: Four Eighteenth-Century Studies* (London, 1954), which includes chapters on Dresden and Berlin.

Carl Philipp Emanuel Bach has been very well served by recent scholarship in English. A new thematic catalogue by E. Eugene Helm promises to supersede earlier ones in scope and authority. Serious work on a complete edition of the composer's works is now under way. Specialized studies in English include a translation of H. G. Ottenberg's biography, *C.P.E. Bach* (Oxford, 1987), a work of undisguised Marxist orientation but still the only biography in English; D. Schulenberg's dissertation *The Instrumental Music of Carl Philipp Emanuel Bach* (Ann Arbor, 1984), laudable for its attempt to evaluate Bach's music on its own terms without reference to an 'evolving' Classical style; R. W. Wade's exhaustive source study, *The Keyboard Concertos of Carl Philipp Emanuel Bach* (Ann Arbor, 1981); and the less intensive, stylistically orientated chapters on Bach and Hasse in P. Drummond, *The German Concerto: Five Eighteenth-Century Studies* (Oxford, 1980).

The major treatises of the period by Bach, Quantz, and Kirnberger have appeared in English translation, and virtually all important theoretical, practical and journalistic works are available in facsimile reprints. B. S. Brook's edition of *The Breitkopf Thematic Catalogue: the Six Parts and Sixteen Supplements, 1762–1787* (New York, 1966) should also be mentioned here.

Other facets of north German musical life are not well documented in English. For a history of the melodrama one must still rely on E. Istel's *Die Entstehung des deutschen Melodramas* (Berlin and Leipzig, 1906) and J. van der Veen's *Le mélodrame musical de Rousseau au romantisme: ses aspects historiques et stylistiques* (The Hague, 1955). The great monument on German song in the period remains M. Friedländer's *Das deutsche Lied im 18. Jahrhundert* (Stuttgart and Berlin, 1902/*R*1970). For Reichardt's life and music the principal modern study is W. Salmen, *Johann Friedrich Reichardt: Komponist, Schriftsteller, Kapellmeister und Verwaltungsbeamter der Goethezeit* (Freiburg and Zurich, 1963). Two major studies in the area of eighteenth-century aesthetics with an emphasis on Germany are H. Goldschmidt, *Die Musikästhetik des 18. Jahrhunderts* (Zurich, 1915) and W. Serauky, *Die musikalische Nachahmungsästhetik im Zeitraum von 1700 bis 1850* (Münster, 1929).

Chapter X

Haydn at the Esterházy Court

LÁSZLÓ SOMFAI

> He did not know himself how celebrated he was abroad, and he heard of it only occasionally from travelling foreigners who visited him. Many of these, even Gluck, advised him to travel to Italy and France, but his timidity and his limited circumstances held him back; and if he spoke a word about it in the hearing of his Prince, the latter pressed a dozen ducats into his hand, and so he abandoned all such projects again.[1]

> My Prince was content with all my works, I received approval, I could, as head of an orchestra, make experiments, observe what enhanced an effect, and what weakened it, thus improving, adding to, cutting away, and running risks. I was set apart from the world, there was nobody in my vicinity to confuse and annoy me in my course, and so I had to be original.[2]

Among the prominent musical geniuses of the Enlightenment, Joseph Haydn (1732–1809) was the only one who, at least formally, spent more than three-quarters of a productive life covering more than five decades as a musician to a noble family. Thus he might be called a 'court musician', a Kapellmeister serving at a provincial court outside Vienna. This courtly status was, however, anachronistic if we consider the role played by the composer in the general development of European music – because, from at the latest the 1780s until the turn of the century, Haydn was probably the single most influential and individual contributor to the formation of the style of instrumental music: and this at a time when publishers and musicians in Paris, Amsterdam, London and elsewhere had as yet little reliable information about him or about his activities. Why, then, did he continue in this outmoded position until the end of his life? Did he perhaps consciously lead a double life and, from the safety and financial security of a court musician's status, after a time work almost exclusively for external consumption? Furthermore, how could Haydn, for the bulk of the year living in the provinces (in Eisenstadt or Eszterháza), cut off even from Vienna, exert a more enduring influence on the public (and partly also on the composers) of Europe's musical centres than the leading composers who resided there?

This situation, of exceptional interest from the viewpoint of the history of culture, can be understood only in its proper chronological context, in the light of the changing relationships between the ruling prince and his musician, and, no less important, by distinguishing clearly between 'local' musical forms and those for 'export'.

THE ESTERHÁZY FAMILY AND HAYDN

Though the Esterházy name entered the general history of culture only in the decades when its bearers had Haydn as a musician, the family was by that time already on the decline, although not by any means economically. The Esterházy *Fideikommiss* (trust fund) – an indivisible property passed on through the male line together with the title of ruling prince – was the largest Hungarian noble realm, with vast lands and numerous castles, country seats and town mansions.

The prince's annual income was around 700,000 gulden, while the incomes of the six Hungarian nobles whose wealth came closest ranged from about 300,000 to 450,000. Among those who were the wealthiest in the Austrian empire, Prince Esterházy was one of the most powerful millionaires in Vienna, alongside the princes Liechtenstein and Schwarzenberg. The decline of the Esterházys therefore was manifested rather in the domain of creative power and influence upon the nation's history. The Esterházys' great seventeenth-century forebears, in particular the palatine Nikolaus (1582–1645), first prince of the dynasty, and the palatine Paul (1635–1712), were still able, as both war-lords and politicians, to range a considerable part of the nobility on their side in matters of Hungarian import. Their role in this capacity was no doubt inglorious, but it was significant; after all, it was owing to Prince Paul's ascendancy that, after the removal of the Turks and the failure to realize the Bethlen and Rákóczi families' dream of national independence, an act had to be passed providing for the permanent rule of the Habsburgs instead of an autonomous Hungary. This was the palatine Paul who, in 1687, was made a prince of the Holy Roman Empire and who in his capacity as poet and cantata composer was by no means undistinguished.

By comparison, the Esterházys who were Haydn's first princely masters, though excellent men – university graduates, brave soldiers, fit for diplomatic service, cultured and possessing a knowledge of languages, as well as accomplished on several musical instruments – did not rank with their grandfather in the art of living. Their estates, situated mostly on the borders of Austria and Hungary, were an empire within the Empire. No longer could they hope to regain the full support of the patriotic Hungarian nobility. At court Hungarian had been replaced by German as the official language as early as their childhood and princes Paul Anton and Nikolaus 'the Magnificent' chose Italian and German wives respectively. In the imperial capital they naturally emphasized their leading position among the Hungarians, receiving with satisfaction honours and titles from Maria Theresa, but they preferred to spend their time at their provincial residences. They particularly rejoiced in the reception of distinguished visitors from far away, especially from France. All of this should not be disregarded when considering the western-orientated artistic aspirations and hospitality of the Esterházys in the middle of the eighteenth century and that Haydn could live for decades on Hungarian soil without knowing the Hungarian language.

Haydn was musician to four Esterházy princes; but a study of the chronology shows that he had sustained relations with only two of them.

1761	1 May, Haydn (29 years old) engaged by Prince Paul Anton (1711–62) as vice-Kapellmeister; for the greater part of the year the household was resident at Eisenstadt;
1762	18 March, death of Prince Paul Anton; he was succeeded by his younger brother, Prince Nikolaus 'the Magnificent' (1714–90);
1766	3 March, death of the Oberhofkapellmeister Gregor Joseph Werner; Haydn became Kapellmeister; the household, together with most of its musical activities, now gradually moved to Eszterháza (finished by 1784), though the administrative headquarters remained in Eisenstadt;
1776–	many performances of opera given each year at Eszterháza;
1790	28 September, death of Prince Nikolaus; his son and heir, Prince (Paul) Anton (1738–22 Jan 1794), disbanded the orchestra and the opera company but retained Haydn symbolically as Kapellmeister; he was succeeded by his son;
1791–2, 1794–5	Haydn's visits to England; between them he stayed in Vienna and composed;
1795	Prince Nikolaus II (1765–1833), installed June 1794, revived the musical establishment in 1795, and later the theatre, making Eisenstadt again the centre;
1796–1802	Haydn lived for most of the time in his own house in a suburb of Vienna, but wrote a mass annually for the name day of the princess, travelling to Eisenstadt for a month or more for the performance;
1802–	part of the work of the 70-year-old Haydn was taken over by the vice-Kapellmeister Johann Nepomuk Fuchs; in 1804 Johann Nepomuk Hummel succeeded Haydn as Kapellmeister;
1809	31 May, death of Haydn.

Of his total of 49 years in the service of the Esterházys, the last nineteen were more relaxed for Haydn: the five years spent visiting England were virtually paid leave; in the remaining seven active years his service was symbolic (his only regular duties were the annual composition and performance of a mass); and the final seven were those of old age and retirement, in Vienna, of the celebrated but weary master. Thus the actual 'court musician' service, when considered from the productive aspect, was confined to slightly less than 30 years when Haydn was chiefly in the service of Prince Nikolaus. This was also the period when he developed into a composer of distinct individuality and his reputation spread across Europe.

HAYDN'S CONTRACTS AND HIS EARLY ESTERHÁZY YEARS

Although Haydn's period of service with Prince Nikolaus was the most enduring and creatively the most important contact between the composer and the family, the credit for discovering the 29-year-old composer for the Esterházys belongs to Prince Nikolaus's brother, Prince Paul Anton. He was not especially taken with the production of oratorios and masses at Eisenstadt by the modest ensemble under the Kapellmeister, Gregor Joseph Werner, who was responsible for the music in his mother's household. He was acquainted with new, chiefly Italian, music and from 1750, while he was Austrian Minister Extraordinary at the court of Naples, he had collected opera scores. From 1757 the Italian violinist and composer Luigi Tomasini had been employed by him as *valet-de-chambre* and in 1759 he engaged the tenor Carl Friberth, who became a kind of musical and theatrical manager and later wrote Italian librettos for Haydn.

It may have been Friberth who brought Haydn to the prince's attention. At that time Haydn was in the service of Count Morzin as his music director at Lukavec in Bohemia and at his palace in Vienna. Whether because Haydn had married without his master's permission or because financial difficulties had forced the count to dismiss his musicians, Haydn was free in Vienna. Although in his old age the composer remembered the engagement by Prince Paul Anton as having taken place in 1760, the formal contract was signed, in Vienna, no earlier than 1 May 1761. Initially there was a 'trial period' during which Haydn began work on the three symphonies with themes suggested by Prince Paul Anton (nos.6–8: 'Le matin', 'Le midi' and 'Le soir') and, with Haydn's help, new musicians were engaged. This took from April to June, after which the Kapelle, by then under the sole control of Haydn as vice-Kapellmeister, had thirteen members; these, including Haydn himself (who played the violin and conducted the non-vocal works with violin in hand), were: five violinists (one of them also a viola player), one cellist, one flautist, two oboists, two bassoon players (one of them also the double bass player) and two horn players. To these were added occasionally, in all likelihood, two or three other musicians, either from Werner's ensemble at Eisenstadt or from among the prince's valets who played an instrument, since uniforms were tailored for sixteen musicians.

Haydn himself was classed not among the prince's servants but among the house officers. The wording of the oft-quoted contract of 1761 ('Convention and Rules for Behaviour of the *Vice-Capel-Meister*'), when judged by eighteenth-century standards and keeping in mind a realistic assessment of the position in the hierarchy and the immense personal power of a prince of the Holy Roman Empire, is not in fact humiliating, as it is sometimes thought to be.[3] According to the text, set out under fourteen headings:

> 2. . . . his Serene Princely Highness is graciously pleased to place confidence in him, that as may be expected from an honourable house officer in a princely court, he will be temperate, and will know that he must treat the musicians placed under him not overbearingly, but with mildness and leniency, modestly, quietly and honestly . . . and the said Joseph Heÿden[4] . . . shall follow the instructions which have been given to them, appearing neatly in white stockings, white linen, powdered, and either with pigtail or hair-bag, but otherwise of identical appearance.
> 5. . . . [Haydn] shall appear daily (whether here in Vienna or on the estates) in the *antichambre* before and after midday, and inquire whether a high princely *ordre* for a musical performance has been given . . .

Haydn had to settle the quarrels of his musicians (no.6), look after the instruments (no.7), rehearse the expensively trained female singers (no.8) and so on. A point that has been considered to be demeaning is:

> 4. . . . The said *Vice-Capel-Meister* shall be under permanent obligation to compose such pieces of music as his Serene Princely Highness may command, and neither to communicate such new compositions to anyone, nor to allow them to be copied, but to retain them wholly for the exclusive use of his Highness; nor shall he compose for any other person without the knowledge and gracious permission [of his Highness].

A new contract, dated 1 January 1779 and replacing the original one of 1761, outlined Haydn's duties under six headings in an incomparably more liberal form, as can be seen:

> *Tertio*: The party of the second part [Haydn] agrees to perform any music of one kind or another in all the places, and all the times, to which and when H. Highness is pleased to command. *Quarto*: The party of the second part should not, without special permission, absent himself from his duties, nor from the place to which H. Highness ordered the musicians. *Quinto*: Both contractual parties reserve the right to cancel the agreement.[5]

In return for the expropriation, at least initially, of his entire creative and working capacity, the contract of 1761 assured Haydn a basic salary of 400 gulden, with an additional 182 gulden 30 kreuzer for food and board and the supply of a uniform. In 1762 Prince

Nikolaus raised the basic salary to 600 gulden, by no means a small sum when it is considered that Werner's salary remained 400 gulden until his death, or that in 1765, in contrast with the annual 782 gulden 30 kreuzer received by Haydn, Friberth and Tomasini were paid only 482 gulden 30 kreuzer and 432 gulden 30 kreuzer respectively and other good musicians were earning less than 350 gulden a year. This should be compared with the salaries of the prince's highest-paid employees: thus Peter Ludwig von Rahier, the estate director, received 2200 gulden plus the equivalent of about 400 gulden in produce; the prince's chief judge and the master of the forests received 800 gulden plus the equivalent of 40 gulden and 900 gulden respectively. A further comparison proves less favourable: the Viennese imperial Hofkapellmeister's salary ranged from 1200 to 2500 gulden, while that of the great Johann Joseph Fux was 3100 gulden. When, in accordance with Prince Nikolaus's will and testament, Haydn later received a retirement pension of 1000 gulden (increased by 400 by the new prince), in the growing inflation of the 1790s this was an amount equivalent to the salary of a much younger Viennese Kapellmeister, but given to Haydn after many decades of service. Of course, by that time his office was merely a sinecure, since he was free to dispose of his compositions as he wished.

Returning to the year 1761 and to his first years in the service of the Esterházy family, it is hardly an exaggeration to connect with this period Haydn's coming to maturity as a composer and the formation of his character and way of life. It is true that he was already 29 years old, but the previous decade of adult musicianship had been filled with ceaseless adaptation and attempts to seize every opportunity. Neither in the 'years of starvation' (Haydn) that followed the period as a boy chorister at St Stephen's Cathedral in Vienna, nor during the years of teaching which, for the sake of subsistence, took the place of years that would normally have been spent studying, nor yet during the brief musical directorship held under Count Morzin had Haydn had the opportunity to become truly individual, either personally or musically. The position of Esterházy vice-Kapellmeister, on the other hand, not only meant security but also considerable moral and artistic responsibility, and a challenge. In this area he had nobody to share his cares with. As for his new wife, it soon became apparent that she was narrow-minded and insensitive to her husband's art, as well as vain; nor did she ever bear him a child. Haydn was lonely, not only in his private life but in the end also among his new-found musical colleagues. Though he was naturally reserved, his position obliged him to win over, teach and direct the musicians entrusted to him without being too familiar. By all accounts he wore willingly the musicians' prescribed uniform (whose colour and decoration was several times altered, especially in the 1760s). The portrait in oil

58. Joseph Haydn: portrait (c1762–3) by Johann Basilius Grundmann, destroyed in World War II (the composer is shown wearing the blue uniform with silver trimmings of the vice-Kapellmeister of the Esterházy household)

with which the prince's painter Johann Basilius Grundmann first immortalized Haydn (*c*1762–3) shows him in a blue uniform with silver trimmings.

Being ready to serve at all times showed itself in a certain meticulousness in Haydn's outward appearance, which struck visitors even in his old age. His biographer Albert Christoph Dies noted that

> Love of order seemed as inborn in him as industry. The former was to be observed, as also his love of cleanliness, in his person and in his entire household. He never received visits, for instance, if he were not first fully clothed. If he were surprised by a friend, he tried to get at least enough time to put on his wig.[6]

Physically he was unprepossessing. Griesinger, his other contemporary biographer, said that

> Haydn was small in stature, but sturdy and strongly built. His forehead was broad and well modelled, his skin brown, his eyes bright and fiery, his other features full and strongly marked, and his whole physiognomy and bearing bespoke prudence and a quiet gravity.[7]

Dies also noted that

> The lower half of his body was too short for the upper, something commonly to be seen in small persons of either sex, but very noticeable in Haydn because he kept to the old fashion of having his trousers reach only to the hips and not above the waist.[8]

Socially, though not well versed as a conversationalist, Haydn stood the test of any situation. At the Esterházys' he quickly learnt the set conventions and forms of discourse which he was later able to put to good use, mainly in England. ('I have associated with emperors, kings and many great people, and I have heard many flattering things from them, but I would not live in familiar relation with such persons; I prefer to be close to people of my own standing', he told Griesinger in his old age.) From the beginning he was bold and astute on behalf of his musicians, as attested for instance by his letter of 9 September 1765 to Prince Nikolaus. Although the 'Papa Haydn' of the musicians and their filial affection towards him are more typical of the last years, under the fourth prince, even earlier, when only a vice-Kapellmeister, he managed to win the support of the musicians, who sided with him unreservedly. Meanwhile, he repeatedly suffered from the overbearing personality of the estate manager, formerly a military man, Peter Ludwig von Rahier, and his increasing popularity occasioned bitter complaints from the elderly Kapellmeister Gregor Werner, who, lacking any better pretext, laid the blame for disorder and indiscipline upon the young Haydn (in a letter to the prince in October 1765). Werner's letter persuaded Prince Nikolaus to make provision for looking after scores and instruments and for greater organization in the work of the musicians: this took the form of an order entitled *Regulatio Chori Kissmartoniensis*. Haydn also received instructions as a composer:

> Haydn is urgently enjoined to apply himself to composition more diligently than heretofore, and especially to write such pieces as can be played on the gamba [baryton], of which pieces we have seen very few up to now; and to be able to judge his diligence, he shall at all times send us the first copy, cleanly and carefully written, of each and every composition.[9]

It is this paragraph calling him to account that caused Haydn in 1765, as proof of diligence and productivity, to compile retrospectively an outline thematic catalogue of his works (known as the 'Entwurf-Katalog') which he afterwards continued to keep fairly regularly.

The *Regulatio* and Werner's death soon afterwards represent the end of the first period of Haydn's relations with the Esterházy court (1761–5). During this time he had organized his musicians and turned his compositions and his service to good account with his master. The most important musical forms of this period were the symphony and the concerto and vocal compositions written for special occasions. In general, it was not unusual for an eighteenth-century court composer to reflect his master's preferences in some of his pieces; nor was it unusual to include solo sections designed to give an opportunity to the best instrumentalists to excel in accordance with their abilities, while at the same time fashioning works that brought out his own compositional originality. Even so, the famous trilogy of symphonies (nos.6–8, mentioned above) written for the début of the orchestra established under Haydn's direction is one of the most brilliant stylistic essays Haydn ever composed. He had, for example, to remember the 'Italian' taste of his first master, whose recently catalogued music collection contained Vivaldi's *Il cimento* (op.8), which includes the four concertos portraying the four seasons of the year. It can hardly be coincidence that in these symphonies Haydn echoed the style of the Italian concerto grosso by using different soloistic combinations; or that he used fully the operatic style in a recitative-like violin solo played by himself; or that by composing programmatic movements with titles like 'Sunrise', 'Tempest' and so on, he demonstrated his knowledge of the tradition. In the midst of such consistent stylization the modernity of Haydn's own style was evident in, for example, his enormously energetic first movements and his characteristically individual minuets.

Though the complexity and sophistication of this trilogy was not maintained in succeeding symphonies, the yearly output of which

59. The hall where concerts were held in the Esterházy palace at Eisenstadt

averaged about four in this period, symphonies were a representative genre in the Esterházy concerts given in Eisenstadt and Vienna, and occasionally in the residence at Kittsee near the Hungarian capital, Pozsony (Pressburg, now Bratislava). Haydn, taking pleasure in experimentation, offered a rich assortment: symphonies beginning with a fast movement, or, in the *sonata da chiesa* style, beginning with a slow one; others with a part for one or more solo instruments; purely orchestral works; some of a simpler, Italian operatic-overture (*sinfonia*) type; and others using a Gregorian plainsong melody (Symphony no.30, 'Alleluja') – all were to be found among the symphonies of this period.

Related to the symphony were kindred forms, the concerto and the divertimento, their closeness lying mainly in the performing forces and style. Apart from at least half a dozen concertos (now lost) written for the musicians at Eszterháza, there is a superb horn concerto perhaps intended for Joseph Leutgeb, later Mozart's horn player; two violin concertos, probably written for Tomasini, the leader of Haydn's orchestra; and a cello concerto (rediscovered in the 1950s), one of the ornaments of the literature for the instrument, from which we can imagine what manner of cellist the Kapelle had in the person of Joseph Weigl. The symphonies are supplemented by interesting divertimentos, including a cassation in D major for strings and four horns, probably dating from 1763 (Haydn had four horn players only in the years 1763, 1765 and 1767; the 'Hornsignal' symphony, no.31, dates from 1765). These 'neighbouring' groups of works had in turn their related genres. In addition to the usual solo concertos there are concertinos and divertimentos for harpsichord and three string instruments, whose relatively easy keyboard parts were most probably played by Haydn. The larger divertimentos for mixed groups of instruments have their genre relatives in the wind divertimentos entitled *Feldparthie*, in which clarinets also occasionally appeared (Haydn used clarinets in symphonies only in London). The baryton compositions mentioned in the *Regulatio* belong to a later period, as we shall see.

Haydn's composing developed at a tremendous pace, his ideas already rich and concise in the instrumental works of the first Esterházy years. There were of course popular and even humorous features in these pieces. Even so, the style was rather *für Kenner* ('for connoisseurs') than for *Liebhaber* ('amateurs'). The ensemble's small number of players and the transparent sound suitable for it, as well as the musical intelligence of the important person – the prince – sitting in the audience, provided an opportunity for Haydn to develop a concise form of construction exceptional for the time which avoided repetitions and abounded in original effects. Thus what Haydn told Griesinger in his old age was really so: 'I could . . . make experiments, observe what enhanced an effect, and what weakened it . . . I had to be original'.

In contrast to the purely instrumental music, the vocal works were called upon for festive occasions. Apart from a *Te Deum*, very popular at the time (written perhaps for the inauguration of Prince Nikolaus in 1762), and *contrafacta* church works (vocal pieces from other genres set to new words), Haydn's Italian cantatas and earliest surviving stage works would be the ones which, were they a part of today's concert life, might give a true picture of the 'courtly' compositions of this first period. The partly surviving intermezzo-like *La Marchesa Nespola*, entered in Haydn's catalogue (1762), apparently reflects Prince Paul Anton's taste; Haydn's arias were probably heard between the prose dialogues of a troupe of Italian actors from Pressburg. The first true opera by Haydn was *Acide*, a *festa teatrale* composed in 1762 but not heard before the wedding ceremony of Prince Nikolaus's eldest son in 1763; it was performed again in revised form after the lapse of a decade. In it the 'Maestro di Cappella', as Haydn's title appears on the printed libretto, proved to be more gifted at that time in writing dramatic accompanied recitative than arias. The three Italian cantatas of 1763–4 are real occasional works: two of them were to celebrate the name day (6 December) of Prince Nikolaus (the words of *Qual dubbio ormai* even mention the prince's recent honours), while the third, *Da qual gioja improvvisa*, was the welcome for the prince on his return from the coronation of Joseph II in Frankfurt in 1764. These otherwise somewhat formal cantatas contain a number of attractive harpsichord solos, performed of course by Haydn as a personal gesture or compliment which was not self-evident in such occasional compositions.

ESZTERHÁZA AND HAYDN'S MIDDLE ESTERHÁZY YEARS

It is interesting to note that when in April 1764 Prince Nikolaus attended the coronation of Joseph II as King of the Holy Roman Empire in Frankfurt – on which occasion his expensive entourage dazzled even Goethe (*Aus meinem Leben, Dichtung und Wahrheit*, 1811–22) – he did not think it suitable to take with him the Kapelle directed by Haydn. Perhaps at that time music still occupied a humble place in his grand schemes, or his most pressing tasks lay outside the field of music since he knew it to be in good hands. He was preoccupied with the idea of creating a spectacular and luxurious paradise devoted to the arts and entertainment, rising like a mirage from the flat marshland of the steppe. He had decided to rebuild the hunting lodge at Süttör, earlier his favourite residence, and to alter the surroundings. That he wanted to establish a kind of 'petit Versailles de l'Hongrie' virtually in competition with the grand castles of Austria was evident from the beginning. (The prince,

60. The Eszterháza Palace in 1791: engraving by János Berkeny after Szabó and Carl Schütz (a gypsy band plays in the foreground)

contrary to earlier assumptions in the Haydn literature, did not go to Versailles before the main building of the Eszterháza castle was completed in 1767, but before the 1781 rebuilding.) The redesigning of the earlier structure of the castle, which had been designed by A. E. Martinelli, was entrusted to the renowned Viennese architect Melchior Hefele, whose plans and model of 1765, prepared under the prince's personal supervision, were realized surprisingly quickly through the expenditure of huge material resources and manpower. By 1766 the castle was partly habitable and Prince Nikolaus issued his decrees from the residence, called Eszterház (written with varying orthography). Building continued, costing approximately thirteen million gulden, for about a decade and a half.

The opera house was finished in 1768, together with a music house to accommodate the Kapelle, which moved there for the season, and the companies of actors and, later, the increased number of opera singers. There was also a rehearsal room. In 1772, when the second theatre, the marionette theatre decorated in grotto style, was complete the large-scale visits began. Numerous smaller buildings now stood in the vast park, as well as fountains etc, providing settings for the various events, while game reserves were available for guests who wished to hunt. Finally, in 1784, after having erected a new opera house to replace the first one, which in 1779 was destroyed by fire, Prince Nikolaus decided that his creation was finished and he published the famous 'Description', *Beschreibung des Hochfürstlichen*

Schlosses Esterháss, illustrated with the celebrated engravings and sketches (fig.62 below).

The whole Eszterháza site had an almost surreal quality which is conveyed in passages from the travels of a certain Baron Riesbeck:

> What increases the magnificence of the place is the contrast with the surrounding countryside. Anything more dull or depressing can hardly be imagined. The Neusiedler See, from which the castle is not far removed, makes miles of swamp and threatens in time to swallow up all the land right up to the Prince's dwelling, just as it has already swallowed up huge fields containing the most fertile land which has been laid out. The inhabitants of this country look for the most part like ghosts, and in Spring they almost always get cold fever. One has figured out, that with half the money the Prince spent on his gardens, he could not only have dried out the swamp but regained as much land again from the lake . . . Unhealthy as is the country, especially in Spring and Autumn, and although the Prince himself is attacked by cold fever, he is firmly persuaded that in the whole wide world there is no more healthy and pleasant place. His castle is quite isolated, and he has no one about him except his servants and the strangers who come to admire his beautiful things . . .
>
> His orchestra is one of the best I ever heard, and the great Haydn is his court and theatre composer. For his curious theatre he keeps a poet whose ability to fit large subjects into the theatre, and whose parodies of serious pieces, are often very successful. His theatrical painter and decorator is an excellent artist, although he can display his talent only on a small scale. In short the operation is small, but the outward trappings are on a very large scale. He often engages a troupe of players for several months at a time, and apart from some servants he is the whole audience.[10]

This travel report, issued in 1784, probably exaggerates in some respects; and neither the shady social background to the grand creation nor the prince's gradually increasing bouts of depression are mentioned in the Hungarian verse reports favoured by the prince (for example, György Bessenyei's long poem *Eszterházi vigasságok* of 1772 or Márton Dallos's poetic description of 1781), nor in the French brochure published for the Empress Maria Theresa's visit to Eszterháza (*Relation des fêtes données à sa majesté l'impératrice* . . ., September 1773) and the *Excursion à Esterhaz en Hongrie en mai 1784* (virtually an official tourist guide). Moreover, it must have been a strange and to some extent oppressive routine for Haydn to go every day to this enormous, symmetrical edifice rising from the otherwise empty plain, and to be on call daily for various wishes and commands. Perhaps one of its side effects shows itself in the sense of proportion and symmetry of form especially evident in the string quartets from the period 1770–72, with their perfectly balanced sequence of movements.

With the ever-lengthening summer seasons at Eszterháza Haydn's duties and output increased considerably during his second period there (1766–75). As Kapellmeister, since the death of Werner, he was also responsible for the church music at the castle at Eisenstadt. To this charge we owe the series of very important, relatively long masses belonging to the type known as the 'cantata mass' – the *Missa Cellensis* (1766); *Missa in honorem BVM* (*c*1768–9), the 'Great Organ Mass', so called on account of the organ solos included in it, since Haydn was now officially court organist, an appointment for which he received a separate payment; and the *Missa Sancti Nicolai* (1772), which was of course in honour of Prince Nikolaus.

For the time being Haydn and his wife continued to live in Eisenstadt, where they bought a house in 1766. Twice burnt down but

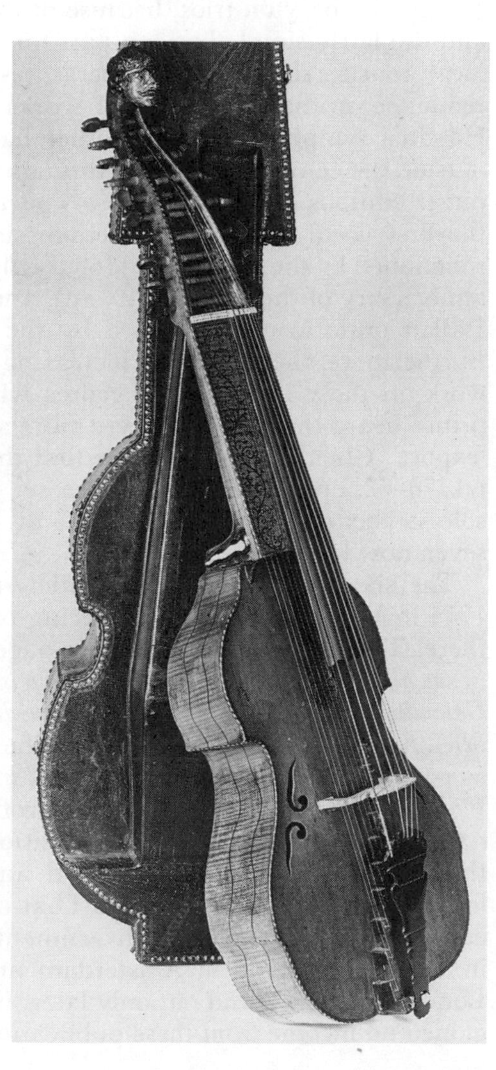

61. Baryton by Johann Joseph Stadlmann, Vienna, 1750, once in the possession of Prince Nikolaus Esterházy

quickly rebuilt, with the prince's help, it was a two-storey country-town house, where they had a maidservant. (It still stands, now a Haydn museum.) Eszterháza, however, became increasingly the scene of Haydn's main activities, and the three principal genres for the court music from 1766 to 1775 were symphonies, baryton trios and opera: the symphonic output was still considerable (about three works a year); Haydn composed about 114 baryton trios and other works for the baryton (a bass string instrument simultaneously bowed from above and plucked from behind by the left thumb), for which the prince had become excessively enthusiastic; and opera became increasingly important – five new Italian operas and two German marionette operas were given and *Acide* was revised. Of the three genres, the baryton trios, because of the instrument's curiosity value and the fairly simple baryton part for the prince, remained typically local music; similarly the operas, especially the first half-dozen, remained primarily occasional works for the Esterházy residence. Haydn's symphonies, on the other hand, were already well known outside the court in the 1760s, through the work of hack-copyists and pirate editions. Apart from these 'courtly' works there soon appeared the first vocal compositions commissioned from other sources (but sanctioned by the prince): in 1768 the *Applausus* cantata, written for an anniversary of the Abbot of Zwettl, and in 1775 *Il ritorno di Tobia*, an Italian oratorio commissioned by the Vienna Tonkünstler-Sozietät Furthermore, there came an increasing emphasis in Haydn's creative work on those instrumental genres which – no matter whether the prince heard them or not – were more and more obviously written for 'export'. Chiefly, these were the first three sets of real string quartets (*c*1770–72, opp.9, 17 and 20, each set containing six works) and the solo keyboard sonatas (*c*1765–73, at least fifteen works, including seven now lost).

The six sonatas for harpsichord written in 1773 were printed in 1774 in Vienna, before the flowering of music publishing had begun there. The dedication on the title-page was addressed to the prince (*a sua altezza serenissima del sacro romano imperio principe Nicolo Esterházy di Galantha* etc . . . *L'autore Giuseppe Haydn Maestro di Capella pref. A. S. Ser.*). A special section of the dedication referred to the prince not only as patron and an active performer of music (*della Musica tutta, non già Violino, e dal Baritono*), but also as proficient in the art (*Professore più esperto*). This was the first printed edition (Haydn was 42 years old by this time) that can be considered an authorized one. It was not followed by another until 1780. That other works of his (mainly the early string quartets, called divertimentos) were published from 1764 in Paris, from 1765 in Amsterdam and a couple of years later in London also, he found out only later, if indeed he ever knew: Haydn gained no income from these publications or from the Leipzig firm of

Breitkopf, whose annual catalogue, including thematic incipits, from 1763 offered copies of his works, obtainable either in manuscript or in printed form.

The first contemporary reviews come from the mid-1760s, as yet mostly of the instrumental pieces written before Haydn's Esterházy service. The majority were favourable, though sometimes they show signs of disapproval from conservatives. In the *Wienerisches Diarium* of 18 October 1766 (see Chapter IV above) he is lavishly praised for the beauty, order, clarity and fine and noble expression of his music. Haydn sent the score of his *Stabat mater* (1767) to one of the most eminent composers in Vienna at that time, Johann Adolf Hasse, of whose appreciation he was immensely proud. On the other hand, he was incensed by the knowledge that 'In the chamber-music style I have been fortunate enough to please almost all nations except the Berliners'. In his autobiographical sketch of 1776 (written for the publication *Das gelehrte Österreich*) he vented his annoyance with the Berliners throughout a whole paragraph, and it is not impossible that the fugal finales and other requisites of the learned style that figure in the 'Sun' Quartets (op.20) are directly connected with the criticism from Berlin in 1771 by a certain Herr Stockhausen. From this is evident not only Haydn's vanity regarding non-professional dismissals of his works but also the fact that he generally won appreciation for compositions performed in the prince's presence and that at the beginning of the 1770s he could feel that his artistic efforts, innovations and surprises did not fail to have their effect upon connoisseurs.

Through the 'Farewell' Symphony (no.45), all of whose movements are equally unusual and splendid in style and structure, we learn accidentally how with it Haydn managed to intercede on behalf of his musicians to counter the prince's suspected intentions of keeping them longer at Eszterháza than usual.[11] But there are at least half a dozen equally extraordinary and original symphonies from that time (no.44 in E minor, no.52 in C minor, no.46 in B, no.54 in G etc) which – along with the best chamber works of the period – also presuppose a reception worthy of Haydn's highest ambitions as a composer. However attractive the explanation according to which Haydn was inspired by a general European 'Sturm und Drang' movement or sentiment (basically literary in origin) to compose these particularly intense works, it cannot be the case. Their surprisingly new style and manner was created by an ambitious composer now fully equipped who before a receptive and select audience he knew very well, was able to give form to deep emotions, caprices and associations in a manner that was unprecedented and eloquent, and who, as his biographer noted in his old age, 'had portrayed moral characters in his symphonies'. Haydn was thus probably being sincere in 1776 when he said of Prince Nikolaus, 'in whose service I wish to live and die'.

He threw himself no less ambitiously into opera composition. In this his hands were tied by a number of factors. The choice of subject and librettist was probably a privilege of the prince. Haydn had further to content himself with a small number of soloists, a stage of limited dimensions and the small, though splendid, chamber orchestra at his disposal – in other words he could write chamber operas only. Had he had the dramatic vocation of a composer like Gluck, which he did not, he would have had to leave the Esterházys in order to be able to work for a real theatre and a large public. He himself acknowledged this in retrospect in a letter of 1787 replying to a request for an *opera buffa* for Prague:

> all of my operas are far too closely connected with our personal circle (Esterház, in Hungary), and moreover [elsewhere] they would not produce the proper effect, which I have calculated in accordance with the locality. It would be quite another matter if I were to have the great good fortune to compose a brand new libretto for your theatre. But even then I should be risking a good deal, for scarcely any man can brook comparison with the great Mozart.[12]

If we do not measure him against Mozart and do not try at all costs to find out why Haydn's theatrical music could not match in popularity the successes of the Italian masters fashionable at the time (Piccinni, Paisiello, Cimarosa etc), we must still value these works highly, as examples of chamber opera or 'residential' opera. An adaptation of a Goldoni libretto, *Lo speziale*, inaugurated the Eszterháza opera house in 1768, gaining success also in Vienna in 1770 when it was performed by the Esterházy Kapelle. *Le pescatrici* (performed 1770) and *L'infedeltà delusa* (1773), staged during Maria Theresa's only visit to Eszterháza, seemed expressly to promise Prince Nikolaus, in their extraordinary delicacy of musical elaboration and the vividness of their comic scenes (use of dialect, disguises etc), that he had found the house opera composer he needed for his grand designs.

Opera was after all the chief artistic spectacle among the various musical offerings during the visits of the princely and royal guests. As 'total art' it ranked alongside the large-scale garden fireworks, the gala dinner or the ball, about which the outside world had detailed information, chiefly from the reports in the *Pressburger Zeitung*.

OPERA AND HAYDN'S LATER ESTERHÁZY YEARS

The third period (1776–84) of Haydn's service as a court musician and of his compositional output was determined by the start of regular operatic performances. Prince Nikolaus had tired of the baryton by

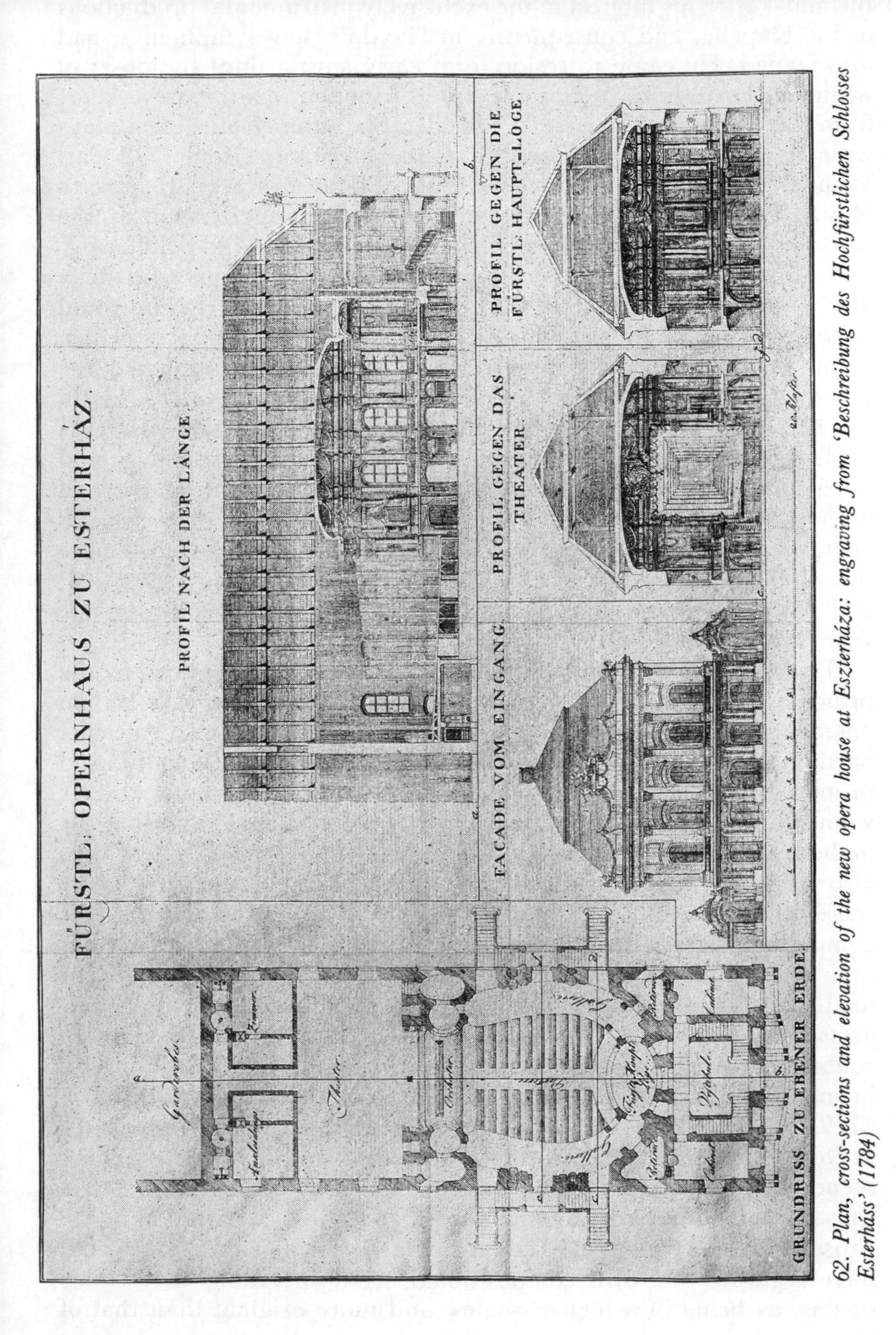

62. *Plan, cross-sections and elevation of the new opera house at Eszterháza: engraving from 'Beschreibung des Hochfürstlichen Schlosses Esterháss' (1784)*

the mid-1770s; his interest in the exclusively instrumental productions of the Kapelle, and consequently in Haydn's new symphonies, had also waned. He came to reside from early spring until the onset of winter at Eszterháza, taking pleasure in the various theatres. Apart from the marionette theatre, a considerable number of spoken plays were given by first-class German troupes of actors (from 1772 Carl Wahr's, from 1778 Franz Diwald's). These troupes brought to Haydn, who wrote much incidental music for their performances, the works of the great playwrights: Shakespeare, Goethe and Schiller.

It is very doubtful whether, from 1776, after discharging his strict duties and having completed his quota of composition, Haydn would have had any time for self-education. The opera performances, which within a few years became a really large concern, burdened the Opernkapellmeister with an immeasurable amount of work. Haydn was helped in the recasting of librettos by the stage manager (who was in charge of printed librettos) and by the set designer, the copyist and others, but one should pause to consider that for one and a half decades he rehearsed and conducted the premières of nearly 70 operas, each lasting a whole evening, as well as many revivals – more than 1000 performances in all. The annual average was between 90 and 100 performances, the record being 125 operatic evenings in one year (1786).

Haydn's work began by his playing over the scores obtained by the prince's agents and recomposing them as necessary, so that Italian operas by Piccinni, Anfossi, Sacchini, Salieri, Righini, Paisiello, Sarti, Gazzaniga, Gassmann and others should provide singable and proportionally brilliant roles for each singer (a maximum of six women and six men, among them highly paid Italians) and that the orchestra should sound as exquisite as Haydn required. There thus also occurred some compositional intervention in virtually every score: the addition of wind parts, the writing of new coloraturas, the composing of new arias ('insertion arias') etc. All this took place not only before a first performance but also when a new singer arrived, or for the revival of an opera years later. A good number of these new arias were written to give Mrs Luigia Polzelli, who had a small, soubrette voice, an enhanced effect on stage. (She was a pretty brunette, the wife of an elderly violinist who came to Eszterháza in 1779, to whom Haydn was undoubtedly amorously attached.) Haydn's musical alterations (mostly deleting, cutting and shortening scenes and arias) clearly show – though he never said so himself – that he worked impatiently and with a good deal of irritation in the cause of these fashionable Italian opera performances.[13] He would have regarded his own compositional style, including that of his operas, as being of a higher quality and more original than that of Cimarosa's generation.

63. Performance of an opera on an oriental subject, possibly in the original Eszterháza opera house (destroyed by fire in 1779): gouache by an unknown artist

During this decade Haydn served his prince as a composer only by writing operas. Almost every year saw a première: in 1777 *Il mondo della luna* (perhaps revived too often today); in 1778 a marionette opera, *Die Feuersbrunst*; in 1779 *La vera costanza*, originally written for Vienna but not performed there because of intrigues; and in the same year, *L'isola disabitata*, an *azione teatrale*. This last had to be presented in the marionette theatre, as the opera house burnt down on 18 November 1779. After being rebuilt it reopened in 1781 with *La fedeltà premiata*, a *dramma pastorale giocoso* displaying alternately *buffo* and pastoral scenes. The work for 1782 was a *dramma eroicomico, Orlando paladino*, one of Haydn's most interesting stage works; and finally, in 1784, *Armida* (an *opera seria*) brought to a close the series of operas written for the prince. These last works were regarded highly not only at Eszterháza (54 performances of *Armida* were given for the prince in the first season): some also reached Vienna, where they were given at the Kärntnerthor or other theatres, sometimes in a German adaptation. After the second performance of *Armida* Haydn wrote proudly to his publisher: 'I am told that this is my best work up to now'.

After January 1780 Haydn had a permanent publisher, the Viennese firm Artaria. At last the opportunity had arrived for Haydn himself to select and prepare his works for the press, at the same time receiving some payment instead of seeing copy-workshops make a profit from pieces intended for sale to the musical public (as happened in the case of the keyboard sonatas in 1766). He published keyboard sonatas for amateur music-lovers (op.30, dedicated to Caterina and Marianna von Auenbrugger, 1780), German lieder (1780–81), a new cycle of string quartets that left their mark on European composition (op.33, 1781, 'written in a new and special way [style]') and, from 1785, the increasingly fashionable accompanied sonatas for keyboard with violin and cello, today called piano trios. These published compositions were no longer intended for the milieu of princely music-making, but for amateur musicians who were becoming more important in Vienna and all over western Europe – musicians who bought fortepianos for their wives and daughters, who wanted to sing songs that they liked to their own accompaniments, and who, not being able to improvise ornaments and cadenzas themselves, happily learnt those written by the composer. Haydn even revised his notation, making it simpler and less ambiguous, for non-professional musicians or ones not trained by him to understand clearly how to perform his works.

From about 1780 he began to correspond with firms other than Artaria and with editors and concert managers in London and Paris. Not a few embarrassments resulted from his selling a work to his Viennese publisher and to several other firms at the same time. His apartment in the music house at Eszterháza (he had disposed of his house in Eisenstadt in 1778) was regularly visited not only by ambitious students (like Ignace Pleyel who, with a scholarship from Count Ladislaus Erdődy, had been Haydn's pupil and lodger in Eisenstadt, *c*1772–7) but also by a series of visitors and musicians from abroad curious to see a celebrity. In all certainty he took it in bad part that his music did not receive the recognition it deserved at the Viennese imperial court: Joseph II had clear reservations about Haydn's style. However, in the 1780s there were indications from all over Europe that the younger generation of composers regarded him as their example in instrumental music, especially the symphony and the string quartet, and that his works were also very successful with the public. Particularly pleasing to him was the fact that Mozart, with whom at that time he became personally acquainted, dedicated a set of six new quartets to him in 1785.

While the prince chained Haydn to himself more and more selfishly as an opera conductor, by the 1780s the composer had undoubtedly outgrown his master and his private artistic world. In 1781 the op.33 string quartets were received enthusiastically by the future Tsar Paul II and his wife in Vienna and in 1785–6 Haydn wrote symphonies to commissions from Paris and elsewhere. Cádiz commissioned him to write instrumental movements to 'The Seven last Words of our Saviour on the Cross'; the King of Naples requested and received pieces for his favourite instrumental curiosity, the *lira organizzata* (a kind of hurdy-gurdy, with organ pipes and bellows); and in London the Professional Concerts could boast works by Haydn. Maybe it was also a sign of the times that Haydn, otherwise deeply religious, in 1785 was admitted to the masonic lodge 'Zur wahren Eintracht'; in the process of separating himself gradually from the narrow Esterházy world and preparing good connections for his future journeys abroad, this event had a symbolic value too.

At this point we should examine the compositions of the fourth period (1785–90), the years when Haydn was active as a conductor of opera but composed no new works in the genre. If we recall the main genres of the four periods in Haydn's output, then it is apparent that (apart from a few late insertion arias) by this time he was writing practically nothing for Eszterháza (see table X.1).

Table X.1 HAYDN'S COMPOSITIONAL OUTPUT, 1761–90

	1761–5	*1766–75*	*1776–84*	*1785–90*
works for Eszterháza	symphonies concertos divertimentos cantatas	symphonies baryton trios masses operas	opera (symphonies)	(insertion arias)
works for 'export'	—	string quartets sonatas (cantatas, oratorios)	sonatas lieder string quartets	string quartets symphonies piano trios (special commissions)

In the last years spent with Prince Nikolaus, now past 70 and becoming even more morose, Haydn grew increasingly impatient with his lack of freedom to travel to Vienna and with the other restraints of his situation. As he complained at the beginning of the 1790 season on his return from a sojourn in Vienna: 'I did not know if I was a *Capell*-master or *Capell*-servant . . . It is really sad always to be a slave . . . I am a poor creature! Always plagued by hard work, very few hours of recreation, and friends?'. Thus he wrote to Marianne von Genzinger, 23 years younger than himself, the wife of Prince Esterházy's Viennese doctor, and for whom he felt warm friendship. To her he addressed one of the most beautiful works he composed shortly before going to London, a sonata in E flat (HXVI: 49) for fortepiano with a fine intimate style ('it is rather difficult but full of feeling').

From the psychological aspect of creativity, we can still find benefits in Haydn's relative isolation, even in the late 1780s, the years of his preparation for foreign tours. In the 'Paris' symphonies (nos.82–7), in the three series of string quartets written in 1787–90 (opp.50, 54–5 and 64) and in a whole series of instrumental pieces intended for western Europe, Haydn composed with immense ambition and inexhaustible invention for a remote public and, of course, for musicians there as well. Since he did not directly experience the reasons for the success of his works, but only heard news of it, he had no opportunity to rest on his laurels and for his work thus to become routine. In each set of pieces he included several examples of what he considered both effective and original, that he hoped would appeal to his 'imaginary public'. Contemporaries accurately observed this remarkable poetic and technical variety. Ernst Ludwig Gerber, in his *Historisch-biographisches Lexicon der Tonkünstler* (Leipzig, 1790–92), said that:

> When we speak of Joseph Haydn, we think of one of our greatest men: great in small things and even greater in large; the pride of our age. Always rich and inexhaustible; forever new and surprising, forever noble and great, even when he seems to laugh. He gave to our instrumental music, and in particular to quartets and symphonies, a perfection that never before existed . . . He has the great art of appearing already known in his movements. Through it, despite all contrapuntal tricks that are found therein, he is popular and attractive for every amateur.[14]

In 1790, while Haydn and his opera company were preparing a performance of Mozart's *Le nozze di Figaro* at Eszterháza, Prince Nikolaus died in Vienna, on 28 September, after a short illness. Before long, Haydn was en route to England to become the star of one of the most successful composer tours of all time. On his return from his two journeys to England (1791–2 and 1794–5), formally resuming in 1796 the post of Kapellmeister with the Esterházys, he was no longer the court musician he had been at Eszterháza. He wrote music for a much wider audience, and if he still identified himself with a community in the stricter sense, then it was with his whole nation, almost in the nineteenth-century sense of the word and its implications. His fourth prince, Nikolaus II, would have liked to have had Haydn's services as court musician in the same way as the earlier Prince Nikolaus, but there was no likelihood of this happening, especially since Haydn's patron was the prince's musical wife, Princess Maria Hermenegild, rather than Nikolaus II himself. She was the one who arranged for the aged master, exhausted from strenuous work on the two late oratorios (*The Creation* and *The Seasons*) and now unable to compose, to be able to live in his house near Vienna without financial difficulties during his last years, which were afflicted by war and inflation.

It is, in all probability, a symbolic reference to these years and to his relationship with his princely master that led Haydn, in 1800 when he published his own edition of the score of *The Creation* (whose alphabetical subscription list, printed in the volume, was headed by the Empress of Austria, the King and Queen of England and more than a dozen other high-ranking notabilities), to put his honorary doctorate from Oxford ('Dr. der Tonkunst') in the first place, the membership of the Swedish Academy second, and third, as the last of his titles, the fact that he was Kapellmeister (in actual service) of the Esterházys.

NOTES

[1] G. A. Griesinger, *Biographische Notizen über Joseph Haydn* (Leipzig, 1810), trans. V. Gotwals in *Haydn: Two Contemporary Portraits* (Madison, 1968), 17.

[2] ibid, 17.

[3] The contract is reproduced, in translation, in H. C. Robbins Landon, *Haydn: Chronicle and Works*, i: *The Early Years, 1732–1765* (London, 1980), 350–51.

[4] Contemporary versions of the spelling of Haydn's name are confusingly manifold. Haydn himself, with very few exceptions, used the form 'Joseph Haydn' or 'Josephus Haydn' when signing letters, petitions etc (the abbreviation 'Jos.', or 'J.', and occasionally the form 'Doctor Haydn' are found more often after his journeys to England), while the greater part of his compositions are signed in Italian as 'Giuseppe Haydn' or later 'di me giuseppe Haydn'. The forms 'Franz Joseph', frequently found in the English Haydn literature, together with the spelling 'Josef', are without foundation.

It should be noted that the consistent use of a single orthographical form for names was not a feature of the time. The Esterházy princes, who were cultivated men, themselves wrote not only 'Esterhazy' but also 'Esterházy' or 'Eszterházy'. In Haydn's letters the spellings 'Esterhazy' and 'Estorhazy' appear (with inflections, 'Esterhazischer', 'Estorhazischer'). Eszterháza, the name given to the site of the Süttör hunting lodge (today found as Fertőd, in Hungary), which Haydn wrote as 'Estoras' or 'Esterhaz' ('Esteras'), appears in princely documents, printed librettos, brochures etc as 'Eszterház', 'Eszterhas', 'Esterháss', 'Esteráz' etc.

[5] Landon, ii: *Haydn at Eszterháza, 1766–1790* (London, 1978), 42–3.

[6] A. C. Dies, *Biographische Nachrichten von Joseph Haydn* (Vienna, 1810), trans. V. Gotwals in *Haydn: Two Contemporary Portraits* (Madison, 1968), 202.

[7] Gotwals, *Haydn*, 51.

[8] ibid, 201. For a comparison of the portraits of Haydn see L. Somfai, *Joseph Haydn: his Life in Contemporary Pictures* (London, 1969).

[9] Quoted in Landon, i: *The Early Years, 1732–1765*, 420.

[10] Riesbeck's and other descriptions are quoted in Landon, ii: *Haydn at Eszterháza, 1766–1790*, 98ff.

[11] See J. Webster, *Haydn's 'Farewell' Symphony: Analysis and Interpretation* (Cambridge, in preparation).

[12] Landon, ii: *Haydn at Eszterháza, 1766–1790*, 702.

[13] Haydn's conducting scores for these performances are discussed in D. Bartha and L. Somfai, *Haydn als Opernkapellmeister* (Mainz, 1960).

[14] Landon, ii: *Haydn at Eszterháza, 1766–1790*, 750.

BIBLIOGRAPHICAL NOTE

Historical background, archive documents

For historical, social and economic matters the large and comprehensive chapters in H. C. Robbins Landon's *Haydn: Chronicle and Works*, i: *The Early Years* (London, 1980), 304–42, and ii: *Haydn at Eszterháza, 1766–1790* (London, 1978), 23–39, contain most of the documents in English. Specialized studies in German can be found in the exhibition catalogue *Joseph Haydn in seiner Zeit* (Eisenstadt, 1982), especially R. Sandgruber's 'Wirtschaftsentwicklung, Einkommensverteilung und Alltagsleben zur Zeit Haydns', 72ff. The Esterházy archive documents are published in two major studies, J. Harich's 'Haydn documenta, 1–5', *Haydn Yearbook*, ii–viii (1964–71), and J. Tank's 'Die Dokumente der Esterházy-Archive zur fürstlichen Hofkapelle in der Zeit von 1761 bis 1770', *Haydn-Studien*, iv/3–4 (1980), 129–333. For a comparison of the various portraits of Haydn and their authenticity regarding the composer's features see L. Somfai's *Joseph Haydn: his Life in Contemporary Pictures* (London, 1969).

Eszterháza: architecture and theatre

In addition to H. C. Robbins Landon's *Haydn: Chronicle and Works*, the best background information on the spoken plays performed at Eszterháza, the theatrical groups and the theatre buildings is to be found in M. Horányi's *The Magnificence of Eszterháza* (London, 1962). For the supposed impression of the whole place and edifice on Haydn's psychology and work see L. Somfai's 'Haydn's Eszterháza: the Influence of Architecture in Music', *New Hungarian Quarterly*, xxiii (1982), no.87, pp.195–201.

Music

For a comprehensive account of Haydn's life and work J. P. Larsen's study *The New Grove Haydn* (London, 1982) is suggested; it has a work-list by G. Feder. The texts of Haydn's first two biographers, Albert Christoph Dies and Georg August Griesinger, are published in translation in V. Gotwals's *Haydn: Two Contemporary Portraits* (Madison, 1968). Detailed descriptions of the musical sources of the operas conducted by Haydn at Eszterháza, including lists of his copyists and watermarks of the music paper, are included in D. Bartha and L. Somfai's *Haydn als Opernkapellmeister* (Mainz, 1960). Details of the genres of Haydn's own operas are in G. Feder's 'Opera seria, Opera buffa und Opera semiseria bei Haydn', *Opernstudien: Anna Amalie Abert zum 65. Geburtstag* (Tutzing, 1975), 37–55.

Chapter XI

London: a City of Unrivalled Riches

WILLIAM WEBER

Public musical life of the modern sort emerged first and foremost in eighteenth-century London. In concert life above all, London set the pace for European cities. Italy, of course, had spawned opera – the original form of public music – and France (or rather Paris) developed the most important early public concert series, the Concert Spirituel. But by the second half of the century London had a multitude of musical riches such as no other city could rival. Its Italian opera was among the best; its concert offerings were the most numerous and varied; its musicians developed precocious entrepreneurial skills; and musical taste took a new direction: the revering of old music in performance. These activities looked ahead to the nineteenth century. By 1800 there had been knit together a fabric of musicians, organizations, publics and tastes that were recognizably modern in ways that those of 1700 were not.

The beginning of the period under discussion is best defined to start with the arrival of an adventurous new set of musical figures – chiefly Felice de Giardini, J. C. Bach and C. F. Abel – in the 1750s and early 1760s. It reaches a climax in the legendary Handel Commemoration of 1784, and ends with the tempering of musical activity that came during the European wars in the 1790s.

SOCIAL AND POLITICAL CONDITIONS

An important reason why London musical life moved ahead so rapidly was that absolutism was never established as a defining principle of the English state. After the Restoration, the royal house was constrained by powerful moral and political restraints upon its social or cultural extravagence. While Charles II tried to dress his court in fancy French fashions, he was unable to dominate upper-class life in anything like the manner of Louis XIV or the Habsburg monarchs of the time. Queen Anne remained aloof from the theatre for moral as much as for medical reasons, and was thus quite different from her royal predecessors. Accordingly, musicians began to shift their attention away from the court to the wealthy homes and public places of London. Roger Bannister, a court violinist who was passed over when French talent was preferred, mounted what are usually regarded as the first public concerts for paying customers in his rooms in 1672. Henry Purcell, who came from a long line of royal servants and musicians, went so far as to present his *Te Deum* and *Jubilate* – a genre almost always written for court celebrations – at the meeting of a private club, the St Cecilia Society, in 1694.

The importance of musical life at court gradually declined. During the first half of the eighteenth century musicians continued to compete for appointments to the King's Music and the Chapel Royal, especially for their guaranteed financial rewards. George Frideric Handel became well known for his anthems for the coronation of George II in 1727, and his rival Maurice Greene for the odes he wrote for royal birthdays. But by the 1760s new works of that sort rarely attracted much attention; the Chapel Royal had ceased to be much in the public eye, and concerts could now provide a more stable income than before. The prominent theatre composer Samuel Arnold was head of the King's Music, but he made his career by running the Academy of Ancient Music for over a decade and putting together pasticcio oratorios for the theatres.[1]

A critical factor behind the growth of public performances in the late seventeenth and early eighteenth centuries was the weakness of government control. In almost all major cities the court or the state restrained the number of such events with monopolies essential to absolutist rule. In Paris, for example, the Académie Royal de Musique (in effect, the opera house) had authority over all musical events and limited the number of public concerts.[2] In London, however, the Lord Chamberlain's Office controlled the taverns and public rooms but not the individual events that went on within them. It regulated the theatres much more closely because their repertory often had political overtones and because they involved much larger financial investments than concerts. Musicians thus enjoyed exceptional freedom because such factors did not come into play. The growing demand for music also had something to do with this, for songs and instrumental numbers became as popular as the plays in theatres by the turn of the eighteenth century.[3]

Direct aristocratic and royal patronage receded more rapidly in London than on the Continent. In the sixteenth and seventeenth centuries fewer noble households kept musical retinues in England than in Austria or Italy. As far as it is known, eighteenth-century aristocratic families in England rarely kept bands of musicians on their estates or in their London town houses, as was still done by several leading ducal families in Paris for most of the century. The short life of the one well-known aristocratic band, that of James

Brydges, Duke of Chandos, at Cannons in the late 1710s and early 1720s, illustrates the weakness of such music-making in the British Isles.[4]

London musical life accordingly grew out of entrepreneurship, rather than state or municipal authority of the sort central to musical life on the Continent. Indeed, it was not until well into the twentieth century that government sponsorship became a major factor in London's public musical life. In fact governmental reticence may have worked to the detriment of nineteenth-century English musical culture, preventing the development of either a high-powered national conservatory or symphony orchestra.[5] But in the eighteenth century the London musical community prospered from the good works of individual musicians; it was their business acumen and ability to sense developing markets that stimulated so dynamic a musical world.

Entrepreneurship and rising competition also increased in the field of music printing and publishing during the eighteenth century. While there was no state monopoly for music publishing in England as in most continental countries, John Walsh the elder (*d* 1736) was the instrument maker for the king and became the leading English publisher with only limited competition during his lifetime; but by the middle of the century many new firms sprang up that rivalled his son, John Walsh the younger, and his successor William Randall, and no single press dominated to the extent that the Walshes had done earlier. At the start of the nineteenth century there emerged another group of firms – Chappell, Novello, Boosey and Cramer, most of them still active today – which brought the English publishing industry to a peak in its international leadership.[6]

The growth of the music business was part of the larger development of a consumer market in England after the late seventeenth century. The purchase of domestic items grew rapidly as small producers identified markets among both wealthy and middle-class homes, selling 'a brass pot for the kitchen shelf, a colourful pair of striped stockings, or a knitted Monmouth cap'.[7] Just as the Wedgwood family hawked pottery and John Packwood sold shaving utensils, so musicians (many of whom were businessmen as much as performers) stimulated a burgeoning market for printed music, instruments, concert tickets and music lessons.[8]

The commercial power of both publishing and concert-giving can be traced to the growth of home music-making among the aristocracy and the prosperous middle class. If singing or mastering an instrument was a highly valued but exceptional accomplishment in the 1600s, from the early eighteenth century it became an increasingly common domestic activity, and eventually a basic part of growing up. First the harpsichord and then, from the 1760s, the piano became a

64. The Cowper and Gore Families: painting (1775) by Johann Zoffany (the square piano is of the type manufactured by the London maker Johannes Zumpe)

customary item of furniture in wealthy households. The lawyer and prominent composer John Marsh revealed how music-making was taken for granted in his day when he wrote in his diary in 1783:

> On the next eve we drank tea at the Plumptres', with the Oxendons, Robinsons, Pugetts and Hammonds; after which a card-table was set for the whist players, and those, who preferred music, were to adjourn to the music room, where Miss Plumptre and Miss Dynoke played, accompanied by me on the fiddle.[9]

We note that Marsh, like many other men, took an active part in music-making. Many aristocratic men sang, played the flute, joined music clubs, collected manuscripts and ran concert series; a few (Marsh, for example) were serious composers. Lord Chesterfield did of course admonish his son not to study music,[10] but such disdain for music derived from a long-standing rhetorical tradition of casting moral aspersions on music and should not be interpreted too literally. If high-born families feared that too much music-making would expose their sons to bad company or the lesser social orders, many young men probably liked music for that very reason.

Domestic music-making played an important role within what

social historians call family formation. While musical activities do not seem to have served as marriage markets at this time – as many soirées musicales did in the following century – musical gatherings were one of the main places where families met and planned their futures. We can glimpse the social role of music-making in *A History of the Adventures of Arthur O'Bradley*, a novel of 1771 by John Potter, a moderately wealthy man-about-town who was the Gresham Lecturer in 1761. He portrays O'Bradley coming from an 'ancient family', attending a 'public' (i.e. exclusive) school, but then being thrown out of the house by his father. O'Bradley proceeds to make his way in the world by playing the harpsichord in wealthy homes:

> We had concerts and assemblies after the races were over, and as I was considered as the Handel of the place, I generally played at the harpsichord; to which my poor father paid more attention than he would have done to the music of the spheres . . . I was the constant companion of the family and the partner of their amusements. All the return they asked, was the compliment of a lesson on the harpsichord to please them and their friends.[11]

Courting the daughter of the family then lands him in prison.

The burgeoning of the music business affected the music itself in important ways. There was nothing new, of course, in writing or printing the music people wanted to hear. But by the late eighteenth century this was done in an increasingly manipulative manner, and musical genres appeared that can be considered distinctly 'commercial' as their predecessors cannot. One such tendency was shaped by the need to write down to the performing level of amateurs, partly because standards of virtuoso playing were advancing so rapidly and partly because there were so many more amateurs. This 'amateur' music was devoid of complex or sophisticated harmony and counterpoint. 'In a sense accompanied keyboard sonatas were the commercial music of later eighteenth-century Europe. Intended primarily for convivial domestic amusement, they had to be simple enough for amateurs to play, and nothing further was expected of them but pleasing tunes and standard harmonizations.'[12] Thus did Muzio Clementi come to write his three two-movement accompanied sonatas of opp.2, 3 and 4 in the 1770s. John Marsh was also referring to this kind of music in the passage from his diary cited above.

A second tendency was towards a much keener sense of musical fashion. The growth of the consumer market brought a heightened awareness of fashion to many people's lives during the eighteenth century. Regarding the marketing of women's dress:

> this new fashion world was one in which entrepreneurs were trying deliberately to induce fashionable change, to make it rapidly

> available to as many as possible and yet to keep it so firmly under their control that the consuming public could be sufficiently influenced to buy at the dictate of *their* fashion decisions.[13]

Such a play upon fashion can be seen in the fads for programmatic pieces on popular topics – J. C. Bach's variations on 'God Save the Queen', for example, or the piano and percussion piece *Battle of Prague* written in 1790 by the Bohemian František Kocžwara. The latter piece set off such a craze that publishers scrambled not only to publish pirated copies, but also to produce imitations for all kinds of instruments.[14]

By the end of the century publishers knew much better how to ride the waves of fashion than they had done at the beginning. They devised a more commercial method of selling editions of sheet music by providing subscribers with a packet of pieces every month. They expanded their arrangements of well-known works for the use of increasingly varied instruments. The invention of lithography around 1800 provided a means of attracting the eye as well as the ear in tempting customers. The faster diffusion of periodicals and sheet music further increased sales. Operas, especially comic ones, became much more quickly and more widely known than before, and stimulated a cycle of fads. All this culminated in the cult for Gioachino Rossini and its astounding commercial success from the 1820s.

It would be much too facile to attribute the growth of musical life to a 'Rise of the Middle Class', that *deus ex machina* of social history. If anything, social historians now see a resurgence of the English nobility in the course of the eighteenth century. Much of the economic dynamism and expansion of wealth during the century came from this class, since noblemen were among the entrepreneurs of mining, metalworking, urban real estate and modernized farming. To a certain extent the class tightened its ranks. There was increasing intermarriage among peerage families as the century progressed, a higher proportion of bishops appointed from that class and a keener sense of class identity generally.[15] But another aspect of the aristocratic resurgence was a broadening of its social and cultural leadership. By mid-century, peerage families had begun to accept the contact with plebeians that public schools and universities gave their sons, for they now sensed that 'the rough and tumble of a public school was the best preparation for public affairs'.[16] To be aristocratic meant that one was engaged in public life. In musical life, too, the aristocracy was a major source of leadership and innovation. Members of that class engaged themselves in many reaches of it, and the brilliance of their way of life afforded an increasing glamour to concerts and opera during the period.

The London bourgeoisie also played an important role in this

65. Johann Christian Bach: portrait by Thomas Gainsborough (1727–88)

history, contributing a size and breadth to the public that was crucial for its commercial scale. The bourgeoisie and noblemen did not stand worlds apart in musical life. Just as there were close professional and economic links between noblemen and lawyers, merchants and clergymen, so the expansion of concert life depended on the network of ties between these groups. In the early nineteenth century, it is difficult to distinguish between bourgeois and aristocratic – indeed, gentry – musical tastes.[17] Nor was the nobility invariably the leader in matters of taste. Even though aristocrats were the ultimate arbiters of taste, some important new tendencies (such as the appreciation of old music) began largely among the middle class.

It is important to remember that when speaking of the middle class in the musical life of this period, one is still mostly concerned with its upper reaches. Few people who could afford a keyboard instrument were not among the well-off families in business and the professions. The democratization of musical life had yet to come; the clerk and the shopkeeper might sing part-songs or buy used instruments, but for the most part they had to wait for further breakthroughs in printing for cheap sheet music to be sold at their economic level.

The vitality of public life in the last decades of the century had political origins. At the start of the century the severe partisan disputes between Whig and Tory had divided society deeply and made public life extremely uneasy. Even though Robert Walpole brought a measure of political stability during the 1720s, the aristocratic oligarchy that supported him was still fearful of the Jacobites (those who called for the return of the Stuart Pretender) and therefore acted with considerable caution politically. But when this threat was proved impotent in the Great '45 – the attempted overthrow of the Hanoverian monarchy in 1745 – the country's élite found a unity and a confidence such as they had not enjoyed since before the Civil War. Public musical life, like the 'public' schools, flourished in this political context.

From the late 1760s to the mid-1780s, however, was a time of political troubles. Soon after the coronation of George III, disputes arose between the king and members of the Whig oligarchy who feared that he was exceeding his authority. The onset of the revolution in America gave a sharp focus to this struggle, and at one point the king even considered abdication. At the same time a more popularly based dissident movement formed behind the highly-born John Wilkes following his arrest and imprisonment for sedition in 1763. Composed of middle-class and artisan activitists, it raised serious questions about the reform of parliament and civil liberties, and awakened popular political feelings in ways that were to continue into the nineteenth century. In the midst of all this the Gordon Riots erupted in 1780. These were disturbances over the issue of Catholic Emancipation during which noblemen (including some of the leading musical amateurs) were torn from their carriages by mobs. Thus did aristocratic, middle-class and artisan movements shake the established political order in late eighteenth-century England.[18]

One can see the impact of the political unrest in the musical writings of John Hawkins. A magistrate in the Middlesex Quarter-Sessions during the 1760s, Hawkins put many of Wilkes's followers into prison and came away from the experience beset by a dread of political anarchy. His musical taste had a similar dogmatic conservatism. At the beginning of his history of music, he warned that most concerts were 'the means of recreation to a gaping crowd' and that:

> the prevalence of a corrupt taste in music seems to be but the necessary result of that state of civil polity which enables, and that disposition which urges men to assume the character of judges of what they do not understand; . . . and when the ignorant become the majority, what wonder is it that, instead of borrowing from the judgement of others, they set up opinions of their own.[19]

As we shall see, the taste for old music was far from being a democratic force.

London musical life must also be understood in terms of its urban environment. By the middle of the eighteenth century London had become a metropolitan centre without rival, having grown far more than any other major city in the previous century, especially in comparison with the national population. While France had more than four times the population of England, Paris was half the size of London. What this meant most of all for musical life was an extraordinary concentration of the nation's wealthy families, and thus a sharp stimulus to cultural activity. Moreover, in London the upper classes were suburbanized unusually early. At the start of the century they began moving west of the City of London or to outlying villages, and the fashionable shops and entertainments took up a new position in the West End and Westminster. Musical life was no longer focussed on courtly buildings in the urban centre, as was the case in Paris, Berlin and Rome.[20]

Yet one cannot talk about London musical life in isolation from that in provincial towns. London was closely linked to the provincial cities. Indeed, England was the most integrated country in the Western world, both politically and economically. For all the centralization achieved in France since the reign of Louis XIV, its provincial cities were independent economic centres, much more so than their counterparts in England, and the country had many more remote backwaters. London did not dominate the provincial cities: it was linked to them, and they to each other, in a set of economic and cultural networks. Developments in transport and communications reinforced the integration of English society and musical life. By 1770 almost all the major cities had turnpikes that cut the travelling time between them significantly. Provincial newspapers became established widely – 35 by 1765 – which both widened and accelerated the diffusion of news and tastes.[21]

Provincial musical life thrived under these influences.[22] During the century over a hundred local music societies that performed both instrumental and vocal music were established in towns and cities of many sizes and regions. Generally made up of amateurs and one or two local professionals, usually led by an organist and choirmaster, they met in the assembly rooms often attached to an inn that were the focus of local social and cultural life. While leading businessmen and members of the gentry tended to dominate the clubs, their members often included men from the lower levels of the middle class and even from the artisans. According to John Marsh, for example, the members of a music society in the Hampshire town of Romsey included a scrivener, a tallow-chandler, a hairdresser and a minor canon.[23]

There was a great deal of interchange between these clubs and London's musical life. The reverence for the concertos of Arcangelo Corelli developed chiefly in the provinces, and Charles Avison made his reputation as a composer and musical commentator without

66. Gertrud Elisabeth Mara singing at a concert in the Assembly Rooms, Bath, c1795: watercolour by Thomas Rowlandson

leaving Newcastle upon Tyne, in the far north-east. The music societies were, of course, private in that most of them opened their doors to the general public (and to women) only several times a year. But the line between public and private was not sharp in towns like this. John Marsh seems always to have had access to music meetings in his travels, and one suspects that good musical hands were usually welcome.

All this was part of an explosion in entertainments – indeed in cultural activities generally – in eighteenth-century England. In the course of the century, the size and the number of theatres expanded; balls became a standard fare in assembly rooms; and horse racing (122 tracks by 1722) now took its modern form. Most of these events were entrepreneurial in nature and increasingly commercial in their management. They also worked closely together. As one reads in the story about Arthur O'Bradley, during the week when the assizes (the royal law courts) were held in a town, there were usually horse races, balls, concerts and myriad private musical gatherings.[24]

OPERA

During the second half of the century (as had been mostly true of the first) operas with Italian texts were given only at the King's Theatre in the Haymarket, and those in English at Drury Lane and Covent Garden. The King's Theatre was the first central opera hall in a national capital to be fully under commercial rather than court management. While the royal opera companies in France, Austria and Prussia had in effect been made municipal institutions by 1750, they continued to have court patronage. In Vienna, especially, the schedule of the opera still revolved around the birthdays and name days of members of the royal family.[25] Few such trappings of absolutist opera ever arrived in London. While the attendance and benevolence of the royal house was essential to the King's Theatre, it was run on an independent, commercial basis earlier and more fully than was the case in the other major capital cities. The informal role of the court made the management of the London company unstable; from the arrival of Italian opera at the start of the century it depended upon the financial support of wealthy gentlemen, which was often barely sufficient.[26]

By 1750, too, the growing complexities of running the opera had led to the withdrawal of noblemen from its day-to-day management. While they put up capital, they no longer played a central role such as they did in the Royal Academy or in the 1730s company dubbed the 'Opera of the Nobility'. Management was now put chiefly into the hands of the more businesslike musicians. We can sense a nostalgia for the older aristocratic leadership in a pamphlet from about 1760, *A Fair Enquiry into the State of Opera in England*. 'While the Nobility were pleased to honour the operas with their direction, the Representations were elegant in the highest degree', it said, since 'those honourable Persons had no views but for the improvement of the Entertainment.' None the less, 'since that Period Operas have declined . . . when the performers undertook the Opera for themselves, they lost, because, being foreigners, they were imposed upon' (pp.5 and 8).

Yet the Italian opera was still the plaything of the most wealthy noblemen, illustrating an important element in the continuing power of the aristocracy in English society. Italian opera was unquestionably the most popular entertainment among London's élite. Aristocrats did of course go to the English theatres, and some works performed there became quite popular among them, most prominently Thomas Arne's *Artaxerxes* (1762). But as was true of all the main halls in the national capitals, going regularly to the opera was the focal point of a very prestigious and public way of life, especially among those who lived the most fashionably – the *beau monde*. The King's Theatre seems to have had a socially less diverse public than was the case in

Paris and most Italian theatres, principally because it had few cheap seats in the gallery. A newspaper suggested the theatre's élitism in 1790:

> The disposition of the boxes – the lighting and security from fire – the tickets numbered for each box, to prevent servants keeping places – the limitation of their number – the commodiousness and cheapness of the pit for the people – and the exclusion of the mob from the galleries . . . render it the most admirable and best regulated theatre in Europe.[27]

Opera life continued outside the hall, for wealthy or aristocratic families brought the leading singers into their London homes and out to their country estates to perform and to socialize with them to a certain extent. While aristocrats generally no longer had permanent musical retainers in their homes, they served as patrons to musicians in a powerful if less direct way. They exerted pressure upon the opera's administration in the choice of composers and singers and thereby had a profound influence on what happened in London's concerts and in its publishing industry.

While stories abound about people doing many things other than listening at the opera, we should not regard taste for Italian opera as essentially unmusical in origin. The singing at the King's Theatre is generally thought to have been as good as, if not better than,

67. Riot at a 1763 performance of Thomas Arne's 'Artaxerxes' at Covent Garden, caused by the decision to stop the half-price rule for those entering the theatre at the interval: engraving

anywhere outside the leading Italian halls, and the theatre, though distant from the Austro-Italian vortex of the opera world, exerted a major influence on it. Someone who rented a box for a season heard a great deal of opera, and often had a very keen taste for what was thought good or bad in the music and the voices of that time. There was good reason why Charles Burney devoted so much of his *General History of Music* (1776–89) to tracing the progress of Italian opera.[28] Taste for this music was of a fine and mannered sort, whose principles, which escape many modern critics and historians, are spelt out in Chapter II above. That these principles seem foreign to many modern listeners is no reason to dismiss them as alien to serious artistry.

The repertory of the King's Theatre was often a decade behind its German or Italian counterparts in the arrival of important new works, since England was much further from the main routes in the diffusion of operas.[29] *Opera buffa*, which appeared in Italy as early as the 1730s, did not become a prominent part of the London opera schedule until 1761–2, when Baldassarc Galuppi's *Il filosofo di compagna* and Niccolò Piccinni's *La buona figliuola* arrived. Moreover, the repertory was almost exclusively by Italian composers. One would not have expected works by Haydn or Mozart to have been performed there in the eighteenth century since their works rarely left German-speaking countries, but the relative lack of interest in Gluck until the end of the century suggests that taste there was more circumscribed than in Paris. The tradition of the Grand Tour, indeed the close links of English with Italian culture generally, orientated the repertory towards such composers as Antonio Sacchini, Felice de Giardini, Niccolò Piccinni and Pietro Guglielmi. The singers none the less had more diverse backgrounds, most prominently the Italian Gasparo Pacchiarotti, the German Gertrud Elisabeth Mara and the English Nancy Storace.

The repertory of the King's Theatre was essentially progressive in regard to the evolution of musical style. *Opera seria*, set to stories from mythology or ancient history, played upon themes of war, love, honour and treachery that had some meaning for noblemen, many of whom were statesmen or military officers. But the genre remained conservative in the development of its musical and dramatic style; *opera buffa*, on the other hand, took the lead in the development of the *galant* or early Classical style. By the 1770s half the repertory at the King's Theatre was *buffa*, and by 1790 three-quarters. The 'reform' of opera in dramatic terms, however, was less prominent in London than in Paris. The opera public in the English capital did not have as strong an intellectual component, and while works in the new idiom by Nicolò Jommelli and Gluck were performed, they did not elicit a powerful response from their audiences.

During the late eighteenth century the King's Theatre began to develop a considerably more stable repertory than had been the case in the first half of the century. It had formerly been the practice for a small number of works to be performed frequently and then discarded after one or two seasons. But by the end of the century, revivals had become fairly common, including works in both *opera buffa* and *opera seria*, making the repertory larger and of more diverse age than ever before. If Piccinni's setting of *La buona figliuola* led the list of revivals – 112 performances in 22 seasons between 1767 and 1810 – Paisiello's *Elfrida* (an *opera seria*) was next – 59 times in eight seasons. Thus was established the modern practice of a continuing repertory. These works were not called 'classics' – great pieces deserving immortality – but a practice was established that eventually led to such high reverence for old music. Indeed, works by Gluck were revived in a number of seasons during the 1790s and 1800s, and the admiration accorded to them suggested the first glimmerings of devotion to a great composer from the past in England's Italian opera theatre. But the opera world was not ready for revivals of works from very far back. Handel was lionized in concert life, and a few numbers from his operas were commonly done there, but the only effort to put on a complete work on stage was a pasticcio entitled *Giulio Cesare in Egito* offered in 1787. One cynic claimed it was done only to get the king back into the King's Theatre.[30]

English opera entered a strong period in the 1760s, chiefly due to the popularity of Thomas Arne (1710–78). Having made his reputation in all-sung opera with *Rosamond* in 1733, he extended his reputation for that kind of writing in the early 1760s with *Thomas and Sally* and *Artaxerxes*, a full-scale *opera seria* setting Metastasio's libretto in English translation. Moreover, his 1762 pasticcio with spoken dialogue *Love in a Village* started a craze for opera of this sort. It included songs by him and William Boyce written for Vauxhall Gardens, arias from recent Italian operas and from Handel's *L'Allegro* and *Susanna*, and the adaptation of an instrumental work by Geminiani. If *Artaxerxes* stimulated three imitations – all-sung English operas – then *Love in a Village* led composers for the King's Theatre to imitate it as well. The production of Piccinni's *La buona figliuola* as *The Accomplished Maid* at Covent Garden in 1766 shows how the Italian and English musical theatres interacted to a great degree.

What followed was the beginning of a long lapse in the prominence of English opera, comic or tragic. The most popular English operas were revivals considerably reworked, chiefly *The Beggar's Opera* and Arne's *Comus* and *Love in a Village*. The most well-received recent ones were those in the comic genre by Samuel Arnold, by the elder and younger Thomas Linley and by William Shield. The London opera was essentially to be a place of imports for a long time.[31]

CONCERT LIFE

London's concerts in the half-century after 1750 suggest much that was to continue through the middle of the nineteenth century, and in some ways into the twentieth. These changes related closely to the evolution of London as a metropolis. In 1700 the concert world was small, mostly consisting of clubs meeting in taverns; the emphasis was on the informal and the impromptu. Concerts were the poor relations of opera, lacking both the scale of entertainment and concentrated élite public found at the King's Theatre. But by 1780 concerts took place in bigger halls, annual subscription series were the focus of attention and large-scale orchestral concerts had made their appearance. The role of newspapers is indicative. In 1700 advertisements and notices of concerts were sporadic and brief; in 1780 not only were advertisements a necessity for almost any concert of significance, but also reviews of the most interesting events were published. Concerts were now a growing commercial concern and success, not the pastime of a few amateurs and their musician friends.

Concerts had grown out of informal music-making in the taverns, and during the first half of the eighteenth century many became organized as clubs. Among the most important were the Castle

68. The great room of the Pantheon (built in 1772; burnt down in 1792) during a masquerade: engraving (1773) by Charles White

Concerts, founded about 1715 in the City and eventually held at the Castle Tavern, and the Philharmonic Society, begun about 1730 at the famous Crown and Anchor in Arundel Street. A more historically orientated repertory was offered by the Academy of Ancient Music (or, for its first few years, 'Vocal Music'), founded in 1726. The growth of London's public life passed these organizations by after 1750, however. While the Castle Concerts lasted into the early 1780s, they were not widely known outside their small clientèle, and the Academy of Ancient Music was transformed into a public concert series in the 1780s. Clubs instead became places where amateurs pursued specialized interests; how that was done in the Madrigal Society and the Catch Club is discussed below.[32]

At the beginning of the century public concerts were small and poorly organized. They were given to fairly small audiences, often of no more than 200 people, and were usually one-off affairs. The main halls provided what permanence there was: the York Buildings in the Strand and Hickford's Rooms, the name for halls first in James Street then Brewer Street. These rooms also offered a wide range of events – banquets, balls, masquerades, auctions and meetings. If such occasions often had musical numbers, the concerts sometimes offered other attractions. Entertainments at the Stationers' Hall in the 1710s, for example, often included country dancing along with a musical programme, and vaudeville numbers were common at provincial events.[33] Roger North, the former lawyer of Charles II, complained that at concerts in the York Buildings everything

> was without designe or order; for one master brings a consort with fuges, another shews his guifts in a solo upon the violin, another sings, and then a famous lutinist comes forward, and in this manner changes followed each other, . . . and a gabble and bustle while they changed places.[34]

A larger and more elegantly appointed set of halls appeared in the second half of the century, and with them a more stable and ordered approach to concert-giving. Hickford's Rooms remained in use throughout the 1760s (Mozart and his father held a benefit concert there in 1764). The main hall there was 50 by 30 feet in size, but the new ones – Almack's, the Hanover Square Rooms and the London Tavern – were about 90 or more by 30, seating 800–1000 people and therefore probably about twice the capacity of the older halls.[35] An even bigger standard came with the Pantheon in 1772. Erected in prosperous Oxford Street and displaying imposing colonnades and a rotunda, it held over 2000 people and was called 'the wonder of the eighteenth century and of the British Empire' by the historian Edward Gibbon (fig.68).[36]

With the help of these halls concerts began to play a considerably

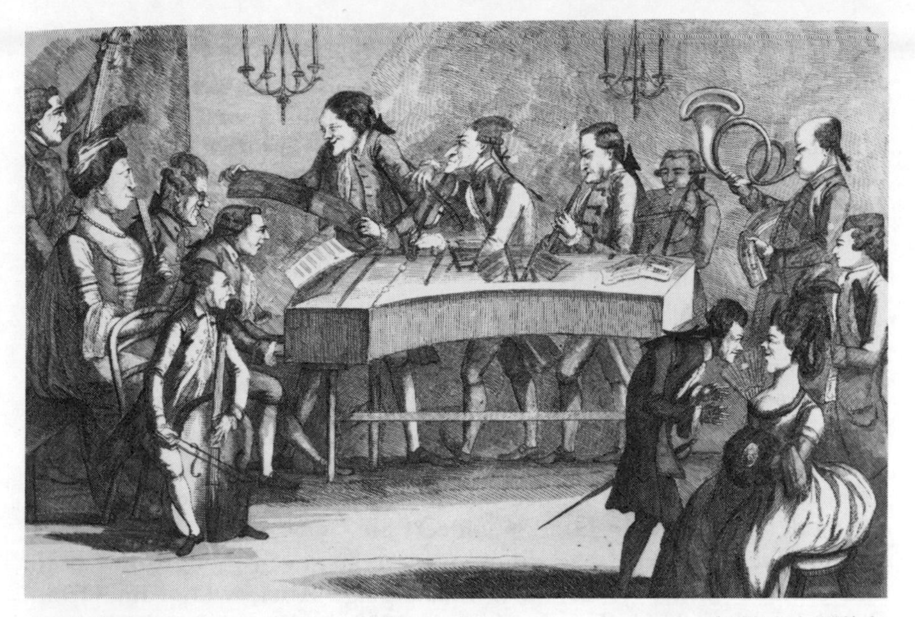

69. A Sunday Concert at the home of Charles Burney: satirical engraving (published 1782) by C. Lorraine Smith; among the performers are F. Bertoni (piano), Cervetto the younger (cello), and behind them (l to r) Cariboldi (double bass), Hayford (oboe), Pacchiarotti (castrato singer), Salpietro (violin), J. C. Fischer (oboe), ?Langani (violin), Pieltain (horn), with Charles Burney gossiping in the foreground

more imposing role in London cultural life than they had done previously. They now rivalled the opera with a great deal of snob appeal. While the halls continued to offer other sorts of events – the Pantheon, indeed, was a kind of indoor pleasure garden – they were now chiefly associated with their musical occasions. All but the Pantheon (which burnt down in 1792) continued in use until the middle of the nineteenth century.

The Hanover Square Rooms quickly became the most important hall in London after its opening in February 1775. Designed chiefly for concerts, it was owned by musical figures, originally C. F. Abel and J. C. Bach, who put on their concert series there, and Giovanni Gallini, the ballet-master (later manager) of the King's Theatre. The room was lit by candles set behind translucent paintings by West, Cipriani and Gainsborough, and in 1804 the hall was enlarged and a grand set of boxes was constructed for the royal family. The rooms were identified chiefly with the Handelian Concert of Ancient Music, with orchestral concerts that grew out of the Bach–Abel series and with the Philharmonic Society after its founding in 1813.

Concert life achieved this new prominence also from the appearance of a new generation of violinists, musicians who assumed a powerful social and musical leadership. The most important of them, the Italian Felice de Giardini, arrived in London in 1751; the others were from diverse countries, as their names suggest – Niccolo Pasquali, Carl Stamitz, F.-H. Barthélemon, Richard Hay, Pieter Hellendaal and Wilhelm Cramer. These violinists turned away from the concerti grossi of Corelli, whose influence had shaped the development of string music in England since the turn of the century. They modelled their music instead upon the virtuoso style for the solo instrument begun by Giuseppe Tartini and Antonio Vivaldi and developed by the Sammartini brothers, Giovanni in Milan and Giuseppe in London. By the early 1760s works in the new genre dominated instrumental music in England.

Giardini knew particularly well how to get ahead. He wrote several works for the opera, published his own music, ran a series of concerts at Hickford's, dabbled in oratorio performances and was accepted more freely in upper-class social life than any other performer of the time. In his wide-ranging, prestigious career one can see the start of the modern virtuoso in London concert life.[37]

J. C. Bach and Abel had different interests, even though they both had studied under J. S. Bach in Leipzig. Abel, who came from Dresden and settled in London first, in 1759, had an unusual career as one of the few viola da gamba players in his time. He wrote little vocal music and was appointed musician to Queen Charlotte. Bach, who had been at the Prussian court, was much more skilled and up to date in his style, and he chiefly concerned himself with opera and was an important teacher (Mozart was among his pupils). They none the less began putting on concerts together in 1764, in 1765 taking over a series that had been started by the shrewd singer and businesswoman Theresa Cornelys at Carlisle House, Soho Square. The programmes mixed concertos, overtures and symphonies with arias from Italian operas. Their main novelty was introducing Londoners to recent German instrumental music, and by the early 1780s Haydn's symphonies were represented frequently. Bach and Abel also drew some extremely fine musicians to London, especially from Germany.

In founding this series, Bach and Abel laid down a milestone in the history of London concert life. While sets of concerts had been run by subscription before (by Handel and Geminiani, for example), tickets had been sold mostly for individual events, and none had become as imposing as this series. In 1767 Bach and Abel moved from Mrs Cornelys's rooms to the more spacious Almack's, and in 1775 to the new hall in Hanover Square. The concerts drew an unusually high-class public and radiated a special chic. Enticed by lists published in newspapers of the aristocrats in the audience, people scrambled to get subscriptions to the fifteen concerts each year. The opera now had a rival.

While the concerts did not become permanently established, they were the first in a succession of series that were central to London musical life. Bach and Abel were not very shrewd businessmen and they experienced financial difficulties from the late 1770s; Bach died unexpectedly in 1782 and his partner withdrew from the series a year later. But a group of gentlemen subscribers kept the series going as the Hanover Square Wednesday Concerts, and then a committee of musicians ran it as the Professional Concerts until the mid-1790s. The series had an impact on many other concerts. It stimulated competing series at Hickford's and the Pantheon, and both the Academy and the Concert of Ancient Music were influenced by its example to some extent (see below).

Johann Peter Salomon brought the development of subscription concerts to an early peak. Salomon was a violinist in the Professional Concerts who, when excluded from the ensemble in 1786, started his own series. In 1791 he succeeded in bringing Haydn to London, as Bach and Abel had tried to do a decade before. The visit (repeated in 1792 and 1794) brought German instrumental music, and specifically the symphony, to the fore in English musical life and made orchestral music the rival of vocal pieces in public taste. Though opera arias remained central to the repertory of such concerts, the deep respect for Haydn's symphonies helped shift the focus of concert life in an important respect.[38]

Another development in the concert life of this period was the consolidation of the 'benefit concert'. This sort of production was not new, since it had been the practice of many an English or foreign

70. The Hanover Square Rooms: watercolour (1831) by Thomas Shepherd

musician to give a programme once a year for his or her own benefit. Leading opera singers had offered the most popular such attractions, generally in the theatres at the end of the social season. After 1750 the rise of eminent instrumentalists – Giardini and Cramer most of all – added to the lustre surrounding such concerts, and the generic term 'benefit concert' became established. Several such major events were put on every week in the season between March and mid-June, most commonly at the Hanover Square Rooms or a hall in Dean Street.

They were not recitals, however. Often called 'A Grand Concert of Vocal and Instrumental Music', these concerts offered a variety of performers, and the sponsor usually appeared in only a few of the ten to twenty numbers. An instrumental ensemble (varying widely in both size and ability) would support the soloists. Glamour and fashion were a top priority. Many people went out of social obligation because the sponsor had taught them or performed for them, and the audiences were usually not made up of the most musically well-educated amateurs. One senses the mood of these gatherings in the advertisement by one Signor Swanberg for a benefit concert at the Freemasons' Hall in 1783: 'the music will be entirely new, and the best and most capital performers, both for vocal and instrumental parts, are engaged by the manager'.[39]

A few musicians made a lot of money from benefit concerts. A fairly popular artist might take in £100, then pay each member of the ensemble a guinea and each soloist three or four guineas. In 1780 the much sought-after soprano Sarah Harrop attracted 2102 people to her annual benefit in the Pantheon and came away with over £1000, £300 more than the previous year.[40] Concert programmes drew on more varied genres and performing forces than is conventional today. Vocal music was always to be expected; only in some provincial towns might one hear entirely instrumental pieces. Chamber and orchestral works were done together. Even solo keyboard pieces were played alongside orchestral works. In 1776 J. C. Fischer performed a sonata for harpsichord at such an occasion, and in 1789 Pieter Hellendaal played a harpsichord lesson at one in Cambridge.[41]

But the format of programmes was quite strict. After an opening overture or symphony (the terms were still used interchangeably), vocal and instrumental works would alternate, and pieces in the same genre would rarely follow each other. Male and female soloists usually alternated as well in the sequence of vocal numbers. The names of composers were often not mentioned in the programmes, partly because the soloists were the main attraction but also because the pieces might not be known to the organizer until the performance. The concertos were usually by the soloists and the vocal numbers were the prerogative of the singers (and were generally well known to the audience anyway). Swanberg opened his concert with an overture

71. Advertisement from 'The Times' (16 May 1791) concerning Haydn's benefit concert to be given that day

HANOVER-SQUARE.

MR. HAYDN respectfully acquaints the Nobility and Gentry, that his CONCERT will be on This Day, the 16th of May.

Part I. New Grand Overture, Haydn. Aria, Signora Storace. New Concertante for Violin, Oboe, Flute, and Obligata, Messrs. Salomon, Harrington, and Caravoglio – Haydn. New Aria (with Oboe and Bassoon Obligata) Signor David—Haydn. Concerto Violin, Signor Giornovichi.

Part II. (By particular desire) the new Grand Overture, Haydn, as performed at Mr. Salomon's first Concert. Sonata, Signor Pacchierotti—Haydn. Concertante for Piano Forte and Pedal Harp, Mr. Dusseck and Madame Krumpholtz. Duetto, Signor David and Signor Pacchierotti. Finale, Haydn.

Doors to be opened at Seven, and begin exactly at Eight o'Clock.

Tickets, at Half-a-Guinea each, to be had of Mr. Haydn, No. 18, Great Pulteney-street, Golden-square; at Messrs. Longman and Broderip's, Cheapside and Haymarket; and at Mr. Bland's Music Warehouse, No. 45, Holborn.

and closed it with a symphony; the first part included two unspecified airs, a concerto by Cramer and a 'Grand Concerto' by Abel for violin, oboe and cello. The second part included a symphony by J. C. Bach, concertos for cello and oboe probably by Swanberg and two unspecified vocal numbers.

It is too easy for us to smile at these programmes, for they seem miscellaneous, unserious and much too long. Yet they had a quite coherent shape; indeed, they tended to be more patterned than modern ones and had greater homogeneity in the age and stylistic definition of the music. Programmes might run for three hours because it was expected that some people would move among various theatres and concert halls in order to take in performances that were of special interest to them. That custom arose in part from a casual attitude towards programmes and works of art, but also from the accessibility of the halls to one other, and therefore from the greater integration of urban life in that society than in modern times.

Like benefit concerts, pleasure gardens reached the peak of their development during the late eighteenth century. Since the late seventeenth century there had been many places of general resort for food, drink and entertainment, most of them either on the Thames or at a spa with curative waters. Vauxhall Gardens in Lambeth was begun as early as 1661 and Sadler's Wells in Clerkenwell in 1684; Ranelagh was a latecomer, founded in Chelsea in 1742. Concerts in bandstands dated back to the gardens' inception, but larger quarters for music, both outdoors and within rotundas, were built in the middle of the eighteenth century. By the 1750s the concerts held three nights a week from late spring to early autumn were some of the most popular musical events in the metropolis. The hour of seven-thirty or eight o'clock anticipated modern practice, later than the six o'clock still normal at the opera. The fireworks were as important as the music; the order of firing was published daily in the newspapers ('a battery of maroons, two Fierloni wheels, a grove of Chinese fire trees . . .').[42] The social class of the public was more varied than at most public concerts, for the city's élite were joined by people from the middle classes and even occasionally by artisans. Prostitutes found customers there, and one had to watch one's purse.

The pleasure gardens were the ancestors of many later, casual concerts – the promenade concerts of the 1830s and 1840s, the Proms (begun at the turn of the twentieth century) and the summer 'bowl' concerts found in cities throughout America. The orchestra of 20–24 members was highly respected, being one of the few permanent bands outside the theatres. Most prominent London composers wrote songs (or even extended vocal pieces) for Vauxhall or Ranelagh, including Arne, J. C. Bach and William Shield. In the 1790s the programmes at Vauxhall began with a fairly serious first half, with a symphony (most commonly by Haydn), an overture (often by Handel) and a concerto or two (featuring a popular organist such as James Hook). The second half was mostly of vocal music in a lighter vein, including sentimental strophic ballads. English music received more exposure here than at any other well-known concerts and was composed not only by the gardens' own composers (Arne, Hook and John Worgan), but also by Jonathan Battishill, Samuel Arnold and Joseph Baildon. It is regrettable that the mixture of light and serious genres did not survive during the dogmatic nineteenth century.

ANCIENT MUSIC

London musical life of the late eighteenth century also anticipated the future by inaugurating a cult for old music, or 'ancient music' as it was called. Before that time music had normally been new by definition, for it was unusual for works more than two or three decades old to be performed, and even less usual for them to be revered. The English pioneered this extension of taste into the past. While instances of the preservation and performance of old music may be found in many parts of Europe during the eighteenth century, nowhere else did it go as far as it did in England, and especially in London.[43]

A set of independent traditions in the performance of old works had taken root at the start of the century. One was a cult for Henry Purcell.[44] Following his death in 1695, theatres continued to offer his music to *King Arthur* and other plays; singers kept his songs in their repertories; publishers continued to issue his catches; and, perhaps most important of all, his *Te Deum* and *Jubilate* were the first works by a dead composer to persist in the repertories of many church music festivals in London and the cathedral cities. Purcell may not have been revered as highly as Handel, but no other composer of the late seventeenth century, English or otherwise, had so many kinds of

72. Concert at Vauxhall Gardens: watercolour (c1784) by Thomas Rowlandson (Mrs Weischel sings from the 'Moorish-Gothick' Orchestra, while Dr Johnson, Boswell and possibly Mrs Thrale eat in the supper box below)

73. The Rotunda at Ranelagh Gardens: painting (1754) by Canaletto (the orchestra is under the canopy to the right of the picture)

music performed after his death. He became closely linked to the national music tradition; the ritual of performing Handel's oratorios indeed grew from the tradition that became established for Purcell's *Te Deum*.

An even more reverential, though narrower, cult surrounded Arcangelo Corelli.[45] In Italy and Germany the performance of his works did not persist long after his death in 1713, but in England his concertos became a *sine qua non* for many provincial music societies. These works became so popular because, while of the highest artistic quality, they were easy for amateurs to play – an important factor at a time when eighteenth-century composers began writing increasingly difficult virtuoso music for the violin. The belief grew up that Corelli's music came closer to perfection than any other of its kind. John Hawkins told how Henry Needler, a highly skilled amateur performer and a member of the Academy of Ancient Music, formed a circle of musical friends on the very day when an edition of the concertos arrived; they were so transported with the sight of such a treasure that they played all twelve at one sitting.[46] During the 1720s and 1730s there was a music shop in London called Corelli's Head. Charles Burney summed up all this in 1789:

> The concertos of Corelli seem to have withstood all the attacks of time and fashion with more firmness than any of his other works . . .; the effect of the whole, from a large band, so majestic, solemn, that they preclude all criticism, and make us forget that there is any other music of the same kind existing.[47]

Even though Corelli's concertos disappeared from concert programmes in London after about 1750, they were still played regularly in provincial concerts, along with those of Handel and Geminiani, throughout the nineteenth century.

The third cult for old music – for Elizabethan masses, motets and madrigals – is where the term 'ancient music' originated. This taste grew up chiefly among musicians in the Chapel Royal and the cathedrals, where old works were revived after the Restoration and came to be seen as a great national tradition. By the 1710s sixteenth-century music had come to be known as 'ancient music', a term borrowed from the study of antiquity. (While in literary and scientific contexts it was still used to mean the music of ancient Greece or Rome, the Elizabethan meaning became primary.) One product of this movement of taste was the publication (three volumes in 1760, 1768 and 1773) of *Cathedral Music*, a compendium of English church music since the Elizabethan Age, developed by a long line of musical scholars and completed by William Boyce.[48]

It was no coincidence that the country where banking and commerce developed so prodigiously also set up a conservative new order of musical taste. The devotion to Corelli and Handel grew out of the processes of social and political change taking place during the eighteenth century, and in part were a reaction against them. From the outset, writings on ancient music were inspired by a distrust of the commercial direction music had taken, bringing about a desire for more solid foundations of taste than could be produced by the whims of fashion. The High Church clergyman and polemicist Arthur Bedford articulated this point of view in his *Great Abuse of Music* (1711), as did Roger North writing during the 1720s and 1730s in his eulogies to Corelli and other composers of the old school. John Hawkins continued this moralistic point of view on musical taste in his history, and William Jones of Nayland, a music theorist and a conservative political writer of the same period, argued that the performance of great works from the past would work against the vices of luxury and degeneracy.[49]

The most important early milestone in the evolution of this taste was the founding of the Academy of Ancient Music in 1726. By the early 1730s its unusual repertory – all vocal music, some of it *a cappella* – had become focussed on madrigals and sacred music of the sixteenth century, especially the music of Palestrina. Apart from the Sistine Chapel in the Vatican no other place is known where these sacred works were performed regularly during the eighteenth century. The club also offered a good deal of music of the seventeenth century and of its own time, though the latter works tended to be conservative or academic in style.[50]

Though initially quite prominent in London musical life, the society faded into obscurity after the death of its founder, J. C. Pepusch, in 1752. During the 1780s the club was changed into a public concert society not unlike the Bach–Abel series. Meeting in the Freemasons' Hall rather than in the club room of a tavern, it enlisted a strong body of prosperous middle-class subscribers and developed a less esoteric but still historical repertory. Little music of the sixteenth century was performed any more; works by Handel, Purcell and Corelli were now combined with recent pieces by such composers as Haydn, Pleyel, Sacchini and Cherubini. Its performances seem to have ended when the health of its director Samuel Arnold declined in 1796.

Two societies that retained an interest in sixteenth-century music were the Madrigal Society and the Catch Club. The Madrigal Society began informally in the early 1740s within a circle of men who took up singing madrigals regularly. Led by John Immyns, the amanuensis of Pepusch and lutenist to the Chapel Royal, they formed themselves as a club but remained much more private and less well known than the Academy. The members seem to have included singers from the metropolitan choirs and shopkeepers and clerks from the City, some

74. The Catch Singers, (l to r) Sir William Howe, Lord Howe, Lord George Germain and Lord North: satirical engraving (published c1776) (the satirist's choice of catch singing to make political points suggests how prominent the pastime had become among the upper classes by the 1770s)

of them probably dissenters whose psalm tradition had links with sixteenth-century music. The society exerted a powerful influence on the music historian John Hawkins, for his musical upbringing was essentially at its meetings, leading him to view the mainstream of musical life from the outside and from a rather jaundiced moral perspective. During the last decades of the century, however, high-born gentlemen began joining the club, and by the 1830s it had achieved great prominence as one of the leading specialized organizations in musical life. It is still in existence today.[51]

The Madrigal Society and the Catch Club illustrate the aristocratic resurgence social historians now see in the second half of the century. The founding of the Noblemen and Gentlemen's Catch Club in 1761 was led by John Montagu, the Earl of Sandwich. His long and complex political career, primarily in the Admiralty, ended in ignominy as he tried to defend the embattled George III in the American War of Independence, and when his mistress was murdered by a jealous suitor in the streets of London in 1780. None the less his political life linked him with a wide variety of important gentlemen, many of whom joined the club. They met weekly in the Thatched House Tavern, from February to June, to dine, to listen and then to join in the singing. Though essentially a social club – the quality of the claret is a matter of special concern in its minutes – it obtained many of the best of London's singers and heard not only catches but also sixteenth-century madrigals and canons and newly-composed glees. In most years it conducted a contest for the best settings of texts in various genres. It, too, is active today.[52]

Montagu played a part in founding the Concert of Ancient Music and the Catch Club, suggesting how a stricter division of labour was developing within private and public musical societies as the century progressed. The Ancient Concerts, as they were often called, had no formal links to the Academy of Ancient Music even though the series owed an intellectual debt to it. Begun in 1776, and in existence until 1848, it was probably conceived on the model of the Bach–Abel series but became much more firmly established, developing a more stable form of management.[53] The concerts were directed by a committee of gentlemen directors, most of them peers of the realm and active amateur performers or music collectors. Most of the work was done, however, by the music director Joah Bates. The son of a Halifax innkeeper, he had rapidly climbed the social ladder under Montagu's protection. He and his wife Sarah Harrop socialized among the aristocracy, and in 1787 the programmes named him as a subscriber rather than music director, even though his role among the players did not change. That kind of snobbery permeated the series from the start. During the 1780s the nobility and other titled persons made up 30 to 40 per cent of the subscribers, and the rest of the subscriptions were meted out carefully. During the nineteenth century such social exclusiveness was practised by the leading symphony orchestras in the major European capitals, and in London by the Musical Union, the distinguished chamber-music society founded in 1845.

Handel's music was the core of the programmes, providing generally half to two-thirds of each season's pieces. Complete works were rarely presented; since the series was defined as a public concert rather than as a club, its programmes were organized around short pieces in the manner of most concerts. The repertory was none the less quite sophisticated. It paid limited attention to the old Handelian favourites; instead of repetitions of *Messiah* and *Judas Maccabaeus*, the series featured arias from the operas and selections from *Jephtha* and *Samson* and even the little-known *Susanna* and *Semele*. Even though the concerts were socially exclusive, they helped to perpetuate an otherwise little-known section of Handel's music in a secular context.

The Ancient Concerts were the first public series to define its repertory as a 'canon' of great works from the past. Bates and the directors redefined the term 'ancient music' to mean any piece at least twenty years old. They drew together the various strands of old music that had been performed independently since earlier in the century – Purcell, Corelli and sixteenth-century madrigals (though unlike the Academy, with no sacred polyphony). To this they added opera arias or sacred works by such composers as Cimarosa, Pergolesi, Jommelli, Hasse and J. C. Bach. English music was also represented to a modest extent by the concertos of Avison, sacred works of Boyce and recent glees by the early eighteenth-century composer John Travers.

If the Ancient Concerts and the Catch Club demonstrate the aristocratic resurgence during the late eighteenth century, the host of tavern clubs that also appeared suggests the growing strength of the middle-class public for music. Most were essentially public concert series focussed on ancient music. The Anacreontic Society (1766–94), which met at the Freemasons' Hall, seems to have started out as a social club of dinner and glees, similar to the Catch Club in style but with a less exalted membership. By the 1780s, however, recent overtures and concertos are to be seen on its programmes. The Glee Club, begun in 1788, also had programmes of the ancients and moderns, including many sixteenth-century madrigals sung by high-ranking professionals. The Handelian Society had a similar base in a tavern, complete with dinner, but offered programmes influenced instead by the Ancient Concerts. Amateur groups also began to appear in this period, chiefly in the Caecilian Society, begun in 1785 for the singing of hymns and anthems, probably with a largely dissenting clientèle. Finally, a club of professional musicians appeared in 1798 in the Concentores Society, where members were admitted upon demonstrating their ability, as the rules put it, in writing 'correct counterpoint' in the old polyphonic style.[54]

But 'ancient music' found its widest exposure in the performance of Handel's oratorios in annual festivals – most dramatically of all in the legendary Commemoration of Handel in 1784. The tradition of music meetings grew up in the late seventeenth and early eighteenth centuries at cathedral services held annually to support hospitals or pension funds for choristers or clergy. Performance of orchestrally accompanied works at these services made them a highpoint in the year for the cathedral choirs, and the settings of the *Te Deum* by Purcell and Handel became standard repertory. After the middle of the century, however, the ritual – which is what it had indeed become – was expanded drastically in its scale. This was done first in Salisbury in 1748 and then most significantly in the Three Choirs' Festival which was rotated among the cathedrals of Worcester, Gloucester and Hereford. The oratorios of Handel were now usually presented in assembly rooms rather than the cathedral, and the addition of evening concerts with contemporary secular music extended most of the festivals to two or three days. In many cases these events coincided with the arrival of the royal law courts (the assizes) or the local race meetings. By the 1780s events of this sort had spread well beyond the cathedral cities into Anglican parishes throughout England and dissenting chapels in the north.[55]

The 1784 Handel Commemoration in London put such ceremony on a much grander and more cosmopolitan plane. While the jubilees for Shakespeare's birth were the main precedent for the festival, the five days of music-making in Westminster Abbey and the Pantheon essentially grew out of the customs of the cathedral cities. The festival was initiated and conducted by the directors of the Concert of Ancient

Music, whose social prestige had a great deal to do with the success of the venture. Three concerts were originally planned, but so many people attended the first events (close to 4000 for *Messiah* in the Abbey), that two of the programmes were repeated.[56]

One has to recall that the Commemoration came at the end of over ten years of bitter turmoil in English politics. In effect it served as a celebration of the new political stability after the election of William Pitt as prime minister. His supporters and detractors together acclaimed the festival as a sign that the English political system had worked and that peace had returned to Westminster. Speaking of the event, the *Public Advertiser* declared that 'it was little less than what may be called the Constitution which accomplished this great effort'.[57]

In the process Handel became an English national institution. Though it was recognized that he wrote in an international style, his music took a ritual role within a national tradition even stronger than had been (indeed, still was) the case with the music of Purcell. George III became the leading national Handelian in the aftermath of the Commemoration, patronizing the Concert of Ancient Music for the rest of his life and spending his final years continually writing programmes for its use.

Was this a religious event? One can argue that the Commemoration was a festival to a new religious unity in English life. Eighteenth-century English politics must be understood in religious terms; the main divisions in society often surfaced in religious issues, interacting closely with the conflict between Whigs and Tories throughout the 1750s. After the disappearance of the Jacobite threat and the coronation of the iconoclastic George III in 1760, Tory gentry swung behind him, and the Church of England once more had a powerful role at the summit of English politics and society. Thus in celebrating the triumph of the constitution the Commemoration also celebrated the triumph of the established church. In what better place might that be done than Westminster Abbey? A related religious and political process happened in the English parish church. For example, psalms were revived in the Anglican church after being expelled as a dissenting practice; as the modern versions were accepted by people from different religious persuasions, music began moving back closer into church life.[58]

*

With the 1790s came a brief period of decline in the development of London's musical life. The French Revolution brought a cautious and more inward-looking mood to public life; the war with France, especially the commercial blockade after 1806, hindered the travel of performers from the Continent and limited the popularity of the productions at the King's Theatre. The pleasure gardens lost much of their clientèle, partly because urban development encroached upon them and partly because taste for their simple pleasures was waning in the face of commercialized entertainment. By 1800 musical life was quieter and much more focussed on clubs than it had been ten years earlier.

After the conclusion of the wars, however, it did not take long for London music life to flourish once more. The opera was revived by many glamorous new singers, the Philharmonic Society took up where the Professional Concerts had left off, and the city's many resident and visiting instrumentalists inaugurated the era of grand virtuosity. The English capital's musical pre-eminence was reasserted.

We have seen how the city's musical culture developed in advance of the other capitals for rather unexpected reasons – more through the aristocracy than the middle class, and more from an existing state of urban growth than the new industrialization. But this is precisely what social historians see as primary in English history generally. They have found that industrialization affected society less than has often been thought and that there was a profound conservatism in English life that resisted the development of industrial might after the middle of the nineteenth century. The continuing power of aristocratic values hindered the growth of English industry after its precocious early period.[59] It is thus no surprise that this same country pioneered the reverence of music from the past – a conservative tradition in which it is still a powerful force.

NOTES

[1] On court musical life, see J. Harley, *Music in Purcell's London: the Social Background* (London, 1968), 16–20, and 'Music at the English Court in the Eighteenth and Nineteenth Centuries', *ML*, l (1969), 332–51; D. J. Burrows, *Handel and the Chapel Royal during the Reigns of Queen Anne and King George I* (diss., Open U., 1981); and R. McGuiness, 'The Origins and Disappearance of the English Court Ode', *PRMA*, lxxxvii (1960–61), 69–82.

[2] M. Brenet, *Les concerts en France sous l'ancien régime* (Paris, 1900), 159–63 and 355–65; similarly for Leipzig, see A. Schering, *Musikgeschichte Leipzigs* (Leipzig, 1926), iii, 413–14, 483–4 and 600–01.

[3] C. Price, *Music in the Restoration Theatre* (Ann Arbor, 1979), 106–7 and passim.

[4] W. Woodfill, *Musicians in English Society from Elizabeth to Charles I* (Princeton, 1953); B. S. Brook, *La symphonie française dans la seconde moitié du 18e siècle* (Paris, 1962), i, 181 and passim; C. H. C. and M. I. Baker, *The Life and Circumstances of James Brydges, First Duke of Chandos* (Oxford, 1949); for recent work on Cannons, see G. Beeks, ' "A Club of Composers": Handel, Pepusch and Arbuthnot at Cannons', *Handel Tercentenary Collection*, ed. A. Hicks and S. Sadie (London, 1987).

[5] C. Ehrlich, *The Music Profession in Britain since the Eighteenth Century* (Oxford, 1985).

[6] W. C. Smith and C. Humphries, *A Bibliography of the Musical Works Published by John Walsh, 1721–1766* (London, 1968); J. Walsh, *A Catalogue of Music Published by John Walsh and his Successors* (London, 1953); W. C. Smith, 'John Walsh and his Successors', *The Library*, 5th ser., iii (1949), 291–301; F. Kidson, W. C. Smith and P. W. Jones, 'John Walsh', *Grove 6*; and D. W. Krummel, 'Printing and Publishing of Music', *Grove 6*.

[7] J. Thirsk, *Economic Policy and Projects: the Development of a Consumer Society in Early Modern England* (Oxford, 1978), 8.
[8] N. McKendrick, J. Brewer and J. H. Plumb, *The Birth of a Consumer Society: the Commercialization of Eighteenth-Century England* (Bloomington, 1982).
[9] Journal of John Marsh, *GB-Cu* Add.7757, ix (1783), 832.
[10] P. D. Stanhope, 4th Earl of Chesterfield, *Lord Chesterfield's Letters to his Son and Others* (London, 1929), 97. Marsh indeed noted in his journal in 1774, after an evening over a new edition of the letters, that 'I found myself interested in the peculiarity of his opinions' (vi, 1774, 486).
[11] J. Potter, *The History of the Adventures of Arthur O'Bradley* (London, 1772), i, 2, 186 and 190.
[12] L. Plantinga, *Clementi: his Life and Music* (London, 1877), 51. For a somewhat later period, see N. Temperley, 'Domestic Music-Making in England, 1800–1860', *PRMA*, lxxxv (1958–9), 31–48.
[13] McKendrick, 'Commercialization and the Economy', 43.
[14] A. Loesser, *Men, Women and Pianos: a Social History of the Piano* (New York, 1954), 243–4.
[15] N. Ravitch, *Sword and Mitre: Government and Church in Eighteenth-Century France and England* (The Hague, 1966); J. Cannon, *The Aristocratic Century: the Peerage in Eighteenth-Century England* (Cambridge, 1984).
[16] Cannon, *Aristocratic Century*, 43.
[17] N. Temperley, 'Ballroom and Drawing-Room Music', *Music in Britain: the Romantic Age, 1800–1914*, ed. Temperley (London, 1981), 116–21; W. Weber, 'The Muddle of the Middle Classes', *19th-Century Music*, iii (1979–80), 175–85.
[18] J. Cannon, *Aristocratic Century*; L. Colley, *In Defiance of Oligarchy: the Tory Party, 1714–60* (Cambridge, 1982); and J. C. D. Clark, *English Society, 1688–1832* (Cambridge, 1985).
[19] *HawkinsH*, ii, 806. On the political and judicial side of his career, see B. H. Davis, *A Proof of Eminence: the Life of Sir John Hawkins* (Bloomington, 1973).
[20] E. H. Wrigley, 'A Simple Model of London's Importance in Changing English Society and Economics, 1650–1750', *Past and Present*, xxxvii (1967), 44–70; and G. Rudé, *Hanoverian London, 1714–1808* (Berkeley, 1971).
[21] P. J. Corfield, *The Impact of English Towns, 1770–1800* (Oxford, 1982).
[22] S. Sadie, 'Concert Life in Eighteenth-Century England', *PRMA*, lviii (1958–9), 17–30; and M. Tilmouth, 'The Beginnings of Provincial Concert Life in England', in *Music in Eighteenth-Century England: Essays in Memory of Charles Cudworth* (Cambridge, 1983), 1–18.
[23] Marsh, *Journal*, v (1772), 194 and 391. On the music societies, see also A. Hutchings, *The Baroque Concerto* (London, 1959).
[24] J. H. Plumb, 'The Commercialization of Leisure', *Birth of a Consumer Society*, 265–85.
[25] F. Hadamowsky, 'Barocktheater am Wiener Kaiserhof mit einem Spielplan (1625–1740)', *Jb der Gesellschaft für Wiener Theaterforschung* (Vienna, 1955), 7–117.
[26] F. C. Petty, *Italian Opera in London, 1760–1800* (Ann Arbor, 1980); C. Price, 'The Critical Decade for English Music Drama, 1700–1710', *Harvard Library Bulletin*, xxvi (1978), 245–66; and J. Milhous and R. Hume, 'Opera Finances in London, 1674–1738', *JAMS*, xxxvii (1984), 567–92.
[27] *Woodfall's Register* (15 April 1790), 4.
[28] *BurneyH*, iv, chaps.1, 3, 5–9; K. Grant, *Dr Burney as Critic and Historian of Music* (Ann Arbor, 1983), chap.8; R. Mount-Edgcumbe, *Musical Reminiscences, Containing an Account of the Italian Opera in England from 1773* (London, 1824); and M. Kelly, *The Reminiscences of Michael Kelly of the King's Theatre and Theatre Royal, Drury Lane* (London, 1826; ed. R. Fiske, 1975).
[29] On repertory, see Petty, *Italian Opera in London*.
[30] Mount-Edgcumbe, *Musical Reminiscences*, 55.
[31] R. Fiske, *English Theatre Music in the Eighteenth Century* (London, 1973).
[32] R. Elkin, *The Old Concert Rooms of London* (London, 1955); A. Carse, *The Orchestra in the Eighteenth Century* (London, 1940); H. A. Scott, 'London's Earliest Public Concerts', *MQ*, xxii (1936), and 'London Concerts from 1700 to 1750', *MQ*, xxiv (1938); and M. Tilmouth, 'Some Early London Concerts and Music Clubs, 1670–1720', *PRMA*, lxxxiv (1957–8), 13–26.
[33] M. Tilmouth, 'A Calendar of References to Music in Newspapers Published in London and the Provinces (1660–1719)', *RMARC*, i (1961).
[34] R. North, *Roger North on Music*, ed. J. Wilson (London, 1959), 353.
[35] Elkin, *Old Concert Rooms*, 44; A. H. King, 'The London Tavern: a Forgotten Concert Hall', *MT*, cxxvii (1986), 383.
[36] Elkin, *Old Concert Rooms*, 65.

[37] S. McVeigh, *The Violinist in London's Concert Life, 1750–84: Felice Giardini and his Contemporaries* (diss., U. of Oxford, 1979); and Hutchings, *The Baroque Concerto*.
[38] C. F. Pohl, *Mozart und Haydn in London* (Vienna, 1867/*R*1970); and C. Roscoe, 'Haydn and London in the 1780s', *ML*, xlix (1968), 203–12.
[39] *Morning Chronicle* (4 Feb 1783), 1.
[40] Henry Bates to Mrs Fury (21 March 1780), copy in Papers of A. H. Mann, Cambridge Musicians, *GB-Ckc*.
[41] *Morning Chronicle* (26 April 1776); A. H. Mann Papers, Cambridge Concerts, copy of *Cambridge Chronicle* (14 Nov 1789). On the pleasure gardens, see 'London', *Grove 6*; M. Sands, *Introduction to Ranelagh* (London, 1946); and C. Cudworth, 'The Vauxhall "Lists" ', *GSJ*, xx (1967), 24–42.
[42] *Morning Chronicle*, Marylebone Gardens (3 Aug 1771).
[43] See W. Weber, 'The Contemporaneity of Eighteenth-Century Musical Taste', *MQ*, lxx (1984), 175–94; and 'The Intellectual Bases of the Handelian Tradition, 1759–1800', *PRMA*, cviii (1981–2), 100–14.
[44] R. Luckett, ' "Or Rather our Musical Shakepeare": Charles Burney's Purcell', *Music in Eighteenth-Century England*, 59–78.
[45] O. Edwards, 'The Response to Corelli's Music in Eighteenth-Century England', *Studia musicologica norvegica*, ii (1976), 51–96.
[46] *HawkinsH*, ii, 806.
[47] *BurneyH*, ii, 442.
[48] H. D. Johnstone, 'The Genesis of Boyce's "Cathedral Music" ', *ML*, lvi (1976), 26–40; C. Dearnley, *English Church Music, 1650–1750* (London, 1970); and P. Lovell, ' "Ancient" Music in Eighteenth-Century England', *ML*, lx (1979), 401–15.
[49] *HawkinsH*, Preliminary Discourse and Conclusion; and W. Jones, *Treatise of the Art of Music* (Colchester, 1784), preface. On Jones, see Clark, *English Society*, 218–21 and 247–9.
[50] J. Doane, 'The Academy of Ancient Music', *Musical Directory* (London, 1794), 76–86; H. D. Johnstone, *The Life and Work of Maurice Greene (1696–1755)* (diss., U. of Oxford, 1967); *BurneyH*, ii, 749, 775 and 987; and *HawkinsH*, ii, 673, 805, 837, 860–61 and 885.
[51] J. G. Craufurd, 'The Madrigal Society', *PRMA*, lxxxii (1955–6), 33–46; *HawkinsH*, ii, 886–7.
[52] V. Gladstone, *Story of the Noblemen's and Gentlemen's Catch Club* (London, 1930); *BurneyH*, ii, 106; and *HawkinsH*, ii, 915.
[53] J. E. Matthew, 'The Ancient Concert, 1776–1848', *PRMA*, xxxiii (1906–7), 55–79; and W. Weber, 'Intellectual Bases of the Handelian Tradition, 1759–1800'.
[54] Pohl, *Mozart und Haydn in London*, ii, has the most comprehensive overview of these and other societies.
[55] W. H. Husk, *An Account of the Musical Celebrations on St. Cecilia's Day in the Sixteenth, Seventeenth and Eighteenth Centuries* (London, 1857, 3/1862); and B. W. Pritchard, *The Musical Festival and the Choral Society in England in the Eighteenth and Nineteenth Centuries* (diss., U. of Birmingham, 1968).
[56] C. Burney, *An Account of the Musical Performances in Westminster Abbey and the Pantheon in Commemoration of Handel* (London, 1785); H. D. Johnstone, 'A Ringside Seat at the Handel Commemoration', *MT*, cv (1984), 632–8.
[57] *Public Advertiser* (27 May 1784), 2; see also W. Weber, 'The 1784 Handel Commemoration as Political Ritual', *Journal of British Studies*, xxvii (1989), 43–69.
[58] N. Temperley, *The Music of the English Parish Church* (Cambridge, 1979), i, chaps.5–7.
[59] M. J. Wiener, *English Culture and the Decline of the Industrial Spirit, 1850–1980* (Cambridge, 1981).

BIBLIOGRAPHICAL NOTE

Social history

Useful general histories of England in this period are J. H. Plumb's *England in the Eighteenth Century* (Harmondsworth, 1950/*R*1963) and W. Speck's *Stability and Strife: England, 1714–60* (London, 1977); the key monograph in recent work is J. Brewer's *Party Ideology and Popular Politics at the Accession of George III* (Cambridge, 1976). For contrasting views on the evolution of society – did the middle class really rise? – see R. Porter's *English Society in the Eighteenth Century* (Harmondsworth, 1982), J. Cannon's

Aristocratic Century: the English Peerage in the Eighteenth Century (Cambridge, 1984), J. Sharpe's *Early Modern England: Social History, 1550–1760* (London, 1987), J. C. D. Clark's *English Society, 1688–1832* (Cambridge, 1985), and the critique of Clark by J. Innes in *Past and Present*, cxv (1987).

Little new writing has appeared in recent years on London in the second half of the century. For early work, see M. D. George's *London Life in the Eighteenth Century* (London, 1925) and G. Rudé's *Paris and London in the Eighteenth Century* (London, 1952) and his *Hanoverian London, 1714–1808* (Berkeley, 1971). For a model social study, see N. Rogers's 'Money, Land and Lineage: the Big Bourgeoisie of Hanoverian England', *Social History*, iv (1979).

Music

On Italian opera, see F. C. Petty's *Italian Opera in London, 1760–1800* (Ann Arbor, 1980) for a detailed chronology, D. Nalback's *The King's Theatre, 1704–1867* (London, 1972) for general history, and M. Kelly's *The Reminiscences of Michael Kelly* (London, 1826; ed. R. Fiske, 1975), and R. Mount-Edgcumbe's *Musical Reminiscences* (London, 1824) for useful sources. There is a welcome new edition of R. Fiske's *English Theatre Music in the Eighteenth Century* (London, 1873, 2/1987). On the pleasure gardens, see M. Sands's *Introduction to Ranelagh* (London 1946) and C. Cudworth's, 'The Vauxhall "Lists" ', *GSJ*, xx (1967), 24–42. For the more extensive work done on early eighteenth-century Italian opera, see n.26.

For a bundle of useful material on the music meetings throughout England, with an emphasis on Birmingham, see B. W. Pritchard's 1968 thesis at the University of Birmingham, *The Musical Festival and the Choral Society*, and his 'The Provincial Festivals of the Ashley Family', *GSJ*, xxii (1969). On the 1784 Handel Commemoration see H. D. Johnstone's 'A Ringside Seat at the Handel Commemoration', *MT*, cxxv (1984), 632–8, and W. Weber's 'The 1784 Handel Commemoration as Political Ritual', *Journal of British Studies*, xxvii (1989), 43–69.

On orchestral concerts and musicians, begin with the still useful works by A. Carse, *The Orchestra in the Eighteenth Century* (London, 1940), R. Nettel, *The Orchestra in England* (London, 1948), and C. F. Pohl, *Mozart und Haydn in London* (Vienna, 1867/*R*1870). For newer material, see L. Plantinga's *Clementi: his Life and Music* (London, 1977); S. Sadie's 'Concert Life in Eighteenth-Century England', *PRMA*, lviii (1958–9), 17–30; H. C. Robbins Landon's *Haydn: Chronicle and Works*, iii: *Haydn in England* (Bloomington, 1980); and A. H. King's 'The London Tavern: a Forgotten Concert Hall', *MT*, cxxvii (1986), 383.

The study of English musicians is blessed by an excellent set of articles in *Grove 6*, but see as well the pieces Mollie Sands contributed on a variety of subjects to the *Monthly Musical Record* in its last fifteen years, and the opening of Cyril Ehrlich's vital *Music Profession in Britain since the Eighteenth Century* (Oxford, 1985). See as well Simon McVeigh's useful thesis from Oxford in 1979, *The Violinist in London's Concert Life, 1750–84: Felice Giardini and his Contemporaries*.

Eighteenth-century English musical life was not deeply engaged with literary life, but see none the less R. Lonsdale's *Dr Charles Burney: a Literary Biography* (Oxford, 1965), K. Grant's *Dr Burney as Critic and Historian of Music* (Ann Arbor, 1983) and B. H. Davis's *A Proof of Eminence: the Life of Sir John Hawkins* (Bloomington, 1973). Nicholas Temperley shows the close relations between musical life and religion in *The Music of the English Parish Church* (Cambridge, 1979).

Chapter XII

Stockholm in the Gustavian Era

ANNA JOHNSON

STOCKHOLM THROUGH THE PRISM OF BELLMAN'S SONGS

In the songs of Carl Michael Bellman (1740–95), Stockholm of the late eighteenth century is seen as through a bright prism – refined Rococo pastels, as well as shrewd drawings with revealing details. Bellman, 'the Nordic Anachreon', was the genius of Swedish poetry and an excellent performer of his own songs. As royal secretary he was just as welcome at the court as in the bourgeois salon or the tavern. Hence, in his poetry, he swiftly moves from one milieu to another, at ease in every social stratum. He depicts a world of music and dance – in countryside manors, brothels and alleys of 'The Town between the Bridges'.[1]

Stockholm is a city on water, whose islands and peninsulas span the Baltic and Lake Mälaren. In the eighteenth century ships from all over Europe made port there (Epistle no.33):[2]

> Hurrah! A blast on the waldhorn! Susanna sings, the breezes frolic and the waves heave and sway. – Shove off!
>
> Splendid isle,
> I awhile
> Will flee from thy joys,
> Thy tumult, stir and noise;
> All thy proud palaces.
> Blow your horn, Movitz – Yes!
> See our boat
> Bravely float!
> 'Mid schooners and yachts the Spanish trader note
> Puts to sea
> Gallantly!
> In Cádiz and Dublin soon she'll be.

With about 70,000 inhabitants, eighteenth-century Stockholm was still quite provincial, surrounded by forests and villages. On the shores of Brunnsviken, in the grounds of Djurgården or at rural taverns like Fiskartorpet (the Fisherman's Hut), Bellman and his friends met for pastoral, bacchanalian amusements (Epistle no.71):

Ulla, my Ulla, what sayst to my offer?
Strawberries scarlet in milk and wine!
Or from the fishpond a carp may I proffer,
Or from the fountain a rill crystalline?
See from their hinges thy portals nigh broken
Scarce can the flowery breeze resist;
Show'rs in the heavens new sunshine foretoken,
As thou seest!

Isn't it divine, say, this our Fisher Cot?
Divine, yea, be it spoken!
And these solemn oak-trees, proudly row on row
All greenly blow!
Where the quiet reaches
On the inlet flow,
There afar off, between ditches,
Meadows, lo!
Isn't it delightful, all this verdant show?
Divinely so! Divinely so!

But on the whole, life in Stockholm was far from divine. It was a crowded, poor and exceedingly dirty town. The mortality rate was almost twice as high as in the rest of the country – in fact it was close to that of Paris, which was the worst in Europe. Rousseau's affirmation of the superiority of rural life had a starkly factual basis. With an increasing number of factories in ancient, densely built-up quarters on the islands, Stockholm was a miserable compound of old and new. For the factory workers in particular, social conditions were often appalling. In the 1770s and 1780s famine, tuberculosis and plagues raged through the town. Death was omnipresent (Epistle no.81):

Mark how our shadow, mark, Movitz, mon frère,
One small darkness encloses;
How gold and purple that shovel there
To rags and rubbish disposes.
Charon beckons from tumultuous waves,
Then thrice this ancient digger of graves;
For thee ne'er grapeskin shall glister!
Wherefore, my Movitz, come help me to raise
A gravestone over our sister.

The little bell echoes the great bell's groan;
Robed in the door the precentor,
Noisome with quiristers' prayerful moan,
Blesses those who enter.
The way to this templed city of tombs
Climbs amid roses' yellowing blooms,
Fragments of mouldering biers,
Till black-clad each mourner his station assumes,
Bows there deeply in tears.

In this insular town, brothels and taverns were neighbours to the royal palace. Even if social and economic inequalities between the wealthy merchants and the simple shopkeepers were considerable, the distances between their homes were short and the gaps between the classes no longer insurmountable. It was a time of intensified social and cultural mobility among the four Estates. A middle class of intellectuals, gentry, merchants and bureaucrats gained strength, cutting through the old social barriers. Despite poverty, filth and famine, musical life in Stockholm flourished as never before in a process of sweeping transformation.

There were also lively contacts between the great political and cultural centres in northern Europe – Copenhagen, St Petersburg and Stockholm – with an exchange of ideas, musical styles and artists.[3] Many prominent composers and musicians alternated between the royal courts in these capitals. In the second half of the century, public concerts became highly fashionable. For more than a century Italian opera had dominated the scene even in these northern countries, mostly through visiting Italian troupes. At the end of the eighteenth century it was overshadowed by French *opéra comique*, which gained immense popularity in St Petersburg, as well as in Stockholm and Copenhagen. More significant than this shift from Italian to French, however, were the signs of a growing, pre-Romantic nationalism in comedies, Singspiels and ballets – for the first time a striving for a national idiom in music outside the great cultural powers of central Europe. The contacts between these powers were far more dramatic and controversial politically than culturally. For centuries they had been involved in a struggle for supremacy in the Baltic region. At the end of the eighteenth century this combat was in the hands of two magnificent sovereigns: Catherine the Great of Russia and Gustavus III of Sweden. Both also left their stamp on the cultural policies of their countries.

GUSTAVIAN OPERA

The so-called 'Gustavian era' in Swedish history is framed by two *coups d'état*. In August 1772, after one year as king, Gustavus III successfully mounted a bloodless revolt against the council and the two parties of the parliament, long since weakened by internal conflicts. Overnight he reached his goal: restoration of royal power. For two eventful decades (1771–92) he was the supreme ruler of Sweden and Finland, as the object first of enthusiasm, then of increasing opposition and finally of hatred. In March 1809 his son and successor Gustavus IV Adolf was arrested and deposed after a war and a peace treaty, through which Sweden lost the entire province of Finland. A new constitution was adopted which transferred power to the parliament and the council. The Gustavian era

75. Interior of the Drottningholm Theatre, built for Lovisa Ulrika, mother of Gustavus III, in 1766

was conclusively brought to an end.

The reign of Gustavus III was the most glorious in the history of Swedish culture. His aspiration was to place his country among the great powers of Europe and himself among the foremost of enlightened monarchs. He knew how to use the virtually unlimited power he had gained through his revolt and was indeed the director of political as well as cultural life. Never were opera and theatre so efficiently used for political propaganda, nor were practical politics ever such a well-directed drama as in the hands of Gustavus III, 'the Theatre King'.

Under the guidance of his mother, the cultivated and arrogant Lovisa Ulrika, sister of Frederick II of Prussia and a friend of Voltaire, he was brought up on French literature and Enlightenment thought. In spite of this strong French orientation, he ardently dedicated himself to creating a national culture; his ideas permeated musical life in Gustavian Stockholm and gave it a distinctive contour on the map of European music. He himself was active as author of numerous Swedish theatre and opera pieces, as actor (until the court and the French ambassador protested about such behaviour from a crowned head), as producer and as the most generous patron of the arts – far too generous, in the eyes of his political opponents.[4]

Gustavus III was not primarily interested in music; his goal was a national theatre. The 'harsh and vulgar' Swedish language was, however, unacceptable for the sophisticated, French-speaking aristocracy. For the realization of his national programme he chose opera as the most efficient vehicle:

> What means, then, must one take to establish a Swedish theatre? By beginning with the means that in other countries is usually the end: grand opera. An opera that has pleasant music, a well-drilled ballet, smart costumes, pretty and well-painted scenery, has so much to attract the eye, the ear and the other senses, that they are all entertained at the same time. Gradually one becomes accustomed to the language; its hardness is softened by music; words and expressions become lighter until finally one is reconciled to one's own tongue.[5]

During the first years of his reign Gustavus III founded the Royal Academy of Music (1771) and the Royal Swedish Opera (1773). This was the first opera house in northern Europe to give regular performances in the vernacular, not merely of Singspiels and vaudevilles, but also of great, heroic operas. Such a policy – operas in the vernacular, performed by a professional, native ensemble – was in itself remarkable for this part of Europe, where operatic ventures were traditionally dependent on visiting French or Italian troupes. More radical, however, was his invention of a new repertory. In the following years a number of Swedish operas were created, often at the initiative of the king himself, and in many cases they were even drafted and directed by him. Some were closely dependent on continental models, but national elements gradually increased.

Many of these operas were staged at the Drottningholm Theatre, which Gustavus III inherited from his mother in 1777 (fig.75). Built in 1766, it is one of the few surviving European Baroque theatres, with pastel interior, a very deep stage with pairs of side-wings and superb machinery. After the assassination of Gustavus III it was closed and out of use for over a hundred years. When finally 'rediscovered' in the twentieth century, it was untouched, with the original sets on stage and the machinery intact.

The first theatre ordered by Lovisa Ulrika was in fact the Confidence, built at the castle of Ulriksdal in 1753 and often used by the royal family. Here, for instance, the opera *Proserpina* by Joseph Martin Kraus was first performed (in a concert version) in 1781, and much appreciated by the king. Like the Drottningholm Theatre, the Confidence was closed after the death of Gustavus III. In the nineteenth century it was used as a hunting lodge, but finally restored and reopened as an opera house in the 1980s.

At the castle of Gripsholm a theatre in a quite different style of architecture was built – a classical amphitheatre in white, gold and green. It was a *petite scène* for the private theatre performances of the court, with the royal family as actors. But this was not enough for the kingly projects. In the centre of Stockholm a grand new opera house was erected (inaugurated in 1782), with Carl Fredric Adelcrantz as architect; it was one of the most elegant examples of Gustavian classicism, technically well equipped with advanced stage machinery. This building was in use for a century until it was pulled down in the 1890s to make room for the present opera house.

The first production by the Royal Swedish Opera, *Thetis och Pelée* (*Les noces de Thétys et Pélée*), presented in January 1773, was based on a libretto by Fontenelle, revised and translated. It is significant that the music for this premier Swedish opera was written by an Italian, Francesco Antonio Uttini (1723–95). From 1755 he was contracted by the court as leader of an Italian opera troupe (dissolved after some years) and as *maître de chapelle*. For his cultural projects Gustavus III could draw on brilliant native writers, artists and singers; for the music, however, he was dependent on foreign, mainly German, composers.

All through the Gustavian period French *opéra comique* by Grétry, Monsigny, Piccinni and others, all in Swedish translations, formed a prominent and very popular part of the repertory. The new realism in the depiction of scenes of middle-class life was received with special enthusiasm. 'Never has any piece been so well received; it seems as if people would rather watch the adventures of men than of gods', G. J. Ehrensvård, director of the Royal Opera, wrote after the first performance of Grétry's *Lucile*. And Anna Maria Malmstedt, the young translator, saw the plot of this opera as a contribution to the emancipation of women: 'I hope that as a result of the enlightenment of Gustavus III's reign . . . women too will gain more scope for their abilities than they have hitherto been granted'.

A strong dependence on the French tradition is also evident in some of the new operas composed for the Swedish stage. Uttini, for instance, made another contribution with his music to Sedaine's *Aline, reine de Golconde* (1776). In 1782 the new opera house in Stockholm was inaugurated with *Cora och Alonzo*, a Swedish version of Marmontel's novel *Les Incas*, set to music by the Dresden composer Johann Gottlieb Naumann (1741–1801), who visited Sweden twice and wrote three operas for Gustavus III.[6] Within its exotic frame, this work is a proclamation of religious tolerance and an idealization of freemasonry, ten years before Mozart's *Die Zauberflöte*. In this it serves as a confirmation of current political principles, like so many other Gustavian operas and spoken dramas. In 1781, a year before the opening performance of *Cora*, Gustavus III had put through a law allowing greater religious freedom.

76. Scene from Gluck's 'Orfeo ed Euridice', presented in Swedish by the Royal Opera in 1773: painting by Pehr Hilleström the elder

Most influential, however, were the 'reform' operas of Gluck. As early as November 1773, one year before the Paris version, *Orfeo ed Euridice* was presented in Swedish (with the part of Orpheus sung by a tenor). It was a tremendous success, the first in a series of excellent Gluck productions during the reign of Gustavus III (*Iphigénie en Aulide* was staged in 1778, *Alceste* in 1781, *Armide* in 1787 and *Iphigénie en Tauride* in 1783, all in Swedish translations). Stockholm was a stronghold for Gluck's music at this time and his 'reform' operas became the stylistic ideal for Gustavian works.[7]

In the 1780s classicism became fashionable in all forms of art in Sweden. The interest in Roman antiquity was fostered by Gustavus III who in 1783–4 spent half a year in Italy with his retinue of artists and architects, eagerly studying the excavations in Rome, Paestum and Pompeii. After returning to Sweden, he commissioned a new palace at Haga outside Stockholm (never completed), pavilions and interiors in classical style. His intentions were realized in architecture, monuments and sets for the royal stages by the French artist Louis Jean Desprez. This eccentric genius among European stage designers arrived in Sweden in 1784 on the invitation of Gustavus III and remained there until his death in 1804. His set designs for the Gluck performances and the new, national operas were outstanding.

The royal park at Haga, Gustavus III's favourite residence during

77. Opening of the song 'Frjäriln vin gad Synspa Haga' from Carl Michael Bellman's collection 'Fredmans sånger' (1791)

his last years, was depicted by Bellman in one of his most beloved songs (*Fredmans sånger* no.64; see fig.77):

O'er the misty park of Haga
In the frosty morning air
To her green and fragile dwelling
See the butterfly repair;
E'en the least of tiny creatures
By the sun and zephyrs warm'd
Wakes to new and solemn raptures
In the bed of flowers form'd.

In thy leas, O royal Haga,
Many a fair and grassy space!
Proud the swan upon thy waters
All her gleaming grace displays.
In the forest's distant chambers,
Where the echoing axes call,
E'en the granite stones are moulded
And the birch and pine-tree fall.

Lo! Brunnsviken's tiny naiads
All their golden horns upraise,
As a white cascading fountain
Over Solna's church tower plays.
'Neath thy green and leafy arbours,
On these trim and gravell'd aisles,
Where the filly trots, the farmer
At thy charms, O Haga, smiles.

How delightful 'tis to savour
Within a park so rare,
Both a royal monarch's favour
And the greetings of the fair!
Ev'ry glance his eye dispenses
Ask of gratitude a tear;
E'en the sullen in his sorrow
Must at Haga find new cheer.

Gustavian classicism culminated in the opera *Aeneas i Carthago* by Joseph Martin Kraus (1756–92), the most prominent among Gustavian composers. Kraus came to Sweden in 1778 as a young, unknown composer after studies in Mannheim and Göttingen. When, after years of poverty, his opera *Proserpina* was performed at court, Kraus became assistant conductor at the Royal Opera and was later appointed Kapellmeister. During the period 1782–6 he made a long study tour through Austria, Italy and France (commissioned by Gustavus III), where he met and made friends with Albrechtsberger,

Haydn and Gluck. 'J'y reconnais Kraus. Quelle profondeur de pensées – quel talent classique', Haydn later said of one of Kraus's 'Sturm und Drang' symphonies. In addition to operas Kraus's output includes symphonies, chamber music and songs in an individual, pre-Romantic style.

The libretto for *Aeneas i Carthago* was written by the poet Johan Henrik Kellgren, based on a draft by the king, and the sets were sketched by Desprez. It is a grandiose, five-act work with choruses, ballets, pantomimes and brilliant solo arias, set to music by Kraus in his personal synthesis of classical grandeur and expressive 'Sturm und Drang'. Initially, this work was intended for the inauguration of the new opera house in 1782, but 'Dido' (the prima donna Caroline Müller) suddenly left the country, escaping her creditors, and Kraus's opera was abandoned. Neither the composer nor his royal Maecenas was ever to hear this masterpiece. When *Aeneas* was at last – and then miserably – performed in 1799, they were both dead. The new regime received this inheritance from the late monarch with frosty reluctance.

Opera in Stockholm thus became a melting-pot of national and continental trends, of Rococo, Classicism and a growing Romanticism. In what sense, then, were the so-called 'national Gustavian operas' actually 'national'? Obviously not in the sense that a Swedish style of music was created. There were only some initial attempts in that direction. It may be more judicious to think in terms of a particular Gustavian *Vermischter Stil*, with influences from French and Italian opera, and with Gluck's music as the ideal.[8]

National ideas were manifested by other means. As we have seen, a native ensemble and Swedish librettos were important starting-points. More significant for Gustavian opera and theatre, however, is the fact that many of these works were based on national subjects. In 1773 the Italian Abbé Domenico Michelessi had exhorted Swedish authors to pay attention to the history of their own country: 'The truth of Swedish history is more amazing than the novels of other people'.[9]

This was a decisive and remarkable step. Indeed, the comic Singspiel with spoken dialogue, folk scenes and folk-music allusions was a fresh, new genre, popular in several parts of Europe in the late eighteenth century – in Germany, Austria, Poland, Russia and not least in Denmark. But grand, heroic operas based on subjects from a country's history or legends, written in the vernacular (*Der Freischütz, Prince Igor, Boris Godunov, Halka* etc), belong to the national Romanticism of the nineteenth century. Even Mozart adhered to the form – and the language – of the Italian *opera seria* for his heroic operas. His German works are comic Singspiels, although with *Die Zauberflöte* he broke all the barriers of the genre.

Gustavus III was fascinated by his country's history. He wrote several plays and operas on national subjects and other writers followed his lead. Most spectacular were the two heroic operas drafted by the third Gustavus about his predecessors and namesakes on the throne, Gustavus Wasa and Gustavus II Adolf. From early childhood Gustavus III was taught to see these heroes of Swedish history as his ideals and himself as their successor and peer: throughout his life he played the part of 'the third Gustavus'. Thus the operas about these absolute rulers also served as manifestations of his own sovereignty and as efficient, strategic tools for both foreign and domestic policy.

Gustaf Wasa (1786) was obviously meant to be the true national opera of Sweden – and so it was for more than a hundred years. The production was the most magnificent during the Gustavian era, and the greatest public success. The libretto was versified by Kellgren on a prose draft by Gustavus III, the music was composed by Johann Gottlieb Naumann and the set designed by Desprez, a mobilization of the best resources in Stockholm at that time. Naumann considered it his best opera. It has continuous music with an overture of French grandeur, large choruses, ensembles, accompanied recitatives, ariosos and arias in various forms. The intensity of his music was further strengthened by the dramatic force of Desprez's sets. Indeed, the German composer and the French artist gave their utmost in this patriotic Swedish opera.

78. Stage design by Louis Jean Desprez for Act 3 of Johann Gottlieb Naumann's opera 'Gustaf Wasa', first performed at the New Opera House, Stockholm, in 1786

Historically, Gustavus Wasa, who was elected king in 1523, was the leader of a successful war of liberation against Danish supremacy and the founder of Sweden as a sovereign state. For Gustavus III, Denmark was still the hereditary foe and Gustavus Wasa the perfect propaganda symbol when, in the 1780s, he secretly mobilized against the southern neighbour. The opera focusses on the relation between the monarch and his people, especially the aristocracy. In a hymn to freedom – the best-known part of the opera – the loyalty of the gentry is praised. In contrast, the Danish King Christian is frankly characterized as a cruel tyrant. The effect was the desired one. Witnesses to the first performances report of agitating shouts from the parterre – 'beat them, beat them' – and the young crown prince raising his fist against the Danish army on the stage.

In this atmosphere of chauvinism Gustavus III convoked the parliament, to receive sanction and support for his policy. But the four Estates were not as willingly directed as the opera chorus. For the first time he met persistent opposition, especially from the nobles, and had to abandon his controversial project – at least temporarily.

The second great opera on a national hero, *Gustav Adolf och Ebba Brahe*, was first performed in 1788. Like the previous one, it was a collaboration between Gustavus III, Kellgren and Desprez. The composer this time was the German organ virtuoso Abbé Georg Joseph Vogler (1749–1814), who in 1786 had been contracted by the Swedish king as 'direktör av musiken'.[10] This is a work of a different character, in plot as well as in music, created in a hardening political climate. As a result of the confrontations with the aristocracy, Gustavus III more openly appealed to the peasantry. In the new opera, Gustavus II Adolf is characterized as the noble, unselfish father of his country, beloved by the people. As the scenery alternates between the palace and a small fishing village, so the continuous music varies between sublime *opera seria* and light sections inspired by folk music. For the second act Vogler creates a charming scene of folk tunes, choruses and dances – a precursor of the national operas of the nineteenth century. (Vogler later became the teacher of Carl Maria von Weber and of Meyerbeer – a direct link between the Gustavian and German national operas.)

Some months after the opening performance of *Gustav Adolf och Ebba Brahe*, war was declared between Sweden and Russia. After serious Swedish losses a conspiracy against Gustavus III was discovered among his officers. As in the opera, the king now had to rely on the loyalty of the peasantry. In the footsteps of Gustavus Wasa he went to Dalecarlia (since the Middle Ages a stronghold of peasant power), appealing to the people there for armed support, and like the sixteenth-century monarch he attained his goal. The conspiracy was crushed and the losses turned into modest victories.

Thus in most of the Gustavian operas and spoken plays dramatic tension is focussed on the relation between the great hero and the common people ('the heroic' and 'the popular' are often fundamental ideas within national arts). Gustavian opera represents, in its own way, the transition in the late eighteenth century from the old *opera seria*, with its heroes from ancient history or mythology, by way of the classical grandeur of Gluck, to a growing Romanticism with its cult of the people. These transformations are clearly reflected in the different stylistic layers of the Gustavian operas: in the late Neapolitan *seria* style of Uttini, the Italian-German *empfindsamer Stil* of Naumann, the very personal fusion of Gluck and 'Sturm und Drang' in Kraus's music, the programme music and the folk music pastiches of Vogler. It is significant that a national idiom is first noticeable in folk scenes, as in *Gustav Adolf och Ebba Brahe*. Obviously Vogler's ambition here was to create music which not only sounded 'popular', but even sounded 'Swedish'. It seems, however, far more difficult to create a national musical idiom for the heroic ideal and the Gustavian composers never attempted that.

During the last decades of the eighteenth century the Royal Opera in Stockholm met increasing competition from a private company, the Stenborg Theatre.[11] Its repertory was dominated by French *opéra comique* (in Swedish translation), by Swedish Singspiel and spoken plays. Some parody vaudevilles were very successful, produced as direct counterparts to the heroic operas. Thus *Gustaf Wasa* was matched by the Singspiel *Gustav Ericsson i Dalarna*; *Thetis och Pelée* became *Petis och Thelée* etc. The shepherd and the shepherdess in Handel's *Acis and Galatea* are transformed in the Swedish parody *Casper och Dorothea* into a German shoemaker and a Djurgården tavern madam. Polyphemus, the cyclops, has taken the guise of a school-teacher and the chorus consists of boatswains, waffle-makers and schoolboys. In these light genres the perspective is reversed. The grand hero of the serious opera is seen through the eyes of common people and deprived somewhat of his *gloire*. The milieu of these plays was often a middle-class home or a rural village, and thus the representation of Swedish society is broadened. The music, however, was strongly dependent on French models. Even if it was more popular than the music of serious opera, it was hardly more national.

This repertory reached a broad, middle-class audience. It is, however, characteristic of the socio-cultural structure of Stockholm at this time that it was just as popular among the upper classes, not least those of the court. The Stenborg Theatre often successfully competed for the same audience as the Royal Opera – indeed, in many cases with the same composers, librettists, singers and stage designers, and with royal support. Carl Stenborg was a star among the singers of the Royal Opera, creating such parts as Pelée, Orpheus, Gustavus Wasa and Gustavus Adolf. Finally he was allowed by his royal protector to act on his own stage as well and his theatre was given a monopoly in *opéra comique*, the most profitable genre.

PUBLIC CONCERTS, SECRET ORDERS, PARLOURS AND TAVERNS

The first public concert in Stockholm was held as early as 1731 – long before the Gustavian era – on the initiative of Johan Helmich Roman (1694–1758), 'the Father of Swedish music'. He was the first Swedish composer of high international stature, with a long list of works in the late Baroque and *galant* styles. Few individuals were more crucial to the development of music in eighteenth-century Sweden than Roman. As Kapellmeister and teacher of a generation of Swedish musicians he laid the foundations for an expansion of musical life and he did for sacred music what Gustavus III was later to do for opera. In his anthems he wanted to prove 'the pliability of the Swedish language to church music'. With public concerts he opened new opportunities for the royal orchestra outside the closed circle of the court. It is significant, though, that the first series of concerts was given at the House of Nobles: the audience still belonged to the highest ranks of society.

This period in Swedish history, known as 'the Age of Liberty' (1720–72), was a time of political agitation, utilitarianism, increasing manufacture and a rising, prosperous middle class. It was, furthermore, a distinguished era for Swedish science, with such figures as Carl von Linné, Anders Celsius and Emanuel Swedenborg. In this atmosphere of economic growth and cultural hunger, a public musical life rapidly developed. In the middle of the century concert series, such as 'the concerts of the cavaliers', were regularly presented by court musicians or by amateurs, usually in collaboration. Most such ventures had a charitable purpose, the customary social welfare of the eighteenth century.

During the reign of Gustavus III this sector of music expanded further, alongside the intense operatic activities. The quality as well as the quantity of musicians and singers gradually increased. One of the objects of the Royal Academy of Music was to serve as a conservatory – an intention which was very slowly realized. The court orchestra was still the only professional orchestra in Sweden so it was often used for concerts, just as the singers of the Royal Opera were soloists at these events.

The most sensational performances were given by Abbé Vogler, who toured all over Europe, from St Petersburg in the north to Cádiz in the south, as an organ virtuoso. For several years he lived sporadically in Sweden, taking an active part in musical life as composer, conductor, teacher, theorist and organist. His organ

79. Chamber music in an aristocratic salon: painting (1779) by Pehr Hilleström the elder

concerts were chiefly famous for his brilliant improvisations and unusual programme music, some of it with colourful titles, for example *The Siege of Jericho*, *Mortal Lamentation of the Moors in Morocco*, *Painting of Shepherds' Merriness, interrupted by a Thunderstorm*.

In a small town like Stockholm, the same clique of artists and musicians met again and again in the fashionable upper-class salons, where a refined taste for chamber music developed. Native composers could also contribute to these genres of more modest proportions. Thus the first Swedish string quartets were written in the 1760s or 1770s by Anders Wesström (*c*1720–81), one of the most skilful violinists of his time and a pupil of Tartini; he was highly individual as a composer but eccentric and destructive, ending his life in abject poverty. Quartets in a more Classical style were composed by Johan Wikmanson (1753–1800), a civil servant and organist. Like his friend Kraus, he was a great admirer of Haydn and this is openly revealed in his music. Symphonies by Haydn and Mozart appeared in the concert repertory in Stockholm from the 1780s, together with music by, among others, Roman, Handel, Pergolesi, Graun, Uttini and Kraus. (On the other hand, the first performance of a Mozart opera, *Die Zauberflöte*, did not take place until 1812.)

In concerts, but even more so in private music-making, the solo lied was much esteemed. Among accomplished amateur musicians this was the favourite genre, and several Swedish composers contributed to it. Even immigrants like Kraus and Vogler made excellent settings of Swedish texts. The demand for chamber music is also reflected in a number of editions, for example of quartets, keyboard arrangements and solo songs. In 1788 Olof Åhlström received a monopoly in music

80. Carl Michael Bellman playing a cittern (?cithrinchen): portrait (1779) by Per Krafft the elder

printing in Sweden. During the following decades he published several musical 'journals', with such titles as *Musikaliskt Tidsfördriv* ('Musical pastime') and *Skaldestycken satte i musik* ('Poems set to music'), which were not magazines but serially issued anthologies of music.

Throughout the eighteenth century membership of academies and orders was highly popular, either of international orders like the freemasons or local ones such as Utile Dulci and Par Bricole. Music was often an indispensable part of their ceremonies, for which a stream of occasional poems and compositions was produced. Among the members of these societies were practically all the leading writers, artists, composers and musicians in Stockholm, as well as members of the royal family. Thus Gustavus III and his brothers were freemasons, as were Uttini and Naumann. From 1759 the masonic lodges in Stockholm regularly gave charity concerts in support of their orphanage. Utile Dulci was primarily a literary society but it also had a 'musical areopage' which gave private and public concerts and assembled an extraordinary music collection.

Among all these solemn societies Carl Michael Bellman founded a satirical order of his own – Bacchi Orden – for which he wrote an extensive collection of drinking-songs, *Bacchi Tempel*. Bellman was the supreme performer of his own songs, improvising the accompaniment on his cittern, imitating voices and instruments – cello, flute, fiddle, horn – 'indeed every instrument, to perfection'. He also appeared as an actor in *divertissements* and comedies at the court or in private assemblies. In his diary, Johan Gabriel Oxenstierna, a young nobleman and poet, described an evening in December 1769 with Bellman and his friends:

> Bellman has founded an order in honour of Bacchus, to which no-one can be elected who has not publicly lain in the gutter at least twice. Sometimes he calls the members together to dub a new knight, after a meritorious candidate has come forward. Tonight he holds a Requiem over a dead knight, in verses set to opera tunes. He sings himself and plays the zither. His gestures, his voice, his playing, which are unrivalled, heighten even more the pleasure that one obtains from the verses themselves. They are always beautiful and contain thoughts, sometimes comic, sometimes sublime, but always new, always strong, always unexpected, over which one cannot but be amazed and, finally, dissolve in admiration or in laughter.

The art of musical parody (setting song texts to existing melodies) was much esteemed during the eighteenth century, not least in France and Sweden. Bellman's parodies were in a long tradition, forming one of the richest legacies of Swedish music and one that has lasted to the present day.[12] In Bellman's songs this art reached a peerless culmination. Kellgren wrote in his preface to *Fredmans epistlar*:

> Never before were the arts of poetry and of music so well matched. It is not the verses which are put to that music, nor the music which is composed to those verses; they have so enhanced each other, have become one beauty, that one can scarcely perceive which, when missing, would detract most from the other's perfection: the verses, to be properly understood, or the music, to be properly heard.

Bellman chose his tunes from various types of instrumental music, from popular French chansons, *opéra comique*, serious opera and Swedish folksongs.[13] Many are also found in the fiddlers' music books and the large bulk of broadside melodies: indeed, his selection gives a good idea of the most popular repertory at the time. Like many vaudeville poets, Bellman was musically illiterate although he was an excellent musician. Many of his songs were notated and arranged by his friends Åhlström and Kraus.

In 1790 and 1791 *Fredmans epistlar* and *Fredmans sånger*, Bellman's most important collections, were at last published by Åhlström. In these song cycles Bellman creates a world of his own – a shimmering and stinking Stockholm populated by a gallery of eccentric Gustavian figures, seen in the light of ancient mythology. His poems bear an almost Shakespearean ambiguity of marvellous fantasy and sharp realism. And, like Gustavian opera, they show a peculiar fusion of Rococo, Classicism and Romanticism. But in contrast to opera, this is a world of anti-heroes, of simple burgers, soldiers, grave-diggers, innkeepers and whores. We meet Fredman, 'once a respected Royal Watchmaker, now without watch, workshop or stock'; Ulla Winblad, 'nymph and priestess in the temple of Bacchus'; Father Berg, 'painter of wallpapers and virtuoso of several instruments'; Movitz, 'constable and cellist'; Mollberg; Jergen Hunchback; Jeanna 'who lost her ruby'; Lotta and Sophia.[14] They all play instruments, dance and drink. In Epistle no.3 'to each and all of the sisters, but more especially to Ulla Winblad', Father Berg blows his horn and Ulla is dancing:

Father Berg his horn is blowing,
See, the pretty nymph is going,
Merrily in the ball!
See at Jergen's courtly scraping
Father Berg astonish'd gaping;
His notes demented fall.
Hurrah, see Ulla dancing!
Cuffs of lace her wrist enhancing!
Father, veil and frills! Entrancing!
White her legs!
See lamps and lamplight glow!

In the air the waldhorns mumble,
All around me sirens tumble.
Here by Apollo's side.
Ulla Winblad, dearest sister!
Witty, gay, who can resist her?
Each day thou art a bride!
Hurrah, hear Ulla singing,
Fröja's temple loudly ringing;
Fiery darts see Cupid flinging.
Drunken I
In Charon's wherry lie.

Thus in Bellman's songs we glimpse a musical world outside the institutions and official, upper-class society, and it is a world which is just as vital and dramatic. We hear broadsheet ditties, bagpipes and keyed fiddles. Other sources report a rivalry between fiddlers, organists and court musicians and quarrels about the right to play at lucrative private celebrations, weddings and funerals. Obviously there were no borderlines between the different musical spheres, nor between written and oral traditions. Poems by the most prominent writers were frequently spread as broadsheets. Many manuscripts of fiddlers' pieces include dance music composed by organists or by musicians of the court orchestra, tunes which the nineteenth-century collectors labelled 'genuine' Swedish folk music.

*

After years of increasing royal despotism the political opposition – especially among aristocrats and officers – exploded in hatred and Gustavus III was assassinated by conspirators in March 1792. Mortally wounded, he was at last given the leading, heroic part in a tragedy more fantastic than any author could ever invent: the 'theatre king' murdered by masked assassins during a ball in his own opera house. In his final role Gustavus acted with great dignity and magnanimity, gently and mercifully. Amid the general horror at the terrible deed, political opposition to the royal despot turned into sympathy. In the end he stood, like the kings in his national heroic operas, at the centre of the stage, surrounded by his devoted, mourning people. No wonder Verdi saw in this a supreme plot for an opera (*Un ballo in maschera*). Even his funeral took the form of a well-directed drama, with scenery more appropriate to an opera stage than to a church. The funeral cantata by Joseph Martin Kraus represents the aptly impressive climax of Gustavian music, in heroic opera style, with all the grandeur and serenity of Gluck's music and with outbursts of intense 'Sturm und Drang' expressiveness.

The assassination of Gustavus III marked the end of an era, politically as well as culturally. The new regime was indifferent to the ideas of a national culture and openly hostile to the Gustavian coterie of poets, artists and musicians. After some years of drastically reduced activity, the Royal Opera was closed and the singers, dancers and musicians were dismissed. The young king, with the symbolic name Gustavus IV Adolf, even wanted to demolish the opera house where his father had been murdered.

Within a few years the most prominent of the Gustavian composers and artists were dead or had left the country. Joseph Martin Kraus died of consumption, at the age of only 36, some months after the royal funeral. Bellman was taken into custody – in the royal palace, where so many times he had been invited by Gustavus III – because of his perpetual debts. Desprez was neglected as an artist and died in poverty. From Germany Johann Gottlieb Naumann wrote to a Swedish friend:

> I still have a constant pull towards Sweden, which I would gladly see again one day; but I doubt if I should be welcome there. So many changes and disasters have happened there during my absence. My *Gustaf Wasa*, which I have never seen or heard, would give me great pleasure to see, hear and myself conduct. If the old king had lived, that would very likely have happened – but now everything has passed away with him.[15]

When Sweden rose after the Napoleonic wars and the exacting peace treaty in 1809, society had thoroughly changed. Slowly a new musical life developed, no longer dominated by an almighty sovereign but by prosperous upper and middle classes, by 'Kenner' and 'Liebhaber'. It was time for 'the discovery of the people' and for a new nationalism.

NOTES

[1] For a fascinating description of Stockholm in the Gustavian era see P. B. Austin, *The Life and Songs of Carl Michael Bellman* (Malmö and New York, 1967).

[2] The verse quoted in this chapter is from Bellman's song collections *Fredmans epistlar* (1790) and *Fredmans sånger* (1791), translated by P. B. Austin.

[3] During the eighteenth century Copenhagen and Stockholm were still the two capitals of the Nordic countries. Until 1814 Norway was a part of Denmark, while Finland from the Middle Ages until 1809 belonged to Sweden. Hence these 'provinces' had no court music of their own and no professional orchestras. On the other hand, an upper- and middle-class music rapidly developed in these as in many other parts of the Nordic countries during the eighteenth century, with professional town musicians, public concerts and private music-making.

[4] For a penetrating investigation of theatre repertories in Sweden during the reign of Gustavus III see M.-C. Skuncke, *Sweden and European Drama 1772–1796* (Uppsala, 1981).

[5] G. J. Ehrensvård was the first director of the Royal Swedish Opera (1773–6); his diary (published in 1877) gives valuable information about the cultural policy of Gustavus III.

[6] Besides his two sojourns in Stockholm, in 1785–6 Naumann also visited Copenhagen where he wrote music for a Danish version of Orpheus. An account of Naumann's operas for the Nordic countries is given in R. Engländer, *Johann Gottlieb Naumann als Opernkomponist* (Leipzig, 1922).

[7] For information about the Swedish productions of Gluck's operas see R. Engländer, *Joseph Martin Kraus und die gustavianische Oper* (Uppsala, 1943), 27–37; and K. Hansell, 'Gluck's *Orpheus och Euridice* in Stockholm from 1773 to 1786: Performance Practices on the Way from *Orfeo* to *Orphée*', in *Gustavian Opera: an Interdisciplinary Reader in Swedish Opera, Dance and Theatre, 1771–1809* (Stockholm, 1989).

[8] Engländer, *Joseph Martin Kraus*, 53–85.

[9] From Michelessi's introductory speech at Kungliga Vetenskapsakademien (Royal Academy of Science) in Stockholm in 1772. The Italian Abbé Domenico Michelessi belonged to the same group of learned classicists as Calzabigi, Algarotti and Durazzo, taking active part in opera reform. Michelessi, who lived in Stockholm during the 1770s, contributed to the first Swedish performance of Gluck's *Orfeo* in 1773.

[10] A short remark by Vogler gives interesting information about the attitude towards text declamation and performing at the Swedish Opera: 'In Stockholm no opera is staged before all the actors and actresses have declaimed the entire work in a special rehearsal, after the manner of a tragedy; this is the true touchstone, if the singer can have the music taken away and yet remain an actor' (trans. from Engländer, *Joseph Martin Kraus*, 33–4).

[11] Skuncke, *Sweden and European Drama*, 49–60.

[12] There are thorough analyses of the musical parody technique in Bellman's songs in J. Massengale, *The Musical-Poetic Method of Carl Michael Bellman* (diss., Uppsala U., 1979).

[13] Massengale, *The Musical-Poetic Method*, 18 and 151–206.

[14] Bellman gives a short description of his characters in the introduction to *Fredmans epistlar*.

[15] Letter to Per Frigel, librarian at the Royal Academy of Music, Stockholm (27 Jan 1797); published in Engländer, *Johann Gottlieb Naumann*, 403–4.

BIBLIOGRAPHICAL NOTE

Historical-social background

An informative survey of the Scandinavian countries and their status in the European political scene during the late eighteenth century is presented by H. A. Barton in *Scandinavia in the Revolutionary Era, 1760–1815* (Minneapolis, 1986). It is a comprehensive study, emphasizing economic and cultural developments as well as domestic and foreign policy. Parliamentary development and foreign affairs are further examined by M. Roberts in *The Age of Liberty: Sweden 1719–1772* (Cambridge, 1986) and by M. F. Metcalf in his dissertation *Russia, England and Swedish Party Politics 1762–1766: the Interplay between Great Power Diplomacy and Domestic Politics during Sweden's Age of Liberty* (Stockholm U., 1977).

The radical social and economic changes of eighteenth-century Swedish society are thoroughly examined by S. Carlsson in several works. See for example his article 'Sweden in the 1760s' in *Sweden's Development from Poverty to Affluence, 1750–1970*, ed. S. Koblik (Minneapolis, 1975), or his dissertation, *Ståndssamhälle och ståndspersoner 1700–1865: studier rörande det svenska ståndssamhällets upplösning* ('Social class and the élite, 1700–1865: studies of the dissolution of the Swedish class system') (Lund U., 1973). A magnificent standard work on the history of ideas and science in Sweden is S. Lindroth's *Svensk lärdomshistoria* (Stockholm, 1975–81).

An early French monograph on Gustavus III is A. Geffroy, *Gustave III et la cour de France* (Paris, 1867). The first full-length biography of Gustavus III in English was published in 1894 by R. N. Bain, *Gustavus III and his Contemporaries (1742–1792): an Overlooked Chapter of 18th-Century History (from Original Documents)* (New York, 1970). It is an eloquent work, but now obviously out of date. For a recent, brief biography of Gustavus III, see O. Warner, 'Gustavus III, King of Sweden', *History Today*, xvi/2 (1966), 103–10. The major monograph in Swedish is B. Hennings, *Gustav III* (Stockholm, 1957). A brilliant analysis of the enigmatic personality of Gustavus III is presented by E. Lönnroth in *Den stora rollen: Kung Gustav III spelad av honom siälv* ('The grand role: King Gustav III played by himself') (Stockholm, 1986). In his article 'Gustav III and the Enlightenment', *Eighteenth Century Studies*, vi/1 (1972), A. Barton discusses the influence of Enlightenment ideas on Gustavus III and his political actions. This topic is also examined in some French articles: M. Launay, 'J.-J. Rousseau et Gustave III de Suède', *Revue de littérature comparée*, xxxii (1958), 496–509, and G. von Proschwitz, 'Gustave III et Voltaire', in *Rousseau et Voltaire en 1776–1778: Nice 1979*, 135–147; see also von Proschwitz's *Gustave III de Suède et la langue française* (Göteborg and Paris, 1962).

The final conspiracy against the Swedish monarch and his assassination in 1792 is related by G. Sahlberg in *Murder at the Masked Ball: the Assassination of Gustav III of Sweden*, trans. P. B. Austin (London, 1974), first published as *Den aristokratiska ligan* (Stockholm, 1969).

A thorough monograph on one of the most remarkable and influential personalities of the Gustavian era is A. Barton, *Count Axel von Fersen: Aristocrat in an Age of Revolution* (Boston, Mass., 1975); it describes von Fersen's position in Swedish policy, his participation in the American revolutionary war and his involvement in the French Revolution and it contains a detailed bibliography of works on Scandinavian history during the late eighteenth century.

Literature, theatre and the visual arts

A standard reference work in English on Swedish literature is A. Gustafson's *A History of Swedish Literature* (Minneapolis, 1961). Some of Gustavus III's literary works were published in French a few years after his death: *Collection des écrits politique, littéraires et dramatiques de Gustave III, roi de Suède; suivie de sa correspondance, édition procurée par Jean-Baptiste de Chaux* (Stockholm, 1803–5). Several collections of his letters have been published. The major critical edition is *Gustave III par ses lettres*, ed. G. von Proschwitz (Stockholm and Paris, 1986), which contains a detailed bibliography. See also 'Lettres de Gustave III à la comtesse de Boufflers et de la comtesse au roi', *Actes de l'Académie nationale des sciences, belles-lettres et arts de Bordeaux* (Paris, 1898).

The literature by and about Carl Michael Bellman is extensive. His works (including music to all song texts) are published in a standard critical edition: *Carl Michael Bellmans skrifter* (Stockholm, 1921–). A most fascinating and comprehensive biography (with many Bellman songs translated into English) is P. B. Austin's *The Life and Songs of Carl Michael Bellman* (Malmö and New York, 1967). Of special interest for musicologists is J. R. Massengale's dissertation, *The Musical-Poetic Method of Carl Michael Bellman* (Uppsala U., 1979).

Continental influences on Swedish theatre are examined by M.-C. Skuncke in her dissertation *Sweden and European Drama 1772–1796* (Uppsala U., 1981). Valuable information on Swedish artists of the Gustavian era is found in P. Lespinasse's *Les artistes suédois en France au 18ᵉ siècle (1695–1804)* (Paris, 1929) and in L. Schudt's *Italienreisen im 17. und 18. Jahrhundert* (Vienna and Munich, 1957). Swedish drawings from the eighteenth century are published in the volume *Svenska teckningar 1700-talet* ('Swedish drawings from the 18th century') (Stockholm, 1982). A brief, richly illustrated trilingual introduction to the work of the most prominent Swedish artist of the Gustavian era is *Johan Tobias Sergel: Skulpturer och teckningar/Sculptures and Drawings/Skulpturen und Zeichnungen*, with a preface by S. Å. Nilsson (Uddevalla, 1980). The stage designer and artist Louis Jean Desprez, so important for the development of Gustavian opera, is the subject of two major monographs by N.G. Wollin, *Desprez en Italie* (Malmö, 1935) and *Desprez en Suède* (Stockholm, 1939). A scholarly and beautifully illustrated work is G. Hilleström's *Drottningholmsteatern förr och nu: The Drottningholm Theatre Past and Present*, trans. J. Stewart (Stockholm, 1980).

Music

There is no standard work on Swedish music history in general or on the Gustavian era in particular. However, a good survey is provided by the anthology *Gustavian Opera: an Interdisciplinary Reader in Swedish Opera, Dance and Theatre, 1771–1809* (Stockholm, 1989), containing several illuminating essays on different aspects of Gustavian culture. A thorough study of eighteenth-century instrumental music in Sweden is S. Walin's *Beiträge zur Geschichte der Swedischen Sinfonik* (diss., Uppsala U., 1941). There are several publications on individual eighteenth-century composers in Sweden. An excellent monograph on Johan Helmich Roman, 'the father of Swedish music', is I. Bengtsson's *J. H. Roman och hans instrumentalmusik* (diss., Uppsala U., 1955), with penetrating analyses of his musical style and an extensive English summary.

Joseph Martin Kraus is the subject of several publications. Major works are R. Engländer, *Joseph Martin Kraus und die Gustavianische Oper* (Uppsala, 1943); B. van Boer jr, *The Sacred Music and Symphonies of Joseph Martin Kraus* (diss., Uppsala U., 1983); and I. Leux-Henschen, *Joseph Martin Kraus in seinen Briefen* (Uppsala, 1978). Also informative are V. Bungardt, *Joseph Martin Kraus: ein Meister der klassischen Klavierliedes* (Regensburg, 1972); the reports from a series of international Kraus symposia: *Joseph Martin Kraus: ein Meister im gustavianischen Kulturleben*, ed. H. Åstrand (Stockholm, 1980); *Joseph Martin Kraus in seiner Zeit*, ed. F. W. Riedel (Salzburg and Munich, 1982); and *Kraus und das gustavianische Stockholm*, ed. G. Larsson and H. Åstrand (Stockholm, 1984). For valuable information on Gustavian opera see also R. Engländer's *Johann Gottlieb Naumann als Opernkomponist* (Leipzig, 1922).

One of the few native Swedish composers of the late eighteenth century is the subject of C.-G. Stellan Mörner's *Johan Wikmanson und die Brüder Silverstolpe* (diss., Uppsala U., 1952). Critical editions of Swedish music are published in the series Monumenta Musicae Sveciae; volumes have been issued containing works by, among others, Roman, Kraus, Wikmanson and Vogler. In Musica Sveciae, a major anthology of Swedish music recordings (in preparation), the Gustavian composers will be well represented; the recordings are supplemented by informative booklets.

Chapter XIII

Spain in the Enlightenment

C. H. RUSSELL

With the coming to power in Spain of the French Bourbon family at the beginning of the eighteenth century, the doors to Spanish society and culture – long closed to many developments of Spain's European neighbours – were flung open to admit a torrent of new ideas, philosophies and cultural trends. Philip V, the grandson of Louis XIV, introduced the Spanish court to the latest rage in France – the *contredanse*, the *danse à bal* and the *danse à deux*. All members of high society were expected to be familiar with the latest dances and their steps. French fashions, hairstyles and courtly manners found their way into Spanish life. French neo-classical thought set in motion a series of reforms in the Spanish theatre and in literature. Italian operatic and virtuoso instrumental styles rapidly inundated the Iberian peninsula. The passion for opera shared by Philip V and his son Ferdinand VI not only helped to shape tastes in the Spanish musical theatre but also left its indelible mark on sacred music. The inclusion of Italian theatrical styles in sacred compositions provoked a score of polemics. In fact, the issue of morality as it related to all of these foreign influences was hotly debated. These foreign intrusions met with stubborn resistance in some Spanish circles, especially among the middle class which flourished under the new economic policies of Charles III. New organizations and forms of public diversion arose. Nationalism – initially generated largely by middle-class concerns – permeated the entire fabric of Spanish society as the century progressed.[1]

THE CHURCH

A social history of music must first concern itself with patrons. Traditionally, three social institutions had promoted the composition and performance of music – the church, the court and the theatre; to these a fourth was added in the eighteenth century – the middle class. Unquestionably, in Spain the largest of these (with the most employees) was the church. Unlike some European countries, which had a multitude of sacred musical centres of equal importance, one metropolitan centre, Madrid, dominated the Spanish musical landscape at this time. It served as the model for the cathedrals and monasteries in the outlying provinces. A position in any of the three royal chapels in Madrid – the royal chapel (Capilla Real) and those of the monasteries of the Incarnation (Encarnación) and the Royal Discalced nuns (Descalzas Reales) – was a veritable prize: the salaries were high; a post at any of them brought fame and prestige; and furthermore a church composer's presence in the capital enabled him to compose for the theatre as well. Links with institutions in the provinces further strengthened the influence of the capital: Toledo Cathedral had extremely close ties with the Descalzas Reales; the affairs of the Encarnación in Madrid were administered from Santiago de Compostela; Palencia repeatedly drew its musicians and influence from Madrid; and there are other examples of such links. In short, Madrid was the hub of cultural life, with influence radiating out to the provinces.[2]

Musical life in the Capilla Real underwent several significant changes in the course of the eighteenth century. A fire at the Royal Alcázar on Christmas Eve 1734 destroyed the music archive. Philip V commissioned many new works from composers such as Joseph de Torres Martínez Bravo, Antonio Literes, José Nebra and Francesco Corselli (or Courcelle), to begin rebuilding a basic repertory of sacred music. Ferdinand VI (reigned 1746–59) similarly dedicated much attention to rebuilding the archive. In 1750 he had numerous chant books copied to replace those lost in the blaze. He also initiated several notable reforms of the Capilla Real: in 1747 he established a code of behaviour to restore discipline among the chapel musicians – their conduct had sunk to an inadmissible level of rowdy and indecent behaviour. Ferdinand conceded an important new privilege to his subjects in 1753 by making the chapel a parish church, thus allowing them access on a daily basis. The 'New Order' of 1756 greatly enlarged the musical resources of the chapel and its progressive policies provided the musicians with such benefits as accident insurance, a retirement plan and increased salaries.[3]

Composers in Spain employed by the church were remarkably mobile, moving freely from post to post in a highly competitive job market. This fluid movement of composers across the Iberian peninsula worked against the formation of insular 'schools' or regional styles. The most highly coveted posts included the cathedrals at Salamanca (which brought with it close and lucrative associations with the university), Santiago (with opportunities to augment the already high income through ties to the university, prebends and frequent functions outside the cathedral), Seville and Toledo. The positions in the Canary Islands were also sought for their respectable salaries and idyllic climate.

Throughout the century the church was concerned with a series of moral questions concerning music. Many church officials were appalled at the Italian recitative-and-aria type of music creeping into the Spanish liturgy and they railed against the appearance of this theatrical style. Juan Francisco de Sayas, for instance, launched a series of diatribes against the Italians in his *Música canónica, motética y sagrada* (Pamplona, 1761): in criticizing the homophonic Italian style he stated that 'the music that is called fashionable has neither craft, nor concept, nor corresponds to the [appropriate] feeling' and 'that music presently in fashion is violent harmony, not conforming in any way with the purpose for which it is used'.[4]

One of the most influential reformers of the late eighteenth century was Francisco Javier García Fajer, *maestro de capilla* of La Seo at Saragossa (Zaragoza) from 1756 until his death in 1809, often referred to as 'El Españoleto'. For some time the Spanish liturgy had included selections in the vernacular called *villancicos*. They replaced the Latin responsories and by the mid-eighteenth century they often had an operatic flavour, replete with recitatives and homophonic arias. García Fajer regarded these *villancicos* as an intrusion of the theatre into God's church and he initiated a movement that advocated their total exclusion. He was effective. An impressive list of cathedrals banned the use of any romance language (and thus the *villancico*) from the liturgy: Santiago, Granada, Pamplona, Málaga, Santander, Cádiz and Jaén.

The Court

The second major patron of the arts was the court. Ferdinand VI shared his father's passion for music and the arts. Domenico Scarlatti was in the employ of his wife, María Barbara Braganza. The famous Italian castrato Carlo Broschi, better known as Farinelli, remained one of the most important and influential men at court even after Philip V's death in 1746. Philip's widow, Isabel (Elisabetta Farnese), attempted to retain Farinelli in her service but was overruled by the newly crowned Ferdinand VI, who not only retained Farinelli but augmented his role in cultural affairs. Farinelli was made director of the royal entertainments and initiated an impressive series of performances in the royal sites of the Buen Retiro and Aranjuez. The lavish style with which he enticed Europe's top performers is recorded in his manuscript *Fiestas reales en el reinado de Fernando VI*.[5] Artists were granted eight days with meals and lodging during rehearsals at the royal sites, while rehearsal time in other theatres was normally confined to two days. If the elegantly furnished accommodation was not to a virtuoso's liking, he or she could find lodging elsewhere and be fully reimbursed. Carriages were supplied to allow the artist to make visits to the country, pay social calls or go to Mass.

Perhaps the most spectacular events under Farinelli's guidance

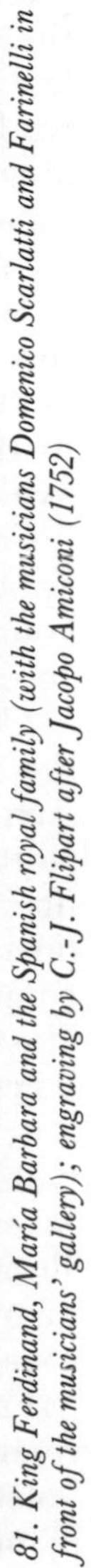

81. King Ferdinand, María Barbara and the Spanish royal family (with the musicians Domenico Scarlatti and Farinelli in front of the musicians' gallery); engraving by C.-J. Flipart after Jacopo Amiconi (1752)

were the elegant boat excursions that he planned for the royal couple and their court during their spring residences of 1752–7 at Aranjuez. A stunning regatta of ornately decorated boats took short journeys up and down the Tagus. The music on these occasions must have been as lavish as the rest of the entertainments. Farinelli sang, often accompanied by the king himself or by the queen. On numerous occasions the queen and Farinelli sang duets. These regal expeditions also featured fishing and the hunting of wild boar, deer, foxes and other wildlife that were roused and frightened towards the banks by the king's servants. For the evening of 17 July 1757 Farinelli arranged a breathtaking display in which the boats and river banks and the branches of the trees were illuminated by 40,000 candles.[6]

Italian influence soon dwindled. When Charles III assumed the throne in 1759 he quickly made known his love of hunting and his apathy towards opera. One of his first acts was to send Farinelli back to Italy, although with his full salary. Yet if Charles III was not an avid music-lover himself, he nevertheless took great care to see that his children received the best music education available. In 1761 he appointed the great Italian violinist Felipe Sabbatini to instruct the young Prince Charles (who was to become Charles IV) and secured José Nebra as clavichord teacher for him and for Prince Gabriel.[7]

Under the protection and patronage of Charles III's sons, musical life continued to flourish. Gabriel had a concert hall, the Casita de Arriba, constructed in the centre of El Escorial. It consisted of two storeys under a domed ceiling; the public was seated on the ground floor and the performers on the floor above, which had small windows open to the public below. Gabriel surrounded himself with music at court. He sponsored music academies in his own quarters, at which Haydn's music was often performed. At El Escorial Padre Antonio Soler, who had arrived in 1752, soon impressed the royal family so much that Charles III appointed him master of music for the princes Gabriel and Luis Antonio. Not surprisingly, a large proportion of Soler's publications bear the inscription 'composed especially for Prince Gabriel'. Soler had had constructed a special type of keyboard instrument, with the tone divided into nine parts, to illustrate for his royal student the differences between a major and a minor semitone.[8]

Prince Luis Antonio's small court, called the 'Prince's Room', rivalled his brother's; if Gabriel had access to the accomplished Padre Soler at El Escorial, Luis Antonio could claim in his employ an artist of no less brilliance – Luigi Boccherini. The Italian was initially invited to Spain in 1770 by the French ambassador of Luis Antonio's brother Charles, but Luis Antonio was the fortunate one who actually obtained Boccherini's services at Aranjuez that same year. Luis Antonio's death in 1785 left Boccherini and his fellow court musicians unemployed and in a precarious financial state. Charles agreed to pay their wages for six months while they were searching for new posts. Oddly enough, he did not assimilate Boccherini into his own court when he ascended to the throne in 1788, but continued with his previous master of music (clearly of lesser talent), Gaetano Brunetti.[9]

The nobility of Spain had personal courts that rivalled the crown's. Superb musical performances often graced the palaces of the Duke of Osuna and the Duke of Arcos.[10] No court, however, surpassed that of the house of Alba; Spain's finest musicians performed at the musical evenings organized by Fernando de Silva (the twelfth Duke of Alba) and his son Francisco de Paula de Silva (the Duke of Huescar). Fernando was responsible for putting many of the Spanish intelligentsia in contact with the artistic and philosophical trends of Spain's European neighbours. While serving as the ambassador to Paris under Ferdinand VI he became acquainted with Jean-Jacques Rousseau.[11] The secretary of the embassy during his stay was none other than Ignacio de Luzán, Spain's most influential neo-classicist. Their artistic precepts so impressed the duke that he became one of the leading proponents of neo-classicism in Spain upon his return. Ramón de la Cruz, the first librettist successfully to incorporate neo-classical principles into the zarzuela (a dramatic form including singing and dancing with spoken dialogue), was under the duke's protection.[12] The younger Duke of Huescar was no less enthusiastic in his patronage of the performing arts. Musical performances at his palace inspired scores of imitators attempting to replicate the rich quality and quantity of those gatherings. The list of composers represented at them reads like a 'who's who' of eighteenth-century Spanish composition. Works by such masters as Luis Misón, Antonio Guerrero, Manuel Canales and Blas de Laserna were standard fare. Tragically, the bulk of musical scores for these concerts was destroyed by two fires: the first, in 1795, consumed the libraries of the houses of Villafranca and Alba; and a disastrous fire during the Spanish Civil War obliterated the Alba archives.[13]

One of the most colourful purveyors of taste was the Duke of Huescar's daughter, the Duchess María Teresa Cayetana of Alba. She had a flamboyant and eccentric flair – she was a stunning beauty, had amorous affairs with bullfighters and sponsored boisterous *tertulias* in the middle of the night in the Prado. Foreign fashion did not excite her. She rejected the refined customs generally associated with the aristocracy and adopted instead the language, dress and fashion of the Spanish commoner. She effectively promoted these values among the Spanish nobility and it was not long before her chief cultural competitor, the Countess-Duchess of Benavente and Osuna (María Josefa Alonso Pimentel), was also playing the role of the Spanish *maja*.[14]

The Countess-Duchess of Benavente was herself an independent spirit; she was a good huntress and would often climb mountains and hike alone. She enjoyed the company of writers, philosophers and artists. The latest fashions from Paris and London filled her wardrobe. Only the Duchess of Alba and Queen Maria Luisa of Parma (wife of Charles IV) matched her importance as a principal definer of artistic taste and fashion. It was she who introduced many of Haydn's compositions to Spain and she so adored his music that she had her representative in Vienna, Carlos Alejandro de Lelis, negotiate a contract with Haydn in which he was to send copies of his new works directly to her, from 1783 to at least 1789. She surrounded herself with talent: Tomás de Iriarte and Ramón de la Cruz composed for her theatre. Her orchestra included some of Spain's best instrumentalists, including José Lidón and Luigi Boccherini, who became her orchestra director after he failed to obtain a post under Charles IV.[15]

THE THEATRE

Dramatic activities in Madrid revolved around three principal theatres. The Teatro del Príncipe and Teatro de la Cruz were well-established public theatres devoted primarily to dramas from Spain's golden age: the works of Lope de Vega, Calderón de la Barca and Tirso de Molina were still perennial favourites in the very buildings that had seen their premières centuries earlier. The theatres had remained in their original condition – open-air constructions with a central patio surrounded by windows and balconies belonging to the neighbouring residents – until their demolition and reconstruction in the early eighteenth century (the Cruz theatre was rebuilt in 1738, the Príncipe in 1744). A third, Teatro de los Caños del Peral, opened in Madrid in the early eighteenth century. It was dedicated almost exclusively to performances of Italian opera and Philip V afforded the theatre extremely generous financial and political privileges that assured its success in the early years; but it too was demolished and reconstructed, in 1737. By 1739, however, the regular scheduling of opera performances had already ceased and the theatre closed its doors, except for an occasional opera, concert or masked ball.

The Príncipe and Cruz, being public theatres, relied on popular support to maintain operation. But the court relied on these theatres as well. The two entities – court and theatre – developed a type of symbiotic relationship. The public theatre benefited from the relationship (at least early in the century) because the king bore the financial burden of mounting expensive zarzuelas. After opening at the palace, a zarzuela moved to one of the public theatres to play for several performances. Thus the public theatres were spared the risk of enormous production costs when they had no assurance that they could recoup their investment. (Later in the century, however, the court was unwilling to finance zarzuela productions, which forced them to become entirely self-supporting through box-office receipts.) In addition, the performers received extra payments for part-time employment in palace productions. However, the crown depended heavily on the public theatres. The actors needed for the *autos sacramentales* (one-act sacred plays performed especially on the feast of Corpus Christi) were normally drawn from the companies performing at the Cruz and Príncipe theatres. The palace needed to draw on their talent for its own productions, for it had no resident, full-time theatre troupe. Lastly, the public theatres supported local charities: one third of their total profits was distributed to charitable causes.[16]

A series of important reforms in the second half of the century transformed the two theatres, especially with regard to their musical resources. In 1765 small orchestras became a standard fixture instead of an occasional luxury. The Count of Aranda instituted several changes in 1767: he encouraged more cooperation between the two theatres and declared that the two companies must alternate in the use of each other's halls. The orchestra moved from behind the curtains on stage to its modern position in front of the audience. On stage, theatre flats or screens replaced curtains. Musicians and actors were first granted permission to mount productions for their direct

82. Masked ball in the Teatro del Príncipe: painting (c1770) by Luis Paret y Alcázar

financial benefit during the summer nights in 1768, a privilege that spawned a new flurry of musical activity and concert life. Music became more firmly established as an essential part of the theatre troupes in 1768, when the post of 'company musician' appeared on the companies' rosters and payrolls. The job entailed teaching the necessary music to the actors, guiding the dance steps, assisting with rehearsals and copying parts when the copyist was ill. The roster of Manuel Martínez's company of 1778 at the Teatro de la Cruz mentions a new post of elevated importance entitled 'company composer'. The holder had to compose the music for all productions. The staggering magnitude of that task can be gathered if one considers that Pablo Esteve y Grimau (who was appointed in 1778) had to compose in that year alone music for at least 72 *tonadillas* (short plays treating comic subjects, involving several singing characters) and scores for the Spanish comedies and zarzuelas and for French tragedies. Not surprisingly, both Esteve and Laserna (who was appointed company composer to the other theatre) began almost immediately to complain of unrealistic expectations.[17]

In the last decade of the eighteenth century, theatres were disrupted by several events. Leandro Fernández de Moratín and the board of censors set out to rid the Spanish stage of any works that abused the neo-classical principles that they cherished so dearly. Their campaign, in the course of which they compiled a list of over 600 prohibited works that included most of the masterpieces by Tirso, Lope and Calderón, had a disastrous effect. Another equally radical policy, although of a different bent, was instituted in 1799 by the board of theatrical reform. Resentment towards the importing of foreign culture (especially Italian opera) had finally reached such a pitch that the board banned the mounting of any dramatic piece in any language other than Castilian and made it mandatory for all performers to be Spanish as well. The policy reflects how much public and official opinion had changed since the century's first years, when Italian opera was so passionately promoted by Philip V and his court.[18]

Two dramatic forms unique to Spain, the zarzuela and the *tonadilla escénica*, captured the underlying social currents that were shaping eighteenth-century Spanish society. The zarzuela was an elaborate theatrical production, usually in two acts, that alternated sung numbers and spoken dialogue. Until the second half of the eighteenth century it dealt with allegorical or mythological topics, but the withdrawal of the crown's financial underwriting of production costs later in the century necessitated changes in the genre itself. The zarzuela abandoned mythological topics for popular, folklike ones, beginning with Ramón de la Cruz's and Antonio Rodríguez de Hita's *Las labradoras de Murcia* (Príncipe, 1769). After all, the financial risk was now entirely the theatre's and the indigenous folklike scenes drawn from daily life were more likely to please the paying public than Greek mythology. Neo-classical precepts affected zarzuela plots, beginning with Rodríguez de Hita's and de la Cruz's *La Briseida* (1768), which was commissioned by the Count of Aranda who zealously championed neo-classical thought in the Iberian peninsula. The first successful union of neo-classical ideals with national characteristics occurred in de la Cruz's and Fabián García Pacheco's *El buen marido* of 1770. It is neo-classical in that it adheres to the three classical unities, it does not rupture dramatic verisimilitude and it attempts to instruct the audience with a moral lesson. At the same time, popular Spanish values are captured by its setting in the streets of Madrid and its characters drawn from everyday life. Even Italian opera is represented in the virtuosity of certain musical numbers and recitative sections.[19]

Few artistic genres have captured the new aesthetics of the middle class more perfectly than the *tonadilla escénica*, a literary-musical production that flourished from about 1750 to 1800. Normally performed between the acts of a Spanish drama or *comedia*, *tonadillas* were satirical yet true-to-life, depicting everyday scenes with such characters as street vendors, magicians, soothsayers, gypsies, bullfighters, poets, musicians, soldiers, guards and bandits. By far the two most common character types to appear were the abbot and the *majo*. The audience would roar as the pious church father broke into a jovial song-and-dance routine. The other indisputable favourite was the Spanish *majo* who, through his sharp wit and biting ridicule, would have great fun at the expense of the Italian fops and French dandies. He was the theatrical manifestation of Spanish resentment towards foreign cultural invaders.[20]

The middle class loved *tonadillas*. Academies frequently included them in their programmes. The nobility, too, became infatuated with them as the century progressed. This was a result of the shift from foreign, affected and over-refined mannerisms to values considered natural, folklike or indigenous to Spain. There are abundant examples of the enthusiasm of high society for *tonadillas*. They were standard fare at the king's residence in Aranjuez. The Countess-Duchess of Benavente and the Countess of Peñafiel repeatedly staged them at their private functions. The Count of Artois, the French ambassador to Spain, was so taken by them that he requested that one of his favourites (*Los viajantes*) be performed between the acts of the drama he attended on 4 August 1782.[21] Beaumarchais was also an avid fan of the genre. He had been in Madrid from spring 1764 to spring 1765 and after his return to Paris he wrote back to a business associate, frantically pleading with him to locate the stack of *tonadillas* he had mislaid.[22]

The nobles squirmed rather than applauded, however, whenever the *majos* or *majas* on stage aimed their satirical barbs in their direction. One of the most graphic instances was a *tonadilla* composed by Luis Misón in which the acclaimed singer 'La Caramba' strolled on to the stage dressed as an elegant noblewoman, only to portray the nobility in an extremely unflattering light. Misón's work so enraged the Countess-Duchess of Benavente and the Duchess of Alba that he had to flee to avoid both prosecution and the wrath of the Duke of Arcos, who had amorous ties with the offended ladies.[23]

SOCIAL REFORM AND THE MIDDLE CLASS

The complexion of Spanish society in the eighteenth century was the result of two driving forces: the economic and political reforms instituted by Charles III and the introduction of radically different attitudes regarding socially acceptable behaviour. The Spanish economy flourished under Charles III's farsighted economic policies. One of the important products of that healthy economy was a burgeoning middle class with the time and new-found wealth to pursue such interests as the arts and music. Not coincidentally, then, two new entities sprang up – the *concert spirituel* ('sacred' concert) and the academy – that enabled this new public to enjoy the musical pleasures previously reserved for the court. During Lent, opera and staged representations were forbidden because of the solemnity of the

83. Chamber musicians: pen and ink sketch by Manuel Tramullas (1751–91)

season. Opera or theatre companies therefore began to organize public performances of unstaged musical works known as *concerts spirituels* for this off-season, to ease the performers' financial hardship while the theatre was closed.[24] The Duke of Hijar petitioned the crown for permission to produce *concerts spirituels* in Madrid at the Caños del Peral theatre in 1786 as a way to raise money needed for the hospitals' board. Financially they were a huge success and almost immediately the other two theatres in Madrid organized their own.[25] *Concerts spirituels* were also inaugurated in Barcelona and Valladolid in the final years of the century.[26] The other new development was the establishment of public concerts or academies. During the hiatus between opera seasons several enterprising musicians from the opera companies organized academies at various locations in the capital.[27] Before the crystallization of a viable paying audience the existence of such academies would have been unthinkable.

Many citizens also delighted in the masked balls and other public dances that had become commonplace in Madrid's public theatres by the mid-1770s. They were festive occasions lasting from eleven o'clock at night until four in the morning, with serving tables of soups, roast foods and cold cuts. They were not exclusive, closed affairs for the nobility but granted free access to the middle class. Again, Charles III (who sponsored these dances) revealed his concern for the well-being and pleasure of his subjects.[28]

Curiously, however, Charles III was unsympathetic to music publishers, a group that was attempting to meet the needs of the new middle-class market. Prospective publishers petitioned the crown for permission to establish a music press in Spain, but they met with apathetic responses or even open antagonism.[29] Thus Spain never developed the publishing houses capable of addressing the new amateur market or of disseminating Spanish music beyond its borders. Most Iberian music, regardless of merit, was imprisoned in manuscript form. In spite of these conditions, a handful of publications did see the light and were most often directed towards this new audience of the *aficionado* or amateur. Early in the century Pablo Minguet y Yrol published a number of small books (usually extremely condensed summaries and blatant plagiarisms of other authors' work) that claimed to teach almost any instrument or dance without the need for an instructor, and he was quite successful in reaching the middle-class musician.[30] Similarly, numerous guitar books appeared at the end of the century, all directed towards the new amateur market.

The position of music in university studies changed dramatically in the eighteenth century as a result of Charles III's expulsion of the Jesuits in 1767. The Society of Jesus owed its allegiance directly to Rome, not Madrid. The Jesuits therefore stood as an impediment to Charles III and his desire to develop a strong secular government, headed by the monarchy and free of church intervention. (Charles III was not the first European ruler forcibly to remove the Society of Jesus from his realm; the Jesuits were expelled from Portugal in 1759 and from France in 1762.) The Jesuits' monopoly of Spanish education evaporated with their expulsion and almost immediately educational instruction shifted its emphasis from religious concerns and antiquated scholasticism to a preoccupation with modern sciences and empirical thought. Although this reform may have been beneficial in many ways, music studies did not fare well. Charles IV's reforms of 1807 removed music from the university altogether. Another unfortunate repercussion of the Jesuits' expulsion came with the forced exile of Spain's first modern music historians, Esteban de Arteaga and Antonio Eximeno. Their best works were published far from Spanish soil.[31]

The second force reshaping Spanish society was the introduction of radically different attitudes regarding socially acceptable behaviour. Before the turn of the century the home was a fortress rarely penetrated by non-family members; women rarely left home. The Bourbons permanently altered this way of life: for the first time friends were received at home as a common occurrence and women would leave their homes daily to display their expensive carriages or stroll along the streets to talk to friends and to show off new clothes.[32] This dissolution of the extreme privacy of the home, coupled with the desire to display private wealth in a public fashion, helped to bring about two new cultural phenomena – the *tertulia* and the *sarao*. The *tertulia* consisted of an evening of intellectual discussion on the latest trends in the arts, philosophy and modern sciences and would often include a concert. *Tertulias* could take place at a nobleman's palace, an individual's home or even a public gathering place. The *sarao* differed from the *tertulia* in that it concluded with group dancing. The ability to dance and familiarity with the latest steps became indispensable for anyone hoping to circulate in high society. What better way to show off wealth and social skills than with an ostentatious evening replete with extravagant refreshments and a spectacle of music followed by a dance.[33]

The women's role in Spanish society had changed strikingly with Bourbon rule. Not only did the walls of her home no longer imprison her, but the behaviour expected of her while within those walls had also been altered. It became nearly obligatory for a woman of high society to take private instruction in singing, playing an instrument and dancing. Often the instructors were French or Italian, and the fashions and styles they promoted were usually foreign.[34]

As in the theatre, so in domestic affairs: resentment of the wholesale import of culture grew as the century progressed. The Spanish middle

84. The Fandango: frontispiece from C. A. Fischer's 'Voyager en Espagne aux années 1797 et 1798' (1801)

class, in particular, ridiculed the upper class's seemingly insatiable thirst for anything and everything new and foreign. José de Cadalso y Vásquez captured this view in his *Cartas marruecas* (1793) when he asked:

> How does the powerful man of this century spend his money? Two chamber servants, elegantly dressed and combed, wake him; he has an exquisite mocha coffee in a cup carried from China via London; he puts on the finest shirt from Holland, later a coat of good taste woven in Léon, France; he reads a book bound in Paris; he dresses to the instruction of a French tailor and hairdresser; he goes out with a carriage that has been painted where the book was bound; he goes to eat his hot meals in dishes produced in Paris or London and his fruits and sweets on plates from Saxony or China; he pays a master of music and another of dance, both of them foreigners; he attends an Italian opera (well or poorly performed) or a French tragedy well or poorly translated; and when it is time to go to bed he is able to say this prayer, 'I give thanks to heaven that all my activities of today have been directed to send out of my homeland as much gold and silver as has been in my power'.[35]

The character that appeared in the late eighteenth century demonstrating the extent to which middle-class values had affected artistic trends – the *majo* – was the antithesis of the foreign dandy or fop (the *curatoco* or *petimeter*). He valued the indigenous and traditional; he detested artificial courtesies, preferring real passion to courtly rules and foreign mannerisms. Goya captured the *majo* in his canvases. As we have seen, the *majo* was one of the principal character types on the Spanish stage; the rowdy spectators (*mosqueteros*) in the theatre's open patio delighted in scenes where the *majo* made fools of the foreigners. Dance, too, was transformed by popular values. Gradually the French *danse à deux*, minuet and contredanse (so fashionable at the beginning of the century) fell from favour and by the final decades were replaced by the traditional dances of the *majos*, such as the fandango, bolero, *seguidilla* and *tirana*.

Spain shared many of the cultural developments of the Enlightenment that pervaded the entire continent of Europe. Neo-classical precepts imported from France gradually appeared in Spanish theatrical works. To the traditional sources of musical patronage – church, court and theatre – was added the increasingly powerful middle class. New cultural outlets developed to address this new middle-class audience. Public performances and dances abounded. An appeal to simplicity and natural expression (devoid of obtuse or over-refined mannerisms) became the aesthetic goals in the arts.

The enormous resentment caused by imported cultural trends and the resulting nationalism that took hold were primarily the reaction to the cultural upheaval that accompanied the institution of a new dynasty. The Bourbons transformed Spanish attitudes towards daily life and brought with them Italian opera, French dance and the instrumental styles that were fashionable across Europe. But in the Iberian Peninsula these foreign styles were charged with political and social overtones not present (or at least not to the same degree) in other European countries. Their presence galvanized debate and public concern over the preservation of indigenous Spanish culture, particularly among members of the middle class. Thus by the end of the century Italian opera had been formally banned, French dance had fallen from favour and the common Spanish *majo* had ascended to a primary role as the cultural ideal.

NOTES

[1] See A. Martín Moreno, *Historia de la música española: siglo XVIII* (Madrid, 1985), especially pp.288–388; C. E. Kany, *Life and Manners in Madrid: 1750–1800* (Berkeley, 1932/*R*1970), 268–338; and C. Martín Gaite, *Usos amorosos del dieciocho en España* (Barcelona, 1972).

[2] Martín Moreno, *Historia*, 27–90; A. Araiz Martínez, *Historia de la música religiosa en España* (Madrid, 1942), 162–77; J. Subirá, 'La música en la capilla y monasterio de las Descalzas Reales de Madrid', *AnM*, xii (1957), 147–66; and J. Subirá, 'La música en la Real Capilla Madrileña', *AnM*, xiv (1959), 207–30.

[3] Martín Moreno, *Historia*, 29–30, 43–9, 50–56.

[4] F. J. León Tello, *La teoría española de la música en los siglos XVII y XVIII* (Madrid, 1974), 226–37.

[5] For a modern edition see Carlo Broschi Farinelli, *Fiestas reales en el reinado de Fernando VI*, ed. C. Morales Borrero (Madrid, 1972).
[6] E. Cotarelo y Mori, *Orígenes y establecimiento de la ópera en España hasta 1800* (Madrid, 1917), 101–90, especially pp.182–3; and Farinelli, *Fiestas reales*, 61–86.
[7] Martín Moreno, *Historia*, 235, 249.
[8] S. Rubio, *Antonio Soler: Catálogo crítico* (Cuenca, 1980), 23–4.
[9] Martín Moreno, *Historia*, 240–44.
[10] ibid, 258–65.
[11] J. Subirá treats Rousseau's and the Duke of Alba's extensive correspondence in *La música en la Casa de Alba* (Madrid, 1927), 89–98.
[12] Martín Moreno, *Historia*, 266.
[13] Subirá, *La música en la Casa de Alba*, p.xix.
[14] Martín Moreno, *Historia*, 310–11.
[15] Countess de Yebes, *La Condesa-Duquesa de Benavente* (Madrid, 1955), especially pp.81–107; and N. A. Solar-Quintes, 'Las relaciones de Haydn con la Casa de Benavente . . .', *AnM*, ii (1947), 81–104.
[16] W. M. Bussey, *French and Italian Influence on the Zarzuela: 1700–1770* (Ann Arbor, 1982), 6, 7, 52, 78.
[17] J. Subirá, *La tonadilla escénica: sus obras y sus autores* (Barcelona, 1933), 128–32; J. Subirá, *La tonadilla escénica* (Madrid, 1928), i, 321; and R. E. Pellissier, *The Neo-Classic Movement in Spain during the XVIII Century* (Palo Alto, 1918), 97.
[18] Subirá, *La tonadilla escénica: sus obras y sus autores*, 82, 184; and Martín Moreno, *Historia*, 369–70.
[19] Bussey, *French and Italian Influence on the Zarzuela*, 98–165.
[20] Subirá, *La tonadilla escénica: sus obras y sus autores*, 11–12, 42–3; and J. Subirá, *La participación en el antiguo teatro español* (Barcelona, 1930), 55–6.
[21] Subirá, *La tonadilla escénica*, i, 261–7.
[22] ibid, i, 276–7; and Subirá, *La participación*, 67.
[23] Subirá, *La tonadilla escénica*, i, 267.
[24] ibid, i, 267–8; and Cotarelo y Mori, *Orígenes y establecimiento de la ópera*, 310.
[25] Martín Moreno, *Historia*, 316; Cotarelo y Mori, *Orígenes y establecimiento de la ópera*, 300.
[26] Martín Moreno, *Historia*, 320–21.
[27] Lists of founders and addresses for numerous academies are found in Subirá, *La tonadilla escénica*, 267, and Cotarelo y Mori, *Orígenes y establecimiento de la ópera*, 310.
[28] Martín Moreno, *Historia*, 306–7.
[29] ibid, 247, 262, 397.
[30] For information concerning Minguet's publications see C. H. Russell, *Santiago de Murcia: Spanish Theorist and Guitarist of the Early Eighteenth Century* (diss., U. of North Carolina, Chapel Hill, 1981), 143–54, especially n.14 and n.19.
[31] Martín Moreno, *Historia*, 299–301, 435–9.
[32] Martín Gaite, *Usos amorosos del dieciocho en España*, 286.
[33] Martín Moreno, *Historia*, 289; Martín Gaite, *Usos amorosos del dieciocho en España*, 36–8; and Kany, *Life and Manners*, 268–89.
[34] Martín Gaite, *Usos amorosos del dieciocho en España*, 41.
[35] Martín Moreno, *Historia*, 292.

BIBLIOGRAPHICAL NOTE

Historical-political background

The best social history of this period is still J. Sarrailh's *La España ilustrada de la segunda mitad del siglo XVIII*, translated into Spanish by A. Alatorre (Mexico City, 1957); the best histories in English are R. Herr's *The Eighteenth-Century Revolution in Spain* (Princeton, NJ, 1958) and C. E. Kany's *Life and Manners in Madrid: 1750–1800* (Berkeley, 1932/*R*1970). C. Martín Gaite's eloquent and perceptive study of amorous customs in eighteenth-century Spain. *Usos amorosos del dieciocho en España* (Barcelona, 1972), is indispensable for those interested in Spanish secular music or dance of the era. W. N. Hargreaves-Mawdsley's *Eighteenth-Century Spain 1700–1788: a Political, Diplomatic and Institutional History* (London, 1979) is well-documented and thorough; in *Spain under the Bourbons, 1700–1833: a Collection of Documents* (London, 1973) the same author has compiled and translated a wealth of government documents, royal decrees and other primary source material. This latter publication – which deals exclusively with official documents – is complemented by an anthology of contemporaneous anecdotes and travellers' accounts found in *Viajes de extranjeros por España y Portugal*, compiled, annotated and translated into Spanish by J. García Mercadal (Madrid, 1962).

The Bourbon monarchs and their policies are the subject of J. D. Bergamini's *The Spanish Bourbons: the History of a Tenacious Dynasty* (New York, 1974). C. Petrie deals admirably with the reign of Charles III in *King Charles III of Spain: an Enlightened Despot* (London, 1971). Several important studies of the reign of Ferdinand VI are found in *La época de Fernando VI: Ponencias leídas en el coloquio conmemorativo de los 25 años de la fundación de la Cátedra Feijoo* (Oviedo, 1981): see F. Aguilar Piñal, 'Sobre la política cultural de Fernando VI', 297–314, and J. M. Caso González, 'La Academia de Buen Gusto y la poesía de la época', 383–414. Another important publication pertaining to Ferdinand VI's reign is Carlo Broschi Farinelli's *Fiestas reales en el reinado de Fernando VI*, ed. C. Morales Borrero (Madrid, 1972).

Concerning iconography of the period, see F. Sopeña Ibañez and A. Gallego Gallego, *La música en el Museo del Prado* (Madrid, 1971). This study of paintings in the Prado Museum that depict musical scenes is lavishly illustrated and contains valuable cross-references to other art histories.

Music: general studies

The most comprehensive and articulate treatment of Spanish music in the eighteenth century is A. Martín Moreno's *Historia de la música española: siglo XVIII* (Madrid, 1985); it is well-documented, thoroughly researched and clearly organized and it provides the most useful and extensive bibliography to date. J. López-Calo provides an excellent and concise summary of sacred and secular music practices in eighteenth-century Spain in 'Barroco-estilo galante-clasicismo', *España en la música de occidente*, ii, *Salamanca 1985*, 3–29. Another recent contribution to eighteenth-century Spanish scholarship is the collection of papers delivered at the II Congreso Nacional de Musicología (*Bicentenario de la muerte del P. Antonio Soler: Madrid 1983*); most of these papers appear in *Revista de musicología*, viii/1 (1985). Still of substantial value are J. Subirá's *Historia de la música española e hispanoamericana* (Barcelona, 1953) and G. Chase's *The Music of Spain* (New York, rev. 2/1959).

F. J. León Tello provides exhaustive analysis and commentary for nearly every Spanish theoretical work from the era in *La teoría española de la música en los siglos XVII y XVIII* (Madrid, 1974). León Tello summarizes some of his main theses and observations in 'Introducción a la estética y a la técnica española de la música en el siglo XVIII', *Revista de musicología*, iv/1 (1981), 113–26. For an investigation of the influence of French dance and Italian instrumental music in Spain see C. H. Russell's 'Imported Influences in 17th- and 18th-Century Guitar Music in Spain', *España en la música de occidente*, i, *Salamanca 1985*, 385–403, and C. H. Russell's *Santiago de Murcia: Spanish Theorist and Guitarist of the Early Eighteenth Century* (diss., U. of North Carolina, Chapel Hill, 1981).

Church music

An important investigation of the sacred musical practices in late eighteenth-century Spain is M. Pilar Alén's 'Las capillas musicales catedrálicas desde Carlos III hasta

Fernando VII', *España en la música de occidente*, ii *Salamanca 1985*, 39–49. An adequate summary of Spanish sacred music is A. Araiz Martínez's *Historia de la música religiosa en España* (Barcelona, 1942). For activities in Madrid see J. Subirá's 'La música en la capilla y monasterio de las Descalzas Reales de Madrid', *AnM*, xii (1957), 147–66, and his 'La música en la Real Capilla Madrileña y en el Colegio de Niños Cantorcicos', *AnM*, xiv (1959), 207–30. For the best account of Francisco Javier García Fajer and his reforms see J. J. Carreras López, *La música en las catedrales en el siglo XVIII: Francisco J. García 'El Españoleto' (1730–1809)* (Saragossa, 1983).

Court music

A. Martín Moreno's *Historia . . . siglo XVIII* contains the best overview of Spanish music at court. J. Subirá's *La música en la Casa de Alba* (Madrid, 1927) gives a fascinating and well-researched account of musical life of the house of Alba; for a discussion of the house of Benavente see Countess de Yebes, *La Condesa-Duquesa de Benavente: una vida en unas cartas* (Madrid, 1955), especially pp.81–107, and N. A. Solar-Quintes, 'I. Las relaciones de Haydn con la Casa de Benavente; II. Nuevos documentos sobre Luigi Boccherini; III. Manuel García intimo: un capítulo para su biografía', *AnM*, ii (1947), 81–104. Most of the sources cited below also deal extensively with music at court.

Theatre music

The best accounts in English of the Spanish theatre during the eighteenth century are W. M. Bussey, *French and Italian Influence on the Zarzuela: 1700–1770*, Studies in Musicology, no.53 (Ann Arbor, 1982), and C. E. Kany, *Life and Manners in Madrid*, 290–338. Other excellent accounts of theatres and their activities include E. Cotarelo y Mori, *Orígenes y establecimiento de la ópera en España hasta 1800* (Madrid, 1917); Cotarelo y Mori, *Colección de entremeses, loas, bailes, jácaras y mojigangas desde fines del siglo XVI a mediados del XVIII* (Madrid, 1911); Cotarelo y Mori, *Historia de la zarzuela: o sea el drama lírico en España, desde su origen a fines del siglo XIX* (Madrid, 1934); J. Subirá, *La tonadilla escénica: sus obras y sus autores* (Barcelona, 1933); Subirá, *La tonadilla escénica* (Madrid, 1928); and Subirá, *La participación en el antiguo teatro español* (Barcelona, 1930). X. M. Carreira has published two articles that contain much primary documentation and shed much light on the theatre in the provinces: 'Orígenes de la ópera en Cádiz: un informe de 1768 sobre el Coliseo de Operas' and 'La tasa y regulación del Colisea de Operas y Comedias fabricado por Setario (La Coruña, 1772)', *Revista de musicología*, x/2 (1987), 581–99 and 601–21.

The polemics surrounding the moral and immoral aspects of the Spanish theatre are discussed at length in A. Martín Moreno's *El Padre Feijoo y las ideologías musicales del XVIII en España* (Orense, 1976); of great value are the appendices listing the different polemics and their participants. In addition, the relevant texts for these disputes are quoted in Cotarelo y Mori, *Bibliografía de las controversias sobre la licitud del teatro en España* (Madrid, 1904).

Chapter XIV

Philadelphia: a City in the New World

NICHOLAS E. TAWA

English colonists belonging to the religious Society of Friends, commonly known as Quakers, founded Philadelphia in 1681. During the next 120 years, while the vast majority of Americans lived on farms or in villages, Philadelphia experienced rapid growth, and this ensured music-making beyond the simplest sort. Shortly after the mid-eighteenth century, Philadelphia's population numbered about 40,000 – making it one of the largest English-speaking cities in the British Empire. By the year 1800, its population had grown to 70,000. In the infant United States, only New York City, with 60,000 inhabitants, came close to this figure.[1]

As the city grew, it added Scots-Irish Presbyterians, members of the Church of England and German Lutherans, among others, to the original Quaker settlers. Before long, secular music, especially that for the musical stage, became a matter of contention mostly between the stricter Quakers and Presbyterians, who wanted to contain its expansion, and the more artistically orientated members of the Church of England, who fostered it. As early as 1716, the Quaker leadership was warning people about 'going to or being in any way concerned in plays, games, lotteries, music, and dancing'.[2] Yet, whatever the opposition, the most significant reasons why music failed to flourish in Philadelphia during the first half of the century were the lack of leisure and disposable income and a dearth of such urban inhabitants who could support recreations beyond the execution of simple songs and dances. Stage plays, concerts, opera, 'and all such formal and sophisticated entertainment require a settled and urban life to support them'; therefore 'theatres had to wait for society to become settled and reasonably sophisticated'.[3]

MUSIC IN WORSHIP

The surviving records of religious music in Philadelphia begin before those of secular music. Quakers used no music in their worship, unlike the German Pietists who settled in Pennsylvania in 1694. They had brought a small organ with them, which was lent to the Gloria-Dei Church in Philadelphia in 1703. It is significant that Justus Falckner, the church's pastor, had written two years before to Heinrich Mühlen of Holstein asking for an organ in order to foster sacred music and thereby to interest people in joining the congregation. He insisted that it would 'tend to attract many of the young people away from the Quakers and sects to attend services where such music was found, even against the wishes of their parents'.[4]

Christ Church of the Anglicans had an organ in 1728, the Moravian Church had two organs by 1743, St Joseph's Catholic Church had one in 1748 and St Peter's, an Anglican church, had one in 1763. In 1763 there was agitation among Presbyterians for improving the singing during worship by using an organ.[5] That required an organist, professional or amateur. For example, James Bremner, a professional musician, crossed the Atlantic in 1763 to become the organist at St Peter's and, in 1767, at Christ Church. He soon returned to England, however, and an amateur musician temporarily replaced him. In the Christ Church vestry minutes for 10 December 1770 is the comment:

> Mr. church-warden [Francis] Hopkinson having been so obliging as to perform on the organ at Christ Church during the absence of Mr. Bremner, the late organist, the vestry unanimously requested of him a continuance of this kind office, until an organist should be appointed, or as long as it should be convenient and agreeable to himself. Mr. Hopkinson cheerfully granted this request.[6]

Various witnesses attest to the frequent singing of psalms and hymns in the home, particularly during times of religious fervour. When the charismatic preacher George Whitefield arrived from England in 1738 and began preaching his doctrine of Calvinist evangelism in Philadelphia, he attracted enormous crowds. Benjamin Franklin wryly remarked that everyone was 'growing Religious so that one could not walk thro' the Town in an Evening without Hearing Psalms sung in different Families of every Street'.[7]

Whether the singing was accomplished or not, Franklin did not say. We know from others that in church it was not always pleasing to hear. Some could not sing at all, others sang conflicting versions of the sacred tunes. Organs, a few people hoped, would improve matters. Nevertheless, more needed to be done, so instruction in singing from printed music began. At mid-century several teachers of psalmody from New England conducted singing schools in Philadelphia. The Connecticut-born Andrew Adgate is known to have taught a singing school that included psalmody in 1760. The next year he compiled and published, in Philadelphia, *Urania, or A Choice Collection of Psalm-Tunes, Anthems and Hymns*, several of them by native American composers. The same Francis Hopkinson who filled in as organist at

Christ Church also undertook, with the help of one William Young, to instruct 'the children of the united congregations' of Christ and St Peter's Church in 1764.[8] Twenty years later, Adgate founded an Institution for the Encouragement of Church Music, then started a Free School for Spreading the Knowledge of Vocal Music (later called the Uranian Academy). Education and sacred choral concerts were its objectives. One concert, on 4 May 1786, employed an Academy chorus of 320 singers and an orchestra of 50 musicians; among the works performed were some by native Americans – James Lyon and William Billings.[9]

Most of Philadelphia's non-Quaker families remained conservative in their musical tastes throughout the century. For singing at home, or for study in singing school, hymns and psalms were their staple musical fare. They attended public concerts of sacred music but were much less keen to hear secular music unmixed with sacred and their attendance at theatrical performances was rare.

AMATEUR MUSIC-MAKING

There is every reason to believe that teaching non-sacred music had begun earlier than teaching psalmody. By 1728 dancing instruction was available in Philadelphia's boarding-schools; the next year a dancing-master, Samuel Perpoint, was named. In 1730 the *Pennsylvania Gazette* first advertised a music teacher, the sister of a Mr Thomas Ball, just arrived from London, who taught 'Singing, Playing on the Spinet, Dancing, and all sorts of Needle Work'. By March 1749, John Beals, also from London, was offering instruction in the violin, oboe, flute and dulcimer, 'by note', both in his studio and in the homes of students who wanted privacy. He also expressed his willingness to play the violin 'at the Assembly Balls and all other Entertainments'. The same James Bremner mentioned as organist at Anglican churches in Philadelphia started a morning music school in 1763 to instruct young ladies in the harpsichord and guitar, and an evening one to instruct young gentlemen in the violin, German flute, harpsichord and guitar.[10]

During the American Revolution musical instruction was greatly curtailed; soon after hostilities ended, however, a number of fine musicians arrived in Philadelphia and began teaching. Most notable among them was the composer, music director and pianist Alexander Reinagle:

> Upon peace being concluded . . . he emigrated to this country . . . settling in Philadelphia as a teacher of music, in which capacity he was employed by the most respectable families and the principal boarding schools in or near the city. Not only the fashionable songs from England, as he received them, but others of a higher quality,

> and even Italian airs, did he arrange, in an easy and familiar style so as to make them attainable by his pupils.[11]

During the first two-thirds of the century Philadelphia printers mostly issued books on psalmody. As early as 1729, Benjamin Franklin had reprinted the seventh edition of Watts's Psalms of David in order to improve psalmody and religious singing. Printers also did a thriving trade in broadsides of ballad texts to be sung to existing tunes; they were cried on the Philadelphia streets by hawkers and sold in large quantities.[12] In the main, secular music, like songs and dances or variations on popular airs for keyboard, had to be imported directly from England by music-lovers. Printers' shops and one or two stores probably also sold London music publications. For example, the *Pennsylvania Gazette* of 27 December 1759 mentions a Michael Hillegas who offered for sale from his house not only instruments but also an assortment of music, including solos, overtures, concertos, sonatas and duets for various instruments, music books, self-instruction books and songs.[13]

Only after the Civil War did the local publication of secular music in sheet-music or songbook format begin. John Aitken and Thomas Dobson were publishing music in 1785, Moller and Capron in 1791 and Benjamin Carr in 1793. By the end of the eighteenth century there were at least ten Philadelphia music publishers.[14] Mostly from the British Isles, they issued scarcely anything by native Americans; they published some music by foreign composers resident in America and a great deal of music currently fashionable in England. One notes the claim printed with Charles Dibdin's *Jack at the Windlass* (published by Benjamin Carr in Philadelphia *c*1793) that at Carr's establishment 'may be had all the newest music reprinted from European publications'. (An international copyright law was still a hundred years in the future.)

The music was intended almost entirely for amateur musicians. If the singer was musically illiterate, he or she learnt the tunes by ear and purchased 'songsters' containing only the words. If an accompanying instrument was not available, the singer might buy a songbook containing a collection of songs with a single-line melody for each lyric.. For those who possessed a keyboard instrument the songs were issued individually as sheet music with a simple two-staff accompaniment and sometimes, as an extra, with the melody transposed into a convenient key for execution by a flautist. For much of the century the harpsichord was the accompanying keyboard instrument. In 1775, however, John Behrent advertised in Philadelphia that he had 'just finished an extraordinary instrument, by the name of the Piano-Forte, made of mahogany, being of the nature of a Harpsichord with hammers and several changes'. Twelve years later, Charles

Taws began to make pianos in Philadelphia.[15] Other piano manufacturers followed, and many imported pianos appeared in Philadelphia music shops during the 1780s and 1790s.

Owning a keyboard instrument and taking lessons in playing it, and taking singing lessons, were also usually confined to the well-to-do, and to young women in particular. A knowledge of music was seen as a fashionable and genteel accomplishment. In 1794 Susanna Rowson wrote of industrious tradesmen who, when they could afford it, decided that their daughters 'must be *genteelly* educated'. Among the accomplishments these young women had to acquire was 'the very fashionable one of jingling the keys of the harpsichord with great velocity, though perhaps out of time and out of tune'. Rowson further observed that most of these young women, unless they had 'an independent fortune', would have 'neither the time or opportunity' to continue their music-making in later life. Yet, Rowson admitted, education in cooking, sewing, keeping house and managing servants was not enough if one were to be accepted as a gentlewoman. She mentioned a Miss Withers who, 'to the fine arts . . . was a perfect stranger. Music, dancing, or drawing, has no charms for her, nor had she the least idea of the pleasures resulting from a well informed, elegantly cultivated mind'.[16]

Musical accomplishments could help a woman to win a husband. The noted Philadelphia physician Benjamin Rush, in a letter to Lady Jane Wishart Belsches dated 21 April 1784, reported that his wife 'knows that she owes her conquest in part to . . . [her] singing "The Birks of Endermay" the first evening I was introduced to her . . . [and in this fashion] she opened an avenue to my heart'.[17] Once won, a husband might be kept faithful through music. Elizabeth Griffith, in 1796, wrote some advice to young married women of Philadelphia, describing music as one of the 'most winning accomplishments . . . necessary to preserve the lover in the husband'.[18]

In a century when public amusements were limited, entertainment was inevitably confined to the family circle and took the form of dancing, singing and performing on such instruments as the harpsichord or piano, flute and guitar. When visiting each other, people often took music with them as a contribution to an evening's entertainment.[19]

In the 1740s there was a Philadelphia 'Musick Club', comprising amateur male musicians, at which 'one Levy played a very good violine [*sic*], one Quin bore another pritty good part; Tench Francis played a very indifferent finger upon an excellent violin'. When the College of Philadelphia (later the University of Pennsylania) needed music for its commencements and convocations, male and female amateur musicians, including Francis Hopkinson, volunteered their services. In 1771 a depressed Hopkinson found his musical companions reduced to almost none and wrote to one of them, Governor Penn, then in England:

> Music is at present in a very deplorable Condition here – Sigr. *Gualdo* lies in Chains in one of the Cells of the Pennsylva. Hospital; and poor *Butho* was kill'd a few Weeks ago by a Fall from his House – Except *Forage* and myself I don't know a single Votary the Goddess hath in this large city.[20]

The *Journal* of Sally Wister, the sixteen-year-old daughter of a rich Philadelphia Quaker merchant, describes some evenings in her home in 1777. It also demonstrates that not all Quaker families were adamantly opposed to music, particularly within the confines of the home and after mid-century. In October she and her cousin Liddy were seated at a table looking at a book when Major William Stoddert joined them, asking: 'Pray, ladies is there any songs in that book?' 'Yes, many', came the reply. Begged to sing, they refused: 'Liddy, saucy girl, told him I cou'd. He beg'd and I deny'd; for my voice is not much better than the voice of a raven'. A few days later 'arriv'd two officers, Lieutenant Lee and Warring, Virginians . . . Lee sings prettily and talks a gret deal; how good turkey hash and fry'd hominy is – (a pretty discourse to entertain the ladies)'. In December she was visited by a young man, Robert Tilly, who brought his German flute with him. His playfulness, however, annoyed her:

> I am vex'd at Tilly, who has his flute, and does nothing but play the fool. He begins a tune, plays a note or so, then stops. Well, after a while he begins again; stops again. 'Will that do, Seaton? Hah! hah! hah!' He has given us but two regular tunes since he arriv'd. I am passionately fond of music. How boyish he behaves.[21]

Music-making in the homes of Quakers is also mentioned by the Marquis de Chastellux. On 11 December 1780, he visited the home of Dr William Shippen and enjoyed a musical soirée: 'Miss Rutledge played on the harpsichord, and played very well. Miss Shippen sang with timidity, but with a pretty voice. Mr Otto, secretary to the Chevalier de La Luzerne sent for his harp; he accompanied Miss Shippen, and also played several pieces'. Chastellux was given the opportunity to observe what men sang when the women were out of the parlour. Three days after visiting the Shippen house he had dinner at the home of James Wilson. After dinner, the women retired and

> Mr [Richard] Peters, the Minister of War, gave the signal for mirth and jollity by favouring us with a song of his own composition, so broad and unrestrained that I shall dispense with giving either a translation, or a selection of it here. He then sang another, more chaste and more musical; this was a very fine Italian *cantabile*. Mr Peters is unquestionably the minister of two worlds who has the best

> voice and who sings best both the pathetic and the *bouffon* – a fact doubtless unknown in Europe and one which could not have been guessed at there. I was told that the preceding year there were still some private concerts at Philadelphia, where he sang among other comic pieces, a burlesque part in a trio which was in itself very pleasing, and which he seasoned with all the humorous strokes usual on such occasions.[22]

Another Sally, Benjamin Franklin's daughter, sang and demonstrated commendable proficiency at the keyboard – so much so that Francis Hopkinson recommended in 1765 that her father should purchase a better harpsichord. Without question, she participated in spontaneous evening social entertainments featuring music. Note Benjamin Franklin's comment on Philadelphia musical life, made in a letter to Polly Stevenson dated 6 May 1786:

> As to public amusements, we have neither plays nor operas, but we had yesterday a kind of oratorio, as you will see by the enclosed paper; and we have assemblies, balls and concerts, besides little parties at one another's houses, in which there is sometimes dancing, and frequently good music; so that we jog on in life as pleasantly as you do in England; anywhere but in London, for there you have plays performed by good actors. That, however, is, I think, the only advantage London has over Philadelphia.[23]

Many of these 'little parties' were in the home of Mrs John Penn. After visiting Philadelphia in January 1784 Francesco de Miranda stated: 'Mrs John Penn has a private concert in her home once a week, at which the best musicians in the city gather. The room is small, and, necessarily, the orchestra and company'.[24]

Spontaneous 'little parties' with singing and instrumental performances also took place on porches or benches placed in front of Philadelphia houses and on picnics or 'frolics' during the warm summer months. In winter there was music on sleigh rides to outlying taverns. We should bear in mind that Philadelphians felt so cramped in their small eighteenth-century houses that they resorted to a surprisingly recurrent street and tavern life.[25] Another form of outdoor music-making which, to judge from irate letters to newspapers, annoyed older Philadelphians, was the nocturnal serenading of young women by enamoured young men. John Durang narrated one such incident that happened in 1785:

> Previous to my leaving Philad'a I engaged our band of music [of the Old American Company] and serenaded a young lady for whom I had an honorable sincere attachment. Tho' music hath charmes to melt the savage brest, to soften rocks and bend the knotet oak, yet it had not charmes enough to melt the heart of the guardian of my love who watched her so close that we could not bid farewell by the hand.[26]

The 'band' referred to comprised professional theatrical instrumentalists, not amateurs.

CONCERTS AND THEATRE

The earliest recorded public concert in Philadelphia was given by John Palma in 1757. From then on, though sporadically, professional musicians arranged concerts, usually by subscription, often assisted by amateur musicians. Songs, operatic arias, choruses, overtures, movements from concertos and sonatas composed by European musicians resident in America or by composers who were the centre of London's attention, like Handel, Geminiani, Arne and Johann Stamitz, made up the programmes before the American Revolution in 1775. After the Revolution the number of professional musicians from Europe in Philadelphia increased and public concerts became more frequent. Resident foreign-born composers like Alexander Reinagle, Henri Capron and John Moller performed their own works and added others by noted contemporary European composers, among them Johann Christian Bach, Joseph Haydn and Niccolò Piccinni.[28]

Public concerts were of less importance to Philadelphian music-lovers, however, than staged drama with music. The former interested a small circle of educated and relatively sophisticated men and women; the latter drew music-lovers from all walks of life. Although favourite songs and arias were presented at concerts, Philadelphians preferred to hear them within the context of a staged drama, or as adjuncts to one. The theatre was the most engaging public entertainment offered to Philadelphians; it was able to move people, however unsophisticated, and yet it retained a hold on the affections of those with more cultivated tastes. Comic or satirical repartee, clever dances and brief, tuneful, strophic ditties of a popular or traditional nature characterized the English ballad operas that made up a major portion of the theatrical fare of eighteenth-century America. Even when serious dramas like the plays of Shakespeare or Sheridan were performed, songs were heard between the acts and were sometimes interpolated into them. Moreover, after the presentation of a straight drama, it was customary to give a ballad opera of modest length as an afterpiece.

For the first few decades of the colony's existence, the Quakers, abetted by many Presbyterians and Lutherans, saw themselves as the moral conscience of the town. Although they might not wish to infringe on people's freedom of conscience, they felt the need to censor what they considered depraved public behaviour. In their eyes the theatre was a reprehensible amusement and an enticement to wickedness that had to be discouraged.[29] Important aspects of developing American civilization are revealed in the long (and eventually successful) struggle to establish a theatre in Philadelphia: the increase of commerce and wealth in a major seaport town, the growth and changing complexion of the population and the increasing cultural exchange with Europe.

As early as 1700, the Pennsylvania Assembly found it necessary to prohibit 'stage-plays', 'masks' and 'revels', thus indicating that some form of theatre must have existed nineteen years after Philadelphia's foundation. When Benjamin Franklin left Philadelphia for England in 1724 he travelled with James Ralph, who, in 1730, wrote *The Fashionable Lady*, the first ballad opera written by a native American.[30]

The years 1749 and 1750 saw the brief appearance of the Kean and Murray Company of players at William Plumstead's warehouse in King Street. Among the musical offerings were *The Beggar's Opera*, *The Devil to Pay*, *Flora* and *Damon and Phillida*. In January 1750 the *Recorder* of Philadelphia warned that a continuation of the company 'would be attended with very mischievous results', causing the Board to order 'the Magistrates to take the most effectual measures for suppressing this disorder'.[31]

In 1752 the newly-arrived Lewis Hallam 'Company of Comedians from London' appeared in Williamsburg and New York. A group of Philadelphia gentlemen went to New York and pressed Hallam to bring his company to Philadelphia, promising him a favourable outcome in spite of Quaker antagonism. At the same time, Governor Hamilton was petitioned to grant permission for the company's appearance, which he did after receiving an assurance that nothing 'indecent or immoral' would be staged. A season of 24 performances began on 25 April 1754, after which the company left for the West Indies.[32]

Lewis Hallam died, and David Douglass, who married Hallam's widow, reorganized the players (soon to be known as the American Company) and returned to the North American continent in 1758, appearing in Philadelphia in 1759. From then until the eve of the American Revolution, the American Company made appearances in Southwark, just beyond the town's limits.[33]

Two or three performances a week, beginning at six o'clock, were the norm. Affluent theatre-goers sent servants a few hours beforehand to reserve their seats. Dandies wandered backstage and even onstage to exchange pleasantries with female actors awaiting their entry cues – a practice that ended in 1761 after many complaints from the audience. Gentlemen-performers, playing for their own enjoyment, assisted the professionals in the orchestra. This is made clear in a notice printed in the *Pennsylvania Gazette* for 30 November 1769:

> For the future, the days of performance will be Tuesday and Friday. The Orchestra, on Opera Nights, will be assisted by some musical

Persons, who, as they have no View but to contribute to the Entertainment of the Public, certainly claim a Protection from any Manner of Insult.[34]

The insult usually came from the gallery, where a rowdy element ensconced itself and on occasion made free to pelt the better-dressed audience below, the orchestra and the stage with eggs, apples and other missiles.

Whenever the American Company appeared in Philadelphia there were accolades from theatre-goers and protests from the upholders of strict morality. For example, during the 1766–7 season, a 'gentleman contributor' wrote a letter to the *Pennsylvania Gazette*, saying he spoke for himself and others who enjoyed witnessing *Love in a Village*:

I must beg leave to inform the Public, that the pleasing LOVE IN A VILLAGE is done here beyond expectation and must give real Delight to every Person void of Ill-Nature [!] . . . Miss Wainright is a very good singer, and her Action exceeds the famous Miss Brent. Mr. Hallam exceeds everything in the Character of Hodge; and Mr. Woolls almost equals Beard in Hawthorn. Miss Hallam deserves universal Applause and Encouragement. I could wish to see the House better filled whenever this justly applauded Entertainment is exhibited.

In contrast, on 10 November 1773, a person signing himself 'Philadelphus' attacked the players in the pages of the *Pennsylvania Gazette*, stating:

It is a matter of real sorrow and distress to many sober inhabitants of different denominations to hear of the return of those strolling Comedians, who are travelling thro' America, propagating vice and immorality. And it is much to the disreputation of this City that more encouragement should be given them here than in any other place on the Continent.[35]

It was partly in response to the sanctimonious yet money-grubbing dominant class of Philadelphia that a pseudonymous Andrew Barton of Philadelphia wrote a comic opera which exacerbated the situation. Entitled *The Disappointment, or The Force of Credulity*, the work was to be produced by the American Company on 20 April 1767. Existing tunes are indicated for eighteen song lyrics in the libretto. However, owing to the coarse language, biting satire and ridiculing of prominent residents for being greedy and stupid, the authorities banned its production.[36]

Controversy over the theatre was suspended on 20 October 1774 when the Continental Congress in Philadelphia passed a resolution to end every manner of public entertainment because of the unsettled times. Theatre productions ceased for the duration of the war, except

85. Interior of the Chestnut Street Theatre, Philadelphia: engraving from 'The New York Magazine' (1794)

for the activities of the British during their occupation of Philadelphia in the winter of 1777–8, when officers and their wives staged a few performances which some Philadelphian citizens did not hesitate to attend. Even after the war, Philadelphia's religious conservatives succeeded in discouraging theatrical performances, aided in part by postwar economic and emotional impoverishment and by remembrance of those who had recently suffered and died to achieve independence.

Nevertheless, by 1785 Lewis Hallam jr and John Henry had returned with a reorganized American Company, now renamed the Old American Company, and had reappeared in Southwark with scenes from plays and ballad operas. These were deceptively described as concerts or moral and entertaining lectures, in order to circumvent the objections of moralists. The company included an orchestra of about twelve musicians led by Philip Phile.[37]

The claim of moral lectures notwithstanding, the Old American Company could not always control the behaviour of the gallery rowdies. During the Philadelphia Constitutional Convention of 1787, prominent Americans, including George Washington, went out to Southwark for relaxation and sometimes found only unpleasantness. One evening, in spite of Washington's presence with a guard of honour, 'the house could not be kept in reasonable order', stated John Durang in his memoirs:

> As soon as the curtain was down, the *gods* in the galleries would throw apples, nuts, bottles and glasses on the stage and into the

> orchestra. That part of the house being always crowded it was hard to discover the real perpetrators . . . Vociferating with Stentorian lungs 'Carlisle's march,' 'Cherry Charlotte's jigg,' 'Mother Brown's Retreat.' These were the names of notorious characters with their slang and flash appellations [namely whores], as given by the rowdies of that day.[38]

In 1789 certain prominent citizens (among them General Walter Stewart, Major T. I. Moore, William Temple Franklin, Dr Joseph Redman, James Crawford and John West) formed themselves into the Dramatic Association and submitted a consequential statement of rights to the Pennsylvania legislature. The association insisted that 'the prejudices of those of their fellow citizens' opposed to the theatre and 'every other amusement' were 'contrary to the laws of conscience and virtue', and that the prohibition of theatrical entertainments should cease.[39]

The law was changed and soon afterwards came competition. The Old American Company could not continue its dominance of the stage. Thomas Wignall and Alexander Reinagle, with their own company of excellent singer-actors from London and an orchestra of around twenty musicians, opened the new and sumptuous Chestnut Street Theatre, which seated 2000 people and closely resembled the Theatre Royal in Bath. In February 1794 the Chestnut Street Theatre's first dramatic presentation was mounted, Samuel Arnold's English opera *The Castle of Andalusia.* The next year, Rickett's Amphitheatre opened with ambitious circus productions that included song, dance and musical scenes.[40] Until the end of the century, Philadelphians were assured a steady diet of public musical entertainments, in concerts that included instrumental and vocal works, or in stage presentations of various kinds. These included songs introduced into spoken drama, entire English operas, scenes extracted from English operas and independent musical skits.

One looks in vain for native Philadelphians who composed during the eighteenth century. An occasional song was printed with text by 'a lady' or 'a gentleman'; but music was almost always by an immigrant musician. This accounts for the relative importance of Francis Hopkinson – lawyer, signatory to the Declaration of Independence, poet and amateur musician and composer. On 21 March 1781 his *America Independent, or The Temple of Minerva* was performed, a kind of oratorio for which Hopkinson produced the text but probably not the music. The occasion was a reception for Washington at the residence of Chevalier de La Luzerne, the French minister. A song for which he wrote the text and music, *My days have been so wondrous free*, dates from 1759. In 1788 he published *Seven [recte Eight] Songs for the Harpsichord or Forte Piano*, with a dedication to George Washington.[41] The music is unexceptional but pleasant, in the current English song style, and 'composed in an easy, familiar style, intended for young practitioners on the harpsichord or forte piano'. A copy was sent to Jefferson, who was in Paris. He wrote back to Hopkinson:

> Accept my thanks . . . and my daughter's for the book of songs. I will not tell you how much they have pleased us nor how well the last of them [*The trav'ler benighted and lost*] merits praise for its pathos, but relate a fact only, which is that while my elder daughter was playing it on the harpsichord, I happened to look towards the fire and saw the younger one all in tears. I asked her if she was sick? She said 'no; but the tune was so mournful'.[42]

It is possible that Jefferson intended no more than a nice compliment to the composer.

As late as 1800, Philadelphians still depended on imported compositions and foreign-born professionals for their musical recreation. Nevertheless, although founded in a wilderness, the city could point 119 years later to private and public musical activities that rivalled those of any city in England, except for London. This in itself was a remarkable achievement.

NOTES

[1] C. Bridenbaugh, *Cities in Revolt: Urban Life in America, 1743–1776* (London, 1971), 5 and 216; and R. B. Nye, *The Cultural Life of the New Nation, 1776–1830* (New York, 1960), 124.

[2] L. C. Madeira, *Annals of Music in Philadelphia and History of the Musical Fund Society*, ed. P. H. Goepp (Philadelphia, 1896), 17.

[3] L.B. Wright, *The Cultural Life of the American Colonies* (New York, 1957), 178.

[4] J. T. Howard, *Our American Music* (New York, 4/1965), 17–18.

[5] Madeira, *Annals*, 18, 21 and 24; Howard, *Our American Music*, 19.

[6] O. G. Sonneck, *Francis Hopkinson . . . and James Lyon* (Washington, 1905), 29.

[7] B. Franklin, *Autobiography*, ed. L. W. Labaree and others (New Haven, 1964), 175–6.

[8] Sonneck, *Francis Hopkinson*, 31.

[9] ibid, 57; Howard, *Our American Music*, 105.

[10] Sonneck, *Francis Hopkinson*, 12–13, 17, 23 and 27–8.

[11] See the *Boston Euterpeiad* (19 Jan 1822), 170.

[12] Bridenbaugh, *Cities in Revolt*, 179.

[13] Sonneck, *Francis Hopkinson*, 23.

[14] H. Dichter and E. Shapiro, *Early American Sheet Music: its Lure and its Lore* (New York, 1941/*R*1970 as *Handbook of Early American Sheet Music, 1768–1889*, 166, 177, 187, 216, 224, 226, 233, 236, 244 and 248.

[15] Madeira, *Annals*, 47.

[16] S. Rowson, *Mentoria*, ii (Philadelphia, 1794), 64–5 and 86–93.

[17] *Letters of Benjamin Rush*, i, ed. L. H. Butterfield (Princeton, 1951), 328.

[18] Mrs Griffith, *Letters Addressed to Young Married Women* (Philadelphia, 1796), 42–5.

[19] R. Nettel, *Seven Centuries of Popular Song* (Denver, 1956), 161; see also N. E. Tawa, 'Secular Music in the Late Eighteenth-Century American Home', *MQ*, lxi (1975), 511–27.

[20] See Bridenbaugh, *Cities in Revolt*, 194; Sonneck, *Francis Hopkinson*, 30–31, 40–41 and 46.

[21] *Sally Wister's Journal*, ed. A. C. Myers (Philadelphia, 1902), 91–2, 107–8 and 125.

[22] Marquis de Chastellux, *Travels in North America in the Years 1780, 1781 and 1782*, i, rev. trans. H. C. Rice jr (Chapel Hill, 1963), 170 and 176.

[23] Bridenbaugh, *Cities in Revolt*, 398–9; *'My Dear Girl', the Correspondence of Benjamin Franklin with Polly Stevenson, Georgiana and Catherine Shipley*, ed. J. M. Stifler (New York, 1927), 202–3.

[24] *The New Democracy in America: Travels of Francesco de Miranda in the United States, 1783–84*, trans. J. P. Wood, ed. J. S. Szell (Norman, Oklahoma, 1963), 56.
[25] N. E. Tawa, *Sweet Songs for Gentle Americans: the Parlor Song in America, 1790–1860* (Bowling Green, Ohio, 1980), 27; S. Warner jr. 'Colonial Philadelphia', in *Urban America in Historical Perspective*, ed. R. Mohl and N. Betten (New York, 1970), 42.
[26] *The Memoirs of John Durang*, ed. A. S. Downer (Pittsburgh, 1966), 21; see also Tawa, *Sweet Songs*, 28.
[27] Howard, *Our American Music*, 27–8; Madeira, *Annals*, 31–2; and Sonneck, *Francis Hopkinson*, 43–4 and 53–5. For a detailed description of public concerts in early Philadelphia during the entire eighteenth century, see O. G. Sonneck, *Early Concert-Life in America (1731–1800)* (Leipzig, 1907/*R*1978).
[28] Howard, *Our American Music*, 71–110; Madeira, *Annals*, 36–7; O. Sonneck, *Suum cuique* (New York, 1916), 48.
[29] Wright, *Cultural Life*, 69.
[30] Franklin, *Autobiography*, 89–96; T. C. Pollock, *The Philadelphia Theatre in the Eighteenth Century* (Philadelphia, 1933), 4.
[31] Madeira, *Annals*, 26–7; O. Sonneck, *Early Opera in America* (New York, 1915), 14–15.
[32] Madeira, *Annals*, 28–9; Pollock, *Philadelphia Theatre*, 7–9.
[33] Madeira, *Annals*, 29–30; Pollock, *Philadelphia Theatre*, 13–17.
[34] Sonneck, *Early Opera*, 24–5.
[35] Pollock, *Philadelphia Theatre*, 21–2; Sonneck, *Early Opera*, 49.
[36] S. L. Porter, 'Ballad opera', *Grove A*.
[37] *The Memoirs of John Durang*, ed. Downer, 20.
[38] ibid, 27–8.
[39] Pollock, *Philadelphia Theatre*, 47.
[40] Madeira, *Annals*, 39; *The Memoirs of John Durang*, ed. Downer, 43.
[41] R. Crawford, 'Hopkinson, Francis', *Grove A*; Sonneck, *Suum cuique*, 46–7.
[42] Letter of Jefferson to Hopkinson, from Paris, dated 13 March 1789; see *The Papers of Thomas Jefferson*, xiv, ed. J. P. Boyd (Princeton, 1958), 649.

BIBLIOGRAPHICAL NOTE

Historical and cultural background

Four books give scattered but valuable information about eighteenth-century Philadelphia, including political and religious attitudes, social and population change and cultural development. A useful starting-point is D. J. Boorstin's *The Americans: the Colonial Experience* (New York, 1958). A chapter on eighteenth-century Philadelphia, S. B. Warner jr, 'Colonial Philadelphia: the Environment of Private Opportunity', is included in *Urban America in Historical Perspective*, ed. R. A. Mohl and N. Betten (New York, 1970), 32–48. Three invaluable books on the cultural growth of the cities along the Atlantic seaboard are L. B. Wright, *The Cultural Life of the American Colonies, 1607–1763* (New York, 1957); C. Bridenbaugh, *Cities in Revolt: Urban Life in America, 1743–1776* (London, 1971); and R. B. Nye, *The Cultural Life of the New Nation, 1776–1830* (New York, 1960).

Contemporary commentaries

References to music-making in Philadelphia are found only now and again in the letters, journals and autobiographies of the time. Among them are B. Franklin's *Autobiography*, ed. L. W. Labaree and others (New Haven, 1964); *Sally Wister's Journal*, ed. A. C. Myers (Philadelphia, 1902); *Letters of Benjamin Rush*, i, ed. L. H. Butterfield (Princeton, 1951); and Marquis de Chastellux, *Travels in North America in the Years 1780, 1781 and 1782*, i and ii, rev. trans. H. C. Rice jr (Chapel Hill, 1963). Two men who were professionally involved with the cultural life of eighteenth-century Philadelphia have written about their experiences: see *The Diary of William Dunlap*, ed.

D. C. Barck (New York, 1969), and *The Memoir of John Durang*, ed. A. S. Downer (Pittsburgh, 1966). Insights into cultural life during the second half of the century are provided in the poems of Susanna Rowson, *Miscellaneous Poems* (Boston, 1804), and the novels of Charles Brockden Brown, for example *Ormond* (New York, 1799).

Music

Essential and reliable information on musical life in eighteenth-century Philadelphia is contained in the writings of O. G. Sonneck, especially *Francis Hopkinson . . . and James Lyon* (Washington, 1905/*R*1965); *Early Concert-Life in America (1731–1800)* (Leipzig, 1907/*R*1978); *Early Opera in America* (New York, 1915/*R*1963); and *Early Secular American Music*, rev. W. T. Upton (New York, 1964). Knowledge about music in the home is difficult to come by. Most useful are N. E. Tawa, *Sweet Songs for Gentle Americans: the Parlor Song in America, 1790–1860* (Bowling Green, Ohio, 1980); 'Music in the Washington Household', *Journal of American Culture*, i (1978), 19–43; and 'Secular Music in the Late-Eighteenth-Century American Home', *MQ*, lxi (1975), 511–27.

Books exclusively on Philadelphia are L. C. Madeira, *Annals of Music in Philadelphia and History of the Musical Fund Society*, ed. P. H. Goepp (Philadelphia, 1896); T. C. Pollock, *The Philadelphia Theatre in the Eighteenth Century* (Philadelphia, 1933); and R. A. Gerson, *Music in Philadelphia* (Philadelphia, 1940).

Chronology

MUSIC AND MUSICIANS	POLITICS, WAR, RULERS
1740 C. P. E. Bach (1714–88) moves to Berlin in Frederick the Great's service. The *Twelve Grand Concertos* op. 6 of George Frideric Handel (1685–1759) published. Matthias Georg Monn (1717–50) writes the first four-movement symphony. *A Musical Dictionary* by James Grassineau (*d* 1767) published, the first work of its kind.	**1740** War of Austrian Succession: Prussia, France and Bavaria against Austria and England (–1748). Death of Frederick William I of Prussia; succeeded by his son Frederick II ('the Great'). Death of Emperor Charles VI of Austria; succeeded by his daughter Maria Theresa. Death of Empress Anna of Russia; succeeded by her great-nephew Ivan VI, an infant of three months. Death of Pope Clement XII; succeeded by Benedict XIV.
1741 *Goldberg Variations* by Johann Sebastian Bach (1685–1750) published (1741–2). *Deidamia*, Handel's last opera, given in London. *Artaserse*, the first opera of Christoph Willibald Gluck (1714–87), given in Milan. The Madrigal Society founded in London by John Immyns (*d* 1784). Antonio Vivaldi (63) dies, Vienna; Johann Joseph Fux (80) dies, Vienna.	**1741** Empress Elizabeth usurps the Russian throne.
1742 *Messiah* by Handel given, in Dublin. The first keyboard sonatas of Carl Philipp Emanuel Bach published. The Berlin Opera opened by Frederick the Great with *Caesar und Cleopatra* by Carl Heinrich Graun (*c*1703–1759). Mannheim opera house opens with *Meride* by Carlo Pietro Grua (*c*1700–1773). Ranelagh Pleasure Gardens open.	**1742** Charles VII of Bavaria elected Holy Roman Emperor. Prague occupied by Bavarian and French troops.
1743 Handel's *Samson* performed, London.	**1743** Maria Theresa crowned Queen of Bohemia. George II is the last European monarch to ride into battle at the head of his troops, at Dettingen. Mme de Pompadour becomes Louis XV's mistress and for over 20 years influences French politics and diplomacy.
1744 Handel's *Semele* performed, London.	**1744** Frederick the Great invades Saxony.
1745 *Platée* by Jean-Philippe Rameau (1681–1764) given at Versailles. Johann Stamitz (1717–57) becomes Konzertmeister at the Mannheim court.	**1745** Death of Charles VII of Bavaria; succeeded by Maximilian Joseph. Maria Theresa's husband, Francis Stephen of Lorraine, elected Holy Roman Emperor. Second Jacobite Rebellion (–1746). Prince Charles Edward Stuart attempts to gain the English throne but is defeated at Culloden (1746).
1746 Gluck visits London, where his *La caduta de'giganti* is given. Wilhelm Friedemann Bach (1710–84) appointed organist at the Liebfrauenkirche, Halle.	**1746** Death of Philip V of Spain; succeeded by Ferdinand VI. Death of Christian VI of Denmark–Norway; succeeded by Frederick V.
1747 Handel's *Judas Maccabaeus* performed, London. Bach visits Frederick the Great's court at Potsdam; his *Musical Offering* published.	
1748 Bach's B minor Mass assembled (1747–9). The Holywell Music Room, Oxford, opened (the first room built specifically for music).	**1748** Treaty of Aix-la-Chapelle ends the War of Austrian Succession, with Austria having lost Silesia to Prussia.

LITERATURE, PHILOSOPHY, RELIGION	SCIENCE, TECHNOLOGY, DISCOVERY	FINE AND DECORATIVE ARTS, ARCHITECTURE
1740 Completion of *A Treatise on Human Nature* by David Hume (1711–76). *Pamela, or Virtue Rewarded*, an epistolary novel by Samuel Richardson (1689–1761) published. Louis, Duc de Saint-Simon (1765–1755), composes his *Memoires* of Louis XIV (–1750).	**1740** Dijon Academy of Science founded. The circumnavigation of Lord Anson (1697–1762) in the *Centurion* (–1744).	**1740** Palace of Dos Aquas, Valencia, remodelled (–1744).
	1741 Stockholm Academy of Science founded.	
1742 In *Cartas eruditas* (–1760) Benito Feijoo (1767–1764) contributes to the intellectual emancipation of Spain.	**1742** Anders Celsius (1701–44) proposes a centigrade thermometer.	**1742** Jacques Dubois (1693–1763) becomes a master cabinet maker; his style represents the culmination of the Rococo. William Hogarth (1697–1764) paints *Marriage à la Mode* (–1746). *Diana Resting after her Bath* by François Boucher (1703–70).
1743 *The Mourning Turtle Dove*, poems on the death of her husband by Hedwig Charlotta Nordenflycht (1718–93), published.	**1743** Copenhagen Academy of Science founded.	**1743** The pilgrimage church of Vierzehnheiligen begun by Balthasar Neumann (1687–1753). Capo-di-Monte porcelain factory established in Naples.
1744 George Berkeley (1685–1753) publishes *Siris*, a scientific and philosophical meditation. Third edition of *Scienza nuova* by Giambattista Vico (1668–1744), the first survey of the social evolution of mankind.		**1744** The Abbey of Ottobeuren, the masterpiece of Michael Fischer (1692–1766), begun. Dominkus Zimmerman (1695–1766) begins the pilgrimage church of Die Wies.
	1745 Invention of the 'Leyden jar' for storing electricity by Pieter van Musschenbroek (1692–1761).	**1745** Chelsea porcelain factory, the first in England, established. Sanssouci Palace, Potsdam, begun by Georg von Knobelsdorff (1699–1753).
		1746 Antonio Canaletto (1720–75) arrives in London.
		1747 St Andrew's Cathedral, Kiev, begun by Bartolommeo Rastrelli (1700–71). Strawberry Hill, Twickenham, begun by Horace Walpole (1717–97) in the Gothic style.
1748 Charles-Louis de Secondat, Baron de Montesquieu (1689–1755), publishes *De l'esprit des Lois*, the first great synthesis of political economy. *Der Messias* (completed 1773) by Friedrich Gottlieb Klopstock (1724–1803) appears anonymously, inaugurating a new era in German poetry.	**1748** Osmosis discovered by Abbé Nollet (1700–1770). Discovery of the ruined city of Pompeii.	**1748** Lancelot ('Capability') Brown (1716–83) plans his first independent landscape garden design, at Warwick Castle.

MUSIC AND MUSICIANS	POLITICS, WAR, RULERS
1749 Handel's *Solomon* performed, London. Rameau's *Zoroastre* given, Paris.	
1750 J. S. Bach (65) dies, Leipzig.	**1750** Death of John V of Portugal; succeeded by Joseph I. Britain joined Austro–Russian alliance, hostile to Prussia.
1751 The violinist and composer Felice Giardini (1761–96) settles in London. Francesco Geminiani (1687–1762) publishes *The Art of Playing on the Violin*, the first advanced violin manual.	**1751** Frederick II of Sweden dies; succeeded by Adolphus Frederick.
1752 Handel's *Jephtha* performed, London. Johann Joachim Quantz (1697–1773) publishes his *Versuch einer Anweisung die Flöte traversiere zu spielen*. The Querelle des Bouffons begins, Paris.	
1753 Ignaz Holzbauer (1711–83) appointed Kapellmeister at Mannheim. Jean-Jacques Rousseau (1712–78) publishes his *Lettre sur la musique française*. C. P. E. Bach publishes vol.i of *Versuch über die wahre Art, das Clavier zu spielen* [vol.ii, 1762].	
1754 Johann Stamitz visits Paris. *Il filosofo di campagna* by Baldassare Galuppi (1706–85) given, Venice.	**1754** Anglo–French war in north America.
1755 William Boyce (1711–79) appointed Master of the King's Musick to George II. *Cephalus and Procris* by Francesco Araia (1709–*c*1776), the first opera sung in Russian, given in St Petersburg. C. H. Graun's *Montezuma* to a libretto after Frederick the Great given; his *Der Tod Jesu* performed, Berlin. Thomas Cahusac (*d* 1798) founds probably the first instrument-making business in London.	**1755** Lisbon devastated by an earthquake.
1756 Leopold Mozart's *Versuch einer gründlichen Violinschule* published.	**1756** Seven Years' War. Frederick the Great invades Saxony. Austria now allied to France and Russia against Prussia and Great Britain. Britain and France fighting for colonial territories.
1757 First public concert in Philadelphia. Domenico Scarlatti (71) dies, Madrid; J. Stamitz (39) dies, Mannheim.	**1757** Battle of Leuthen: Frederick the Great's defeat of Austria regarded as his greatest military triumph. France defeats Britain at the Battle of Plassey in India.
	1758 Death of Pope Benedict XIV; succeeded by Clement XIII.
1759 Joseph Haydn (1732–1809) enters the service of Count Morzin, Lukavec. *Ippolito ed Aricia* by Tommaso Traetta (1727–79) given, Parma. Handel (74) dies, London.	**1759** General Wolfe captures Quebec for Britain; by 1760 French rule in India and Canada virtually ended. Charles III, ruler of the Two Sicilies, becomes King of Spain on the death of Ferdinand VI.

LITERATURE, PHILOSOPHY, RELIGION	SCIENCE, TECHNOLOGY, DISCOVERY	FINE AND DECORATIVE ARTS, ARCHITECTURE
1749 *The History of Tom Jones, a Foundling* by Henry Fielding (1705–54) establishes the novel of action in England.	**1749** Publication of the first of the 36-volume *Histoire naturelle* in which George Buffon differentiates the sciences of anthropology, geology and archaeology.	
	1750 Göttingen Academy of Science founded.	**1750** Giovanni Battista Tiepolo (1696–1770) commissioned to decorate the archbishop's palace at Würzburg. *Robert Andrews and his Wife* painted by Thomas Gainsborough (1727–88). Battersea Enamel factory set up.
1751 Denis Diderot (1713–84) edits the *Encyclopédie*, in 17 volumes (–1772); it advocates a secular morality, undermining the supernatural sanctions on which the *ancien régime* is based.		**1751** Ecole Militaire, Paris, begun by Jacques Ange Gabriel (1698–1782).
	1752 Gregorian Calendar adopted by Great Britain. Benjamin Franklin demonstrates lightning to be electricity.	**1752** Royal Palace at Caserta, Naples, the last great Italian Baroque palace and the largest 18th-century building, begun by Luigi Vanvitelli (1700–1733).
	1753 Carl Linnaeus (1707–78) publishes *Species plantarum*, followed in 1758 by the tenth edition of *Systemae naturae*, the starting-points of botanical and zoological nomenclature.	**1753** St Nicholas, Prague, completed.
		1754 The Winter Palace, St Petersburg, begun by Rastrelli. Thomas Chippendale the Elder (1718–79) publishes *The Gentleman and Cabinet-maker's Director*.
1755 Publication of *A Dictionary of the English Language* by Samuel Johnson (1709–84).		**1755** Louis-François Roubiliac (1705–52) completes his statue of Newton. François Boucher appointed Director of the Gobelins tapestry works. Johann Winckelmann (1717–68) publishes *Reflections on the Imitation of Greek Works of Art in Painting and Sculpture*.
1756 Edmund Burke (1729–97) publishes *A Philosophical Enquiry into the Origin of our Ideas on the Sublime and Beautiful*, the first English treatise on aesthetics.		**1756** The French royal porcelain factory moved from Vincennes to Sèvres.
1757 Mikhail Vasilyevich Lomonosov (1711–65) copiles the first systematic Russian grammar.	**1757** The *Elementa physiologiae* (–1766) by Albrecht von Haller (1708–77) initiates the science of physiology.	**1757** The Panthéon, Paris, begun by J. G. Soufflot (1713–80).
1758 Publication of *Historia del Famosa Predicor Fray Gerundio* by Jose da Isla (1703–81), a successful satire on Spanish bombastic oratory [vol.ii, 1768].	**1758** Reappearance of Halley's comet as predicted by Edmund Halley (1656–1742) after its last appearance in 1682.	
1759 Voltaire, pseudonym of Francois-Marie Arouet (1694–1778), publishes *Candide*.	**1759** Munich Academy of Science founded.	**1759** The British Museum opened to the public.

MUSIC AND MUSICIANS	POLITICS, WAR, RULERS
1760 Piccinni's *La buona figliuola* (*La Cecchina*) given, Rome. The firm of Breitkopf, Leipzig, issue the first published thematic catalogues.	**1760** Berlin occupied by enemy troops for a few days in October. Death of George II of Britain; succeeded by his grandson George III.
1761 Haydn engaged by Prince Paul Anton Esterházy as vice-Kapellmeister. The Noblemen's and Gentlemen's Catch Club founded in London.	
1762 J. C. Bach (1735–1782) leaves Milan and settles in London. *Orfeo ed Euridice* by Gluck given in Vienna. Geminiani (74) dies, Dublin.	**1762** Death of Empress Elizabeth of Russia; succeeded by Peter III, who is deposed after a few months by his wife, Catherine II.
1763 Wolfgang Amadeus Mozart (1756–91) plays in Paris and before the court at Versailles. Florian Leopold Gassmann (1729–74) succeeds Gluck as Vienna court ballet composer. Liebhaber-Concerte, Leipzig, founded.	**1763** The treaties of Hubertsburg and Paris end the Seven Years' War, with Prussia retaining Silesia and British supremacy established in India and Canada. Augustus III ('the Strong'), Elector of Saxony and King of Poland, dies; succeeded by his grandson Frederick Augustus in Saxony and puppet rulers in Poland.
1764 Mozart plays in London. Rameau (79) dies, Paris.	**1764** Defensive alliance between Prussia and Russia as a first move in the peaceful partition of Poland.
1765 Bach–Abel concerts founded in London [succeeded by the Professional Concerts (1783–93)].	**1765** Death of Francis Stephen of Lorraine. His son Joseph II becomes co-ruler with Maria Theresa and Holy Roman Emperor. Leopold, younger brother of Joseph II, becomes Grand Duke of Tuscany. The Stamp Act for taxing the American colonies is passed by the British Parliament but repealed after protest 'No taxation without representation' in 1766.
1766 Haydn becomes full Kapellmeister to Count Esterházy. The theatre at Drottningholm, near Stockholm, built.	**1766** Death of Frederick V of Denmark–Norway; succeeded by Christian VII.
1767 George Philipp Telemann (86) dies, Hamburg; C. P. E. Bach succeeds him as Kantor and music director there. Gluck's *Alceste* first performed in Vienna. Leeds Festival, the first in a British industrial city, founded.	
1768 J.-J. Rousseau's *Dictionnaire de musique* published. The opera house at Eszterháza inaugurated with Haydn's *Lo speziale*.	
1769 Luigi Boccherini (1743–1805) settles in Madrid.	**1769** Death of Pope Clement XIII; succeeded by Clement XIV.
1770 The Concert des Amateurs, Paris, founded (*c*1770). Liebhaberkonzerte, Berlin, founded. Giuseppe Tartini (77) dies, Padua.	**1770** Marriage of the French dauphin (later Louis XVI) to the Habsburg Archduchess Marie Antoinette.

LITERATURE, PHILOSOPHY, RELIGION	SCIENCE, TECHNOLOGY, DISCOVERY	FINE AND DECORATIVE ARTS, ARCHITECTURE
	1760 Academies of science founded at Verona and Turin.	**1760** Allan Ramsay (1713–84) made painter-in-ordinary to George III.
1761 Publication of *Contes Moraux* by Jean-François Marmontel (1723–99).	**1761** John Harrison's (1693–1776) fourth marine chronometer for measuring longitude successfully tested at sea. The Bridgewater Canal laid out by James Brindley (1716–72), a major contribution to the Industrial Revolution (completed 1767).	**1761** The foremost German Classicist painter, Anton Mengs (1728–79), summoned to Madrid as director of the royal tapestry works. Matthew Boulton (1728–1809) sets up a metalware factory in Birmingham.
1762 The influential *Du contrat social* and *Emile*, treatises on politics and education by Jean-Jacques Rousseau (1712–78) are published. Carlo Goldoni (1707–93), prolific Venetian playwright, settles in Paris. Publication of *Fingal* by James Macpherson (1736–96) which, with *Temora* and the 'translated' works of Ossian, profoundly influences the Romantic movement.		**1762** Robert Adam (1728–92) and his brothers remodel Syon House according to their concept of total interior design (–1769).
		1763 Thomas Affleck (*d* 1795) emigrates to New York where he becomes the leading cabinet maker in the Chippendale style. Benjamin West (1738–1820) settles in London and becomes the first American artist of international reputation.
1764 Anonymous publication of *The Castle of Otranto*, the first Gothic novel, by Horace Wimpole (1717–97).	**1764** Spinning Jenny invented; perfected in 1766 by James Hargreaves (*d* 1778).	
	1765 James Watt (1736–1819) adds a separate condenser to Newcomen's steam engine.	**1765** *Essays on Painting* published by Denis Diderot (1713–84).
1766 Christoph Martin Wieland (1733–1813) writes *Geschichte des Agathon* (–1767), a landmark in the development of the modern psychological novel. Publication of *The Vicar of Wakefield* by Oliver Goldsmith (1730–79).	**1766** Henry Cavendish (1731–1810) discovers that hydrogen is an element of air. The circumnavigation of Louis de Bougainville (1729–1811) in the *Boudeuse* (–1769).	**1766** *The Swing* painted by Jean Honoré Fragonard (1732–1806). George Stubbs (1724–1806) publishes *The Anatomy of the Horse*, revolutionizing animal painting.
1767 The publication of *Phädon*, an essay on the immortality of the soul, brings Moses Mendelssohn (1729–86) to the forefront of European intellectual life.		**1767** Sir John Wood (1728–81) builds Royal Crescent, Bath (–1775).
	1768 Captain James Cook's (1728–78) first circumnavigation, in the *Endeavour* (–1771). Peter Simon Pallas (1741–1811) travels in Asia on behalf of Russia (–1774).	**1768** The Royal Academy of Arts founded by George III with Joshua Reynolds (1723–92) as president. The first aquatints are created by Jean-Baptiste Le Prince (1733–81).
1769 Publication of the poem *Les saisons* by Jean François, Marquis de Saint-Lambert (1716–1803).	**1769** Richard Awkwright (1732–92) invents the roller-spinning water loom. Transit of Venus which provides the incentive for scientific work and exploration.	
	1770 Captain Cook lands at Botany Bay, proving the existence of Australia. James Bruce (1730–94) visits the source of the Blue Nile.	

MUSIC AND MUSICIANS	POLITICS, WAR, RULERS
1771 Publication of *The Present State of Music in France and Italy* by Charles Burney (1726–1814) followed in 1773 by *The Present State of Music in Germany, the Netherlands, and United Provinces.*	**1771** Death of Adolphus Frederick of Sweden; succeeded by Gustavus III. Russia completes the conquest of the Crimea.
1772 Haydn's so-called 'Sturm und Drang' symphonies, nos.43–7, written. Vienna Tonkünstler-Sozietät founded by Gassmann. J. C. Bach visits Mannheim for performances of his *Temistocle.*	**1772** First Partition of Poland between Prussia and Russia. Hieronymus, Count of Colloredo, Prince-Bishop of Gurk, elected Prince Archbishop of Salzburg.
1773 Foundation of the Royal Swedish Opera by Gustavus III.	
1774 Antonio Salieri (1750–1825) succeeds Gassmann as court composer and conductor of the Italian opera in Vienna. James Hook appointed organist and composer at Vauxhall Gardens, London. *Esemplare ossia saggio fondamentale pratico di contrappunto* by Padre Martini (1706–84) published [ii, 1775]. Gluck goes to Paris and gives *Iphigénie en Aulide* and *Orphée.* Baldassare Galuppi (78) dies, Venice. Nicolo Jommelli (69) dies, Naples.	**1774** Death of Louis XV of France; succeeded by his grandson Louis XVI. The first continental congress in the American colonies meets in Philadelphia and passes the Declaration of Rights, drawn up by Thomas Jefferson (1743–1836). Death of Pope Clement XIV; Pius VI elected the following year.
1775 Hanover Square Rooms opened in London. Johann Adam Hiller (1728–1804) founds the Musikübende Gesellschaft, Leipzig.	**1775** Battle of Bunker Hill, the first outbreak of hostilities in the American War of Independence, which continues until the surrender of General Cornwallis at Yorktown in 1781.
1776 John Hawkins's *History* and vol.i of Charles Burney's published. The Burgtheater in Vienna taken over by Joseph II's court. The Ancient Concerts begin, London.	**1776** 4 July, American Declaration of Independence. The Portuguese colonies in South America organized into one unit with Rio de Janeiro as the capital.
1777 Mozart visits Mannheim.	**1777** Death of Joseph I of Portugal; succeeded by Maria I. Death of Maximilian Joseph of Bavaria; succeeded by Carl Theodor, Elector Palatine.
1778 Mozart visits Mannheim and Paris. The Mannheim musical establishment moves to Munich. Teatro alla Scala, Milan, opens with Salieri's *L'Europa riconosciuta.* Joseph II establishes the Deutsches National Singspiel at the Vienna Burgtheater. Thomas Augustine Arne (77) dies, London.	**1778** Partition of Bavaria which leads to the War of Bavarian Succession between Austria and Prussia, 1778–9; Carl Theodor moves his court to Munich.
1779 Gluck's *Iphigénie en Tauride* given, Paris. Piccinni's *Roland* given, Paris. William Boyce (77) dies, London.	
	1780 Death of Maria Theresa; Joseph II becomes sole ruler of the Habsburg lands.

LITERATURE, PHILOSOPHY, RELIGION	SCIENCE, TECHNOLOGY, DISCOVERY	FINE AND DECORATIVE ARTS, ARCHITECTURE
1771 The first *Enclyclopaedia Britannica* issued by a 'Society of Gentlemen in Scotland'. Emmanuel Swedenborg (1688–1772), Swedish scientist, mathematician, philosopher and mystic, publishes *Vera Christiana Religio*, the most comprehensive exposition of his philosophy.		**1771** The Pavillon de Louveciennes by Claude-Nicolas Ledoux (1736–1806) begun, the first building in France in the neo-classical style throughout.
	1772 Captain Cook's second voyage of discovery, in the *Resolution* (–1775).	
1773 Suppression of the Jesuits by Pope Clement XIV, after a campaign by European monarchs.		
1774 Johann Wolfgang von Goethe (1749–1832) publishes his epistolary novel *The Sorrows of Werther*, the first novel of the 'Sturm und Drang' movement. *Letters* to his son by Lord Chesterfield (1694–1773) published posthumously, becoming a handbook of gentlemanly behaviour. Gottfried Bürger (1747–94), one of the Hainbund poets, publishes his ballad *Lenore*.	**1774** *Experiments and Observations on Different Kinds of Air* by Joseph Priestley (1733–1804) demonstrates that plants immersed in water give off gas (oxygen). George Bogle (1746–81) visits Tibet to establish relations between Tibet and British India.	**1774** Thomas Gainsborough moves to London and begins to paint society portraits.
	1775 James Watt perfects the steam engine.	**1775** Josiah Wedgwood (1730–95) first produces Jasper ware, the perfect ceramic body for neo-classical ornaments. Adams brothers erect Portland Place, London.
1776 Adam Smith (1723–90) publishes *An Inquiry into the Nature and Causes of the Wealth of Nations* which revolutionizes economic theory. Edward Gibbon (1737–94) publishes the first volume of his *History of the Decline and Fall of the Roman Empire* (–1788).	**1776** Captain Cook's third voyage, in the *Resolution* (–1780); he is killed in Hawaii in 1779.	**1776** George Romney (1734–1802) paints the portrait of Richard Cumberland.
	1777 Oxygen named by Antoine Lavoisier (1743–94).	
1778 Publication of *Evelina*, an epistolary novel by Fanny Burney (1752–1840).		**1778** Joseph Wright (1743–97) has his first exhibition at the Royal Academy. Bust of Benjamin Franklin modelled by Jean-Antoine Houdon (1741–1828), acknowledged as the leading portrait sculptor in Europe.
	1779 Samuel Crompton (1753–1827) perfects the spinning 'mule' – a cross between Hargreaves's Jenny and Arkwright's water frame spinning machine. The first cast-iron bridge erected at Ironbridge, Shropshire, designed by Abraham Darby and John Wilkinson.	
1780 Publication of *An Introduction to the Principles of Morals and Legislation* by Jeremy Bentham (1748–1832).		**1780** Caughley pottery, Shropshire, makes the first known willow-pattern plate.

MUSIC AND MUSICIANS	POLITICS, WAR, RULERS
1781 Mozart's *Idomeneo* given in Munich; he leaves the service of the Archbishop of Salzburg and settles in Vienna. Haydn's op.33 string quartets published. The Concert de la Loge Olympique instituted in Paris. Leipzig Gewandhaus opens, with Hiller as conductor.	**1781** Joseph II abolishes serfdom in Austria; his edict of toleration reduces power of the church.
1782 Mozart's *Die Entführung aus dem Serail* given, Vienna. *Il barbiere di Siviglia* by Giovanni Paisiello (1740–1816) given, St Petersburg. *Versuch einer Anleitung zur Composition*, vol.i by H. C. Koch (1749–1816) published [ii, 1793] Pietro Metastasio (84) dies, Vienna. J. C. Bach (46) dies, London.	
1783 Prague opera house (the Estates Theatre) built by Count Nostitz, opens. Johann Adolf Hasse (84) dies, Venice.	**1783** Great Britain formally recognizes American Independence.
1784 Wilhelm Friedemann Bach (73) dies, Berlin. Mozart composes six piano concertos, Vienna. Grétry's *Richard, Coeur-de-Lion* given, Paris. Stephen Storace (1763–96) gives quartet party, Vienna: Dittersdorf, Haydn, Mozart, Vanhal. The first Handel Commemoration held, Westminster Abbey and the Pantheon, London.	**1784** William Pitt the younger (1759–1806) wins British general election.
1785 Caecilian Society founded, London. Mozart's six string quartets dedicated to Haydn published.	
1786 Mozart's *Le nozze di Figaro* given, Vienna. Haydn's Paris Symphonies (nos. 82–7) given, Paris. Earliest surviving example of a grand piano by John Broadwood (1732–1812).	**1786** Death of Frederick the Great of Prussia; succeeded by Frederick Wilhelm II.
1787 Mozart's *Don Giovanni* given in Prague. Salieri's *Tarare* given in Paris (in Vienna, as *Axur, rè d'Ormus*, 1788). Samuel Arnold (1740–1802) begins his complete edition of Handel (abandoned in 1793, with 180 parts issued). Gluck (73) dies, Vienna.	**1787** Federal government established in the USA. France declared bankrupt.
1788 Mozart writes his last three symphonies, nos.39 in E♭, 40 in G minor and 41 in C ('Jupiter'). The Glee Club founded, London. C. P. E. Bach (74) dies, Hamburg.	**1788** Death of Charles III of Spain; succeeded by Charles IV. The first convict settlement established at Botany Bay, Australia.

LITERATURE, PHILOSOPHY, RELIGION	SCIENCE, TECHNOLOGY, DISCOVERY	FINE AND DECORATIVE ARTS, ARCHITECTURE
1781 Publication of the *Critique of Pure Reason* by Immanuel Kant (1724–1804), which contains the root of his philosophical system. Johann Christoph Friedrick von Schiller (1759–1805) publishes his first drama, *Die Raüber*. Emperor Joseph II introduces religious toleration to the Habsburg lands.	**1781** William Herschel (1738–1822) discovers the planet Uranus.	**1782** Carl Gustav Pilo (1711–93) paints *The Coronation of Gustavus III*. Charles Wilson Peale (1741–1827) opens the first art gallery in the USA, exhibiting his portraits of personalities of the Revolutionary War.
	1783 First demonstration of hot air and hydrogen balloons by the Montgolfier brothers. Royal Society of Edinburgh formed.	
1784 The Methodists, led by John Wesley (1703–91), break away from the Church of England. Johann Gottfried von Herder (1744–1803) writes his monumental *Ideas on the Philosophy of the History of Mankind* (–1791).		**1784** *The Oath of the Horatii* painted by Jacques-Louis David (1748–1825), one of the landmarks in the history of neo-classicism.
	1785 William Withering (1741–99) publishes his conclusions on the use of digitalis in medicine.	**1785** The design by Thomas Jefferson (1743–1826) for the State Capitol in Richmond, Virginia, for the first time applied the classical temple form to a monumental building.
1786 Publication of *Poems* by the American Philip Freneau (1752–1832). Gustavus III founds the Swedish Academy, giving particular encouragement to literature. Publication of *Poems, chiefly in the Scottish Dialect* by Robert Burns (1759–96). Goethe travels in Italy (–1788), where he conceives the ideal of a classic literature.	**1786** Uranium discovered by M. H. Klaproth (1743–1817). Early attempts at gas lighting in England and Germany.	**1786** Marie-Louise Vigée-Lebrun (1755–1842) paints *Marie Antoinette in a Satin Dress with a Rose*.
1787 *The Vision of Columbus*, an epic in heroic couplets, published by Joel Barlow (1754–1812), American diplomat and poet.	**1787** First ascent of Mont Blanc, by Horace Saussure.	**1787** Sir Henry Raeburn (1756–1823) returns to Edinburgh and becomes the leading portrait painter in Scotland. Juan de Villaneuva (1739–1811) designs the Prado, Madrid, as a Museum of Natural History. *Cupid and Psyche* (–1793), a marble by Antonio Canova (1757–1822), shows how sculpture can be freed from an architectural setting.
	1788 Linnaeus Society founded. Joseph Lagrange (1736–1813), foremost mathematician of the era, publishes *Mécanique analytique*.	**1788** Humphrey Repton (1752–1818) sets up as a landscape gardener and is soon the acknowledged leader of his profession. Karl Longhaus (1732–1808) builds the Brandenburg Gate, Berlin (–1791).

MUSIC AND MUSICIANS	POLITICS, WAR, RULERS
1789 *Philadelphia Harmony*, a book of popular American and European sacred music, published. Daniel Gottlob Türk (1750–1813) publishes *Clavierschule*. For a performance of the oratorio *Hiob* by Carl Ditters von Dittersdorf (1739–99), citizens are first able to buy tickets for the Berlin court opera.	**1789** 5 May, the first meeting of the Estates-General in France for more than 150 years; 14 July, the Storming of the Bastille marks the beginning of the French Revolution; 4 August, Declaration of the Rights of Man proclaimed by the newly formed French National Assembly; 5 October, the Paris mob march to Versailles and force the royal family to go to Paris.
1790 Mozart's *Così fan tutte* given, Vienna. Concert Spirituel, Paris, founded in 1725, closes down.	**1790** Death of Emperor Joseph II; succeeded by his brother Leopold II, Grand Duke of Tuscany.
1791 Mozart's *La clemenza di Tito* given, Prague, and *Die Zauberflöte*, Vienna; he dies (35). Haydn's first visit to England (–1792): symphonies nos.93–8.	**1791** The National Assembly in France becomes the Legislative Assembly.
1792 Ludwig van Beethoven (1770–1827) settles in Vienna. *Il matrimonio segreto* by Domenico Cimarosa (1749–1801) given, Vienna. Berlin Singakademie founded by C. F. C. Fasch (1736–1800). Teatro La Fenice, Venice, opens.	**1792** Assassination of Gustavus III of Sweden by dissatisfied nobles; succeeded by Gustavus IV. Death of Leopold II of Austria; succeeded by Francis II. Overthrow of the French monarchy. France declared a republic, 22 September.
	1793 Execution of Louis XVI on 21 January, followed by that of Marie Antoinette on 16 October. Britain, the Netherlands, Spain, Portugal, Naples, Tuscany and the Holy Roman Empire declare war on France. Second Partition of Poland. The Terror in France ends after the death of Robespierre in July 1794.
1794 Haydn's second visit to England (–1795): symphonies nos.99–104.	
1795 Beethoven's first two piano concertos performed, Vienna. Paris Conservatoire founded.	**1795** The Directoire in France (–1799).
1796 The first two of Haydn's late masses composed, Vienna.	**1796** Death of Empress Catherine II of Russia; succeeded by Paul I.
1797 Haydn's op.76 string quartets composed. *Médée* by Luigi Cherubini (1760–1842) given, Paris.	**1797** Death of Frederick Wilhelm II of Prussia; succeeded by Frederick Wilhelm III.
1798 Haydn's *The Creation* given, Vienna. Beethoven's op.13 piano sonata ('Pathétique') written. First collected edition of Mozart's works begun.	**1798** Battle of the Nile; Horatio Nelson plays a leading part in the destruction of the French fleet.
	1799 The Consulat in France (–1804) with Napoleon Bonaparte as First Consul. Income tax first introduced in England.

LITERATURE, PHILOSOPHY, RELIGION	SCIENCE, TECHNOLOGY, DISCOVERY	FINE AND DECORATIVE ARTS, ARCHITECTURE
1789 Alexander Nikolayevich Radishchev (1749–1802) publishes his *Journey from St Petersburg to Moscow*, attacking autocracy and serfdom. William Jones (1746–94) translates the Sanskrit drama *Sakuntala* into English.	**1789** Antoine Lavoisier produces his first memoir on respiration and laid the foundations for the study of metabolism. Gilbert White (1720–93) publishes *A Natural History of Selborne*. Alessandro Malaspina (1754–1810) explores the north-west coast of America (–1794).	**1789** William Blake (1757–1827) publishes *Songs of Innocence* with a new method of illuminated printing. Francisco Goya (1746–1828) becomes court painter to Charles IV of Spain.
1790 Nikolai Mikhaylovich Karamzin (1766–1826), the first Russian writer to gain an international reputation, publishes *Letters of a Russian Traveller*.	**1790** Lisbon Academy of Science founded.	
1791 James Boswell (1740–95) publishes *The Life of Samuel Johnson*. Tom Paine (1737–1809) publishes *The Rights of Man* in reply to Burke's *Reflections on the French Revolution*.		**1791** Charlotte Square, Edinburgh, laid out by Robert Adam. Thomas Sheraton (1751–1806) publishes *The Cabinet-maker and Upholsterer's Drawing Book* (–1794), used extensively both sides of the Atlantic.
1792 Josef Dobrovsky (1743–1829) publishes *History of the Bohemian Language and Literature*.		**1792** The Alexander Palace, Tsarkoe Selo, begun by Giacomo Querenghi (1744–1817), a gift from Catherine II to the future Alexander I (–1796).
1793 Vincenzo Monti (1754–1828) writes *Bassvilliana*, a poem in *terza rima* on the French Revolution.		**1793** The Louvre opens as the first national art gallery in Europe.
1794 Publication of *The Mysteries of Udolpho* by Ann Radcliffe (1764–1823), the leading exponent of the Gothic novel.	**1794** Ecole Polytechnique in Paris founded, the first of its kind in Europe.	
	1795 Mungo Park (1771–1806) explores West Africa and the River Niger. James Hutton (1726–97) publishes *Theory of the Earth* outlining the science of geology.	
		1796 The silversmith Paul Storr (1771–1844) sets up business in London. The fantastical Fonthill Abbey begun by James Wyatt (1746–1813). J.M.W. Turner (1775–1851) exhibits his first work in oils, *Fishermen at Sea*, at the Royal Academy.
		1797 *A History of British Birds* published (–1804) with woodcuts by Thomas Bewick.
1798 *Lyrical Ballads* by William Wordsworth (1770–1850) and Samuel Taylor Coleridge (1772–1834) appear; the beginning of the Romantic movement in English literature.	**1798** Edward Jenner (1749–1823) publishes his theory of vaccination against smallpox. William Herschel discovers the infra-red radiation in the light of the sun. Lithography invented by Alois Senefelder (1771–1835).	
1799 Schiller completes his *Wallenstein* trilogy, his finest drama.	**1799** The Rosetta Stone discovered in Egypt.	**1799** Blake paints *The Adoration of the Magi;* the satirical *Coprichos* of Francisco Goya (1746–1828) etched.

Index

Page numbers in *italics* refer to captions to illustrations.

Index

Index